# A HARMONY OF THE GOSPELS

# A HARMONY OF THE GOSPELS

*The Story of the Messiah*

An Expanded, Interpretative Paraphrase of a Chronological Harmony of the Four Gospels, with Cross References, Supplementary Notes, and Indexes

BRADLEY GALAMBOS

authorHOUSE®

*AuthorHouse™*
*1663 Liberty Drive*
*Bloomington, IN 47403*
*www.authorhouse.com*
*Phone: 1-800-839-8640*



*Published by AuthorHouse 04/14/2012*

*ISBN: 978-1-4685-4828-0 (sc)*
*ISBN: 978-1-4685-5104-4 (hc)*
*ISBN: 978-1-4685-5103-7 (e)*

*Library of Congress Control Number: 2012902547*

# CONTENTS

*To Janice*

# — INTRODUCTION —

This book contains a harmony of the Gospels—that is, the four Biblical records of the life of Jesus have been merged into a single account. This way, the entire Gospel story can be read in one place at one time, without the reader constantly flipping pages to read each separate account, constantly trying to harmonize the different versions. However, while such harmonies already exist, this book is unique in that the stories and messages of the Gospel are paraphrased and explained in simple language—in a commentary-like style—as though such explanations were a part of the original text. In short, this book may be described as is indicated in its subtitle:

**An Expanded, Interpretative Paraphrase of a Chronological Harmony of the Four Gospels, with Cross References, Supplementary Notes, and Indexes**

As a bit of an explanation, I will discuss briefly each portion of this book.

**Harmony:**

As indicated, this harmony of the Gospels is the merging together, in a single account, of the four different versions of the Gospel record—Matthew, Mark, Luke, and John. And, because the Ascension of Jesus is described in Acts 1:2-12—which is really an extension of Luke's Gospel record—I have included these verses as part of the Gospel account. It could be said, then, that the final result of this harmony is a *fifth* version of the Gospel story.

Of course, when there is just one version of a particular part of the Gospel record, writing the *Harmony* (the easy-to-recognize, one-word name I've given the book) was a fairly simple procedure. But when the record is increased to two, three, and even four accounts, significant difficulties can quickly arise. For example, it is surprising to discover how many differences there are among the various accounts. To be sure, most of the variations are minor, but in a case or two, the differences are quite significant.

Furthermore, I wanted to make sure that not a single concept of any one verse was missed. All the discrepancies between the texts had to be carefully analyzed. Ultimately, decisions were made as to which concepts should be included in the final text, as well as how they should appear.

The making of the *Harmony* was further complicated by the fact that there appear to be some stories, teachings, and parables that have been duplicated. Bible scholars are divided as to whether there were such duplications during the ministry of Jesus, or whether these are various descriptions of the same event. I considered it likely that Jesus repeated Himself to different people, in different places, and under different circumstances. This is not at all surprising. In fact, such duplication is to be expected. Indeed, it is very unlikely that Jesus said a certain thing only once during His ministry! That being the case, the reader will find a few stories that read almost identically to others, some teachings that are similar to others, and a few parables that are repeated. But, in the interest of being faithful to the *entire* Gospel record, I have included most of these apparently duplicated things as separate events. However, in a situation or so, I did consider such duplications to be really the same event. In any case, I have made note of such within the *Harmony.*

Altogether there are 89 chapters in the four Gospels combined, comprising no less than 3,780 verses (when the 12 verses from Acts are added in). But, in the final analysis, I trust that every essential thing that was written by the Gospel recorders has been accurately included within the *Harmony*. And, in this particular version of the Gospel record, there are nearly 180 separate events in the story of Jesus. Each of these events is listed separately and titled under a combination of either sections or sub-sections within the 18 chapters of the *Harmony*. Also, the *Harmony* is written in a chapter-and-verse-style, like that of any regular Bible. Additionally, to aid the reader in the study of this book, the various paragraphs contained herein are separated by extra spacing, so that the footnoting at the end of each paragraph is easier to distinguish and read.

**Paraphrase:**

I put the words of the various texts into modern English. To make the *Harmony* read smoothly, I dropped some repetitive words as well as a number of connecting phrases that one finds in the regular Biblical record in the original Greek. On the other hand, because a reader might use the *Harmony* as a reference book—that is, to study only one particular portion or story of the Gospel record at a time—I included certain explanatory phrases that may seem slightly repetitive to the one who might be reading the book from cover to cover as a complete story.

And, to give variety, I mixed up the varied names and appellations referring to Jesus, such as Lord, Savior, Christ, Master, Messiah, etc. Often the word I chose was not the one in the original text, but the meaning remains the same. And, throughout the entire *Harmony*, I capitalized any word (such as Savior, Lord, etc.) or pronoun (such as He, His, etc.) that directly refers to Jesus, or to God.

**Expanded Interpretive:**

Beyond paraphrasing the texts, in various ways I have added a great many brief comments that seek to interpret further the record of the Gospel. In effect, then, this book might accurately be called a "light" commentary. I did this because so many of the events—and especially the actual teachings of Jesus—in the Gospel record are so deeply profound, that when one reads them quickly, it is so easy to miss the powerful message which is borne by them. For this reason, I expanded on the original text by adding brief explanations—and in some cases, summaries—to the text. While this has resulted in a great expansion of the Gospel text, an overall understanding and appreciation of the message of the Gospel story is hugely enhanced.

But, I have, with some exceptions, made effort to make sure that I did not *in most cases* add a lot of extra wording to the text. I did this because I wanted to preserve as much as possible the "flavor" and uniqueness of the brief Biblical record. On the other hand, there were a fair number of times that a reasonably large number of words—and sentences, or even paragraphs—had to be added in order to give a proper interpretation to the texts. Quite often, I *embedded* these comments—whether brief or more extensive—within the texts themselves. These insertions generally include two types of commentary:

- I have included distances between most of the cities and provinces so the reader can visualize where these places were located relative to each other. Occasionally, too, I refer to specific dates and times that are, of course, not in the original text.

- I added many thoughts that help explain things that the average reader might not know, or that might be difficult to understand. I wanted to make sure that no concept was overlooked that needed to be explained further. Most of the time, in these cases, I have added just a few words, or phrases here or there. And, to preserve the flow of normal prose, no reference is made to the fact that these comments are added to the text. However, sometimes I added whole sentences. Most often, these added comments have been written to blend into the text, as though they were a part of the original account. A good number of these comments were placed at the end of paragraphs; some are interspersed throughout the text; quite often, they are at the beginning a paragraph.

On many other occasions, my added comments are somewhat lengthy. These usually include comments mostly composed of more than one sentence. In these cases, I added them to the *Harmony* in separate, fully-indented paragraphs. There are nearly 700 such paragraphs within the *Harmony.* They are called Explanatory Notes. These Notes are entirely my own comments, and are not in any way a part of the Biblical record. The *Harmony*, though, is constructed in such a way that the story line flows almost without interruption when one reads the book *with* or *without* the Explanatory Notes included.

In spite of these commentary insertions, I did not moralize or sermonize in these Explanatory Notes. I want the reader to draw his or her own moral conclusion as to the message a particular Gospel story may convey. I also, in most cases, made effort not to include additional thoughts that are not a part of, or are not implied by, the original text.

Furthermore, in my interpretations I did not use flowery words or colorful adverbs or adjectives. Adding these types of words would detract from the general style of the original text. However, if the context of a verse, or the choice of the original word used implied a stronger word, I felt free, in that case, to use a more powerful word. It should be noted, too, that I used a variety of words as synonyms for verbs such as "said," and "answered." But in any case, I sought a word that was reasonably implied by the intent of the text.

Additionally, when quoting Jesus and most other people, I often included extra words as though they were actually spoken by them. In these cases, I enclosed the entire remarks—*both original and added*—in quotation marks. However, by referring to the original Scriptural account (by using the footnotes at the bottom of the pages), the reader can easily determine which of these words were added.

In the process of writing the *Harmony,* I became aware of various concepts that are thematic to the ministry of Jesus. I included these thematic concepts in two places within the book—once near the beginning and then again near the end.

Furthermore, I tried to make the Gospel story "gender neutral." This means that on most occasions I used the phrases "he or she" or "his or her," and so forth, in interpreting various Biblical quotes, when in the original text only "he" or "him," etc., may be mentioned.

And finally, I thought that placing the tedious list of the "begats" in the main text of the *Harmony* would detract from the overall readability of the book. So, the two versions of Christ's genealogy—recorded by Matthew and Luke—are placed in the Supplementary Notes section of the first chapter.

**Chronological Timeline:**

In the *Harmony*, I have placed the various events of the life of Jesus on a timeline to show how they relate to one another chronologically. In the vast majority of cases, the Gospel records of Matthew, Mark, Luke, and John do not have such a time perspective—or at least a perspective that is obvious to the reader.

Also, interspersed throughout the *Harmony*, I included, by direct reference, different timeline segments in the Lord's public ministry. This means that I divided the three-and-a-half-year public ministry of Jesus into seven six-month segments, previewing and reviewing each time segment when it appears in the book. Then, near the end of the *Harmony*, I added a final review of the Lord's entire ministry.

In regard to chronology, I must say that the general and specific timing of the overall Gospel story, as well as of its various events, is not at all easy to determine. Actually, that is hardly surprising. This is because the dates that we are familiar with—B.C. ("before Christ") and A.D (Latin for "in the year of the Lord")—were determined many years after the actual events they represent took place. The problem was, of course, to determine the actual B.C. and A.D. dates of the various events in the life of Jesus, compared with the contemporary dating of the time. This involved the changing of known dates—often based on the reigns of various rulers—to the supposed dates of B.C. and A.D. The complexity of this procedure is significant, considering the fact that, in the ancient world, a number of often competing dating methods were used! So today, after much, much research, the *best* of modern scholarship has now determined that the original designation of the year of the birth of Christ (where B.C. ends and A.D. begins) was actually off by several years. In fact, no one really knows for sure what the exact date was. In reality some guesswork has had to take place to make such a determination.

I am not an expert in chronology. That being the case, I was almost totally dependent upon the work of others when I assigned various dates to the life and ministry of Jesus. So, for some very good reasons—well beyond the scope of discussion of this book—I have used the date 4 or 5 B.C. for the birth of Jesus, and A.D. 31 for His death. What is most important, though, is not the exact dating of the life and ministry Jesus as it relates to our time period, but rather, how the dates of certain events relate to each other. (See more on this in the Acknowledgement and Sources section near the back of this book.)

*One final note on chronology:* In the final Part of the *Harmony* (Chapters 14-18), when I referred to a particular date in the *Jewish* calendar (such as Nisan 9, etc.), I reckoned it according to Biblical timing: that is, "sunset to sunset" to determine when a day began and when it ended. However, when I referred to a particular day of the week according to *our* reckoning (Sunday, Monday, etc.), I figured the beginning and ending of each such day based on the usual "midnight to midnight" timing that we are accustomed to.

## Cross-References:

This feature of the *Harmony* is similar to the marginal texts one might find in many Bibles, yet on a lesser scale. The purpose of the cross-references in this book is to provide added Scriptural insight and foundation to the overall understanding of the Gospel story. Also, when certain events either are similar to, or may be related to other events in the Gospel record, these cross-references provide easy access to such events. Overall, there are about 1,600 of these cross-references in the *Harmony.*

## Supplementary Notes:

Within the main text of the book, I did not discuss, as any regular commentary might do, the various options faced in making a decision as to any particular interpretation of the text. Instead, I first determined what I thought the text was saying, and then I wrote it down from that sole perspective. This is because I wanted to preserve as much of the original thought of the text as possible, while, at the same time, provide an easy-to-read interpretive paraphrase of the Gospel record. A number of times, though, I did discuss some of the issues of interpretation I had to confront in making certain interpretations. These discussions are found in the Supplementary Notes located at the end of the various chapters. The notation for such notes is found as a superscripted letter of the alphabet placed within parentheses. Altogether, there are almost 450 of these Notes.

At the end of the *Harmony,* in the last Supplementary Note in Chapter 18, I listed a few things that really surprised—or even shocked—me when I was in the process of writing the book.

**Indexes:**

There are three large Indexes at the end of the *Harmony:* (1) a Chronological Index; (2) an Alphabetical Index; and (3) a Scriptural Index. First, the Chronological Index consists of the various chapter titles, sections, and sub-sections of the book, along with their Scriptural references and dating, so that the readers of the *Harmony* can easily follow the entire chronological timeline of the story of Jesus. Second, the Alphabetical Index contains a multitude of events and people, as well as sayings of Jesus, which are a part of the Gospel record. By using this index, the reader can quickly find where such events, people, and sayings can be found in the *Harmony.* And third, the Scriptural Index—made up of the 1,818 footnotes of the book, which are located at the bottom of most pages of the *Harmony*—serves as a very powerful tool to help the reader find in the *Harmony* the many verses of the Gospel account as they are recorded in the Bible. And, this index can be used to locate in the Bible a certain portion the *Harmony* may be referring to.

## — The Two Main Ways This Book Can Be Used —

First, the *Harmony* can be read as one might read a *biography* from cover to cover, much like the way one would read the Gospel story in any Bible. One can do so by either skipping the Explanatory Notes, or by reading the entire *Harmony,* including these Notes. In either case, as I've said before, the *Harmony* mostly reads as a seamless story.

Second, the *Harmony* can also be used a *reference work*—that is, as one might use a commentary—to quickly find and study one or more of the separate parts of the story of Jesus. However, in this case, this commentary is constructed in such a way that the comments are a part of the original text.

But to use the *Harmony* as such a reference work requires that the reader can easily find his or her way throughout the book in the search for a desired item, or quickly look up something in the Bible. Therefore, in the back of this book, under "Features for Using the *Harmony* as a Reference Book," tools which the reader can use to easily accomplish this task are listed in alphabetical order. It is suggested, though, that even if the reader does not plan on using the *Harmony* as a reference book, he or she would, at least, take a look at the rich resources these features can provide. But in any case, should someone be reading the *Harmony* from cover to cover and come across some unfamiliar symbol or insertion, this same list can provide an explanation for that puzzling item.

# — PREFACE —

Could it be that the One who was known as Jesus of Nazareth, born over 2,000 years ago, was really God, even the Creator of the heavens and the earth? Could He actually be the Savior of the world, the One who would be known as the Messiah of mankind? Well, the four writers of the Gospel story, and hundreds of millions of those who have believed their record, certainly think so!

To them it doesn't make any difference that millions of others in the world don't believe in the Biblical story of Jesus. Instead, their faith in the Man, Jesus, as the Messiah of the universe, is unshakeable. They, accordingly, have placed their trust in the words and works of His ministry. To them, the life of Jesus was wrapped up in the kind of miraculous things one might expect from One who is truly divine. The unexplainable is not a cause for them to doubt. Rather, the very real mysteries of the life of Jesus actually serve as a reason to accept Him as the Messiah.

To be sure, the entire Bible is a book that is based upon the incredible and the unfathomable. To true believers, the words of the Scriptures have served to open their minds to accept the unexplainable. Whether those who place their faith in Jesus as the Messiah look out into the great expanse of the universe, or peer into the microscope to find the hidden components of the tiniest cell, the amazing things of nature merely reveal the challenging mysteries of God upon which their faith is cast. For example, in Psalm 19:1, those who believe are directed to accept the reality of God's existence by viewing the majesties of the universe, when they are told that "the heavens declare the glory of God." And then, in Psalm 139:14, these same believers are commanded to trust in God's creative power by simply observing the marvelous workings of their own bodies, when they are told that they are "fearfully and wonderfully made." To them, if the mind-boggling wonders of the extended universe can be observed in the night sky, and the fantastic intricacies of the human body can be seen with or without a microscope, why is it so hard to believe that there is a creator God who revealed Himself to humanity, to save them from their sins? Why, then, is it so difficult to accept the story of the Gospel writers as being the absolute and genuine truth?

But beyond that, when one considers how truly limited the actual ministry of Jesus was, and yet how extensive its impact has become, there is then even more reason to believe in its miraculous, yes, even divine nature. For, it was for only three and half years—probably 42 months—that Jesus worked and ministered. Indeed, during His lifetime His influence extended over only a tiny portion of the earth's land mass and its population. And yet, today, who can seriously question the dramatic impact and extent of the movement of Christianity?

Of course, those who truly believe in the ministry of Jesus also believe that its broad influence is the result of another miracle. To them, the success of the Christian faith is not simply the result of the ministries of the Lord's twelve disciples and their subsequent followers whom the He left behind to work for Him in His behalf. Instead, their dramatic success was the result of the infusion of the Lord's divine, miracle-working power through the Holy Spirit who has empowered their ministry.

The story of Jesus—often called the Gospel's "good news"—is the unfolding of the many events in the life of the Man from Nazareth. His miracles inspire the heart; His teachings empower the mind; His sacrifice encourages the soul . . . and even changes the character.

In this book, the simple yet profound story of Jesus is told yet once more. It still has the power to change people for ever. Someone has said that the story of Jesus was the "greatest story ever told." Well, from my perspective, it is *still* the "greatest story ever told"!

— Bradley Galambos

The Messiah's ministry was a fulfillment of an Old Testament prophecy of the prophet Isaiah:

> God said, "Behold, I have chosen My Servant, the Messiah. He is My Beloved Son, the One in whom I have taken great pride. I will place My Holy Spirit in His life. And through the Spirit, He will preach justice and fairness to the peoples of the whole world, including the heathen. He will not be noted for loud debates with His enemies. Neither will He will make a big noise shouting out in the streets. Instead, a bruised reed"—the refuse of society—"He will not cast away. A smoldering wick"—the weak and struggling of the world—"He will not ignore or criticize. Rather, His goal will be to provide justice to those who feel defeated, so that they can taste victory for themselves. As a result, all the peoples of the world—from every circumstance and background—will have good cause to hope in the power of His Name." [Isaiah 42:1-4]

(As quoted from Matthew 12:17-21 in the *Harmony*.)

# Part I

*Beginnings:*

*From the Birth of Jesus*

*Through The Lord's First Miracle*

*(6 B.C.-A.D. 28)*

# Chapter One

## The Early Years of the Messiah—

**From the Mission of the WORD, to Jesus Grows Up in Nazareth**

**(Autumn, 6 B.C. - Autumn, A.D. 27)**

### The Mission of the WORD!
### (John 1:1-5, 9-14, 16-18)

### — The WORD as God, Creator, and Light {John 1:1-5, 9}

Throughout all eternity—even before the origin of any created thing—the WORD already existed. In fact, there was never a time that both the WORD and God did not dwell together in harmony. In addition to that, the WORD was also Himself fully God, possessing every divine attribute. To state it again, even before the world was created, the WORD was already in total and intimate partnership with God, even forever and ever. Furthermore, everything that has been made was personally fashioned by the WORD. In truth, nothing which has been created came into existence without His personal, hands-on involvement—not even one thing! [Genesis 1:1; Psalm 33:6, 9; Colossians 1:15-17; *Harmony* 16:101, 107/][(a)] [1]

To be sure, then, the WORD was the origin of all Life—in fact, He was Life itself! And in reality, the WORD still continues to be that never-ending source of Life. [Genesis 2:7] Additionally, this same Life also imparts the Light of Truth to all mankind. And finally, this Light of Truth constantly shines into the world to dispel the darkness of sin and falsehood. [*Harmony* 4:12; 11:42, 80] And there is no way that the darkness has been able to snuff out the brightness of that Light. Obviously, too, the darkness is not able to appreciate the Light's true beauty. Furthermore, the WORD is the Light of truth, who, when He came into

---

1 John 1:1-3

the world, had the potential to change dramatically every individual who lives on the earth. [*Harmony* 11:115][2]

## — The WORD as Savior {John 1:10-14, 16, 17}

Now the WORD lived for some time in the world that He had created. But most of His created beings did not recognize who He was, or what marvelous things He was able to do for them. The WORD also came to minister to His own people—the ones who should have recognized immediately who He was, and, consequently accepted Him. However, for the most part, they, too, rejected Him! [*Harmony* 12:123/4; 14:150] But, those few who did accept Him, and were willing to place their entire trust in Him as their Savior, to them the WORD imparted the privileged authority to become the children of God. Of course, their birth as children was not of the physical body. Neither was it of mere human passion, nor of the will of any man. Rather, it was the result of the miracle-working, spiritual power of God permanently to change their innermost being. [*Harmony* 11:60][3]

But to accomplish this miracle, the WORD for a time took upon Himself a human body of flesh, and personally lived here on earth among mankind. Fortunately, some of the people among whom He lived were determined to understand His ministry fully. They were totally committed personally to observe and reflect His perfect, glorious life, for His was a life full of the glorious virtues which exist uniquely in One who has come from the very presence of God. [*Harmony* 16:45] His life was also filled with God's favor and truth. And because of the fullness of His beautiful character, those who followed Him received an ever-increasing measure of His life-altering greatness within their own lives. This resulted in a continual, positive transformation of character within those who accepted Him. [*Harmony* 16:72, 73][(b)] [4]

The WORD also came to give new meaning and power to the Law of God. Now, the actual words of the Law were given by God through Moses. [Exodus 20:2-17] But a deeper understanding of the words of the Law, as it relates to the true religion of the heart, was explained by Jesus Christ—the WORD. [*Harmony* 5:19] Indeed, this broader spiritual meaning of life—which also includes the grace

---

2 John 1:4, 5, 9
3 John 1:10-13
4 John 1:14, 16

of forgiveness and the reality of a converted, victorious life—can be appreciated and experienced completely only through the continued ministry of the WORD. [*Harmony* 5:19/1, 2][5]

## — The WORD Speaks on Behalf of God {John 1:18}

Now it is a fact that no sinful being has ever seen God's face at any time. However, as previously said [*Harmony* 1:1], not only was He Himself divine, the WORD, for eternity, dwelt in the actual presence of God. And thus, when He lived among the people of the world, He did so as One who uniquely and intimately knew God. Therefore, He was able to demonstrate, by His lifestyle and words, a complete and full knowledge of the character of the Almighty. [Hebrews 1:1, 2][(c) 6]

> The WORD, then—the Man, Jesus—was, in a very real sense, the "VOICE" of God, to be clearly heard by mankind throughout the earth. Simply put, that is why He is called the "WORD!"

## The Recording of the Gospel Story (Luke 1:1-4)[(d)]

A few people have taken it upon themselves to tell the complete story of the life and ministry of Jesus, the Christ. They have compiled, from various sources—such as eyewitness accounts and those who had been preaching the words of Jesus—the details of the things that He accomplished while living among mankind. These have included, not only the specific facts of the Lord's life and ministry, but also the things He taught regarding God and His character.[7]

> Among the recorders of the story of Jesus, three of these compilers—Matthew, Mark, and John—were eyewitnesses to most of the things which Jesus did. Two of them—Matthew and John—were among His twelve closest disciples, who shared with others what they had learned directly from their Lord. One of the compilers—Luke—received his story from others who had communicated to him the events of the Lord's life.

---

5 John 1:17
6 John 1:18
7 Luke 1:1, 2

So, from various sources, of both the written and spoken word, these few authors delivered the Gospel story for all to read and hear. Thus, it seemed to be a good idea to carefully research these facts—starting even before the Lord's ministry began, and continuing up through His ascension into heaven—and write them down in their proper order. In doing so, and by determining their accuracy, all may know for certainty the exact truth about the things that are being taught regularly regarding the work of the Lord and Savior, Jesus, the Christ—the Messiah of all mankind![8]

## Two Miracle Babies
## < Autumn, 6 and 5 B.C. >
## (Luke 1:5-80)

### — Gabriel Gives Zacharias Some Good News
### < Autumn, 6 B.C. >
### {Luke 1:5-25}

> At this time in history—over 2,000 years ago—the Roman Empire ruled large portions of the world. Included in this was the nation of Israel, which was, in a practical sense, "occupied" by the Empire. The Empire allowed its subjected nations a certain amount of autonomy. In the case of Israel, while still under the control of Rome, the nation had a king. His name was Herod the Great. He was not a Hebrew by nationality, but he had been converted to Judaism. However, he was hardly a faithful Jew. [*Harmony* 11:58/]

It was during the days of Herod the Great, king of Judea [*Harmony* 1:61], that there lived a priest by the name of Zacharias. His wife, Elizabeth, also belonged to the distinguished family of Aaron, Israel's first High Priest. Both Zacharias and Elizabeth lived the kind of righteous lives that were pleasing to God. This meant that they were determined to live in complete harmony with the spirit and principles of the Ten Commandment Law of Scripture. [Exodus 20:2-17] They also conformed their lifestyle to all the important Jewish religious rituals of the day. However, they had no children, for Elizabeth had always been barren. Furthermore, they were both elderly—indeed, well beyond normal child-bearing age.[9]

---

[8] Luke 1:2-4

[9] Luke 1:5-7

Zacharias was a man of prayer. He had persistently prayed that he and his wife would have a child. But it now appeared, because of their age, that such a request would never be honored. Zacharias also prayed that the promise of the coming Messiah would soon be fulfilled.

Now, Zacharias was of the daily service order of the priesthood named Abia, which had been established by King David over a thousand years before. [1 Chronicles 24:1-19] On a particular day, Zacharias received a high, once-in-a-lifetime honor. He was chosen by the casting of lots—which is like the throwing of dice—to enter the Temple of God in Jerusalem to burn incense on the golden altar. This random selection process was necessary because there were so many priests in each order that it was impossible for each one to serve at his regularly appointed time. As he entered the Temple, Zacharias was dressed in a long white robe with a white turban on his head. [Exodus 28:40-43] And, as Zacharias was burning incense at the appointed hour of prayer, a multitude of people were praying outside in the court of the Temple. The rising smoke of the incense, which entered the Most Holy Place directly behind the altar where Zacharias stood, symbolized the prayers of the people ascending into the presence of God.[10]

At that exact moment, an angel from the Lord suddenly appeared, standing at the right side of the Altar of Incense! Seeing the angel, Zacharias was understandably deeply distressed and overwhelmed with fear. But the angel comforted the priest, by saying, "Don't be afraid, Zacharias, because your prayers both for a son and the coming of the Messiah have been heard by God. As a result, your wife, Elizabeth, will give birth to a son, and you must name him John"—which means, "Jehovah is gracious." "Consequently, Zacharias," the angel continued, "in your old age, your son will give you great joy and gladness! And many others will also rejoice at his birth. This is because God will consider your son to be a great man, and that he will do an equally great work for the Lord. However, he must not drink fermented wine, nor liquor of any kind." This indicated that John was to be a Nazirite, meaning "a separated one." A Nazirite was an individual who was uniquely consecrated by a vow to the Lord. Besides not drinking anything made from grapes, Nazirites never cut their hair during the time of their commitment to their vow. Most Nazirite vows were temporary in nature. [Numbers 6:1-21; *Harmony* 2:5/] However, in the case of John, he was

10 Luke 1:5, 8-10

to be a Nazirite for life. "In addition," the angel added, "your son will be filled with the Holy Spirit . . . even before he is born![11]

"And, during his ministry," the angel continued, "your son will preach a message of repentance which will inspire many of God's people to turn their hearts back to the Lord, their God. You see, your son will definitely be the forerunner of the Messiah, the Lord. Indeed, your son will minister in the spirit and power of Elijah the prophet." [Malachi 4:5, 6; *Harmony* 2:41] (Now, Elijah was an Old Testament prophet whose work led to a great, though temporary, spiritual reformation in Israel.) [1 Kings 17-2 Kings 2][12]

Then the Lord's angel concluded, saying, "Zacharias, your son will function as Malachi suggested: 'to unite together, once more, the heavenly Father with His children—the people of Israel.' [Malachi 4:6] But more than that, he will lead the way before the coming of the Messiah. In that regard, many of those who have been living wicked lives will have a complete change of thinking and attitude. Indeed, they will wisely switch from their sinful lives to lives of righteousness, so that they will be prepared for the arrival of the Messiah. As a result, many divided families will be brought back together again in a great spiritual revival which will sweep over the nation of Israel."[(e) 13]

> For many years, the Hebrew people had been looking forward to the arrival of the Messiah. The word Messiah comes from a Hebrew word, meaning, "the Anointed One." (In the Greek language, the word for Messiah is "Christ.") It was the dream of the entire nation of Israel that an individual would be "anointed"—or specifically chosen by God—to lead them to national greatness and peace. As a consequence, they would be victorious over their enemies. [Isaiah 9:6, 7] (The angel who communicated with Zacharias told him that his son would not be the actual Messiah, but that he would prepare the way for the coming of this Messiah.) [Isaiah 11:1-5][[1]]
>
> However, there was to be a deep spiritual aspect to the ministry of the coming Messiah. He would lead the people to experience something much more important than national and political greatness. Instead, he would lead them back to their God—to reconcile them, in harmony

---

11 Luke 1:11-15
12 Luke 1:16, 17
13 Luke 1:17

and peace, with their Creator. In short, the Messiah would cleanse them from their sins, and restore righteousness within their lives.[2]

But Zacharias protested the angel's promises, exposing his doubts regarding the news that the angel bore. He questioned, "How can I be sure this will happen as you say? Remember, both my wife and I are far too old to be having a child!"[14]

The angel responded, "My name, indeed, is Gabriel, the angel who is constantly in the presence of God." (To be sure, Gabriel was a powerful angel who served as a special heavenly messenger for the Lord. [Daniel 8:16-26; 9:21-27; *Harmony* 1:18-23]) Gabriel continued with his message to Zacharias, declaring, "You can count on the truthfulness of my message when I announced this good news to you of the upcoming birth of your son. And why? Because I received it directly from God Himself! And it was He who sent me to communicate this message to you. Therefore," Gabriel warned Zacharias, "because you have doubted my words, as a punishment, you will not be able either to speak with your mouth, or hear with your ears, until my prediction of the birth of your son comes to fruition in the natural course of time."(f) [15]

Meanwhile, the people outside the Temple grew impatient and wondered why Zacharias was inside the Temple longer than the usual, carefully prescribed time. According to tradition, before they were allowed to leave for home, they had to wait for the priest to come out of the Temple, and pronounce a benediction upon them. However, when Zacharias finally appeared, he was unable to speak to them, just as the angel had declared. Because of his inability to speak, he was not able to pronounce the customary blessing upon them. Nevertheless, through various gestures, he tried to explain to the people what had happened to him while he was in the Temple. The crowd assumed, based upon his efforts to communicate with them, that Zacharias had seen some kind of vision from God.[16]

Within a few days, when his Temple service in Jerusalem was completed, Zacharias returned to his home. Soon after, Elizabeth became pregnant, just as the angel had predicted. For the first five months of her pregnancy, Elizabeth remained in seclusion, carefully to prepare her heart for the solemn task of raising

---

14 Luke 1:18

15 Luke 1:19, 20

16 Luke 1:21, 22

her son to be the forerunner of the Messiah. Without a doubt, though, Elizabeth was thrilled with the prospect of having a child, for she said, "I am so thankful that the Lord has seen fit to give me a child. In doing so, He has removed from me the shame and humiliation of being barren." In ancient days, barrenness was considered a sign of great misfortune, perhaps even a divine curse. [*Harmony* 1:20][17]

**— Gabriel Gives Mary Some Great News**
**< Spring, 5 B.C. >**
**{Luke 1:26-38}**

In the sixth month of Elizabeth's pregnancy, God sent the angel Gabriel [*Harmony* 1:15] to Nazareth, a city in the northern province of Galilee of the nation of Israel. There, he was to visit a certain young, unmarried woman. Her name was Mary. She was legally engaged to a man named Joseph. Both Mary and Joseph were direct descendants of David, Israel's most famous king.[(h)] [18]

When Gabriel entered Mary's house, he greeted her with the words, "Rejoice, you honored one of God! You have received a special measure of God's grace. Indeed, may the Lord be with you! Among all the women of the world you are especially blessed by God." Mary, understandably shocked by these incredible words from the angel, tried to figure out what this strange greeting might mean.[19]

"Now don't be afraid, Mary," Gabriel continued, "for God looks with great kindness upon you!" Then, getting to the purpose of his mission, the angel stated, "Consider this: You will become pregnant and give birth to a Son. You shall name your Son, 'Jesus'"—which means, "Jehovah is salvation." "And," the angel went on, "your Son will be great. He will be recognized as the Son of the Highest One in heaven. [*Harmony* 1:22] In fact, the Lord God will restore, through Him, the kingship of His father, David. And furthermore, your Son will reign over the house of Jacob—the nation of Israel—forever. Indeed, His kingdom will never end!" [*Harmony* 1:40, 51] (It was commonly taught in Israel that the Messiah would be known as the Son of David, and that He would re-establish David's kingship.)[20]

---

17 Luke 1:23-25
18 Luke 1:26, 27
19 Luke 1:28, 29
20 Luke 1:30-33

Even though Mary believed the angel, she was puzzled as to how this seemingly impossible miracle would take place. Thus she asked, "But how can this be? I have never been with a man! I'm a virgin!" [*Harmony* 11:46][21]

The angel answered, "The Holy Spirit will come upon you! Your pregnancy will take place by the power of the Most High God who will spread over you. Your Son will be holy. You see, then, that's why, as I have said, 'He will be called the "Son of God."' [*Harmony* 1:20] In addition, Mary, your relative, Elizabeth, even though she is very old, is also pregnant with a son. [*Harmony* 1:17] For many years it has been said of her that she was barren, but now she is already in her sixth month! Mary, when God declares that something will happen, nothing is impossible!" [*Harmony* 1:38, 40][(g)] [22]

In summary, Gabriel meant that Jesus, as the "Son of the Highest One in heaven" [*Harmony* 1:20], would be the "Son of God." And, by restoring the "kingship of His father, David" [*Harmony* 1:20], Jesus would also be the "Son of Man." Clearly, by possessing this dual nature—being both the "Son of God" *and* the "Son of Man"—Mary's Child would be none other than the long-looked-for Messiah! And, the Messiah's kingdom—which would last forever—would be both spiritual and temporal in nature. [Isaiah 61:1-4][[1]]

But in what sense was Jesus the "Son of God"? Before His conception in the womb of Mary, Jesus was fully God. He was equal to God. He was God. He was not, in any way, less than God. [*Harmony* 1:1; Isaiah 9:6] But when His essence was placed in Mary's body, the Lord took upon Himself another role. From that moment, until His ascension into heaven after His resurrection, He would be subservient to God, the Father. Thus, during His time on earth, God would be called His "Father." [Philippians 2:5-11] And, throughout His human existence in this world, as the "Son of God," Jesus was dependent upon God as His "Father," just as any human being might be dependent upon an earthly father. In that sense, then, Jesus was called the "Son of God."[[2]]

All the members of the Godhead—Father, Son, and Holy Spirit [*Harmony* 18:88]—were involved in this marvelous plan which Gabriel described to Mary. First, miraculously and inexplicably, the essence of one Person

---

21 Luke 1:34

22 Luke 1:35-37

of the Godhead—the One called the "Son"—was to be placed within the womb of Mary, to grow as a baby in her body! Second, this miracle would happen through the power of the Holy Spirit—another Person of the Godhead. In addition, the Holy Spirit, who descended upon Jesus at His baptism, would be His constant companion and help throughout His entire life. Third, the remaining Person of the Godhead—the one known as the "Father"—would be in control of the Lord's life while He dwelt on this earth. Once more, then, that is why Jesus would be known as the "Son of God."[3]

Again, Gabriel told Mary that her Son would be the promised Messiah! Indeed, He would be more than a mere human being—He would, in fact, be divine! He would be the Son of God. Nevertheless, He would also be the Son of Man, being conceived in Mary's womb. Thus, the designations, "Son of God" and "Son of Man," would both accurately and equally apply to Him. Without question, Mary's Baby would possess a totally unique nature. From Mary, He would be human. From the work of the Holy Spirit within her, Jesus would be divine. The union of the human and divine natures—often called the Incarnation—would be a miracle of indescribable proportions! [*Harmony* 3:91/][4]

Completely awed, Mary blurted out, "Look at me! I am only the humble servant of the Lord. I am ready for you to do with me as you wish!" At that instant, the angel disappeared from her sight.[23]

### — The Mothers of the Two Miracle Babies Meet
### < Spring, 5 B.C. >
### {Luke 1:39-56}

A short time later, Mary rushed to the hilltop region of Judea, probably about 65 miles south of Nazareth. There, in an area near Jerusalem, Israel's largest city, she arrived at the town where Zacharias and Elizabeth lived. Mary entered the house of Zacharias, and greeted Elizabeth, his pregnant wife. And, as soon as Elizabeth heard the greeting, the baby growing within her womb, jumped![24]

The pregnant mother, inspired by the Holy Spirit, cried out with a loud voice, "Mary, of all women you have received a special blessing from God, who has also placed a blessing upon the Child growing in your body! How can it

23 Luke 1:38
24 Luke 1:39-41

be that you, the mother of my Lord, should honor me by visiting in my home? Imagine this: At the very second I heard your greeting, the baby growing within my own body jumped for joy! Indeed, Mary, everything that has been told to you regarding the Child within you will happen because you have believed the angel when he spoke to you."[25]

> By these glowing words, Elizabeth declared that Mary was, in fact, the mother of the Messiah. But more than that, by calling Mary's Baby her "Lord," Elizabeth prophetically confirmed that the Baby in Mary's womb was, indeed, the "Son of God"!

Amazed by these words, Mary jubilantly responded, "My soul greatly uplifts the Lord in praise! My spirit exalts God, my Savior, because He has showered me, His humble servant, with honor even though I have nothing good to give back to Him! So, indeed, for that reason, all generations, from this moment forward, will consider me to be especially honored. This is true because the Mighty One has done majestic things for me. Holy is His name!"[26]

Mary continued, declaring, "God's mercy will abide with unceasing generations of those who seek to personally know Him. To be sure, our God has performed awesome deeds with His arm. He has shattered those who considered themselves to be great in their own minds. He has toppled rulers off their thrones, while, at the same time, lifted up the afflicted ones who are humble in their hearts. With tasty food, He has fed to complete satisfaction the rejected ones who are hungry. And those, who have hoarded everything for themselves, He has sent away with hunger pains. He has shown compassion to His servant, Israel, because He never forgets the commitment of mercy He has made to us, His people. It was just as the Lord promised to Abraham, our fathers, and to us: that He would take care of His people forever." [Genesis 12:1-3][27]

After this amazing meeting of the two mothers, both pregnant with their miracle babies, Mary stayed with Elizabeth throughout the next three months. Mary did not return to her home in Nazareth until after Elizabeth's baby was born.[28]

---

25 Luke 1:41-45
26 Luke 1:46-49
27 Luke 1:50-55
28 Luke 1:56

**— The Birth of John the Baptist**
**< Summer, 5 B.C. >**
**{Luke 1:57-80}**

Finally, the time arrived for Elizabeth to give birth to her son. Hearing of the birth of her baby, both her neighbors and relatives recognized that the Lord had obviously shown great mercy to the elderly mother. They rejoiced with her in her good fortune.[29]

On the eighth day after the baby's birth—when all Hebrews boys were circumcised [Leviticus 12:3] and officially named—Elizabeth's relatives were sure that the child's parents would call him Zacharias, in honor of his aged father. In fact, that's what they were already calling him. But his mother protested, "No! No! You are to call him John!"—a name which means, "Jehovah is gracious."[30]

However, the relatives debated with her, saying, "But there is no one in your family with that name. So why are you going to use the name John for your baby?" Then Zacharias's relatives used signs to communicate with him because he was still unable to hear or speak. They asked him which name he, as the father, desired for the son of his old age. [*Harmony* 1:15][(i)] [31]

After signaling for a writing tablet to be brought to him, he clearly wrote the words, "John is his name!" All the relatives were truly surprised that both Zacharias and Elizabeth were in total agreement as to what the boy's name should be. And, as soon as Zacharias made it clear that the baby's name would be John, his mouth was opened and the old priest was able both to speak and to hear again. The first words he spoke were those of praise to the Lord! Accordingly, a profound sense of awe and wonderment settled upon everyone living in the area.[32]

From that moment on, the details of the miraculous birth of John were repeatedly discussed throughout the entire hill country of Judea. The people kept thinking of the baby, John, saying in utter amazement, "Who must this child be? What will be his future?" Among the people, there was no question that the Lord was with the baby and his parents in a most unusual way. [*Harmony* 2:18][33]

---

29 Luke 1:57, 58
30 Luke 1:59, 60
31 Luke 1:61, 62
32 Luke 1:63-65
33 Luke 1:65, 66

About that time, Zacharias, under the complete control of the Holy Spirit, began to prophesy regarding the soon-coming Messiah. He, alluding to Old Testament prophecies, cried out, "Praise to the Lord God of Israel [Psalm 41:13; 106:48], for He has come to us in the time of our distress and has worked out redemption for His people by sending them the Messiah. He has raised up the authoritative Horn of Salvation and victory for us through the dynasty of King David, His servant." [Psalm 132:17] (In Jewish thought, a horn represented power and authority.) "Indeed," Zacharias continued, "this is what God declared by the mouth of the holy prophets from ancient days. God has promised us many things. He has promised us deliverance and salvation from those who wish to do us harm. He has promised us freedom from the domination of all those who truly despise us. He has fulfilled His promises to our fathers to show mercy toward us. Indeed, He has promised never to forget His sacred covenant of mercy—the one which He swore to our father, Abraham. [Genesis 12:1-3; Psalm 105:8, 9] This is to make sure that we, when delivered from the oppression of our enemies, shall be able to serve Him without being afraid of those who would do us harm. He has also removed from us the oppressive guilt of our many sins. To be sure, we will live fearlessly, filled with complete consecration and righteousness. And we will dwell in God's presence for the rest of our lives." All these things that Zacharias mentioned referred to the blessings that would occur when the Messiah would arrive.[34]

And then, speaking directly to his infant son, Zacharias declared, "And you, my little child, will be known as the prophet of the Most High, because you will lead and prepare the way before the presence of the Lord, even the Messiah, who is to come. This child of mine is the one who will explain to the Lord's people the truth of salvation. [Isaiah 40:3] He will reveal to Israel what it means to have complete forgiveness of, and total cleansing from, all their sins." [*Harmony* 2:3][35]

Concluding his prophecy, Zacharias added more words regarding the coming Messiah by declaring, "Because of the deepest, most tender mercy of God, we will see, as it were, the Rising of the Sun in our nation"—which is the coming of the Messiah. "For, when He arrives, He will shine as the bright morning sunlight upon those who have been fearfully cowering in the black darkness of sin and despair, even within the bleakest shadow of death. [Isaiah 9:2] In doing so, He

---

34 Luke 1:67-75

35 Luke 1:76, 77

will guide our feet onto the correct and straight path of peace which the Lord has provided for us."[36]

With such a prospect and blessing, it is not surprising that the child John grew up with a strong intellect, a keen sense of righteousness . . . as well as possessing an independent spirit![37]

## The Birth and Infancy of the Messiah
## < 5 and 4 B.C. >
## (Matthew 1:1-2:23; Luke 2:1-40; 3:23-38)

### — An Angel Visits Joseph
### < Summer or Autumn, 5 B.C. >
### {Matthew 1:18-25}

Now the circumstances surrounding the birth of Jesus—the Messiah—had the potential to cause considerable trouble. For even though Mary, the future mother of Jesus, was legally engaged to marry a man named Joseph, she became pregnant before they were officially married. Of course, as Mary had already been told, this pregnancy was the result of the work of the Holy Spirit. That is, the conception of her Child was not the result of the action of any man. [*Harmony* 1:22; 11:46][38]

However, no one in Nazareth, not even Joseph, knew this astounding fact. So when Mary's pregnancy became obvious, her husband-to-be, who was a fair and morally principled man, did not want to expose Mary to ridicule. Neither did he desire that she face a possible public trial and be accused of adultery. [Deuteronomy 24:1] Therefore, Joseph thought that perhaps the best thing to do would be to break off the engagement quietly—by a divorce—and have Mary sent away to give birth to her Baby secretly. A divorce was necessary, for in those times an engagement was a legal commitment, bound by law. To break this commitment, as Joseph was considering doing, required a legal action to nullify the engagement.[39]

But while Joseph was in the process of considering what would be the best course of action in this confusing situation, he was interrupted by an angel from

---

36 Luke 1:78, 79
37 Luke 1:80
38 Matthew 1:18
39 Matthew 1:19

the Lord who appeared to him in a dream. The angel declared, "Joseph, son of David, do not be afraid to take Mary as your wife! Her pregnancy is the result of a miracle of the Holy Spirit. It is not the result of the action of any man! [*Harmony* 1:22] Mary will give birth to a Son, and you shall name Him, Jesus"—which means, "Jehovah is salvation"—"for He is the One who will save His people from their sins." [*Harmony* 1:20][40]

> By this message to Joseph, the angel clearly established the fact that the Baby in Mary's womb was Israel's long-awaited Messiah. Furthermore, as the angel indicated, the primary purpose of the ministry of Jesus, as the Messiah, would be to bear upon Himself the sins of His people. [*Harmony* 2:49, 53]

Now all these things occurred as a fulfillment of a prophecy given by the Lord through the prophet Isaiah, who said, "Behold, the virgin shall conceive a Child in her womb, and she shall give birth to a Son, and they will give Him the title Emmauel," which means—in the Hebrew language—"God with us." [Isaiah 7:14][(j) 41]

> This prophecy clearly indicated that the Baby—the promised Messiah—would be divine in nature, and that, while He lived on the earth, it would be as though God were dwelling among mankind.

So Joseph awakened from his sleep and did exactly what the angel instructed him to do. Accordingly, he married Mary immediately. However, he would have no intimate relations with her until she gave birth to her first-born Son.[42]

### — The Messiah Is Born
### < Autumn, 5 B.C. >
### {Luke 2:1-7}

It was in those days that Augustus, the Roman Caesar, issued a decree that a census registration—probably for taxation purposes—was to be taken in every place where Rome was in control. This decree included the land of Israel. This registration first occurred while Cyrenius was the governor of Syria.

---

40 Matthew 1:20, 21

41 Matthew 1:22, 23

42 Matthew 1:24, 25

Caesar's decree required that people return to their city of ancestral origin for the registration.[43]

Because both Joseph and Mary were of the house and family of David [Romans 1:3], they needed to travel over 70 miles to Bethlehem of Judea, the birthplace of David, to comply with the decree. Bethlehem was about five miles due south of Jerusalem, the main city of Israel. Thus it was that Joseph left Nazareth in Galilee and began to travel south with Mary, his pregnant wife.[44]

Mary was in the last stages of pregnancy. And soon after their arrival in Bethlehem, the time of her Son's birth approached. Because there was no room for the couple to lodge in an inn, they stayed in an animal stable! While there, Mary gave birth to her first-born Son. She wrapped Him in strips of cloth—the usual garb for infants—and, for His first bed, she laid Him in a manger—a common feeding trough for animals![45]

## — The Angels Visit the Shepherds
## < Autumn, 5 B.C. >
## {Luke 2:8-20}

That night, in the nearby countryside, there were shepherds staying in the fields, taking turns tending their flocks of sheep. [*Harmony* 11:110] Suddenly, an angel of the Lord appeared to the shepherds. In fact, the angel's brightness filled entire sky with a brilliant light that lit up the countryside. Not surprisingly, the shepherds were very frightened by this glorious display.[46]

But the heavenly messenger tried to comfort them by declaring, "Don't be afraid! For, listen, I announce to you some very good news! It will cause great joy, not just for you, but for all peoples everywhere. For today, in the city of David—Bethlehem—there has been born for you the Savior, who is the Christ"—the Messiah—"even the Lord! And this will be the indication to you that you have found the right Baby: You will find the Infant wrapped in strips of cloth . . . lying in a manger!"[47]

---

43 Luke 2:1-3
44 Luke 2:4, 5
45 Luke 2:5-7
46 Luke 2:8, 9
47 Luke 2:10-12

Instantly appearing with the angel was a multitude of others angels—in number, about the size of an army. They praised God, declaring, "May there be great honor to God who dwells in the heavens! And on earth, may God's favor and peace abide with men who possess a positive attitude toward both God and mankind!"(k) [48]

When the angels disappeared back into the heavens, the shepherds excitedly said to one other, "Indeed, let us go right away to Bethlehem! We must see this thing that has occurred which the Lord has revealed to us!"[49]

So they quickly made their way to Bethlehem and searched out the stable where Mary, Joseph, and the Baby, were staying. There, they found the Child as He lay in the manger. After observing the Child for awhile, they left and told everyone about the things that they had seen. They also proclaimed the message they had heard from the angel regarding the Baby—that He would be the promised Messiah. Those who heard the testimony of the shepherds greatly marveled at what they described. From that time onward, the shepherds continued to tend their flocks, constantly giving glory and praise to God for all the things that they had both seen and heard. They were happy that events had taken place just as the angel had described to them. They were very excited that they had been privileged to the see the infant Messiah. However, Mary secretly cherished these things within her heart. She often meditated deeply upon all that had happened and what it might mean.(l) [50]

> Why would the Son of God, the Savior of the world—the Messiah—when born, have to be placed in a manger? First, the humble birth of Jesus would give hope to those who are poor and downtrodden. And, second, as Jesus explained as an adult, He came to serve mankind, not to be served. [*Harmony* 16:19, 20] His humble life bears testimony to this fact. There would be plenty of time in eternity for the Lord to live again in the glory of His Father. [*Harmony* 16:116] But until then, His humble origins and life would be an inspiration to the weak and distressed, as well as an object lesson to all that the greatness of life is found in serving others rather than being served.

---

48 Luke 2:13, 14

49 Luke 2:15

50 Luke 2:16-20

## —Jesus Is Circumcised
## < Autumn, 5 B.C. >
## {Matthew 1:25; Luke 2:21}

After eight days, Jesus was circumcised according to Jewish law. [Leviticus 12:1-3] Circumcision had its roots in the founding of the Hebrew nation under Abraham. [Genesis 17:9-14; Exodus 12:48] This rite gave Jesus all the privileges and responsibilities which male Israelites possessed. It was at that time the Baby was officially named Jesus. This was the same name that the angel Gabriel had commanded both Mary and Joseph that the Child should be called, even before His conception. [*Harmony* 1:20, 40][51]

## —Jesus Is Dedicated in the Temple
## < Autumn, 5 B.C. >
## {Luke 2:22-38}

Forty days after the birth of Jesus, according to Mosaic law [Leviticus 12:1-8], the time of Mary's ceremonial purification as a mother had expired. [Leviticus 12:4] So the family made their way five miles north to Jerusalem to dedicate the Child to God. It was written within the law of the Lord that "every first-born male that opens the womb shall be dedicated unto the Lord as holy." [Exodus 13:2][52]

Because of his economic circumstances, Joseph brought the required offering of those who were poor. This was in accordance with the law of the God, which said that the poor could bring for a baby dedication, "a pair of turtledoves, or two young pigeons." [Leviticus 12:8][53]

Now it so happened that there was a man in Jerusalem whose name was Simeon, who was known to be righteous and faithful in his religion. He had been awaiting eagerly for the arrival of the Messiah. The Messiah was commonly referred to as the "Consolation of Israel," for it was expected that the Christ would give "comfort" to the entire nation. Additionally, the Holy Spirit, who had filled Simeon's life, had revealed to him that he would not die until he personally saw, with his own eyes, the Lord's Messiah—even the Christ, the Anointed One of the Lord.[54]

---

51 Matthew 1:25; Luke 2:21

52 Luke 2:22, 23

53 Luke 2:24

54 Luke 2:25, 26

Simeon was especially led by the Holy Spirit to be in the Temple area that day when Joseph and Mary, according to the law [Exodus 13:2], brought Jesus in for the dedication service. Taking Jesus in his arms, Simeon praised the Lord, and tearfully declared, "Ah! Now, my Master, You can allow Your servant to die in peace, as you have spoken! For my eyes have seen Your Salvation, the One whom You have made ready and ordained to be seen by all peoples of the earth. For He shall be a Light to reveal the truth to the Gentiles—indeed, unto the entire world. [Isaiah 9:2; 60:1-3] At the same time, He will give honor and praise to Your own people, the Israelites."[55]

Both Joseph and Mary were literally stunned by the extraordinary words which Simeon spoke regarding their Child! Then, Simeon pronounced a blessing upon them and added to Mary, "Please note: This Child has been selected for a very special purpose. Because of Him, many in Israel will stumble and fall in their sinful condition, while others will be lifted up toward heaven by the conversion of their hearts. He will act as a 'sign,' as it were, sent from God for people either to accept or to reject. In their doing so, in the end, the secret thoughts of many hearts will be revealed." [*Harmony* 7:15][56]

> The future ministry of Jesus would serve as a time of testing for the people of the world. Those who accepted His ministry would be saved. Those who rejected it would be lost. It is in this sense that His ministry would be a "sign" to every person who would be confronted with its terms, either to accept or reject it.

"But, Mary," Simeon added cautiously, "I also tell you that a huge sword will be driven deep into your soul!" Here, Simeon was speaking of the future crucifixion of Jesus and the severe pain it would certainly cause the heart of Mary. [*Harmony* 17:127][(m)][57]

While Simeon was making these predictions, Anna, a prophetess, the daughter of Phanuel, of the tribe of Asher, arrived in the Temple area. Anna's husband had died just seven years after their marriage. In fact, she had been a widow for 84 years, making her well-over 100 years old! Anna never left the

---

55 Luke 2:27-32

56 Luke 2:33-35

57 Luke 2:35

Temple grounds. Instead, she served there constantly, fasting and praying during both the morning and evening services of the Temple.(n) [58]

At that very moment, overhearing Simeon's blessing, she approached the family of Jesus. Under the inspiration of the Holy Spirit, Anna immediately recognized Jesus as the promised Redeemer. As a result, she praised the Lord with words of thanksgiving. And, afterward, with great joy, she constantly shared this news with all those who would come to the Temple complex. Anna declared to those eagerly anticipating the coming of the Messiah that she had seen the actual Messiah with her own eyes! She made it clear that it was He who would save them from their sins and ultimately restore Jerusalem to national and moral greatness.[59]

## —The Genealogy of Jesus(o)
## {Matthew 1:1-17; Luke 3:23-38}

It should be noted that Jesus, as a human being, came from a very good family tree. Being a Hebrew, this was quite important. Of course, His human ancestry began with Adam. Through both His earthly father, Joseph, and mother, Mary, Jesus was related to Abraham, the father of the Hebrew people. Jesus was also a part of the royal bloodline of Israel—including King David—as well as many other well-known rulers of the Jewish nation's history. [*Harmony* 11:25][60]

## — The Visit of the Magi
## < Winter, 4 B.C. >
## {Matthew 2:1-12}

Some time after Jesus was born in Bethlehem of Judea, while Herod the Great was the king [*Harmony* 1:9], wise men—known as the Magi—traveled from a nation far to the east of Israel. [*Harmony* 11:25/][61]

> The wise men came from perhaps as far as 800 miles away, maybe from the nation of Persia. They were experts in the known sciences of the day—especially that of astrology, and the general study of the stars and other heavenly bodies.

---

58 Luke 2:36, 37

59 Luke 2:38

60 Matthew 1:1-17; Luke 2:23-38

61 Matthew 2:1

As soon as the Magi arrived in Jerusalem, they began to ask around, "Where is the One who has been born King of the Jews? We have been following His star ever since it first arose in the east. The star has led us here . . . and we have come to worship the King!"[62]

> A divinely appointed star had been placed in the heavens, marking the event of the birth of Jesus. And it was this star that the wise men had observed and followed as it moved across the sky. The Magi, who regularly and carefully watched the heavens, noticed the star's mysterious appearance. They were familiar with the Scriptural prophecy which said, "There will rise a star out of Jacob"—that is, from the land of Israel. And also, a "Scepter"—symbolizing a king—"shall appear out of the land of Israel." [Numbers 24:17] This prophecy further predicted the ultimate victory of Israel over its enemies. The wise men assumed that this would happen as the result of a King who would take control of the nation. Ultimately, this King would lead his nation in the victories which were predicted in the prophecy. Therefore, the Magi came, wanting to worship this new, conquering King. And, because the wise men were following the star, they could travel only at night. This meant that it must have taken them quite a long time—perhaps weeks, or even months—to travel the distance from their home country to Israel. But they were undeterred in their desire to find this new King.

When it came to Herod's attention that these wise men were asking questions around town, he was very concerned, because an apparent rival to his throne now existed. Even the entire city of Jerusalem was upset because there was no telling to what lengths the extremely jealous—and notoriously cruel—Herod might go to destroy this potential usurper to his throne![63]

Herod brought together all the nation's head priests and those who were especially trained in the Scriptures. He earnestly inquired of them just where this potential King, or Messiah—the Christ—was to be born. They boldly replied, "Why, He is to be born in nearby Bethlehem of Judea! This has been predicted by the prophet Micah, who said, 'And you, Bethlehem in Judea, you are in no way the least important among the leading ruling cities of the nation. For from within your midst will appear a Ruler who shall be the Shepherd of Israel—that is, the Messiah.'" [Micah 5:2; *Harmony* 11:25] The Messiah, of whom Micah

62 Matthew 2:1, 2

63 Matthew 2:3

wrote, and the so-called "King of the Jews," mentioned by the wise men, was one and the same Person.[64]

Upon hearing this, Herod privately called for the Magi and interviewed them to ascertain from them the precise time when they had first observed the star. [*Harmony* 1:70] Then, secretly lying to them, he sent them on to Bethlehem, instructing them, saying, "Please go and search carefully for this Child. And when you have found Him, report back to me, so that I, too, may go and worship Him!" [*Harmony* 1:68][65]

Having heard the king's instructions but unaware of Herod's true motives, the wise men made the five-mile trip to Bethlehem, which is where the eastern star continued to lead them. In fact, it directed them to the place where the Child was located, for amazingly, the star stopped directly over the precise spot where the Baby lay! Noticing that the star had ceased its movement, the Magi were completely overjoyed and thrilled, for their long search for the Messiah King was finally accomplished![66]

When they entered the house, they saw the Child with His mother, Mary. Immediately, they prostrated themselves on the ground before the Baby and worshipped Him. They, opening their treasure chests, presented to Him kingly gifts: gold, frankincense, and myrrh.[(p) (q) 67]

> Gold, of course, has been considered valuable throughout all recorded history. Frankincense is a white resin from the frankincense tree which grows in only a few locations in the Middle East. When burned, it gives off a pleasant aroma. In Bible times, it had significant commercial value. Myrrh is a resin from an equally rare tree. In the case of myrrh, though, not only does it have a pleasant aroma when burned, but it was considered in ancient days to have medicinal value. Thus, it was a worthwhile commodity either to possess or to sell.

Before having a chance to bear the news of the Baby to King Herod [*Harmony* 1:65], the wise men were directed by God in a dream not, under any

---

64 Matthew 2:4-6
65 Matthew 2:7, 8
66 Matthew 2:9, 10
67 Matthew 2:11

circumstances, to return to the king. So accordingly, using a different route, they returned to their own country, avoiding Jerusalem altogether.[68]

It is puzzling why the Jewish leaders, who knew where the Messiah was to be born [*Harmony* 1:64], never sought, as did the wise men, to see the Baby for themselves. Why is this? No doubt, they had heard the amazing story of Zacharias, a fellow priest. [*Harmony* 1:11-17] Certainly they must have heard about the testimony of the shepherds [*Harmony* 1:46, 50], and that of Simeon and Anna. [*Harmony* 1:52-59] And, they were obviously well aware of the experience of the wise men. [*Harmony* 1:62-65] So then, why did they not check out the story for themselves? Their pride was the problem! They were offended that God had bypassed them and communicated the Gospel story to humble shepherds. And in the case of the wise men, the Jewish leaders considered them to be nothing more than foreigners—that is, non-Jews. Thus, in the minds of these leaders, the Magi were merely heathen men. The hard-hearted attitude of the leaders of Israel was already manifested within their lives even while Jesus was yet a baby! This persistently negative attitude would play a huge role in the Savior's extremely problematic relationship with the Jewish leaders throughout His entire ministry.[1]

Thus far, in the life of Jesus, His future ministry as the Messiah was confirmed by a number of individuals and sources. First, there was Gabriel, who was sent by God, to both Zacharias [*Harmony* 1:11, 12] and Mary [*Harmony* 1:20], to declare the truth regarding who Jesus would be. Second, an angel—perhaps Gabriel—communicated the same message to the Lord's earthly father, Joseph. [*Harmony* 1:40, 41] Third, both Zacharias [*Harmony* 1:34-36] and Elizabeth [*Harmony* 1:25], under the inspiration of the Holy Spirit, verified the same message. Fourth, the angels who appeared to the shepherds declared the truth of the Lord's calling as the Messiah. [*Harmony* 1:47, 48] Fifth, Simeon [*Harmony* 1:54-56] and Anna [*Harmony* 1:59], both inspired by God, explained the Messiah's work and ministry. In addition, there were the miraculous circumstances surrounding the birth of both Jesus [*Harmony* 1:21, 22, 40-42] and John. [*Harmony* 1:11-15, 22] Sixth, the wise men followed the amazing star that was, itself, a fulfillment of prophecy, thus confirming the Gospel story. [*Harmony* 1:62] In short, the evidence

[68] Matthew 2:12

> pointing toward the Baby Jesus as the Messiah was quite overwhelming, powerful, and convincing.[2]

**— The Family of Jesus Flees Into Egypt**
**< Winter, 4 B.C. >**
**{Matthew 2:13, 14, 16-18}**

As soon as the Magi left, an angel from the Lord suddenly appeared to Joseph in a dream. The angel urgently commanded, "Get up and get moving! You must take the Child and His mother with you and quickly escape into Egypt. And stay there until I tell you otherwise. You must do this because Herod is actively planning to find the Baby in order to kill Him!" [*Harmony* 1:63, 65, 66, 68] Immediately obeying, Joseph gathered up Jesus and His mother, and leaving that night, began to head toward Egypt which was about 250 miles to the southwest.[69]

When Herod figured out that the Magi had tricked him, he was beside himself with rage and indignation. Therefore, he sent soldiers to kill all the male children of Bethlehem and its surroundings, who had reached their first birthday. Herod's selection of this age was based upon the information he had obtained from his interrogation of the wise men regarding the precise time when the star which they had followed first appeared in the heavens. [*Harmony* 1:65] It had been approaching a year since the star first appeared.[(r)] [70]

The horrendous slaughter of the babies by King Herod was predicted, in part, by the prophet Jeremiah, who wrote, "A voice is heard in Ramah"—which is a town fairly close to Bethlehem. "Also there is heard great weeping and wailing. It is the sound of Rachel lamenting an awesome loss. She absolutely refuses to be comforted, because her children are all dead." [Jeremiah 31:15][(s)] [71]

> When the nation of Judah—the "Rachel" in the prophecy—went into Babylonian captivity in 586 B.C., many of the nation's young children died. The wailing of their mothers back then was *similar* to the weeping of the mothers who lost their sons as the result of Herod's cruelty during the time of Jesus.

---

[69] Matthew 2:13, 14
[70] Matthew 2:16
[71] Matthew 2:17, 18

**—Jesus and His Family Return to Nazareth**
**< Summer, 4 B.C. >**
**{Matthew 2:15, 19-23; Luke 2:39, 40}**

Jesus and His parents remained in Egypt until Herod died. Then, at that point, the Lord's angel appeared once more to Joseph in a dream and commanded, "Get up now! Take both the Child and His mother and return to the land of Israel, for those who have tried to snuff out the life of the Baby are now all dead."[72]

So Joseph began his return trip to Israel. However, he had heard that Archelaus was king in his father, Herod's, place. Joseph was afraid to return to Judea, because Archelaus was particularly noted for his cruelty, even worse than his father's—if that were possible! In addition to that, through yet another dream, he was strongly warned not to settle in Judea. And because he had previously concluded all the ceremonies required by the law of the Lord—that is, the Child's circumcision [*Harmony* 1:51] and dedication [*Harmony* 1:52-59]—Joseph bypassed Judea altogether and returned directly to the northern province of Galilee, to their home village of Nazareth. The entire trip, from Egypt to Galilee, was well over 300 miles to the northeast.[73]

When the family of three left Egypt, after Herod's death, it was a fulfillment of the prophecy of Hosea which said, "Out of Egypt I have called My Son." [Hosea 11:1][(t)] [74]

When Joseph and his family arrived back in Galilee, they settled permanently once again in their own town of Nazareth, thus fulfilling some prophecies which had suggested, "He, the Messiah, will be called a Nazarene"—that is, one who is from Nazareth.[(u)] [75]

While living there, Jesus continued to grow and mature. He was strong in body and personality, exhibiting an unusual amount of wisdom for His age. Also, it was obvious that the favor of the Lord was clearly present within His life.[76]

72 Matthew 2:15, 19, 20
73 Matthew 2:21, 22; Luke 2:39
74 Matthew 2:15
75 Matthew 2:23; Luke 2:39
76 Luke 2:40

## The Childhood and Young Manhood of Jesus
## < Spring, A.D. 9-A.D. 27 >
## (Luke 2:41-52)

### — Jesus' First Passover Visit
### < Spring, A.D. 9 >
### {Luke 2:41-50}

Jesus' parents would customarily, on a yearly basis, make the 70-mile trip south to Jerusalem to celebrate the Passover, the first of the yearly Jewish Festivals.[77]

> The Passover was a celebration of the time in the history of the Hebrews when they were freed from Egyptian bondage. [Exodus 12:1-51] This celebration, correctly understood, also looked forward to the time when the Messiah would arrive, and free Israel—even the whole world—from the slavery of sin. [1 Corinthians 5:7]

When Jesus reached the twelfth year of life, He was able, for the first time, to attend the Passover with His mother and father. Traditionally, this was the time in a Jewish boy's life when he could begin to participate in many of the customs of the nation's religion, including the public celebration of the Passover festival.[78]

At the conclusion of the full week's celebration of the feast, when the family was heading back northward to Nazareth, Joseph and Mary noticed that the young Jesus was not with them. They were not aware that He had remained in Jerusalem. Instead, they figured that He must be somewhere in the midst of the large, crowded caravan of pilgrims heading back home with them. So for a day they did not seem to worry. But after that day's journey, when they still did not see Him, they began to search seriously for Him among the various relatives and friends. But neither Mary nor Joseph was able to find the Child! Therefore, they headed back to Jerusalem to continue their search for Him there.[79]

On the third day, after looking for Him everywhere, they finally found Jesus in the Temple complex. There He was, sitting within a circle of especially learned teachers of the Law. He was listening to what they were saying. He was also asking them challenging questions. All of the religious leaders in His presence

---

77 Luke 2:41, 42
78 Luke 2:42
79 Luke 2:43-45

were amazed at the depth of the young Person's understanding of the Scriptures, as well as the intelligent answers He gave to their pointed questions. When His parents saw this, they, too, were just as astonished.[80]

Nevertheless, Mary, who had been very upset because Jesus had been missing for such a long time, questioned Him. She asked rather reprovingly, "My Child, why have you done this to us? Look! Your father and I have been franticly searching for you. We have been so very worried!"[81]

But Jesus calmly responded to His parents with childlike simplicity, saying, "But why were you looking for Me? Don't you know that it is necessary for Me to be doing My Father's work in His Temple?" However, His parents had no clue what He meant by such an explanation, especially the part about doing His Father's work. What could that mean? they wondered. [*Harmony* 2:71/][82]

> These are the first recorded words of Jesus. In them, it is clear that He already knew that the God of heaven was His Father! This indicated that Jesus, at the tender age of twelve, was aware of the fact that He and the God of heaven had a special relationship—that He was, in fact, the Son of God. His parents, though, quite surprisingly—considering what had been told to them regarding their Child [*Harmony* 1:20, 40]—remained puzzled by the words of their young Son.

**—Jesus Grows Up In Nazareth**
**‹ Spring, A.D. 9—Autumn, A.D. 27 ›**
**{Luke 2:51, 52}**

After the excitement of that first Passover, Jesus obediently went back with His parents to Nazareth, and continued to subject Himself to them. In the meantime, Mary secretly treasured within her heart the things which Jesus had said to them while in the Temple, vividly recalling each detail of what had happened there. What could all this mean? she continually asked herself. [*Harmony* 2:71/][83]

For Himself, Jesus continued to progress. He also grew mentally strong, possessing an unusual amount of wisdom. He also matured physically. And both

---

80 Luke 2:46-48
81 Luke 2:48
82 Luke 2:49, 50
83 Luke 2:51

the favor of God and of His fellow citizens of Nazareth was showered upon Him.[84]

> For about the next eighteen years, Jesus remained in Nazareth with His family, living in all but complete obscurity. In fact, there is absolutely no additional Biblical record of what Jesus did during that time period except a passing reference to the fact that He was a carpenter, the same occupation as His earthly father, Joseph. [*Harmony* 8:60]

**Supplementary Notes:**

**(a)** **[1:1]** The record says that Jesus (the WORD) was both *with* God and that He *was* also, Himself, God. This would indicate that there are at least two individuals who are part of the divine Godhead. No doubt this includes the One called the *Father* and the other One known as the *Son*. From other sources (*Harmony* 18:88), we know that there is also a third Person to this Godhead, the One known as the *Holy Spirit*.

**(b)** **[1:4]** The sentence that reads, "His was a life full of the glorious virtues which exist in One who has come from the very presence of God," is based on the interpretation of the word, and its concept, that is translated in the KJV as "only begotten." How did I arrive at this long interpretation from a single expression? There are two basic meanings of the phrase "only begotten." (1) It can refer literally to one who has been the first and only individual, born to someone. This is *not* the best meaning of this phrase as it applies to Jesus. (2) The second meaning is more apropos. In this case, it refers to the rights and privileges of the one who is the first born and/or the only child within a family. Of course, Jesus, in heaven, was not born. He always existed as God. Instead it refers to Jesus in His *incarnate*—or human—state. As One who knew God in an intimate way in heaven, when He came to this earth, He was unique in nature. There was no one like Him—before or after! Why? First, He knew God the Father, for He was with the Father. Second, even as a human being, He had a unique knowledge of God. He also possessed the power of God, for He was God. And His privileges as God—even as a human being—were unique and unparalleled throughout the history of the universe. It is because of this sense of the meaning of the phrase, "only begotten," that I translated and interpreted the text as I did.

---

[84] Luke 2:52

**(c)** **[1:6]** The sentence reads: "And thus, when He lived among the people of the world, He did so as One who uniquely and intimately knew God." The expression that is so interpreted in the verse, is the same word used, as is described in **Note "b"** above.

**(d)** **[1:6/+]** Luke originally wrote his book for Theophilus, a friend of his (referred to as "most excellent Theophilus" in Luke 1:3, KJV). Rather than referring to Theophilus in the text of the Gospel *Harmony*, I have mentioned him only here in the Supplementary Notes. However, the basic message which Luke wrote to Theophilus, outlining his motivation for the writing of his book (Luke 1:1-4), is recorded within the main text of the *Harmony* as *generally applying* to anyone who might be reading it.

**(e)** **[1:13]** The verse seems to indicate a revival of the relationship between *human* fathers and their children. That is quite appropriate. However, in a broader sense, it could also refer to the relationship between God—as a *Father*—and His *children*—the human race. I chose, therefore, to incorporate this additional concept into the *Harmony*.

**(f)** **[1:15]** Luke seems to indicate that Zacharias's relatives repeatedly tried to communicate with him. If he could hear, such repeated efforts to communicate with him would not be necessary. Therefore, it appears that Zacharias was both dumb *and* deaf. However, the record mentions specifically only his inability to speak. In the *Harmony*, though, I mentioned both.

**(g)** **[1:18]** Clearly, Joseph was of the house of David. But was Mary? While there is no direct statement as such, the following texts strongly hint at this possibility: Acts 2:29, 30; 13:23; Romans 1:3; 2 Timothy 2:8. They speak of Jesus being of the seed of David. It is doubtful that this truth would apply only to Joseph, who was *not* the *actual* birth father of Jesus. But if Mary was, indeed, also of the house of David, these verses would truly apply. Accordingly, I put it as such into the *Harmony*.

**(h)** **[1:22]** It is often said that Jesus and John the Baptist were cousins. From the Biblical record, it seems they may have been. This possibility is based upon the KJV translation of a Greek word in Luke. The KJV translates the word—referring to the relationship between both Jesus and John's mothers—as being that of a *cousin*. Actually, the word is best translated as *relative*, rather than *cousin*. This means that though Jesus and John were probably cousins, the precise relationship between the two is unknown.

**(i)** **[1:31]** See **Note "f"** above.

**(j)** **[1:41]** The methodology of Matthew in quoting Old Testament references and describing them as being "fulfilled" by various parts of the ministry of Jesus provides a challenge for Bible scholars. These so-called prophetic fulfillments (in Matthew 1:22, 23; 2:15, 17, 18), appear, on the surface, not to apply as Matthew uses them. In other words, he *seems* to be *misapplying* the Old Testament Scriptures. In my opinion, there is no completely satisfying answer to this apparent dilemma. However, there are two possible explanations that are *reasonable.*

The **first** explanation is based upon a principle called *primary* and *secondary* prophetic applications. The primary application is what the original prophecy meant to the one who wrote it, and to whom it was directly written. The secondary application is what the prophecy might mean to those to whom the prophecy was not originally written.

The prophecy of Matthew 2:15 is an example. In the original prophecy (Hosea 11:1), the Lord referred to the time when He led the children of Israel—His "son" in the prophecy—out of Egypt during the Exodus. Again, this is the *primary* or *main* application. However, in Matthew 2:15, the Gospel writer used it to refer to Jesus, the "Son" of God, being called out of Egypt after the death of Herod. This is a *secondary* or *lesser* use of the prophecy. Even though this may not be satisfying to some, this is a principle that is used a number of times in the Bible. Apparently, this is what Matthew did. But there must be a strong word of caution: This procedure can be used only by a prophet writing under inspiration, such as in the case of Matthew. One can readily see how disastrous things can become if any one of us would start using this principle as we choose! There would be no limit to what could be proved from the Bible. So, while the principle of the primary and secondary use of Bible prophecy may be valid, it must be remembered that it is valid only for those who wrote the Bible, where New Testament writers quote Old Testament writers. That is the only safe course to follow.

The **second** explanation is to suggest that Matthew used the prophecies as *illustrations* of certain things in the ministry of Jesus. In the case of Matthew 2:15, Matthew is, in effect, saying, "*Just* as God led the nation of Israel—His 'son'—out of Egypt during the Exodus, *He also* led Jesus—His 'Son'—out of Egypt after the death of Herod." Perhaps this is what Matthew meant. But, as in the case of the first explanation, this procedure is to be used exclusively by Bible writers. Once again, it would be disastrous for anyone else to have this liberty. All kinds of concocted theories could be devised if this principle would be used without caution.

**(k) [1:48]** The KJV translation of part of the text "peace, good will toward men," may not be based on the best Greek manuscripts. I chose to follow a more untraditional interpretation based on what many consider to be better manuscripts.

**(l) [1:50]** The reactions of Mary and the shepherds are recorded in the verses, Luke 2:16-20. Verses 17, 18, and 20 record the reaction of the shepherds, while verse 19 records Mary's reaction. For better continuity, I regrouped the reactions—the shepherds' first, and Mary's second—in the *Harmony*.

**(m) [1:57]** In the original text, Simeon's statement regarding the sword that would pierce the soul of Mary is parenthetically inserted in the middle of his statement about Christ's ministry being a "sign" to the world. I thought it best that, in order to highlight the statement regarding the sword, in the *Harmony*, it should be recorded as a separate statement. Accordingly, I have done so.

**(n) [1:58]** It is not clear whether the 84 years refers to Anna's age or her widowhood. It could go either way. If it referred to her widowhood, Anna would be about 100 years old or more! I chose to take this position, because I thought it more interesting to consider!

**(o) [1:59+]** The record of the genealogy of Jesus is found in two places within the Gospels: Matthew 1:1-17 and Luke 3:23-38. These genealogies differ in two major aspects. (1) Matthew traces the Lord's family tree from Abraham *forward* to the time of Jesus; while Luke traces the Lord's family history from Jesus all the way *back* to Adam's creation. (2) There are some names listed in Matthew that are not listed in Luke; likewise, there are some names listed in Luke that are not recorded in Matthew. The differences between these two lists could lead one to think that they are contradictory. It can be quite puzzling! In truth, however, very few people are really concerned in today's world regarding the actual genealogy of Jesus. Besides, a reconciliation of these two lists is not within the scope of the *Harmony*. Accordingly, it is suggested that interested individuals should seek a good commentary that will effectively deal with the issue. Also, because such "begats" can be tedious to many modern readers, I listed them in the Supplementary Notes section, rather than in the main text of the *Harmony*. What follows, then, is a paraphrase of the two versions of the genealogies, first Matthew's, and then Luke's.

**Matthew 1:1-17:** This is the book of the genealogy of Jesus, the Christ: He was the son of David, who was the son of Abraham. Being a son of both Abraham and David was important, for the Messiah was to come from both of these Jewish families. [Genesis 22:18; Isaiah 9:6, 7; 11:1; Acts 2:29, 30; Galatians 3:16] Now, Abraham was the father of Isaac, who was the father of Jacob, who, in turn was the father of Judah and his brothers.[1]

Judah was the father of Pharez and Zarah, whose mother was Tamar. Pharez's son was Hezron, who was the father of Aram. Aram was the father of Amminadab, who was the father of Nahshon, who was the father of Salmon. Salmon's son was Boaz, whose mother was Rahab of Jericho.[2]

In turn, Boaz was the father of Obed, whose mother was Ruth of the book of Ruth. To Obed was born Jesse, who became the father of David, the famous king of Israel. David was the father of Solomon by Bathsheba, one of his wives, who originally was the wife of Uriah, the Hittite.[3]

Solomon, in turn, was the father of Rehoboam, who was the father Abijah, who was the father of Asa, who was the father of Jehosaphat, who was the father of Jehoram, who was the father of Uzziah.[4]

To Uzziah was born Jotham, who was the father of Ahaz, who was the father of Hezekieh, who was the father of Manasseh, who was the father of Amon, who was the father of Josiah, who was the father of Jehoiachin, as well as his brothers. This was at the time of the Babylonian Captivity.[5]

After the Babylonian Captivity, Shealtiel was born to Jehoiachin, and Shealtiel was the father of Zerubbabel, who was the father of Abiud, who was the father of Eliakim, who was the father of Azor, who was the father of Sadok, who was the father of Achim, who was the father of Eliud, who was the father of Eleazar, who was the father of Matthan, who was the father of Jacob.[6]

Jacob's son was Joseph, the husband of Mary. Mary was the mother of Jesus, the Christ—the world's Messiah.[7]

In summary, then, all the generations from Abraham to David are fourteen; and from David to the Babylonian Captivity are another fourteen generations; and from the Captivity to the time of Jesus was an additional fourteen generations.[8]

**Luke 3:23-38:** Jesus was supposedly the son of Joseph—supposedly because Joseph wasn't truly His birth father, but only his earthly father in the sense that he was the one who provided for Jesus. Now, Joseph was the son of Heli, the son of Matthat, the son of Levi, the son of Melchi, the son of Janna, the son of Joseph, the son of Matthathias, the son of Amos, the son of Nahum, the son of Esli, the son of Naggai.[9]

Naggai was the son of Maath, who was the son of Mattathias, the son of Semei, the son of Joseph, the son Judah, the son of Joananes, the son of Rhesa, the son of Zerubbabel, the son of Shealtiel, the son of Neri, the son of Melchi, the son of Addi, the son of Cosam, the son of Elmodam, the son of Er.[10]

Er was the son of Joses, who was the son of Eliezer, the son of Jorim, the son of Matthat, the son of Levi, the son of Simeon, the son of Judah, the son of Joseph, the son of Jonan, the son of Eliakim, the son of Melea, the son of Menam, the son of Mattatha, the son of Nathan, the son of David, the king.[11]

David was the son of Jesse, who was the son of Obed, the son of Boaz, the son of Salmon, the son of Nahshon, the son of Amminadab, the son of Admin, the son of Aram, the son of Hezron, the son of Pharez, the son of Judah, the son of Jacob, the son of Isaac, the son of Abraham, the father of the Hebrew people.[12]

Abraham was the son of Terah, the son of Nahor, the son of Serug, the son of Reu, the son of Peleg, the son of Eber, the son of Salah, the son of Cainan, the son of Arphaxad, the son of Shem, the son of Noah of the days of the Flood.[13]

Noah was the son of Lamech, the son of Methusaleh, the son of Enoch, who walked with God. Enoch was the son of Jared, the son Mahaleel, the son of Cainan, the son of Enosh, the son of Seth, who was the third son of Adam, who himself, was as it were, the son of God![14]

**1. Matthew 1:1, 2**
**2. Matthew 1:3-5**
**3. Matthew 1:5, 6**
**4. Matthew 1:7, 8**
**5. Matthew 1:9-11**
**6. Matthew 1:12-15**
**7. Matthew 1:16**
**8. Matthew 1:17**
**9. Luke 3:23-25**
**10. Luke 3:26-28**
**11. Luke 3:29-31**
**12. Luke 3:32-34**
**13. Luke 3:34-36**
**14. Luke 3:36-38**

**(p)** **[1:67]** The word translated as *house* in the verse refers to a real house, not a stable. Considering the fact that the wise men arrived a good deal of time after the birth of Jesus (Matthew 2:7, 16), it is unlikely that Jesus was still in the stable and/or the manger. Assuming that there would later be "room in the inn," it is hard to conceive that people would have long allowed a baby to remain in a manger! Unfortunately, though, such a possibility messes up Christmas Nativity scenes!

**(q)** **[1:67]** Traditionally, it is said that there were three wise men (or Magi). However, the Bible does not give the actual number. There were at least two, but the exact number is unknown—in fact, there might have been many more! It has been suggested that the number three was chosen because the Magi brought three gifts to Jesus: gold, frankincense, and myrrh; this actually, though, proves nothing.

**(r)** **[1:70]** The Jews used inclusive reckoning for aging. This means that a child was considered one year old at birth—that is, in his or her first year. Thus, a two-year-old would refer to any child who has reached his or her first birthday. In the *Harmony*, I have stated it as such.

**(s)** **[1:71]** (Please first see **Note "j"** for added help.) This is a most confusing use of Bible prophecy. This prophecy in Jeremiah originally referred to the anguish that mothers must have felt when the nation of Judah was taken captive in 586 B.C. *That* prophecy is based, in part, on the story of Rachel in Genesis 35:18, who died in the same area while giving birth to her son, Ben-oni—meaning, "son of my sorrow." So, Jeremiah partially used the Rachel story as a basis for his prophecy. Thus, the Matthew 2:17, 18 prophecy is a *secondary* use of the Jeremiah prophecy, which is also based, in a *secondary* sense, on the Rachel story! To state it again: the mothers of Bethlehem wept when their children were killed by Herod, in the same way that the mothers of Judah wept when the nation was taken captive in 586

B.C. In turn, this event was similar to the weeping of Rachel just before she died, knowing that she would not see her son, Ben-oni (later named Benjamin), grow up. Still confused? In that case, read a good commentary that explains Matthew's method of using Bible prophecy.

**(t)** **[1:74]** See **Note "j"** above.

**(u)** **[1:75]** There are no Old Testament texts which say this. This fact causes a bit of a dilemma for Bible scholars. It is possible, however, that Matthew is referring to some prophecies, oral or written, that were not a part of Scripture, the references of which we have no present knowledge.

# CHAPTER TWO

## THE EARLY MINISTRY OF JESUS—

**From the Ministry of John the Baptist, to the Lord's First Miracle**

**(Autumn, A.D. 27 - Spring, A.D. 28)**

### The Ministry of John the Baptist
### < Summer and Autumn, A.D. 27 >
### (Matthew 3:1-12; Mark 1:2-8; Luke 1:80; 3:1-18; John 1:6-8, 15, 28)

John, the son of Zacharias and Elizabeth [*Harmony* 1:29-32], was now about 30 years old. He was living secretly in the desert places, away from the masses, waiting to hear from the Lord. At last, John received God's official call to begin his public ministry, which began in the fifteenth year of the reign of Tiberius Caesar, the Roman emperor. It was in the spring of the year A.D. 27. At that time, Pontius Pilate was the governor of the province of Judea, which was located in southern Israel. The northern and eastern portions of the nation—Galilee and Peraea—were under the rulership of the tetrarch, Herod Antipas. (A tetrarch was a ruler on a slightly lower level than that of a king.) His brother, Herod Philip, was tetrarch of Ituraea and Trachonitis, areas north and east of Galilee, respectively. And finally, Lysanias was tetrarch of Abilene, which was located east and south of Ituraea. All of these areas were under the control of the Roman Empire. The High Priest of Israel was Joseph Caiaphas, who had replaced his father-in-law, Annas.[1]

Obeying the command of the Lord, John revealed himself to the people and started to preach the Word of God in the desert areas of Israel. This included the wilderness section of Judea, west of the Jordan River. It also included the Bethany region of Peraea, east of the Jordan, just north of the Dead Sea. This latter area was about 25 miles northeast of Jerusalem.[(a)][2]

---

1 Luke 1:80; 3:1, 2

2 Matthew 3:1; Mark 1:4; Luke 1:80; 3:3; John 1:28

In his preaching, John emphasized the necessity of baptism. This baptism ritual—performed by immersing an individual in water—symbolized repentance, which is a change of one's thinking, that, in turn, leads to a dramatic alteration of a person's lifestyle. Also, baptism illustrated the forgiveness and the washing away of one's sins. [Romans 6:2-6] John specifically declared, "You need to repent, for the kingdom of heaven has come close to you." This meant that the gift of salvation was immediately available for all those who wished to receive and experience it. [*Harmony* 1:35; 2:19, 22, 30, 47; 14:56; 16:17/][3]

John was the one whom the Old Testament prophet, Malachi, had indicated would come. Malachi—as though God was speaking directly to the coming Messiah—had declared, "Watch carefully! I am sending My personal emissary before Your face, who will prepare the way before You." [Malachi 3:1] Specifically, this prophecy predicted that John would prepare the way for the coming of the promised Messiah. Also, another Old Testament prophet, Isaiah, prophesied in his scroll, saying of John and his ministry, "The voice of one who, like a loud-sounding trumpet, is crying out in the desert places, declaring, 'Clear the way for the coming of the Lord'"—that is, the Messiah. "'Make sure His paths are straight. Every crevasse will be filled up. Every mountain and hill will be leveled off. All the sharp curves will be made straight. And the bumpy roads will be made smooth. And in the end, all mankind shall clearly observe the saving power of the Lord at work.'" [Isaiah 40:3-5; *Harmony* 2:68/2; 10:72; 12:123/5; 16:86][(b) 4]

> As in the case of Malachi's prophecy, Isaiah's prediction referred to the work of John in preparing the Jewish people for the coming of the Messiah and His ministry. In ancient days, when a king was traveling, soldiers would prepare the roads for the monarch as he proceeded on his journey. The rough places would be made smooth. Sharp turns were rounded off, and high hills were flattened. This elaborate procedure, performed for earthly kings, was illustrative of the preparation needed for the coming of the heavenly King—the Messiah. That is, John's ministry was to prepare the hearts of the people, by repentance, forgiveness, and transformation, to receive the message of the Messiah when He would soon arrive.[1]

---

3 Matthew 3:1, 2; Mark 1:4; Luke 3:3

4 Matthew 3:3; Mark 1:2, 3; Luke 3:4-6

For years, the Hebrew people had been looking for the Messiah. [*Harmony* 2:38] It was the nation's hope that the Messiah would restore the glory of the kingdom of David. Ever since the time of David's reign, and that of his son, Solomon, Israel went through one tragedy and humiliation after another. For nearly a millennium after the reign of these two kings, the Hebrew people's dream of international greatness had turned into a nightmare. Initially, there was the split of the country into two smaller nations during the reign of Solomon's son—Israel in the north and Judah in the south. [1 Kings 12:1-24; 2 Chronicles 10:1-19] Next, there were years of apostasy, leading to the embarrassing captivities of both nations, first Israel [2 Kings 17:1-41], and then Judah. [2 Kings 25:1-30; 2 Chronicles 36:10] The glorious Temple, designed by David and built by Solomon, was demolished. [2 Chronicles 36:17-21] Even after a restoration of the southern kingdom of Judah, true national greatness never materialized. There were constant problems and wars with surrounding nations. Most galling of all, in the days of Jesus, Israel was under the nearly complete domination of the Roman Empire.[2]

Thus, the Hebrew people longed for the arrival of the Messiah, who would, according to their understanding of the promise of God [Isaiah 61:4-9], restore their nation to the political greatness and influence that it had enjoyed during the days of David and Solomon. At least, that was the hope of the majority of Israelites. However, there were some in the nation who knew that Israel's fall from greatness was the result of their own failure, as a people, to remain faithful to God and His laws. They further knew that there was no hope that the nation would ever re-establish itself as a great country until it rejected its shameful apostasy and returned fully to God. To these people, the coming of the Messiah would provide an opportunity for Israel to be restored to a high level of spiritual morality and righteousness, rather than national greatness. [Isaiah 61:1-3] National glory would follow, they believed, only if the people first turned back to God. Thus, whether the Hebrew people looked for a Messiah who would lead them to national greatness or to spiritual purity or both, the entire nation was desperately longing for the Messiah's appearance.[3]

But most importantly of all, the Scriptures predicted that the Messiah would bear the sins of the world. He would be the Redeemer of the peoples of the entire earth, even the Savior of the whole world. [Isaiah

53:4-6, 10-12] While most Jews seemed to care little for this aspect of the work of the Messiah, it was, in fact, His most important function. Fortunately, there were some in Israel who did care very deeply about this facet of the Messiah's ministry. [*Harmony* 2:4/3, 4][4]

And so it was at this precise time that John the Baptist began his work of calling people to repentance. Indeed, the impact of his ministry upon the nation—and ultimately the world—would be nothing short of dramatic.[5]

Now John was different from just about anyone else preaching the Word of God at that time. John's physical appearance was similar to that of the prophets of Old Testament days, rather than that of the Jewish priests of his day, with their ornate attire. His clothing was constructed from the cloth made from camel's hair. John had a crude leather belt tied around his waist. His diet consisted of locusts—that is, the pods of carob trees—and wild honey. [*Harmony* 8:5/, 23, 30] [(c) 5]

John was a Nazirite from birth. [*Harmony* 1:11] The word "Nazirite" means one who is "devoted" or "separate." The vows of a Nazirite included a complete refusal to drink anything made from grapes. Also, Nazirites never cut their hair during the time of their vow. Because he was a Nazirite from birth, John's hair and beard must have been very long, and, no doubt, rather shaggy looking! But, despite his rough exterior, his preaching of repentance was like a breath of fresh air to the common people of Israel. It was a message that they were not used to hearing from their other religious teachers . . . but it was a message they desperately needed to hear.[(d)]

John's preaching was so powerful that people actually left the comfort of the cities and villages and went out into the wilderness to hear him preach! Indeed, a constantly swelling multitude of people from Jerusalem, Judea, and the area around the Jordan River came out to see John. So many came to listen to him that it seemed as though the entire population of Judea and Jerusalem, at one time or another, heard John preach! John baptized, by immersion, many of these listeners as the result of their acknowledgement of their sins. [*Harmony* 2:3, 19; 8:24] Consequently, John became popularly known as "John the Baptist."[6]

---

5 Matthew 3:4; Mark 1:6

6 Matthew 3:1, 5, 6; Mark 1:4, 5

> Now, it was a practice among the Jews to baptize Gentiles—that is, non-Jews—who wished to accept the Jewish religion. What was unique about John's ministry, however, was that he was primarily calling Jews to repentance and baptism. This was not the norm! Jews, for the most part, because they were Jews, did not think that conversion, symbolized by baptism, was necessary for them. In short, they did not believe that they needed to repent as did the heathen Gentiles. They believed that salvation was given to them by divine right and natural birth. Because they were born as Jews, they believed that their nationality was sufficient for salvation. Further, they believed that they could save themselves by their own efforts. Nevertheless, John called the Jews to repentance. He emphasized that they, like all peoples, needed to repent and change their lives through the power of God. Accordingly, the Jewish people came by droves to receive forgiveness and be baptized.

When the Jewish leaders were told excitedly of the ministry of John, they went out to listen to him for themselves. Among those who came to see what all the excitement was about was a large contingent of the religious hierarchy of the nation, especially the Pharisees and Sadducees. Some of them came just to observe. But some came to be baptized themselves.[7]

> Now the Pharisees were the religious conservatives of that day. Their beliefs were very legalistic. The Sadducees, a smaller group than the Pharisees, were the liberals. They were so liberal that they even doubted the reliability of most Scripture. As might be expected, these two groups of religious teachers were rivals.[1]

> And the losers in this power struggle were the common people. The extreme views of these two religious philosophies left the masses confused and bewildered. On one hand, the Pharisees taught a religion that was hardly more than a list of "do's and don'ts." The list of regulations and rules was so long and oppressive that the people languished in guilty despair and utter frustration. While the Pharisees most likely claimed to depend on God for their salvation, the truth was that they actually relied upon their own works as well as on their national birth as Jews. On the other hand, the Sadducees were so unsure of the truthfulness of most Scripture that their teachings were more political and secular than spiritual. It was as if from the Pharisees the people received too much

7 Matthew 3:7

religion, and from the Sadducees not enough! What were the people to do? That is why the sound, inspired, and deeply spiritual preaching of John attracted so many followers. John and his ministry was the primary topic of conversation around the entire nation of Israel. From the perspective of the Pharisees and Sadducees, they were losing their grip on the people. [*Harmony* 5:22, 22/; 13:57][2]

It so happened that, in order to appear that they were in accord with the many people who viewed John as a great spiritual man, perhaps even a prophet, these leaders acted as though they were equally excited about what John was preaching and doing. In fact, some of the Jewish leaders even asked John to baptize them. However, most of these people were quite insincere![8]

So on every occasion when John saw within the crowds of those who came to hear him phony, insincere people—especially these hypocritical Jewish leaders who were coming to observe or to be baptized—he was very distressed. That is why he cried out to them in extremely blunt language, "You children of vipers! Who has warned you to flee from the anger of God's judgment which is coming upon you as a result of your transgressions? If you really want to repent of your sins, then you need also to change your wicked lifestyle. That is the only way that you will be able to prove to God that you are truly sincere in all your requests for baptism." [*Harmony* 7:11; 14:64][9]

John added, "Yes, I know what you're thinking. You say, 'We are the children of our father, Abraham.' Well, don't even think that way! Being a child of Abraham does not save you . . . even though that is what you think! Let me tell you, it would be easy for God to create children of Abraham from these stones that you see lying about in this desert! [*Harmony* 11:61-66] The truth is that this very moment God is judging you. And His judgment is like an axe, already slicing into the roots of trees that have failed to produce good fruit. Yes, that is the kind of judgment which will befall those of you who do not bear the fruit of genuine conversion. And don't forget that, as I have just implied, every tree that does not bear good fruit is chopped down and tossed into the raging fire. So then, you had better watch out if you like worthless trees don't bear the fruit of righteousness and conversion within your lives!"[10]

---

8 Matthew 3:7
9 Matthew 3:7, 8; Luke 3:7, 8
10 Matthew 3:9, 10; Luke 3:8, 9

Many people hearing such words from John—on this and similar occasions—were convicted deep within their hearts. These individuals, therefore, would question him, asking, "If this is true, what then are we supposed to do?"[11]

John would answer them, saying, "Let the man who possesses an extra shirt, share it with one who has none. Let the one who has food, give to those who are hungry."[12]

On occasion, tax-collectors came to John seeking baptism. Now these tax collectors were usually Jews who were working for the Romans, assessing taxes upon their fellow countrymen. They were often noted for unethical behavior. So, when coming to John for baptism, these tax-collectors would ask, "Then, teacher, what should we do?"[13]

John would reply to them, saying, "Obviously, assess no more in taxes than you are required by law to collect. In short, stop cheating the people!"[14]

> Some other Jewish men served as soldiers, working directly for Rome. Because they had the authority of the empire behind them, these soldiers could be quite oppressive, taking unfair advantage of the people. Feeling that they did not make enough in wages, they often would force their fellow citizens to give them extra money. In general, many of these soldiers made life miserable for the people. And, because these soldiers had the power of Rome on their side, most citizens of the nation were afraid to protest against their evil practices.

When soldiers, under conviction, came to John for baptism, they would question him, asking, "And what about us? What are we to do?"[15]

John would reply, "Don't threaten people for the purpose of extorting money from them. Don't falsely accuse people. Yes, stop making life miserable for them by exerting your martial authority over the citizens of your own nation. Be satisfied with your wages. In short, stop your constant complaining!"[16]

---

11 Luke 3:10
12 Luke 3:11
13 Luke 3:12
14 Luke 3:13
15 Luke 3:14
16 Luke 3:14

As the result of listening to these bold, powerful words of warning and rebuke, all the people were in great expectation, wondering if John might be the promised Messiah! Accordingly, they questioned him in this regard. But John clearly denied that he was the Messiah. Rather, he declared that the Messiah was to come after him, and, further, that the Messiah would be superior to him. John explained, "I've been asked this question many times. I'll tell you what I've been saying all along. The Messiah is the One of whom I have always spoken when I said, 'The One who comes *after* me is of a much higher rank than me, because He existed *before* me.'" [*Harmony* 2:19, 50][(e)] [17]

> Here John recognized the fact that the Messiah would be divine in nature—that is what he meant when he said that the Messiah "existed" before him. Now, as far as this world was concerned, Jesus was actually younger than John by six months. [*Harmony* 1:18, 22] Therefore, John was talking about the Lord's existence in heaven *before* His birth on this earth. [*Harmony* 1:1-6]

In summary, then, even though John was born as the result of a miracle [*Harmony* 1:11-15, 33] and called by God as a prophet, he was not the Messiah. Rather, he was the man whose testimony would constantly bear witness of the "true Light" who would come after him. [*Harmony* 11:42] When the Messiah—the true Light—actually came, the people would believe in Him in direct response to John's ministry and preaching. John recognized that he was not himself the Light, but was to bear witness to the Light. [*Harmony* 2:45][(f)] [18]

"Now, regarding what I'm doing," John continued to explain, "I baptize with the water of repentance, which symbolizes the change of people's thinking and the complete cleansing of sin from their lives." [*Harmony* 2:3, 6] Then, discussing the work of the coming Messiah, John added these words, "However, there is One who will follow after me who is much more powerful than I. In fact, I'm not worthy to stoop down to untie the strings of His sandals. Neither am I worthy even to remove His sandals, and carry them for Him!" [*Harmony* 2:17, 47] In Jewish culture, handling the sandals of others was the most menial task of a slave. John was, in effect, saying that he was unworthy to be even a common slave of the coming Messiah. Then, continuing to discuss the Messiah, John added, "And it is He who will completely immerse you in the power of the Holy Spirit, which is like a mighty, purifying fire, cleansing all of you from your unrighteousness,

---

17 Luke 3:15; John 1:15

18 John 1:6-8

so as to change your lives permanently for the better. Yes, I baptize you with water . . . but the Messiah will baptize you with the cleansing 'fire' of the Holy Spirit. [*Harmony* 3:33; 8:25; 12:2][19]

"With a pitchfork of judgment in His hands," John went on, using another illustration, "the One who will follow after Me will totally clean up His threshing floor. With the pitchfork He will separate the valuable wheat from the worthless chaff. The grain—His true followers—He will store in His 'barn,' which, so to speak, is His eternal kingdom. However, the chaff—those who refuse to accept Him—He will cast into a fire that will never go out until it finishes its work of total destruction!" [*Harmony* 7:34, 35; 12:2][20]

> Here John referred to the ministry of the Messiah who would, in the final judgment, separate the wicked from the righteous. To make his point, John compared the judgment to a farmer who separates the good grain from the chaff. This was done by casting the grain and the chaff into the air with a pitchfork. The heavier grain fell to the ground, but the lighter chaff blew away in the wind. Then the farmer gathered the grain into his barn, but the remnants of the chaff were piled together to be burned. So it will be in the time of the judgment.[1]
>
> During his ministry, the words of counsel John gave his listeners was primarily practical in nature. In short, he taught that people were to treat one another with compassion and fairness. The people were to change their lifestyles and attitudes, not only toward God, but also toward their neighbors. To be sure, in the Jewish religion of the time there was a huge emphasis on obeying God, but there was little or no focus upon caring for others, especially the so-called heathen. In summary, John's message was very different from the things that the Jewish religious leaders had taught the people.[2]

In addition to all these words, John gave much more solid counsel and spiritual advice to the people as he explained to them the primary principles of the Gospel message which he had been commissioned to preach.[21]

—

19 Matthew 3:11; Mark 1:7, 8; Luke 3:16

20 Matthew 3:12; Luke 3:17

21 Luke 3:18

## *The Timeline of the Ministry of Jesus, Segment ONE: Autumn, A.D. 27 — Spring, A.D. 28*(g)

Very soon now, the ministry of Jesus, the true Messiah, would begin. The public ministry of Jesus lasted for about three and a half years—from the Autumn of A.D. 27, through mid-Spring, A.D. 31. It began at His baptism and ended at His ascension into heaven.[1]

Jesus clearly had a three-fold objective to complete during His ministry. First and of primary importance, He was to serve as the "Lamb of God" [*Harmony* 2:49] who would die a substitutionary death for the sinners of the world. This means that Jesus died so that forgiven sinners need not be lost for eternity. [Isaiah 53:4, 5] Indeed, all those who accepted His death by faith could be assured of the gift of eternal life. Second, the Lord needed to present before the world a set of eternal teachings that would serve as the doctrinal and lifestyle-altering foundation of the Christian Church. In short, this would be called the "everlasting Gospel." [*Harmony* 5:1-86; Revelation 14:6, 7] And third, Jesus needed to prepare a group of followers who, when He left this earth, would successfully take the Gospel message to the whole world. [*Harmony* 18:88] By their doing so, a large number of people could be made ready for His Second Coming at the end of the world. [*Harmony* 15:11] Of course, in addition to this, there were many other things that the Lord accomplished and taught during the course of His ministry.[2]

The three and a half years of the Lord's public ministry can be divided into seven segments of time of about six months apiece. During each of these segments, Jesus accomplished certain objectives that contributed effectively to His overall ministry as the Messiah of the world. In reality, the Lord organized His ministry in a very specific way. That is, He had a definite plan of action. At every point throughout His ministry, He knew exactly what He was doing and why.[3]

The first such segment (1/7)—Autumn, A.D. 27 through Spring, A.D. 28—as far as the Gospel record is concerned, began with the Lord's baptism and concluded with His first miracle in Cana of Galilee. Also, during this six-month time period, Jesus was tempted in the wilderness, and called His first disciples to follow Him. However, the details and events that are found in the Gospel record during this first six-month segment are actually quite limited.(h) [4]

**Thematic Preview of the Ministry of Jesus:**[i]

Of all the things Jesus taught, there were some that became *thematic* during His ministry—that is, they were the things that He *repeatedly* emphasized.[5]

In this regard, throughout His ministry Jesus constantly stressed the Gospel message in two ways. First, He shared some specific *doctrinal teachings* with the people which would serve as a sure foundation of belief. And second and more importantly, the Lord gave *practical advice* to His followers which they could use in their everyday lives as they sought to live out the principles of the Gospel which He taught them.[6]

Related to these areas of doctrine and practical advice, there were two main things that the Lord taught over and over again. First, He discussed often the reality of His extremely close and eternal relationship with God—the One whom He called His "Father." [*Harmony* 3:86-99] This, without question, was the Lord's *number one theme* throughout His ministry. Second, the Savior discussed at some length the meaning and nature of what He alternately called the "kingdom of heaven" or the "kingdom of God." From the Lord's perspective, there were two parts to this "kingdom." First, there was what could be called the "kingdom of grace." This "kingdom" dealt with the spiritual relationship each individual should have with Jesus as his or her personal Savior. This relationship included forgiveness of sins, growing in grace, and ultimate victory over sin. Second, there was what could be called the "kingdom of glory." This dealt with the final establishment of the Lord's eternal, glorious kingdom at His Second Coming. Very often the Lord used the vehicle of parables when explaining either aspect of this "kingdom." [*Harmony* 7:22-35][7]

In conjunction with the "kingdom of heaven" or the "kingdom of God," the Lord emphasized the concept of the final judgment at the end of the world. This was a recurring theme during His ministry. In connection with that, the Lord always stressed the importance of making a positive decision for the Gospel message. And of course, He never wanted His followers to delay making such a decision. [8]

Because of that, it is hardly surprising that Jesus spent most of His time teaching those aspects of the Gospel that would be of greatest benefit to His followers. These were the things His followers could use or understand on a day-to-day basis during their lives as they continued to make decisions that would affect their ongoing relationship with Him and the Gospel He taught. They included at least seven specific items:[9]

First: The Lord emphasized the need of His followers to understand the deep spiritual nature of the Law. A proper understanding in this matter ultimately leads to true obedience of the whole Law of God. Jesus stressed this concept—what could be called observing the "spirit of the Law," as opposed to just simply keeping the "letter of the Law." Even though, in the Gospel record, Jesus never actually used the phrase "spirit" or "letter" of the Law, He nevertheless used different words to emphasize the basic meaning of this concept time and time again. Without doubt Christ's primary exposition on this subject is found in His famous "Sermon on the Mount." [*Harmony* 5:2-84][10]

Second: Even though early in His ministry Jesus taught His followers the importance of believing in Him as the Messiah, it was near its end that He made it increasingly clear that a mere intellectual belief would not be sufficient. Instead, He emphasized the necessity of His followers to have a personal, one-on-one, growing experience with Him—something that could be called an "abiding" relationship with the Lord. [*Harmony* 16:71-75][11]

Third: Christ spent much time instructing His followers—especially His closest disciples—in the art of sharing their faith with others so that the Gospel would be spread ultimately to the entire world. This emphasis included the proper caring attitude His followers needed to have in their relationship with those whom they might be ministering to at any particular time. This included at first the Jews and finally the Gentiles—or non-Jews. With this, the Lord discussed the utmost importance of His followers being faithful to their calling to share the Gospel message with others. He also talked about what would be required for all His disciples to be ready for His Second Coming.[12]

Fourth: The Lord gave considerable practical advice as to how His followers were to co-operate with their fellow workers or disciples in the work of the Gospel ministry, no matter how difficult the circumstances might become.[13]

Fifth: The Savior constantly sought to uplift the hope of those who had been treated badly by society. This included the poor as well as those who were viewed as "sinners." Additionally, the Lord uplifted the role of women in society. In so doing, Jesus endorsed the positive influence that women should have within His body of believers. [14]

Sixth: Jesus spent significant time trying to correct several misunderstandings the people had regarding His ministry. Two areas were of major importance. One: The Lord talked a lot about the "suffering" aspect of the Messiah's work—a part of His ministry that was terribly misunderstood and neglected. Two: Jesus devoted considerable time trying to explain the true meaning of His miracle-working power which was such a large part of His public persona. This was the theme of His dramatic, decision-making "Bread of Life" presentation which would affect the rest of His ministry. [*Harmony* 9:29-49][15]

Seventh: The Lord's ministry—mostly noted for its healing, teaching, and preaching—included a large social aspect. That is, Jesus immensely enjoyed socializing with all types of people. By doing that He elevated the value of humanity's need for socialization based upon love and appreciation for one another.[16]

All these things, and many more of a like nature, kept the Lord very busy during the three and a half years of His ministry as He related dramatically to the people around Him.[17]

Throughout the Lord's lifetime, He ministered to four basic groups of individuals. First, there were the Jewish leaders. This relationship was never positive! Second, there were His disciples. These disciples included, of course, the closest of His followers, commonly called the "Twelve." But there were many other disciples who were a part of His extended group of followers. The Lord always expected a lot of His disciples. However, whenever they fell short of His expectations for them—which were often—He showed a good deal of patience toward them. Third, there were the common people of the Jewish nation. This included a very large number of people—often called a "multitude." The Lord exhibited a great deal of patience toward these individuals. They had been misinformed by the Jewish leadership regarding the truth of the Gospel message. It would take much time for them to re-learn the truth. Accordingly, He moved slowly with them. And fourth, Jesus ministered to a fair number of Gentiles—or non-Jews—during His ministry. He was often amazed by the high quality of faith they exhibited in Him. The Lord's relationship with this group, was with a few exceptions, quite positive.[18]

—

## The Lord's Baptism
## < Autumn, A.D. 27 (1/7) >
## (Matthew 3:13-17; Mark 1:1, 9-11; Luke 3:21-23)

Under the power of the Holy Spirit, John the Baptist labored tirelessly in preparing many people's hearts for the appearing of the Messiah. Now, the time for the coming of the Messiah—the Christ—was imminent. So it was at this precise time that Jesus left the town of Nazareth in the province of Galilee, some 65 miles to the north, and headed toward the place at the Jordan River where John was baptizing. [*Harmony* 2:2, 3] The ministry of Jesus, as the promised Messiah, the Son of God, was about to begin![(j)] [22]

After arriving at the very place where John was in the process of baptizing many people, Jesus came out from within the crowd, and asked John to immerse Him in baptism also.[23]

> John had been previously informed by God that the Messiah would personally come to him. In fact, John had been given a specific detail that would make it very clear to him that it was, indeed, the Messiah. The detail was that John would see the Holy Spirit, visibly and openly, descending upon the Savior. [*Harmony* 2:22/, 51]

As Jesus requested baptism, John looked into His face. John sensed the Lord's holy and perfect character. Accordingly, he thought that this Person standing before him was *most likely* the Messiah. However, because John had not yet seen the Holy Spirit visibly falling on Jesus—the thing that God had told John would happen to the Messiah when He appeared to him [*Harmony* 2:51]—John couldn't be absolutely sure if this Man was actually the Messiah. Perhaps a bit unsure of what to do, John initially resisted the Savior's request for baptism by declaring, "No! Rather it is I who should be baptized by You! So why do You come to me to be baptized? I am quite unworthy to baptize someone as righteous as You!"[(k)] [24]

But Jesus insisted, firmly stating, "Please do it this way. It is the right thing for us to perform all the acts of righteousness"—including all rituals, such as baptism—"which God would have us to perform." [*Harmony* 11:16/][25]

---

22 Matthew 3:13; Mark 1:9; Luke 3:21
23 Matthew 3:13; Luke 3:21
24 Matthew 3:14
25 Matthew 3:15

> Why did Jesus, perfect as He was, request to be baptized? First, the Lord's baptism would serve as an example to all others who needed to do the same. It would encourage them to be baptized themselves. If Jesus was willing to be baptized, certainly they should be too! Second, Christ's baptism would also serve as a ritual symbolizing the "anointing" of His life by the Holy Spirit as He began to fulfill His work and ministry as the Messiah of the world. In fact, the word "Messiah" means "the anointed one." [*Harmony* 2:27]

Understanding this line of reasoning—at least partially—John agreed to immerse Jesus. Accordingly, he baptized the Lord in the Jordan River.[26]

After Jesus was baptized, as He began to come up out of the water, He prayed for the outpouring—or "anointing"—of the Holy Spirit to come mightily upon Him. As a result of His petition, something incredible happened. [*Harmony* 2:25/] Both Jesus and John saw the heavens split open, and the Holy Spirit in the clear shape of a dove suddenly appeared. With the flapping of its wings, it lowered itself and settled upon the Lord's head. This indicated that Christ and His ministry were anointed by the power of the Holy Spirit. If that wasn't enough, at that same moment, the voice of God was heard coming directly from heaven, declaring, "You are My Son, the Beloved Chosen One! With You I am very delighted and extremely pleased!" [*Harmony* 2:30, 33/, 50; 10:67][(l)] [27]

> It is hardly surprising then that at this point John had no doubt whatsoever that Jesus was, in fact, the Messiah. The appearance of the Holy Spirit was the exact sign he had been told to look for when the Messiah was to be anointed as the Savior of the world! [*Harmony* 2:23/, 51][1]

> At the Lord's baptism—at the time when He was officially anointed as the Messiah—the entire Godhead was present. The Father spoke. The Son, Jesus, of course, was baptized and anointed. And the Holy Spirit in the form of a dove appeared as the One who had anointed Him.[2]

Thus began the Gospel story of the public ministry of Jesus, the Son of God. He was about 30 years old at the time. According to Jewish custom, it was at the

26 Matthew 3:15; Mark 1:9; Luke 3:21
27 Matthew 3:16, 17; Mark 1:10, 11; Luke 3:21, 22

age of 30 that a Hebrew man was considered to be old enough to bear the full responsibilities of ministry in public life.[28]

## The Temptations of Jesus in the Wilderness(m) (n) (o)
## < Autumn, A.D. 27 (1/7) >
## (Matthew 4:1-11; Mark 1:12, 13; Luke 4:1-13)

Filled with the Holy Spirit from His anointing experience at His baptism [*Harmony* 2:22-27], Jesus immediately left the area of the Jordan River. The Holy Spirit quickly directed Him into the part of the wilderness which was west of the river. There, still led by the Spirit, the Lord lived among the wild animals of the desert. Jesus needed this time of privacy to prepare Himself, in close communion with His Father, for the ministry which lay ahead of Him. The Savior spent 40 days and 40 nights in the wilderness, fellowshipping with His Father. But during that entire time, He was tempted and tested by Satan, the devil, who had intruded himself upon Jesus and this special time with His Father.(p) [29]

Satan—also known in the Scriptures as the Devil—was originally called Lucifer, the "son of the morning." He had been the top-ranking angel in heaven. But he had rebelled against God and His government. [Isaiah 14:12-14] A large portion of the angelic host joined Lucifer in his rebellion. After a grand struggle in heaven, they were cast down to this earth. Ever since being thrown out of heaven, Satan has sought to destroy the relationship of trust God has worked to preserve between Himself and His created beings. [Revelation 12:3-10] To accomplish his goal, the devil has always challenged God's honesty, making Him out to be a liar. [Genesis 3:3-5] Unfortunately, a significant portion of humanity has permanently joined Satan in his rebellion. Moreover, the devil has constantly pointed out the many flaws and shortcomings of God's people—those who have tried to remain faithful to the Lord. In fact, that is why the devil received his new name, Satan—the "adversary." [Zechariah 3:1] In short, then, the devil has challenged both the love of God and the faithfulness of His people.[1]

When Satan was thrown out of heaven, it was the result of a great struggle between God and the devil. When Jesus—a member of the Godhead—came to this earth to be its Messiah, the devil saw this as

---

28 Mark 1:1; Luke 3:23

29 Matthew 4:1, 2; Mark 1:12, 13; Luke 4:1, 2

a great opportunity to get back at God and especially at Jesus. It was Jesus—also known as Michael—who had fought with Satan in heaven just prior to his expulsion from there. [Revelation 12:7-9] Satan, then, viewed this time with Jesus in the wilderness as a renewal of his battle with the Lord. When the struggle took place in heaven, the devil was on God's ground, so to speak. But when Jesus came to this earth, He was now on the devil's "turf." This time the devil was determined to come out as the victor![2]

If Satan could get Jesus to sin—just once—then the plan of salvation—the work and ministry of the Messiah—would be totally shattered. Obviously much was at stake for both God and humanity. For thousands of years—ever since mankind's first sin [Genesis 3:1-6]—the devil had been planning and scheming to be ready for this, his golden moment of opportunity![3]

Initially, the devil's method was to distract the Savior from His close communion with His Father while He was in the wilderness. Satan hoped that such a distraction would cause the Lord's firm trust in His heavenly Father to falter and weaken. And should this happen, the devil believed he would have a good chance to tempt Jesus into sinning. But during the Lord's 40-day sojourn in the wilderness, Satan failed spectacularly with this intention. Indeed, Christ's connection with the heavenly Father was too strong for the devil to break, even in the slightest.[4]

However, during this entire time, Jesus ate nothing because He wanted to have His heart focused solely on His Father's will for Him and His upcoming ministry. So, after fasting during the entire 40-day period, Jesus was famished. Taking advantage of the Lord's obvious hunger, the devil used it as a basis for a strong temptation. Accordingly, the tempter challenged Jesus, by saying, "You must be hungry! So then, if You are really the Son of God—the 'Beloved Son' in whom He delights [*Harmony* 2:27]—then prove it by commanding that these stones which You see scattered around You, be turned into loaves of bread! That way, You can eat and nourish Your starving body. And, more than that, it is by turning these stones into bread that You can establish to Yourself whether You are *truly* God's Son or not. Take care of Yourself, Jesus! Certainly Your so-called Father doesn't want You to die of starvation . . . or does He?"(q) 30

30 Matthew 4:2, 3; Mark 1:13; Luke 4:2, 3

This first temptation, ingeniously fabricated by Satan, had at least three aspects. First, a little over a month before—at the Lord's baptism—Jesus' heavenly Father had openly declared that the Lord was His "Beloved Son." [*Harmony* 2:27] The devil used these same words to tempt Jesus. *If* Jesus was really the Son of God, the devil argued, then He should prove it to Himself by turning stones into bread which He desperately needed to eat. By this temptation Satan wanted Jesus to actually test the words of His Father to see whether they were true or not. Second, the devil, in this temptation, was implying that the Father did not care enough for Jesus to preserve His life. This was the devil's reasoning: If God loved Jesus so much, why was He willing to allow Him to die of starvation? By this part of the temptation, Satan wanted to raise doubts in the mind of Christ regarding the Father's supposed love for His Son. Third, the devil took advantage of the Lord's true physical need for food. He tempted Jesus in an area where He was clearly vulnerable—that is, He needed to eat . . . and soon!

But the Lord answered back to the devil, firmly declaring, "No! For it is written in the Scriptures, 'Man does not live solely by eating bread to fill his stomach. Rather, he is to be sustained by every single word that God speaks. That is true food for the soul.'" [Deuteronomy 8:3][31]

In effect, Jesus was saying, "If God wills for Me to die of hunger, then I will die. I am fully committed to His will for Me. If I am His Son—and I fully believe that I am—then He will take care of Me. That is what He said to Me [*Harmony* 2:27], and I completely believe His *words*. I will live by them. In any case, I will not use My power as God's Son to save Myself—a power by faith I believe I possess!"[1]

Indeed, while Jesus was on the earth, He was to live by faith, in total submission to the will of His Father. [*Harmony* 11:174; 16:107] To make stones into bread would violate this principle. Further, Jesus would not allow His famished condition to be the cause of disobeying His Father. By resisting this temptation, Jesus showed that His faith and trust in His Father were unshakable. Indeed, the Lord totally submitted His will to that of the Father. Jesus had triumphantly passed the test. God's word—His promise—was sufficient for the Lord.[2]

31 Matthew 4:4; Luke 4:4

Next, Satan crafted another temptation to use on Jesus. The devil included at least two components to this new temptation: First, because Jesus had expressed such a strong confidence in His Father, the devil chose to test Jesus to see to what extent He would go in proving His unflinching trust in the Father. That is, would He be willing to dramatically test the Father's love for Him? Second, Jesus had also shown a firm, unwavering reliance upon the Word of God by quoting a portion of the Scriptures in response to the devil's first temptation. [*Harmony* 2:31] So, in the next test, the devil decided he would also use the Word of God as part of his temptation of the Lord.[3]

So Satan took the Lord into the holy city, Jerusalem, and set Him on top of the outer rim of the roof of the Temple—the highest portion of the building. "Now then," Satan declared, "if You really are the Son of God—as You have so eloquently claimed—then jump off the roof! Don't be afraid to do so, for the Scriptures, which You like to quote [*Harmony* 2:31], also say, 'God will command His angels to take good care of You, and they will catch You up in their hands, so that You will not crush Your foot against a rock.' [Psalm 91:11, 12] By faith, You can be assured that Your Father will save You from death . . . that is, if You possess such a faith!"[32]

If Jesus had jumped off the Temple, He would have acted in a way clearly outside the will of His Father, for God had not directed Jesus to do such a thing. To state it another way, by jumping off the Temple, Jesus would have had to disobey His Father. This means that for Jesus to expect God to protect Him, especially when He clearly was acting outside the specific will of God, would have been presumptuous.

Without hesitation, Jesus replied to the devil's temptation, saying, "The Scriptures that you have quoted may be true. But I've quoted the Scriptures before, so I'll quote them again. For they also say in a certain place, 'You are not to put pressure on the Lord your God by testing His love for you.' [Deuteronomy 6:16] Yes, it would be wrong—against My Father's direct will—for Me to test His love for Me by forcing Him to save Me."[33]

By jumping off the Temple, Jesus would be doing more than proving to Himself that He was truly the Son of God. Again, He would also

---

32 Matthew 4:5, 6; Luke 4:9-11

33 Matthew 4:7; Luke 4:12

be presumptuously "forcing" the Father to deliver Him from a potential tragedy that God had not directed Him to face. Jesus would be testing God to prove by a miracle the truthfulness of the words that the Father had declared to Jesus just over a month previously. That is when, at the Lord's baptism, He had declared that Jesus was the Son of God—His Beloved Son. [*Harmony* 2:27] Faith is to believe without absolute proof. Presumption is to require absolute proof. Also, faith is to have a firm trust which results in obeying the will of God. Presumption is to find an excuse to test God's love by disobeying the will of God.[1]

The devil had quoted a portion of Scripture in his effort to tempt Jesus to sin. He used the text in such a way that could have led the Lord to misunderstand the meaning of Scripture. But, in response to Satan, Jesus also quoted the Word of God. By doing so, the Lord showed that the Word of God needed to be understood correctly by comparing Scripture with Scripture so that true meaning of truth could be comprehended accurately.[2]

Now that the first two temptations had failed to accomplish the devil's purpose, he devised yet a third temptation. This temptation would have just one simple emphasis. The devil dropped the issue of the Lord's faith in His Father as well as the foundation of Scripture in the life of Jesus. He no longer even mentioned the matter of whether Jesus was the Son of God or not. It was as if the devil were saying to the Lord, "It's just between You and me now. No more Scripture. No more about Your supposed heavenly Father. We will settle this issue—just between the two of us." Specifically, in this last temptation, Satan focused on the humanity of Jesus, and the Lord's natural human tendency to avoid, if possible, the severe suffering and anguish it would take to secure salvation for the world. Suffering, as part of the plan of salvation, was an important issue to Jesus. He would mention it often. Not surprisingly, it was something He as a human being would wish to avoid. [*Harmony* 17:4][3]

It was then that the devil carried Jesus to a very high mountain. He showed Him within an instant of time all the kingdoms of the world. He showed the Lord all the glorious splendor of the nations of the entire earth. Then, he declared to Jesus, "See all these kingdoms? Well, I will give them all—along with all their power and beauty—to You! And . . . I will make it easy for You. You will not need to suffer in order to accomplish Your mission here on earth—the suffering that Your Father has planned for You! No! In fact, I will hand over to You complete authority to rule this world. It will be yours! You see, authority over the entire earth has been given to me to use as I desire. And I have the power to give it to whomever I choose. However, there is something You must first do for me: You must fall down on Your face and give Your allegiance to me—right here and now! If You do, this earth will be yours! I will give it to You! It's just that simple!" [*Harmony* 17:4][34]

> The devil implied that if Jesus did not go along with his demand, he would make life miserable for Him. On the other hand, the devil indicated that if the Lord complied with his demand, then he would just walk away and let Jesus alone. Of course that was a bold-faced lie! He never had any intention of doing any such thing! But, nevertheless, that is what the devil said he would do.[1]
>
> Certainly Satan was committed to making life very difficult for Jesus. And that is exactly what he did during the Lord's entire ministry. Based upon what the devil was planning to do in order to upset the ministry of Jesus, it was as though, that during this third temptation—combining both truth and exaggeration—he was telling Jesus this: "From Your family You will receive only misunderstanding. [*Harmony* 7:1; 11:1-3] I'll make sure of that. From Your home town of Nazareth, You will receive hatred. They will even try to kill You! [*Harmony* 4:4-10] From the people of Israel You will receive, at best, inconsistent support. They will be interested only in Your miracles and not in Your teachings. [*Harmony* 3:9; 9:28-33, 50] From Your own disciples, for the most part, You will receive betrayal [*Harmony* 17:17, 18], denial [*Harmony* 17:26-29, 40-44], and frustrating misunderstanding. [*Harmony* 10:86, 87] From the Jewish leadership You will receive extreme, unrelenting hatred [*Harmony* 11:171] and finally . . . agonizing and painful death. [*Harmony* 17:115, 116] And, when You hang in humiliation on the cross, You will think that even your heavenly Father has rejected You. [*Harmony* 17:129] At that very moment, You will think that everything You have suffered wasn't worth the anguish. Your ministry will appear to You to be a complete failure. Yes indeed, I'll make life miserable for You. But, if You will only admit that I am the true ruler of this world by

---

34 Matthew 4:8, 9; Luke 4:5-7

worshipping me—here in secret, with no one looking on—then I'll walk away from You and leave the world to You. No suffering! No anguish! No rejection! And no agonizing death! It's Your call! It's Your choice!"[2]

Yes, by worshipping the devil in secret, Jesus would be trying to bypass the plan the Father had in mind for Him as the Savior of the world. True faith required that the Lord submit *totally* to the will of His Father. And in doing so, the Savior, in the natural course of things, would suffer unmercifully as the Sin Bearer of the world. But here, through this third temptation, the devil sought to get Jesus to try to accomplish the plan of salvation without directly obeying God's will. But this obviously was completely unacceptable. Furthermore, one can never worship the devil and get anything truly valuable in return. The price is always high: the cost of one's soul! The devil can never be believed or trusted.[3]

Jesus' response to the third temptation was unequivocal, "Get out of here, Satan! You are filled with lies! Away from Me! For it is written, 'You shall give total allegiance to the Lord your God *alone*, and serve *only* Him.'" [Deuteronomy 6:13][35]

Whatever Jesus needed to suffer for the cause of the Gospel, He was willing to bear. He would take no shortcuts. He would take the tough road. He would still trust His Father. He would continue to rely on the Word of God. He firmly believed that He was truly the Son of God. Besides, as the Lord well knew, the devil had no real control over the world. And that being the case, Jesus would worship and serve only His Father and submit to His will—the real Owner of the world—no matter what the price might be . . . and no matter what the devil might claim. [*Harmony* 17:3/]

The devil failed on these three occasions to induce Jesus into sin. He was unable to get the Lord to desert His heavenly Father and His will for Him. Accordingly, Satan left the Lord until another opportune time would arise to tempt Him further. When the devil was gone, angels immediately surrounded the Lord to strengthen and encourage Him. They resuscitated Him, assisting Him in recovering from the privations and struggles He had just experienced.[36]

---

35 Matthew 4:10; Luke 4:8

36 Matthew 4:11; Mark 1:13; Luke 4:13

The nature of the three temptations of Jesus was something that Satan had designed specifically for Him. They were unique to Him. After all, would any normal human being be truly tempted to turn stones into bread, jump off a building to test God's protecting power, or to really think that worshipping the devil would result in receiving the authority to rule the entire world? In general, the devil's temptations of individuals are based upon what makes a person the most vulnerable. For sinful human beings, the devil uses temptations that appeal to the weaknesses of character each person might possess. But where would Jesus be vulnerable? He had no weaknesses of character. However, there were areas where Jesus *was* vulnerable. What were they? They were primarily three-fold, paralleling each of the three temptations.[1]

First, He was tempted to use His divine power to find out for certain if He truly possessed miracle-working authority as the Son of God. Not only that, He would be able to feed His starving body, fulfilling a survival instinct. As the Son of Man He had laid aside His divine power and was totally submissive to the will of His Father. [Philippians 2:6-8] But He understood and experienced this arrangement solely by faith. By turning the stones to bread, He would be able to ascertain on His own whether He truly was the Son of God. However, His relationship of faith and trust in His Father would have been broken. In that case, He would have sinned, and the plan of salvation would have been ruined.[2]

Second, Jesus was tempted to test His Father's love for Him by forcing God to protect Him as His Beloved Son. By jumping off the Temple roof, He would make God save Him, or else. After all, the devil reasoned with Him, would His so-called Father *really* let Him die? Of course not! But again, His faith would be based on disobedience rather than obedience. Faith must always be based upon obedience, never on disobedience.[3]

Third, the Lord was tempted to bypass the incredible struggles He would face while completing the work of the plan of salvation. Yielding to this temptation would appear to release Him from an unbelievable amount of suffering. It would also free Him from a constant submission of His will to that of His Father. What a relief that would appear to be! Worshipping the devil for just a second—in secret—with no one looking on would seem to be so much easier than the persistent struggle He knew He must face as the Savior of the world. But Jesus refused to yield to the temptation of seeking an easier path other than that of faith and obedience—the one that the Father had chosen for Him.[4]

Fortunately, Jesus successfully resisted all three temptations. In all three cases, the basis of His victory was His reliance upon the words of God which formed the foundation of His unshakable faith in the will of the Father.[5]

## Jesus Officially Begins His Ministry
## < Late Autumn, A.D. 27 (1/7) >
## (John 1:19-51)

### —John the Baptist Is Questioned by the Jewish Leaders
### < Late Autumn, A.D. 27 (1/7) >
### {John 1:19-28}

Because of John the Baptist's unusual popularity with the people, the Jewish Council in Jerusalem—the Sanhedrin [*Harmony* 17:36/1, 2]—sent a group of religious leaders to question him closely. This delegation was composed of priests and other Levites. [*Harmony* 11:156][(r)] [37]

The priests belonged to the tribe of Levi, and of the most important family in that tribe, that of Aaron. [Numbers 3:6-13] The priests were the ones who ministered directly in the sacrificial system of the Jews. The Levites were also from the tribe of Levi. However, they were from other families of that tribe. While they worked in and around the Temple, caring for the building and other responsibilities, they were not permitted to work directly with the sacrifices. So it was that this important delegation made their way into the wilderness where John was preaching and baptizing. They were concerned about the negative impact his ministry might have upon their jealously guarded power and control over the common people. What would John have to say regarding himself? And would he say something they could use to weaken his influence with the people?

When arriving where John was baptizing [*Harmony* 2:3], the delegation of Jewish leaders asked of him, "Who are you? Do you claim to be the Christ, the promised Messiah?" [*Harmony* 2:4/2-4][38]

---

37 John 1:19
38 John 1:19

Without hedging, John answered their question honestly and forthrightly by stating unequivocally that he was not the Messiah. He exclaimed, "No indeed! I am not the Christ!"—the Messiah. [*Harmony* 3:29][39]

Next they asked, "Well, then, if you are not the Messiah, who do you claim to be? Do you perhaps consider yourself to be Elijah, the prophet whom Malachi predicted would come to precede the Messiah?" [Malachi 4:5] Many Jews believed that before the Messiah would appear, Elijah would return from heaven [2 Kings 2:11] to announce His coming, just as Malachi had seemingly predicted. [*Harmony* 2:49/][40]

Once more he denied it by saying, "No! I'm not Elijah." While John did the work of Elijah as Malachi had predicted, he was not the actual *person* Elijah—he only functioned in the "spirit and power of Elijah." [*Harmony* 1:12][(s) 41]

"Well, then," they continued to ask, "are you that 'Prophet' spoken of by Moses?" [Deuteronomy 18:15; *Harmony* 11:25][42]

> There was a difference of opinion among the Jews as to who this "Prophet" of whom Moses had written would be. Some thought he would be the actual Messiah. Some believed that he would be a special prophet—perhaps even a resurrected Moses—who would arrive to lead the way before the coming Messiah.

"No!" was John's terse reply to this question.[43]

"So," they continued, "if you claim to be none of these special individuals, then please tell us who it is that you actually claim to be! Who are you? We need to give an answer to the Sanhedrin. Tell us then, what do you say in defense of yourself?"[44]

With determination, John answered, "I am a voice crying out in the wilderness, saying, 'Make straight the road for the coming of the Lord'—that is, prepare the way for the coming of the Messiah, as was spoken of by the prophet Isaiah."

---

39 John 1:20
40 John 1:21
41 John 1:21
42 John 1:21
43 John 1:21
44 John 1:22

[Isaiah 40:3] Indeed, John was the "voice" that would proclaim the coming of the "WORD!" [*Harmony* 1:1; 35; 2:18, 49/; 3:29; 10:72/][45]

Now those who had been sent to question him were Pharisees [*Harmony* 2:7/1, 2], the Jewish conservatives. They were concerned that John was functioning without proper authority in his preaching and baptizing. Of course their concern was hardly sincere. Instead, they were selfishly worried that John's ministry might impinge upon their own influence with the people. So they asked him, saying, "Who do you think you are? If you not the Christ, or Elijah, or that Prophet, then, by what authority do you baptize? Why is it that you baptize people? Indeed, who are you? Who gave you such authority? There's one thing we know for certain: we didn't give it to you!"[46]

Without directly answering their questions, John replied, "I have only been baptizing with water." [*Harmony* 2:3] At that very moment John saw Jesus standing in the crowd. The Lord had just returned from His 40 days of temptation in the wilderness. [*Harmony* 2:29-36] Looking at Jesus, John added, "However, there is Another who is standing here in your midst. You are not yet acquainted with Him. Yet, He is the One I said would come after me. And, as I've also said before, I am not even worthy to untie His sandal's strap. [*Harmony* 2:19] Indeed, He is the One who really counts." [*Harmony* 2:19; 10:72] This final response effectively ended the discussion between John and those who had been sent to question him. [*Harmony* 2:49][(t)] [47]

> The Jews did not recognize that John was talking about Jesus as the One who was standing in the crowd near them. Neither did Jesus openly respond to John's declaration regarding Him. In fact, Jesus was waiting for John officially and publicly to announce Him to the people.

This interrogation of John took place at Bethany, which was at one of the fords on the Jordan River, some 25 miles from Jerusalem, on the eastern side of the river. It was there that John was baptizing at the time. [*Harmony* 2:2][48]

---

45 John 1:23
46 John 1:24, 25
47 John 1:26, 27
48 John 1:28

## —John Declares Jesus to be "The Lamb of God"
## < Late Autumn, A.D. 27 (1/7) >
## {John 1:29-34}

The next day, after the Jewish delegation had returned to Jerusalem [*Harmony* 2:37], John the Baptist noticed Jesus again. This time the Lord was coming toward him. It had been but a brief period of time since the Lord's wilderness temptations. [*Harmony* 2:29-36] It was now clear to John that God expected him to *publicly* introduce Jesus to the masses as the coming Messiah, something he had failed to do the previous day. [*Harmony* 2:47] So, looking intently at the Lord, John openly and loudly declared for all to hear, "Attention everyone! Have a good look! Here He is: The Lamb of God, who is to bear upon Himself all the sins of the world!" [*Harmony* 1:40/; 2:53; 3:28; 8:25; 10:72; 13:33; 14:121/5; 16:5/, 25/; 17:3/, 134/][49]

> In what sense was Jesus—the Messiah—the "Lamb of God"? In the Scripture-based Hebrew religion, sacrificial animals—especially lambs [Exodus 12:3-10]—symbolized the ministry of the coming Messiah who would literally take the sins of the world upon Himself. [Isaiah 53:4-12] Clearly John recognized that Jesus was the Messiah, and thus would carry upon Himself the sins of the world as its Savior. [*Harmony* 1:40, 45] Jesus as the Messiah would suffer for the sins of all those on the earth. However, this concept of suffering was, for the most part, very foreign to the beliefs of the Jews as it related to the ministry of the Messiah. They did not understand that the Messiah would need to suffer and die for the sins of the world—including their own! [Isaiah 53:4, 5, 10, 11; *Harmony* 10:84, 85] For the most part, they saw only His glory as a conquering king, not His agony as a suffering sacrifice.

John continued, "See, this is He of whom I have previously told you, 'After me will come a Man of a much higher rank than me, because He existed before me.'" [*Harmony* 2:17] John, of course, was speaking of the Lord's pre-existent state as the WORD who was with God, and who was God. [*Harmony* 1:1][50]

"I must confess that I did not, at first, recognize who He was," John further explained. "But I knew that at some point He would be revealed to the nation of Israel. That's why I've been baptizing people in water—to prepare their hearts

---

[49] John 1:29

[50] John 1:30

for His coming. That is my calling and my authority." [*Harmony* 2:3] John continued to testify of the events he had witnessed, saying, "But when I actually baptized Him, I saw the Holy Spirit descend upon Him in the shape of a dove, and the dove remained upon Him. [*Harmony* 2:22-27] As I have just said, I did not at first recognize Him, but when God first sent me to baptize with water, He said to me, 'The One on whom you see the Holy Spirit lowering itself, and remaining there, He it is who will baptize people with that same Holy Spirit.'" Here John clearly indicated that the ministry of Jesus, as the Messiah, would be distinguished by the obvious and dramatic power of the Holy Spirit working through Him. [Isaiah 61:1][51]

"So then, when I saw all this actually happen before my own eyes," John added, "I knew for certain that this Man was the Son of God! [*Harmony* 1:22/1-3] I bear witness to these facts, that they have taken place just as I have described them to you."[52]

> Without any question, John's testimony that Jesus was the long-awaited-for Messiah [*Harmony* 2:4/3, 4 ] was abundantly obvious and unmistakable! John the Baptist had effectively introduced Jesus, the Messiah, to the people. [*Harmony* 2:23/]

**— Jesus Calls His First Disciples**
**< Late Autumn, A.D. 27 (1/7) >**
**{John 1:35-51}**

The next day, John the Baptist was standing with two of his disciples, Andrew and another man, also named John. This other John—the later author of the Gospel of John—was the son of Zebedee, a fisherman. Once again, as he had done the day before [*Harmony* 2:49], John the Baptist looked intently at Jesus as He walked by. John declared a second time, "Look! The Lamb of God!" When they heard these words, John's two disciples left his side and began to follow after Jesus. [*Harmony* 1:40/; 3:28; 8:25][(u)][53]

The Lord turned around and saw them following Him. And He asked them, "What is it that you want?"[54]

---

51 John 1:31-33
52 John 1:34
53 John 1:35-37, 40
54 John 1:38

They answered, "Rabbi"—the Hebrew word for *teacher*—"where do You live?"[55]

Jesus replied, "Come and see for yourselves." Andrew and John went with Him and saw the place where He was staying. They remained with Him for the rest of the day, for it was already about 4:00 in the afternoon.[(v) 56]

Now, Andrew had a brother named Simon. As soon as he could, he found Simon, and told him excitedly, "We have found the Messiah!" [*Harmony* 2:4/3, 4] The Hebrew word, *Messiah* means, in the Greek language, the *Christ*—or the *Anointed One*. [*Harmony* 2:25-27] So, Andrew took Simon to meet Jesus.[57]

Looking intently at Simon, and peering into his eyes, as though He were reading his soul, Jesus declared to him, "I know that your name is Simon, the son of Jonah. But from now on, I will call you Cephas." The name Cephas is an Aramaic word which means in the Greek language, *"Peter"*—that is, a stone, or rock. (In spite of different theories, it is not at clear why Jesus gave Simon this nickname.)[(w) 58]

> Aramaic was the *spoken* language by Jesus, and of course, by all the people in that area of His day. However, people *wrote* in Greek! The Aramaic language had its roots with the Aramaean people who lived in northern Mesopotamia and Syria. In the days of Jesus, the people of Israel spoke what can be called Palestinian Aramaic. After the Babylonian captivity, 600 years before Christ, Aramaic ultimately replaced Hebrew as the spoken language of the Jews. However, there are similarities between the two languages. Today, Aramaic is a dead language.

The following day, the Lord decided to leave for Galilee, some 75 miles to the north. When He arrived there, He saw a certain man named Philip. Jesus said to him, "Follow Me!" Now Philip was from the city of Bethsaida, a fishing village on the Jordan River, near the northern coast of the Sea of Galilee. This village was also the home town of Peter and Andrew. Philip was the first person to whom Jesus directly said, "Follow Me!" [*Harmony* 4:50; 9:4][59]

---

55 John 1:38
56 John 1:39
57 John 1:40-42
58 John 1:40, 42
59 John 1:43, 44

Next, Philip found his friend, Nathanael, sitting under a fig tree. [*Harmony* 2:65] Philip excitedly said to him, "We have found the One of whom Moses talked about in the Law. [Deuteronomy 18:15] And He is the One about whom the prophets of Scripture wrote—indeed, the Messiah! His name is Jesus. He's from Nazareth, and His father's name is Joseph."[60]

Nathanael was from Cana, which was less than ten miles from Nazareth. So, upon hearing that Jesus was from that village, and knowing of that town's less than stellar reputation, Nathanael replied with some scorn, "Can any good thing really come out of Nazareth? No! I don't think so!"[61]

Undeterred by Nathanael's negative response, Philip answered him, "Come and check Him out for yourself! Then decide!" Accordingly, Nathanael went to see Jesus for himself.[62]

As the Lord saw Nathanael coming toward Him, He made the firm observation, "Look at this! Now here's a genuine Israelite: a man who is honest, and free of false pretenses!"[63]

Overhearing this observation of himself, Nathanael inquired of the Lord, "How is it that You think You know me? Why, we've never met before!"[64]

"Ah!" Jesus answered, "Even before Philip told you about Me, I saw you sitting under that fig tree." [*Harmony* 2:60][65]

The Lord's miraculous knowledge of Nathanael and his actions truly startled the man. So he blurted out, "Rabbi,"—Teacher—"You are indeed the Son of God! You must be the King of Israel—the Son of David, even the Messiah! [*Harmony* 2:4/3, 4; 6:10/] Nobody else could know the things that you know, unless He was the Messiah."[66]

> Nathanael recognized Jesus as both the Son of God and the Son of David—that is, the Son of Man! [*Harmony* 1:22/1-4] The fact that Nathanael recognized that Jesus was both divine and human this early

60 John 1:45, 48
61 John 1:46
62 John 1:46
63 John 1:47
64 John 1:48
65 John 1:48
66 John 1:49

in the Lord's ministry shows just how deep was his knowledge regarding the true nature of the promised Messiah.

Jesus answered Nathanael, "Do you believe in Me simply because I knew you were sitting under a fig tree? Trust Me . . . if you stay with Me, you will see far greater things than that!"[67]

Then the Lord, still speaking to Nathanael, added, "Of certainty, from now on, you will see, as it were, heaven's gates thrown open and angels going up and down upon the Son of Man." [*Harmony* 3:95][68]

By this cryptic illustration, reminiscent of Jacob's Old Testament dream [Genesis 28:10-22], Jesus referred to the impressive nature of His own ministry. It would be as though the angels of heaven would be constantly working at His bidding. Some angels would be going into heaven to bear messages there, calling for heaven's assistance for spiritual power and healing. Other angels would be coming from heaven, carrying messages to the earth which would influence and change people's lives, both spiritually and physically. In effect, the ministry of Jesus, in the work of saving people, would keep the communication lines "hot," as it were, with busy activity between heaven and earth. He was the vital link. Further, based upon this illustration, it is clear that the angels of heaven had a major role to play during the ministry of Jesus, no doubt including the performance of His miracles. [Hebrews 1:14][1]

There can be no real doubt that these five men—John, Peter, Andrew, Philip, and Nathanael—were originally disciples of John the Baptist. John's ministry, as it related to "clearing the way before the Lord"—the Messiah [*Harmony* 2:4]—obviously bore significant and positive fruit.[2]

## The Lord's First Miracle: Turning Water Into Wine at Cana ‹ Late Autumn, A.D. 27 (1/7) › (John 2:1-12)

A couple of days later a wedding took place in Cana, located in the province of Galilee. Cana was about 13 miles west of the Sea of Galilee. Mary, the mother of Jesus, was in attendance. Jesus, along with His fledgling group of disciples, was also invited. (In general, the word "disciples" indicated people who closely

---

67 John 1:50
68 John 1:51

followed the teachings of someone.) At the time, Jesus had five such disciples: Andrew, John, Peter, Philip, and Nathanael. This is the first time in the Gospel record that the followers of Jesus were called *disciples.*[(x)] [69]

During the lengthy wedding feast that lasted for several days, the supply of wine ran out. When Mary was informed that the wine was gone, she hinted that Jesus should do something about it, for she simply said to Him, "Jesus, they have no more wine."[70]

But He, with respect, answered her, "Mother, what does that have to do with either you or Me? What do you expect Me to do about it? Besides, My time to publicly declare Myself as the Son of Man has not yet arrived."[(y)] [71]

> These rather strong words by Jesus were intended to send a message to His mother. She was not to be in charge of His ministry. He had been a faithful son. He had obeyed her. [*Harmony* 1:83] But now that His ministry had begun, it was important that she recognize that Jesus had to make His own decisions regarding His public work. From now on, it was to be His relationship with His heavenly Father that would be paramount in decision-making—not His relationship with His mother. [*Harmony* 1:82]

But in spite of the Lord's apparent rebuff of His mother, Mary told the servants, "Whatever He tells you to do . . . do it!"[72]

Now, standing nearby, were six empty stone water pots that were to be used for the various Jewish ceremonial washings at the feast. [*Harmony* 10:1-13] Altogether, the pots could hold about 160-180 gallons of water! Even though Jesus had clearly indicated to His mother that He did not wish to solve the wine shortage problem, nevertheless, to strengthen the faith of Mary and His disciples, He went into action.[(z)] [73]

"Fill the pots with water, right to the top!" He told the servants. They did as the Lord commanded. "Now," He continued, "pour out some of their contents, and take it to the headmaster of the feast"—the one charge of the feast. This,

---

69 John 2:1, 2
70 John 2:3
71 John 2:4
72 John 2:5
73 John 2:6, 7

they also did. When the headmaster tasted the water, it had miraculously become fresh, unfermented wine! But he did not know where it had come from. Of course, the servants knew, but they didn't tell him.[(aa)] [74]

The headmaster called the bridegroom and said to him, "Under normal conditions, during a wedding feast they serve the best wine first. And when everyone has had a good deal to drink, then they bring out the poorer quality wine to consume. But for some unexplained reason, you have saved the best wine for the last!"[75]

So it was in Cana that the Lord performed His first miracle during His ministry. By doing so, He revealed His glorious power to the people. But more importantly, His new disciples had further proof to believe that He was, indeed, the Messiah.[76]

> The Lord's first miracle was performed in part to enhance a social event. This is the first of a number of occasions that Jesus would be directly involved in social activities. [*Harmony* 8:1-4; 12:19, 90; 14:1] This indicates that the Gospel experience includes other things besides spiritual preaching and teaching.

After the wedding feast was over, Jesus went with His mother, step-brothers [*Harmony* 7:1], and disciples to Capernaum, which was about 20 miles from Cana, on the northwest side of the Sea of Galilee. There He stayed a few days. [(bb)] [77]

## Supplementary Notes:

**(a)** **[2:2]** The best evidence reveals that Bethany is in reality the preferred name of the location of John's ministry over that of Bethabara (as is found in John 1:28 in the KJV). Accordingly, I went with Bethany.

**(b)** **[2:4]** In Mark's version (Mark 1:2, 3), he gives credit to Isaiah for the whole reference. However, verse 2 is really a quote from Malachi 3:1, while verse 3 is a quote of Isaiah 40:3. In the *Harmony*, I also gave proper credit to Malachi.

---

74 John 2:7-9
75 John 2:9, 10
76 John 2:11
77 John 2:12

**(c) [2:5]** The Greek word for "locusts" (in John the Baptist's diet) could refer to either the plant or the insect. While the preponderance of evidence would favor the insect over the plant, I, nevertheless, chose the plant over the bugs! I have a hard time, I guess, believing that John would have eaten so many insects for a large part of his diet! Though locusts and other insects were an important source of protein in Africa, they did not form a major part of the diet in Israel. Nevertheless, locusts—the insect—are listed as being "clean" (or edible) in Leviticus 11:22.

**(d) [2:5/]** The Nazirite vow is explained in Numbers 6:1-21. The word Nazirite means "to separate." In our modern society, the Nazirite vow seems so strange! But, apparently, in Bible times it made much more sense to those living then.

**(e) [2:17]** Part of this paragraph is based upon John 1:15 in addition to Luke 3:15. The reference in the Gospel of John seemed to fit the context, so I included it here. As to when John the Baptist actually made such a statement is not clear. However, I felt it was better to include it where I did as opposed to keeping it with the other John 1 statements.

**(f) [2:18]** This paragraph is based upon John 1:6, 8. (See note above to explain its insertion here.)

**(g) [2:21+]** This is the first of eight insertions in the *Harmony* that places the events of the three-and-a-half-year ministry of Jesus on a "timeline," divided into seven six-month segments. (The eighth insertion is at the end of the seventh segment.) The other segment insertions can be found in the following locations: Segment Two, *Harmony* 3:0; Three, *Harmony* 3:33/2; Four, *Harmony* 3:71/; Five, *Harmony* 6:17/; Six, *Harmony* 10:0; Seven, *Harmony* 11:0; and Eight, *Harmony* 18:99/1-21.

**(h) [2:21/4]** This segment has the designation 1/7 for its "Segmental Placement" number. (See "Segmental Placement" in the "Features for Using the *Harmony* as a Reference Book" section near the back of this book for more information.)

**(i) [21:21/4+]** The "Thematic Preview of the Ministry of Jesus" parallels the "Thematic Review of the Ministry of Jesus" (*Harmony* 18:99/8-21). (For more information on how the "Thematic Preview" and the "Thematic Review" are to be used, please refer to "Thematic Preview of the Ministry of Jesus" and "Thematic Review of the Ministry of Jesus" in the "Features for Using the *Harmony* as a Reference Book" section near the back of this book.)

**(j) [2:22]** A major prophecy dealing with the arrival of the Messiah is located in Daniel 9:24-27. I believe that Jesus determined His arrival at the Jordan to be baptized by John, in fulfillment of this prophecy. This is a rather complicated prophecy and its interpretation is well beyond the scope of the *Harmony.* It should be noted that this interpretation is based upon a *historical* theory of interpretation, and not a *futurist* theory. I suggest the reader consult a good commentary that uses the *historical* theory of interpretation, though such a commentary may be hard to find!

**(k) [2:24]** Because Jesus and John the Baptist were relatives (*Harmony* 1:22), and because the mothers of both the Lord and John had communicated with each other (*Harmony* 1:24-28), a couple of logical questions could be asked: Could Jesus and John have known each other? And, that being the case, could they have discussed each other's missions with one another? I suppose it's *possible,* but I consider it highly unlikely. The way the story reads, I would think that such a prior communication with each other did not take place. And, it seems that John's mother, Elizabeth, did *not* tell her son that his relative, Jesus, was to be the Messiah. While this might be surprising to some, the way the story reads, I consider it the most likely scenario.

**(l) [2:27]** In Matthew's version of the baptism story, the voice of God speaks *to the people,* while both Mark and Luke have God speaking directly *to Jesus.* I chose Mark and Luke's version for the *Harmony.* I felt that having God speak directly to Jesus would be the best way of presenting the story, wherein Jesus would, as He began His ministry, receive a direct word of encouragement from His Father. Of course, the people could "listen in," as it were, on what the Father said to His Son; but, I thought, Jesus would be especially blessed by the experience if the Father spoke directly to Him.

**(m) [2:28+]** Determining the devil's purpose in devising each of the three temptations, as well as to why they would be particularly tempting to Jesus, is, in my opinion, quite challenging. The first—turning stones to bread—was easiest to understand. Jesus was hungry, *and* He would certainly like to know *if* he was truly the Son of God. But, being tempted to jump off a building to test God's love for Him (the second temptation), and to really think that to privately worship the devil (the third temptation) would gain Him the whole world, presents a stronger challenge. In the *Harmony,* I did my best, but I am still open to additional ideas.

**(n)** **[2:28+]** There are two versions of the Lord's temptations in the wilderness. In Matthew, the second temptation involved Jesus jumping off the Temple, while the third temptation called for Jesus to worship the devil. In Luke's account, these two temptations are switched. I have followed Matthew's version for the *Harmony,* considering it the most likely sequence.

**(o)** **[2:28+]** Here's an intriguing question: In what physical form did the devil appear to Jesus when he tempted Him in the wilderness? Did he "appear" only as a voice? If he appeared as an angel, did he appear as an angel of light (2 Corinthians 11:14), or of darkness? Or perhaps, did he appear in some other form? Unfortunately, we don't have a clear Biblical clue as to the answer to these questions. For myself, I strongly suspect that he appeared as an angel of light. I suppose, it really doesn't matter. To be sure, the only thing that does certainly matter is that the Lord successfully resisted the devil's temptations, so that the plan of salvation could ultimately be secured!

**(p)** **[2:29]** Would the Holy Spirit really lead Jesus into the wilderness to be tempted by the devil—as the record seems to read in Matthew's account—thus making it appear as though the Spirit was working in conjunction with the devil? I really don't think that is its meaning. Rather, as I see it, the Lord was directed by the Spirit to enter the wilderness to spend time with the Father. And, *while He was there,* the devil tempted Him. I think this makes much more sense and I have interpreted the *Harmony* accordingly.

**(q)** **[2:30]** In Matthew's account, the devil tells Jesus to turn *stones* (plural) into loaves of bread. However, in Luke's version, the devil tells Jesus to turn a *stone* (singular) into a loaf of bread. I chose Matthew's version as the one for the *Harmony.*

**(r)** **[2:37]** The Sanhedrin was the highest legal authority of the Jewish nation. Among other things, it served in practical terms as the nation's court of law. A description of some its functions and practices can be found throughout Chapter 17 of the *Harmony.*

**(s)** **[2:41]** John denied being Elijah as his ministry is described in the Malachi text. In reality, though, Jesus clearly declared that John's ministry *was,* in fact, the fulfillment of that prophecy (Matthew 17:11-13). Of course, John was not the exact person named Elijah, but rather he came *in the power of Elijah*. When John denied that he was Elijah, it is not clear what he had in mind. He could have meant that he was *not* the *actual* person Elijah (as above). Or he could have meant that he did *not know* that his ministry was a fulfillment of that prophecy. Or maybe John was just being modest. For myself, I suspect that John's point was that he did not claim to be the actual person Elijah who had come down from heaven. But in any case, we really do not know why John responded the way he did. In the *Harmony*, I just let his statement stand as he spoke it.

**(t)** **[2:47]** The text does not actually say Jesus was that very moment standing in the crowd. However, based upon the context, such an interpretation is possible. In fact, the impact of John's words would be much more effective if John actually saw Jesus standing there. Accordingly, in the *Harmony* I recorded it that way.

**(u)** **[2:53]** Andrew's name is mentioned. The name of the other disciple is not mentioned. Following the normal practice of John—the author of the Gospel of John—(John 21:20-23, etc.), he did not include his own name in his book (*Harmony* 18:83-86, etc.) It seems logical to most scholars, then, that this second disciple was John. Accordingly, that is the way I recorded the event in the *Harmony*.

**(v)** **[2:56]** (See above.)

**(w)** **[2:58]** It is often suggested that Jesus nicknamed Simon as "Peter"—a "stone" (as opposed to "Rock")—to indicate his unstable character. While this may be true, I am not convinced. In truth, we really don't why Jesus called him Peter.

**(x)** **[2:69]** The "third day" is a Jewish idiom that refers to the day after tomorrow. Thus, in the *Harmony*, I use the phrase "a couple of days later" at the beginning of the text, which means the same thing.

**(y)** **[2:71]** In this text, Jesus addressed His mother as "Woman." In the *Harmony*, I changed it to "Mother." In the times of Jesus, to address one's mother as "woman" was a sign of respect. Nevertheless, even knowing this, I was still uncomfortable using the word that way in the *Harmony*. It sounds so foreign, even disrespectful, in our usage of the word today! So that is why I changed the word to "Mother."

**(z) [2:73]** As implied in the text, the Jews were big proponents of all types of ceremonial washings and purifications. For more detail on this subject see *Harmony* 10:1, 2.

**(aa) [2:74]** The Greek work for "wine" can refer to *either* fermented *or* unfermented wine (or grape juice). I find it difficult to believe that Jesus actually made an alcoholic beverage, which, at a marriage feast could easily have led to public drunkenness!

**(bb)[2:77]** It is clear from the Gospel record that Jesus had both brothers and sisters (Matthew 13:54-56), as found in *Harmony* 7:1; 8:60; 11:2. (See additional information there.)

# Part II

*Public Ministry:*

*The Judean*

*and*

*Galilean Ministries*

*(Passover, Spring, A.D. 28-*

*Passover, Spring, A.D. 30)*

# CHAPTER THREE

## THE JUDEAN MINISTRY OF JESUS—

**From the First Cleansing of the Temple, to the Lord's Defense Before the Sanhedrin**

**(Passover, Spring, A.D. 28 - Passover, Spring, A.D. 29)**

—

***The Timeline of the Ministry of Jesus, Segment Two: Spring, A.D. 28 — Autumn, A.D. 28***[(a)]

The first six months of the Lord's ministry—Autumn, A.D. 27 through Spring, A.D. 28—had concluded. About three more years of His work yet remained. The first six months began with His baptism. Very soon after that, the Lord was tempted for 40 days in the wilderness. Upon His return from the desert, John the Baptist declared that Jesus was the "Lamb of God." Immediately after that, Jesus began the process of selecting certain individuals to become His disciples. A short time later, Jesus officially began His public ministry by performing His first miracle: turning water into wine at the wedding feast at Cana.[1]

The Lord's main focus of this first six-month segment of His ministry was establishing a firm relationship with His Father—during the 40-day wilderness experience—as well as forming a strong foundation of trust with a portion of those who would become His closest disciples. Overall, it was a "getting started" time for Jesus and His ministry.[2]

No doubt Jesus did a number of other things during these six months, but the Gospel record does not mention any more of them.[3]

During the second segment of six months (2/7)—beginning with the Passover of A.D. 28—Jesus cleansed the Temple for the first time, and had a night meeting with Nicodemus. Jesus also began His first significant and extended public work of ministry. It was in the southern province of Judea. After leaving Judea,

Jesus headed toward the northern province of Galilee to begin a work there. On His way, He met with a woman—a Gentile, or non-Jew—at Jacob's well. So then it could be said that His Judean ministry lasted around six months—from the Spring of A.D. 28, to the Autumn of that year. As was true with the first six-month segment of Christ's ministry, the Gospel record contains relatively few details regarding the events that took place during this time period.(b) [4]

—

## The Lord Begins His Ministry in Judea
## < Passover, Spring, A.D. 28 (2/7) >
## (John 2:13-3:36)

### — The First Cleansing of the Temple(c)
### < Passover, Spring, A.D. 28 (2/7) >
### {John 2:13-25}

In the spring of A.D. 28, when it was time for the Jews to celebrate the Passover, Jesus journeyed over 80 miles south from Capernaum in Galilee to Jerusalem in Judea. When He entered the Temple court in the Holy City, He noticed a number of people were selling oxen, sheep, and doves on the spot. There were also moneychangers seated there. [*Harmony* 14:44, 45][1]

> The Jews provided these animals for the Passover visitors to use for their required sacrifices. This way, travelers would not need to suffer the inconvenience of bringing animals along with them on the long trip there. Instead, they could purchase them at the Temple. However, there was a sinister side to this arrangement. The animals could be purchased only with a special "Temple coin"—a coinage which had to be procured at an increased rate of exchange from the "moneychangers." In other words, there was a significant profit to be made at the expense of the people who were in town for the sole purpose of worshipping their God! Additionally, the animals themselves were extremely overpriced. But even though the people knew that they were being cheated, many were still willing to pay exorbitant prices because of the convenience involved. The motives behind the entire practice were displeasing to the Lord. In addition, such a procedure obviously detracted from the worshipful atmosphere of the Temple.

---

1 John 2:13, 14

Jesus fashioned a whip of small cords made from reeds, and with it, drove out all those who were selling the animals. He also cast out the moneychangers and even the animals themselves, including all the sheep and oxen. He overturned the tables, dumping the coins onto the floor. And to those who were selling the doves, He cried out, "Take these birds out of here . . . now! Stop making My Father's house a place of common merchandise!" [*Harmony* 14:150/2][2]

This episode reminded the Lord's disciples of the Old Testament text which read, "Enthusiastic love for Your house"—the Temple—"has overwhelmed Me." [Psalm 69:9][3]

Reacting to the stern command of Jesus, the Jewish leaders indignantly challenged Him, saying, "Who do you think You are? What sign"—or miracle—"can You perform as evidence to prove that You have the authority to throw the moneychangers out of the Temple as You have just done?" [*Harmony* 12:150/2; 17:36][4]

In a flash, Jesus replied, "Annihilate this Temple and within three days I will restore it to its original condition." [*Harmony* 7:14][5]

Shocked by the Lord's reply, the Jews retorted, saying, "That's impossible!" Pointing at the Temple, they added, "Why, it took no less than 46 years to build this Temple in the first place. So how is it that You can rebuild it again in a mere three days? Such utter foolishness!"[(d)] [6]

> Obviously, the Jewish leaders had no clue what Jesus meant by these words. To them, it was nothing more than a ridiculous, arrogant declaration.

But of course Jesus was describing His body as a "temple." Indeed, the Lord's body and ministry, in part, were symbolized by the Temple building itself. So, when Jesus made His prediction, He was, in fact, referring to the resurrection of His body three days after His crucifixion—events which would take place three years into the future. [*Harmony* 18:50] And, it was only when this prophecy was literally fulfilled at the resurrection, that His disciples fully understood what He

---

2 John 2:15, 16
3 John 2:17
4 John 2:18
5 John 2:19
6 John 2:20

meant by this declaration. This helped confirm their belief in the Old Testament prophecies regarding the ministry of the Messiah [Psalm 16:8-11; Acts 2:24-28], as well as Jesus' own words about His work.[7]

> On the surface it might appear that the Lord's reference to destroying the Temple and the rebuilding of it in three days was irrelevant to the question which the Jewish leaders had posed to Him regarding His authority for casting out the moneychangers. But the Lord's cryptic response was significant. From the Savior's perspective, the greatest evidence of His authority as the Messiah would be demonstrated when He was resurrected from the dead. Of course, at the present moment, the Jewish leaders did not recognize that fact. But when Jesus was actually resurrected, they would understand it very well! [*Harmony* 18:31][1]
>
> Also, the cleansing of the Temple symbolized the restoration of the understanding of the true meaning of the Temple and its services, which were, in reality, a symbolism of the entire plan of salvation. For example, the Altar of Burnt Offering [Exodus 27:1-8] represented the cross. The Altar of Incense [Exodus 30:1-8] symbolized the prayers of God's people. The Ark of the Covenant [Exodus 25:10-22] represented God's Throne. And it was, after the death and resurrection of the Lord, that a fuller understanding of the Christian faith was accomplished. By both the death and resurrection of the Lord, the true power of God would be revealed—the power both to forgive sins, and to impart eternal life to those who repent of their sins. Both of these principles were illustrated in the Temple and its services. Indeed, a clearer understanding of salvation, which had been lost for many years, was restored by the death and resurrection of Jesus.[2]
>
> Again, by making His prophecy regarding the rebuilding of the Temple—that is, His body—in three days, He was predicting both His death and resurrection. Later on, the disciples who loved Him and the Jewish leadership who hated Him would know that the Lord clearly knew His future, and what would happen to Him. Once more, by making this prophecy . . . and miraculously fulfilling it, Jesus demonstrated Himself to be the Messiah![3]

---

[7] John 2:21, 22

> Already this early in His ministry the Jewish leaders were aligned against Jesus. Their mindset was one of rebellion and a refusal to listen to reason—especially from the Lord Himself. In truth, by their own choice, it was already too late for the Jewish leadership as a group to accept Jesus as the Messiah and follow His words! As individuals, a few might accept Him. But as a group, the choice for outright rejection was very early on firmly set in place. [*Harmony* 14:150-154][4]

During the remaining time of the Passover season, Jesus stayed in Jerusalem. Many believed that He was the Messiah because of the miracles which He performed during that time period. However, the details of these miracles are not recorded in the Gospel story. [*Harmony* 3:10, 68][8]

Throughout this time, Jesus refused to allow Himself to be placed under the control of the people because He did not trust them to be in charge of His ministry or actions. He knew that people could be quite fickle: One day they might be willing to proclaim Him as King while the next day they might want to kill Him! No one needed to explain this strange paradox to Jesus because He understood the true nature of sinful humanity. [*Harmony* 2:34/][9]

> The so-called cleansing of the Temple was the first of many, many confrontations Jesus would have with the leaders of Israel during the course of His public ministry. And certainly it is no exaggeration to say that this first confrontation did not go well! During the next three years, relations would never get any better between Jesus and the Jewish leaders. In fact, things would only worsen. [*Harmony* 11:175][1]
>
> Why did Jesus, so near the commencement of His ministry, choose to cast the moneychangers out of the Temple, thus causing great tension between the Jewish leaders and Him? There are at least two good reasons for the approach Jesus used.[2]
>
> First, as the true Messiah, Jesus had the right and authority to declare what was either appropriate or inappropriate to take place in the Temple. Indeed, as the Messiah of Israel, He had to take a stand, which He emphatically did. Moreover, by casting out the moneychangers, Jesus was able—at least for a brief time—to restore to the Temple and its services to the sanctity of proper public worship. But beyond that, by His

8 John 2:23

9 John 2:24, 25

action the Lord made an official public declaration—though somewhat indirectly—that He was the Messiah. Further, He was sending a notice to both the Jewish leaders and the common people that He was in charge, and not they.[3]

Second, the style of worship that usually took place in the Temple presented the public face of the Jewish religion and its beliefs before the peoples of the world. The entire process of selling animals in the Temple area was extremely offensive to the Lord. Jesus could not remain silent! The entire system of public worship which regularly transpired in the Temple symbolized various aspects of the plan of salvation. Thus, among other things, the selling of animals in the Temple area severely tainted the people's understanding of that plan. In casting out the moneychangers, the Lord attempted to present before the people a correct understanding of the truth regarding the plan of salvation. As the Messiah, He had not only the right but also the divine responsibility to do so.[4]

### — The Night Visit of Nicodemus
### < Passover, Spring, A.D. 28 (2/7) >
### {John 3:1-21}

Now there was a certain Pharisee named Nicodemus who was a ruler of the Jews. [*Harmony* 11:38; 17:36/2; 18:8] Being called a "ruler of the Jews" means that he was a member of the Hebrew Council, the Sanhedrin. Nicodemus had been watching closely the actions of Jesus—such as the cleansing of the Temple [*Harmony* 3:1-7]—and listening carefully to His words. He had marveled at the Lord's miracles. [*Harmony* 3:8] He was intrigued by the possibility that this young Teacher was the Messiah of Bible prophecy. But, not wanting to reveal his suspicions to his doubting fellow rulers—who were still quite agitated over the Lord's casting out of the moneychangers from the Temple—he made a secret visit to Jesus by night. Nicodemus wanted to debate the theology of the Biblical teaching regarding the soon-coming Messiah. He also wanted to explore with Jesus the possibility that He *might* be that Messiah.(e) (f) [10]

Seeking to impress Jesus, Nicodemus began by complimenting Him, saying, "Rabbi,"—that is, "Teacher"—"it is obvious to us that You have come as a teacher from God, and at His direction! For no one can perform the kind of the miracles

[10] John 3:1, 2

which You have been doing, unless, of course, He has received special power from God."[11]

> Nicodemus hinted that he thought Jesus *might* be the Messiah. On the other hand, when he called Jesus a "teacher" rather than the Messiah, Nicodemus was expressing some doubt as to whether Jesus actually was the Christ. However, Nicodemus was hoping that the Lord might declare Himself to be such. If the Lord would do that, then he could enter into a theological debate with Jesus on the matter.[1]

> Jesus, reading Nicodemus's thoughts, ignored these words of intended flattery from the Pharisee. He knew that Nicodemus sought a more personal understanding of His ministry—that is, the kind of understanding that would give new meaning to his *personal life.* But Jesus also knew that Nicodemus was very hesitant to discuss openly the subject of his dire need and desire for personal conversion. To do so would make it appear that Nicodemus had some fault in his life that needed to be corrected—something he would be very slow to admit to Jesus, whom he considered, at least for the time being, his inferior. Of course, at that moment, an intellectual debate over various theological points—the type of discussion that Nicodemus wanted—would not solve the deep spiritual problems which the Pharisee had in his heart. So it was that, while Nicodemus desired for himself a change of heart, he refused to admit such to Jesus or even to himself! To be sure, while the Pharisee believed he was living a righteous life, his experience was not filled with the kind of peace and satisfaction he would have thought such a life should produce. In short, Nicodemus was living a confused, contradictory life.[2]

In response to Nicodemus, Jesus, getting directly to the point, declared, "It is an absolute fact that unless a man is born again from above he will not be saved in the kingdom of God!"[12]

> In effect Jesus was saying, "A person, in order to be saved, must first experience a complete life-changing repentance of heart and mind. [*Harmony* 2:3; 4:2] This means that what's really essential for *you*, Nicodemus, is to experience the power of conversion in *your* life, before

---

11 John 3:2

12 John 3:3

you can even begin to think that you are able debate with Me the issue regarding the mission of the Messiah."[1]

Nicodemus well understood the spiritual nature of the Lord's statement. But in spite of the deep longing within his heart, as a faithful Jew he was upset that Jesus had suggested that he, from among the cream of the Jewish people, actually needed to be converted. After all, from his Jewish viewpoint, he was well on his way to salvation! Nicodemus believed that because of this, he was well prepared for a debate with Jesus on theological points. Of course, Jesus saw it the opposite way![2]

Responding to Jesus, Nicodemus ridiculed His declaration about the new birth as though Jesus meant it to be literal. Nicodemus said, "That doesn't make sense! How can a man be born when he is already an adult? Do you really think that he can enter a second time, as a baby, into his mother's womb? That's impossible! Ridiculous!"[13]

Actually, Nicodemus did *not* believe that the Lord was really saying he needed to enter again into his mother's womb. But because Nicodemus did not wish to discuss freely with Jesus the emptiness he felt within his own heart, he tried to make light of the Lord's statement so as to effectively sidestep the issue.

Ignoring Nicodemus's incredulous words, Jesus continued to drive home His spiritual point by declaring further, "Yes, with great certainty, I tell you again, that unless one is born of both the water and the Holy Spirit, one simply cannot be saved in the kingdom of God! That is, one must be baptized by water, which is a symbol of the transforming power of conversion"—the new birth—"which takes place in the life of everyone, *including you,* who is truly touched by the energy of the Holy Spirit." [*Harmony* 2:3][14]

Among the Jews, baptism by water was performed when a non-Jew was converted to Judaism. But Jews themselves usually were not baptized. They felt no necessity to do so. This was especially true of many of the Jewish leaders—including Nicodemus—who considered themselves the most righteous and blameless of anyone. But Nicodemus did, in fact, need the kind of baptism which John the Baptist was offering in the

13 John 3:4

14 John 3:5

Jordan River. More importantly, he needed to experience the conversion of the heart that baptism symbolized.

"Being born in the flesh," Jesus continued, "as you were as a baby, is one thing. Of course, that is not what I'm talking about! But being born of the Holy Spirit is a *spiritual* thing, which is clearly My point! So then, there is no need for you to act amazed when I said, 'You must receive the spiritual birthing from above.'"[15]

Here, by powerful words, Jesus strongly implied that Nicodemus needed a conversion experience . . . just like non-Jews!

"To illustrate My point: It is like the wind," the Lord continued with His explanation. "It blows wherever it wishes. Of course, you can hear its sound, but you do not know—or see—where it comes from. Neither do you know—or see—where it's going. But you can see its effects! It is the same way with those who are born again of the Holy Spirit. While you cannot literally see the Holy Spirit working within people, you can certainly see its dramatic impact in the lives of those who have been influenced by its power. And, Nicodemus, that's exactly what you need in your life!" [*Harmony* 7:9][16]

Once more, Nicodemus was stung by the clear statement that he, a highly respected and law abiding Jewish leader, needed such a conversion experience.

Nicodemus, to show his displeasure at the words of Jesus, pretended that he did not understand what Jesus' words meant. So he said, "I don't really understand what You are talking about. How does that make any sense?"[17]

Here a definite conflict was taking place between Jesus and Nicodemus. On one hand, Nicodemus believed that he did not need conversion. And to show his displeasure at the suggestion that he needed to be converted, he acted as though the Lord's reference to the "new birth" actually meant to be born again in his mother's womb. On the other hand, Jesus was relentless in His determination to inform Nicodemus that he did, in fact, need the "new birth" experience. Yet ironically, at the same time, Nicodemus felt a huge emptiness in his heart. But the really sad part

---

15 John 3:6, 7

16 John 3:8

17 John 3:9

was that, while Jesus sought to satisfy that need, the Pharisee, because of pride, continued strongly to resist.

But Jesus, not allowing Nicodemus off the hook, replied, "You call yourself a teacher in Israel? Yet, how is it that you do not understand even these basic concepts of salvation? Nicodemus, the reason that you are struggling with this idea is that you have not yet experienced it for yourself! Let Me tell you the truth: Those of us who understand the meaning of the new birth, and how it is activated in the lives of people are quite able to explain it to others. But those who have not yet experienced it—such as you—are neither able to grasp it for yourself nor to explain it to others. You see, in your own case, throughout your life and teaching, your knowledge has been merely theoretical and not personal. You talk a good story, but you don't live it! That is why you seem to be confused about My words which I've spoken to you. And that is also why you seem to reject them. In short, you refuse to understand it because your refuse to actually experience it!"[18]

All his life Nicodemus had tried to earn salvation by the *outward* performance of righteous deeds. However, he had never experienced true conversion, which changes the heart from *within*. [*Harmony* 10:13]

"The really sad part is," Jesus added, "if you are not able to comprehend or accept the simple, basic, elementary concepts of how a person is saved—such as I have illustrated to you by describing the wind [*Harmony* 3:16]—how will you be able to understand or accept the heavier, more profound concepts of heavenly things? This includes such things as the theology of the coming of the Messiah—the kind of thing you want to discuss with Me."[19]

Again, Nicodemus had wanted to debate the various points of the Scripture regarding the coming of the Messiah. He wanted to compare his views of who or what the Messiah would be with those of the Savior. He was curious to see if Jesus would enter into such a debate, and perhaps, claim to be the Messiah by proving it to him by convincing arguments . . . or, even better yet, a miracle! But Jesus would neither enter into such a debate nor work such a miracle. At that moment, Nicodemus needed something much more important: personal conversion. That would continue to remain the Lord's focus with the Jewish leader.

---

[18] John 3:10, 11

[19] John 3:12

Jesus continued, chiding Nicodemus, "No one can perfectly understand the things of heaven unless he's been there. Only one of the two of us has been to heaven—and that is, the Son of Man. Of the two of us, He is the only one who has come from heaven. So only He can truly understand the things of heaven and speak with total accuracy regarding them. Thus, you should not attempt to debate these issues with Me. Rather, you should concentrate on understanding the basic, so-called earthly concepts of salvation . . . such as how to be saved! Your discussion with Me has made it obvious that these things are difficult enough for you to grasp! So then, focus on them." [*Harmony* 9:40/][20]

> Nicodemus, as a teacher in Israel, thought that he had the right to challenge Jesus and to debate with Him. Nicodemus, heavily trained in the judgmental thinking of the Pharisees, thought that he was on an equal footing with the Lord, if not superior to Him. Jesus had to make it clear that, in spite of his intense training, Nicodemus was hardly prepared, either spiritually or intellectually, to actually debate and argue with the Creator of heaven and earth, those issues which he had neither comprehended nor experienced!

Jesus added words of encouragement: "However, these rudiments of the gift of salvation can be easily understood . . . should you try. They can be compared to the Scriptural story about when many of the children of Israel were bitten by snakes, and how Moses placed a model snake on a stick and lifted it up in the wilderness. [Numbers 21:6-9] Do you remember that story? Well, as you know, those who gazed at that snake were healed of the poisonous bites. In a similar manner, the Son of Man will someday be lifted up, and all who place their confidence and trust in Him and what He has done for them will not suffer eternal death but rather secure eternal life." [*Harmony* 17:125, 126][21]

> Of course, when He mentioned the Son of Man being "lifted up," Jesus spoke about His ultimate death on the cross. And, it is by faith—"gazing" as it were upon Jesus, and considering carefully what He did for the world as He hung on that cross—that all sinners can secure the hope of eternal life. It is by placing one's personal confidence and trust in what Jesus secured on the cross as the world's Sin Bearer, that salvation can be truly understood and effectively experienced. This is what Nicodemus needed to understand—especially for himself. And sadly, it was precisely

---

20 John 3:13
21 John 3:14, 15

this that Nicodemus—in spite of his religious training—did not comprehend!

"It was because God the Father loved the world with so much passion," the Lord added, "that He gave His only Son as a Gift to the world. And, whoever maintains a resolute trust in Him will not suffer eternal death, but rather, bask in the joys of eternal life. It follows, then, that the Father did not send His Son into the world to function primarily as its condemning judge. No! Instead, the Son came so that the world might have the opportunity through Him to be spared from eternal death. The basis of salvation, then, is faith in what the Son of Man can do for all the sinners of the world who have placed their trust in Him. [*Harmony* 13:77/; 14:148][(g)][22]

"So then, everyone who trusts in the Son will not be condemned in the judgment. On the other hand, I should add, those who refuse to trust in Him are already condemned. And why is this? It is because they have refused to trust in the name of God's only Son—the only One who can provide salvation for them. Belief in the Son, then, is the key, the very basis of salvation. Those who truly believe will be saved. Those who do not believe will be lost. It is just that simple! Again, true belief in the Son is the foundation of salvation." [*Harmony* 3:89][(h)][23]

It should be noted, here, that the word "belief" entails much more than a mere intellectual belief in Jesus. It obviously includes a deep emotional commitment to the cause of the Lord, which clearly involves a personal one-on-one relationship with the Savior.

"In fact," the Lord continued, "this is what will ultimately lead to the condemnation of many in the world during the judgment: That is, as the Light of the truth of the Gospel message shines brightly into the world, most evil men will continue to love the darkness of sin in preference to the Light of salvation. And why is that? Because sin has such a bewitching power over them! To say it once more, when people are controlled by sin, they despise the Light. They do not desire to come into the Light of truth, because the Light will expose their sins which they love so much. Consequently, they would rather run from the Light and remain sinners. Indeed, they refuse to be changed by the power of the Gospel." [*Harmony* 3:33; 11:42] Jesus concluded His discussion with Nicodemus by adding, "On the other hand, those who desire to live constantly by the energy

22 John 3:16, 17
23 John 3:18

of the Light of truth will receive readily the benefits of its brightness. In short, they will accept and embrace the Light. The power of God will enable them constantly to live righteously as it continually transforms them."(i) 24

> Nicodemus had much to consider after his night visit with Jesus was completed. But it would take some time before it would bear fruit. [*Harmony* 11:30; 18:6-9][1]
>
> In His night conversation with Nicodemus, Jesus outlined essential concepts which need to be understood and experienced by anyone who is seeking to receive the gift of eternal life. First and foremost, one must be born again from above. Pure and simple, this refers to the transformation of one's life—that is, the conversion of the human mind through a thorough experience of repentance. Second, one should be baptized as a public confession of what has been transpiring in the inner life. Third, this transformation in the life comes as a result of the continual working of the Holy Spirit within the converted individual. Fourth, the work of the Spirit—both in conversion and transformation—takes place when one has a relationship of faith with Jesus. It is by beholding the life and character of Jesus that this transformation occurs. This relationship of faith is illustrated by the Lord's reference to the coming to, and the remaining in, the "Light of truth." [*Harmony* 3:24] This exemplifies the continual progress of the spiritual growth of one who remains constantly in the presence of the Lord.[2]

## — John the Baptist Defends the Lord's Ministry in Judea < Spring through Winter, A.D. 28 (2/7) > {John 3:22-36}

Soon after this, Jesus and His disciples—Andrew, John, Nathanael, Peter, and Philip—began a ministry that expanded out from Jerusalem into the larger part of the southern province of Judea. For some time they ministered in the area, with the Lord's new disciples baptizing many people.[25]

John the Baptist—also in Judea at the time—continued his ministry of baptizing and teaching. Specifically, he was working in Aenon near Salim, which was in the northeast part of the province. There was a good deal of water there, making it possible to baptize by immersion the many people who continued to

24 John 3:19-21

25 John 3:22; 4:1, 2

come to see him. (Of course, this was well before John had been cast into prison. [*Harmony* 3:69-71])[26]

At this time, some of John's own disciples entered into a discussion with certain of the Jewish leaders regarding the meaning of ceremonial washings involving the use of water. The Jews had an elaborate system of man-made physical washings—purely ceremonial in nature—that were purported to cleanse their souls from sin. Of course, these washings were foolish. Later on in His ministry, Jesus would directly address this system of washings. [*Harmony* 10:1-8][27]

> Not surprisingly, during this discussion that took place between John's disciples and the Jewish leaders, the subject of baptism by immersion was raised. This discussion would naturally include the purpose of baptism, for baptism was a physical washing of sorts that symbolized the true cleansing of the soul. Obviously, John's disciples strongly defended their master's ministry. This discussion caused to rise to the surface a point of irritation that they had harbored for some time. Specifically, they were concerned that Jesus and His disciples were conducting a ministry similar to theirs. In short, they considered the ministry of Jesus to be unfair for, in a sense, it was in competition with John's own work. It so happened that their discussion with the Jewish leaders about the meaning of baptism helped solidify their thinking that John's baptizing ministry belonged exclusively to him, and to no one else . . . including Jesus. After all, they reasoned, John was there first! [*Harmony* 3:34]

Some of John's disciples came to him and said, "Teacher, guess what? We have heard that the One named Jesus, who was with you when you were ministering on the eastern side of the Jordan River—the One whom you have declared to be the 'Lamb of God' [*Harmony* 2:49, 53]—is Himself baptizing individuals. And, many, many people are going to Him . . . and not you. Is that fair? Is that right?" [*Harmony* 3:34][28]

John explained, "A man can do only what the God of heaven has called him to do. This is certainly true in my case. Remember, you have heard me declare, 'I am not the Messiah!' [*Harmony* 2:39] but rather 'I have been sent to lead the way before Him.' [*Harmony* 2:45] Isn't that right? Again, I can do only what God has

---

26 John 3:23, 24

27 John 3:25

28 John 3:26

called me to do—nothing more! My work, then, was to prepare the way for His ministry, to help to make it more successful. You see, in the end, it is *His* ministry that truly counts . . . not mine"[29]

"Look at it this way!" John continued, "In a marriage, it is the groom who gets the bride. The best man is the one who only stands up for the groom, listening to what the groom has to say, and so forth. Obviously the best man *never* gets the bride! Nevertheless, the best man is happy for the groom and, during the marriage ceremony, delights to hear every word which the groom utters. That is his satisfaction. I repeat: It is the groom, never the best man, who gets the bride. In a similar way, I am more than happy for the groom—who, in this case, is Jesus, the Messiah. It is He who is to get the 'bride'—that is, all those who are now following after Him. I am just the 'best man,' so to speak. Thus, as in the case of the groom and the best man, the Lord's successes result in my joyous pleasure. In short, then, He must increase in popularity and influence, while I must decrease in those same things! Does that make sense to you? [*Harmony* 8:6][30]

"Furthermore," John added, "Jesus, the Messiah, originally came from heaven. [*Harmony* 1:1] This simple fact makes Him much more awesome and important than those of us who have come into existence by the natural, human way of this world. Thus I, who am from the world, am able to speak merely of earthly things. But because Jesus has come from heaven, therefore He is greater than everything and everyone who is earthly. [*Harmony* 1:6] So then, what He has seen and heard of the things which have happened in heaven, He has shared with us here on the earth. Because of who He is and where He has come from, He has done just that. Obviously, I cannot.[31]

"Sadly, so few have been willing to accept the truths which Jesus has presented to them—so few as to make it seem that no one has received Him! But those few who have received the Lord's message, have verified it"—that is, have shown it to be the truth—"by the depth of their conversion experience. It is as if they have placed their stamp of approval upon the ministry of Jesus when they were converted through the power of the words which He has spoken to them. Indeed, they have authenticated it in their own lives![32]

---

29 John 3:27, 28
30 John 3:29, 30
31 John 3:31, 32
32 John 3:32, 33

"Let Me say it once more, the Messiah—Jesus—has been sent from God," John concluded. "Because of that, He is able to speak the exact words of God. Furthermore, there is no limit to the power of the Holy Spirit in His life." [*Harmony* 2:19] (The entire Godhead, then—the Father, the Son, and the Spirit—were involved in the ministry of Jesus.) "Yes, indeed," John continued, "based upon what we have seen, there can be no doubt that the Father loves the Son, and consequently, has placed everything under His controlling authority. Because of this, those who continue to believe and put their trust in the Son of God will receive eternal life! On the other hand, those who do not place their trust in the Son, and accordingly, remain rebellious in their lives, will not receive everlasting life. It is certainly true that in the judgment the wrath of God will be hurled against them who have remained in their sins . . . and God's wrath will crush them! [*Harmony* 3:22-24] In summary, then, there is no one on this earth, including me, who has the authority which the Messiah alone possesses. Do you see that?"[33]

> By these powerful words, John was able partially to assuage the concerns of his disciples who were questioning the divine authorization of the ministry of Jesus. However, they continued to have lingering doubts.[1]

—

## *The Timeline of the Ministry of Jesus, Segment Three: Autumn A.D. 28 — Spring A.D. 29*[j]

The first full year of the Lord's ministry was concluded, with two and half years yet remaining. During the first half of that year—Autumn, A.D. 27 through Spring, A.D. 28—Jesus was baptized, was tempted in the wilderness, called His first disciples, and performed His first miracle in Cana. The second half of that first year—Spring, A.D. 28 through Autumn, A.D. 28—included events surrounding the Savior's trip to the Passover celebration in Jerusalem. While in Jerusalem, Jesus cast out the moneychangers from the Temple and had a night visit with Nicodemus. This was followed by a relatively brief public ministry in the southern province of Judea. In fact, this was the only sustained length of time Jesus spent ministering in Israel's most populous province. Most of the rest of the Lord's time was spent elsewhere. In the Gospel record, there are only a few actual details given of the Lord's ministry in Judea. This six-month

---

33 John 3:34-36

period concluded with a controversy that arose when John the Baptist's disciples jealously questioned the Lord's ministry.[2]

In the next six-months segment (3/7)—Autumn, A.D. 28 through Spring, A.D. 29—Jesus concluded His ministry in Judea and headed toward the northern province of Galilee to begin a ministry there. On the way to Galilee, Jesus stopped in Samaria and visited with a woman—a Samaritan—at Jacob's Well. This was a significant event for it would mark the first recorded time that the Lord worked with a non-Jew. The impact of this fact would ultimately have a far-reaching effect upon His ministry as well as on the combined ministries of His followers. At the conclusion of this time-period, Jesus healed a certain nobleman's son.(k) [3]

—

## A Sojourn Into Galilee
## < Winter, A.D. 29-Spring, A.D. 30 (3/7) >
## (Matthew 14:3-5; Luke 3:19, 20; John 3:23; 4:1-54)

### — The Conversion of the Samaritan Woman at Jacob's Well
### < Winter, A.D. 29 (3/7) >
### {John 4:1-42}

Even though Jesus did not personally baptize people, His disciples did. In fact, they baptized many more converts than even John the Baptist. When the Pharisees discovered this fact, they tried to use it to their advantage. [*Harmony* 3:27, 27/] Because they were very nervous about the ministries of both Jesus and John, they sought to foster the natural jealousy of John's disciples toward the ministry of Jesus. However, John tried to prevent the jealousy of his disciples toward the Master from becoming a major problem [*Harmony* 3:25-33], but to no avail. So, in order to prevent the conflict from boiling over, Jesus decided to allow John to minister alone in Judea. Thus, Jesus left the southern province and returned to Galilee to begin a ministry there. On His way to that northern province, He purposefully chose the road that required travelers to pass through the province of Samaria.[34]

> Samaria was sandwiched between Galilee to the north and Judea to the south. Nearly 1,000 years before, the original nation of Israel was divided into two kingdoms: Israel was to the north, composed mainly

---

[34] John 4:1-4

of nine and half tribes. Judah—later Judea—was to the south, primarily made up of two and half tribes. Israel's capital was the city of Samaria, and Judah's capital was Jerusalem. Often the entire northern nation of Israel was called Samaria. Unfortunately this northern kingdom was noted mainly for its extreme apostasy. Thus, as a result of God's judgment, it was completely destroyed by the Assyrian Empire some 700 years before the birth of Jesus. Most of the people of the region were carried into exile. But, in order to keep the land from becoming desolate, Assyria transplanted a number of people from Syria, Babylonia, and northern Mesopotamia into the region. Of course, they brought with them their own pagan religions. The region of Samaria of Christ's day was once a large portion of that northern kingdom of Israel, filled with the descendants of those pagan transplants. [2 Kings 17:24][1]

After the passing of many years, the Jewish religion of the southern kingdom of Judea influenced the pagan religions of Samaria, leading to a blending of their various religious beliefs. Ultimately, the Samaritans of the north wanted to be accepted by the Jews of the south. However, the Jews refused to allow them to be a part of their religion, for they considered the Samaritans' religious teachings to be heretical in nature. This rejection gave rise to a bitter hatred between the two nations, which, by the time of Jesus, was quite profound. Even though the two religions were surprisingly similar to each other—including a belief in a soon-coming Messiah [*Harmony* 3:49, 52]—the two nations were constant enemies of each other. Distrust was rampant. The Samaritans at one time even had their own rival temple built on Mount Gerizim in Samaria. Though this temple no longer existed during the Lord's lifetime, the Samaritans still celebrated the Passover on that mountain. Relations continued to deteriorate between the two nations. In fact, they hardly ever communicated with each other. Often Jewish travelers heading north or south, would bypass Samaria so as to avoid the Samaritan people altogether. [*Harmony* 11:68, 122, 133/, 157][2]

On His way through Samaria, Jesus stopped near the city of Sychar at the foot of Mount Gerizim by the plot of land that Jacob had given to his son Joseph. A well was located there. It had been dug personally by Jacob. Thus it was commonly known as "Jacob's Well." The Samaritans honored Jacob in their religion to the same extent that the Jews reverenced his grandfather, Abraham.

Jesus was thirsty and weary, so He sat at the well. Meanwhile, His disciples went into Sychar to purchase some food for it was noon.[35]

While He was resting there, a Samaritan woman came to fetch water from the well. Jesus asked her, "Please give Me something to drink." [*Harmony* 10:14/][36]

Knowing of the very strained relationship that existed between Jews and Samaritans, the woman asked incredulously, "How is it that You, a Jew, would ask me, a Samaritan—a woman no less—for a drink of water?" The woman was especially surprised—for a Jewish man to talk with a Samaritan woman simply was not done![37]

Jesus calmly yet dramatically answered, "If you truly understood the gift of salvation given by God, and who it was that has asked you for a drink of water, you would have asked Him instead, and He would have given you living water!" [*Harmony* 11:24] Here, Jesus used water as an illustration of the transforming power of the Gospel that He, as the Savior of the world, was willing to impart to the woman.[38]

While the woman realized that Jesus must have been talking about something other than just common water in a well, she had a hard time grasping what precisely He meant by such a declaration. Therefore she commented, "Sir, I see that You have nothing to use by which to draw water. The well is deep. So how can You draw for me this so-called 'living water' from this well? Do you actually claim to be more powerful than our father Jacob who dug this well in the first place? He drank water from it. And from it, he also quenched the thirst of his sons and his cattle. So then, if our national hero, Jacob, drank just ordinary water from this well, then how can You get this so-called 'living water' from it? I don't understand!"[39]

> Obviously the woman was unclear as to what Jesus meant. She thought that the Master was suggesting that He could perhaps miraculously transform the common water of Jacob's Well into some kind of miracle "living water"! She wondered that if Jacob, her national hero, could draw

---

35 John 4:4-6, 8
36 John 4:7
37 John 4:9
38 John 4:10
39 John 4:11, 12

only ordinary water from the well—to drink for himself and to give to other thirsty people and cattle—than how could this Jew—someone normally despised by Samaritans—get so-called "living water" from the same well? Again, it made no sense to her at all. [*Harmony* 11:24; Revelation 14:7]

The Lord tried to clarify His point by deliberately moving the emphasis away from the *literal* water in the well to the *spiritual* water of life. He said, "Everyone who drinks of the water in this well will get thirsty again—just as Jacob did. But whoever drinks of the water which I am indeed able to provide, will never get thirsty again! In fact, the water which I give will be like a gushing fountain of water that is constantly bubbling up within a person to impart eternal life!"[40]

Of course, Jesus was speaking of the power of the Gospel to permanently change people's lives. The "fountain" represented the Gospel's power to perpetually inspire a person to seize and experience the blessings of eternal life. Even though the woman began to understand that Jesus was probably talking about something other than literal water, she still did not fully comprehend the true meaning of the Lord's promise. So she continued to wonder where this special type of water of which Jesus spoke could be obtained—certainly not from Jacob's Well! Then where was it to be found? Clearly the woman had a hard time distinguishing between common water from a well and the "water" that imparts eternal life.

Exposing her continued confusion regarding the precise meaning of the words of the Lord, the woman asked Him, "Give me this water, sir. Just where can I find it? This way I will not get thirsty again, neither will I ever need to come out here and go through the tedious process of drawing water from this well ever again. That would be wonderful!"[41]

Clearly, the woman still did not grasp the deeply spiritual intent of the Lord's statement. Only partially did she get the Lord's meaning. For the most part, she wanted Jesus to provide some special, *literal,* yet miraculous water for her from some undefined location, so that she would no longer need to draw literal water from Jacob's Well again.

40 John 4:13, 14
41 John 4:15

By now, Jesus realized that in order to get through to the confused woman, He needed to intensify her need for a *spiritual* change. This way, she would get her mind off of *literal* water, and focus it upon spiritual drink. So, Jesus totally changed the subject by saying to her, "Go, call your husband to come here."[42]

The woman answered the Lord's command by declaring, "But I have no husband!"[43]

"Ah! You have spoken the truth when you said you have no husband," Jesus boldly responded. "For you have had five husbands! And the one who you are presently living with is not really your husband at all! Isn't that right? Yes, you have declared the truth when you said, 'I have no husband!'" Here, Jesus exposed her life of sin, based upon a number of illicit relationships which she had had.[44]

> By this exchange, Jesus accomplished two things. First, He was finally successful in getting the woman to sense a need for a spiritual change in her life so that she would truly desire the living water He had promised her. Her focus was no longer on drinking literal water from Jacob's Well—or any such well for that matter. Second, because the Lord miraculously knew a hidden fact of her life, the woman began to comprehend that He was much more than a mere human being.

So she boldly commented in return, "Sir, I can see that You are a prophet!" But instead of reaching out at that moment to Jesus for the transforming power of the Gospel in her life, she changed the subject by asking Him a theological question. By doing so, she made it clear that she desired to avoid discussing the subject which Jesus wanted to share with her. This way she would not need to confront her sinful life. Accordingly, the woman queried, "Our fathers have worshipped here on Mount Gerizim, and you Jews say that people ought to worship on Mount Zion in Jerusalem. So which one is the right place? As a prophet, what do You say?" [*Harmony* 3:48][45]

The Lord replied, "As far as truth is concerned, the Jewish religion, properly understood, has the correct understanding of salvation. You Samaritans worship something which you do not really understand. But we Jews know what we worship. However, for now, ma'am, that isn't the point. Please believe Me, the hour

---

42 John 4:16
43 John 4:17
44 John 4:17, 18
45 John 4:19, 20

is coming when you Samaritans will find the truth of the Gospel by worshipping God *neither* on Gerizim, *nor* on Mount Zion in Jerusalem!"(l) [46]

> Jesus declared that the truth of the Scriptures was better understood by the Jews rather than Samaritans. Nevertheless, He wanted the woman to move her focus away from discussing points of theological difference between the two nations and their religions. Rather, He wanted her to redirect her interest to the basic conversion of her heart.

Jesus continued, "Once more, what is of paramount importance for you to know is that the hour is coming—and even now has arrived—that the true worshippers of God will seek to worship the Father in spirit . . . and then in truth. These are the ones whom the Father seeks to worship Him. Yes, doctrine—for example, the *truth* of *where* to worship—is important. But, the *spirit*—the reality of a personal, heart conversion—is just as important. In fact, God requires both."(m) [47]

The Lord concluded His point by explaining, "God is a spiritual being. That is, He is not limited by the mere location of certain buildings and mountains—the kind of thing which has been concerning you. [*Harmony* 3:45] Because of that, true worshippers must *first* worship Him with the 'spirit'—that is, a desire for complete conversion. This is totally separate from specific places of public worship and mere doctrinal truths. It is only after you are converted—that is, to worship God in 'spirit'—that you should concern yourself about the 'truth'—that is, upon which mountain you should worship. Indeed, God wants both things from those who worship Him: spirit and truth. But the spirit—conversion—must come first!"(n) [48]

> In summary, Jesus wanted the woman for the time being to focus solely on her personal salvation—that is, the "spirit." Once she found the gift of eternal life, then she could focus upon where to worship—the "truth." Until she figured out the proper sequence, she would remain confused and unchanged by the Gospel.

Sensing that Jesus might be the Messiah, the Samaritan woman, hinting at that possibility, further commented, "I know that the Messiah, the One called

---

46 John 4:21, 22

47 John 4:23

48 John 4:24

the Christ, is coming. And when He comes He will tell us plainly everything we need to know." [*Harmony* 3:34/2][49]

In a short, powerfully dramatic statement, Jesus verified her suspicions. He frankly declared, "I am! Yes, it is I, the One who is speaking to you right now!" [*Harmony* 11:105][50]

At that very instant, the disciples interrupted the conversation by returning from the city. They were shocked and amazed that Jesus, against the cultural customs of the day, was actually talking with a despised Samaritan—and a woman, no less! But not one of them had the nerve to say to the woman, "What is it that you want?" or to Jesus, "Why are You talking to that Samaritan woman?"[51]

A bit overwhelmed by all that had happened to her, and unsure of the attitude of the returning disciples, the woman immediately left her water pitcher at the well and hurried back into the city. She excitedly informed its inhabitants, saying, "Come with me and see a Man who knows everything that I've ever done! Do you suppose He might be the Christ? I think so!" [*Harmony* 3:34/2] Intrigued, they immediately went with her to see this unusual Person for themselves.[52]

After the woman had left the well, the Lord's disciples, knowing that Jesus had not eaten anything for some time, strongly urged Him, saying, "Rabbi, please eat something!"[53]

"No," He responded, "I have been eating plenty of nourishing food which you know nothing about!"[54]

Puzzled by the Lord's response, the disciples asked each other, "No one has brought food to Him, have they? Of course not! Who around here would have given Him food to eat?"[55]

---

49 John 4:25
50 John 4:26
51 John 4:27
52 John 4:28-30
53 John 4:31
54 John 4:32
55 John 4:33

Hearing their comments to each other, Jesus replied, "Actually, the 'food' which really satisfies Me is to do the will of the Father who has sent Me to complete His work." [*Harmony* 16:107][56]

In Israel, the planting season started in the fall, with the harvest in the springtime. Accordingly, using this as an illustration, Jesus added, "Haven't you been saying, 'There are still four months until the harvest season comes next spring'? On the contrary, I must tell you to lift up your heads and look out over the fields. They are already white with ripened grain for the harvest!" [*Harmony* 8:37; 11:134][57]

> Of course, Jesus referred here to the harvest of souls. The land of the Samaritans was considered a place where it was virtually impossible to spread the Gospel. Yet within a short period of time the woman had been converted and was herself already in the process of sharing her conversion experience with many others! In fact, as the disciples looked out over the fields before them, they could see the people of Samaria already coming through the fields to see Jesus for themselves! Indeed, then, the fields were already "white" for the harvest.

Jesus continued, "At this moment those who are reaping the harvest are being handsomely paid for their labor of gathering the 'grain' of souls for eternal life. Indeed, the one who plants the seed and the one who harvests the grain are able to rejoice together as a team."[58]

> Here in this brief parable the "grain" represented those who had received the gift of eternal life, such as in the case of the Samaritan woman. The "planters" represented the work of Jesus while the "reapers" represented the ministry of His disciples. The "handsome payment" that both the planters and the reapers receive was the indescribable joys of seeing people accept the gift of eternal life. Such would be case of the work of Jesus and His disciples, then and in the future.

The Lord concluded, "No truer words have been spoken, 'One sows and another reaps!' I have sent you to labor in the field of ministry which John the Baptist and his disciples have sown. He and his disciples have labored hard, and

---

56 John 4:34

57 John 4:35

58 John 4:36

your many recent baptisms [*Harmony* 3:25] have shown that you benefited greatly with comparably little effort from what they had already accomplished."[59]

> And in the future there would be even greater results—through the preaching of the Gospel—as the culmination of the labor that Jesus had begun in places such as Samaria. [Acts 1:8; 2:41, 47; 5:14] Thus, the disciples would benefit greatly, not only from the labors of John the Baptist, but from the work of their own Lord and Leader as well.

And so it was that from that city there were many Samaritans who believed in Jesus because of the simple testimony of the woman at Jacob's Well who said, "He told me everything I've ever done." The Samarians who came to see Jesus were so impressed by what they saw in Him that they implored the Savior to remain with them for awhile. So for two days He stayed with them, teaching the Gospel message. As a result, many more believed in Him because of the words which He spoke directly to them.[60]

The converted Samaritans summarized their reaction to Jesus by telling the woman, "We no longer believe in Him simply because of what you said to us. No! Rather, we now believe because we have heard Him for ourselves. We are now convinced that this Man is for certain, the Savior of the world—even the Messiah!"[61]

> It should be noted that the contrast between the receptive nature of the Samaritans and negative, hostile attitude of the Jewish leaders was striking. [*Harmony* 3:1-6][1]

> And, in working with the woman at the well, Jesus demonstrated a high level of wisdom, succeeding not only in breaking down her prejudice, but also, in a relatively short period of time, in leading her into a conversion experience. First, by asking her for a drink of water, He was successful in counteracting a huge amount of prejudice that a Samaritan might normally have against a Jew. Second, when the Lord talked about the "living water," He was seeking to create within the woman a desire for a change in her sinful life. Third, even though at first the woman did not fully understand what He was saying to her, Jesus relentlessly continued to find a way to create that need. Fourth, when the woman finally

---

59 John 4:37, 38

60 John 4:39-41

61 John 4:42

grasped what the Lord was saying—despite having tried to change the subject from her personal salvation to that of theology—Jesus was not deterred in His determination to create within the woman a necessity for change in her life. Fifth, when she finally admitted to a need in her life, He quickly supplied the remedy by sharing the power of the Gospel with her, by revealing Himself to her.[2]

The stories of the Samaritan woman and Nicodemus [*Harmony* 3:10-24] can be analyzed for their contrasts and similarities. Nicodemus was a so-called pious man. In contrast, the woman of Samaria was a sinner. Nicodemus was a part of the church that supposedly taught the truth. The woman belonged to a religion that did not know the truth. Nevertheless, they both needed conversion and transformation of life. They both were reluctant to face the reality of their sinful lives. Both tried to evade the truth of their condition by wanting to discuss theology rather than personal conversion. In both cases, though, Jesus was able to get through to them. However, in the case of Nicodemus—the religious leader—it took two years. [*Harmony* 18:8] In the case of the Samaritan woman—the sinner—it happened almost immediately. Not only was the woman converted, but she quickly shared her faith with others so that they, too, might be converted.[3]

### —Jesus Heals the Nobleman's Son
### < Winter, A.D. 29 (3/7) >
### {John 4:43-54}

After completing His two-day ministry in Samaria, Jesus continued on His journey toward Galilee. [*Harmony* 3:34] When arriving there, Jesus did not stop in His home town of Nazareth. Jesus knew that He would not be well received there. [*Harmony* 4:4-10; 8:59-62] This fact led Him to comment that "a prophet is usually not honored in own country." So He traveled on to other cities within the province of Galilee where the people were receptive to Him and His ministry. Consequently, Jesus labored in those areas. Some were even excited to accept Him as the promised Messiah. These people had watched Jesus closely when they were in Jerusalem for the previous year's Passover. [*Harmony* 3:1-9] They continued to be intrigued by what He was saying and doing. These Galileans were curious to see if the Lord would do many of the same things—especially perform miracles—in their own province that He had done in Judea. They did not have long to wait.[62]

In His Galilean travels, Jesus returned to Cana, which was eight miles north of Nazareth. Cana was the place of His first miracle. It had been a little over a year since He had turned water into wine at the wedding feast. [*Harmony* 2:69-77] There was in the town at this time a certain nobleman—a Jew—who was an assistant to Herod Antipas, the tetrarch—a ruler—of Galilee. This particular nobleman's son was very sick. The youngster was back in his home town of Capernaum, about twenty miles to the northeast. Hearing that Jesus was in the area after His return from Judea, the nobleman went to find Him. He begged Jesus to come down to Capernaum and heal his son, for the lad was near death.[63]

Jesus sensed that the nobleman had limited faith in Him. He further knew that the nobleman would exercise complete faith in Him only if He were to heal his son. This man's faltering faith was characteristic of the people of Galilee at large. Jesus, therefore, said to him—as well as to the people who were listening in—"Unless all of you first see convincing signs and miracles from Me, you will not place your trusting faith in Me. That's not acceptable!" Jesus wanted them to believe in Him before He performed a miracle rather than just after. [*Harmony* 13:56][64]

The nobleman, realizing that his son would probably die because of his own lack of faith, immediately committed himself to the Lord, and continued to beg Jesus to heal the boy. He said to Jesus, "Lord, you just must come to see my little one before he dies . . . you just must come!"[65]

But instead of going with the nobleman to Capernaum, Jesus wanted him to trust by faith that the child would be healed without the Lord actually going to see him in person. So it was with compassion that Jesus answered the nobleman, saying, "Go your way then . . . your son lives!" Believing with a renewed, energized faith, the nobleman fearlessly returned to Capernaum without undue haste, confident that his son would be healed, just as the Lord had promised.[66]

---

62 John 4:43-45
63 John 4:46, 47
64 John 4:48
65 John 4:49
66 John 4:50

And, sure enough, the next day, as the nobleman neared his home, his servants came out to meet him. They brought good news, saying, "Your son is alive and well!"[67]

The nobleman asked as to the exact time the boy began to get better. The servants informed him, "Why, it was yesterday, at 1:00 o'clock in the afternoon when the fever vanished." The nobleman was not at all surprised for it was the same hour that Jesus had told him, "Your son lives!" This man and his entire family continued to believe in Jesus and became His followers. Now, this is the second recorded miracle that Jesus performed in Galilee—besides those, of course, He had performed in Judea. [*Harmony* 3:8] The first Galilean miracle Jesus had performed had been the turning of water into wine at Cana. [*Harmony* 2:69-77; 6:2][(o)] [68]

### —John the Baptist is Imprisoned
### < Spring, A.D. 29 (3/7) >
### {Matthew 14:3-5; Luke 3:19, 20; John 3:23}

John the Baptist continued his preaching and baptizing ministry in Aenon, near Salim in eastern Samaria, west of the Jordan River. But at some point he moved his ministry to the eastern side of the river into the province of Peraea. While John was there, Herod Antipas, tetrarch over Peraea, had John arrested, bound in chains, and thrown into prison.[(p)] [69]

This occurred because John had spoken out, reproving Herod for divorcing his wife so that he could marry Herodias, his half-brother Philip's wife. This divorce, because of the way it took place, caused quite a scandal among the people of Israel. John, as a prophet of God, felt compelled to call Herod down for this wicked action. Not surprisingly, this rebuke angered Herod and Herodias when John publicly addressed the tetrarch, saying, "It is not lawful or morally right for you to have Herodias as your 'wife.'" Herod, raised with an understanding of the Jewish religion, including its principles on divorce [Leviticus 18:16], knew this was true. Nevertheless, in order to please Herodias and calm his own anger, Herod had John imprisoned.[70]

---

67 John 4:51
68 John 4:52-54
69 Matthew 14:3; Luke 3:20; John 3:23
70 Matthew 14:3, 4; Luke 3:19

But this was not the first time that John had made a public condemnation of some of Herod's actions. In fact, John had often rebuked the tetrarch for various evil things he had done. So, when John spoke against this morally repugnant marriage, it was the last straw for Herod. The tetrarch was a very wicked man. Thus it was, when he threw John into prison, it was the latest in a long list of evils he had committed against the people he ruled. Initially, Herod wanted to kill John, but he was afraid of what the people would do if he followed through with this desire, for many of them considered John to be a prophet. If Herod had executed John, a significant number of his passionate followers might begin to riot. Herod certainly did not want to face this prospect. So he did nothing more at that time than to put John in prison, as bad as that was. [*Harmony* 10:43/; 12:87/2][71]

—

### *The Timeline of the Ministry of Jesus, Segment Four: Spring, A.D. 29 — Autumn, A.D. 29*[(q)]

A full eighteen months had passed since Jesus began His ministry in the fall of A.D. 27. During the first six months of this period—Autumn, A.D. 27 through Spring, A.D. 28—Jesus was baptized, was tempted in the wilderness, and called His first disciples. He had also performed His first miracle in Cana. It was a "getting started" time for Jesus. The next six months, the middle part of the Lord's first eighteen months of ministry—Spring, A.D. 28 through Autumn, A.D. 28—included a visit to the Passover in Jerusalem. While there, the Lord cleansed the Temple. This event was followed by His night visit with Nicodemus. For the next several months, the Lord, along with His disciples, ministered in Judea. This ministry involved preaching and baptizing. Overall, though, the impact of Lord's ministry in Judea was quite limited. Jesus began the last six-month segment of the first year and a half of His ministry—Autumn, A.D. 28 through Spring, A.D. 29—by visiting in Samaria—with the woman at Jacob's Well—on His way to begin a ministry in Galilee. Next, Jesus worked for some months in Galilee. During that time, He healed the nobleman's son. All told, the recorded events and details of that first eighteen months of Christ's ministry are very few in number, especially during the last six-month segment. No doubt the Lord probably spent a significant portion of this time period instructing His growing group of disciples.[1]

---

71 Matthew 14:5; Luke 3:19, 20

There were yet another two years remaining in the ministry of Jesus—from the Spring of A.D. 29, through the Spring of A.D. 31.[2]

During the next six-month segment (4/7)—the Spring, A.D. 29, through the Autumn of A.D. 29—Jesus had a major encounter with the Jewish leaders over a miracle He performed on the Sabbath day. The Lord then returned to Galilee to begin a much extended and extremely successful ministry in that province. His popularity among the people there reached a fever pitch. His reputation as an outstanding teacher, preacher, and healer grew exponentially. During this time, the Lord organized and consolidated the group of His closest followers, who became known as the "Twelve." He also gave His most famous sermon—commonly known as the "Sermon on the Mount." This sermon stated the principles upon which His Gospel ministry was based. In all, it was an extremely busy time for the Master. In fact, it was one of the most fruitful and productive time-periods of the Lord's entire ministry. It was a time when the Lord's work was going full steam ahead.(r) [3]

—

## Jesus at the Passover Again
## < Spring, A.D. 29 (4/7) >
## (John 5:1-47)

### — The Healing of the Invalid at the Pool of Bethesda
### < Spring, A.D. 29 (4/7) >
### {John 5:1-15}

It was time once again for the Jewish festival, the Passover. Accordingly, Jesus traveled the approximate 80 miles from Galilee to Jerusalem to attend this celebration.(s) [72]

Now, there was near the Sheep Gate in the city near a pool named, in the Hebrew language, Bethesda, which probably meant "house of olives." This pool was 55 feet long, 12 feet wide, and surrounded by five arches. Under these arches lay a great many sick and infirm people. Among them were those who were blind, lame, or had withered extremities. There was a traditional belief that an angel from God came down at certain times to the pool and stirred up the water. It is not clear if this tradition was based on fact or whether it was—as is more likely—just a mythical belief. But according to the tradition, whoever was the

72 John 5:1

first to enter the pool after it rippled would be healed of whatever infirmity or disease he or she suffered from.[73]

There was a certain man lying there who had for 38 years suffered from paralysis. When Jesus saw him lying there, He knew that the man had been in this condition for a very long time. The Lord asked the paralytic, "Do you want to be healed?"[74]

The paralyzed man replied, "Sir, I have no one to help me into the water when it's rippling. While I'm trying to get into the water first, there's always someone else, stronger than I, who is able to get in before I can." The man was hinting that if Jesus would stay with him, He could ease him into the water the next time it rippled. If this Stranger would do that for him, the paralytic would be satisfied.[75]

But of course, Jesus did not need the rippling of the water—real or imagined—to heal the man. So instead, ignoring the implied request of the paralytic, Jesus said in a commanding tone, "Rise up! Take up your mat and walk!" Inspired by these firm words, the crippled man stood up, rolled up his mat, and began to walk again. He had been instantly healed. [*Harmony* 8:23][76]

Now it was on the seventh day of the week, the Sabbath, that Jesus healed the paralytic. A short time later, when the Jewish leaders saw that the man was carrying his mat on the Sabbath—which was a violation of a man-made law of theirs—they reprimanded him. "It's the Sabbath," they said. "The carrying of a mat is strictly forbidden by the law! You should know that!"[77]

However, the man defended himself by explaining, "It was He—the Man who made me well—who commanded me, 'Take up your cot and walk.' So naturally, I obeyed Him!"[78]

"Who was that Man who said, 'Take up your mat and walk'?" they sternly demanded of the healed paralytic. But he had no idea who it was who had healed him. Jesus was no longer in the area, for He had, without fanfare, disappeared

---

73 John 5:2-4
74 John 5:5, 6
75 John 5:7
76 John 5:8, 9
77 John 5:9, 10
78 John 5:11

into the large crowd. So the cured paralytic was unable to point Jesus out to the Jewish leaders, and neither was he able to name Him. [*Harmony* 11:12][79]

Sometime later Jesus found the man in the Temple area and said to him, "Look! You are now quite well! Stop your sinful lifestyle that caused your paralysis in the first place, or something even worse will come upon you!" [*Harmony* 4:43][80]

> Because of his previous sinful life, the man had become diseased. The disease ultimately led to his paralysis. This was the reason why the Lord strongly encouraged him to change his lifestyle.

Upon hearing these words, and finding out it was Jesus who had healed him, the man looked up the Jewish leaders. He informed them that it was a Man named Jesus who had healed him and directed him to carry his mat, even though it was the Sabbath day.[81]

### —The Lord's Defense Before the Sanhedrin
### < Spring, A.D. 29 (4/7) >
### {John 5:16-47}

The Jewish leaders were very upset when they found out that it was Jesus who had healed the paralytic on the Sabbath. This was the second time that the Lord had a direct confrontation with the leaders of Israel. The first time was when, a year before, He had cast the moneychangers out of the Temple. [*Harmony* 3:1-9; 11:30][82]

> Now Jesus, by His actions, had challenged one of the most significant controls the leaders of Israel exercised over the people: that is, the way the seventh-day Sabbath was to be kept. The Jewish leaders and scribes had encumbered the reasonable and logical seventh-day Sabbath commandment [Exodus 20:8-11] of the Ten Commandment Law [Exodus 20:2-17] with a great many un-Biblical, even ridiculous restrictions. This had the effect of making Sabbath-keeping an oppressively heavy burden for the Jewish people. Jesus sought to remove these man-made restrictions from the Sabbath. In fact, this was just the

---

79 John 5:12, 13

80 John 5:14

81 John 5:15

82 John 5:16

first of a number of occasions that the Jewish leaders would have cause to tangle with Jesus regarding this specific issue.(t) [1]

In both situations—the cleansing of the Temple and the healing of the paralytic on the Sabbath—a power struggle was taking place. It was between the human leaders of Israel and the Divine One who was thought by many to be the Messiah. While it was true that the leaders of Israel were desirous of having the Messiah arrive among them, they wanted a Messiah who would agree with their ways of thinking and action. To state it bluntly, they did not approve of the way Jesus was conducting His ministry. For, instead of publicly agreeing with them and endorsing their leadership, He was openly challenging some of their pet ideas. In doing so, He was undermining their authority with the people. This they could not tolerate![2]

So strongly did they disagree with the methods of Jesus that, before long, they developed an ever-increasing passion to kill Him! They started persecuting Jesus by publicly condemning Him. Furthermore, they had Jesus arraigned before the Sanhedrin court—the highest Jewish legal authority in the nation—to give, if He could, an explanation of His supposed Sabbath-breaking.(u) [83]

The defense that Jesus gave before the Sanhedrin at the time of His arraignment contains the most complete statement found anywhere in the Gospel record regarding His own concept of who the Messiah was to be. In addition, Jesus clearly defined the extent of His personal relationship with His Heavenly Father. This relationship formed the basis upon which the Lord's authority to teach, heal, and declare truths of all kinds was founded. This relationship with His Heavenly Father would be a recurring theme throughout His entire ministry.

When arraigned before the court, the Lord was questioned regarding His rationale for healing the paralytic on the Sabbath. He boldly answered, "My Father is working within the world, even now. He has never ceased His work to keep the world operating . . . even on the Sabbath. And accordingly, I, Myself, work! Thus, as the Father works, so do I, His Son."(v) [84]

In effect, Jesus was saying to the court, "My Father originated the Sabbath. What He chooses to do on that day, I as His Son am empowered to do.

83 John 5:16
84 John 5:17

Furthermore, God, in a sense, 'works' on the Sabbath to keep the world running. He doesn't take a day off."

After hearing these strong words, the members of the Sanhedrin were even more passionately determined to kill Him. [*Harmony* 4:1] Their desire to murder the Lord was based not only upon His healing of the paralytic on the Sabbath [*Harmony* 3:72-81]—and thus breaking their Sabbath laws—but also the fact that He called God His own Father. In doing so, He made Himself equal with God. This they considered blasphemous, a religious crime worthy of death. [Leviticus 24:15, 16; *Harmony* 11:10][(w) 85]

But the Jewish leaders had a greater reason for wanting to kill Jesus than punishing Him for the supposed sin of blasphemy. If Jesus were truly divine, then how could they effectively challenge His pronouncements? How could they argue with One who was equal with God? They would have no choice but to submit to the Lord's authority. In short, in the process, they would have to abandon their own opinions. Therefore, there was no way that these Jewish leaders would, from their own perspective, give in to this young upstart of a Man.

So, understanding the true feelings that the Sanhedrin had against Him, Jesus repeated, "It is an absolute fact that the Son can do nothing of His own volition, unless He first has seen what the Father has done. So whatever the Father does, the Son has the authority to do, and in the same way. Indeed, the Father loves the Son and continues to reveal to Him what He should be doing. In fact, the Father will show the Son greater things to do than just the healing of the paralytic—things that will be so astounding that you will be completely amazed when you see them!" [*Harmony* 11:9, 17][(x) 86]

Again, by claiming that God was His Father, Jesus was in reality claiming divinity for Himself. Clearly it was as the angel had told Mary and Joseph: Jesus would be called the Son of God. [*Harmony* 1:22, 41] Also, Jesus was insinuating that by rejecting Him the Jews would be rejecting the Father who, in the first place, gave Jesus the authority to do the things that He did. Further, the Lord claimed that His miracle-working power was the result of fulfilling the will of His Father. And because

85 John 5:18
86 John 5:19, 20

of that, there would be no limit to the miracles He would perform, including ultimately even resurrections. [*Harmony* 13:1-30]

To illustrate what He meant, Jesus added, "For example, the Father has the power to raise people from the dead and restore them to life. In the same way, the Son also has the power to give life to anyone He chooses to resurrect from the dead." [*Harmony* 8:17/][87]

The Lord's point was dramatically clear: The power to resurrect people, which the Jewish leaders obviously believed belonged only to God the Father, also belonged to Jesus, His Son!

Jesus continued, "Furthermore, the Father judges no one. Instead, He has given the right of judging all mankind to His Son—something He will certainly do at the end of the world. [*Harmony* 15:51] Because of this, all the world ought to honor the Son in the same way that they willingly honor the Father. To state it bluntly: If one does not properly honor and respect the Son, he is refusing likewise to honor the Father who sent Him and gave Him His authority. Do you see the logic of that?"[88]

Once more, Jesus claimed divinity for Himself, making it clear that if anyone rejected Him, they were also rejecting God the Father. Thus Jesus was claiming three prerogatives for Himself that only God possessed: the ability and authority to heal people, even on the Sabbath; the power to resurrect the dead; and the authority to pass final judgment upon mankind.[1]

There were some in the nation of Israel who believed that the Messiah, when He came, would possess such powers. They also believed that He would be divine in nature. However, there were many more who believed that even though the Messiah would be a conquering king, He would be a mere human being, with no special divine powers within Himself. Thus some in the Sanhedrin persistently refused to accept the Lord's claim of divinity, for to do so would require them to accept the Lord's words and actions. It would also require them to change their opinions regarding the true nature of the Messiah—that is, whether or not He would be divine. They were too entrenched in their preset ideas to do either.[2]

---

87 John 5:21

88 John 5:22, 23

Jesus continued to be insistent on this point: "I tell you, it is a fact that anyone who hears and believes My word and consequently, totally trusts in the Father who sent Me [*Harmony* 13:28] will have eternal life. Such a person will not be condemned in the judgment, but rather, will escape from the condemnation of eternal death to the promise of everlasting life." [*Harmony* 3:23; 11:45][89]

By these words Jesus stated that an acceptance of the true nature of His relationship with the Father was essential for eternal life. But to believe that Jesus was the Son of God must involve something *more* than mere intellectual assent. It must also be *practical* in nature. This required that all true believers be transformed by the power of the Holy Spirit dwelling within them. In other words, true belief must lead to a real change in people's lives, attitudes, and characters. [Romans 12:1-3]

To prove that His authority as the Messiah came directly from the Father, once again Jesus claimed for Himself the greatest power that God possessed: the power to give life! That is why Jesus added, "It also an undeniable fact when I tell you that the hour is approaching—and even now is here—when the dead will actually hear the voice of the Son of God . . . and they shall live—not just spiritually, but also physically! For just as the Father has life within Himself, the Father has given to the Son the authority to have life within Himself. The Father has the power to resurrect the dead. Accordingly, the Son too has that same power!"[90]

During His ministry, Jesus would resurrect at least three persons. [*Harmony* 6:20-23; 8:9, 17-19; 13:1-30] Also, at Jesus' own resurrection two years hence, a number of saints would be resurrected. [*Harmony* 18:33] This is what Jesus meant when He said that "the hour is approaching and even now is here" when the dead would hear the voice of the Son of Man and live again. Of course Jesus was referring also to the great resurrection at the end of the world. [1 Thessalonians 4:16, 17]

Jesus continued, "Furthermore, the Father has given full authority to the Son to execute His judgments because He is not only the Son of God but also the Son of Man." [*Harmony* 1:22/4][(v)] [91]

89 John 5:24
90 John 5:25, 26
91 John 5:27

> Jesus, by this declaration, was revealing His unique role in the plan of salvation—that is, His nature was both human *and* divine. And because of that, He had both the authority of God—as the "Son of God"—and a special understanding of the weaknesses of humanity—as the "Son of Man." This characteristic—totally unique to Jesus—was at the very foundation of the Biblical teaching as to who the Messiah would be. From the Lord's perspective, then, the Messiah must be divine . . . but He must also be human. No one else could be the Messiah, for no one else—ever—had this special dual nature. The Jewish leaders never accepted this fact regarding Jesus. And, of course, the Lord's authority as the Son of Man was valid only if He was also the Son of God, for it was His divinity—His position as God's Son—that empowered Him and gave Him credibility as the Son of Man. That is, a mere human being never could, and never would, have such power or authority. [*Harmony* 1:22/4]

"Don't be surprised, or shocked!" the Lord continued, still speaking of the resurrection. "The hour is coming when all those who are in their graves will hear the voice of the Son of God and they shall be resurrected. Those who were righteous in this life will be resurrected to enjoy the pleasures of eternal life. And those who were evil in this life will be resurrected to face condemnation in the final judgment."[92]

> Here Jesus mentioned the Biblical teaching of the two resurrections—one for the righteous, and the other for the wicked. The one for the righteous will take place at the Second Coming of Jesus. The one for the wicked will take place a thousand years later, after the so-called Millennium has ended. [Revelation 20:1-5][1]

> The Lord's point was that in the case of the two resurrections He had the full authority in the final judgment, to give eternal life to whomever He determined was worthy. He also had the full authority to condemn to eternal death those He found to be unworthy. These two resurrections of which Jesus spoke—the resurrection of the righteous and the wicked—will be a part of the final judgment process that will take place at the end of the world. Here Jesus combined the Messiah's authority both to resurrect the dead and to be the final Judge of the world. [*Harmony* 15:51][2]

---

92 John 5:28, 29

But Jesus wanted the Jews to understand that His authority to judge the world was not something that He claimed for Himself. Rather, it was something that the Father had given to Him. So He further explained, "As I have said, I can do nothing on My own. [*Harmony* 3:88] As I hear, so will I judge. And you can count on the fairness of My judgment because I do not seek My own will but rather the will of the Father who sent Me to judge. If it was just My own word upon which I base My actions, you might have good reason to doubt the truthfulness of what I say. However, there is Another who bears witness of Me—the Father—and He gave Me My authority. And I know what He says regarding Me is the truth."[93]

> Simply put, Jesus was saying, "If you believe in the God of heaven, you must also believe in Me, for My authority to act was given to Me by My Father. I do not act on My own." Of course as God [*Harmony* 1:1] Jesus could on His own act by His own authority. But in His incarnate state as God's Son—as a human being, that is—He was subservient to the will of His Father. [Philippians 2:5-8] And it was the will of the Father, Jesus maintained, that He as the Messiah should exercise such power. Thus, the mere fact that Jesus could perform miracles clearly proved that the Father had given Him the power to do so.

Jesus continued, "You sent people to question John the Baptist. [*Harmony* 2:37-47] Right? Remember, that John bore witness to the truth of who I am. But the witness that really counts is not the one that John—or any other man—gave of Me, but rather the one that comes from the Father who is the Almighty God! Now I do you a favor when I make this clear to you. By believing in this explanation I've given, you might have the opportunity once more to believe the words of God and be saved, as opposed to rejecting Me—as you are doing this very moment—and be lost."[94]

> Again, the Lord's authority to act was based not upon what John said of Him—as good as that might be. Rather it was based upon what the God of heaven and earth, the Father, said of Him. And when did that happen? No doubt Jesus was referring in part to the time right after His baptism, when the Father declared Jesus to be His Son. [*Harmony* 2:27]

---

93 John 5:30-32
94 John 5:33, 34

"Concerning John the Baptist, his witness was like that of the fire of a burning torch," Jesus continued to explain. "And for a short time you were happy to bask in that light. For a brief while, many of you listened to John, perhaps even believed in him—even though by now most of you have ended up rejecting him. [*Harmony* 12:123/5] But the light of John's ministry and the witness which he bore of Me, as great as it was, was pale compared to the real witness that exists of My genuineness. What do I mean? John's words were just that: *words!* But the Father has given Me *works* to perform as part of My ministry—I'm speaking here of My miracles. So when I successfully work miracles—such as the healing of the paralytic [*Harmony* 3:72-81]—they effectively testify of the fact that it was truly the Father who has sent Me. Simply put, unless My Father gave Me the authority to work miracles, I could not perform them. Certainly you can see that!"[95]

> In His incarnate state, Jesus was given by the Father works to do and miracles to perform. Further, God gave Jesus the full authority to perform these works and miracles as He saw fit. And when Jesus did so, it proved to anyone who was sincere in heart and attitude that Jesus was the Messiah, acting on the full authority of God in the performance of His miracles. Of course, beyond His miracles, the Lord's words, character, and teachings bore strong witness to the truthfulness of who He was, and that it was His Father who had sent Him. [*Harmony* 2:68, 68/]

Jesus went on, saying, "In addition, the Father—the One, again, who has sent Me—has Himself borne witness regarding Me. And how has He done this? While you cannot now hear the actual words of God, nor can you see His form, you can hear His voice if you choose. It is softly speaking within your heart through your conscience. But unfortunately you have refused to hear His word, neither is His word dwelling within you, because you have rejected Me, the One whom He has sent." [*Harmony* 7:9][96]

> The gentle persuasion of the conscience through the power of the Holy Spirit—combined with the powerful evidence of the Lord's miracles—was sufficient in itself to convince the Jews that Jesus was the Messiah. But they ignored the impressions of their consciences. Instead, they sought to kill Jesus rather than accept Him as the Messiah who had been sent from God. [*Harmony* 7:9, 10][1]

---

95 John 5:35, 36

96 John 5:37, 38

> Here Jesus claimed the full power of the Godhead as the testimony of His authority. First, Jesus claimed that the Father gave Him His authority. Second, Jesus Himself claimed that the Father's authority was indeed in His life. And third, Jesus claimed that the Holy Spirit through the power of the conscience had truly verified the ministry of Jesus.[2]

"Yes—and beyond all that—I know you boast about the fact that you are great students of the words of Scripture," Jesus added. "Indeed, you constantly investigate and search them because you think that by doing so you will earn for yourself eternal life. [*Harmony* 12:123/7] But, ironically, it is in these same Scriptures that you will find the truth that directly declares who I am! And yet you persistently refuse to come to Me in faith so that you might receive eternal life." [*Harmony* 12:148/][97]

> There was still another proof that Jesus was the Messiah: the words and prophecies of the Scriptures. Had the Jews studied the Word of God as should have, they would have accepted Jesus as the true Messiah of prophecy. The Scriptures rightly understood revealed all the characteristics of the Messiah. They revealed His divinity and humanity as well as His relationship with the Father. They revealed all the things that He did and all the things that were done to Him—all this and more. If the Jews had only studied the Scriptures as they should have done they would not have ended up rejecting Jesus. Instead, in their research of the Word the Jews had a tendency to read into the Scriptures their own pre-conceived ideas—only those that would verify their own beliefs.

To emphasize the utter foolishness and tragedy of the Jews' position in rejecting Him, Jesus further added, "Of course, the success of My ministry is not dependent upon any praise you might give Me. No, indeed! Yes, you can be sure that I know what you are thinking . . . and I know that you do not have a genuine love for God who wishes to dwell within you. And it's a shame! I have come in My Father's name, and yet you reject Me. If, however, another person with your own mindset would come in his own name, claiming to be your leader,"—or the Messiah—"you would instantly accept him! That makes no sense whatsoever! Why is it that you are so willing to believe in someone who gives glory solely to himself—by comparing himself to sinners—while you refuse to believe in Me? Why is it that you seek praise from one another, and yet are so cavalier in your

---

97 John 5:39, 40

refusal to seek God's praise? Why do I say that? For, to be sure, God would pay you honor if you would accept Me, for it is His will for you to do so! When you obey God, He honors you! Certainly you can understand that! Why is it, then, that you do not seek praise and honor from God, which is the only praise in the long run that really counts?"[98]

Jesus concluded by saying, "However, I do not need to condemn you before the Father. Rather, the one who accuses you is none other than Moses. That's right, Moses! It is in his Law and your allegiance to it that you have placed your hope of eternal life. Isn't that true? But if you really believe in Moses, as you claim, you would have no recourse but to believe in Me, for he wrote concerning Me. Throughout his writings, he constantly alluded to the work and ministry of the Son of God. However, if you refuse to believe Moses, then how is it possible that you would actually believe in Me?"[99]

> By this, Jesus referred to a direct statement of Moses [Deuteronomy 18:15], as well as to the many allusions to Jesus found in the ritual services and symbols recorded in his writings.[1]
>
> To summarize, in His monologue with the Sanhedrin, Jesus methodically outlined the reasons why they should accept Him as the true Messiah. First, when Jesus spoke or acted, He did so with the full authority of God, the Father. This authority did not come from within Him. It was given to Him from the Father. Second, the things He did were the same kinds of things that the Father had done. In other words, the Lord's actions were consistent with the will and actions of the Father. Jesus did not act on His own account. His actions were never embarrassing to the Father. They only gave glory and honor to Him. Third, the kind of things that Christ did could be performed only by the power of God. For example, to resurrect people was a demonstration of a power that no mere mortal could claim! In fact, all the Lord's miracles, including His ability to read the thoughts of people, were the result of the power and authority of the Father in His life. Fourth, as the Messiah, Jesus would ultimately judge the world. God would never give any mere human being that kind of power. Fifth, Jesus claimed for Himself the unique nature of being at the same time both human and divine. He was the Son of God. He was also the Son of Man. As the Son of God, He had the full power

---

98 John 5:41-44

99 John 5:45-47

and authority of God and, as the Son of Man, He intimately understood the weaknesses of humanity. There can be no doubt that Jesus claimed for Himself this characteristic of the Messiah. Again, no other person who has ever existed has had such a nature. Sixth, the Lord's authority as the Messiah was further confirmed by four different sources: One: John the Baptist as the forerunner of Jesus verified through his testimony that Jesus was the Messiah. Two: The testimony of the miracles of Jesus as well as His character under the power of God clearly showed that He was the Messiah. Three: The testimony of the Holy Spirit impressing human hearts of the truthfulness of the Lord's ministry, demonstrated that Jesus was the Christ. And four: The testimony of the Scriptures—especially the writings of Moses—regarding the coming of the Messiah, the Person He would be, and the things He would do—clearly demonstrated that Jesus fulfilled those prophecies.[2]

While Jesus never directly said to the Sanhedrin, "I am the Messiah," when He claimed to be the Son of God, He was in effect claiming to be the Messiah. That is what He meant, and there can be no real doubt that is what the members of the Sanhedrin understood Him to be saying.[3]

With two years left in the ministry of Jesus, the Jewish leaders, had they been willing to follow the specific, point-by-point advice the Lord gave them that day, had ample time left to repent and to obey the Lord. They certainly had enough time in which to observe the ministry of Jesus, and, under the conviction of the Holy Spirit, could have changed their negative attitude toward the Lord and accepted Him as the true Messiah of Bible prophecy. To be sure, they could have forestalled the tragedy of their rejection of His ministry. [*Harmony* 14:132] Unfortunately, they wasted their golden opportunity.[4]

Indeed, in spite of all this evidence, the Jewish leaders for the most part rejected Jesus as the Messiah and His work as Messianic. Not only did they reject Him, they also sought to kill Him! Jesus had no real choice but to seek another, more fruitful place in which to minister than Judea. He would move on to Galilee and elsewhere.[5]

Finally, this confrontation between Jesus and the Sanhedrin would greatly affect the remainder of His ministry. Most of the members of this Jewish court would earnestly seek to kill Jesus. The Lord's relationship with them, while never good, would only worsen. They would be a constant irritant to the Lord in His ministry wherever He might be laboring at any given time.[6]

**Supplementary Notes:**

**(a) [3:0+]** This is the second of eight insertions in the *Harmony* that places the events of the three-and-a-half-year ministry of Jesus on a "timeline," divided into seven six-month segments. (The eighth insertion is at the end of the seventh segment.) The other segment insertions can be found in the following locations: Segment One, *Harmony* 2:21/; Three, *Harmony* 3:33/2; Four, *Harmony* 3:71/; Five, *Harmony* 6:17/; Six, *Harmony* 10:0; Seven, *Harmony* 11:0; and Eight, *Harmony* 18:99/1-21.

**(b) [3:0/4]** This segment has the designation 2/7 for its "Segmental Placement" number. (See "Segmental Placement" in the "Features for Using the *Harmony* as a Reference Book" section near the back of this book for more information.)

**(c) [3:0/4++]** A number of scholars believe that there was just one cleansing of the Temple rather than two as the Gospel record seemingly implies. I think that there were, indeed, two such cleansings. For more on this subject, refer to **Note "p"** in Chapter 14.

**(d) [3:6]** To figure the actual dating of the 46 years the Jews said it took to build the Temple is impossible to verify from the evidence available. Because of that, I made no special comment on this in the *Harmony.*

**(e) [3:10]** The description of Nicodemus as a "ruler of the Jews," appears to indicate that he was a member of the Sanhedrin. Thus I said so in the *Harmony.*

**(f) [3:10]** See *Harmony* 2:7/1, 2 for a definition of a Pharisee.

**(g) [3:22]** It is unclear whether John 3:16-21 is a continuation of Jesus' discussion with Nicodemus, or whether it contains John's *personal commentary* on the meaning of what happened during the discussion between Jesus and Nicodemus. In the *Harmony,* I chose to make it a part of what Jesus said.

**(h) [3:23]** (See above.)

**(i) [3:24]** (See **Note "g"** above.)

**(j) [3:33/+]** This is the third of eight insertions in the *Harmony* that places the events of the three-and-a-half-year ministry of Jesus on a "timeline," divided into seven six-month segments. (The eighth insertion is at the end of the seventh segment.) The other segment insertions can be found in the following locations: Segment One, *Harmony* 2:21/; Two, *Harmony* 3:0; Four, *Harmony* 3:71/; Five, *Harmony* 6:17/; Six, *Harmony* 10:0; Seven, *Harmony* 11:0; and Eight, *Harmony* 18:99/1-21.

**(k) [3:33/3]** This segment has the designation 3/7 for its "Segmental Placement" number. (See "Segmental Placement" in the "Features for Using the *Harmony* as a Reference Book" section near the back of this book for more information.)

**(l) [3:46]** I thought that the record sounded clearer if I were to switch verses 21 and 22. Doing so (something I've done rarely in the *Harmony*) does not, in my opinion, change the message of the Lord contained therein. In fact, I believe it greatly enhances it.

**(m) [3:47]** I spent a great deal of time analyzing the meaning of the phrase "spirit and truth" as contained in the record. I am firmly convinced that a detailed definition of these two words greatly enhances the overall meaning of the Lord's words to the woman. While some may question my definition and interpretation, I am very comfortable with it.

**(n) [3:48]** (See above.)

**(o) [3:68]** The text says that the healing of the nobleman's son was the Lord's second miracle, with the turning of water to wine being the first. (*Harmony* 2:69-77) Of course, Jesus performed miracles during His Judean ministry (*Harmony* 3:8), the details of which are not included in the record. So then, the healing of the nobleman's son was not really his second *overall* miracle. What, then, does the text mean? John said this miracle was the second miracle He performed *"when he was come out of Judaea into Galilee"* (John 4:54, KJV)—that is, *after* He began His Galilean ministry. Why John thought it important to mention this fact is not clear. *Perhaps* John considered the Lord's Judean ministry was of small significance as compared to His Galilean ministry. Possibly, too, because the details of the miracles of the Lord's Judean ministry are not recorded, while the details of the first two miracles of His Galilean ministry are mentioned, John made the statement that he did. In any case, it is clear from the record that the Lord performed miracles in Judea *between* His "water to wine" and the "nobleman's son" Galilean miracles.

**(p) [3:69]** The texts do not say that John had moved into Peraea when Herod arrested him. However, John must have been in that area, for Herod would have not had the authority to arrest John elsewhere. That's why I added the idea in the *Harmony* that John went into "Peraea."

**(q) [3:71/+]** This is the fourth of eight insertions in the *Harmony* that places the events of the three-and-a-half-year ministry of Jesus on a "timeline," divided into seven six-month segments. (The eighth insertion is at the end of the seventh segment.) The other segment insertions can be found in the following locations: Segment One, *Harmony* 2:21/; Two, *Harmony* 3:0; Three, *Harmony* 3:33/2; Five, *Harmony* 6:17/; Six, *Harmony* 10:0; Seven, *Harmony* 11:0; and Eight, *Harmony* 18:99/1-21.

**(r) [3:71/3]** This segment has the designation 4/7 for its "Segmental Placement" number. (See "Segmental Placement" in the "Features for Using the *Harmony* as a Reference Book" section near the back of this book for more information.)

**(s) [3:72]** The text says that there was a "feast" in Jerusalem, but it does not say it was the Passover. However, it is a very reasonable assumption that the Passover is being referred to. Accordingly, I have done so in the *Harmony.*

**(t) [3:82/]** For more information about the man-made Jewish Sabbath laws, see *Harmony* 4:51/1, 2; 11:89/.

**(u) [3:83]** The record does not indicate that Jesus appeared before the Sanhedrin, the Jewish court. However, in the light of all the facts, it very likely that is what happened. An appearance before the Sanhedrin provided the usual forum for such a formal discussion and defense as is so dramatically described in the record. The *Harmony* reflects such a likelihood.

**(v) [3:84]** (See above.)

**(w) [3:85]** See **Note "u"** above.

**(x) [3:86]** See **Note "u"** above.

**(y) [3:91]** Perhaps some might think I've gone too far in my interpretation of this verse—saying that Jesus claimed in it to be *both* the "Son of God" *and* the "Son of Man"—but I don't think so. In the previous verse (John 5:26), by using the words "Son" and "Father," Jesus, from my perspective, clearly referred to the fact that He was indeed the *"Son of God."* Thus His reference to the "Son of *Man*" in the verse 27, *connected* to His reference to the "Son of God" in verse 26, allows for the strong interpretation that I made in the text. I am more than comfortable with it.

# Chapter Four

## The Early Galilean Ministry of Jesus—

**From the Opening of the Lord's Galilean Ministry, to the Official Appointment of the Twelve Disciples**

**(Spring, A.D. 29 - Late Summer, A.D. 29)**

**The Lord's Ministry In Galilee**
**< Spring, A.D. 29 (4/7) >**
**(Matthew 4:12-22; 8:14-17; Mark 1:14-34; Luke 4:14-41; 5:1-11)**

**— The Opening of the Lord's Galilean Ministry**
**< Spring, A.D. 29 (4/7) >**
**{Matthew 4:12; Mark 1:14, 15; Luke 4:14, 15}**

When the members of the Sanhedrin formally rejected Jesus—after He had defended His ministry before them [*Harmony* 3:82-99]—it was extremely difficult for the Lord to continue His work in Judea, laboring directly under the noses of the Jewish leaders who were determined to kill Him. [*Harmony* 3:85] Furthermore, the casting of John the Baptist into prison by Herod [*Harmony* 3:69-71] might embolden the Jews to try to have the same thing done to Jesus. Therefore, the Lord, when He heard of John's imprisonment, decided to leave Judea altogether and work for the time being in the province of Galilee, over 70 miles to the north. [*Harmony* 10:14][1]

When He arrived in Galilee, the Master began to preach the Gospel message by declaring, "The time has been fulfilled! The kingdom of God is now at hand! Repent and believe in the Gospel!" [*Harmony* 2:3; 3:12; 4:13; 8:41][2]

> In effect He declared, "The prophecies predicting the coming of the Messiah have been fulfilled. [Such as Daniel 9:24-27] Yes, the time for

---

1 Matthew 4:12; Mark 1:14; Luke 4:14

2 Mark 1:14, 15; Luke 4:14

> the arrival of the Messiah has come! All who so desire can now receive the power of the good news of the Gospel message of God's kingdom within their lives! And the message is this: Repent—that is, change your way of thinking through the power of the Holy Spirit—so that your lives may be molded to conform to the will of God. [Romans 12:1, 2] All this can be accomplished by trusting in the promises of God's grace which He has abundantly granted to you." [2 Peter 1:4]

Consequently, the Lord's ministry in Galilee was marked with great success. The power of the Holy Spirit was clearly with Him. Christ's fame spread like wildfire throughout the entire province. As He regularly taught in many synagogues—the Jewish churches—all the people constantly praised the high quality of His ministry. [*Harmony* 4:63-66][3]

### — The Lord's First Rejection in Nazareth
### < Late Spring, A.D. 29 (4/7) >
### {Luke 4:16-30}

> Nazareth was, of course, the home town of Jesus where He had spent most of His life. It had been 18 months since the Lord had last been there. [*Harmony* 2:22] In fact, Jesus had not been back there since He began His public ministry. Several months before, Jesus had bypassed Nazareth on a previous journey to Galilee because he knew that He would be rejected there. [*Harmony* 3:62] The attitude of the Nazarenes was negative. No doubt they would want Jesus to perform some miracles to impress them. But the Lord never worked miracles merely to amaze people.

Because it had been some time since Jesus had visited Nazareth, on this occasion the Lord decided to stop in the town wherein He had been raised. And, as was customary for Him, He went into the synagogue on the seventh-day Sabbath to worship. Jesus' ministry of teaching and healing was well known to the people of Nazareth. Therefore, as a somewhat famous former resident of the town, He was asked to read from the Scriptures and give the morning sermon. Accordingly, the Lord requested from the deacon that the scroll of Isaiah be brought to Him. As was usually done, He stood up, unrolled it to particular portions, and began to read from it. Speaking in Hebrew, He read the words, "The Holy Spirit of the Lord is upon Me. Therefore, He has anointed Me"—as

---

3 Luke 4:14, 15

the Christ—"to peach the Gospel message to the poor. He has also sent Me to heal those whose lives have been shattered, to preach deliverance to those who have been prisoners to sin, to give new sight to the spiritually blind, to give freedom from pain to those who have been bruised with guilt to the depth of their souls, and to proclaim the coming of the Messianic Gospel age of God's favor, which He has abundantly bestowed upon them." [Isaiah 61:1, 2; 58:6][4]

> However, Jesus did not include in His reading that portion of Isaiah 61:2, which read that the Messiah would proclaim "the time of vengeance of our God." This particular portion of the prophecy referred to the time, at the end of the world, when the Messiah would establish His eternal kingdom that would dramatically replace the kingdoms of this world. Often, this destruction of earthly principalities is referred to as the "kingdom of glory." [*Harmony* 7:23/; 13:43/] This event would not take place until Jesus came the second time. [*Harmony* 15:51-58] Jesus did not quote this part of the prophecy because it would not be fulfilled during the time of His first coming. Unfortunately, the Jews emphasized this portion of the prophecy rather than the part that Jesus actually quoted. In other words, the Jews emphasized the wrong part of the prophecy! The Lord's emphasis, though different from that of the Jews, was the correct one. It would not be until the people of the world had had a chance to experience the part of the prophecy that Jesus actually quoted—that is, the spiritual aspects of the Gospel work—that the second part—the establishment of the Messiah's eternal kingdom of glory—could take place. The Lord's emphasis, no doubt, ultimately disappointed the listeners in the Nazareth synagogue.

Rolling up the scroll again, Jesus handed it back to the deacon. According to Jewish custom, the Scriptures were read while standing. The delivery of the sermon was given from a sitting position. So, accordingly, the Lord sat down to address the congregation with comments on what He had just read. They all, with great anticipation, were intently looking at Him. During His sermon, Jesus explained how the Messiah would fulfill every aspect of the Isaiah Scriptures He had just quoted. After speaking on the subject for awhile, Jesus concluded by declaring, "This very day, the Scriptures which I have read, have been fulfilled within your hearing of My voice . . . in this very place!"[5]

---

4 Luke 4:16-19

5 Luke 4:20, 21

> The Isaiah Scriptures which Jesus quoted [Isaiah 58:6; 61:1, 2], were understood by all to refer to the ministry of the Messiah. Thus, there could be no doubt as to what Jesus was saying: He was clearly, and unmistakably, claiming that He was the long-awaited Messiah. But when the Lord declared that the details of the prophecy He quoted were fulfilled in their presence, they were offended. But why were they offended? Because He had declared that *they* were poor in the Gospel hope. Furthermore, that *they* were blind to the truth, and that *they* were captives to sin! From the Jewish perspective, such a statement certainly could be applied to the heathen of the world. However, the people in the synagogue that day were obviously averse to having such words applied directly to them, members of God's chosen nation of Israel, no less! Furthermore, the people in Nazareth that day had doubts as to whether Jesus was truly the Messiah. He would have to do something more to convince them—such as performing a miracle—than just declaring it to be so, by merely preaching a sermon, in which He seemed to condemn them!

On one hand, the listeners in the synagogue were deeply impressed by the gracious way that Jesus spoke, and by the words which He used to communicate with them in the early part of His sermon. Indeed, by their own observation, the good things that they had heard about His ability to communicate were certainly true. Accordingly, they expressed to each other, during the early portions of His sermon, their general approval of what He said. But, on the other hand, they were offended that He, one of their own, would dare suggest, as He did in His concluding remarks, that they needed to be converted just like the heathen of the world around them. Moreover, they had known Jesus from infanthood. Thus, they had considered Jesus to be nothing more than just one of them—certainly not the Messiah! Therefore, they said, with puzzlement to one another, "He is just the son of Joseph, isn't He?" [*Harmony* 8:60] From their viewpoint, in order for them to accept Him as being someone greater than an ordinary human being—such as the Messiah, sent from God—He would have to convince them by personally performing a miracle or miracles in their presence. But, again, Jesus never worked miracles just to remove people's doubts. This occasion was no exception.[6]

Instead, Jesus responded to their doubting words by commenting with sadness, "No doubt you will quote this common saying to Me: 'Physician, heal

---

6 Luke 4:22

yourself!' As it is ironic for a physician to have to heal himself, so it is for Me to have to prove Myself to the people of My own home town!"[7]

Jesus continued with even stronger words, saying, "And then you will add, 'Whatever miracle that we have heard was done in Capernaum'"—that is, the healing of the nobleman's son [*Harmony* 3:62-68]—"'you must do here in Your home town, in order for us to believe that You are really the Son of God, as You seem to claim to be!'[8]

"But, sadly," the Lord concluded, "I must, in truth, tell you that no prophet is accepted in his own home town! However, I must also tell you another truth: There were many widows in Israel during the days of Elijah. Remember when God shut up the heavens for three and a half years [1 Kings 17:1; 18:1], causing a great famine over the land? Well, during that time Elijah was not sent to an Israelite widow, was he? No! Instead, Elijah was sent to Zarephath, in the foreign, so-called heathen land of Sidon, to a widow there. [1 Kings 17:8-24] Moreover, there were many lepers in the days of Elisha the prophet [2 Kings 7:3], yet not one of them was healed, except Naaman of Syria, of another so-called wicked nation! [2 Kings 5:1-19] Isn't that right? So, here's My point: Just because you think you know Me doesn't mean that you will receive some special favor from Me. Because I am from your town doesn't mean that I will perform a miracle for you to satisfy your curiosity. Rather, faith in Me is what is essential—something that you obviously lack. Instead, I will minister to those who accept Me by faith, and not those, such as you—even though you are of my home town—who are always demanding a miracle from Me. Those who believe in Me without a miracle are the very ones for whom *I will* work a miracle."[9]

> The Lord's point was unequivocal: The power of God had bypassed them, the people of Jesus' own home town, because they had demonstrated no faith in Him as the Messiah. Instead His miracle-working power was to be shown to those who did not know Him as well, but nevertheless had shown sufficient faith in Him, even though they were not of His own home town.

Clearly comprehending the intent of the Lord's words, the people in the synagogue were filled with uncontrollable rage. They rose up and dragged Him

---

7 Luke 4:23
8 Luke 4:23
9 Luke 4:24-27

out of the synagogue toward the edge of the city. They shoved Him toward the precipice of the limestone cliff which was a part of the hill upon which the town was built. They were intending to cast Him over the edge, to kill Him. But He disappeared miraculously from their midst! This freed the Lord to go on His way in safety. [*Harmony* 2:34/; 8:59-62; 11:77, 78, 171, 175; 14:21/5][(a)] [10]

A question begs to be answered: Why would the people of the Lord's own home town be so angry with Jesus that they would actually try to kill Him? When Jesus referred to the faith of the woman of Zarephath and Namaan of Syria, the people's anger was kindled. They were indignant that Jesus would praise Gentiles—outright heathen in their minds—while, at the same time, condemn them. Their offended spirit, under the influence of the devil, quickly grew into rage. And this rage led to thoughts of murder! And finally, these thoughts led to violent actions. Had Jesus praised them, and condemned their non-Jewish enemies, and then worked a few miracles, they would readily have accepted Him. Because Jesus did not do this, their pride was wounded. Their sense of national greatness was offended. They wanted to kill the messenger for they hated the message so much. Such is the power of sin when cherished in the human heart! But, even at that, it is still hard to comprehend how the people of His own home town would actually try to kill Him. Additionally, it is almost incomprehensible that at one moment, the people were praising Him, and at the next moment, they were trying to murder Him! [*Harmony* 3:62; 8:59-62]

### —Jesus Moves to Capernaum
### < Late Spring, A.D. 29 (4/7) >
### {Matthew 4:13-17; Luke 4:31}

The Lord had no real option but to leave Nazareth. Thus, Jesus chose as the base of His ministry, Capernaum, which was situated on the northern bank of the Sea of Galilee. This was about 25 miles northeast of Nazareth, and it would remain the center of the Lord's work for the next year and a half.[11]

Capernaum was a wise choice to serve as the Lord's headquarters. This town was primarily a Jewish city, even though many Gentiles lived there. It was located close to the Sea of Galilee, making it easy for the Lord to

10 Luke 4:28-30

11 Matthew 4:13; Luke 4:31

travel by boat to other villages of that province. Also, Capernaum was located on a major road that ran east and west, thus making it possible for travelers who heard of the work of Jesus to share with others the details of His ministry. And, the fact that Peter, one of the Lord's disciples, had a home in Capernaum made it easier for Jesus to find a place to rest when necessary.

Capernaum was located within the ancient boundaries of the tribe of Naphtali which no longer existed, while Nazareth was located in the area of the old tribe of Zebulun. The Lord's choice of Capernaum of Galilee to serve as the base of His ministry fulfilled a prophecy of Isaiah which reads, "The lands of Zebulun and Naphtali, which are beside the Galilean sea, beyond the Jordan River, in Galilee, is where many Gentiles"—or non-Jews—"live. The people of that region were sitting in darkness, but they saw a bright Light. It was upon those who were sitting there, under a dark shadow of death and despair, that the Light of the truth of righteousness suddenly flashed." [Isaiah 9:1, 2] Indeed, Jesus was the Light of truth and freedom that would dissipate the darkness of sin, deception, and slavery to evil. [*Harmony* 1:2][12]

While in Capernaum, Jesus continued His ministry. Its theme, from that time onward, was based upon the same words He previously spoke [*Harmony* 4:2]: "Repent, for the kingdom of God is at hand." That is to say: "Change the way you think, so that you will be ready to receive the ever-present power of the Gospel into your lives." [*Harmony* 2:3; 4:2][(b)] [13]

### — The Disciples Are Called by the Sea[(c)]
### < Late Spring, A.D. 29 (4/7) >
### {Matthew 4:18-22; Mark 1:16-20; Luke 5:1-11}

One day Jesus was walking by the edge of the Sea of Galilee. There He saw two of His disciples, Simon Peter and his brother Andrew. They lived in Capernaum and were fishermen. Even though they had been following Jesus for about eighteen months [*Harmony* 2:53-58], they occasionally went back to their former occupation of fishing. On this particular day, as the brothers were casting their large net into the sea, Jesus called out to them, "Come! Follow after Me! And I will now teach you how to 'fish' for people!" The time had arrived for them to follow the Lord on a full-time basis as His permanent disciples.

12 Matthew 4:13-16
13 Matthew 4:17

So accordingly, without hesitation, they left their nets and followed after Him. [*Harmony* 13:86][14]

A little further on, the Lord saw John, also one of His followers for the past eighteen months. [*Harmony* 2:53-58] He was with his brother James. They were sitting with their father Zebedee in his boat, along with hired servants. They were all repairing their nets. Jesus quickly called out to James and John as He had done to Simon and Andrew. At His words, the two brothers left their father and the hired servants and followed after Jesus. [*Harmony* 13:101][15]

> Even though all four men followed Jesus that day, they still from time to time would return to their familiar work of fishing, perhaps unsure as to whether they really wanted to work with Jesus on a permanent, full-time basis or not.[(d)]

Sometime later, a large crowd was pressing close in on the Lord as He was teaching the Word. He was standing by the Lake called Gennesaret—which is another name for the Sea of Galilee. At that moment, Jesus spied two boats on the shore of the lake. They were empty because their owners were washing their fishing nets. He climbed into one of the boats, which happened to belong to Simon Peter. He asked Peter to push the boat a little distance out from the shore. And, from this safe distance, as the Lord sat down on the edge of the boat, He was able to teach the multitude gathered there. [*Harmony* 7:22][16]

When He finished His teaching, Jesus said to Peter, "Put out for deeper water, and let down your nets for a catch."[17]

But Peter answered, "Master, we have been trying to catch fish all night long, but without success. As experienced fishermen, we know that nighttime is the best time for fishing. Nevertheless, because You have asked us, we will cast down our nets once more, even though it is the daytime."[18]

After doing so, they caught so many fish that the bulging nets began to tear! They had to signal for their partners, James and John, who were the fishermen in the other boat, to come and provide them assistance. After they had hauled all

---

14 Matthew 4:18-20; Mark 1:16-18

15 Matthew 4:21, 22; Mark 1:19, 20

16 Luke 5:1-3

17 Luke 5:4

18 Luke 5:5

the fish aboard, there were so many fish that both boats were completely filled, and even threatened to sink![19]

When Peter realized that an incredible miracle had just happened, he fell on his knees at the Lord's feet and declared, "Depart from me! I am a sinful and unworthy man, My Lord!" Incredible awe and amazement seized the fishermen because of the miracle that they had just witnessed. This included James and John, the sons of Zebedee, who were partners with Peter in the other boat.[20]

But Jesus, trying to reassure Peter, told him, "Don't be afraid! From now on, you will be taking men alive! Yes, instead of catching fish, which soon die, you will catch men, who will live forever!"[(e)] [21]

So when they brought their boats to the shore—this included all four: Andrew, Peter, James, and John—they decided finally to leave their fishing occupation behind and follow Jesus as His full-time disciples. From that moment on, there would be no turning back for any of them.[22]

### — The Healing of the Demoniac in the Synagogue
### < Late Spring, A.D. 29 (4/7) >
### {Mark 1:21-28; Luke 4:31-37}

Soon after the call by the sea [*Harmony* 4:14-22], Jesus, with His disciples, could be found in the synagogue—or Jewish church—in Capernaum each seventh-day Sabbath. On a particular Sabbath, as He was teaching the people in the synagogue, the congregation was quite astonished at His words. The Lord taught them as One who possessed great spiritual insight and persuasive authority—which was very different from the scribes and the empty spiritual platitudes which they regularly taught in the synagogues![23]

On this particular occasion, there suddenly appeared a man who was possessed of a demon. The devil in the man cried out with an extremely loud voice, "Aha! Let us alone! What do we have in common with You, Jesus of Nazareth? Have

---

19 Luke 5:6, 7, 10
20 Luke 5:8-10
21 Luke 5:10
22 Luke 5:10, 11
23 Mark 1:21, 22; Luke 4:31, 32

You come to destroy us? I know who You are—You are the Holy One of God, even the Messiah!"[24]

> One the most unusual features found in the ancient world was the fact that some people were literally possessed by devils. For those living in most of the world today, this phenomenon is hard to comprehend. Nevertheless, the Gospel record states categorically that some people were, indeed, possessed by a demon or demons. And one thing is certain: The fact that Jesus met demon possession head on—and was victorious—certainly made it abundantly clear to the people that He possessed a most unusual power. There was no doubt that His ability to cast out demons was well beyond that of any ordinary person. [*Harmony* 6:15; 7:2, 3][(f)]

Jesus rebuked the demon, "Muzzle yourself! Come out of that man!" [*Harmony* 4:30, 65] The demon threw the man into the crowd surrounding him, severely wrenching his body. And, after one more ear-piercing scream, the demon came out of the man without doing him any further harm. [*Harmony* 9:28/][25]

> When casting the devil out of the man, Jesus refused to allow the demon to say anything more. Having a demon verify His claim to be the Messiah would cause additional prejudice to be leveled against Him—something He did not need! In that case, His critics would charge that the demon knew Him because He was under the demon's control. In fact, that is exactly what His critics would later accuse of Him of being. [*Harmony* 6:17; 7:3]

Amazement gripped the people as they variously questioned each other. They exclaimed, "Who is this Man, called Jesus?" "What new thing is this Man teaching?" "What power there must be in His words, for, it is with authority that He commands even unclean spirits to come out of the possessed . . . and they obey Him!" "Unbelievable!" And so, that very day, the report of the great works of Jesus spread quickly throughout all the countryside of Galilee. [*Harmony* 4:47, 62/3][26]

---

24 Mark 1:23, 24; Luke 4:33, 34

25 Mark 1:25, 26; Luke 4:35

26 Mark 1:27, 28; Luke 4:36, 37

## — Peter's Mother-in-Law Is Healed, and Other Sick Are Healed that Evening < Late Spring, A.D. 29 (4/7) > {Matthew 8:14-17; Mark 1:29-34; Luke 4:38-41}

As soon as Jesus healed the demoniac, He arose and left the synagogue and headed toward Andrew and Simon Peter's home. Coming along with Him were James and John, two of His other disciples. When they arrived, they found out that Peter's mother-in-law was sick in bed, in the grip of a high fever. The disciples immediately urged Jesus to do something to help her.[27]

Jesus went to where she was lying. He stood over her and touched her hand. Next, firmly taking hold of the woman's hand, He raised her up, and commanded the fever to leave her. Instantly, the fever fled from her! And then, on her own, she quickly arose and served all of them a meal![28]

That evening, after the sun had set, marking the close of the Sabbath, a number of people came to the house. They had heard of the miracle in the synagogue earlier that day [*Harmony* 4:23-26], and brought a large number of sick people so that the Lord might heal them too. In fact, so many people came that it was as though the entire city was at the door! Many of the people were suffering from various diseases. There were others who were demon-possessed, just like the man who had been healed in the synagogue.[(g)] [29]

Laying His hand on each of them, one at a time, Jesus healed them all, even though there were many of them. He also cast out many demons through the power of His word. When the devils were thrown out, some shouted as they left, declaring, "You are the Son of God—the Messiah!" However, Jesus refused to allow the demons to say another word, for they knew that He was the Christ. [Harmony 4:25, 65][30]

> Again [*Harmony* 4:25, 25/], for Jesus to be publicly declared as the Messiah by demons was not a good thing for His ministry, which was already under scrutiny by many of the Jewish leaders in the area. They would falsely and viciously accuse the Lord of being in partnership with demons. [*Harmony* 7:3]

---

27 Matthew 8:14; Mark 1:29, 30; Luke 4:38

28 Matthew 8:15; Mark 1:31; Luke 4:39

29 Matthew 8:16; Mark 1:32, 33; Luke 4:40

30 Matthew 8:16; Mark 1:34; Luke 4:40, 41

This healing episode—among many others—was implied by Isaiah, the prophet, who wrote, "He took upon Himself our weaknesses, and thus, carried away our sicknesses." [Isaiah 53:4] Because of that, He was able to understand human frailties and infirmities. But more than just understanding human weaknesses, Jesus was able to heal those afflicted by various diseases, completely restoring them to wholeness.[31]

## The Lord's First Major Evangelistic Galilean Tour < Late Spring through Late Summer, A.D. 29 (4/7) > (Matthew 4:23-25; 8:2-4; 9:2-9; 12:1-21; Mark 1:35-2:14; 2:23-3:19; Luke 4:42-44; 5:12-28; 6:1-16)

### — The Beginning of the Lord's First Galilean Evangelistic Tour < Late Spring, A.D. 29 (4/7) > {Matthew 4:23-25; Mark 1:35-39; Luke 4:42-44}

The next morning, sometime after 3 a.m., Jesus arose. He left the house, found a private place, and began to pray. Later, Peter, along with the other disciples, looked around for Him. When they finally found Him, they said, "Everyone is looking for You!" Indeed, though it was still early, the crowds were already searching for Him! They wanted to see and experience more of His healing miracles. When they found Him, they pressed in close, making it difficult for the Lord to move. In fact, the multitude grabbed hold of Him, begging Him to stay in their midst, so that He could continue His healing ministry among them.[(h)] [32]

To their chagrin, Jesus said, "No! My disciples and I must go into the other villages of Galilee. That is the right thing for us to do. I need to preach the Gospel of the kingdom in those places too. Remember, I have been sent here to the earth for that exact purpose. We can't spend all of our time here in just one place, no matter how well things may be going in Capernaum." So, He and the disciples went to the other synagogues around the entire province of Galilee. There, the Lord preached and taught the Gospel of the kingdom. He also cast out many demons.[(i)] [33]

In the course of His ministry, Jesus visited many of the nearly 200 towns of the densely populated province of Galilee. Jesus continued to heal people of every imaginable disease and sickness. Those who were brought to Him for healing

---

31 Matthew 8:17

32 Mark 1:35-37; Luke 4:42

33 Matthew 4:23; Mark 1:38, 39; Luke 4:43, 44

included the demon-possessed, the insane, those suffering from chronic pain, and those who were paralyzed. He had the ability to heal them all, no matter what their physical or mental problems might be! As a result, the good news regarding His work traveled far and wide, even to the foreign nation of Syria, to the northeast. Large crowds of people from the entire province of Galilee followed Him, as well as from Decapolis—the place known as the Ten Cities—well to the southeast of the Sea of Galilee. People came from Judea, Jerusalem, and even from as far away as Peraea, east of the Jordan River. [*Harmony* 6:18; 8:39][(j)] [34]

> The Savior's extended missionary and evangelistic tour of Galilee is often called the Lord's "First Galilean Evangelistic Tour," which lasted for several months. [*Harmony* 6:18; 8:39; 9:54/][[1]]
>
> The conclusion of this first Evangelistic Tour of Galilee roughly marked the halfway point of His entire public ministry. The recorded details of His earlier ministry are far scantier than those of the second half of the Lord's public ministry.[[2]]

**—Jesus Heals His First Leper**
**< Summer, A.D. 29 (4/7) >**
**{Matthew 8:2-4; Mark 1:40-45; Luke 5:12-16}**

While Jesus was visiting one of the cities of Galilee on His evangelistic tour of the province, a man with leprosy approached Him. [*Harmony* 13:40-43][(k)] [35]

> What the Bible calls leprosy was a dreaded disease of ancient days. It was a malady that started on the skin and then spread deeper into the flesh of the body. It was considered by the ancients to be extremely contagious. Accordingly, they felt it necessary to quarantine those afflicted with the disease. No one wanted to get close to a person with leprosy, let alone touch those suffering with this disease. Should an uninfected person ever come near a leper, the leper was required to cry out, "Unclean! Unclean!" [*Harmony* 4:36] To make matters worse, leprosy was considered by many Jews to be a physical punishment from God for some sin in the life of the sufferer. Thus, this disease was thought to have had both physical and moral implications, and anyone suffering from this dreaded malady was thought by some to be unworthy of healing. Leprosy was so prevalent that God, through Moses, gave an elaborate description of the

34 Matthew 4:23-25
35 Matthew 8:2; Mark 1:40; Luke 5:12

various forms of the disease and how it must be controlled. [Leviticus 13 and 14]

This particular leper who found Jesus had an especially severe case of leprosy. In fact, the disease had covered his entire body. Against the rules that lepers were to avoid contact with others [*Harmony* 4:35/], he walked boldly right up to the Lord, and fell on his face to worship Him. Then rising to his knees, the leper pleaded, "If You are willing, I know that You can cleanse me from my leprosy!"[36]

Notice that the leper, when asking Jesus to heal him, expressed a reservation, saying, "*If* you are willing." This was because he was unsure that the Lord would be willing to heal him of such a horrible disease commonly thought to be a divine punishment for a sinful life.

Filled with compassion, Jesus stretched out His hand toward the leper and, deliberating ignoring society's taboo, actually touched him! The Lord declared, "Yes! I am quite willing! Be clean!" At the sound of the Lord's voice, the leprosy vanished from the man, leaving him completely clean! [*Harmony* 4:62/4; 8:23][37]

By healing the leper, Jesus clearly indicated that He would be willing, not only to cleanse someone of leprosy, but also to remove the supposed moral defect that caused the illness in the first place. Jesus, as the Messiah, was not afraid to have close contact with a leper. By this action, considering the mindset of the times, He also implied that He was not afraid to have an equally close contact with even the most despised sinners.

Then the Lord sent the former leper on his way, with these stern instructions, "See to it that you tell no one what I did for you! Go directly—right now—and show yourself to the priest for his approval. Be sure, also, to present the prescribed offering as thanks to God for your cleansing as Moses commanded. [Leviticus 14:2] Such an offering will serve as clear proof to the priest and the people that you have been truly healed. If you do this, then your healing will be accepted by the priest as genuine."[38]

The Lord's strongly worded command to the leper to remain silent regarding the details of his cleansing was important for the leper to follow. There were several reasons for this command. If the news regarding the

36 Matthew 8:2; Mark 1:40; Luke 5:12

37 Matthew 8:3; Mark 1:41, 42; Luke 5:13

38 Matthew 8:4; Mark 1:43, 44; Luke 5:14

> power of Jesus to heal leprosy was widely known, many lepers would flock to Jesus. Were this to happen, people needing to see Jesus for reasons other than leprosy would be so afraid of contracting the disease that they would stay away from Him altogether. Also, Jesus did not want His ministry to be known solely as a disease-healing work. This would greatly detract from His spiritual ministry. And, furthermore, according to the law it was a priest who was to inspect a person claiming to be healed from leprosy. In order for a priest not to be prejudiced against a truly healed leper, it was important that he be unaware that it was Jesus who had healed him. This was true because many of the priests were opposed to the work of Jesus. Thus, if they knew Jesus had supposedly healed a leper, the priest might be inclined to refuse to declare that such a person was really cleansed of leprosy. [*Harmony* 4:65/]

Nevertheless, in spite of the Lord's explicit command, the former leper told everyone everywhere about his healing and how it had happened! As a result, many, many people searched out Jesus to be healed of all kinds of diseases. They came from what seemed to be the whole world! For a time, Jesus could no longer enter into a city in a public manner. Instead he had to remain in the more sparsely populated regions. Just to get a little privacy, often He would disappear from the masses altogether to pray in some secret place.[39]

> The healing of the leper and his subsequent spreading the news of his cleansing ended, for all practical purposes, the Lord's first major evangelistic tour of Galilee. [*Harmony* 6:18; 8:39] The crowds of people surrounding Jesus seeking their own healing made it impossible for the Savior to minister adequately to the masses as He desired. Indeed, for a while, He was no longer able to teach the truth of the Gospel effectively to them. Thus, the reasons behind His strong counsel to the cured leper to keep silent about his healing, were, unfortunately, proven to be valid.

### — The Healing of the Paralytic Lowered Through the Roof
### < Summer, A.D. 29 (4/7) >
### {Matthew 9:2-8; Mark 2:1-12; Luke 5:17-26}

In the course of time, Jesus returned secretly to Peter's home in Capernaum. A few days later, the news of His arrival leaked out. As a result, people from all over began to say to one another, "He's at Peter's home!" Accordingly, crowds of

---

39 Mark 1:45; Luke 5:15, 16

people rushed over to the house. In fact, so many came that there was no longer any room left in the house or even at the door! Inside Peter's home, Jesus was preaching and teaching the words of the Gospel to those who were packed into the place.[40]

On this particular occasion, among those in the house were some Pharisees and other teachers of religious law who had come from the various towns of Galilee. There were also some who had come all the way from Jerusalem and Judea, seeking to find fault with what the Lord might say and do. It was clearly evident, nevertheless, that the power of the Holy Spirit was working through the Savior that day to perform miracles of healing, and to touch the hearts of those listening to Him.[41]

At one point during His teaching session, there came a group of four men, carrying a paralyzed man on a stretcher-like bed. This man desperately wanted to see the Lord face to face. Because of the crowded conditions, they were unable to find a way into the house. Most houses of the day had either steps or a ladder leading up to the roof where the family sat in the cool of the evening. The men took the paralytic up onto the flat roof of the building, removed the tiles that were laid over the rafters, and began to lower the man, still lying on his bed, down into the center of the house. He ended up right in front of the Lord![42]

When Jesus saw their faith, He was impressed with their bold action. He knew that the sick man was paralyzed as a result of a very sinful lifestyle. [*Harmony* 3:80] While the man wanted to be healed, he was even more desirous of having his sins forgiven. So, even before the paralytic could say a single word, Jesus said to him, "Be of good courage and comfort, My son! I say to you, man, all your sins are all totally forgiven."[43]

The close-minded Jewish leaders and religious teachers sitting there were shocked by what Jesus said to the paralytic. They began to reason among themselves, saying, "Who does this Man think He is, using such words? He's a blasphemer! How dare He! Who can forgive sins? Certainly not this mere mortal. Indeed, only God can forgive sins!"[44]

---

40 Mark 2:1, 2; Luke 5:17

41 Luke 5:17

42 Matthew 9:2; Mark 2:3, 4; Luke 5:18, 19

43 Matthew 9:2; Mark 2:5; Luke 5:20

44 Matthew 9:3; Mark 2:6, 7; Luke 5:21

At that very instant, Jesus knew by the power of the Holy Spirit the evil thoughts which were in their minds. So the Savior said to them, "Why are you thinking this way with such despicably evil thoughts? Tell Me: Which is easier to say to the paralytic, 'Your sins are forgiven,' or, to say to him, 'Get up! Pick up your stretcher and walk'?" [*Harmony* 4:62/5; 8:23; 9:28/][45]

Of course, on the surface, it was easier for a human being to say, "Your sins are forgiven." In that case, no one would know for sure whether the sins were actually forgiven by God, or not! However, to say, "Pick up your stretcher and walk!" could only be easy if a person were actually able to heal someone such as the paralytic.

Dramatically driving His point home, Jesus, looking directly at the Jewish leaders, triumphantly declared, "Just so you may know with certainty that the Son of Man has the full, God-given authority on earth to forgive sins—." And then, pausing for a second, and turning toward the paralytic, He commanded him, "I tell you: Rise up! Take up your stretcher and walk on home!" Obeying the command of the Lord, the man who had been paralyzed jumped up in front of the whole crowd. Taking his stretcher, he walked out the door and headed toward his home, praising God all the way![46]

Jesus had healed the man before the eyes of His critics. They could have no real doubt that God was with Him. For, if a man, on his own, were to try to forgive the sins of others—and thus truly be a blasphemer—certainly God would not give this same individual the power to heal someone of a dreaded disease—especially such an incapacitating one as paralysis. Thus, the fact that Jesus was able to heal the man dramatically proved that He also had the authority to forgive sins, for the power and authority to heal and forgive must come from the same source: God![[1]]

Further, Jesus boldly used the phrase, "Son of Man" to describe Himself. Among many Jews this specific designation referred to the Messiah. By using it to refer to Himself, Jesus was clearly implying that He was the Messiah. In fact, it was the Lord's favorite title for Himself. Furthermore, by forgiving the sins of the paralytic, Jesus, just as clearly indicated to the Jewish leaders that He was not only the "Son of Man," but also the

45 Matthew 9:4, 5; Mark 2:8, 9; Luke 5:22, 23

46 Matthew 9:6, 7; Mark 2:10-12; Luke 5:24, 25

"Son of God." This means that, as the Son of God, He possessed the divine power and authority to forgive sins.[2]

As far as the crowds were concerned, they were truly amazed by the fact that God would give power to a human being to both forgive sins and heal people. They began to glorify God, saying, "We've never seen anything like this before!" A fearful sense of awe fell upon them as they declared, "We have witnessed some truly unbelievable things today: A Man who can forgive sins, and heal a disease with the mere sound of His voice—even a paralyzed body, no less! It's truly amazing!" [*Harmony* 4:26][47]

Thus Jesus had silenced His critics. By forgiving the paralytic's sins, Jesus took upon Himself the privileged authority of God. By His actions, He claimed to be the Messiah—the Son of God, and also the Son of Man.

### — Levi Matthew Is Called to be a Disciple
### < Summer, A.D. 29 (4/7) >
### {Matthew 9:9; Mark 2:13, 14; Luke 5:27, 28}

Jesus went on another short journey along the coast of the Sea of Galilee, not very far from Capernaum. As usual, a huge crowd of people surrounded Him. So accordingly, He took the time to teach them.[48]

After He finished teaching the people, Jesus headed back home toward Capernaum. As He did so, He passed by a tax office in that vicinity. Sitting there collecting taxes was a certain Jewish man named Levi Matthew, the son Alphaeus.[49]

This particular tax office was located on the main road that led from Syria in the east to the Mediterranean Sea in the west. Herod Antipas, the tetrarch of Galilee, was charging a transportation tax to those who traveled along that road. (A tetrarch was a ruler on a level slightly lower than that of a king.)[1]

Tax collectors, as is true in all ages, are generally disliked by society at large. This was especially true in Jesus' day. Any Jew who collected taxes for the hated Roman government was considered a virtual traitor

47 Matthew 9:8; Mark 2:12; Luke 5:26

48 Mark 2:13

49 Matthew 9:9; Mark 2:14; Luke 5:27

> to the Hebrew people. Thus, tax-collectors were despised by all the citizens of the nation. In addition, many of the tax-collectors of that day were well-known cheaters and extortionists. In fact, the usual word for a tax-collector—publican—was a byword to describe a sinner. These two words, *publican* and *sinner*, were often linked together in normal conversation as referring to all types of wicked people. [*Harmony* 8:3] Indeed, these two words were interchangeable in the thinking of most individuals. [*Harmony* 5:39; 13:59, 108, 109, 109/, 111, 112, 120][2]

Knowing Levi Matthew's heart, the Lord saw something good in this man. He said to him, "Follow Me!" [*Harmony* 2:59] And immediately, the tax-collector arose from his seat, left everything behind, and followed Jesus, becoming one of His regular disciples.[50]

> This was the seventh disciple whom Jesus had called to follow Him on a full-time basis, the others being Andrew, James, John, Philip, Nathanael, and Peter. [*Harmony* 2:53-68] Levi Matthew would ultimately become the author of the Gospel record commonly known as *Matthew*.

**— The Disciples Pluck Grain on the Sabbath Day**
**< Summer, A.D. 29 (4/7) >**
**{Matthew 12:1-8; Mark 2:23-28; Luke 6:1-5}**

One Sabbath day—the seventh day of the week—Jesus and His disciples were walking through a field of ripened grain. Because they were hungry, the disciples picked some of the heads, rubbed them in their hands to remove the hulls, and then ate the kernels. Some Pharisees, spying on Jesus and His disciples, complained to the Lord, saying, "Your disciples are doing something that is illegal to do on the Sabbath day. Look, why is it that they are doing what is clearly forbidden by the Sabbath law?"(l) [51]

> Now, eating grain out of someone else's field was entirely legal. In fact, the law of Moses specifically provided that hungry people could, on occasion, eat grain from someone else's field. [Deuteronomy 23:24, 25] However, the Pharisees protested. But why did they? While it was appropriate to eat grain from another's field, it was not legal, *according to a man-made Jewish law*, to do so on the Sabbath. Based upon a strict, human interpretation of the Fourth Commandment [Exodus 20:8-11],

---

[50] Matthew 9:9; Mark 2:14; Luke 5:27, 28

[51] Matthew 12:1, 2; Mark 2:23, 24; Luke 6:1, 2

> the process of picking and rolling the grain in the hand was considered by most of the Jewish leaders to be a violation of the command to do no work on the Sabbath. To them, it was tantamount to reaping, threshing, and grinding the grain.[1]
>
> The truth is that the disciples did not disobey any of the Biblical laws which dealt with proper Sabbath-keeping. What they violated were *man-made* restrictions that the Jews had created, which had the effect of encumbering the Sabbath with ridiculous and petty regulations. In reality, many of these man-made laws were quite ludicrous in nature. For example, it was unlawful to look in a mirror attached to a wall, or to even light a candle on the Sabbath! It was not legal to carry a handkerchief on the Sabbath day unless it was sewn to one's clothing. To carry one unattached was considered the carrying a burden! The Jews had made Sabbathkeeping nothing more than the burdensome adherence to a long list of prohibitions, many petty in nature. It was all quite unbelievable. [*Harmony* 4:59/, 11:89/][2]

Jesus, strongly defending His disciples, questioned the Pharisees, "What are you talking about? Have you never read the story of David in the Scriptures, when he and his companions, were hungry? It was then that he entered the tabernacle of God—when Abiathar was the high priest—and a priest there gave him the sacred unleavened bread right from the holy table! As you well know, such bread is not allowed to be eaten by anyone except the priests. [Leviticus 24:6-9] To make matters worse, David even gave some of the bread to his companions to eat. Have you never read that? [1 Samuel 21:1-6] Now, you criticize My disciples, and even Me, for the simple, harmless task of picking and eating a little common grain on the Sabbath day. Yet you have given David a pass for what he did. And why have you excused David's violation of the law? You have reasoned that in order for David to survive—which is a greater good—it was all right for him to eat of the consecrated showbread, even though that was clearly a technical violation of that law of God. Isn't that right? But then, on the other hand, My disciples have rolled a few kernels of grain in their hands on the Sabbath, and you charge them with some huge violation of the law. Again, you are willing to give David a break, but do not do the same with My disciples. To feed their hungry stomachs is more important than a small technical violation of one of your Sabbath laws. Again, you forgive David for violating a *Scriptural* law. Yet, at the same time, you refuse to forgive My disciples for the so-called breaking of one of you own *man-made* laws. Therefore, I declare that your accusation against My disciples is unwarranted![(m)] [52]

"Furthermore," Jesus continued, "have you not read in the law, that on the Sabbath day it is appropriate for the priests, while working in the Temple, to do things that would normally be wrong to do on the Sabbath? Yet they are considered innocent of any wrongdoing. [Leviticus 24:8; 1 Chronicles 9:32] And why is this? Because the work of the Temple is of such great importance that a technical violation of the Sabbath commandment is deemed permissible in order for the Temple services to continue to run smoothly. Now, isn't that right?[53]

"But I tell you the truth, there is an issue at stake here that is greater than any man-made regulation you may have decreed to be binding on My disciples!"[(n)] [54]

> Jesus agreed with the concept that the technicalities of Sabbathkeeping were of lesser importance than the true meaning of worship on the Sabbath day. This included the operation of the Temple services. For example, if, in keeping the Sabbath, the priests allowed the functions of the Temple to cease, that would be counterproductive. On this, the Jewish leaders and Jesus both agreed. With that being the case, Jesus implied if that, likewise, in the keeping of the Sabbath, the work of His own ministry would be hindered, little value would be accomplished. Thus, the smooth functioning of His ministry was of much greater worth than the technical violation of any man-made Sabbath law. Beyond that, the Sabbath was intended to be a blessing—not merely a set of laws just for the sake of regulating people's lives, as the Jewish, man-made laws appeared to do. (On the other hand, the Lord's statement here should not be used to excuse clear violations of the Biblical Sabbath commandment [Exodus 20:8-11], so as to destroy the true import of that law.)

In summary, Jesus added, "If you really understood what the Scripture means when it says, 'I desire compassion over sacrifice' [Hosea 6:6], then you would know that allowing My hungry disciples to eat a little food on the Sabbath is more important than your ridiculous holy day restrictions, and further, you

---

52 Matthew 12:3, 4; Mark 2:25, 26; Luke 6:3, 4

53 Matthew 12:5

54 Matthew 12:6

would not have condemned my disciples' actions. I declare that My disciples are innocent of your charges!"[55]

> By quoting this Scripture, Jesus meant that, allowing for some necessary minor technical violations of the Sabbath law—that is, showing *compassion*—was more important than being sticklers for the law, and foolishly restricting the lives of welling-meaning people—that is, requiring *sacrifice.*

The Lord concluded: "The Sabbath was made for the good of mankind—to be a blessing for all the peoples of the world. Man was not created to be a mere showpiece, as it were, in an overly-burdened, restrictive Sabbath. This makes everyone miserable who seeks to honor its sacredness. The Sabbath is to be flexible enough to adapt to the real world! So then, the Son of Man, as the Lord, has the full authority over everything, including the Sabbath day itself. He gave the Sabbath to be a blessing to those whom He created and continues to love. He knows how, at the same time, to honor the Sabbath and bless His people. In other words, if the Son of Man says something is all right to do on the Sabbath, it's all right. In short, His word is final."[56]

> Again, the Sabbath was created to bless mankind. God did not create mankind merely to fit into a Sabbath structure. Again, the smaller technicalities of Sabbathkeeping—as important as they may appear to be—are not more important than the people whom the Sabbath was made to bless.[1]

### — The Healing on the Sabbath of the Man with the Withered Hand
### ‹ Summer, A.D. 29 (4/7) ›
### {Matthew 12:9-14; Mark 3:1-6; Luke 6:6-11}

> The issue of Sabbathkeeping, especially regarding who had the final authority to prescribe proper Sabbathkeeping—Jesus or the Jewish leaders—became a major source of contention between these leaders and Jesus. [*Harmony* 4:51-56] How this issue would be resolved would largely determine whether the Lord would be accepted as the Messiah or not. As far the Jewish leaders were concerned, the Savior must submit to their will on this subject. Unless Jesus did so, He would never cease to incur their wrath. For Jesus, the issue of proper Sabbathkeeping was

55 Matthew 12:7

56 Matthew 12:8; Mark 2:27, 28; Luke 6:5

also important. As Creator, and as the Son of Man, He was determined to restore the Sabbath to the position it originally had. [Genesis 2:1-3] It was to be a blessing to mankind rather than a heavily burdened and overly restricted day. So, this issue would be a bone of contention between Him and the Jews throughout the remainder of His ministry.[2]

On another Sabbath day—some time after the plucking of the grain incident [*Harmony* 4:51-56]—Jesus went into a synagogue in a different place. There, during His session of teaching, He suddenly noticed a man with a shrunken right hand, the result of either disease or accident.[57]

The scribes and Pharisees moved closer to the Lord so that they might carefully scrutinize Jesus to see what He would do in this case. They did not want to miss a thing that they might be able to use against Him, especially as it related to Sabbathkeeping. Indeed, if He were to heal the man on the Sabbath, it would give them further cause to accuse Him of Sabbath lawbreaking. They were even so bold as to ask Him, "Is it lawful to heal on the Sabbath day?" Of course they did not believe so! But to be sure, Jesus knew the evil intentions these Jewish leaders possessed in their hearts.[58]

To make a public issue of the situation, Jesus called out to the man, "Get up and stand in the middle aisle so that everyone can see you!" As the man complied, Jesus said to the congregation—and especially to the Jewish leaders—"I have a single question to ask all of you: Is it consistent with the law to do good, or to do evil, on the Sabbath—to save a life, or to allow one to suffer or die?" Surprised by the Lord's open boldness, they did not know what to say. So they said nothing![59]

> Rabbinical law permitted the helping of someone in a crisis on the Sabbath. However, it prohibited the helping of one with a chronic problem—such as in the case of this man. Such people could, the Jews reasoned, be assisted on another day. Thus, by His question, Jesus challenged this foolish line of thinking. [*Harmony* 4:51/2]

Jesus continued, "What person here who owns a single sheep that has fallen into a ditch on the Sabbath, would not take hold of it and pull it out? Of course all of you would! Isn't that right? To prove My point, your own law allows for this

---

57 Matthew 12:9, 10; Mark 3:1; Luke 6:6

58 Matthew 12:10; Mark 3:2; Luke 6:7, 8

59 Mark 3:3, 4; Luke 6:8, 9

technical violation of the Sabbath commandment. That's true, isn't it? Now, let Me ask you, how much more valuable, then, is this man than a sheep? [*Harmony* 12:74, 92] So, it seems to Me—and I affirm it—that it is quite proper—even according to Scriptural law—to do good on the Sabbath day, such as the potential healing of this man!" Then He looked around at each one of those who were challenging Him. The Lord stared into each face. He was momentarily angry that they, Israel's own leaders, were so unbelievably cruel and narrow-minded. He continued to be grieved at their incredible stone-hardness of heart.[60]

To clinch His point that it was quite acceptable to heal someone on the Sabbath day, Jesus said to the man, "Hold out your hand!" And when the man stretched out his right hand, instantly it was restored to its normal size and function, just like the left one! [*Harmony* 4:62/6][61]

Openly upset and enraged to the point of losing all sense and reason, the Pharisees stomped out of the synagogue in a huff, even before the services were finished. [*Harmony* 12:31] And they, at once, in consultation with the Herodians [*Harmony* 14:85], tried to figure out a way that they might have Jesus killed! [*Harmony* 4:63][62]

> Now the Herodians were a Jewish political party who were normally bitter enemies of the Pharisees. The Herodians sided with King Herod in the political issues of the day. This showed how desperate the Pharisees were to kill Jesus, that they were willing to go into partnership with the hated Herodians. They thought that the Herodians would, perhaps, be able to seek Herod's aid in doing something to have Jesus killed, or, at least, imprison Him as Herod had done with John the Baptist. [*Harmony* 3:69-71] It is ironic that the Jews, on the Sabbath day, plotted the death of Jesus, because the Lord had relieved the suffering of the man with the withered hand on that Sabbath day![1]
>
> An additional point to be considered is that while the healing miracles of Jesus were of real benefit to those who were blessed by them, the Lord had another purpose in performing these miracles. His miracles were also to teach spiritual lessons which would help sinners understand more fully the plan of salvation and show them how to experience it for

60 Matthew 12:11, 12; Mark 3:5; Luke 6:10
61 Matthew 12:13; Mark 3:5; Luke 6:10
62 Matthew 12:14; Mark 3:6; Luke 6:11

themselves. [*Harmony* 11:80] Several of the miracles Jesus performed in His early ministry in Galilee are strong cases in point. [*Harmony* 9:28/][2]

One such example is the healing of the demon-possessed man in the synagogue. [*Harmony* 4:23-26] In this healing, Jesus showed that He had complete control over demons—even the devil himself. The obvious spiritual lesson which can be learned from this miracle is that the Lord has control over all evil, even the weaknesses of character that dwell within the sinner. Thus, the power of the devil's temptations in one's life can be overcome under the influence of the in-dwelling spirit of Christ. [*Harmony* 9:28/][3]

Another example is the miracle of the healing of the man with leprosy. [*Harmony* 4:35-39] In this case, Jesus was unafraid to touch the body of the man afflicted with such a dreaded contagious disease. This clearly demonstrated that the Lord was equally unafraid to associate with sinners. He showed that sinners need not fear to approach Him for His help in their lives.[4]

Yet another example is the story of the paralytic let down through the roof. [*Harmony* 4:42-48] In this story, the power of the Lord to heal the man was proof that He had the authority to forgive his sins. The power to heal and the authority to forgive come from the same source. This made the fact clear that *any* sinner could have confidence in the full authority of Jesus to completely cleanse his or her life from every taint of sin. [*Harmony* 9:28/][5]

And, finally, there is the story of the man whose withered hand was healed in the synagogue on the Sabbath. [*Harmony* 4:57-60] By performing this miracle on the Sabbath, Jesus was clearly emphasizing the spiritual aspects of true Sabbath-keeping—that it was appropriate to do good on the Sabbath.[6]

Thus, in all four of these miracles, the Savior—beyond the actual healings themselves—taught vital spiritual truths. In most, if not all of the Lord's miracles, He taught similar lessons. As the Messiah, He wanted the people to look beyond the actual miracle and understand the spiritual truth He was trying to teach them. In most cases this was just as important as the actual miracle itself. [*Harmony* 9:30][7]

## — The Lord's Popularity in Galilee
## < Summer, A.D. 29 (4/7) >
## {Matthew 12:15-21; Mark 3:7-12}

Aware that many of the Jewish leaders were seeking to kill Him [*Harmony* 4:62], Jesus relocated Himself nearer to the Sea of Galilee, just south of Capernaum, to a place less populated. However, with the news of His mighty preaching and fantastic healings spreading far and wide, an increasingly large multitude continued to follow Him wherever He went. This multitude, of course, came from Galilee. Many people also came from Judea—including Jerusalem—from as far as 80 or more miles to the south. They came, too, from Idumea, which is south of Judea, and from Peraea, which was east of the Jordan River. They even came from the areas of Tyre and Sidon, well to the west. These were cities in Phoenicia on the Mediterranean Sea, northwest of Galilee. Paradoxically, as the hatred of the Jewish leaders toward Jesus increased, His popularity among the common people increased. [*Harmony* 4:3; 12:32][63]

In order to prevent the crowd from crushing Him, Jesus instructed that a boat be constantly readied so that, on a moment's notice, He could enter the watercraft. When He was pushed off shore, the Lord could thus escape the crowd of people pressing in on Him. Jesus had healed many people. Still more were coming to be cured of various painful diseases. Some came just to touch Him, with the hope that a single touch might heal them. In fact, so many people came that some actually stumbled and fell against the Lord as they pushed in on Him! Nevertheless, the Savior was able to heal everyone that needed healing.[64]

Some, possessed of demons, came on their own to be healed, or were brought to Him by caring friends. And whenever the demons recognized that it was Jesus who was about to cast them out, they would cause those who were possessed to fall down before the Lord. The demons would scream out, "You are the Son of God!"—that is, the Messiah. But Jesus strictly forbade the demons to announce to others who He was. In fact, the Lord often demanded of people who had been healed of various other diseases besides demon-possession that they keep quiet about their healing. [*Harmony* 4:30][65]

---

63 Matthew 12:15; Mark 3:7, 8
64 Matthew 12:15; Mark 3:9, 10
65 Matthew 12:16; Mark 3:11, 12

Regarding the casting out of devils, Jesus commanded the demons to keep quiet because His critics would try to claim that He was in partnership with the demons that He had cast out. They would argue that this was the reason that the demons were able to recognize Him. And in the case of general healings, the Lord also wanted to prevent His work from becoming solely a healing ministry. In that case, the Lord would be surrounded by thousands, desiring mere physical healing. This would certainly detract from His ministry of preaching the Gospel to the people at large. [*Harmony* 4:38/]

Overall, the Savior's ministry was a fulfillment of a prophecy of Isaiah, which says, "Behold, I have chosen My Servant, the Messiah. He is My Beloved Son, the One in whom I have taken great pride. I will place My Holy Spirit in His life. And through the Spirit, He will preach justice and fairness to the peoples of the whole world, including the heathen. He will not be noted for loud debates with His enemies. Neither will He will make a big noise shouting out in the streets. Instead, a bruised reed"—the refuse of society—"He will not cast away. A smoldering wick"—the weak and struggling of the world—"He will not ignore or criticize. Rather, His goal will be to provide justice to those who feel defeated, so that they can taste victory for themselves. As a result, all the peoples of the world—from every circumstance and background—will have good cause to hope in the power of His Name." [Isaiah 42:1-4][66]

### — The Official Appointment of the Twelve Disciples[(o)]
### < Late Summer, A.D. 29 (4/7) >
### {Mark 3:13-19; Luke 6:12-16}

It was about that time that Jesus left His disciples in a valley and went up onto a mountain in the hills west of the Sea of Galilee. There, He spent the entire night in prayerful communion with His Father. [*Harmony* 9:14] In the morning, He called for His disciples to come up with Him onto the mountain. Of the many disciples who followed Him, Jesus chose twelve to be His closest apostles—which means, "those who are sent." These twelve—also known as "The Twelve"—were always to be with Him. They would be sent out to preach in His stead or in advance of His arrival. The Lord also gave them both the authority and power to heal all manner of diseases, including the casting out of demons. [*Harmony* 16:21/][67]

---

66 Matthew 12:17-21

67 Mark 3:13-15; Luke 6:12, 13

Here are the twelve disciples the Lord especially chose and empowered:

Simon, whom He had called "Peter"—that is, a "Stone"[68]

Peter was originally from Bethsaida on the northeastern shore of the Sea of Galilee. He later moved to Capernaum, where he lived with his wife. When he was called to be a disciple, his occupation was fishing. He was among the closest of the disciples to Jesus, with James and his brother John being the other two. Peter denied his Lord during His trials. But, 40 days later, he was the leading spokesman on the Day of Pentecost. He played a major role in the early church. Later on, Peter wrote two books of the New Testament, both named after him.

Andrew, Peter's brother[69]

As a brother of Peter, he also was originally from Bethsaida. At the point of his calling to be a disciple, he was in partnership with Peter as a fisherman. Later on, he lived with Peter in Capernaum. He, along with Philip, introduced some Greeks to Jesus during the Passion Week.

James, the son of Zebedee [*Harmony* 4:71][70]

James was a Galilean, and partnered with his brother John and their father Zebedee, as fishermen. Along with John and Peter, he was part of the inner circle of the closest three disciples of Jesus. James was the first of the Twelve to be martyred, about 13 years after the Lord's ascension.

John, James's brother (and, to James [*Harmony* 4:70] and John, Jesus gave the name Boanerges, which means *Sons of Thunder*, for both brothers were noted for their fiery tempers.) [*Harmony* 11:123][71]

John was the younger brother of James, and was associated with him and their father, Zebedee, as a fisherman. He was one of the three disciples who were the closest to Jesus, with James, and Peter being the other two. John often referred to himself as the disciple "whom Jesus loved." John wrote the Gospel of John, the letters 1, 2, and 3 John, and the book of Revelation. He probably was the last of the Twelve to die.

---

68 Mark 3:16; Luke 6:14
69 Mark 3:18; Luke 6:14
70 Mark 3:17; Luke 6:14
71 Mark 3:17; Luke 6:14

Philip[72]

Philip was from Bethsaida in Galilee. Jesus had called Philip early on in His ministry, and he soon introduced Nathanael to Jesus. Philip also assisted Andrew in introducing some Greeks to Jesus during the Passion Week.

Bartholomew—also known as Nathanael[73]

Nathanael was from Cana of Galilee. He was the one who had questioned if a Nazarene—one from Nazareth—was worthy to be the Messiah.

Levi Matthew, the former tax-collector[74]

Matthew, from Capernaum, was a tax-collector when Jesus called him. Matthew may have been the brother of James, the son of Alphaeus, another one of the Twelve. Of course, Matthew was the author of the Gospel of Matthew.

Thomas, also known as Didymus, meaning the "Twin"[75]

Because Thomas's other name was Didymus—the "Twin"—no doubt, he had a twin sibling. Thomas was often concerned about the future suffering and death of Jesus. He was the disciple who was not with the others when Jesus first revealed Himself to them after His resurrection. The phrase "doubting Thomas"—to describe people who are slow to believe—was coined to commemorate that event.

James, the son Alphaeus[76]

Because Levi Matthew's father name was Alphaeus, it is probable that he was Matthew's brother. Nothing else is known of him.

Lebbaeus Thaddaeus, also known as Judas, the son of James[77]

Beside his three names, nothing else is known of this disciple.

---

72 Mark 3:18; Luke 6:14
73 Mark 3:18; Luke 6:14
74 Mark 3:18; Luke 6:15
75 Mark 3:18; Luke 6:15
76 Mark 3:18; Luke 6:15
77 Mark 3:18; Luke 6:16

Simon, a Cananaen—an Aramaic name, meaning the "zealous one"[78]

Simon was also called the "Zealot." The Zealots were a political party that were especially antagonistic to the Romans, and Simon was once a member of that party. Besides his earlier association with the political party of the Zealots, nothing else is known of him.

Judas Iscariot, the one who would become a traitor and betray Jesus[79]

Judas was the son of Simon Iscariot. The name Iscariot probably indicates that Judas was from the village of Kerioth in southern Judea. If this is the case, Judas was, most likely the only disciple who was from Judea, and not Galilee. Also, it very doubtful that Judas was actually selected by Jesus to be one of the Twelve. [*Harmony* 16:21-23] Then why did Jesus include him among the Twelve? Jesus probably allowed Judas to be a part of that exclusive group in order to teach the other disciples a vital lesson, for they, no doubt, were the ones who had pressed Jesus to include him in their fellowship. In time they would all learn that true spirituality was much more important than mere talent and ability.[1]

This official appointment of the twelve disciples took place nearly two years after Jesus began His ministry. They would officially be His disciples for only a little over a year and a half of the Lord's public work. Jesus did not rush their official ordination to become His disciples, because He wanted them to be absolutely sure that they were really committed to being His full-time followers. They, of course, needed to remain faithful, not just for the short period of Christ's own ministry, but, indeed, for the rest of their lives.[2]

## Supplementary Notes:

**(a) [4:10]** I added "limestone cliff" to the record for, as I understand it, such a cliff does exist in Nazareth. This helped explain this detail of the story.

**(b) [4:13]** The phrases "kingdom of heaven" and "kingdom of God" mean the same thing and are quite interchangeable. (See also *Harmony* 7:23/; 13:43/ for a further explanation of the "kingdom.")

---

78 Mark 3:18; Luke 6:15

79 Mark 3:19; Luke 6:16

**(c) [4:13+]** In my opinion, the two basic accounts of the Call of the Disciples by the Lake (Matthew 4:18-22 and Mark 1:16-20—which are virtually identical—*and* Luke 5:1-11) are quite irreconcilable. The Matthew and Mark accounts have Jesus casually walking by the Sea and calling Peter and Andrew at one time, and a little later on, in a similar manner, calling James and John. However, Luke's account is very different. In his record, Jesus is in Peter's boat, and after a miraculous catch of fish, Jesus calls them. In all cases, He uses the phrase, "I will make your fishers of men." It is surprising to me that in a couple of commentaries which I have read, very little effort has been made to reconcile these clear discrepancies. After some consideration, in the *Harmony* I have decided to *suggest* that Matthew and Mark are describing *one* event, and that Luke is describing *another* event that happened relatively soon afterward. It is known that even though Jesus had called these same people 18 months earlier in His ministry (John 1:25-51), they must have, on occasion, gone back to their old occupation of fishing, meaning that they followed Him only on a part-time basis. That is clear from the record. So, it seems reasonable, that, from time to time, Jesus could have repeated His call for them to follow Him on a full-time basis. Again, this is the position the *Harmony* takes, and this theory is expressed accordingly. But the truth remains, we don't know for sure just how the details regarding the Call by the Sea actually transpired. It is quite possible—perhaps even likely—that the discrepancy is really the result of a faulty memory of someone who was responsible for describing the event. In short, I decided to describe both versions of the event in the way that I did (so that the flow of the story is not interrupted), and let readers decide for themselves the actual truth of the matter.

**(d) [4:15/]** (See above.)

**(e) [4:21]** Even though not in the original text, I added the concept of comparing the *death* of fish with the *life* of men. I thought this was an interesting comparison.

**(f) [4:24/]** Such a dramatic situation as described in the account is, in the so-called civilized world, quite foreign to our present-day thinking. Nevertheless, I have been assured by some who know, that similar *modern* demon-possessions do, in fact, exist today in certain parts of the world. Also, some modern scholars suggest that the demon-possessions described in the Bible were really *physical* maladies, not mental or emotional disturbances brought on by literal demon possession, as the record clearly indicates. Personally, I do not subscribe to such an opinion. I believe that the events of the Gospel record are just as they are written. There may have been physical manifestations involved, but this does not detract from the mental and emotional situations—caused by actual demon possession—that are, quite often, so dramatically described.

**(g) [4:29]** According to Biblical reckoning, the Sabbath day ended at sunset (Leviticus 23:32), not at midnight as we are used to separating our days today. Accordingly, I recorded at as such in the *Harmony.*

**(h) [4:32]** The 3 a.m. timing is a *reasonable guess* based upon the phrase in Mark which says "in the morning," as it was commonly used in Bible times.

**(i) [4:33]** In Mark, Jesus used the word "us"—including the disciples—to describe the fact that *they* should minister elsewhere other than Capernaum, while Luke used the word "I" to described the same thing. I considered "us" to be the better choice.

**(j) [4:34]** The Jewish historian of the first century, Flavius Josephus, says that there were some 200 villages in the province of Galilee. While Josephus has been known to exaggerate a bit, I included his figure in the text to indicate just how heavily populated this province probably was.

**(k) [4:35]** It is generally conceded that the leprosy of the Bible is probably different from the disease of today which is also called leprosy (or Hansen's Disease). It is quite possible, though, that the modern leprosy *might be included* among the range of diseases generally called leprosy in the Bible (Leviticus 13 and 14). In any case, the two diseases—Biblical and modern leprosy—and their symptoms, are not necessarily identical. Thus, it is better to *assume* that the two diseases are really different in nature.

**(l) [4:51]** The meaning of the phrase translated "second sabbath" of the KJV (Luke 6:1), is uncertain. It probably means *another Sabbath.* That is why I used the phrase "One Sabbath day" in the *Harmony.*

**(m) [4:52]** The story Jesus told of David eating the showbread is expressed in the Bible in rather long questions. I thought this form of expression to be somewhat awkward to read, so I retold *some* of the story in the form of declarative sentences when I wrote the account in the *Harmony.*

**(n) [4:54]** It is not clear if Jesus referred to *someone* or *something* when He made this statement. I considered *something* to be a better choice.

**(o) [4:66+]** See "Disciples of Jesus" in the "Alphabetical Index" in the back of the *Harmony* to learn more details about each of the twelve disciples.

As an additional note, it is intriguing to me that we really know so little about a number of the disciples upon whom the human foundation of the Christian Church was founded.

# CHAPTER FIVE

## THE EARLY GALILEAN MINISTRY OF JESUS—
**The Sermon on the Mount**

**(Late Summer, A.D. 29)**

**The Sermon on the Mount**[(a)]
**< Late Summer, A.D. 29 (4/7) >**
**(Matthew 5:1-8:1; Mark 3:13, 14; Luke 6:13, 17-49)**

### —Jesus Prepares for His Most Important Sermon
**< Later Summer, A.D. 29 (4/7) >**
**{Matthew 5:1, 2; Mark 3:13, 14; Luke 6:13, 17-20}**

After the appointment and ordination of the twelve disciples—or apostles—Jesus came down from the mountain with them. As soon as they reached the broad plain below, a huge contingent of His other disciples, along with a vast multitude of other people—not only from Galilee, but also from Judea, Jerusalem, and even the seacoast cities of Tyre and Sidon—came to hear more of His words. Of course, many of them were there to be healed of various diseases. Among them were those who were horribly possessed of demons. Accordingly, Jesus healed them all! There were many in that massive throng who tried to touch Him, because they discovered that a healing power was constantly emanating from Him. In each of these cases, those who were able merely to touch Him were cured of their illnesses![1]

When Jesus saw more of these people coming to see Him, He retreated partway up onto the side of the mountain. There, the Lord sat down. The crowd moved up with Him, surrounding Him on the grass. He looked carefully over the multitudes as they sat down with Him. Before Him were the masses who were hungry for the truth of the Gospel, and the healing of body and soul. It had been nearly two years since Jesus had begun His public ministry. And He had been in

---

1 Mark 3:13, 14; Luke 6:13, 17-19

the Galilean region now for almost six months. Jesus was most desirous of making clear to all of them what He required of them to become His true followers. He did not want them to be misinformed. This was especially true of the newly ordained twelve disciples. They must understand clearly the truth regarding His Messianic ministry and its ultimate purpose. So Jesus, looking intently at His disciples, began to speak, teaching them the true Gospel message.[2]

> What Jesus presented to the people surrounding Him that day is commonly called the "Sermon on the Mount." It can be called, too, the greatest sermon that was ever preached. In this presentation, the Lord outlined for His followers the lifestyle principles that would personally motivate His entire ministry. These same principles should also serve as the foundation of the lives of all of the Lord's followers throughout the history of Christianity. This sermon was carefully organized and brilliantly presented. It was not a hodge-podge of various, unrelated ideas. Instead, it was connected, from beginning to end, with sound thought and irresistible logic, calculated to excite all His disciples and inspire them to live better, more fulfilled, and truly righteous lives. Throughout the remainder of His ministry, Jesus would often repeat ideas and concepts from this Sermon.[1]

### — Blessings of Growth for Those Who Accept the Gospel of Jesus: "The Beatitudes"
### < Late Summer, A.D. 29 (4/7) >
### {Matthew 5:3-12; Luke 6:20-23}

Jesus began His sermon by saying,[2]

"Truly fortunate are those of you who are humble to the core of your heart and soul, because the abiding grace of the salvation of God's heavenly kingdom will certainly be yours.[3]

"Truly fortunate are those of you who weep on account of your sins, because you will be comforted by the knowledge that you have been completely forgiven and cleansed of all your unrighteousness. Yes, you may be weeping now because of your sinful condition, but after you are forgiven, you will most assuredly laugh again! [*Harmony* 13:61][4]

---

2 Matthew 5:1, 2; Luke 6:20

3 Matthew 5:3; Luke 6:20

4 Matthew 5:4; Luke 6:21

"Truly fortunate are those of you who have a teachable attitude in your relationship with God, because you will ultimately inherit the new earth that shall be yours forever.[5]

"Truly fortunate are you who are now passionately hungering and thirsting for the divine power of the Gospel within your lives to change and perfect them, because you will, I assure you, in the end be totally satisfied.[6]

"Truly fortunate are you who show compassionate mercy to others through your words and actions, because both divine and human mercy will be shown back toward you.[7]

"Truly fortunate are you who have been transformed to the very depth of your mind and soul, because you will receive the assurance that you will ultimately see God, face-to-face.[8]

"Truly fortunate are you who are able to model the virtue of not only living peaceably with others, but also pursuing a ministry of reconciliation among people, because you will, accordingly, be honored by being called sons or daughters by God, your Father.[9]

"Truly fortunate are you, when, for the sake of the Gospel, you are harassed and persecuted, because you will have the comfort of knowing that your citizenship in the kingdom of heaven is secure.[10]

"Yes—perhaps surprisingly—you are truly fortunate when there are those who hate you. Indeed, they may insult your integrity, chastise you, reject you, even ridicule your name, and turn their backs on you. They may, with malice and evil purpose, charge you with wicked, lying accusations for the sake of the Gospel and of Me, the Son of Man. To be sure, they will besmirch your name. But in the day when these things happen to you, be happy and rejoice . . . yes, even jump for joy when they do these things to you! And why? For you can be assured that your eternal reward is great in heaven. That's the thing that really counts! Remember, too, that the fathers of those who persecute you now are the ones who persecuted

---

5 Matthew 5:5
6 Matthew 5:6; Luke 6:21
7 Matthew 5:7
8 Matthew 5:8
9 Matthew 5:9
10 Matthew 5:10

all the famous prophets who lived before you. Indeed, these persecuted prophets will be a part of God's eternal kingdom . . . and so will you![11]

"All of these things that I have just explained to you are like steps in the Gospel experience. Each step lifts you higher and higher toward God and His will for you and your character development. You may begin as one who feels totally unworthy [*Harmony* 5:3, 4], but you will, ultimately, end up standing up for your faith in the face of extreme persecution. [*Harmony* 5:10, 11] And, as I have just described, you can have the assurance of God's promise and leading at every step of the way, and that salvation is, here and now, truly yours."[1]

**— Woes Upon Those Who Reject the True Gospel Message**[(b)]
**< Late Summer, A.D. 29 (4/7) >**
**{Luke 6:24-26}**

"But there are others who will refuse to accept the Gospel truth that I have just outlined for you. To them I say: Shame on you who think you are rich in the knowledge of your *own* so-called truth of the Gospel, but as a result, are rich only in the materialistic things of this world. Look! Your teachings are dangerously wrong, and your reliance upon the things of this life provides only a false sense of security. I tell you: It will be only in this life that you will receive such comfort, for you certainly will receive nothing from the life to come![2]

"Yes, shame on you who have everything this world supposedly has to offer, thinking that you will never need anything more! You had better rejoice now, for that's all the pleasure you'll be getting as a result of your foolish striving![12]

"Shame on you who think that you have filled your stomachs, so to speak, with everything the world provides, for you, later on, will end up starving with severe hunger pains![13]

"Shame on you who do not take the message of the Gospel, which I preach, as seriously as you should. Rather, you treat it as a joke, or something to laugh

---

11 Matthew 5:11, 12; Luke 6:22, 23
12 Luke 6:24
13 Luke 6:25

at! Believe Me, the day will come that you will be wailing with sadness over your failure to accept it.[14]

"Shame on you if you think that words of human praise are worth all the effort you give to attain them! Think about it! The ancestors of those who praise you used those same words of praise to describe the false prophets who lived in the old days—the false prophets whom God roundly rejected!"[15]

### — God's Plan for You—His People

> "If you would truly accept and experience the message of the Gospel which I share with you today, you shall fulfill God's will for you to minister effectively to others in this world. You are to change the world around you. In brief: The Gospel is to change you . . . and through its power, you are to change others. Let Me give you two illustrations to show you what I mean."[1]

### — To Be the Salt of the Earth
### < Late Summer, A.D. 29 (4/7) >
### {Matthew 5:13}

"Here's the first illustration:[2]

"Primarily, as individual followers of the Gospel, you are to be the preserving and seasoning 'salt' of the earth. This means that, through your subtle influence, you are to permeate, like salt, the lives of those around you. Yes, through your quiet witness to the Gospel's power in your life, you can help change the wrong direction of many, encouraging them to move toward the true Gospel message.[16]

"But, if the 'salt' of your life's influence should become useless—either by your rejection of the Gospel, or by a gradual loss of its influence in your own life—how will you regain its effective 'savor' again? In that case, the 'salt' of your witness, then, will be just as worthless as common salt that has lost its saltiness. And, just as tasteless salt which has lost its seasoning value is thrown away to be trampled underfoot, so your witness will be useless to others and to Me! [*Harmony* 10:105, 106; 12:110][17]

---

14 Luke 6:25
15 Luke 6:26
16 Matthew 5:13
17 Matthew 5:13

"Indeed, how can people who should have understood the Gospel but because of unbelief do not personally accept it, be effective in witnessing to others? It is obvious that such people's effort to share their faith is of no real lasting value to the cause of the Gospel!"[1]

**— To Be the Light of the World**
**< Late Summer, A.D. 29 (4/7) >**
**{Matthew 5:14-16}**

"Now here's the second illustration:[2]

"Primarily, when you, as a corporate body of believers—the church—reflect the truth of the Gospel within your lives, you will become the 'light' of the world. [*Harmony* 11:42] Yes, you are to shine as brightly as the morning sunlight, reflecting the message of the Gospel into the entire world. You are to dispel the nighttime darkness of sin and unbelief. And further, you—the church—are to be like a city on a hilltop, that, when illuminated at night, cannot be hidden. In a similar vein, does anyone who has lit a lamp, place it under a basket, and thus hide its brightness? Of course not! Rather, this burning light is placed on a lamp stand, so that it can give light to everyone in the entire house. This means that you are to be the light which illuminates the entire world! So then, you are to let your light shine into the world, so that all those who see your good works will accordingly give the credit to your Father who dwells in heaven, for He truly is the One who has enlightened you. [*Harmony* 7:36; 12:16, 18, 55][18]

"As your good works are spread abroad, when you share the Gospel message, the people of the world will respond favorably to its influence, and many will, themselves, become a part of its work. And your Father will justly receive the praise and honor because of your good works and actions![1]

"Clearly then, the Gospel is to change not only you, but, through you, the world. Thus, you have been called, not only to your own personal salvation, but to share the Gospel with the whole world." [*Harmony* 18:88][2]

---

18 Matthew 5:14-16

## — The Gospel Will Change Your Lives Forever

"To be sure, when you allow the power of the Gospel to come into your lives, its impact will be nothing short of dramatic. It will radically change the way you think and the way you act. Nothing will remain the same. From now on, a new spiritual energy will animate all your activities . . . as well as your witness to others. Indeed, it will change you through and through."[3]

## — The Gospel Reveals the True Spirit of the Law and the Scriptures
## < Late Summer, A.D.29 (4/7) >
## {Matthew 5:17-20}

"No doubt you have heard My critics say that I have come to abolish the Law and the Prophets—even the entire Scriptures. But nothing could be further from the truth! In reality, I have not come to dismantle the Law and the teachings of Scriptures in any way whatsoever. Rather, I have come to deepen the understanding of the principles of the Law and the Word of God, to present them with even greater meaning than you have previously understood. [*Harmony* 1:5; 12:31/][19]

"This includes the entire meaning of the Law. Nothing is to be excluded. In fact, I have come to explain the inner 'spirit' of the Law that reveals its true purpose. As a final result, your comprehension of the Law will actually be increased and expanded.[1]

"My critics—the Jewish leaders—say that they live righteous lives. But they—sometimes even rigidly—keep only the 'letter' of the Law. That is, they attempt to obey only the actual, precise words of the Law. In reality, they know little or nothing about its 'spirit"—that is, the real, deeper meaning of the Law. Yes, the real meaning of commandment-keeping is what I will teach you to understand. But, let Me make it clear: A revealing of the 'spirit' of the Law does not, in any way, weaken or abolish its 'letter.' In reality, the 'spirit' of the Law actually strengthens the meaning of its 'letter.'[2]

"So then, in spite of what my critics have said about Me, I declare that until heaven and earth disintegrate into nothingness, not even the dotting of a single 'i,' or the crossing of an individual 't,' will be changed in the Law and

---

19 Matthew 5:17

its message, until we are all living in harmony with it in the total perfection of eternity. [*Harmony* 12:140][(c) 20]

> "To put it another way: If I, in My teaching, will not change even a single 'i' or 't' of the Law—that is, the very least of the 'letter' of the Law—you can be sure that I will place even greater emphasis upon the Law's deeper meaning and basic purpose. In fact, because I shall emphasize the 'spirit' of the Law, you can be assured that I will never change the least of the 'letter' of the Law. Certainly, you can see that!

"Whoever, then, would consider diminishing intentionally or inadvertently, even the smallest genuine commandment of the Scriptures, and would have the audacity to influence others to do the same, is in grave, grave danger. For, in the judgment, when the citizens of the kingdom of heaven are chosen, such people will be given the least consideration. On the other hand, whoever obeys and teaches, or influences others to obey every single law of the Scripture, will receive the greatest consideration in the judgment when the citizens of heaven's kingdom are chosen. The former will be lost. The latter will receive a great, eternal reward. Yes, those trampling upon the smallest law will be rejected. And, those honoring the whole Law will be greatly honored.[21]

> "So, you can clearly see that I have not come to destroy the Law—not even the least of it! Instead, I will teach you how to keep the whole Law—indeed, every Scriptural principle—with a greater depth and energy than you have previously experienced. That is my goal and emphasis!

"To put it another way—and this may shock you—I firmly declare to you that if your righteousness does not supersede the supposed righteousness of the scribes and Pharisees—those who claim to have taught and modeled true, perfect obedience of the Law—you simply will not be a part of the kingdom of heaven! [*Harmony* 2:7/1, 2][22]

> "In fact, your trust in the Gospel, which I will teach you, will empower you to obey the Law to a much greater extent than the scribes and Pharisees. They seek to obey only within their own strength, without a complete trust in the power of the Gospel's promises. The power, then,

20 Matthew 5:18
21 Matthew 5:19
22 Matthew 5:20

comes from belief, not from any mere, self-righteous, human effort. They think that as long as their good deeds outweigh their evil deeds, they will be fine. In doing so—if they are lucky—they only keep the 'letter' of the Law, but, in no way do they keep nor understand the 'spirit'—or deeper meaning—of the laws they aspire to obey. Indeed, I have come to expose a much deeper meaning and power of the Law.[1]

"Now, by quoting various portions of the Law within the Scriptures, let Me show you what I mean. I will compare what some of the so-called religious scholars have said about the Law. Then I will tell you what *I say about it*. In doing so, I will show you what the true, deeper meaning of the 'spirit' of the Law is really all about. Let Me begin."(d) [2]

### — The True Meaning of the Sixth Commandment: You Shall Not Kill
### < Late Summer, A.D. 29 (4/7) >
### {Matthew 5:21-26}

"You know that our forefathers, over many generations, have said, quoting the 'letter' of the Sixth Commandment, 'You shall not commit murder.' [Exodus 20:13] To this, religious scholars have added, 'Whoever shall actually commit murder will be hauled into a court of law for proper judgment.' Now that's fine, but they shouldn't stop there! By failing to further expose the deeper meaning of the 'spirit' of this Commandment, they imply that anything short of actual murder is all right! These scholars do not take into account the secret sins of the heart, such as anger and hate, but you must! That is the true 'spirit' of this Commandment.[23]

"That is why *I say to you*, everyone who, without just cause, is maliciously angry with his brother will be considered guilty in the court of God's judgment . . . if not in a court on this earth. While earthly courts usually judge only the open act of murder, God will, in the end, judge the angry heart. As you can see, this approach deals with the true 'spirit' of the Law, not just its 'letter.'(e) [24]

"Yes! In fact, even one's hateful words will be judged! Thus, whoever says to his brother, 'Raca: you empty-headed good for nothing!' ought to be held responsible for this reckless statement before a local court of the church, to answer for these inflammatory words. Furthermore, I say, whoever viciously slanders someone by

---

23 Matthew 5:21

24 Matthew 5:22

such an epitaph as, 'You fool!' will definitely be in grave danger of hell-fire in God's final judgment![(f)] [25]

"It may be that an earthly court that judges such inflammatory words does not now exist. But in a certain sense, it should! The point is that one who is guilty of an actual murder, or of merely being unjustly angry at another person, is in serious trouble with God. The person committing any of these actions will be called to account before some court—if not human, then certainly divine! Yes, the Gospel requires a change of heart, not a mere refusal to actually kill someone. You may escape a judgment in an earthly court of men for your evil thoughts and words, but I assure you, you will not escape God's judgment![(g)]

"Because of this fact, if you should be in the process of bringing a sacrificial gift before the Lord's altar for the forgiveness of your sins, and at that moment remember that your brother has just cause to be upset with you, leave the gift at the altar. Go, and first make peace with your brother. Only then should you come and present your gift to God! As you can see, making peace with others is a required prerequisite for making peace with God. Trying to make peace with God without first trying to make peace with others is not acceptable to the Lord.[26]

"Let me make a comparison: Would you not agree that it is wise counsel for you to make friends quickly with those to whom you owe a debt, before they force you into a court of law for non-payment? Of course it is! For, if you continue with a hostile attitude toward a creditor and refuse to pay your debt to him, he will turn you over to the judge who will administer justice upon you. Indeed the judge will hand you over to the jailer who will throw you into debtor's prison. There, you will have to stay until the last cent of your debt is paid! Clearly then, it would have been far better for you to peaceably settle the issue out of court by working out a satisfactory plan with your creditor. So, in a like manner, deal properly with your anger toward others before God as the final Judge has to pass eternal condemnation upon you for your evil attitude." [*Harmony* 12:66] [(h)] [27]

---

25 Matthew 5:22

26 Matthew 5:23, 24

27 Matthew 5:25, 26

## — The True Meaning of the Seventh Commandment: You Shall Not Commit Adultery < Late Summer, A.D. 29 > {Matthew 5:27-30}

"Now, moving on: You have also heard it said, as the 'letter' of the Seventh Commandment reads, 'You shall not commit adultery.' [Exodus 20:14] Of course, the religious leaders do an acceptable job in punishing those who actually commit the sin of adultery, but they say relatively little about the sin of the heart—the 'spirit' of the Law—that causes one to commit adultery in the first place. That is why *I say to you*, should someone—a man or a woman—look at a person of the opposite sex, and within his or her heart, lusts after that individual, he or she has committed adultery already.[(i) (j) (k) 28]

> "The Gospel deals with the secret sin of the heart, not just with the open sin which the world sees. Yes, the power of the Gospel is all about the transformation of the thinking of a person, not just his or her actions. The teachings of the religious scholars, on the other hand, are shallow, not dealing with the thoughts of the heart as does the true Gospel message. Again, they deal only with the 'letter' of the Law.

"Because this point is so serious, I say that if your right eye should see something—or someone—that causes you to lust in your heart, it would be far better for you to tear out that eye, and throw it away! In that case, it would be more acceptable to lose one part of your body, so to speak, than to have your entire body cast into the fires of hell after the final judgment! In like manner, should you with your right hand touch something which leads you to sin in your heart, I say, slice off that hand, and throw it away! Again, it would be far better to lose that hand, so to speak, than to have it be the cause of your whole body to be burned in hell-fire! [*Harmony* 10:102-104][29]

> "Obviously, I'm not actually suggesting that you mutilate your body by either plucking out your eye, or cutting off your hand! Rather, I'm making an important point. I'm saying that the sin of the heart will be judged by God just as seriously as the sin of an action. It's that important! Indeed, God will judge all the actions *and* the thoughts of mankind, both the deed—the 'letter' of the Law—and the thought—the 'spirit'

---

28 Matthew 5:27, 28

29 Matthew 5:29, 30

of the Law—that might have led to the deed. The power of the Gospel enables you to control your thoughts, not just your actions. That is the true meaning of the Gospel message." [Ecclesiastes 12:13, 14]

**— The Only Justification for Divorce**
**< Late Summer, A.D. 29 (4/7) >**
**{Matthew 5:31, 32}**

"In a similar vein, it has been said, 'Whoever wishes to do so, may send away his wife. However, he should first secure a certificate of divorce.' [Deuteronomy 24:1] While this Scriptural law certainly allows for divorce, some people have shamefully abused it! [*Harmony* 12:141; 13:62-71][30]

"Yes, the law of Moses, because of the hardness of your hearts, may have *allowed* divorce [*Harmony* 13:62-71], but it never was meant to *encourage* it! No, the law of Moses never intended that! However, some so-called religious teachers have interpreted this law so liberally that divorce has been turned into a sad joke. Over the years, divorces have taken place for completely frivolous reasons—such as the burning of a supper meal—that this has become a shocking embarrassment to the cause of God. These interpreters of the law have turned marriage into a mere legal union that can be broken on a whim, not considering the fact that marriage was intended to be a moral, sacred union, sanctioned and recognized by God. Divorce was never the will of God. To ignore this fact is completely wrong![(l)]

"The Gospel that I preach is more virtuous than that! That is why *I say to you*, that anyone who divorces his wife, except in the clear case of marital infidelity, will cause that woman to commit adultery herself when she remarries. And the man marrying such a woman also commits adultery. [*Harmony* 12:141; 13:62-71][(m) 31]

"This is true because the first marriage was not acceptably terminated. Indeed, I declare that divorce is no longer to be considered a possibility, as it was in the old days, for those who simply desire it! And should someone get a divorce for a reason other than infidelity, he or she cannot marry again. Yes, the Gospel message of today seeks to raise all of God's children to a much higher standard. This includes the recognition of

---

30 Matthew 5:31

31 Matthew 5:32

the fact that marriage is divinely instituted and must be treated with an awesome respect and dignity."

**— How to Make Vows**
**< Late Summer, A.D. 29 (4/7) >**
**{Matthew 5:33-37}**

"Next, it has been said by our forefathers, 'You are not to make false vows, but to fulfill your promises which you make to the Lord.' [Leviticus 19:12; Numbers 30:2, Deuteronomy 23:22](n) [32]

"Now, if that was really what people were expected to do and did, that would be fine. To be sure, I have no problem with people making vows as such. The problem, however, is how the vow is ultimately kept . . . or broken, as is so often the case. For, unfortunately, some religious teachers have turned vow-making into a farce. Depending upon what thing a person vows—such as, God, heaven, the earth, Jerusalem, or whatever—ultimately determines whether a vow needs to be kept or not. The scholars say, if a person swears on God or His Name, that vow must be obeyed. However, if a person vows merely on something that belongs to God—such as heaven, the earth, or Jerusalem—that vow may be broken. This is a ridiculous system of degrees of responsibility in vow-keeping.[1]

"The Gospel, once more, has called us to a much higher standard. To be sure, God will hold you to your vows, no matter upon what they are sworn—either Himself, His Name, or anything He has made. God expects honesty in all our commitments! He will hold us to our promises. So, do not think that by vowing on something you perceive to be less than God or His Name, that you will be excused from keeping your vow. I tell you, you won't! Remember, God owns everything and is involved in everything. You cannot escape God's presence.[2]

"Accordingly, *I say:* Don't swear to anything by invoking the name of heaven. And why? Because God will hold you responsible for that vow, for heaven is where He sits on His throne. Don't swear to anything by invoking the earth. And why? Because God will hold you to such a vow, for the earth is His footstool, so to speak. Don't swear to anything by Jerusalem. And why not Jerusalem? Because,

---

32 Matthew 5:33

once more God, our King, will hold you to your promise, for Jerusalem is His own city. It is clear then: No matter whatever you swear upon, you cannot escape God—He is everywhere! [*Harmony* 10:4-7; 14:121-124][(o)] [33]

"But you might say, 'In that case, then, I will swear on my own head and bypass God altogether.' By doing so, you may think that you will escape God's watchful eye. Not so! Remember that your head belongs to God, the One who created you in the first place. It is God—not you—who decrees whether your hair is black or white. That's right, isn't it?[(p)] [34]

"So then, what should you do? Don't make vows! Just say, 'Yes, yes, I will do such a thing,' or, 'No, no, I won't do such a thing.' In short, be honest in everything you say. Do not look for a way out, based upon whatever object you swore upon, to give you an excuse for not fulfilling your promises. Any other man-made approach that provides you an escape from keeping your vows will quickly lead to evil results. Now, you may find a way out of your commitment as far as humans are concerned . . . but not with God. He will hold you personally responsible for all your promises! You can count on that!"[35]

### — The True Meaning of the Laws of Justice: "An Eye for an Eye . . ."<br>< Late Summer, A.D. 29 (4/7) ><br>{Matthew 5:38-42; Luke 6:29, 30}

"Also, you have heard the ancient law which says, 'An eye for an eye, and a tooth for a tooth.' [Exodus 21:24; Leviticus 24:20; Deuteronomy 19:21][36]

> "Now, this law was given to secure justice in a court of law for those who have been wronged. But of course, such a principle must be administered by an impartial court with wise checks and balances set up to secure true and fair justice. These words were not given to be used by a person obsessed with revenge! No, they were not given to be an excuse to exhibit hatred and abuse toward people, just because you feel that you have been wronged by someone. Again, such a statement is not to be used to wreak personal revenge upon one another! The religious scholars, in their effort to get back at those they dislike, have ignored the tenderness and fairness, which we, under the Gospel—and the

33 Matthew 5:34, 35

34 Matthew 5:36

35 Matthew 5:37

36 Matthew 5:38

> Law—need to show toward one another. Such tenderness and fairness is the true 'spirit' of the Law. Instead these people have emphasized only the harsher aspects of the mere legal requirements of justice—that is, the 'letter' of the Law.

"*I say to you*, instead, do not wreak revenge on a person who has done you some wrong. Revenge will have a terrible impact on your soul. Yes, revenge and bitterness will do more damage to you than anything which someone has done wrong to you! So then, *I say* don't, with malice, resist those who have wronged you. For example, should someone slap you on your cheek, it would do a lot less damage to you if you would turn your other cheek and allow that individual to slap that one too! Indeed, reddened, painful cheeks are less harmful than bitterness exploding within your soul! But don't stop there. If someone sues you in court, taking your shirt, give him your coat also. Giving up your coat will do less damage to you than a heart filled with hatred and revenge. And even if a soldier, under the terms of the Roman law, requires you to carry his belongings a mile, *I say*, carry them an extra mile! The aching muscles and sore feet would do less damage to you than harboring hatred toward that soldier. Furthermore, it would be better to give money to someone who has asked to borrow it from you, rather than coldly and without compassion rejecting him. And, while you're at it, don't even ask for anything back! If someone steals from you, you'd be better off not demanding it back in a court of law. Seething with anger will, in the end, destroy your soul. A spirit of generosity will heal a soul . . . just as revenge, most assuredly, will destroy it![(q)] [37]

> "In summary, I'm not saying that seeking justice in a court of law is wrong. But what I am saying is that to be filled with hatred, anger, and bitterness is far worse for your soul than any injustice that has been done to you."

### — The True Meaning of Love: To Love Your Enemies
### ‹ Late Summer, A.D. 29 (4/7) ›
### {Matthew 5:43-47; Luke 6:27, 28, 32-35}

"You have also heard it said, 'You should love your neighbor.' [Leviticus 19:18] But unfortunately, to this simple, straightforward command, some so-called teachers of the law have added the words, 'Hate your enemy.' However, *I say to those of you* who are willing to listen: Love your enemies. Even be good

[37] Matthew 5:39-42; Luke 6:29, 30

to those who hate you! To be sure, it would be wise to place a blessing upon those who curse you. *I say*, even pray for those who may abuse and persecute you! All this is the will of your Father in heaven. And, by doing so, you will prove yourselves to be truly His sons and daughters. Remember, the Father directs the sun to shine on both good and evil people. He gives rain to fall upon both the righteous and the unrighteous. Isn't that right? As His children, you should have the same spirit. You need to treat others the way God treats all His children. This is what the power of the Gospel is able to do for you. This is the true 'spirit' of the Law.[(r) 38]

"In the same vein, if you have a mind to love only those who treat you with love, is there anything special to be gained by that? Even well-known sinners, such as some tax-collectors, do that! [*Harmony* 4:49/2; 13:109/] If you say, 'Hello!' only to your close friends, is there anything unique in having such a mindset? Even the people of the world, who have no true concept of the Gospel, do that. If you show love only toward those who have already shown love to you, there is no credit to be gained by such a thing! Once again, any ordinary sinner does that. If your deeds of kindness are bestowed only upon those who have done, or will do, good to you, what benefit is there to be gained by that? Why would anyone thank you for that? That is the normal practice of sinners! And if your willingness to lend money is limited only to those who you know will pay you back, what virtue is there in such an attitude? Again, why would anyone thank you for that? Instead, that's what you would expect of sinners! Isn't that right? Anyway, all they really want is the interest earned on top of the principal, or the assurance that the borrower might, in the future, lend something to them. As far as you are concerned, you are to lend to others because you have compassion on them, not just to get more interest money in return. Yes, the Gospel calls us to a much higher standard. Once again, that's the 'spirit' of the Law![39]

"Once more, *I say*, love your enemies, and be good to them. Give of yourselves and of the things which you possess to those who need your help. And, expect nothing back from them in return. In that case, you will receive a great reward from God. The Most High will consider you to be His son or daughter. [*Harmony* 12:97, 98] And why is this so important? It's simple! Because He is, Himself, kind to ungrateful and evil people! And, as His children, you need to do the same things as your Father would do.[(s) 40]

---

38 Matthew 5:43-45; Luke 6:27, 28

39 Matthew 5:46, 47; Luke 6:32-34

40 Luke 6:35

"To conclude: The 'letter' of the Law says, 'Don't kill someone'; the 'spirit' of the Gospel that I preach, says, 'Don't even get angry at people.' The 'letter' says, 'Don't commit adultery'; the 'spirit' says, 'Don't even lust.' The 'letter' of the Law says, 'You can get a divorce, if you wish'; the 'spirit' of the same Law says, 'Do everything you can to keep your marriage intact.' The 'letter' of the Law, as explained by some men, says, 'You can look for a way out of fulfilling your vows to God,' however, the 'spirit' of Scriptural Law says, 'Faithfully pay all your vows to God.' The 'letter' of the Law says, 'An eye for an eye'; but the 'spirit' of the Law says, 'It is better to suffer an injustice than to burn with anger and resentment.' And finally, the 'letter' of a man-made law says, 'Hate your enemies'; but the true 'spirit' of God's Law says, 'Love not only your friends but also your enemies.' Indeed, the doctrinal teachings of the scribes and Pharisees—emphasizing only the 'letter' of the Law—have no real power to give you peace and victory over sin. But the true 'spirit' of the Law that I teach—the real Gospel message—changes not only your actions, but, more importantly, your heart. It dramatically and miraculously changes your relationship with your God, as well as your relationship with people. In the end, you will be empowered to treat others the same way that God treats them."[1]

**— In Summary: The True Meaning of Mercy and Perfection**
**< Late Summer, A.D. 29 (4/7) >**
**{Matthew 5:48; Luke 6:36}**

"As you can readily see, to live by the 'spirit' of the Law, as opposed to its 'letter,' requires a totally passionate relationship of love with your God [*Harmony* 14:100-106]—the kind of relationship of which the Pharisees have little or no knowledge. You can certainly see, then, that without such a relationship with God—that is, loving Him with your total being—you will never be able to live by the true 'spirit' of the Law. Indeed, you and your God must be bound together as one so that what His love and mercy is, can also become yours. His character will become yours as you spend more and more time with Him. [*Harmony* 16:71-74] Then, as He loves others, you can love them too. As He is merciful to people, you can also be merciful. [2 Peter 1:2-4] Yes, that must constantly be your objective.[2]

“In summary, then, show mercy to others to the same extent that God shows mercy to them! So *therefore,* in conclusion, your ultimate goal is to be as perfect in your lifestyle and loving attitude toward others, as your heavenly Father is perfect in those very same things. [*Harmony* 5:75/1, 2][(t)] [41]

> “Now, you may not totally reach that standard. Yet such perfection *is* constantly to remain your goal. And, once again, any truly serious attempt to reach out for this objective requires that you have a powerful relationship of love with your God. That’s the key!”[1]

### — The Gospel Will Also Change the Way You Worship God

> “And, as I have already indicated, the power of the Gospel in your life will affect every aspect of your living. This includes not only the way you treat God and people—as I have just described to you—but also the way you worship God, especially in public. Additionally, it affects your motivation in all that you do in your service to the Lord as well as in your ministry to others. Now, I will now give some specific examples of this.”[2]

### — The Proper Motive for Good Deeds
### < Late Summer, A.D. 29 (4/7) >
### Matthew 6:1-4}

“To begin, be careful that when you do good deeds for others, that you don’t do them just to show off in front of people. If that’s what you do, your only reward will be praise from men . . . but I must tell you, there will be none from God who is in heaven. So then, when you give money to the poor, do not blow, as it were, your own horn, so that everyone looks at you when you do your good deed. That’s what the hypocrite actors do. Whether it’s in the synagogue, or in the streets, all that the hypocrite actors really care about is the lofty praise of men! Again, as I have emphatically declared before [*Harmony* 5:15], that’s the only payment they will ever get: the praise of men![(u)] [42]

“*But you,* who desire to follow the Gospel, when you perform your deeds of mercy for others, do it in such an unassuming way that it would be as though your left hand does not know what your right hand is doing! The good news is that your Father will see what you, without any public fanfare, are doing in

---

41 Matthew 5:48; Luke 6:36

42 Matthew 6:1, 2

private, and He will, in His good time, reward you openly." [*Harmony* 15:51-58] (v) 43

## — The Proper Way to Pray
## < Late Summer, A.D. 29 (4/7) >
## {Matthew 6:5-13}

"And, when you pray, please don't be like those hypocrite actors again! They just love to stand in the middle of the synagogues, and on the busy street corners and public squares, so that people will see them and be so impressed with their long, tedious prayers! Well, once again, I can assure you, this will be their only reward! [*Harmony* 14:119][(w) (x) 44]

"*But each of you* who wish to live by the Gospel, when you pray, be humble! Go into your own house, shut the door behind you, and pray there in secret—in your closet, so to speak—with no other person watching you. Once again, the Father will hear your secret prayers, and reward you openly as He sees fit.[(y) 45]

"And, as far as your actual prayers are concerned, don't use repetitive, empty-sounding words and phrases, as do the uninformed sinners of the world who don't know any better! They think that by their using the same words over and over again, God will listen to them. But they are wrong! Remember, God already knows what you need. So, instead, use simple, humble words before Him. Here is a good sample prayer to use when praying to your Father. This is how I want you to pray: [*Harmony* 12:3-15][(z) 46]

"'Our Father who dwells in Heaven, Holy is Your Name![47]

"'May Your final, glorious Kingdom be established, and may Your will be accepted on earth to the same extent that it is totally honored in heaven.[48]

"'Provide for us, on a daily basis, our necessary physical and spiritual sustenance.[49]

---

43 Matthew 6:3, 4
44 Matthew 6:5
45 Matthew 6:6
46 Matthew 6:7-9
47 Matthew 6:9
48 Matthew 6:10
49 Matthew 6:11

"'Forgive us our debt of sin, to the same extent that we have forgiven those who have sinned against us.[50]

"'Help us to stand firm for righteousness, even when we are tempted to sin. Indeed, give us victory over all our temptations. Do not allow us to give in to our evil tendencies.[51]

"'For to You belongs that glorious kingdom of heaven and its victorious power which is the bright, shining hope of eternity, forever! Amen.' Make your prayers that simple . . . and yet, profound."[52]

**— The Requirement for Divine Forgiveness**
**< Late Summer, A.D. 29 (4/7) >**
**{Matthew 6:14, 15}**

"While I'm speaking of forgiveness—as I mentioned in the prayer [*Harmony* 5:50]—remember, if you are willing to forgive others who have wronged you, your Father will also be willing to forgive you for the things that you have done wrong against Him. But the opposite is also true: If you are not willing to forgive others for the offenses which they have committed against you, neither will the Father be willing to forgive your offenses against Him! It's just that simple!" [*Harmony* 10:112-118; 12:8/, 153][53]

**— The Proper Way to Fast**
**< Late Summer, A.D. 29 (4/7) >**
**{Matthew 6:16-18}**

"Let Me address another subject regarding worship: If you are fasting, don't look and act so gloomy and grumpy! Of course, that's what the hypocrite actors do! They go out of their way to look miserable. Indeed, they put on a distorted face so that people will feel sorry for them as they go through their great personal sacrifice of depriving themselves of food! Believe me, as always, that's the only reward they'll ever get. [Harmony 8:5][(aa)] [54]

"*But you,* instead, when fasting, pour joy like celebratory oil all over your heads. Wash your faces, and look happy! This way, it will not appear as though

---

50 Matthew 6:12
51 Matthew 6:13
52 Matthew 6:13
53 Matthew 6:14, 15
54 Matthew 6:16

you are hungry. Thus only God will know you are fasting. That's the way it should be. And, as always, God will reward you openly for what is done in secret within your heart! [*Harmony* 13:59][(bb) (cc) 55]

"In summary: The Gospel I preach is one that provides the proper motive for what you do for the cause of God. This means that when you give your gifts to God, you do so because you love Him, rather than wanting praise from men. When you pray to your Father, you do so to be heard by Him—not to be heard and praised by people. And too, you should be willing to forgive others, to the same extent that God is willing to forgive you. This means that if you want God to forgive you, you must be willing to graciously forgive others. And finally, when you fast, do so privately before God. Don't do it to be seen and praised of men. Of course, the scribes and Pharisees do all these things to be praised by people. Rather, *you* must do them to be accepted by God!"[1]

**— How To Accomplish the Gospel Experience**

"Obviously, to truly experience all the things that I've been talking about—to live by the 'spirit' and not just the 'letter' of the Law, and to have a proper motivation for all we do for the Lord and others—will require a deep, powerful commitment of the heart. You can surely understand that! Yes, you must be completely and totally focused on the transforming power of the Gospel within your life if God is to empower you as He wishes. Without any doubt, it must be the primary emphasis of your life if you are to attain to this standard! And, of course, you must have a strong relationship with your God to accomplish all this."[2]

**— The Proper Attitude Toward Possessions**
**< Late Summer, A.D. 29 (4/7) >**
**{Matthew 6:19-21}**

"It is clear, then, that to reach this objective, you can no longer be in the habit of merely storing up treasures and possessions here on earth as so many others have done. Besides, here on earth, our fragile treasures are subject to being eaten by moths. Even the more durable earthly treasures will often decay or rust. Then, too, thieves can break through the walls of your home and steal those treasurers that were not initially destroyed by either moth or rust! [*Harmony* 12:47, 54][56]

---

[55] Matthew 6:17, 18
[56] Matthew 6:19

"But rather, I say, place your treasure of time, energy, and money in heaven—that is, in the things that are a part of God's heavenly kingdom—the kind of things I've been describing to you. There is no way that a moth, rust, or thieves can do damage to your treasure there! And don't forget: Where your treasure is placed, there the passion of your heart will be also. This means that if your focus is on the things of this earth, then your heart will be earthly. But, if your treasure is in heavenly things, the desires of your heart will, likewise, be heavenly."[57]

**— Your Attitude Toward Heavenly and Earthly Things Is the Key**
**< Late Summer, A.D. 29 (4/7) >**
**{Matthew 6:22, 23; Luke 6:39}**

"Let Me state this concept in another way: The avenue of light to your mind and body is through your eyes. Isn't that right? So it is with the soul. If your 'spiritual eyes'—or passions—are focused on the brightness of heavenly things, then your life will be filled with that brightness. If, on the contrary, your 'spiritual eyes' are focused on the darkness of the things of this world, then, you will be filled totally with that darkness. If what is the 'darkness' of this world should function as 'light' within you, then just imagine how dreary will be that darkness! In short, then, what controls your 'spiritual eyes' will ultimately control your entire life! [*Harmony* 12:18; 14:145][58]

"Just imagine what happens to those who are focused only on the things of this world. Which one of them will be able to lead others to find the truth of the Gospel? To illustrate—by means of a parable—it's like one who is blind trying to lead another one who is equally blind. It's quite impossible, isn't it? And then what will happen? Because neither one knows which way to go, they will both stumble and fall into a ditch! [*Harmony* 10:10][59]

> "Stay focused, then, on the things of heaven and its light, so that you can lead those who are still living in darkness to find that light. That is the goal of the Gospel."

---

57 Matthew 6:20, 21
58 Matthew 6:22, 23
59 Luke 6:39

## — You Must Be Totally Committed to Securing the Gospel Experience < Late Summer, A.D. 29 (4/7) > {Matthew 6:24}

"It's so obvious, isn't it? In the long run, it is impossible to commit yourself to serving two different lords: the 'lord' of this world, or the Lord of Heaven. Each has opposing goals which seek to control your life. In the end, you will either love one and hate the other, or you will cling to one and reject the other. What this means is that you will not be able to serve passionately, at the same instant, both God and the wealth of this world. One of the two will win, while the other must lose. [*Harmony* 12:136][60]

> "To state it succinctly: If you would desire to reach the standard I've placed before you today, you must be focused squarely on the giving of your entire self in a relationship with God in order to attain it!"[1]

## — If You Are Focused on Obtaining the Gospel, You Must Not Worry About Obtaining the Necessities of Life < Late Summer, A.D. 29 > {Matthew 6:25-34}

> "However, the sinners of this world, who don't care at all about the things of eternity, spend much of their time seeking to acquire the things of this life. That is *their* passion. And, while the scribes and the Pharisees claim to care so much about spiritual things, they also spend much of their time and energy acquiring the things and praises of this world. That, without question, constitutes their passion. But you, who truly seek to find the things of eternity and the kingdom of heaven, do not need to be overly concerned about acquiring even the necessities of this life when you are focused on the things of heaven. God will provide for you![2]

"Indeed, I say, don't worry! When you experience the Gospel of which I preach, I can assure you that you do not need to be anxious about what will happen in your life, as to what you will eat or drink. Neither will you need to be worried about what will happen to your body, including what you are to wear. [*Harmony* 12:47][61]

60 Matthew 6:24

61 Matthew 6:25

"Even though food and clothing are important, your life and body are much more important. God knows that, isn't that right? Let Me explain what I mean.[62]

"First, consider for a moment the birds that fly in the heavens. They neither plant seed, nor reap crops to be put into barns. Yet, your Father in heaven provides food for them to eat! Aren't your life and body worth much more than these birds? So then, if God provides for the life-sustaining needs of birds, He certainly will provide for you! Do you see that? Yes, it's that simple! So again I say, stop your worrying! [*Harmony* 12:48][63]

"Second, consider your body: Tell Me! Is all your worrying about your body able to add a foot to your height, or a year to your life? Of course not! [*Harmony* 12:49][(dd) 64]

> "Your worrying doesn't significantly change anything. Instead, it is God who makes your bodies grow, and it is He who gives us the length of our days. Thus, He is the One who will provide the sustenance for our lives! In short, He will take care of you.

"Third, why do you worry about what you are going to wear? Again, God will provide! To give an example: Take a look at the flowering lilies which grow in the field. [*Harmony* 12:50, 51] They do not work nor make their own clothing. Yet I tell you, not even Solomon, decked out in all his splendor [1 Kings 10:1-13, 21] was able to dress himself with such beauty! Therefore, if God so dramatically dresses the grasses in the fields with the beauty of the lilies that grow among them—the grasses that are living one day, and burned as fuel in a fiery furnace the next—will not God much more provide clothing and the other necessities of life for you? Certainly, you are so much more valuable than the plants of the fields! Tell Me: Why are you, then, such 'little-faith' people? [*Harmony* 7:61-66; 9:21; 12:50, 51; 12:36][(ee) 65]

"So don't be wringing your hands and saying, 'What will we eat?' or, 'What will we drink?' or, 'What will we wear?' That's exactly what you would expect the people of the world to do as they anxiously seek after the comforts and necessities of this life. These are the ones who do not understand the message of

62 Matthew 6:25
63 Matthew 6:26
64 Matthew 6:27
65 Matthew 6:28-30

the Gospel. Have some faith! God knows that you—who are seeking the power of the Gospel in your life—need all these things! [*Harmony* 12:52, 53][66]

> "But please don't misunderstand Me. I not suggesting that you shouldn't work hard to provide for yourself. You should not just sit around, waiting for God to provide for you. No! No! Rather, I'm saying that you should not be *obsessed*, as so many in the world are, with providing for themselves. There must be a balance between hard work and faith in God. Certainly you can understand that, can't you?

"Thus, your emphasis should be to first seek eagerly to be a part of the Gospel's kingdom and all its righteousness. Then all these other things that you need will be provided for you. So, don't be so distressed about what will happen tomorrow, for tomorrow will have its own worries. Yes, it's enough to live one day at a time and deal with the troubles of each day when they actually arrive. If you truly experience the Gospel, together with the Lord, you will be able to survive nicely as He helps you to live each day."[67]

### — When You Are Focused on Growing in the Gospel, You Will Not Have Time to Judge Others
### < Late Summer, A.D. 29 (4/7) >
### {Matthew 7:1-6; Luke 6:37, 38, 41, 42}

> "As I have just indicated, growing in the Gospel will consume much of your time. Therefore, you will not have enough time left to spend in judging others. Look out for yourself, and allow God to take care of others.

"Thus, in your relations with people, don't judge others . . . and especially don't condemn them. [1 Samuel 16:7][68]

> "You can't read what's in their hearts—only God can. It is fine to evaluate, based upon the Scripture, the rightness or wrongness of peoples' actions. At times, you will actually need to do this. But in no case are you to judge or condemn the motives of others, which you cannot read. Furthermore, you are not to determine, by your judgment, who is to be saved or lost—again, only God can do that.

66 Matthew 6:31, 32
67 Matthew 6:33, 34
68 Matthew 7:1

"However, if you insist on condemning others, I must warn you that you will, yourself, be condemned. In fact, you will be judged by the same standard by which you have judged others. So indeed, beware! In fact, the extent of your condemnation of others will be matched by God, the righteous Judge, in His condemnation of you! [*Harmony* 10:98, 99][69]

"On the other hand, if you do not, with a critical attitude, judge others, you too, will not be judged. If you don't condemn, you won't be condemned. Forgive someone, and you will be forgiven. Give of your compassion to others, and compassion will be given back to you—from both human and divine sources. In fact, in such a case, the level of compassion that others, including God, will show you shall be awesome. To illustrate, it is like a bowl of flour that has been compressed and shaken, and is even spilling over into your lap! Again, when you show compassion to others, a similar amount of compassion will be literally heaped back upon you. Yes, the way you treat others will, by that same measure, determine how they treat you.[70]

"But to those who are judgmental, I say: Why is it that you search for a tiny sin, like a speck of sawdust in your brother's eye, but are quite unaware of the big sin, like a log, that is stuck your own eye? And furthermore, on what logical basis can you say to that same brother, 'My brother, please allow me to remove that speck of sawdust from your eye,' while, at the same time, that huge log remains embedded in your own eye? What a hypocrite actor you are! Common logic dictates that you should first dislodge the log from you own eye before you can see clearly enough to remove that speck of sawdust from your brother's eye! Isn't that right?[(ff)] [71]

> "But don't misunderstand Me. There will be times in your life when you will meet people who are so completely hardened in sin that they have absolutely no desire to change their sinful lives. They may even challenge your own worthiness to receive the glories of the Gospel into your lives. Be assured, then, that the Gospel does not obligate you to give in to them and to tolerate endlessly their negative lifestyle and attitude. Even though you may care about them, you are not required to devote all your time to them. No, indeed! And why? For many of them, so to speak, are like wild animals that would rip you apart if they could.[(gg)]

---

69 Matthew 7:1, 2

70 Luke 6:37, 38

71 Matthew 7:3-5; Luke 6:41, 42

"No! You are not to give the sacred truths of the Gospel to people who are like 'scavenger dogs,' who would never truly appreciate what you have to offer them. Neither are you to throw the pearls of the Gospel message before those who act like pigs, greedily gulping down the slop of falsehood and hypocrisy! In that case, they will trample the pearls of truth under their feet, while ripping you to shreds. Don't worry about them! But don't condemn them either, for, I promise you, God will take care of them in due course!"(hh) [72]

**— How to Live the Victorious Life**
**‹ Late Summer, A.D. 29 (4/7) ›**
**{Matthew 7:7-11}**

> "Your emphasis, again, must be on determining to stay close to God. In that case, you will be successful in the process of constantly growing within the Gospel message. You will, that is, if you have great faith and confidence in your God. The Gospel experience teaches you that you can trust Him! But you must maintain, by faith, a close abiding relationship with your Father. So, accordingly, you are to ask God for help regularly, and He will give to you what you need.

"You can safely and persistently seek Him, for He will help you find what you are looking for. And, if you keep on knocking, as it were, for His assistance, He will surely open His door of blessing to you. Indeed, everyone who keeps on asking will receive. Each one who keeps on seeking will find what he or she is looking for. And every person who keeps on knocking will see a door opened for him or her. [*Harmony* 12:13][73]

"Look at it this way: Name a single loving human father who would give his own son a stone if he had asked him for a loaf of bread to fill his hungry stomach. Or, should this same son ask his father for a fish to eat, would his father give him a snake instead? Of course not! If then, you—who are subject to the human frailties of sin—know how to give what is truly good to your children when they ask you, just think how much more your perfect heavenly Father will do for those of you who ask Him for the good things of the Gospel! That makes sense, doesn't it?" [*Harmony* 12:14][74]

---

72 Matthew 7:6
73 Matthew 7:7, 8
74 Matthew 7:9-11

### — The Gospel Experience Will Affect the Way You Relate to People
### < Late Summer, A.D. 29 (4/7) >
### {Matthew 7:12; Luke 6:31}

"When you go about acquiring the Gospel experience by the method I've just described to you—by 'asking,' 'seeking,' and 'knocking' [*Harmony* 5:73; 12:13]—you will certainly 'receive' its blessings, and 'find' its power, and the 'door' of salvation will be opened unto you. And when all this happens, it will change your entire life forever. Your relationship with God will grow dramatically. In a similar way, your relationship with people will expand greatly. In fact, there will be a new Gospel principle which will serve as the foundation of your basic relationship with people. And it is this:[(ii)]

"In all your dealings with others, *therefore,* you are to treat people the exact same way that you would wish them to treat you. This concept is firmly based on the principles of the writings of the Law and the Prophets [*Harmony* 14:103]—the Scriptures—and is also the foundation of the Gospel which I teach you today.[(jj)] [75]

"This is the 'Golden Rule,' so to speak, which forms the foundation of our entire relationship with one another. It serves as a test that will measure the depth of your relationship with your God. To be sure, the way you treat people serves as a clear indication of how intimately you know the Lord. [*Harmony* 5:41; 1 John 4:7, 8][(kk)] [1]

"In conclusion, then, there remain two principles upon which My Gospel message is based. First: The standard by which you are to live, as I have said previously, is to be perfect in your lifestyle as God is perfect in His—that is, to live by the 'spirit' of the Law rather than its 'letter.' [*Harmony* 5:41] And, second: The true test of how well you are doing in that regard is whether you are able to treat others as you would have them treat you. The first deals, primarily, with the quality of our love toward, and relationship with, God the Father. And the second deals mainly with the depth of our love toward others. [*Harmony* 5:75] Again, the whole Gospel is based upon these two principles." [*Harmony* 14:102, 103][(ll)] [2]

---

75 Matthew 7:12; Luke 6:31

### — It's Decision Time!
### < Late Summer, A.D. 29 (4/7) >
### {Matthew 7:13, 14}

> "So, now is the time to decide which lifestyle you want. You can either follow the Gospel and its message which I've been describing to you, or follow the phony things that the scribes and Pharisees have been teaching you. Once more, they base *their* Gospel, so to speak, upon obeying only the 'letter' of the Law. They also treat others based solely upon how they *feel* toward one another at any given time—whether it be good or evil. Yes, you must choose what kind of Gospel you want to follow![3]

"But I must caution you: The way of Gospel truth that I've been telling you about is unpopular, because it requires much self-sacrifice. You can enter into it, as it was, only through a narrow gate. On the other hand, the way of falsehood is very popular and enticing, for it appeals to the comfortable weaknesses of human nature. Indeed, its gate is very wide, and the road is very broad . . . but it leads to certain destruction! Unfortunately, there are multitudes who are walking that way! Again, how small is the gate, and how narrow the road that leads to eternal life, and how incredibly few there are who are willing to walk that way! But, you can—if you choose to follow the Gospel way!" [*Harmony* 12:79][76]

### — A Warning!
### < Late Summer, A.D. 29 (4/7) >
### {Matthew 7:15}

> "I need to further warn you: There are people out there who will try to discourage you from making the message of the Gospel I've been teaching a part of your life. They will tell you that their concept of truth is the only one to follow, and that what I've been teaching is wrong! And some of these people will come to you with the stamp of approval of the scribes—in fact, some of them will actually be the scribes! They will give the appearance as of speaking for God, as though they were prophets!

---

[76] Matthew 7:13, 14

"So then, beware of false prophets and teachers. They will come to you dressed in humility like sheep, but they will, underneath that façade, be like plundering wolves bent on destroying you."[77]

**— You Can Distinguish Between the False and True Teachers of the Gospel**
**< Late Summer, A.D. 29 (4/7) >**
**{Matthew 7:16-23; Luke 6:40, 43-46}**

"The good news is you will be able to pick them out by the fruit they bear as the result of their character. As you know, grapes are not picked from thorny blackberry or bramble bushes, and neither do figs grow on thistles. Every good, healthy tree bears good fruit, while dying trees produce that which is of poor quality. The converse is also true: A good tree simply does not bear bad fruit, nor is there any way that a bad tree produces good fruit. So what does a farmer do to a supposed fruit-bearing tree that doesn't produce good fruit? He cuts down that tree and throws it into the fire. In conclusion, then, just as you know the quality of a tree by the quality of the fruit it bears, so you will also know the quality of the teachers you might listen to by the quality of fruit they produce! [*Harmony* 7:11][78]

"Indeed, a good teacher, from the high quality of his Gospel-converted heart, brings forth teachings which match that conversion. But a teacher who has rejected the message of this Gospel I've been teaching you today, will spew forth a doctrine that matches the lowness of his unconverted heart. In short, a teacher has no choice but to speak of that which has filled his heart, whether it is good . . . or evil![79]

"However, there are some—both teachers and followers—who will try to cover up their base weaknesses with flowery words and empty professions of faith. In the final analysis, this means that not every person who has been simply in the habit of saying to Me, 'Lord! Lord!' will be able to enter My eternal kingdom of glory. No, indeed! The only ones who will be able to enter are those who have faithfully followed and practiced the precise will of the heavenly Father. Nevertheless, in the day of the final judgment, many will claim to have a righteous heart by declaring, 'Lord! Lord! Didn't we prophesy, using Your Name?

---

77 Matthew 7:15
78 Matthew 7:16-20; Luke 6:43, 44
79 Luke 6:45

And, in Your Name, didn't we command devils to leave people? Didn't we even work many great miracles by using Your Name? Surely this proves our worthiness to receive eternal life!'[80]

"But, I will tell them emphatically, 'I have never really recognized you as My genuine followers! Go away from Me, you workers of unrighteousness! Tell me, why it is that you have called Me, "Lord! Lord!" but haven't done what I, your Lord, commanded of you? You have not borne the *fruit* of the Gospel that you claim to possess. You have spoken with lying words.' [*Harmony* 12:80, 147][81]

"So it will be for all those who do not follow the Gospel message I teach you today! Please listen to Me, students of Mine: You are not more perfect than your Teacher. It is obvious that good students, after being well trained—as I am teaching you today—will be just like their Teacher, striving to follow Him consistently. Isn't that right?"[82]

### — Conclusion and Appeal: The Parable of the Wise Man and the Foolish Man
### < Late Summer, A.D. 29 (4/7) >
### {Matthew 7:24-27; Luke 6:47-49}

"In conclusion, let Me tell you what you will be like if you ultimately decide to come to Me and obey My words. You will be compared to a man of wise discernment and foresight who has built his house upon solid rock. Yes, he dug the foundation deep to bedrock. And when a storm comes, when the flooding waters begin to rise, smashing against the house, and when the howling winds blow upon the house . . . that house will not come crumbling down. And why? Because it was built upon the rock! Indeed, as in My illustration, your life will be able to withstand the struggles and difficulties of this world, for the foundation of your character is solid.[(mm)] [83]

"On the other hand, those who have an opportunity to listen to My words but refuse to obey them, will be compared to a man who has built his house upon the shifting sands of this world. The rains will come, the floods will rise, smashing into the house, and the winds will blow . . . and that house will surely come crashing down upon him! And how devastating will be its fall! Indeed,

80 Matthew 7:21, 22
81 Matthew 7:23; Luke 6:46
82 Luke 6:40
83 Matthew 7:24, 25; Luke 6:47, 48

as in this illustration, such a life cannot in any way withstand the struggles and difficulties of this world that test the soul."[84]

### —Jesus Concludes His Sermon
### < Late Summer, A.D. 29 (4/7) >
### {Matthew 7:28-8:1}

And thus, Jesus finished His "Sermon on the Mount." The crowd was truly amazed at the tremendous words that the Lord had spoken to them that day. And as He taught them, the obvious truthfulness, authority, and power of the His Words impressed them mightily—nothing like the dogmatic, impractical, and legalistic teachings of their own scribes and Pharisees to whom they were used to listening.[85]

It is not surprising, then, that when Jesus came down from the mountain, great crowds continued to follow Him.[86]

### Supplementary Notes:

**(a) [5:0+]** The Sermon on the Mount is clearly the crowning achievement of the Lord's recorded public pronouncements. In the written Gospel story, it is by far the best and most complete sermon He preached. It is well organized: that is, it has a beginning (or introduction), followed by a clear progression of ideas leading to the concluding appeal—neatly tied together—and all heavily illustrated. But while it is the most complete of all of the Lord's recorded sermons, without a doubt it does not contain all that Jesus said that day. To be sure, it is an *abridged* version of the sermon.

I think, though, that through the addition of *a number of transitions and connecting thoughts*, tying together the items written for us, we have a sermon that is clearly put together in such a way that each idea logically leads to the idea that follows. Conversely, each idea is based upon the idea that precedes it. Thus, from beginning to end, the sermon is a virtually perfect presentation of ideas and concepts. (However, there are two concepts in the Sermon, which, on the surface, do not appear to fit with either the concept preceding them, or the one following them. These will be noted by Supplementary Notes when they appear in the course of the Sermon. I will explain my rationale for the

---

84 Matthew 7:26, 27; Luke 6:49

85 Matthew 7:28, 29

86 Matthew 8:1

way I interpreted each concept, and the way I tied them together with either the concept that preceded or followed it.) To enhance, then, this *abridged* version, I have taken the liberty of adding the aforementioned connecting thoughts, in order to tie the entire sermon together. But, rather than listing these connecting thoughts as my own explanatory comments on the sermon, I listed them as though Jesus, Himself, presented them. This way, the sermon reads from beginning to end as though it were a *virtual transcript* of what Jesus presented that day. I trust that I have done fair justice to the Lord's amazing sermon!

*One important additional thought:* Throughout my interpretation of the Sermon, I quite often compare the "spirit" of the Law with the "letter" of the Law. Jesus did not use these two words; yet He seems to have, over and over, clearly implied these concepts. That is why I liberally use this comparison in my approach in interpreting the Sermon, considering it essential in understanding the main point the Lord was making.

**(b) [5:11/+]** These woes, found in Luke's record, somewhat parallel the Beatitudes (*Harmony* 5:3-11) Jesus might have spoken them in conjunction with the Beatitudes, but I chose to list them separately, thinking that this was the best way to record them.

**(c) [5:20]** The "jot" and "tittle" of the KJV version of this text refer to a couple of letters in the Greek alphabet. The "jot" (probably the Greek "i") is the smallest letter of the alphabet. The "tittle" (perhaps the crossing of the Greek "t") is just a small mark that distinguishes it from the Greek "i". Accordingly, I interpreted the text to read "the dotting of a single 'i' and the crossing of an individual 't'" of our own alphabet.

**(d) [5:22/2]** In this section of the Lord's sermon which follows, He contrasted what the Jewish leaders said on a particular subject with what He, as the Messiah, would say on the same subject. To emphasize this obvious contrast, I *italicized* the Lord's phrase, *"I say to you"* (or similar words).

**(e) [5:24]** (See above.)

**(f) [5:25]** The full intent of this verse is not clear to me. Is Jesus saying that a person who calls someone else a bad name will be judged in a *human* court of law? In truth, some Jewish laws did, in fact, provide punishment for those who slandered others. Perhaps that is what the Lord is referring to here. Or perhaps, He is suggesting that such people *ought* to be so judged. However, one thing *is* very clear: If someone says something evil about someone else, that person will be judged by God—whether or not they appear in a human court of law. In short, in the final judgment, God will hold such people responsible for their words. The world *may* let such people get away with it, but God won't!

**(g) [5:25/]** (See above.)

**(h) [5:27]** In this text, Jesus apparently uses the debtor's prison of His day as an illustration of the need for people to make peace with God.

**(i) [5:28]** The Seventh Commandment deals with the *act* of adultery. However, the Tenth Commandment deals with the *thought of the heart* that leads to adultery. In this text Jesus deals with the *thought* as being the real *sin* committed by the sinner, and thus, He condemned the thought (indicated by the Tenth Commandment), in contrast with just the deed itself (the Seventh Commandment).

**(j) [5:28]** (See **Note "d"** above.)

**(k) [5:28]** In this text, Jesus refers only to the sin of *men* as it relates to adultery. In the *Harmony*, I included it as referring also to *women.*

**(l) [5:30/]** Of all the subjects Jesus addressed during the course of His ministry, He used no stronger words then when He discussed the subject of divorce and re-marriage. Apparently the Lord was very distressed by the lackadaisical attitude of some of the Jewish leaders regarding the issue of divorce and subsequent re-marriage. So strong were the Master's counsels regarding this concept that He *seemed* to allow for no "wriggle room" on the subject. In fact, for years Bible scholars have vehemently debated the various sides of the issue. In this book, I make no real effort to resolve this debate, because such a debate is well beyond the scope of the *Harmony.* Instead, when I interpreted the words of Jesus on this subject, I couched them in expressions that, it seemed to me, represented fairly the obvious strong feelings that Jesus had on the overall subject. And, while I have a personal opinion on the subject, I will allow the readers of this book—and Bible scholars—to debate the particulars of this issue elsewhere. (See *Harmony* 12:141; 13:62-71, along with **Note "h"** in Chapter 13, for more of what Jesus said on the subject of divorce and re-marriage.)

**(m) [5:31]** (See **Note "d"** above.)

**(n) [5:32]** Here and elsewhere (*Harmony* 14:121-124), Jesus expressed His great displeasure in the system of vow-making that was in practice in His day. While such a procedure does not exist in our world today, the principle still applies. That is, if you make a promise to God, plan on keeping it. God will not allow you to get out of your promises. Also, don't make a promise to God, while at the same time already planning a way for you to get out of fulfilling that promise. In short, basic honesty is at stake. Your words count!

**(o) [5:33]** (See **Note "d"** above.)

**(p) [5:34]** Of course, the Lord's statement here was made before the wide-spread existence of artificial hair-coloring!

**(q) [5:37]** (See **Note "d"** above.)

**(r) [3:38]** (See **Note "d"** above.)

**(s) [5:40]** (See **Note "d"** above.)

**(t) [5:41]** While the Lord used the word "therefore" a number of times throughout His sermon, there are *two times* when, in my opinion, the use of this word especially stands out—here and *Harmony* 5:75. After some research and thought, I have come to the strong conclusion that these two uses serve as very important *summaries* in the Lord's sermon. The one used here, deals with how we, based upon a relationship with God, are to reflect the character of God and the way He deals with the various issues He had just listed. (See also **Note "ii"** below, as well as *Harmony* 5:75/1, 2.)

**(u) [5:42]** The Greek word for hypocrite means "actor." That is, hypocrites are really "actors."

**(v) [5:43]** In this and in the next several points the Lord mentioned in His sermon, He contrasted what the Jewish leaders did with what His disciples should do in similar situations. To make this contrast, the Lord used the phrase, *"but you"* (or similar words). To make this contrast stand out, I *italicized* the words, *"but you"* (or the similar words).

**(w) [5:44]** (See **Note "u"** above.)

**(x) [5:44]** The Pharisees were noted for their long prayers—often given in front of people—just to show off to others.

**(y) [5:45]** (See **Note "v"** above.)

**(z) [5:46]** (See **Note "u"** above.)

**(aa) [5:54]** (See **Note "u"** above.)

**(bb) [5:55]** In Bible times, to anoint one's head with oil were, among other things, a sign of joy and thanksgiving.

**(cc) [5:55]** (See **Note "v"** above.)

**(dd) [5:64]** The word in this text can refer to *either* the length of days (long life), or height (how tall someone is). Not knowing which one Jesus might have been referring to, I included *both* concepts in my interpretation of the *Harmony.*

**(ee) [5:65]** The concept, translated as "O ye of little faith" in the KJV is interesting. In reality, in the original Greek, the Lord uses the words "little faith" much like one would use them as a *nickname* to describe those who exhibit "little faith" in something. Accordingly, I interpreted it that way in the *Harmony.*

**(ff) [5:71]** (See **Note "u"** above.)

**(gg) [5:71/]** Because I believe the "Sermon on the Mount" is a completely unified sermon, I really struggled to understand the placement of this concept (explained here and in *Harmony* 5:72, which follows). The meaning was easy enough, but it did not seem to fit here. On the surface, it did not appear to connect with either the idea that preceded it or the one that followed. So, after some time of thinking, I went with the interpretation that I did, considering it the most likely meaning of the concept, in relationship with its placement within the sermon.

**(hh) [5:72]** (See above.)

**(ii) [5:74/]** This concept (as it relates to *Harmony* 5:75), does not seem to fit here in the sermon. The so-called Golden Rule is, of course, very nice, but it does not appear to follow on the heels of *Harmony* 5:73, 74. This fact is made all the more puzzling by the fact that the Golden Rule concept begins with the word "therefore" in the Gospel record. This word clearly implies that the Golden Rule is a natural progression from what *preceded* it. After some consideration, I finally chose the position I took for the *Harmony,* feeling very comfortable with it. I have come to believe, therefore, that the Golden Rule, as Jesus used it in His sermon, is a *test* of how well we are doing in our relationship with God. That is, if we claim to know and love God but do not treat people as the Lord directs, we have fallen far short of God's will for us. And, because it is a test of our relationship with God, it is of major importance to us! I believe, then, that the Lord, in His sermon, placed a large emphasis upon it.

**(jj) [5:75]** (See above.)

**(kk) [5:75/] ** (See **Note "ii"** above.)

**(ll) [5:75/2]** I am convinced that the emphasis that I placed upon the Golden Rule in the *Harmony* is the correct one that the Lord intended it to have. I trust that I have done true justice to the Lord's words! (See also **Note "ii"** above, as well as *Harmony* 5:41.)

**(mm) [5:83]** In the illustration of the wise man, Jesus compares him to *any* individual who ultimately accepts the Gospel. I felt that, to make it more personal, it would be better to compare the wise man to anyone who was *listening that day to Jesus.* Accordingly, in the *Harmony,* I used the word "you" as opposed to a "man."

# CHAPTER SIX

## THE MID-GALILEAN MINISTRY OF JESUS—

**From the Healing of the Centurion's Servant, to the Resurrection of the Widow of Nain's Son**

**(Autumn, A.D. 29)**

**Various Miracles of Jesus**
**< Autumn, A.D. 29 (4/7) >**
**(Matthew 8:5-13; 9:27-34; Luke 7:1-10)**

### — The Healing of the Centurion's Servant[(a)]
### < Autumn, A.D. 29 (4/7) >
### {Matthew 8:5-13; Luke 7:1-10}

After completing His Sermon on the Mount within the hearing of all the people [*Harmony* 5:1-86], Jesus returned to Capernaum. This village served as the base of operations for the Lord's ministry. In that town lived a centurion who was a captain in the Roman army. He, as a captain, was in charge of 50-100 soldiers. This particular centurion had a slave whom he especially loved. Unfortunately, the centurion's servant was critically ill, even at the point of death. He was paralyzed and suffering dreadfully.[1]

The centurion, hearing of the Lord's power to heal the sick [*Harmony* 3:62-68], desired that Jesus would do the same for his beloved servant. However, as a non-Jew, he was reluctant to approach the Lord personally with a request for Him to heal his servant. So, according to the social customs of the times, he sent a delegation of Jewish leaders to plead on his behalf that Jesus come and heal his servant. When the delegation of elders found Jesus, they strongly urged the Master to heal the servant right away. They began their request by saying, "Sir, a certain centurion in this town has a young slave who is very sick, lying paralyzed at his home, suffering horribly in agony. This servant is very special to him—in fact, he treats him as his own son.[(b) 2]

---

1 Matthew 8:5, 6; Luke 7:1, 2
2 Matthew 8:5, 6; Luke 7:3, 4

"Now," these elders continued, "this centurion is certainly unusually deserving of Your granting of his request! This is because, even though he is a Roman, he loves our nation. In fact, it was he who paid for the construction of our city's synagogue!"[3]

Jesus responded in the affirmative, saying, "I will go to his home and heal the centurion's servant." So the Lord began to make His way toward the centurion's home with the Jewish leaders tagging along.[4]

When Jesus was just a short distance from the house, however, the centurion sent some friends to speak further with Him. They said, "The centurion wants us to tell You something. These are his exact words: 'Master, please don't trouble Yourself any more with this matter, for I am not worthy for You to even enter under the roof of my house.'" Nevertheless, Jesus still continued to make His way toward the place.[5]

Seeing that Jesus was fast approaching his home, the centurion himself came out to meet Jesus, declaring, "It is as I have said: I am not worthy for You to enter my house! That is the same reason why I did not come to You in the first place. I am not worthy! Rather, just say the right word and my servant will be healed! For I believe that You have the authority to command that my servant be healed and I know that he will get better! As a soldier, I understand how to take orders. And too, like You, I know how to give orders. Indeed, I have authority over others. I am able to give directions to many soldiers. To one, I say, 'Go!' And he goes. To another, I can say, 'Come!' And he comes. To my servant, I say, 'Do this!' And he does it. So then, in a like manner, just use the right word of authority, and my servant will be healed!"(c) [6]

Hearing this, the Lord was amazed. He turned and declared to the people following Him, "Surely, I must tell you: Nowhere in all of Israel have I ever seen such faith as in this man! I further say to you that there will be many so-called heathen who will come from afar—from the east and west—to eat at the eternal supper table with Abraham, Isaac, and Jacob in the glorious kingdom of heaven. However, at the same time, many of the sons of kingdom"—that is, members of the church—"will be cast into darkness outside the kingdom. In that darkness

---

3 Luke 7:4, 5

4 Matthew 8:7; Luke 7:6

5 Luke 7:6

6 Matthew 8:8, 9; Luke 7:6-8

there will be much weeping and grinding of teeth in anguish, in clear realization of their squandered, wasted opportunities to exercise belief in Me!"[7]

Then, turning back to the centurion, Jesus said to him, "Go! Because of your faith, your servant will be healed just as you have requested." [*Harmony* 10:14/][8]

When the centurion and those with him returned to his house, they found the young servant boy already healed and in good health. Indeed, he had been healed at the very moment that Jesus declared that he would be![(d) 9]

> The Jews said the centurion was worthy of having his servant healed because he had built their synagogue for them. However, Jesus considered the centurion to be worthy because of the extraordinary faith he showed. The Lord recognized the more praise-worthy motive.

### — The Healing of Two Blind Men
### < Autumn, A.D. 29 (4/7) >
### {Matthew 9:27-31}

As Jesus was traveling along, He was just about to enter a house in Capernaum when two blind men who were following Him cried out, "Have mercy on us, Son of David!" At first Jesus appeared to ignore their pleas. Instead, He entered the house and closed the door behind Him. Undeterred, the two men came right up to the house and banged on the door.[10]

> By using the phrase "Son of David" when addressing Jesus, the blind men clearly indicated that they considered Jesus to be the Messiah, for the Jews used this designation to refer to the Christ. [*Harmony* 2:66]

When Jesus answered the door, He said to the blind men, "Do you believe that I have the power to heal your blindness?"[11]

"Oh, yes, Lord!" they answered with firm conviction.[12]

---

7 Matthew 8:10-12; Luke 7:9
8 Matthew 8:13
9 Matthew 8:13; Luke 7:10
10 Matthew 9:27, 28
11 Matthew 9:28
12 Matthew 9:28

Jesus then touched their eyes, saying, "According to your faith, then, it shall be done as you have requested." And instantly they were able to see! But Jesus firmly warned them, saying, "Listen to Me! Do not tell anyone about what I have done for you!" [*Harmony* 8:23; 9:28/][13]

> The Lord gave this command for silence because the news of His miracle-working activities would arouse great animosity against His ministry on the part of many of the Jewish leaders. Thus, His work would be greatly restricted. That is also why He waited to heal the men until He had first entered the house, so that only a few people would witness the miracle.

But in spite of the Lord's command to keep quiet about the healing, the two men left the house and told everyone throughout the countryside what Jesus had done for them.[14]

**— The Healing of a Dumb Demoniac**
**‹ Autumn, A.D. 29 (4/7) ›**
**{Matthew 9:32-34}**

Just as the two recently-healed blind men were leaving the presence of Jesus, a demon-possessed man was brought to Him. As a side effect of his devil possession, the man was unable to speak a word. After Jesus cast the demon out of the man, he was able to speak in a normal fashion again. [*Harmony* 4:24/][(e)] [15]

All the people standing nearby were absolutely amazed at what they had seen. They commented, "Nothing like this has ever been observed to happen in Israel . . . until now, that is!"[16]

On the other hand, many of the Pharisees said, "This Man casts out demons through the power of the ruler of demons—even the devil himself!" [*Harmony* 4:25/][17]

—

13 Matthew 9:29, 30
14 Matthew 9:31
15 Matthew 9:32, 33
16 Matthew 9:33
17 Matthew 9:34

### *The Timeline of the Ministry of Jesus, Segment Five: Autumn, A.D. 29 — Spring, A.D. 30*[(f)]

Two years had elapsed since the Lord began His ministry in the autumn of A.D. 27. During the first six months of those two years—Autumn, A.D. 27 through Spring, A.D. 28—Jesus was baptized, had been tempted in the wilderness, called His first disciples, and performed His first miracle.[1]

During the second six-month section of these first two years—Spring, A.D. 28 through Autumn, A.D. 28—Jesus made a visit to Jerusalem for the yearly celebration of the Passover. While there, He cleansed the Temple for the first time. He also had a night visit with Nicodemus. This was followed by several months of ministry in Judea, the details of which are sparse.[2]

The third six-month segment of these first two years—Autumn, A.D. 28 through Spring, A.D. 29—was spent in Samaria, with the Lord ministering to the woman at Jacob's well, and also with the Samaritans of that area. From there, the Lord went to Galilee to begin a ministry in that province. There, He healed a certain nobleman's son.[3]

Very few events during this time period in the Lord's ministry are recorded.[4]

The final six-month portion of these first two years of ministry—Spring, A.D. 29 through Autumn, A.D. 29—was, according to the record, one of the busiest of the Lord's entire ministry. This time period began with an encounter with the Jewish leaders over His healing of a paralytic on the Sabbath. Appearing before the Sanhedrin, the Lord gave a detailed defense of His ministry, citing a number of convincing theological and practical proofs of His Messiahship.[5]

Then leaving Judea, Jesus began an extensive and dramatic ministry in Galilee. After being rejected in His home town of Nazareth, Jesus chose Capernaum to be His headquarters. He began His work there when He called, by the Sea, His first disciples to join with Him officially on a full-time basis. Soon after that, He healed a demoniac in a synagogue as well as various other people in Peter's home. Next, the Lord started an extended tour of the entire province of Galilee. His early work during this tour was noted for several significant miracles which He performed.[6]

This was followed by a couple of events involving the issue of proper Sabbath-keeping. In spite of the tension this caused with certain Jewish leaders, the Lord's popularity among the common people was nothing short of extraordinary. Literally thousands followed after Him! Later, Jesus ordained twelve of His closest disciples. They would become known as the Twelve.[7]

Immediately after that, Jesus preached His most important sermon, commonly known as the "Sermon on the Mount." This event was followed by several notable healings. The first two years of His ministry had ended.[8]

There were only 18 months of the Lord's ministry left before His crucifixion. This time period extended from Autumn, A.D. 29, through the Spring of A.D. 31.[9]

The next six-month segment of the Lord's ministry (5/7)—from Autumn, A.D. 29, through Spring, A.D. 30—was also very busy time for the Master. He had a second evangelistic tour of Galilee, distinguished by several miracles, including the resurrection of the son of a woman from Nain—the Lord's first resurrection. Of course, He had the usual, off-and-on contentions with various Jewish leaders. (g) [10]

The Lord also had some trouble with His own family. During this time, Jesus began to use parable-telling as a method of communicating the truth of the Gospel. This was especially noted by the Lord's telling of many parables as He sat by the Sea.[11]

Jesus performed a couple of miracles of special note: He healed two demoniacs in Gadara, and raised Jairus's daughter from the dead.[12]

The Savior also dealt with the questionings of the Jewish leaders and the disciples of John the Baptist regarding the Lord's views on both feasting and fasting. Following that, after carefully instructing His disciples, Jesus sent them out, two-by-two, to minister on their own. Near the end of this time period, John the Baptist was brutally murdered.[13]

Finally, Jesus faced a major crisis in Galilee regarding the nature of His ministry and miracles. This crisis was brought to focus through the incidents of the feeding of the 5,000, the Lord's walking on water, and the His teaching of the "Bread of Life." These events marked a serious—and regrettably, negative—turning point in His ministry. But overall, it was one of the busiest and most fruitful six-month segments of the Lord's entire ministry.[14]

—

## The Beginning of the Lord's Second Galilean Evangelistic Tour[h]
## < Autumn A.D. 29 (5/7) >
## (Matthew 9:35; Luke 7:11-17; 8:1-3)

### —Jesus Starts His Second Galilean Evangelistic Tour
### < Autumn, A.D. 29 (5/7) >
### {Matthew 9:35; Luke 8:1-3}

A short time later [*Harmony* 6:15-17], Jesus began traveling again from one village to another, and from one city to another, throughout the province of Galilee, proclaiming and preaching the joyous Gospel of the kingdom of God. He taught the Gospel truth in various synagogues. He also healed people of all kinds of diseases and illnesses. This is often called the Lord's Second Evangelistic Tour of Galilee. This second tour took place about five or six months after the first evangelistic tour. [*Harmony* 4:34] And a third such tour would begin about three months later. [*Harmony* 8:39, 54/][18]

The Lord's twelve disciples went along with Him on this particular tour. A number of women who had been healed of demons and many diseases also traveled with Him. One was Mary—also known as Magdalene—out of whom, seven times, the Lord had cast demons. [*Harmony* 14:2] Another was Joanna, the wife of Chuza, King Herod's personal steward. And too, there was a certain Suzanna. These and many others were financing the Lord's ministry with their own personal money. [*Harmony* 11:162; 17:136; 18:28][i] [19]

### —The Resurrection of the Widow of Nain's Son
### < Autumn, A.D. 29 (5/7) >
### {Luke 7:11-17}

During the course of the Lord's ministry in Galilee, Jesus was approaching Nain, about 25 miles to the southwest of Capernaum. Following Him were His disciples, along with a large crowd. As He came near the gates of the town, suddenly another sizable group came out of the village. They were carrying a dead man prepared for burial. This deceased was the only child of his widowed mother, who was in the procession.[j] [20]

---

18 Matthew 9:35; Luke 8:1

19 Luke 8:1-3

20 Luke 7:11, 12

Seeing the distress of the widow, Jesus was overwhelmed with compassionate feelings for her. "Stop weeping!" He said to her. The Lord went up to the dead body and touched the bier, and the ones carrying the dead man stopped. Jesus said, "Young man, I tell you: Arise!" The dead man sat up and began to talk! Jesus returned the young man to his mother. [*Harmony* 8:23; 13:14, 30/][21]

A great sense of awe overwhelmed the crowd, and accordingly, they began to praise God, declaring, "Truly a great Prophet has arisen up among us!" Others exclaimed, "God has revealed Himself to His people through this Man's ministry!"[22]

Not surprisingly, the report of this miracle which Jesus performed went like lightning throughout all the province of Judea to the south as well as into the surrounding provinces.[23]

> This particular miracle is unique in the sense that Jesus resurrected the young man on His own, without first being requested by anyone to perform the miracle. This shows the Lord's truly compassionate attitude toward those who were grieving.

## Supplementary Notes:

**(a) [6:0++]** There are some interesting differences between the two accounts of this story. Based upon the context of the each detail, I determined just which course of events I would follow. (See **Notes "b," "c,"** and **"d"** below for specific details in each situation.)

**(b) [6:2]** In Matthew's account, the *centurion* talks with Jesus, while in Luke's account, *messengers from the centurion* talk with Jesus. From the context, it is very clear to me that the latter situation is the better account.

**(c) [6:6]** In Matthew's account the *centurion* talks with Jesus, while in Luke's account, the centurion sends *friends,* in this case, to speak to Jesus on his behalf. I think that the overall context of the story favors that the *centurion* was the one speaking to Jesus.

---

21 Luke 7:13-15

22 Luke 7:16

23 Luke 7:17

**(d) [6:9]** I think the context indicates that, while it was the *centurion* who spoke to Jesus (as indicated in **Note "c"** above), *both* the centurion and his friends (as indicated in Luke's account) found his son alive and well when returning home. Therefore, in the *Harmony* I have recorded it as such.

**(e) [6:15]** See **Note "f"** in Chapter 4 for more information.

**(f) [6:17+]** This is the fifth of eight insertions in the *Harmony* that places the events of the three-and-a-half-year ministry of Jesus on a "timeline" divided into seven six-month segments. (The eighth insertion is at the end of the seventh segment.) The other segment insertions can be found in the following locations: Segment One, *Harmony* 2:21/; Two, *Harmony* 3:0; Three, *Harmony* 3:33/2; Four, *Harmony* 3:71/; Six, *Harmony* 10:0; Seven, *Harmony* 11:0; and Eight, *Harmony* 18:99/1-21

**(g) [6:17/10]** This segment has the designation 5/7 for its "Segmental Placement" number. (See "Segmental Placement" in the "Features for Using the *Harmony* as a Reference Book" section near the back of this book for more information.)

**(h) [6:17/14+]** As written in the Bible, some of the events of both Luke 7 and 8 seem to be out of order. Accordingly, to make the story flow better (as part of the Lord's Second Galilean Tour), I have re-ordered them (I hope accurately) in the *Harmony.*

**(i) [6:19]** It is not clear whether Mary Magdalene was cleansed of seven devils at the *same time*, or whether she was cleansed *seven different times*—thus indicating that Mary repeatedly slipped back into sin. I chose, perhaps arbitrarily, *seven different times* for the *Harmony,* thus dramatically increasing the impact of the story of Mary Magdalene's healing and conversion. (See also **Note "e"** in Chapter 14 of the *Harmony.*)

**(j) [6:20]** In the account, the Greek is unclear whether this event took place the "day after" (as the KJV indicates), or just some indeterminate time later. In the *Harmony,* I chose the latter, and interpreted the verse as reading, "During the Lord's ministry . . ."

# CHAPTER SEVEN

## THE MID-GALILEAN MINISTRY OF JESUS: THE LORD'S BUSY DAY

**From Christ's Family Is Concerned About Jesus, to the Healing of the Demoniacs of Gadara**

**(Autumn, A.D. 29)**

### Jesus Heals a Blind and Dumb Demoniac and Talks About the Unpardonable Sin; the Lord's Mother and Brothers Come to Visit Him

**< Autumn A.D. 29 (5/7) >**

**(Matthew 12:22-50; Mark 3:20-35; 6:3; Luke 8:19-21; 11:14-32)**

**— The Lord's Busy Day**

No doubt, most days during the Lord's ministry were busy. However, a detailed record of any specific day during the course His ministry is quite limited. But, on one particular day, its listing of events is amazingly complete. Indeed, the events of a single period of approximately 30 hours have been recorded in some detail. And without doubt, it was quite a "busy day" for the Lord.[1]

In addition, the events that took place that day—such as the Lord's description of the unpardonable sin, His telling of parables for the first time, His miracle of stilling of the storm on the lake, and the healing of the crazed demoniacs at Gadara—significantly added to the power and character of His overall ministry. In that sense, then, it was more than just any ordinary day during the Lord's work on this earth.[2]

## — Christ's Family Are Concerned About Jesus
**< Autumn, A.D. 29 (5/7) >**
**{Mark 3:20, 21; 6:3}**

The Savior's personal family was concerned about how He conducted His ministry. In this regard, His family consisted mainly of His older half-brothers: James, Joses, Simon, and Judas. [*Harmony* 11:1-4] No doubt these brothers were children of Joseph from a previous marriage. [*Harmony* 7:18] Now, these brothers felt that, with so many people surrounding Jesus on a daily basis, He would quickly wear Himself out. Also, they had heard that when He entered any house, the place would be packed with so many people clamoring for help that He was not able even to eat. Overwhelmed by stories such as these, they decided to go and rescue Jesus from this almost daily experience. They said among themselves, "He is losing His senses! Before long, if He keeps this up, He'll go crazy! He'll lose His mind!" Convincing the Lord's mother, Mary, of the seriousness of the situation, His brothers took her along and went to try to free Jesus from the press of these smothering crowds. [*Harmony* 2:34/2; 7:18-21][(a) 1]

> While the Lord's family might have been well-intentioned and understandably concerned about the Lord's physical and mental condition, they should not have tried to interfere. If they had had more faith in Him [*Harmony* 11:2-3/], they would have allowed Him to conduct His own ministry without attempting to control its direction.

## — The Healing of a Demon-possessed Man
**< Autumn, A.D. 29 (5/7) >**
**{Matthew 12:22, 23; Luke 11:14}**

In the meantime, a man possessed of a demon—which had rendered him both blind and mute—was brought to Jesus for healing. [*Harmony* 4:24/] When the Lord healed him, not only did the demon leave his body, but the man was able to both see and speak again. As usual, the crowds were totally amazed by what they saw. They questioned among themselves, "Do you suppose that this Man who performed this incredible miracle could be the Son of David—even the Messiah?"[(b) 2]

---

1 Mark 3:20, 21; 6:3
2 Matthew 12:22, 23; Luke 11:14

## — Contention with the Pharisees over the Lord's Healing of Demon-possessed People
## < Autumn, A.D. 29 (5/7) >
## {Matthew 12:24-30; Mark 3:22-27; Luke 11:15-23}

On the other hand, when the trouble-making scribes and Pharisees who had come from Jerusalem heard what had happened [*Harmony* 7:2], they declared, "Of course this Man was able to cast out demons . . . but He is able to do so only through the power of Beelzebub—the ruler of demons! In fact, we are sure that Beelzebub actually dwells in Him!" [*Harmony* 4:25/; 7:9/2, 10; 8:49]] To make matters worse, there were yet others who, testing Him, were constantly pestering the Lord to work one miracle after another to serve as proof that His ministry was from heaven and not of the devil. The Lord was in an impossible situation. Whatever He did—work a miracle or not—someone would be upset and falsely accuse Him! [*Harmony* 11:68][(c)][3]

> Casting out demons, commonly called exorcism, was practiced by some of the Jewish religious leaders. When one of their own practiced exorcism, the other Jewish leaders usually accepted their work as being genuine. It would seem, then, that if it was appropriate—as far as the Jewish leaders were concerned—for these exorcists to cast out demons, then it must also be all right for Jesus to do the same. Such a thought was quite logical. But the problem was that the Jewish leaders were very willing to accept as genuine some of their own fellow leaders in the practice of exorcism, while at the same time they hypocritically and unfairly refused to accept the Lord's work of exorcism as legitimate. [*Harmony* 7:5]

So Jesus, able to read their thoughts, came close to them so they would not misunderstand a word He had to say. He then spoke in parables, saying, "Every kingdom that is in rebellion against itself will be destroyed. Every city—or family, for that matter—that does not live in harmony with itself will ultimately fall into disarray. So then, if Satan is the one who is casting out Satan, his kingdom certainly will not be able to remain strong. Now, will it? Indeed, if you are correct in your accusation that I cast out devils through the power of Beelzebub—the master of demons—then Beelzebub would be in the process of destroying himself! And that makes no sense. Don't you agree?[4]

---

3 Matthew 12:24; Mark 3:22; Luke 11:15, 16

4 Matthew 12:25, 26; Mark 3:23-26; Luke 11:17, 18

"Furthermore," Jesus continued, "if I, by Beelzebub—the master of demons—cast out demons, who is it that casts out demons when one of your own associates exorcise people of devils? [*Harmony* 7:3/] Logically, then, if I use Beelzebub to cast out demons, you have no real choice but to admit that they are doing the same! Isn't that right? [*Harmony* 11:68] But I tell you, if you had the nerve to accuse some of your own people of false exorcism, they would certainly be justified in being very angry with you. In fact, you could hardly blame them if they reacted violently to your criticism and, in turn, judged you harshly—and with justifiable anger, I might add—for your condemnation of them! So then, again, why do you criticize Me, but refuse to criticize them? Furthermore, you expect Me, without argument or debate, to accept your condemnation of My ability to cast out a demon. That isn't logical. Tell Me, what are you afraid of?[5]

"But, on the other hand," the Lord went on, "if I truly cast out demons by the power of the Holy Spirit and the strong 'finger' of God, so to speak, then you must admit that the kingdom of God, as evidenced by My ministry, is genuine! Yes, the truthfulness of My ministry has been clearly demonstrated . . . right before your very eyes. Can't you see then, that the purpose of My ministry is to destroy the power and work of Satan . . . not to work in cahoots with him? To do otherwise would be ridiculous!"[6]

> In this discussion with the Jewish leaders, Jesus did not suggest that there aren't false exorcisms. In fact, the Lord warned against false miracles. [*Harmony* 15:18] However, in this case, the Lord was specifically talking about His *own* ministry. He had come to this earth, in a large part, to destroy the power of the devil. That being the case, how foolish it would be for Him to work in concert with Satan!

Jesus continued, saying, "Now to illustrate My point: If a intruder wants to enter the well-fortified house of any man to steal his property, must he not first tie up that man with ropes, and *then* seize his possessions? That's obvious! On the other hand, when the owner of the house is fully armed, he is strong enough to defend his own home against the intruder, and successfully retain his possessions. But, should someone come along who is even stronger than the owner of the house, then what will happen? Well, first, the stronger man will remove the armor and weapons from the man of the house—the defenses in which he has confidently placed his security—and then, second, after tying up the man of the

---

5 Matthew 12:27; Luke 11:19

6 Matthew 12:28; Luke 11:20

house, he will be able easily to snatch away all the homeowner's possessions, and plunder his things. Now, that is exactly what I am doing to Satan! Yes, I am able to overpower the devil and bind him. He thinks he is stronger than I am, but he isn't! Next, I am able to take back the world—his 'house and possessions,' so to speak. Can't you see that by exorcising demons, I am binding the devil and seizing his property—the world—and using it for My own righteous purposes? So then, that is hardly working in concert with the devil, as you accuse Me of doing. Now is it?"[(d)] [7]

> It may seem strange that the Lord would compare His ministry to the evil action of an intruder breaking into someone's house, tying up the owner—that is, the devil—and then stealing his possessions—that is, the world which the devil thinks he owns. Nevertheless, that is exactly what Jesus did in using this illustration. In reality, the world does not belong to Satan. He just tried to seize it from God. And for all practical purposes, the devil has succeeded. But that's only temporary. Through the ministry of Jesus, the Lord snatched the world back from the devil. And, in the end, the Lord will reign over the earth—even the whole universe, as He was meant to do!

"In summary," the Lord concluded, "everyone—including you—who is not with Me in this battle against Satan, is in reality, working against Me! And, anyone who is not with Me in the work of bringing all the people of the kingdom of God together in unity, is, in truth, trying to shatter it, thus causing great chaos among My own people!"[8]

**— The Unpardonable Sin**[(e)]
**‹ Autumn, A.D. 29 (5/7) ›**
**{Matthew 12:31-45; Mark 3:28-30; Luke 11:24-26, 29-32}**

The Lord continued, "Because of what I've been saying to you, I want you to understand something very important. I can firmly assure you that any kind of sin and blasphemy can be forgiven mankind. In fact, all types of abusive language that anyone speaks—even against the Son of God—can be forgiven. However, having said that, to speak ill against the Holy Spirit—to commit blasphemy against the Spirit—cannot be forgiven. To repeat, to speak a word against the Son of Man can be forgiven. But to speak a word against the Holy Spirit *cannot*

---

[7] Matthew 12:29; Mark 3:27; Luke 11:21, 22
[8] Matthew 12:30; Luke 11:23

be forgiven. In fact, it cannot be forgiven in this life nor in the life to come—that is, this sin will remain forever . . . unforgiven!" [*Harmony* 3:96; 12:38][9]

> What does it mean "to speak a word against the Holy Spirit," and to "commit blasphemy against the Spirit"? Why is it that the sin of blasphemy against the Spirit "cannot be forgiven in this life, nor in the life to come"? First of all, blasphemy against the Holy Spirit doesn't refer to a specific sin. Rather, it refers to an *attitude*, or a *mindset.* In short, it means that, because of a stubborn and rebellious heart, one continues to refuse to listen to the Holy Spirit's impression—or voice of the conscience—within the soul. When individuals do that, they have cut off the communication link between themselves and heaven! And because of that broken communication, there will be no forgiveness of any sin they may commit. Why is this? Follow this sequence: Forgiveness comes from God as the result of confessing—or the repenting of—one's sins. [1 John 1:9] And confession, in turn, is the result of responding to the impressions of the Holy Spirit in one's heart. [Acts 2:37, 38] Thus, if someone refuses to listen to the Spirit, then confession and forgiveness, which follow in sequence, are impossible. And, without confession and forgiveness, a person remains in his or her sins. This was what Jesus meant by the sin, or blasphemy, against the Holy Spirit—a sin for which there could be no forgiveness.[1]
>
> In the Lord's day, the Jewish leaders in this story were severely cutting off the impressions of the Holy Spirit in their lives. This is proved by the fact that they actually had the audacity to accuse the Savior of working in concert with the devil! [*Harmony* 7:3] Should they persist in such a condition—that is, refusing to listen to the voice of the Spirit within their hearts—their sins would never be forgiven, and thus they would be lost. Indeed, as Jesus said, the sin of speaking ill of the Lord could be forgiven . . . but only if the Jewish leaders responded positively to the voice of the Holy Spirit within their hearts, condemning their despicable attitude. And this was something that many of them refused to do. In short, they were on the verge of committing the unpardonable sin, because they were refusing to listen to the impressions of the Holy Spirit.[2]

---

9 Matthew 12:31, 32; Mark 3:28, 29

Jesus said these strong words because the Jewish leaders had viciously accused Him by saying, "He has a demon dwelling within Him!" [*Harmony* 7:3, 17][10]

Jesus concluded, "Allow Me to illustrate: A tree will either be good, or it will be bad. With certainty, a tree is known by its fruit, whether it be good or bad. Simply put, if the tree is good, it produces good fruit. If it is bad, it produces bad fruit. So it is with you! You must choose to be like either a good tree, or a bad tree. Sadly, it is clear that you have chosen to be like bad trees. Not only that, but to use another illustration, you are like a pit of poisonous snakes! And anyone close to you will be bitten by the poisonous venom of your hatred and evil. But unfortunately, in a sense, you can't help yourselves! And why? Indeed, the mouth—that is, your mouth—can speak only of those things which have already filled up your heart within you, which, in your case, is constantly only terrible wickedness—like the bad fruit, or poisonous snakes! Yes, you speak only of those things that are already in you!" [*Harmony* 2:9; 5:78][11]

Jesus further added, "In a sense, what's in your heart is like a 'storehouse of treasure.' Now, this 'storehouse' is actually your mindset or attitude, whether it is righteous or wicked. And, depending upon which kind of 'treasure' you have in your heart, the words you speak will be good or evil. This means that a righteous man naturally speaks good words as a demonstration of his righteous mindset, because that is what's already in his heart. Conversely, a wicked man naturally speaks evil things, because that is what's in his heart. So serious am I about this, that I declare that of every vicious or idle word which you have spoken about Me today, you will give a strict account during the day of judgment. For, by the *good* quality of your words which have originated in your heart you shall be deemed worthy. In a like manner, by the *evil* quality of the words you've spoken, you will be condemned in the judgment. And, to be sure, what most of you have been saying about Me today [*Harmony* 7:3] has certainly been malicious! Yes, you will be severely judged because of your words, for your heart, which produced those terrible words, is equally wicked!"[12]

Then, some of the scribes and Pharisees interrupted Him, saying, "Teacher! How dare you! Show us some kind of sign"—or miracle—"to prove to us that you have the authority to say these scathing words to us!" [*Harmony* 10:33][13]

---

10 Mark 3:30
11 Matthew 12:33, 34
12 Matthew 12:35-37
13 Matthew 12:38

The people pressed closer to Jesus to hear what He might say in response to this powerful challenge. Not surprisingly, the Lord refused outright to obey such a command. Accordingly, He replied, "It is a sinful and spiritually adulterous generation—such as yours—that constantly begs for such a miracle! [*Harmony* 13:46] In fact, I refuse categorically to give any such sign to it . . . except the sign of the prophet Jonah, that is. By that I mean, for as 'Jonah was three days in the stomach of the sea creature [Jonah 1:17],' so shall the Son of Man spend three days in the depths of the earth." [*Harmony* 3:5; 10:34/, 55-61, 84, 85; 13:99, 100; 15:59][(f) (g) 14]

> Jesus here referred to the time of His burial, between His crucifixion and His resurrection. [*Harmony* 18:8-10] Of course Jesus provided an abundant number of signs of His authority—that is, His many miracles. [*Harmony* 12:150/4; 13:1-30] The Jewish leaders did not accept them. So then, they would hardly accept an additional miracle as any kind of genuine proof of the Lord's authority![1]
>
> Also, the Lord's prediction was similar to the description He gave of His death, burial, and resurrection at the time of His first cleansing of the Temple. [*Harmony* 3:5-7] In the present situation, Jesus did not give the sign which they had been demanding. Rather, He predicted, in parable form, the details of His death, burial, and resurrection. When the events actually did take place later on [*Harmony* 18:14, 17, etc.], then the "sign" of His resurrection after three days would be clear to them. This, of course, would indeed be the proof of His divinity, and thus, His authority![2]

Jesus, slightly changing the subject, continued, saying, "Men, while I'm speaking of Jonah, let me add this: The citizens of Nineveh will stand up in opposition to this very generation of yours in the day of judgment, and will condemn it! And why? Because, even the people of Nineveh repented after listening to the preaching of Jonah. Isn't that right?" [Jonah 3:1-10] Then, speaking of Himself, Jesus added, "But, look! There is someone much greater than Jonah who is preaching to this generation, in this very place today! Indeed, as Jonah was a 'sign' of repentance to the people of Nineveh, so the Son of Man, and His teachings and miracles, will be a 'sign' of repentance to the people of this generation. This means that you need to listen to and obey the Son of Man, just as the people of Nineveh listened to and obeyed Jonah. Indeed, the citizens of

14 Matthew 12:39, 40; Luke 11:29

Nineveh listened to and obeyed Jonah . . . but, the question is, will you listen to and obey Me? [*Harmony* 1:56; 10:34][(h)] [15]

"Likewise, the Queen of Sheba—from a country south of Israel—will also rise up to oppose this same generation, to condemn it in the judgment! Remember, this queen came from the far reaches of the earth to hear the wisdom of King Solomon. And when she heard the king's wisdom, she was truly impressed!" [2 Chronicles 9:1-12] And once again, referring to Himself, the Lord added, "Yet, think for a moment. Someone much greater than Solomon has shared His wisdom with this generation . . . and you have refused even to listen to Him!" Of course, here Jesus referred directly to Himself.[(i)] [16]

"Now," Jesus continued, "to return to the point I was making regarding blasphemy against the Holy Spirit—that is, refusing to listen to His voice—[*Harmony* 7:9, 10] I wish to tell you a story: There was a certain man out of whom a demon was cast. Well, the expelled demon traveled all over dry land, seeking peace and a new place in which to live. But, alas, he couldn't find another suitable dwelling! After some time spent in fruitless searching, the demon said to himself, 'I shall return to the home'—the man, that is—'in which I first lived.' So, when the demon returned, he found that the 'house'—the man's person—was unoccupied, even swept clean, and placed in order. Then the demon searched out seven other demons even more wicked than himself. And all eight of them entered into the man to dwell within him. Of course, this made the man's situation much, much worse than it was in the beginning. Isn't that right? So that's the way it is with this sinful and wicked generation to whom I am ministering!"[(j)] [17]

> What did Christ mean by this unusual story? The Jews spent much time teaching and being taught how to expel every little sin from their lives. But that wasn't enough. These same people did not understand how essential it was to fill the void left by the expelled sins with the righteousness which comes as the result of the working of the Holy Spirit within their lives through a personal relationship with God. Plainly put: They needed to fill their lives, under the influence of the Holy Spirit, with faith and trust in the Son of Man, which would result in true righteous living. But, by not doing so, their lives were ultimately filled with wickedness once again. And this time, the wickedness was

---

15 Matthew 12:41; Luke 11:30, 32
16 Matthew 12:42; Luke 11:31
17 Matthew 12:43-45; Luke 11:24-26

much worse than it ever was in the first place—even to the extent of committing the unpardonable sin!

### — Jesus Identifies His True Family
### < Autumn, A.D. 29 (5/7) >
### {Matthew 12:46-50; Mark 3:31-35; Luke 8:19-21; 11:27, 28}

At this very moment, as Jesus sat down and was teaching the crowd, the Lord's mother and brothers finally arrived from Nazareth. [*Harmony* 7:1] Standing outside the house, they sent a message by someone in the crowd that they wished to have a private conversation with the Lord. His family was unable to reach Jesus because of the size of the crowd surrounding Him. The messenger spoke to Jesus, saying, "Let me interrupt, Teacher! Your mother and your brothers are standing outside looking for you. They wish to have a private word with You."[(k)][18]

Hearing this message, one of the women in the crowd, speaking of the Lord's mother, Mary, cried out to Jesus, "Blessed is the womb that gave birth to You, and the breasts at which You were nursed!"[(l)][19]

But the Lord answered her, "No! No! Rather, blessed are those who both hear the word of God . . . and do it!"[(m)][20]

Then, directly answering the one who had informed the Master that His family wished to speak with Him, Jesus said, "Who is My mother? And who are My brothers?" Of course, the whole crowd heard the Lord's questions. They wondered what answers to these questions the Lord might be seeking. Then, looking around at all the people seated before Him and motioning with His hands toward them and His disciples, Jesus answered His own questions. He declared, "Look around you! See My mother! And My brothers! For, whoever listens to the word of God, and does the will of My Father in heaven—that person is truly My brother, My sister . . . and even My mother!"[(n)][21]

By this Jesus meant that the strongest type of relationship that a person can have is not the connection of familial blood, but a relationship with God based on faith and obedience. That is what counts most of all. By

---

[18] Matthew 12:46, 47; Mark 3:31, 32; Luke 8:19, 20

[19] Luke 11:27

[20] Luke 11:28

[21] Matthew 12:48-50; Mark 3:33-35; Luke 8:21

making this unusual—even seemingly harsh—comment, the Lord was underscoring the great significance of faith and trust in the life, as opposed to the mere family ties of natural birth, which sometimes can influence people to separate themselves from a vibrant relationship with God.

## The Sermon of Parables Given by the Sea
## < Autumn A.D. 29 (5/7) >
## (Matthew 13:1-53; Mark 4:1-34; Luke 8:4-18)

### — Jesus Teaches by the Sea
### < Autumn, A.D. 29 (5/7) >
### {Matthew 13:1-3; Mark 4:1, 2; Luke 8:4}

Soon after this, Jesus left the house where He had been teaching. He made His way down to the edge of the Sea of Galilee, and there He sat down to continue to teach the people who had followed Him. Before long, however, many more people began to arrive from a number of towns throughout Galilee, wanting to hear the Lord's teachings. So, to accommodate the increasing multitude, Jesus climbed into a boat—as He had done before [*Harmony* 4:16]—and had it pushed a short distance from the shore. From that position, the Lord was able to instruct the people as they stood or sat on the bank. Then, Jesus began to teach them by telling them parables—or stories—to illustrate the many points with which He sought to educate the people.[22]

In the crowd were people of different occupations and backgrounds. This included, among others, merchants, fishermen, and farmers. Some of the farmers in the crowd owned their own properties. Others rented the land which they worked. Also listening that day were women who worked hard in their homes providing for their families. In the parables Jesus told, He used familiar and common things from the varied lives of these, His listeners.

### — The Sower and the Soils
### < Autumn, A.D. 29 (5/7) >
### {Matthew 13:3-9; Mark 4:2-9; Luke 4:4-8}

The Master Teacher began His first parable, by saying, "I want you to listen to this story! Now there was a certain farmer wishing to sow seeds of grain in his field. As He began to scatter the seeds, some of them fell on the hard, beaten

---

[22] Matthew 13:1-3; Mark 4:1, 2; Luke 8:4

roadway which ran beside the field. As soon as the birds noticed the seeds which fell there, they came and ate them up! The few seeds that the birds missed were trampled under the feet of people passing by on the roadway. However, some of the seeds cast by the sower fell on rocky soil. There wasn't much good soil there. Nevertheless, the seeds quickly sprouted and began to grow. But because there was no deep soil in that place, the tiny plants received little or no water. So when the sun came up every day, it soon scorched the young seedlings, causing them to wither and die. It was because of the rocks in the soil that the roots were not able to dig deep enough into the earth. Still other of the seeds from the hand of the sower fell on thorny-infested soil. In this case, when the thorns grew up next to the fledgling seedlings that had sprouted, they choked out the life of the young plants. Like the seedlings in the rocky soil, these young plants also withered and died. Finally, some of the seeds that the sower cast landed on good soil. These seeds soon sprouted and ultimately grew into strong, healthy plants. They produced a very good crop of grain for the farmer. Some of these seeds of grain produced a hundred other kernels, some sixty, some thirty. But all the seeds which fell on the good soil produced!" Then Jesus concluded this parable by adding, in loud words, "Now, if you have ears, you had better have a mind to understand what I have just told you." However, at this time, Jesus gave no explanation as to what this parable meant. He would give its meaning later on that day. [*Harmony* 7:48-52][23]

### — The Wheat and the Weeds
### < Autumn, A.D. 29 (5/7) >
### {Matthew 13:24-30}

> Often in His parables, Jesus used the words "kingdom of heaven," or sometimes the "kingdom of God." This was a phrase He used to explain the concept of the transformation that takes place when a person accepts the power of the Gospel within his or her life. On occasion, though, this phrase in the Lord's parables also referred to the time when Jesus would come back to this earth at the end of the world to establish His eternal, glorious kingdom. There were times, too, in certain parables, when this phrase applied to both of these concepts. The context determined which He referred to in any particular parable. [*Harmony* 4:4; 13:43/]

Jesus began His explanation of the meaning of the kingdom of heaven with another parable, saying to the people, "The kingdom of heaven can be compared

---

[23] Matthew 13:3-9; Mark 4:2-9; Luke 8:4-8

to a certain farmer who planted good wheat seed in his field. At night, while the farmer and his servants were sleeping, his enemy came, and among the good, genuine wheat seeds, planted darnel"—an insidious weed that closely resembles wheat. "Of course, by morning, the enemy was gone. The farmer knew nothing of the evil deed of his enemy. In time, the wheat seedlings sprouted, grew, and began to bear grain. By that time, though, the darnel's presence among the wheat had become obvious.[24]

"Noticing the darnel weeds, the farmer's servants came to him and said, 'Master, is it not true that you planted only good wheat seed in your field? Why, then, are there so many darnel weeds growing among the wheat? Where did these weeds come from?'[25]

"The farmer answered them, 'A rival farmer—no doubt an enemy of mine—must have done this!'[26]

"His servants asked, 'Then do you want us to go among the wheat and pull up the darnel weeds?'[27]

"'No! No! That won't work,' was the farmer's answer. 'For, while you are pulling up the worthless darnel, you will also uproot the good wheat. Instead, allow both the wheat and darnel weeds to grow together until the time of harvest. At that time, I will tell the reapers, "Harvest the crop, and separate the wheat from the weeds. First, gather the darnel into bunches and burn them. Next, gather up the good wheat in bundles and place them in my barn."'" This time, as in the previous parable [*Harmony* 7:23], the Lord gave no explanation of this story. Instead, He explained the parable later on that day. [*Harmony* 7:53-55][28]

**— The Growing Seeds**
**< Autumn, A.D. 29 (5/7) >**
**{Mark 4:26-29}**

Jesus told another parable about seeds, saying, "The kingdom of God can be compared to a man who plants seeds in his field. As time goes by—both day and night—while the man works and sleeps, the seeds sprout and begin

---

24 Matthew 13:24-26
25 Matthew 13:27
26 Matthew 13:28
27 Matthew 13:28
28 Matthew 13:29, 30

to grow. Now, just how the seeds grow is a complete mystery to him! It is as if, all by themselves, the seeds produce crops as an outgrowth from the soil: First, comes the seedling. Next appears the immature head of the grain. And finally, the mature grain in the head develops. But there is one thing the man knows for sure: When the crop is ready, he must quickly gather in the grain with a sickle, for the time of the harvest has come!"[29]

> By this parable, Jesus illustrated the growth of the Gospel experience—the "kingdom of God"—in the life. When a person accepts Jesus as his or her personal Savior, it is as though a seed has been planted in the heart. As time passes, the experience grows and expands—just as the seeds become seedlings. How the life is changed by the Gospel is a mystery to the disciple of Jesus, just as the growth of a seed is a mystery to the farmer who planted it. But, in time, the life is changed for the better by the power of the Gospel, like the seed that is transformed from the original tiny seed to a large, crop-producing plant. And, as the plant is perfect in each stage of its development, so is the life of the follower of the Lord as he or she grows in the Gospel. If the farmer is patient—that is, going about his normal life—he will be rewarded by seeing his plants produce good fruit. In a similar way, if the follower of Christ is patient, over time the power of the Gospel will transform his or her life from that of a sinner to that of a saint. And in the final analysis, that person will be ready to be a part of the establishment of God's eternal kingdom at the end of the world. Having the kingdom of heaven in one's heart is necessary to adequately prepare citizens for the Lord's glorious kingdom—the "harvest" in the story—which takes place at the end the world.

**— The Mustard Seed**
**< Autumn, A.D. 29 (5/7) >**
**{Matthew 13:31, 32; Mark 4:30-32}**

Jesus gave the people yet another parable, saying, "By what illustration can I picture for you the broad extent of the kingdom of heaven? Or, by what parable can I describe its growth? Indeed, to what can I compare and liken it? Well, the kingdom of heaven can be compared to a tiny mustard seed that a certain man planted in his field. Even though the mustard seed is one of the smallest of all seeds a farmer may plant, when the mustard plant is full-grown, it is larger than

---

[29] Mark 4:26-29

all other plants one might grow in a garden. In fact, it will grow as a large as a tree—indeed, up to 12 feet tall, with branches an inch or more thick! So large is that mustard 'tree' and its branches, that the birds of the sky will make nests in it to provide sufficient shade for themselves and their young!" [*Harmony* 7:31/1, 2; 12:76, 155][30]

> This parable emphasized the tremendous capacity of the power of the Gospel—the "kingdom of heaven"—to radically change a person's life. The Gospel's start in the life may appear to be very small at first—even as insignificant as a tiny mustard seed. But, given time—and that's the key—the Gospel will change the entire life. What appeared to be little and weak at the beginning—the original "mustard seed"—will expand into something great in the end—an impressive, full-grown mustard plant. And, as a tiny mustard seed will grow into a virtual tree to support the nesting of birds, in like manner, one who was once alienated from God, weak with sin, can ultimately grow into a saint whose life is victorious over sin. And so powerful will be that victory that the new convert is able to give encouragement and support to others who are likewise seeking to grow in the power of the Gospel. This parable clearly teaches the positive effects of the kingdom of God in one's life, as well as its ultimate influence on others.

**— The Yeast**
**< Autumn, A.D. 29 (5/7) >**
**{Matthew 13:33}**

The Lord presented still another parable, saying, "To what else can I compare the kingdom of God and heaven? The kingdom of heaven can be compared to a relatively small amount of yeast which a housewife took and kneaded into over 34 quarts of bread dough. With time, the yeast completely permeated the dough, causing all of it to rise, and, in the end, producing a great deal of tasty bread." [*Harmony* 12:77][31]

> This parable, similar in impact to the story of the mustard seed [*Harmony* 7:30], focused on the influence of the Gospel—that is, the "kingdom of heaven"—as it, over time, changes every part of the life it touches. It takes a relatively small amount of yeast to cause a large amount of bread

---

30 Matthew 13:31, 32; Mark 4:30-32
31 Matthew 13:33

dough to rise. So it is with the power of the Gospel. Its initial influence, while apparently small, is great in the life if it is allowed, over time, to permeate the entire life. Nothing will be overlooked. Nothing will be untouched. Everything will be changed. So it is in the development of the kingdom of God within the human heart.[1]

In the parable of mustard seed [*Harmony* 7:30], the dramatic *growth process* of the Christian life was emphasized. In the parable of the yeast, the powerful *impact* of the Gospel in the life was illustrated.[2]

**— The Buried Treasure**
**< Autumn, A.D. 29 (5/7) >**
**{Matthew 13:44}**

The Lord told another parable: "The kingdom of heaven is also to be compared to a chest full of treasure that has been buried in a field by some unknown individual. Sometime later, a tenant farmer, plowing the field, discovers the treasure. After he re-buries the chest, the laborer, with great excitement and sheer delight over his chance discovery, sells everything he possesses. With the money, he buys the field for himself so that the treasure he had discovered will be his own possession." [*Harmony* 7:33/][32]

This particular parable shows the great value of the power and influence of the Gospel—the "kingdom of heaven"—in one's life. Once discovered, it becomes the main focus of the true follower of the Gospel. Nothing is worth more to the Lord's disciple than the acquisition of the transforming power of the Gospel. The things of this life, once considered to be of great value, are quickly exchanged for the Gospel experience. Such is the value of possessing the kingdom of God in one's life.

**— The Expensive Pearl**
**< Autumn, A.D. 29 (5/7) >**
**{Matthew 13:45, 46}**

Jesus told yet another parable. He said, "Again, the kingdom of heaven can be compared to a merchant who had a passion to secure expensive pearls. When he found the one pearl of greatest value, he sold all his other pearls—and even his

32 Matthew 13:44

personal possessions—to acquire enough money to purchase the most valuable of all pearls!"[33]

> Like the preceding parable of the treasure found in the field [*Harmony* 7:32], this story emphasized the great value of the Gospel—that is, the "kingdom of heaven"—when it is discovered. The difference between the two parables is that in this one, the pearl's finder was diligently searching for it, while in the previous one, the finder of the treasure in the field came upon it by chance. There are some of the followers of the Lord who discover the power of the Gospel almost by chance. On the other hand, there are disciples who are carefully searching for it. In either case, once the Gospel is found, its finder must be willing to sacrifice everything to acquire it. The kingdom of God in the heart is worth the price—no matter the cost.

**— The Fishing Net**
**< Autumn, A.D. 29 (5/7) >**
**{Matthew 13:47-50}**

The Master gave still another parable, saying, "Once again, the kingdom of heaven is to be compared to a fishing net that is cast into the sea. As it is dragged by the fishermen in their boat, it becomes filled with all kinds of fish. Then the fishermen pull the loaded net onto the beach. Next, they sit on the shore and sort all the fish. The good fish they place into baskets for selling. The useless fish they throw away.[34]

"So it will be at the end of world: The angels will come and separate the wicked people from the righteous ones. The righteous will be saved, but the wicked will be destroyed in the furnace of hell-fire. Ah yes, in that place of destruction there will be sorry regrets on the part of those who are lost. This will lead to weeping and grinding of teeth in utter despair—indeed, a woeful realization of squandered opportunities!" [*Harmony* 12:145/2; 15:51-58][35]

> This parable indicated that, at the end of the world, all the peoples of the earth will face the judgment. Then, the Lord will separate the righteous from the wicked, just as net fishermen separate good and bad fish from each other. This parable taught that this process of separation

---

33 Matthew 13:45, 46
34 Matthew 13:47, 48
35 Matthew 13:49, 50

will take place at the end of the world, at the time of the judgment. Until then, the peoples of the world will mingle together. In the judgment, the angels, at the direction of God, will make the proper distinctions. This parable illustrated both the kingdom of God within the heart, as well as the Lord's glorious kingdom at the end of the world. The former prepares one for the latter. [*Harmony* 13:43/]

**— The Lamp**
**‹ Autumn, A.D. 29 (5/7) ›**
**{Mark 4:21-25; Luke 8:16-18}**

Jesus continued with still yet another parable, saying, "Would anyone who has lit a lamp cover it up with a basket? And would that person then place the light under a bed or couch? No, of course not! You would agree that such a person would place the burning light on a lamp stand, so that anyone needing to see his or her way when entering a darkened house will be benefited by the lamp stand's light. That's quite true, isn't it? Nothing could be more obvious! [*Harmony* 5:18; 12:16, 18, 55][(o) 36]

"This means that the truth of the Gospel that has not been understood in the past will, through My ministry, be revealed in all its brightness for you. You will finally understand it. Thus the apparent secret or enigmatic things of the Gospel will no longer be mysterious, for I will reveal the light of truth to you. If any one of you has ears, you should be careful to follow exactly what I'm saying." The Lord added more words of explanation as He spoke to the people. He said, "Indeed, I must tell you: Be very careful how you relate to the truths I'm presenting to you. Indeed, take time to listen to them carefully! To the same extent that you are willing to listen to Me—and share it with others—I will give you a clearer understanding of the truth. If you respond favorably to that, and continue to share it with others, I will give you even more light! Again, whoever follows what I have said thus far, to that person even more will be revealed. On the other hand, whoever refuses to follow what I've been teaching, will lose even what he or she seems to think he or she now possesses! Now is the time to listen, learn, and share! I've lit your lamp, so to speak. You must allow that light that I've given you to shine to others." [*Harmony* 14:145][37]

---

36 Mark 4:21; Luke 8:16

37 Mark 4:22-25; Luke 8:17, 18

In this strongly worded parable, Jesus emphasized the importance of following the light that had been revealed to the people that day through the medium of parables [*Harmony* 7:22-35], so that more light might be given to them. The parable also focused on the necessity of the Lord's followers to share with others the light which they have received from God. In short, in failing to do either or both—that is, to receive *and* to share—the follower would end up losing the light he or she had already received!

## — The Lord Concludes His Parables
## < Autumn, A.D. 29 (5/7) >
## {Matthew 13:51-53; Mark 4:33}

In addition, the Lord told many more parables than those written in the Gospel record. And when Jesus concluded His parables, He asked the people, "Did you understand what I've been teaching you through these parables and stories?" [*Harmony* 7:42-46][38]

They all answered, "Yes, Lord!"[39]

"Then," Jesus replied, using yet another parable, "each one of you who would teach others the things you have learned today about the kingdom of heaven is to be compared to the head of a family who brings jewelry and trinkets out of the treasure chest of his possessions—the kind of things which show off his great wealth. He displays things both old and new. The older things he has inherited from his ancestors. The newer things he has acquired himself during his lifetime. This parable means that the old, reliable truths that you have heard taught for years will continue to be taught and practiced. But the new truths of the Gospel—those which I've been teaching you today—also need be taught, understood, and put into practice!" And so, Jesus finished His parables for that day.[40]

[38] Matthew 13:51; Mark 3:33

[39] Matthew 13:51

[40] Matthew 13:52, 53

### — The Lord's Purpose of Teaching Through Parables
### < Autumn, A.D. 29 (5/7) >
### {Matthew 13:10-17, 34-36; Mark 4:10-12, 33, 34; Luke 8:9, 10}

On this particular occasion, all the truths the Lord presented to the masses were explained through the method of parable-telling. In fact, He did not communicate with them that day without the use of these stories. He explained the things of the kingdom of heaven through parables in a manner that they might readily understand. It was by the measure of their individual ability that He taught them. All this was in fulfillment of the Old Testament prophecy that said, "I will open My mouth in the form of parables. Through them I will speak of, and reveal those things that have been held 'secret'"—or have been not been properly understood—"since the very beginning of the world." [Psalm 78:2][(p) 41]

Soon after concluding His parables, Jesus sent the crowd home. They went on their way and Jesus was left alone with His twelve disciples and a few other close followers. They returned to the house where they had begun their day. When in the house, the disciples asked Jesus, "Why is it that You have spoken to the crowds today in the form of parables? You've never done that before. And while you're telling us that, could you also explain the meaning of the parable you told regarding the sower and the different kinds of soils?"[(q) 42]

So in the privacy of the house, Jesus first clarified for His disciples the purpose of His new method of sharing the Gospel by telling stories. He said, "To you, My closest followers, has been granted by the Father the privilege to understand, at this very moment, the mysteries of the great truths of the Gospel of the kingdom of heaven and of God which have long been misunderstood. I have presented them to you in a very open manner. This is because you have been willing to open your hearts to know the truth in its fullness and clarity. On the other hand, the vast majority of those who heard My message today have not really opened their hearts to learn the truth as they should have. Because of their dull minds, they have, for the most part, remained unreceptive to the working of the Holy Spirit. Therefore, because of their inability to hear the truths which I have openly revealed to you, the Father has not granted them the full knowledge of the truth at this time. While they partially comprehend the truths that I'm presenting, they are unable to fully understand them. That is, they've heard the

---

41 Matthew 13:34, 35; Mark 4:33, 34

42 Matthew 13:10, 36; Mark 4:10; Luke 8:9

words that I'm speaking, but their comprehension of them is limited." [*Harmony* 16:52, 53][(r) 43]

Jesus continued, "In short, no matter what I tell them, they have refused to understand completely. But to you who have a good understanding of the truth I will reveal yet more information. But unfortunately, those who have refused to understand what I've been saying to them will probably end up losing the little bit of knowledge which they now possess. Therefore, I speak to them in parables. And why? Because . . . maybe . . . the stories I tell will shake up their dull minds to help them to begin to comprehend the truth. Of course they do not understand what I've told them today, but perhaps, in time, the memory of these stories will finally break through the hardness of their thinking. In the meantime, they have claimed to understand completely what I told them [*Harmony* 7:38-40], but they have, in truth, for the most part, actually remained blind to My message."[44]

Jesus reiterated, "Yes, as I just explained, they have said that they truly hear what I've been teaching and that they understand it [*Harmony* 7:38-40], but in reality they don't. Instead, they have willfully remained ignorant to the truth. So for now, the parables must suffice. But because of your positive attitude, you who have been close to Me have been given through the Holy Spirit an understanding of the so-called secret things of the kingdom of God. However, to the rest of them on the outside, for now, all they will get is parables! In short, by their actions and attitude, they have fulfilled what Isaiah prophesied, when he said, 'They keep on hearing, but do not really understand. They keep on seeing but still remain blind. While claiming to see the truth, they really don't see anything it at all, because they willfully remain blind. While claiming to hear the truth, they actually don't hear its message, because they are determined to remain deaf to it. They do this, for, had they really been willing to both see and hear the truth, they might actually return to Me and be forgiven . . . and this they have for the most part refused to do!' [*Harmony* 14:150-154][45]

"'But,'" the Lord continued paraphrasing Isaiah, "'because the hearts of these people have become insensitive to what I have taught them, with their ears they can scarcely make out a single sound of the truth. And, too, they have effectively closed their eyes to truth. Otherwise they would have seen the truth as I have taught it to them. But if they would really see with their eyes, understand with

43 Matthew 13:11; Mark 4:11, 34; Luke 8:10

44 Matthew 13:12

45 Matthew 13:13, 14; Mark 4:12; Luke 8:10

their ears, and allow themselves to truly comprehend with their hearts, then they would sincerely return to Me. And I would heal them of their spiritual sickness.'" [Isaiah 6:9, 10][46]

> The Lord's indictment of those who had listened to His parables that day, but had made little or no effort to understand them, was quite strong. While many people were following Him, very few of them had the real heart to comprehend the true meaning of His ministry. Before long, this misunderstanding of the Savior's work would reach a crisis point. [*Harmony* 9:1-54] And, too, there can be no doubt that many of them were blinded by preconceived ideas or prejudice.

Then directly addressing the Twelve and the other close disciples that were with Him in the house, Jesus concluded by saying, "But as far as you are concerned, blessed are your eyes! And why? Because you clearly see the truth with your eyes, and truly hear with your ears. Ah yes, it is a fact, that many of the prophets and righteous people of the old days wished that they could see what you have been able to observe as you have watched My ministry in action! No, those great men of God were not privileged to see it as you have. Neither did they hear it . . . but fortunately for you, you are able to both see and hear!" [*Harmony* 11:149][47]

### —Jesus Gives His Own Interpretation of the Sower and the Soils
### < Autumn, A.D. 29 (5/7) >
### {Matthew 13:18-23; Mark 4:13-20; Luke 8:9, 11-15}

Next, as the disciples had requested of Him, Jesus explained the parable of the sower and the different kinds of soils. [*Harmony* 7:23, 42] He began by asking them a question. He queried, "Do you not understand the parable of the sower? It's an easy one! If you can't understand this one, how will you understand the other, more difficult parables?[(s)] [48]

"Nevertheless, as you have requested, this is the explanation of the parable: Yes, hear and understand the meaning of the parable of the sower. I am the Sower in the story. And I have sown the seed, which is the Word of the God, the truth of the Gospel. When people hear the true message of the kingdom but do not properly understand it, they are like the soil by the roadside, having hard and unimpressionable hearts. Because of that, the devil quickly comes—like the

---

46 Matthew 13:15

47 Matthew 13:16, 17

48 Mark 4:13; Luke 8:9

birds in the story—and snatches away the truth that has been planted in them. In short, they refuse to believe and be saved. They remain unaffected by the Gospel.[49]

"Similarly, the rocky soil represents those who do not allow the seed of the Gospel truth to dig deep roots within them. Yes, they will quickly receive the truth when they first hear it—even with great joy! But their acceptance of the truth is only temporary, for they have no real personal connection of faith in Me. Because of the rocks, their 'roots,' so to speak, are only shallow. This means that they were excited about the words but not about the One who spoke them. In short, their relationship with Me is only shallow. So then, when troubles, temptation, and affliction—the 'rocks' of My story—arise because of their acceptance of the truth, they quickly stumble and become discouraged. They end up shrinking away from the truth. They believe for only a short time. So it is with many of the people that have listened to Me today. [*Harmony* 16:71][50]

"Likewise," the Lord continued, "the thorn-infested soil represents people who hear and accept the word and begin to grow in the Gospel . . . but they also fall away as did the plants in the rocky soil. In this case, these people's failure is due to the fact that the cares of the world, the challenges and deceitfulness of securing wealth, the pleasures of this life—as well as various other things—before long, like the thorns in my story, choke out the influence of the words of the truth before they are able to bear fruit. These people have had a relationship with Me, but that relationship does not continue to grow as it must. Thus, the weaknesses of their character, over the process of time, begin to stunt their growth in the Gospel. The thorns of sin choke them out before they bear any mature fruit! Unfortunately, too, some who listened to Me today are like the thorn-infested soil. [*Harmony* 16:74][51]

"Finally," the Lord concluded, "the good soil represents those who, within their hearts, honestly and sincerely hear the word and understand it. They fully accept it, and bear the fruit of victory over their sins. They experience significant growth in character development. Their personal relationship with Me continues to grow and flourish. In some, the harvest of character development is a hundred-fold. Some bear sixty-fold. And some bear thirty-fold. They succeed because they never give up, no matter what happens. They may bear different

---

49 Matthew 13:18, 19; Mark 4:14, 15; Luke 8:11, 12

50 Matthew 13:20, 21; Mark 4:16, 17; Luke 8:13

51 Matthew 13:22; Mark 4:18, 19; Luke 8:14

quantities of fruit, dependent upon the depth and breadth of their experience, but they all bear fruit—that's what counts!" [*Harmony* 16:72][52]

> Of course, in the case of the good soil people, Jesus was speaking of His own closest disciples. And too, all the various types of soil refer to all those, who, throughout history, have related in one way or another to the call of the Gospel within their hearts and lives.

**—Jesus Gives His Own Interpretation of the Parable of the Wheat and the Weeds**
**< Autumn, A.D. 29 (5/7) >**
**{Matthew 13:36-43}**

The disciples further questioned Jesus regarding the meaning of another parable which He had told that day. They inquired, "Now explain to us the parable of the wheat and darnel weeds." [*Harmony* 7:24-28][53]

The Lord answered, "Well, the One who plants the good wheat seeds is the Son of Man. The field is the world. The good seed represents the children of the kingdom of heaven"—those who respond positively to the Gospel. "The darnel weeds are the children of the devil"—those who are brought into the church by the devil to confuse and wreak havoc among God's true followers. "Of course, then, the enemy that came by night to plant the darnel is the devil himself. The harvest is the end of the world, with the reapers representing the angels. As the darnel weeds are gathered up and burned in the fire, so shall it be at the end of time. They—the insincere ones, represented by the darnel—are not removed prior to the end of the world. Why is this? For doing so might cause many sincere people, not knowing the true motives of these insincere ones within the church, to misunderstand what is happening, and consequently they become discouraged. That is why the separating of the wheat and the darnel takes place during the time of judgment, and not before."(t) [54]

> It may seem surprising that the devil actually brings people into the church to cause trouble within its ranks, but such, according to Jesus, is the case. Instead of Satan attempting to destroy the church only from without with persecution, he also tries to destroy it from within by bringing false members within the fellowship of true believers.

52 Matthew 13:23; Mark 4:20; Luke 8:15

53 Matthew 13:36

54 Matthew 13:37-40

"Yes," Jesus continued, "it will be at that time that the Son of man will command His angels to gather out from among His true followers those who have been stumbling blocks to others. This includes those who are insincere and those who continue to live lawless lives. All these wicked people will be thrown into hell-fire. And it certainly will be a place of wailing and grinding of teeth in despair. Those who are lost have now realized that they have squandered many opportunities to fully accept the truth! To the eye of man, these unrighteous people may not have appeared to be wicked, but God, who reads the heart, knows the truth. On the other hand, the genuinely righteous ones of the kingdom—obviously represented by the good wheat—will shine like the bright sunshine in their Father's kingdom. So then, I conclude: If you have the willingness to truly listen and understand what I've been telling you, hold fast to what you have learned! In summary then, as you can readily see, during the final judgment, some in the church will be saved while others in it will be lost."[55]

## An Exciting Night and Morning
## < Autumn, A.D. 29 (5/7) >
## (Matthew 8:18-9:1; Mark 4:35-5:21; Luke 8:22-40)

### — The Test of True Discipleship
### < Autumn, A.D. 29 (5/7) >
### {Matthew 8:18-22}

By the time that Jesus finished this private discussion with the disciples regarding the meaning and purpose of parables, a large crowd was beginning to form again. They were interested in getting close to Jesus. Sensing this, the Lord directed that a boat be secured so that He and the disciples could go to the opposite side of the Sea of Galilee. Enough had happened that day. The Lord was tired and needed to rest for a while.[56]

When His disciples were making the preparations for this trip, a certain highly educated teacher of Israel came to talk with the Lord. "Teacher," he declared, "I am willing to follow You wherever You go!"[57]

Jesus tested the man by saying, "The foxes of the field have holes in the ground, and the birds of the sky have nests in which to dwell, but the Son of Man

55 Matthew 13:41-43
56 Matthew 8:18
57 Matthew 8:19

has no place to call His own where He might lay His head! Are you sure, then, that you really want to follow Me?"[58]

> This man desired to follow Jesus, but he was not aware of the sacrifices that it would take to be a faithful disciple. He had been used to the good life and its luxuries. Of course, Jesus would have been more than happy to have such a man follow Him, but He knew that this rich, educated man would have struggles dealing with the privations inherent in following the Lord. He wanted to make sure the man had truly counted the cost of following the Savior. If, after realizing what he must sacrifice to be a disciple, he was still willing to pay the price, that would be fine. If not, the Lord did not want the man to follow Him. Obviously, the man ultimately decided that the cost was too high and did not follow the Lord. The Savior wants all of His people to "count the cost" of following Him. He doesn't want His followers to be disillusioned or unprepared. (A very similar story was repeated later in the ministry of Jesus. [*Harmony* 11:126, 127])[(u)]

Next, a part-time disciple came to the Lord, trying to make excuse as to why he was not able to follow Jesus as closely as he should. He said, "I must first wait until my elderly father dies. Then, after I bury him, I will follow you."[59]

But Jesus answered him, "I say to you: follow Me now. Let those who are 'spiritually' dead bury the 'physically dead.' Don't wait for a more convenient time to follow Me—you need to follow Me now, before you change your mind!"[60]

> This man felt a deep conviction to follow Jesus, and the Lord wanted him to follow Him. But the man was hesitating. He began to make excuses. Jesus wasn't suggesting that the man not be allowed to bury his dead father—that would certainly be cruel! The truth was that the father, while elderly, was not really at the point of death. He might live for some time yet—maybe even for years. Rather, the man was using his father's future death as an excuse as to why he shouldn't follow the Lord at that time. In effect, the Lord was saying: "Don't use the impending death of your father as an excuse to refuse to follow Me. Follow Me now. Let others—those who don't have the burden to follow Me as you

---

58 Matthew 9:20
59 Matthew 8:21
60 Matthew 8:22

do—be responsible for your father's funeral, whenever his actual death occurs. Don't allow any family responsibilities—real or imagined—to keep you from making the decision to be one of My disciples." (A very similar story was repeated later in the ministry of Jesus. [*Harmony* 11:128-130])[v]

**— The Storm on the Lake[w]**
**< Autumn, A.D. 29 5/7) >**
**{Matthew 8:18, 23-27; 13:53; Mark 4:35-41; Luke 8:22-25}**

In time, a boat was prepared for the crossing of the lake [*Harmony* 7:56]. When nighttime approached, Jesus finally succeeded in sending most of the gathering crowd back to their homes. As He entered the boat, His disciples followed after Him. "Let's go over to the other side of the lake," Christ said. Pushing the boat out to sea, they began to make their way across the water. However, there were a number of other small boats filled with many of the insistent crowd actually pursuing them![61]

While the boat was in the midst of the sea, Jesus fell asleep. Suddenly a great storm arose, violently shaking the boat with fierce winds. The waves began to splash over the top of the watercraft and it was quickly filling with water. The boat was on the verge of sinking. The situation was obviously grave. Yet Jesus did not awaken. He remained asleep in the stern of the boat, resting on a cushion. The disciples came to the Lord and awakened Him, with various ones frantically crying out, "Lord!" "Master! Master!" "Teacher, save us! Else we will certainly perish!" "Teacher, don't you care that we are dying?" [*Harmony* 9:14-23][62]

But the Master, now awakened by the disciples' pleadings, gently chided them, "Why are you so afraid, 'little-faiths'?" Then, rising in the boat, He condemned both the wind and the sea for their ill temper, by declaring, "Hush! Be still!" Instantly, both the wind and the sea became perfectly calm! "Why are you so cowardly," He continued, "My, oh my, what has happened to your faith?" [*Harmony* 5:65; 9:21; 12:51][x] [63]

---

61 Matthew 8:18, 23; 13:53; Mark 4:35, 36; Luke 8:22

62 Matthew 8:24, 25; Mark 4:37, 38; Luke 8:23, 24

63 Matthew 8:26; Mark 4:39, 40; Luke 8:24, 25

The disciples were, at the same time, very amazed and yet extremely fearful. They said to each other, "What type of Man is this that even the winds and the waves obey His commands?"[64]

### — The Healing of the Demoniacs of Gadara[(y)]
### < Autumn, A.D. 29 (5/7) >
### {Matthew 8:28-9:1; Mark 5:1-21; Luke 8:26-40}

By morning the boat arrived at the other side of the lake in the region of the Gadarenes. This place, on the eastern side of the lake, was populated mainly by non-Jews. When Jesus and His disciples came ashore, two demon-possessed men descended upon them. For a long time, these two men had not lived in a regular house, but were dwelling naked among the tombs of the local cemetery! Under the control of the demons who dwelled within them, the two men were so dangerous that no one was able to go safely into the area where they were roaming. In fact, these two men were so violent and powerful that it was impossible to tie them up—even with chains! Indeed, even though they had been under guard, they had escaped from the chains and had run into the wilderness. They had literally broken both the chains and shackles! Clearly, no one could control them. Moreover, both night and day they could be heard continually screaming among the graves and on the hillsides as they mutilated themselves with sharp stones. (z) 65

> Demon-possession in the ancient days was fairly common. While in the modern world such a condition is considered unusual, there are places where the kind of demon-possession described in the Scriptures still does take place. Such a condition provided an excellent opportunity for Jesus to have a direct encounter with the devil and his angels—or demons—and come away victorious over the powers of incomprehensible evil.

When Jesus left the boat, the two men, seeing Him from some distance, ran up to Him, fell on their knees, and bowed down before Him. Jesus cast the demons out of the men by commanding, "Come out of these men, you evil demons!"[66]

> Why would the demons in the men cause these sorry individuals to bow down to Jesus? In doing so, it would give the appearance that Jesus was

64 Matthew 8:27; Mark 4:41; Luke 8:25

65 Matthew 8:28; Mark 5:1-5; Luke 8:26, 27, 29

66 Mark 5:2, 6, 8; Luke 8:28, 29

> the master of the demons. This could indicate to the uninformed that the Lord was working in conjunction with the demons—something that would be bad for the Savior's reputation.

While Jesus was commanding the demons to leave the men, they, crying out from within the men, interrupted the command by shouting out, "What relationship do we have with you, Son of the Most High God? Have you come to give us trouble before the final time of judgment arrives when all demons are condemned? [*Harmony* 15:55] We beg of You, please don't torment us now!"[(aa)] [67]

"What is your name?" Jesus asked the demons.[68]

"Our name is Legion—for there are that many of us!" Indeed, this was quite a large number, for a Roman legion could consist of up to 6,700 soldiers![(bb)] [69]

The demons continued to plead with the Lord, asking that He not send them out of the region, nor dispatch them to some prison for devils. A short distance away, there was a herd of hogs feeding on a hill. "If you intend to cast us out of these men, please send us to dwell in that herd of hogs," they begged Him.[70]

> It was clearly against the Jewish religion to raise hogs. [Leviticus 11:4, 7] Therefore there can be no doubt that the people of that region were not Jews. And, as non-Jews, their understanding of Jesus and His ministry was quite limited.

In response to the demons' request, Jesus instantly gave permission, saying, "Go!" All the demons left the two men and entered the hogs. This caused the entire herd of two thousand hogs to go crazy and leap over the steep bank into the sea below, resulting in the drowning of all of the hogs! The men who were tending the hogs ran into the town and the surrounding countryside to inform its residents about what had happened to the demoniacs and the hogs. [*Harmony* 10:14/][(cc)] [71]

---

67 Matthew 8:29; Mark 5:7; Luke 8:28

68 Mark 5:9; Luke 8:30

69 Mark 5:9; Luke 8:30

70 Matthew 8:30, 31; Mark 5:10-12; Luke 8:31, 32

71 Matthew 8:32, 33; Mark 5:13, 14; Luke 8:32-34

The inhabitants of the city—again, mainly non-Jews—swarmed out to see for themselves what had happened to their hogs and the two men. There, they found Jesus. They also noticed the two men, previously possessed of demons, sitting at the feet of the Lord. They were in their right mind, and now, fully clothed. Carefully scrutinizing the two men, the people recognized them as the individuals who had been possessed by the legion of demons. All the people were very frightened by the sight. Once more, those who had witnessed the casting out of the demons explained to the people of the town how the formerly demon-possessed men had been saved from the devils, which had entered the herd of hogs. Of course, the hogs were no longer on the hillside. They were drowned, floating in the water! Then, approaching Jesus, the people of the area of the Gadarenes, still filled with fear and consternation, pleaded with the Lord to leave their region.[72]

> Clearly, the people of that region simply did not know how to handle what they had seen that day. Instead of responding to the miracle in a positive way, they were overwhelmed with fear. They reacted in the only way they could at the time: by demanding that Jesus immediately leave the area. Again, because they were Gentiles, their knowledge of the Gospel and the things of faith were limited. Of course, too, they were upset that all their hogs were dead! It would be only after some time of quiet reflection on the event that they would more adequately appreciate what they had observed that day. Months later, Jesus would return to the area, and the reaction of the people would be altogether different. [*Harmony* 10:23-25]

As the Lord was getting back into the boat, the two men who had been healed of demon possession begged Him to let them go along with Him. However, the Lord did not allow them to come along. Rather, He said to them, "Go back home to your own people and friends, and tell them what fantastic things the Lord has done for you—how He has shown such great mercy to you."[73]

So accordingly, the two men proclaimed in the Decapolis region, south of the land of the Gadarenes, the wonderful things Jesus had done for them. Decapolis, too, was populated primarily by non-Jews, and those who heard their story were amazed. Meanwhile, back in the boat, Jesus crossed over to Capernaum, often called "His own city." It so happened that in Capernaum, many people welcomed

72 Matthew 8:34; Mark 5:14-17; Luke 8:35-37
73 Mark 5:18, 19; Luke 8:37-39

Him back with excitement, for they had been waiting for Him to return. While still by the edge of the lake, He continued to teach the people there.[74]

Thus had ended a day or so in the life and work of Jesus! Indeed, it was an incredibly busy time of ministry, of both teaching and healing!

**Supplementary Notes:**

**(a) [7:1]** As indicated in the *Harmony*, the Lord's brothers were probably older than Jesus, the sons of Joseph from a previous marriage before he married Mary. Thus, these brothers were really step-brothers, and not actually the *blood brothers* of Jesus. I take this position, not because I refuse to accept that Mary, the virgin mother of Jesus, might have had other children later on, but rather, because the Lord's brothers tried to exercise control over Him and His ministry. (See also *Harmony* 11:1-4.) Had they been younger than Jesus, according to the customs of the time, they would have not been so bold as to try to control Him and His ministry.

**(b) [7:2]** The subject of demon-possession is hard for the modern mind to comprehend. In fact, some Bible scholars suggest that there was no such thing, even in Bible times. They further suggest that the demon-possession phenomenon was misnamed. They believe certain physical ailments were misdiagnosed by the people of the time as demon possession. For myself, though, I take the position that demon-possession, *did*, in fact, exist in Bible times, and that the Biblical record accurately describes the various situations. (For more information on this subject, see **Note "f"** in Chapter 4, **Note "y"** in this Chapter, and **Note "q"** in Chapter 10, as well as the various descriptions in the *Harmony* dealing with individual demon-possession stories.)

**(c) [7:3]** Beelzebub, of uncertain meaning, is clearly a derogatory name for Satan. Some suggest that it means, "lord of dung!"

**(d) [7:7]** The meaning of the parable (or illustration) of the strong man of the house protecting his property is hard to put into words. Accordingly, I used a lot of extra words to explain this rather powerful illustration.

**(e) [7:8+]** The subject of the unpardonable sin is confusing to many people. In my opinion, this concept is very often misunderstood. That is why I took a lot of extra space to explain this perplexing sin. I trust that the reader

[74] Matthew 9:1; Mark 5:20, 21; Luke 8:39, 40

will grasp the thrust of what I was trying to say, and that my explanation approximates the truth on the subject.

**(f) [7:14]** I followed the placement of this event as recorded by Matthew rather than by Luke.

**(g) [7:14]** In spite of how it appears on the surface, the phrase, "three days and three nights," is a Hebrew colloquial expression that means *the **parts** of three days* as opposed to a literal 72-hour period made up a *full* three days, composed of both daylight and nighttime! A full explanation and study of this concept, however, is beyond the scope of the *Harmony.* I suggest that interested readers should consult a good commentary which explains this strange but true expression.

**(h) [7:15]** Matthew and Luke's sequence in this event is different. I followed Matthew's. Also, I moved Luke 11:32 up to fit with Luke 11:30 and Matthew's sequence.

**(i) [7:16]** I followed Matthew's sequence of this event as opposed to Luke's.

**(j) [7:17]** (See above.)

**(k) [7:18]** In Matthew, *one person* talks with Jesus about His family wishing to speak with Him; in Mark, *a group* speaks to Him. I followed Matthew's account, thinking it more logical.

**(l) [7:19]** I interjected Luke's account here, considering that it more logically fits here as part of Matthew and Mark's accounts.

**(m) [7:20]** (See above.)

**(n) [7:21]** (See **Note "k"** above.) Thus, in the Lord's response, He spoke to one person, not to a crowd, even though they certainly were listening in.

**(o) [7:36]** Matthew's account is in a "question and answer" format. Luke's account is in declarative sentences. I followed Matthew's account.

**(p) [7:41]** Mark's sequence is different from Matthew's. I followed Matthew's in the *Harmony*.

**(q) [7:42]** Because I consider Matthew's account the most complete and its sequence the most logical, I followed his record in the *Harmony*, fitting the record of Mark and Luke into it.

**(r) [7:43]** (See above.)

**(s) [7:48]** (See **Note "q"** above.)

**(t) [7:54]** In His explanation of the parable of the Wheat and the Darnel Weeds, Jesus does not explain why the farmer refused to have the weeds uprooted before harvest time (*Harmony* 7:27, 28). However, I felt that such an explanation was necessary. So I included it within the text *as though Jesus made the explanation Himself.*

**(u) [7:58/]** The story rehearsed here and the one that follows (see **Note "v"** below), seem to be repeated later on in the ministry of Jesus (*Harmony* 11:127, 130). Some have suggested that the various records describe the same events. Perhaps this is so. However, I constructed the *Harmony* in such a way that the same series of events actually took place on different occasions.

**(v) [7:60/]** (See above.)

**(w) [7:60/+]** I followed Mark's sequence rather than Matthew's, considering it the more logical one.

**(x) [7:63]** The Lord's use of the word "little-faiths" in the *Harmony* text is interesting. (For a fuller explanation of its use and meaning, see **Note "ee"** in Chapter 5.)

**(y) [7:64+]** See **Note "b"** above to learn more about the debate on the subject of demon-possession in the Bible record. For myself, I take the position that the extreme details described in the present story—such as superhuman strength on behalf of the demoniacs, voices crying out, and hogs drowning themselves—indicate that such a possession did, in fact, take place as described in the Gospel record.

**(z) [7:65]** Matthew records that there were *two* demoniacs, while both Mark and Luke mention only *one*. I followed Matthew's account as the most likely possibility.

**(aa) [7:67]** Because I followed Matthew's account (see **Note "z"** above), I, of course, used the pronoun "we" instead of "I" when the demoniacs spoke to Jesus.

**(bb) [7:69]** (See above.)

**(cc) [7:71]** Why would the demons ask to inhabit the hogs? And why did Jesus comply with their request, which ultimately led to the death of the hogs? It would seem that Jesus actually participated in the destruction of the Gadarenes' livelihood. So, why did He do that? The answers to all these questions are unclear. However, I will venture some guesses. It is possible that the demons knew that their transference to the hogs, thus causing the hogs' death, would make their owners upset with Jesus. The fact the owners of the hogs asked Jesus to leave the area, shows that the demons' desire to enter the hogs was a clever suggestion. But, then, why did Jesus, who would hardly be working in harmony with demons, agree to the demons' request? Certainly He wasn't in agreement with their purposes! I would think that Jesus' purpose for sending the demons to into the hogs was quite different from that of the demons. *Perhaps* the Lord's purpose was to teach the hogs' owners that they were too involved in financial pursuits, and that they, steeped in paganism, needed to focus on spiritual issues instead. Also, it is possible that, even though the hogs' owners were not Jews, they most likely knew that the raising of hogs—no doubt to be used as food—was prohibited by Biblical law (Leviticus 11:7). Maybe the Lord wanted them to consider this. But no matter how ambiguous the Lord's purpose was, one thing is clear: Even though on this occasion the owners of the hogs asked Jesus to leave the area, when He returned some months later (*Harmony* 10:23-25), their reaction was much more positive and accepting. In short, then, the Lord's purpose in agreeing to the demons' request seems to have been justified.

# CHAPTER EIGHT

## THE LATER GALILEAN MINISTRY OF JESUS—
**From Matthew's Feast, to the Execution of John the Baptist**

**(Autumn, A.D. 29 - Spring, A.D. 30)**

### Jesus at Matthew's Feast, and Troubles with the Jews and John's Disciples
**< Late Autumn, A.D. 29 (5/7) >**
**(Matthew 9:10-17; Mark 2:15-22; Luke 5:29-39)**

### — Matthew's Feast
**< Late Autumn, A.D. 29 (5/7) >**
**{Matthew 9:10-13; Mark 2:15-17; Luke 5:29-32}**

While in Capernaum, Jesus was invited to a large feast given in His honor. The invitation came from His own disciple, Levi Matthew, the former tax-collector. [*Harmony* 4:48-50] The banquet was to be in Matthew's home. The most conservative of the Jews—the scribes and the Pharisees—somehow found out about this upcoming dinner. So they decided to show up at the banquet just to cause trouble for the Lord. [*Harmony* 12:90-102][a][1]

At the appointed time of the feast, the Lord and His disciples reclined at the dinner table to eat the meal. In addition, at the table with Jesus were a surprisingly large number of tax-collectors and others who were personal friends of Levi Matthew. All these were considered to be "sinners" by the Jewish leaders. However, under Matthew's influence, these tax-collectors were in the process of seeking an understanding of the plan of salvation from listening to the Lord, and accordingly, many were beginning to follow Him. [*Harmony* 13:58-61][2]

---

1 Luke 5:29, 30

2 Matthew 9:10; Mark 2:15; Luke 5:29

The Jewish scribes and Pharisees, as planned, arrived at Matthew's house and invited themselves to the banquet! While there, they noticed the tax-collectors and sinners who were in attendance. The Jewish leaders began to question the Lord's disciples, complaining, "Why is it that both your Teacher and you are eating and drinking at the same table with tax-collectors"—publicans—"and other sinners? It's shameful!" [*Harmony* 4:49/2; 8:30; 9:3/2; 12:111][(b) 3]

When Jesus overheard this question being asked of His disciples, He commented to the Jews, saying, "Healthy people are not the ones who need a physician. Rather, it is those who are sick. Go back to your Scriptures and figure out what this means when it says, 'I want you to show mercy to others. Do more than just offer sacrifices.'" [Hosea 6:6] This meant that to show mercy to people is much more important than just going through the motions of religion or the rote performance of its rituals—something these Jewish leaders were well accustomed to doing. "And remember, too," Jesus added, "I did not come to call to repentance those who already consider themselves righteous and in no need of spiritual help. Instead, I came to call those who know that they are sinners and, therefore, desire to repent and change their lives." [*Harmony* 10:108; 12:112, 113; 14:64][4]

### — A Question Regarding Fasting
### < Late Autumn, A.D. 29 (5/7) >
### {Matthew 9:14-17; Mark 2:18-22; Luke 5:33-39}

Quite coincidently, some of John the Baptist's disciples came to talk with Jesus at about the same time. They found Him at Matthew's feast. There they asked the Lord, "The Pharisees fast. Also, we fast. But your disciples do not. Why is that? In fact, we very often fast and pray long prayers. And it's not just us. The disciples of the Pharisees do the same. But, on the other hand, your disciples seem to eat and drink to their hearts' content! Why is that?" [Harmony 5:54; 13:59][5]

> It was a custom of some of the more conservatives Jews to fast—that is, to refrain from eating. They did that quite often, even twice a week. The Pharisees were well-known for this custom. John's disciples, following in the footsteps of their leader—who was known for his rather abstemious

3 Matthew 9:11; Mark 2:16; Luke 5:30
4 Matthew 9:12, 13; Mark 2:17; Luke 5:31, 32
5 Matthew 9:14; Mark 2:18; Luke 5:33

lifestyle [*Harmony* 2:5]—were accustomed to doing a similar thing. Also, considering the fact that John had been put into prison some months earlier [*Harmony* 3:69-71], they, in mourning, were fasting even more than usual. Accordingly, the Pharisees had privately encouraged John's disciples to question Jesus on this subject, clearly trying to cause trouble for Him. Unwittingly, John's disciples had become accomplices of the Pharisees. No doubt it was the plan of the Pharisees to drive a wedge of discontent between the disciples of John and those of Jesus, thus weakening the influence of the Lord's ministry with John's followers.

Without making any apology for the actions of His followers, Jesus replied to John's disciples through a short parable, saying, "Those who are assisting a bridegroom during his marriage festivities will not mourn as long as the bridegroom is in their presence, will they? Of course not! In fact, they will celebrate with him as long as he's with them. But the time will come when the bridegroom will no longer be there. Then they can fast! Until then, they will be quite happy to be in his presence. And, to celebrate with him in his presence, they will eat and drink to their hearts' content." [*Harmony* 3:30][6]

By referring to the bridegroom's leaving, Jesus was alluding to His future death, when His disciples would be greatly saddened. Then fasting would be more appropriate. But until then, His disciples would continue to celebrate being in His presence—as in the case of the bridegroom parable. Some time earlier, John the Baptist had used a similar illustration in explaining to his disciples his relationship with the Lord. [*Harmony* 3:30] No doubt some of those disciples were present at both occasions.

"To illustrate further, let Me give you another parable," Jesus continued. "No one who is a good seamstress attaches a piece of new cloth to an old garment that is torn, for the new piece of cloth will pull away from the old, weakened piece, causing the tear to become even larger. Besides, the new cloth will not match the old, making the entire garment look ugly."[7]

This parable meant that the old, traditional ways of the Jewish religion—such as constant fasting—were no longer practical nor sensible. Now, with the coming of the Son of Man and His teachings, a

---

6 Matthew 9:15; Mark 2:19, 20; Luke 5:34, 35

7 Matthew 9:16; Mark 2:21; Luke 5:36

new way of thinking must replace the old, tired thinking of the past. The two could not be effectively mixed together.

"To illustrate even further," the Lord added, "people do not put new wine into old wine bottles"—made of dried animal skins—"else the pressure from the new wine, in its fermenting process, will easily burst the old wineskins. To be sure, this breakage will waste the wine as it is spilled out on the ground—to say nothing of destroying the bottles! Rather, new wine is placed into new wine bottles. Then, both the wine and the bottles are preserved. And what does this mean? The truth of the Gospel which I've been teaching must replace the old, tired things that have been taught in the past. This is what I mean by the new wine—My teachings—as opposed to the old wine—the Pharisees' teachings. That is to say, the two opposing doctrines—the Pharisees' and Mine—cannot realistically abide with each other! Now back to My wine illustration for a moment: As is often the case, those who are accustomed to drinking old wine cannot stomach the new. Indeed, those who are used to the old wine do not quickly acquire a taste for the new. Their mind is set against it. In My illustration, the negative attitude of the Jewish leaders is represented by the old bottles. They say, 'We like the old wine better than this new stuff!' Unfortunately, that's the way it is with them: They are so used to teaching and practicing their old, tedious religious philosophies that they are unwilling to accept the new—the good news—which I've been teaching. And when they've heard My teachings, they've 'exploded' . . . like the old wine bottles!"[8]

By these three illustrations—the bridegroom, the cloth, and the wine bottles [*Harmony* 8:6-8]—Jesus sent a powerful message to both the Jewish leaders and John's disciples. To the Jewish leaders, He warned that unless they followed Him and His teachings, they would be shutting themselves off from the truth of the Gospel—the Gospel which they claimed that they were teaching. And to John's disciples, He indicated that they needed to remain faithful to the true message which their leader had taught them from the beginning—the message that had first excited them. [*Harmony* 14:64-66]

8 Matthew 9:17; Mark 2:22; Luke 5:37-39

## Jesus Heals an Invalid Woman and Resurrects Jairus's Daughter
## < Late Autumn, A.D. 29 (5/7) >
## (Matthew 9:18-26; Mark 5:22-43; Luke 8:41-56)

At the very moment when Jesus was saying these things, Jairus, a ruler from the local synagogue, came to Matthew's home, frantically searching for the Lord. As soon as he saw Jesus, Jairus interrupted the feast, fell down at the Lord's feet, and passionately pleaded with Him, saying, "My only little daughter is very sick, even at the point of death! Please come down, I beg of You, and lay Your hands on her. If You do so, I believe that she will be saved from her disease. That way, she will not die! Lord, my daughter is only 12 years old!" Immediately Jesus arose and began to follow him. The Lord's disciples, along with an extremely large crowd, also came along, pressing very close upon Him.[(c)] [9]

On the way, a woman appeared who had heard that Jesus was able to heal diseases. The woman yearned to have Jesus heal her, for she had been suffering from a hemorrhage for 12 years. The woman had said to herself, "If only I could touch His coat, I would be saved and get well!" She had also suffered for some time at the hand of many doctors, spending all of her money on worthless cures. In fact, her condition had only grown worse! This woman came up behind Jesus in the midst of the heavy crowd and touched the fringe of His outer coat. Instantly, the woman felt the power of God surging through her body, stopping the hemorrhage and healing her of the disease![(d)] [10]

At that same instant, Jesus, sensing a healing power leaving His own body, turned toward the crowd and inquired of them, "Who just touched My garments?" But the people all denied it.[11]

His disciples—especially Peter—were amazed at His question and answered, "Master, You can see many people pressing and shoving one another just to be close to You. Why then do You ask, 'Who touched Me?' Any one of hundreds could have touched You. In fact, all of them might have touched You!"[12]

---

9 Matthew 9:18, 19; Mark 5:22-24; Luke 8:41, 42
10 Matthew 9:20, 21; Mark 5:25-29; Luke 8:43, 44
11 Mark 5:30; Luke 8:45
12 Mark 5:31; Luke 8:45

Nevertheless, Jesus insisted, saying, "No! There was someone who touched Me . . . who touched Me with a hand of faith, that is. I know, for I felt healing power leaving My body!"[13]

Accordingly, Jesus continued to look around at the crowd. Soon His eyes focused on the woman who had been healed. The Lord kept looking directly at her, clearly singling her out as the one who had, in fact, touched Him. The woman was well aware of what had happened in her body. Filled with fear and trembling, she came forward to Jesus, fell at His feet, and, in front of the whole crowd, explained her entire story to Him. With compassion, Jesus said to her, "My daughter, be of good courage! Your faith has saved you and made you well! Go back to your home in peace, knowing that you have been permanently healed of that terrible malady!" From that moment on, the sickness that had afflicted the woman was gone forever.[14]

Just about that time, when Jesus was comforting the woman, some servants from Jairius's home arrived on the scene to say, "It's too late! Jairus, your poor little daughter has already died! There is no reason to trouble the Master any more in this matter, is there?"[(e)] [15]

Overhearing this, Jesus said to Jairus, "Don't be frightened about what they have just told you! Only keep on believing in Me! You daughter will be saved and made well. Believe Me!" So they all continued on toward Jarius's home.[16]

Soon, when Jesus arrived at the home of the ruler of the synagogue, they could already hear the sound of flutists playing mournful music, confirming the reality of the girl's death. Indeed, a large crowd had assembled at Jairus's home. They were making a huge commotion as they loudly mourned her death. Entering the house with only three of His closest disciples—Peter, James, and his brother John [*Harmony* 10:62, 63/, 69/; 17:2]—Jesus said to the mourners, "Please leave! Why are you making such a commotion, weeping and wailing so loudly? The girl has not died . . . she is only asleep." They all laughed at the Lord, crassly ridiculing Him, for they all knew that the girl was truly dead. [*Harmony* 13:9, 9/][17]

---

13 Luke 8:46

14 Matthew 9:22; Mark 5:32-34; Luke 8:47, 48

15 Mark 5:35; Luke 8:49

16 Mark 5:36; Luke 8:50

17 Matthew 9:23, 24; Mark 5:37-40; Luke 8:51-53

> Of course Jesus knew that the girl was dead. He was only comparing the girl's death to a sleep. He knew that, considering His divine power [*Harmony* 3:87], it would be just as easy for Him to resurrect this girl as it would be for any person to awaken someone from an afternoon slumber.

Jesus remained insistent that the mourners leave. When they finally went away, Jesus, taking with Him only the girl's parents and His three closest disciples [*Harmony* 10:62, 63/; 17:2], went into the room where the girl lay dead. He took her by the hand and said to her in Aramaic—the common spoken language of the time—"Talitha cum!" which means, "Little girl, My child! I tell you, get up!" [*Harmony* 2:58; 8:23] And the twelve-year-old girl began to breathe again. Indeed, she was raised up alive and well. She began to walk around as though nothing had happened to her! [*Harmony* 13:14, 30/][(f)] [18]

> The recording of the actual Aramaic words Jesus spoke in this story is unusual. Why were they so recorded? After all, Jesus always spoke Aramaic. So then, why are His words transliterated so that the reader of the Gospel story would know their exact sound? It is because, when Jesus resurrected Jairus's daughter, and the story was ultimately spread around, people would want to know the exact words Jesus spoke—words so powerful they could raise the dead! Thus, the actual words, in the language of Jesus, just as He spoke them—"Talitha cum!"— were passed down through history.

Of course, everyone—especially the girl's parents—were greatly amazed at what they had seen. Then Jesus instructed that the resurrected child be given something to eat. He also asked that nothing be said about what they had seen and experienced—that is, they were to keep it secret. This was to prevent those who were opposing His ministry from having greater cause to bring accusations against Him. But in spite of the Lord's strict command, the news of this miracle quickly spread throughout the entire country.[19]

---

18 Matthew 9:25; Mark 5:37, 40-42; Luke 8:51, 54, 55

19 Matthew 9:26; Mark 5:42, 43; Luke 8:56

## John the Baptist's Disciples Question Jesus Regarding His Ministry; Jesus Praises John
## < Late Autumn, A.D. 29 (5/7) >
## (Matthew 11:2-30; Luke 7:18-35)

### —John's Disciples Visit with Jesus
### < Late Autumn, A.D. 29 (5/7) >
### {Matthew 11:2-6; Luke 7:18-23}

John the Baptist's disciples heard about all the things that Jesus was saying and doing. Especially impressive was the Lord's miracle of the resurrection the son of the widow of Nain some weeks earlier [*Harmony* 6:20-23], as well as the resurrection of Jairus's daughter. [*Harmony* 8:17-19] So, John's disciples reported these things to the Baptist in prison, where he had been for the past six months. Just recently, some of John's disciples had visited with the Lord regarding the issue of fasting. [*Harmony* 8:5-8] Without question, these disciples were somewhat doubtful regarding the genuineness of the Lord's ministry. In fact, John himself may have had doubts too. This was not surprising, considering the fact that he was languishing all alone in a subterranean prison cell. [*Harmony* 3:69-71; 8:71][20]

Therefore, John sent two of his most trusted disciples, instructing them to find Jesus. Then they were to inquire of Him, asking, "Are You really the Expected One—the Messiah? Or should we look for someone else to come?" [*Harmony* 8:26/][21]

> This question was truly amazing! Just two years before, John had publicly announced Jesus to be the Messiah—the "Lamb of God." [*Harmony* 2:49, 53] It is clear, then, that John's stay in prison was wearing him down. Doubts regarding who Jesus was had surely crept into his thinking. He was no longer absolutely sure of the Lord's identity. [*Harmony* 8:26, 26/]

So accordingly, when John's disciples found Jesus, they asked Him, "John the Baptist has sent us to You to ask this question, 'Are You really the Messiah, or should we yet look for someone else?'"[22]

---

[20] Matthew 11:2; Luke 7:18
[21] Matthew 11:2; Luke 7:19
[22] Matthew 11:3; Luke 7:20

When they were asking the Lord this question, He was in the process of healing people of various maladies. A number who had been blind were now able to see. Indeed, many were being cured of diseases and afflictions, including demon-possession. Pausing from His work of healing, Jesus said to the two disciples, "Go and tell John what you have personally observed—indeed, the things that you have both seen and heard, such as the blind receiving their sight [*Harmony* 6:10-14] and the lame now walking. [*Harmony* 3:72-81; 4:40-47] Lepers are being cleansed [*Harmony* 4:35-39], the deaf are able to hear [*Harmony* 7:2], even the dead are being resurrected. [*Harmony* 6:20-23; 8:9, 15-18] And, in addition to all this—and even more importantly—the poor are having the good news of the Gospel preached to them." And then, to gently chide John and his disciples for their apparent lack of faith, Jesus added, "Blessed are those who are not offended by what I am doing. Their faith must remain strong. Yes, those who claim to be true believers must not question and doubt the genuineness of My ministry."[23]

## — The Lord Praises the Ministry of John the Baptist <Late Autumn, A.D. 29 (4/7) > {Matthew 11:7-30; Luke 7:24-35}

As John's two disciples left, Jesus turned toward the crowd around Him and began to discuss John the Baptist and his ministry. He asked, "What was it that you went out into the wilderness to see when you heard John preach? [*Harmony* 2:6] Was it simply a reed blowing in the wind? Of course not! Well then, what was it that you went out to see? Was it a man dressed in fancy clothes? No, again! Indeed, as you well know, people dressed in such fancy clothes are living in luxury, dwelling in the palaces of kings—not at all like John!" [*Harmony* 2:5] Jesus asked His question yet a third time, "Really then, what was it that you went out to see? Perhaps a prophet?" Then, answering His own question, the Lord declared, "Yes, indeed! I tell you John was a prophet. In fact, his work was more important than that of any prophet who has ever lived! Yes, this man had a unique work to do which was outlined in prophecy. In truth, John's ministry was predicted in the Scriptures, which say, 'Listen! I am sending My messenger out in front of You'"—that is, the Messiah. "'It is he who will prepare the way for You, the Coming One.' [Malachi 3:1][24]

---

[23] Matthew 11:4-6; Luke 7:21-23
[24] Matthew 11:7-10; Luke 7:24-27

"Yes, it is fact," the Lord continued, "that, among those who have been born of women, there has not arisen one who is greater than John the Baptist! And why is that? Of course, John was a great man in moral character and worth. But, more than that, the message he preached—the imminent coming of the long-awaited Messiah—is the greatest news ever commissioned to be preached by any mortal! Thus, his effective and conscientious preaching of that message—and certainly that is what he did—is what made him great. [*Harmony* 2:19, 49, 53][25]

"On the other hand, those of you who are the least in the kingdom of heaven are greater—or more fortunate—than he is. And why is this? Because, John, the great prophet, who is now languishing in prison, has not had the privilege of seeing My ministry first-hand as you have."[26]

> By this statement Jesus indicated that, had John actually had the privilege of viewing the Lord's work on a first-hand basis, he would not be questioning the validity of the Master's ministry as he presently was. In a sense, then, Jesus appeared to be excusing John's apparent and understandable lack of faith. [*Harmony* 8:21]

"But unfortunately," Jesus added, "many of you who have been following Me are doing so for the wrong reasons. You have been trying to force Me to proclaim Myself the conquering Messiah, as a king over all Israel's secular and political foes. In fact, some have been relentless in this determination. Sadly, this has done a great disservice to the true spiritual nature of the kingdom of heaven which I've been preaching. In fact, this has been the situation from the time that John the Baptist first began his ministry even to this very day! While you want Me to proclaim Myself as King, the prophecies of Scripture regarding the Messiah deal primarily with a spiritual revival in Israel rather than a political revolution as you desire. In fact, the ministry of John was, itself, a direct fulfillment of the Scriptures regarding the coming of Elijah the prophet. [Malachi 4:5] This means that the kingdom of which John preached—and the one of which I've been preaching—is *spiritual* in nature. It is not a literal, secular one, as you think. Hopefully, you will be able to bear the truth in this matter, to understand its true meaning. Let Me make it clear: John and his ministry were a direct fulfillment of the prophecy regarding the coming of Elijah the prophet who would bring a spiritual revival among the Hebrew people. So then, if you truly have ears, you had better listen to, and comprehend what I'm saying! And this means that

---

25 Matthew 11:11; Luke 7:28

26 Matthew 11:11; Luke 7:28

you ought to follow this spiritual message that both John and I have preached." [*Harmony* 12:139][(g)] [27]

> Throughout most of the Lord's ministry—especially in Galilee—many of His followers considered Jesus to be the Messiah. They were anticipating that at some time in the very near future, Jesus would publicly proclaim Himself to be the Messiah, take control of the nation of Israel, and then lead them in triumph over the hated Romans. This was their main—even sole—concept of what the work and ministry of the Messiah should be. So determined were many to have this event take place that they placed heavy pressure on Jesus to do this very thing. [*Harmony* 9:13] Of course, the purpose of the Lord's ministry was not to do any of these things. Rather, His kingdom was to be a spiritual one, to encourage the people to have a closer walk with God in a personal relationship with Him as citizens of this heavenly kingdom. It would only be at the Second Coming of Jesus—at the end of the world—that the temporal aspects of the Messiah's kingdom would become a reality. [*Harmony* 15:51-58] It is a fact that during the time of the Lord's earthly ministry many of the people's misguided emphasis on the political aspects of the Messiah's work severely limited Jesus' spiritual ministry. Therefore, the Lord wanted the people more fully to realize and appreciate the true nature of His work. It would be a challenge to their thinking, but a necessary one. [*Harmony* 9:3/]

After hearing the Lord's declaration regarding the nature of the ministry of John, all of those who had been baptized by him—the common people and the tax-collector types [*Harmony* 14:64, 65]—vindicated by their words and actions the correctness of God's true will for them. Indeed, their open confession of faith in Jesus as the Messiah, their repentance from their sins, and the transformation of their lives, all clearly indicated that God's kingdom was spiritual rather than secular. These facts served as a testimony to the veracity of the true work of both John and Christ, of its deep, spiritual nature, as opposed to it being anything political. However, those who had refused to be baptized by John—such as many of the Pharisees and the scribes—showed that they had clearly rejected the spiritual message which God had in mind for them. [*Harmony* 14:66] Instead, they persistently continued to look for a Messiah who would function according to their own designs and political purposes. They wanted a political revolutionary

---

27 Matthew 11:12-15

who would overthrow the Romans. They reasoned that, should Jesus do this, their own power and influence would be greatly enhanced.[28]

Speaking of this latter class, Jesus added further words regarding their insolent attitudes, saying, "But to what should I compare this generation of people? What are they like? They're like little children sitting and playing in the marketplace. It's like when some of the children cry out to their playmates, saying, 'We played dance music on a flute, and you refused to dance. All right, so you don't want to dance! So instead we sang some mournful funeral songs, and then what happened? You refused to play along and beat your chests in sorrow. No matter what we do, you are never satisfied!'[29]

"And what does this mean?" Jesus asked the people as to the purpose of His parable. "Well," He explained, "on one hand, John the Baptist, in his lifestyle, was hardly noted for hearty eating of food and drinking wine at feasts [*Harmony* 2:5; 8:5], was he? And what did they say of him? They said, 'He has a demon dwelling in him!' All right then," Jesus continued, "the Son of Man comes and enjoys eating and drinking with people, and what do they say of Him? [*Harmony* 8:1-4; 12:111] They've said, 'Look! He is a glutton and a drunkard—a friend of tax-collectors and sinners!' Ah! What can I say, then? You are never happy, no matter what happens or what anybody does! You condemned John, who lived a rather conservative life. You have condemned Me, who has lived a more outgoing, socially-oriented life. You're never satisfied![(h)] [30]

"There is a saying, 'Wisdom is justified of all her children.'" Jesus added, "This means that you must admit that the reality—or 'wisdom'—of My observations is clearly revealed by the facts—or 'children,' so to speak—of what I've presented. Indeed, the real truth regarding this generation's negative attitude has been shown by their deeds. What hypocrisy! Because they have not been satisfied by what either John or I have done, they have missed the entire point of the true, spiritual meaning of the kingdom of heaven. Certainly, too, they have missed out on all its blessings."[(i)] [31]

> The negative attitude of many of the Jews—especially their leaders—toward the ministries of both John and Jesus was clearly

---

[28] Luke 7:29, 30

[29] Matthew 11:16, 17; Luke 7:31, 32

[30] Matthew 11:18, 19; Luke 7:33, 34

[31] Matthew 11:19; Luke 7:35

demonstrated. And, because of that attitude, they never realized the true, spiritual purpose of either John or Christ's labors. They looked for a Messiah that would meet their expectations. And when He did not do so, they rejected both John and Jesus in the process. That being the case, no matter what John taught, or Jesus preached, both ministries were, for the most part, rejected by them. [*Harmony* 14:150-154]

To prove the point He was making, Jesus began to pronounce woes upon the cities where His ministry had been most powerfully manifested, but where the people had refused to repent of their sins. He began, saying, "Shame on you, Chorazin!"—a town located near Capernaum. "Shame on you, too, Bethsaida!" Jesus continued. Bethsaida was a town located on the northern shore of the Sea of Galilee, just east of where the Jordan River enters the lake. [*Harmony* 11:141, 142][(j) 32]

"Alas!" the Lord exclaimed. "If the miraculous deeds of My ministry which have been clearly shown in your presence had also been performed in Tyre and Sidon"—two wicked, Gentile cities in Phoenicia, a number of miles to the northwest of Galilee—"they would, long before now, have sincerely repented of their sins. Yes, they would have humbled themselves by wearing uncomfortable sackcloth and throwing ashes over their heads to show their contrition! In fact, I tell you, the cities of Tyre and Sidon will have an easier time in the day of judgment than you, Chorazin and Bethsaida! [*Harmony* 11:141, 142][(k) 33]

"While I'm at it, Capernaum," Christ added, addressing the city where He had centered His work, "you think that you're the greatest of the Jewish cities here in Galilee, to be exalted even unto the heavens! You think that way, don't you? Admit it! Well, in fact, you will be cast down into the grave! And why? If the miracles which you saw performed within your city limits had been done in Sodom [Genesis 18 and 19], that evil city would still be in existence today. And because of that, I say to you, that Sodom will be treated more leniently in the judgment than you will!" [*Harmony* 11:141, 142][(l) 34]

In spite of the fact that there were many who continued to reject Him, there were those who did accept Him. The Lord, looking around Him, saw some of those who were sincerely following Him. There were His twelve disciples, and, of

---

32 Matthew 11:20, 21

33 Matthew 11:21, 22

34 Matthew 11:23, 24

course, a goodly number of the common people who were eager to listen to His words. All these were a source of great encouragement to the Lord. Becoming overwhelmed with joy regarding this really sizable group of people who were faithful to His Gospel message, Jesus broke forth in praise to God. He declared, "I praise You, My Father, Lord of all heaven and earth. I thank You for hiding, as it were, the things of the Gospel from those who think they know it all"—the so-called wise and intelligent leaders of Israel. "Instead, You have revealed the good news of the Gospel to the 'babes' of the church"—those whom the Jewish leaders thought were not intelligent enough to grasp the truth. "Yet it is they, the so-called ignorant ones, who have accepted Me! Yes, Father, their acceptance of My ministry has been very pleasing to You. Moreover, Father, everything involving the truth of the Gospel You have given to Me, My Father. That is because You know Me better than anyone else does. And likewise, I know You better than anyone else possibly could. And the knowledge that I have of You and of Your love I will give to anyone I desire should receive it. Indeed, I have given this knowledge to those here surrounding Me, who have accepted Me." That is, Jesus freely gave this knowledge of the love of God to those who openly accepted Him as the Messiah. [*Harmony* 16:105-116][35]

Standing there and listening to these words of praise were many people who yet needed to make a decision to follow Jesus. Turning to them, He pleaded with them, saying, "Please come to Me, all of you that are so tired of the legalism of the Jewish scribes—you, who are weighed down with all the foolish man-made laws and restrictions which they have loaded upon you. Come to Me and I will, at last, give you sweet rest. And, in place of that awesome burden, I will ask you to carry a new responsibility. But do not fear, for I will carefully and tenderly teach you how to bear that new burden. You see, I have only your best interest at heart, and I will not act in an arrogant, dictatorial manner when I teach you to bear the truth. No, don't be afraid, for at last, because of Me, you will find true rest for your souls! Yes, there is, as I have said, a burden you must carry when you follow Me. But, I tell you, that yoke of responsibility, compared to the horrid weight of sin and legalism which you've been bearing for so very long, is light and easy to bear, for I will bear it with you! You'll see!"[36]

---

35 Matthew 11:25-27

36 Matthew 11:28-30

## The Third Galilean Evangelistic Tour: The Mission of the Twelve Apostles < Winter to Spring, A.D. 29-30 (5/7) > (Matthew 9:36-11:1; Mark 6:7-13; Luke 9:1-6)

Looking at the large number of the people who were coming to hear Him, Jesus felt deep compassion for them. They were like sheep without a shepherd: tired, scattered, harassed, and weighted down with the burden of sin. [*Harmony* 9:4] They were filled with despair. Indeed, there were many of them who needed help, but it seemed that nobody cared. That is why Jesus said to His twelve disciples, "The potential for a large harvest of souls is very great. Yet, those who are willing to do labor for these souls are oh, so few! Therefore, please beg the Lord of the harvest to throw, as it were, more workers to go into the fields to gather the harvest of souls!" [*Harmony* 3:57; 11:133, 134][37]

Accordingly, Jesus gathered His twelve disciples around Him. And to them, He gave conquering authority to cast out demons, and to heal all manner of disease and sickness of the human body. [*Harmony* 16:65][38]

Next, Jesus sent them out in pairs to minister to those living in Galilee. Their work was to be in addition to His own ministry. This was the Lord's third missionary tour of the province. [*Harmony* 4:34; 6:18; 9:54/] It had been four or five months since the Lord's second such tour had begun, and about nine months since His first tour started. These are the names of the twelve apostles—ones who were "sent"—and their pairings. Indeed, these were the ones whom He commissioned: The first, Simon—more commonly known as Peter—and Andrew, Peter's brother. Second, James and John, the sons of Zebedee. Third, Philip and Bartholomew. Fourth, Thomas along with Matthew, the tax-collector. Fifth, James, the son of Alphaeus and Lebbeus, also named Thaddaeus—the one known as Nathanael. And sixth, Simon, the Zealot, and Judas Iscariot—who is, of course, the one who would betray Jesus. [*Harmony* 4:67-79][(m) 39]

> Up until now—six months or so since their official ordination [*Harmony* 4:67-79]—the disciples had worked as a team in close contact with Jesus. They had learned, on a first-hand basis, how to do the work of

[37] Matthew 9:36-38

[38] Matthew 10:1; Mark 6:7; Luke 9:1

[39] Matthew 10:2-4; Mark 6:7

their Master. Now the time had come for them to work for a while on their own. [*Harmony* 11:133-149]

The Lord gave the Twelve the following instructions: "For now, don't spend your time ministering to non-Jews. Neither do I want you to work in the towns of the Samaritans. Instead, your first work is to minister to those among the Jewish nation who are lost."[40]

Later on, the Lord would send His disciples to minister among non-Jews [*Harmony* 11:133-149] in addition to those of the Hebrew nationality. But on this occasion, as the ones who should already have known the truth of God, the Jews would be given the first opportunity to accept the Gospel.

Jesus continued His instructions to the apostles to preach the Gospel and heal the people. He said, "As you go about your work of ministry, preach the Word by declaring, 'Now is the time to receive the gift of salvation and be a part of the kingdom of heaven and of God.' [*Harmony* 4:2] Heal those who are sick. Raise the dead. Cleanse people of leprosy. Cast out demons. And as I, the Lord, have freely given these gifts of healing to you, discharge these services to others without any anticipation of financial remuneration. Indeed, you are not to demand money for your work so as to make a profit."[41]

Jesus added, "Neither are you to take money with you. You will not need to have gold, silver, or copper coins in your money belt. And, besides what you are wearing, you are not to take a bag with you containing a second set of clothes. And take no extra pair of sandals with you in addition to the ones you are now wearing. In fact, don't take an extra walking stick with you besides the one you already have. Also, don't even take any extra food with you. You see, if you do a faithful work, those with whom you share the Gospel and its power will provide adequate freewill gifts of clothes, food, and money to meet your needs. Again, while you are not to charge for your services, those who are helped by your ministry will freely provide all necessities for you." [*Harmony* 11:136][42]

The Lord further added, "Whenever you enter a town, first find out which one of its citizens is the most respected in that community, and stay at that person's house. Continue to use his home as a base of operations throughout your

40 Matthew 10:5, 6
41 Matthew 10:7, 8; Luke 9:2
42 Matthew 10:9, 10; Mark 6:8, 9; Luke 9:3

visit in that town. Stay there until you are ready to move on to the next village or town. This way you will not be wasting your time just visiting around, on a mere social basis, in the various homes of the community, searching for another place to stay. And, you will more readily be respected by others in each community if you are staying at the home of one who is already well respected in that area. [*Harmony* 11:137, 139][43]

"And, in doing your work of ministry, when you enter someone's home, say, 'May God's peace abide in this house!' If those living in the house accept your work of ministry, then let that salutation of peace remain with them as a blessing to them. On the other hand, should those in any home reject your ministry, or refuse to even listen to you, then your blessing of peace is to return to you. That is, don't worry about wasting your time with such people—reserve your energies and time for those who accept your message. Literally, I say, shake the dust off the bottom of your feet when your leave a certain house or city who rejects you by refusing to hear or receive you. Thus you will bear public testimony of their rejection! But, again, don't be concerned about the rejection. God will, in due course, take care of them. Indeed, it will be better for the wicked cities of Sodom and Gomorrah [Genesis 19:1-29] in the time of judgment than for that home or city that rejects your message of peace!" [*Harmony* 11:138, 140, 141][(n) 44]

> The Lord continued with His counsel. This time, though, He expanded His advice to cover not only this particular mission of the disciples but also the future missions they would have, even years into the future. In fact, His advice applies to the Lord's followers throughout the whole history of the Christian church.

He counseled them, saying, "At times during your work of ministry, things will be tough! No doubt you will think on those occasions that I have sent you out as sheep in the middle of a pack of wolves! [*Harmony* 11:135] In your work with others, I want you to use the kind of wisdom and alertness exhibited by snakes . . . but, at the same time, be as innocent as doves when it comes to the meekness of your character. However, I caution you: Watch out for those who are your enemies. They will turn you over to the city councils and the religious courts. They may even flog you in their churches for what you are preaching! On occasion, you may be forced to appear, in My behalf, before the governors of provinces, and even kings of whole nations! In these cases, you will bear a

43 Matthew 10:11; Mark 6:10; Luke 9:4

44 Matthew 10:12-15; Mark 6:11; Luke 9:5

true testimony to the power of the Gospel in your lives—to both Jews and non-Jews—thus shaming them for their clearly evil intentions.[45]

"Now, in spite of what I've just said, I don't want you to be frightened about what will happen to you when they hand you over to the authorities. Don't even be concerned as to what to say in your defense, for the Holy Spirit, sent from the Father, will tell you what words to speak at the very moment when you need something appropriate to say. Remember, it won't be you who is speaking but the Spirit who will be speaking through you, ministering in your behalf. [*Harmony* 12:39; 15:8][46]

"At times," Jesus added, "when the Gospel is being spread, the negative reaction will be terrible. A man will actually betray his own brother, sending him to death! A father will even turn in his own child! And children will rise up in opposition to their own parents, also sending them to death! At times it will appear to you that everyone in the world hates you because you are My disciples! But if you remain faithful to Me—even to the end—you will be saved in My eternal kingdom.[47]

"So then, if they persecute you in one city, move on to the next one . . . and so on. In truth, you will not be able to visit and serve every person who needs your ministry—within the church and without—before the Son of Man returns to establish His eternal kingdom. [*Harmony* 11:143; 12:39][48]

"Remember," Jesus added, "a student does not receive more honor than the teacher who taught him. Nor is a slave better than his master. Instead, it is necessary for the student to become as much as possible like his or her teacher, and the slave is to obey his or her master. Thus, if they have called Me, your Master of the church, Beelzebub" [*Harmony* 7:3]—the master of demons—"then just imagine what they will say about you who are merely My followers, as members of the church! But above all, I do not want you to be afraid of these people who will seek to kill you. No! Sooner or later the truth of God will be revealed. And, too, the evil nature of their actions, which they have tried to hide from the world, will be made clear for all to see. People may seek to suppress the truth by persecuting you, its messengers. But in the end, all such efforts will surely fail.[49]

---

45 Matthew 10:16-18
46 Matthew 10:19, 20
47 Matthew 10:21, 22
48 Matthew 10:23
49 Matthew 10:24-26

"So then," Jesus continued with His strong words of counsel, "what I've been telling you in darkness, you are to speak in the light. That is, what you, as a tiny group of just twelve disciples have learned from Me in private, will be ultimately trumpeted around the world. Yes, what I've said to you in relative secrecy, will finally be shouted, as it were, from the housetops . . . for everyone, everywhere to hear! [*Harmony* 12:34][50]

"This means, then, that you are not to be afraid at all of those who may be able to kill you in this life but are quite unable to destroy you in the life to come. The worst that they can do is to kill you! If, however, I resurrect you at the end of the world, they will not be able to touch you again! No! Don't fear them at all. Rather, if you are to fear anyone, you should fully respect God and His judgment power. For, it is He who is able, in the final judgment, to completely destroy you—both your body and your life itself—in hell-fire, if you have not been faithful to His calling![51]

"Once again," the Lord said, "don't be afraid. Are not two sparrows sold for a mere penny? And yet, as insignificant as sparrows may appear to you, not one of them falls to the earth in death, without your Father's knowledge or permission! But of course, you are much more valuable to the Father than that, so valuable that the Father keeps track of all the hairs of your head! You can see, then, that you are obviously of much, much greater worth to God than many, many sparrows. So that is why I say, don't be afraid![52]

"It logically follows that if any one of you confesses your faith in Me before the peoples of the world, I will also confess My confidence in you before My Father who dwells in heaven. On the other hand, I must warn those who deny faith in Me before the world, that I will profess no confidence in them before My Father who lives in heaven.[53]

"It is certainly sad, but nevertheless true," the Lord went on, "that the preaching of the Gospel will cause great distress in the world. Many of those who reject it will seek to destroy those who believe. Of course, you already know that when I preach the truth of the Gospel, My enemies have been seeking to kill Me. Isn't that right? Do not expect then that when you, in My footsteps,

---

50 Matthew 10:27
51 Matthew 10:28
52 Matthew 10:29-31
53 Matthew 10:32, 33

preach the Gospel, it will bring peace on the earth. No! Instead of peace, it will produce bloody warfare, so to speak. Indeed, there will be a great struggle between those who reject it and those who accept it—that is, between your enemies and you. For My preaching of the Gospel has been causing—and will continue to cause—people to make decisions that have been turning even close members of families against each other.[54]

"Yes, My ministry will result, in some cases, in people making decisions that will turn sons against fathers, daughters against mothers, and daughters-in-law against mothers-in-law, and so forth. In fact, in many situations, a man's worst enemies will be members of his own family! So be careful! Those who love their mother or father more than Me, are really not worthy of me! Furthermore, those who love their own sons and daughters more than Me, are also not worthy of Me! And why is this? It is because when it comes to choosing between one's family and Me, My true followers must follow Me! Yes, those who are not willing to bear their cross of commitment to Me—even to the extent of the possible loss of family relationships—are really not worthy of Me.[55]

"In summary then," Jesus concluded, "those who seek to preserve their life by rejecting Me, will ultimately lose it anyway in the day of judgment. And, those who are willing to die for Me, will, in the end, receive eternal life. Yes, those who serve Me by following your teachings whatever the cost, will in the end find it to have been worth it all."[56]

> It is certainly true that throughout the course of Christian history there have been many examples of situations that demonstrate the truthfulness of these heavy counsels of the Lord. Many families have been divided and even torn apart when the call of the Gospel has been accepted or rejected by family members.

"But don't worry," Jesus went on, "for it is also true that those who accept what you preach and thus are kind to you, will in effect be accepting Me. And of course, those who accept Me, are in reality accepting the Father who has sent Me. To make a comparison, it is like in the old days when there were those who were kind and friendly to prophets. Such people did these kind deeds to the prophets for no other reason than the fact that they were prophets! And in those cases,

---

54 Matthew 10:34

55 Matthew 10:35-38

56 Matthew 10:39

such people received special blessings from God through the prophets as a 'thank you' for the kindnesses shown to them. [2 Kings 4:8-17] Likewise, if people show respect and kindness to any true disciple of Mine—such as you—just because you are My disciple, a special blessing from God will rest upon each one of them. In fact, all the kindnesses shown to the least of My faithful followers—even including the small act of giving you a cup of cold water to drink—will be favorably recognized by God. They will be rewarded to the same extent if they have shown this kind of favor to a child. Yes, in the judgment, such people will receive a special reward for that simple courtesy. Thus I can assure you that those who are good to you will be rewarded with appreciative kindness at the time of the judgment."[57]

After finishing giving these various instructions and counsels to His twelve disciples, Jesus left the area and continued to teach and proclaim the Gospel in the cities of the province of Galilee. But the Twelve went through some other cities of the province, trumpeting the truth of the Gospel everywhere, declaring that all men should repent of their sins. They cast out many demons. In addition, they anointed many sick people with oil, which resulted in every one of them being healed. [*Harmony* 9:1, 2; 10:87/; 16:65][58]

## The Lord's Second Rejection at Nazareth
## < Spring, A.D. 30 (5/7) >
## (Matthew 13:54-58; Mark 6:1-6)

In the course of the Lord's travels throughout Galilee, He came once more to Nazareth, His home town. This was His second official trip there, the first had been just less than a year before. That initial visit had gone very badly! [*Harmony* 4:4-10] His disciples met with Him there on this second occasion. On one particular Sabbath during this visit to Nazareth, Jesus taught in the local synagogue.[59]

Many people there that day were perplexed by His teaching. They were also puzzled by the miracles which they had heard He had performed elsewhere. They said many accusatory things against Him, including, "Where did this Man acquire all this knowledge of the Scriptures?" "How did He become so wise?" "How is it that He is able to perform so many great miracles as a demonstration

---

57 Matthew 10:40-42

58 Matthew 11:1; Mark 6:12, 13; Luke 9:6

59 Matthew 13:54; Mark 6:1, 2

of His power?" "Why, is not this the local carpenter—even the son of another carpenter—that we have known for so long?" "Is He not the son of Mary, and the brother of James, Joses, Judas, and Simon?" "Are these not His sisters whom we know among us?" [*Harmony* 4:6][(o)][60]

They were offended that a common person, like one of them as they supposed, would possess such ability and demonstrate an apparently divine power in His life. Further, they were upset that Jesus did not show any particular favoritism toward them. In short, they felt slighted. Moreover, they were jealous of His miracle-working power! Knowing their feelings toward Him, the Savior observed wryly, "For some unexplained reason, a prophet is honored everywhere he goes . . . except in his own hometown, among his relatives and immediate family!" Indeed, with some of His own family unsure that He was the Messiah [*Harmony* 11:2, 3], it was not surprising that others in Nazareth doubted the veracity of His ministry.[61]

Because of the town's overall negative, skeptical attitude toward Him [*Harmony* 4:10], Jesus did not perform any great miracle among them, except to heal a few people upon whom He had laid His hands. Not surprisingly, His own hometown's basic rejection of His ministry was a source of great amazement to the Lord. And in the final analysis He had no real choice but to move on to the other villages of Galilee, sadly leaving Nazareth behind. [*Harmony* 3:62][62]

## The Execution of John the Baptist
## < Spring, A.D. 30 (5/7) >
## (Matthew 14:1-4, 6-12; Mark 6:14-29; Luke 9:7-9)

Nearly a year before, Herod Antipas, the tetrarch—or ruler—of Galilee and Peraea, had had John the Baptist arrested and thrown into prison. There John sat, bound in chains. [*Harmony* 3:69-71] The reason for John's imprisonment was that he had had a dispute with Herod over his marital situation. The tetrarch had seduced and married Herodias, the divorced wife of Herod's half-brother, Philip. To accomplish this, Herod had divorced his first wife, the daughter of Aretas, the king of Arabia. Thus, both Herod and Herodias had living spouses whom they

---

60 Matthew 13:54-56; Mark 6:2, 3

61 Matthew 13:57; Mark 6:3, 4

62 Matthew 13:58; Mark 6:5, 6

had divorced. This was contrary to the moral principles of the law. [Leviticus 18:16] And, as a Jew, Herod knew better.[63]

John the Baptist had publicly criticized Herod for this illicit affair, which had become a big scandal throughout the entire nation of Israel. Indeed, John was quite bold in his denunciation of the whole situation, declaring to Herod, "It is not lawful, based on Scriptural principle [Leviticus 18:16], for you to have married your brother's wife the way you did!"[64]

Accordingly, Herodias, embarrassed by John's condemnations, harbored a deep grudge against him. She passionately desired to have the imprisoned John executed. However, she was unable to devise a way to accomplish this purpose. This was because Herod, even though he had had John arrested, was actually afraid of the Baptist! He knew that John was a righteous and holy man. Therefore he refused to have John killed. In fact, he actually protected him while in prison. Furthermore, a bit surprisingly, Herod even enjoyed listening to what John had to say! After some time, Herod wanted to release John, but was perplexed as to how to accomplish this because of Herodias's vendetta against the Baptist. The tetrarch did everything he could to protect John from Herodias's evil, murderous plans.[65]

However, at last, Herodias saw a great opportunity to fulfill her driving passion of having John murdered. She well knew Herod's ego and vanity. So, on Herod's birthday, she invited his lords, army generals, and many of the leading men of Galilee to a party in the tetrarch's honor. Next, Herodias had her daughter come before the king and dance for him. Herod and the guests, who were reclining at the dinner table, were captivated by the sensual performance. Then the tetrarch rashly promised the girl, "Whatever you ask of me, I will give it to you." The girl did not respond. So once more—but this time with even greater insistence—the king promised, with an oath, declaring, "I really mean it! Whatever you ask, I will give it to you—even up to half my kingdom!"[66]

The girl went out of the room to ask her mother, "What is it that I should ask for?"[67]

---

63 Matthew 14:3; Mark 6:17

64 Matthew 14:4; Mark 6:18

65 Mark 6:19, 20

66 Matthew 14:6, 7; Mark 6:21-23

67 Mark 6:24

Herodias gloating, answered with shockingly clear instructions, "You are to say, 'I want the severed head of John the Baptist brought to me on a platter!'"[68]

Quickly returning to Herod, the girl callously demanded, "I want, right away, the head of John the Baptist on a platter!"[69]

Herod was extremely upset because of her ruthless request. But because he had twice made his promise in front of his many guests, he was forced to comply with her demand. So Herod immediately sent an executioner to bring to him the head of John. The executioner went and beheaded John in his prison cell. He brought John's head on a platter and gave it to the girl. The girl then gave it to her mother.[70]

When John's disciples heard what had happened to their beloved leader, they came and took the headless body of John and buried him in a tomb. They also found Jesus and informed Him about the tragedy that had befallen the Baptist. [*Harmony* 8:5, 20-23; 9:2; 10:72/][71]

Some time later, Herod heard of the ministry of Jesus and of how His fame was spreading all over Galilee. The king declared, "I beheaded John. But who is this Man that I hear so much about? I'll tell you what I think: This Man, Jesus, is John the Baptist raised from the dead. That is why He is such a worker of miracles." Then he asked his advisors, "Who do you think this Man, Jesus, is?" [*Harmony* 12:86/][72]

His advisors gave their opinions. Some said, "We agree that he is John the Baptist raised from the dead! That is why He is able to work all these miracles." But others suggested, "He is Elijah!" [Malachi 4:5, 6] Even others said, "He is a prophet—like one of the prophets of the old days."[73]

After considering the matter for some time, Herod became convinced that Jesus was really the resurrected John the Baptist. He kept saying to those around him, "Yes, I am convinced that He is John, the one whom I beheaded! He has risen from the dead! That is why he is such a miracle-worker!" To satisfy himself

---

68 Matthew 14:8; Mark 6:24
69 Matthew 14:8; Mark 6:25
70 Matthew 14:9-11; Mark 6:26-28
71 Matthew 14:12; Mark 6:29
72 Matthew 14:1, 2; Mark 6:14; Luke 9:7, 9
73 Mark 6:15; Luke 9:7, 8

regarding the matter, Herod put forth special efforts to see Jesus for himself, but he was unable to make such an arrangement. Some months later, though, he would get his wish. [*Harmony* 10:48, 49; 17:78-81][74]

**Supplementary Notes:**

**(a) [8:1]** I find it hard to believe that Matthew actually invited the scribes and Pharisees to attend his feast. It seems logical, then, that they just showed up to cause trouble. Accordingly, in the *Harmony*, I expressed it as thus. Apparently, they could be quite intrusive!

**(b) [8:3]** (See above.)

**(c) [8:9]** Matthew says that Jairus's daughter was already dead, while both Mark and Luke say she was near death. I followed Mark and Luke's account as being the most likely situation. However, of the three Gospel recorders—Matthew, Mark, and Luke—only Matthew was actually there when the event took place. Therefore it is surprising that *he* would be the one who was wrong in his recollection! Nevertheless, that appears to be the case.

**(d) [8:10]** As an aside, it is of some interest to note that Jairus's daughter was just 12 years old when she died (*Harmony* 8:9), and the woman was suffering from her disease for the same 12 years! For the daughter of Jairus, then, 12 years was such a very *short* time, while, for the woman, suffering for same 12 years was such a very *long* time!

**(e) [8:15]** Mark declares that a number of people reported the death of the girl, while Luke says there was only one. I went with Mark's account.

**(f) [8:18]** See *Harmony* 2:58/ for a further explanation of the Aramaic language.

**(g) [8:27]** These verses from Matthew are a bit difficult to interpret and translate. After due consideration as to their meaning, I am comfortable with the way I interpreted these verses in the *Harmony*, considering it to be the most logical meaning of what of the Lord was saying.

**(h) [8:30]** Regarding the Jews' negative attitude toward the ministries of John the Baptist and Jesus, Luke's account says that the Lord addressed them *directly* as "ye" (KJV), Matthew's account says Jesus addressed them *indirectly* as

---

[74] Matthew 14:2; Mark 6:16; Luke 9:9

"they" (KJV). I followed Matthew's account. However, in the amplification of the text in the *Harmony* (the last three sentences of the text), I used the word *"you,"* as though Jesus was addressing the Jews directly. This way, I was able to use the impact of *both* accounts in my interpretation.

**(i) [8:31]** For me, the meaning of the phrase, "wisdom is justified of all her children" (Matthew 11:19; Luke 7:35, KJV), is tough to explain. I am satisfied that I arrived at the most reasonable explanation of its intent.

**(j) [8:32]** This concept, even in detail, is repeated in *Harmony* 11:141, 142. While this may be a record of the same event, I take the position that Jesus is repeating Himself here, stating the same thing in another place and under different circumstances.

**(k) [8:33]** (See above.)

**(l) [8:34]** (See **Note "j"** above.)

**(m) [8:39]** Refer to *Harmony* 4:67-79 for a more detailed description of each of these disciples.

**(n) [8:44]** The Lord's injunction regarding *shaking the dust off their feet* seems quite harsh! Again, as I indicated in my interpretation, the Lord will judge such people who reject the Gospel. We are not to be *overly* concerned about them. In my opinion, we would never be able to function adequately if we were to be obsessively worried about *every single* person who has rejected the truth that we have presented to them. Thus, the Lord gave this command to save His followers much agony over being rejected when presenting the truth to others. Such workers are to allow the Lord to bear the major portion of that burden! Instead, the Lord's disciples are to focus their attention and interest mainly upon those who *have* accepted the truth. I think that anyone who has worked with people in this way would readily agree with the point I made in my interpretation. (I should add, however, that this principle the Lord mentioned here does not apply to those of one's own family and friendships—those with whom one has a close, abiding relationship. These, of course, need to be worked with on a continual basis.)

**(o) [8:60]** See *Harmony* 7:1; 11:1-4 for more about the brothers of Jesus. Here, however, we are told that Jesus had sisters as well. As to whether these sisters were younger than Jesus (the children of Mary), or older (the children of Joseph from a previous marriage) is unknown.

# Chapter Nine

## The Later Galilean Ministry of Jesus: Trouble in Galilee—
**From the Feeding of the 5,000, to the "Bread of Life" Teaching**

### (Just Before the Passover, Spring, A.D. 30)

### The Feeding of the Five Thousand
### < Spring, A.D. 30 5/7) >
### (Matthew 14:13-22; Mark 6:30-45; Luke 9:10-17; John 6:1-15)

It was the springtime of the year, when the Jews were soon to celebrate the Passover. The apostles gathered around Jesus to report to Him regarding all the things that they had been doing and teaching. For some time now, they had been working on their own. As they had been visiting and ministering two-by-two [*Harmony* 8:37-58], the disciples had experienced many exciting things which they were now sharing with Him.[1]

After listening to the reports, the Savior knew that His disciples—now also known as "apostles," or "sent ones"—desperately needed a break for a while. They had been very busy laboring for so many people who were coming and going that they hardly had time to rest—or even to eat! Of course, Jesus Himself was weary from His own work. Added to this, the Lord was greatly saddened by news of the recent execution of John the Baptist. [*Harmony* 8:63-71] Considering all these things, Jesus made a recommendation to His disciples: "Why not come with Me to a more deserted place and rest for a while?" So they secretly left by boat for a more secluded spot on the other side of the Sea of Galilee—also called Tiberias—where they could rest. There, near the town Bethsaida on the northeastern coast of the lake, they found a good place to relax. [*Harmony* 9:4][2]

---

1 Mark 6:30; Luke 9:10; John 6:4

2 Matthew 14:13; Mark 6:31, 32; Luke 9:10; John 6:1

However, the massive crowds saw that they were leaving their previous location, and clearly recognized who He was. They followed Jesus and His disciples, for they had seen many of His miracles of healing the sick. Some even ran by foot from the various towns and villages to present themselves, en masse, before the Lord and His apostles. In fact, many of the people, anticipating where He might be going, swarmed to the spot even before Jesus and His disciples arrived there themselves! The Lord and the apostles disembarked and seated themselves on a hillside and watched as the multitudes continued to crowd around them.[3]

> From a human perspective—and certainly from the perspective of the disciples—the Lord's ministry in Galilee was a booming success. For the past 12 months, Jesus had ministered to untold numbers in that province. Huge crowds had followed Him. But the Lord knew better. Yes, many people were following Him . . . but for the most part, they were following Him for the wrong reasons. They were looking to Jesus to be a conquering Messiah to break the yoke of bondage of the Romans. They were obsessed with this goal. The spiritual aspects of the Lord's teachings and ministry were often ignored. Even regarding the Master's miracles there were problems. The people largely looked at Christ's miracles from a purely *physical* standpoint. The healing of the body was the only thing that counted with most of them. In doing so, they missed the spiritual meaning of the miracles—that they illustrated how the Lord was seeking to *heal their souls*. Just recently Jesus had voiced His grave concerns regarding this misunderstanding. [*Harmony* 8:27] Now the time had come for the Master to take control of the problem and address it directly. Jesus would soon perform another miracle, but this time the miracle would be different from any He had previously wrought.[1]
>
> Moreover, the Lord had been in conflict with the Jewish leaders. [*Harmony* 8:3] There was almost no end to the trouble they had caused Him. The worst part, however, was the high level of influence these leaders still enjoyed with the common people, many of whom were presently following the Lord. Thus, considering the fact that a sizeable number of the people were following Jesus for the wrong reasons, and that the Jewish leaders were constantly challenging the Lord's work—often

---

3 Matthew 14:14; Mark 6:33, 34; Luke 9:11; John 6:2, 3

> in front of the people—it was clear to the Lord that He had to confront both the leaders and the common people regarding the true nature of His ministry and His miracles. There was, of course, a high risk that when the people clearly understood the real purpose of His work, many of them might cease to follow Him altogether. Nevertheless, this was a risk that Jesus had to take, no matter what the consequences might be.[2]

Even though bone weary, when Jesus saw the multitudes coming to Him, He was filled with compassion toward them, for they were as sheep without a shepherd, wandering about without a true purpose in life. Thus, any thoughts of resting had to be scrapped. [*Harmony* 9:2] The Lord by now was completely focused on ministering to the people. Knowing what He was going to do later, the Lord, testing one of His disciples, asked Philip, "Where do you suppose we could buy enough bread to feed all these people?" [*Harmony* 8:37] If any of the disciples would know where to purchase enough food, it was Philip, for he was from Bethsaida. [*Harmony* 2:59][4]

Philip answered, "Finding enough bread to feed each one of them with just a little morsel is hard enough. But to buy that much bread would cost at least nine-months' salary! We certainly don't have that kind of money on hand!"(a) [5]

Dropping the subject for a while, Jesus began to teach the crowd many things regarding the kingdom of God. As He usually did, He healed a number of the physically sick among them. The hours passed and evening was fast approaching. The twelve disciples said to Jesus, "There is not much to eat in this deserted place, and the hour is late. We ought to send the people away so that they can scavenge for food in the fields, or perhaps purchase food to eat in one of the surrounding villages. As You can see, they have nothing here to eat. Lord, have them stay overnight in one of the villages nearby."[6]

But Jesus said to them, "They have no need to find their own food! Instead, I want all of you to feed them!"[7]

---

4 Matthew 14:14; Mark 6:34; John 6:5, 6

5 John 6:7

6 Matthew 14:14, 15; Mark 6:34-36; Luke 9:11, 12

7 Matthew 14:16; Mark 6:37; Luke 9:13

"But," the disciples protested, "how can we do that? In the unlikely event that we were to find enough food to feed all these people, it would cost at least two-thirds of a year's wages to pay for it! There's no way we can do that!"[8]

Jesus answered, "How many loaves of bread do you think you might find within this crowd? Go and find out!" Of course, Jesus knew that they would find very little, but He already had a plan in mind.[9]

Presently, they reported back to Him. Andrew, Simon Peter's brother, speaking on behalf of the rest of the disciples, said, "We have found a little boy here who has five small barley loaves and just two fish. That's it! Of course, short of buying food for them, that is hardly enough to feed all these people! There are no fewer than 5,000 men here. And, counting the women and children, there must be, at least, 15,000 hungry people! Master, how can we feed so many people with so little food? It's quite impossible!"[10]

"Bring the loaves and fish to Me!" was the Master's simple response. He further commanded, "Have the people sit down on the grass in groups of 50 or 100!"There was a large area of grass upon which the masses could seat themselves, so the disciples obeyed and the crowd complied with the Lord's command.[11]

Then, taking the bread and the fish, Jesus looked to heaven and blessed the food. After breaking the loaves and the fish into smaller pieces, He handed them to the disciples. In turn, they distributed the morsels to the entire multitude, as much as each desired. And everyone ate until they were filled to complete satisfaction! In fact, there was so much food on hand that there was quite a bit left over. "Gather up the remainder of the pieces. Let nothing be wasted," Jesus commanded. So they collected twelve handbaskets of left-over pieces of the barley bread and fish! Again, the number of those who ate that day was 5,000 men, plus women and children—no doubt a total of about 15,000 individuals! [*Harmony* 9: 26; 10:27-32, 39, 40][12]

> What was the Lord's purpose in feeding the 5,000 that day? He wanted to feed their hungry bodies, but beyond that, He had a much deeper purpose in mind. He wanted to teach the disciples and the crowd an

---

8 Mark 6:37; Luke 9:13

9 Mark 6:38

10 Matthew 14:17; Mark 6:38; Luke 9:13, 14; John 6:8-10

11 Matthew 14:18, 19; Mark 6:39, 40; Luke 9:14, 15; John 6:10

12 Matthew 14:19-21; Mark 6:41-44; Luke 9:16, 17; John 6:11-13

important *spiritual* lesson. [*Harmony* 4:62/2-7] The disciples were soon to face what would appear to them to be an impossible task: to share the Gospel with the whole world. [*Harmony* 18:88] Accordingly, just as the pieces of food were multiplied, He wanted them to realize that the power of God would "multiply" the message of the Gospel, so that anyone who wanted to "eat," as it were, the truth of the kingdom of heaven, could certainly be "filled." Indeed, lives would be changed forever by the power of God. As the disciples shared in the distribution of the food, so they would also share in the distribution of the Gospel message. They were to be organized in their efforts of spreading the Gospel, just as the crowd was requested to sit in groups of 50 or 100. They were also to understand that when the Gospel is shared, it will multiply even more, even beyond their greatest dreams. There would be enough "left over," so to speak, to "feed" even more people with the "food" of the Gospel. The final result would be that the Gospel would go into the whole world, and that there would be many who would be ready for the Lord's Second Coming. Unfortunately, neither the disciples nor the people there that day grasped the spiritual emphasis of the Lord's mighty miracle. Their minds were focused solely on the miracle of the *literal* bread and fish! [*Harmony* 10:31]

At that point, the people, awed by the enormity and implications of the miracle they had just experienced, said to one another, "This Man is certainly the Prophet—the Messiah—the One who is to come into the world!" [*Harmony* 8:27, 27/] The Lord could sense that they were about to seize Him and proclaim Him King. At once the Master demanded that His disciples go back the short distance to Bethsaida, get in the boat which they had left there, and return to the other side of the lake. He stayed behind to dismiss the crowd. [*Harmony* 14:21/][13]

Why did Jesus send the multitude away? Obviously, the crowd, along with the disciples, did not comprehend the spiritual truths the Lord was trying to teach them in the performance of this miracle. They saw its value only as it pertained to *literal* bread and fish. They saw that if Jesus possessed such power, there was no telling how many mighty things He would be able to do. For example, the Lord could give soldiers just a morsel of bread that could miraculously sustain them during long

---

13 Matthew 14:22; Mark 6:45; John 6:14, 15

periods of warfare. This way, they could easily fight the hated Roman occupiers of Israel and Galilee. And should any be injured in battle, the Lord could heal them . . . or even resurrect those who were killed! The possibilities were endless! To make Him King seemed such a logical thing to do. Victory over Rome and the possibility of international greatness that would naturally follow were just a few miracles away! They saw the Messiah only as a conquering king, not as the spiritual leader He truly was. Of course, Jesus would have none of that. Indeed, His purpose on earth was spiritual, not political. Jesus had hoped the people would grasp the deep spiritual purpose of the miracle, but they failed to do so. That is why He had to send the people away, much to the frustration of both the crowd and the disciples . . . as well as to the disappointment of Jesus Himself. [*Harmony* 9:46/2]

## Jesus Walks on Water!
## < Spring, A.D, 30 (5/7) >
## (Matthew 14:23-33; Mark 6:46-52; John 6:15-21)

After dismissing the crowd, Jesus went higher into the mountain to be alone. There He continued to pray deep into the night. [*Harmony* 4:67] Meanwhile, the disciples, after entering the boat, were in the middle of the lake sailing toward Capernaum on its northeastern shore. [*Harmony* 7:61-64][14]

Suddenly a storm arose, causing the boat to be tossed about by a strong, contrary wind and huge waves. While praying a good distance away from them on land, Jesus was shown the disciples struggling with the boat, rowing just to stay afloat in the churning waves. They fought the wind and waves with the boat oars for about three, to three and a half miles. It was at the fourth watch of the night—somewhere between 3 and 6 a.m.[(b)] [(c)] [15]

So Jesus went out to meet the disciples on the lake by literally walking on the water! When all the disciples saw someone approaching them, they were understandably greatly disturbed. Then it seemed as though the One walking on the water might pass them by. They did not, at first, recognize the Person walking toward them. [*Harmony* 9:26] Instead, they gasped, "It's a ghost—a phantom!"

14 Matthew 14:23, 24; Mark 6:46, 47; John 6:15-17

15 Matthew 14:24, 25; Mark 6:48; John 6:18, 19

And they continued to scream out in great fear, thinking—foolishly—that death, in the form of a ghostly spirit, was coming to take them to a certain doom![16]

But at that instant, Jesus reassuringly cried out to them, "Be filled with courage! I AM! Don't be afraid!" The disciples immediately recognized His voice. They now knew the One walking on the water was their Master.[17]

> When Jesus used the phrase, "I AM!" He clearly indicated to them that He was God. For indeed, this was a phrase attributed solely to divinity. [Exodus 3:13, 14; *Harmony* 11:51-55, 76, 77; 16:22]

Obviously, the disciples were comforted somewhat by the words of Jesus. So it was, with a burst of confidence, that Peter called out, "If it's really You, Lord, command me to walk out to You on the water!"[18]

Jesus responded, "Come!" Accordingly, Peter clambered over the edge of the boat, and began to walk on the water to where the Savior was standing! But as the powerful wind continued to blow, waves rose in front of Peter.[19]

Becoming very fearful once again, Peter began to sink into the raging water. "Lord! save me!" the disciple cried out in utter panic.[20]

At that moment, Jesus reached out His hand and took hold of Peter. The Master said to him, "'Little faith,' tell Me, why did you begin to doubt?" [*Harmony* 5:65; 7:61-64; 12:51][(d)] [21]

> Here, Jesus called Peter "little faith." The Lord's use of this "nickname" was to underscore to Peter—and the other disciples—how important it was for them use faith and trust in Him at all times—especially when He was actually in their presence.

Together, Jesus and Peter walked on the water over to the boat. When they reached it, the winds stopped. The disciples were understandably amazed beyond measure by what they had seen. They continued to marvel at the sight. Of course, the disciples were excited to have Jesus join them in the boat. Accordingly, all

---

16 Matthew 14:25, 26; Mark 6:48-50; John 6:19

17 Matthew 14:27; Mark 6:50; John 6:20

18 Matthew 14:28

19 Matthew 14:29, 30

20 Matthew 14:30

21 Matthew 14:31

fell down and worshipped the Lord, declaring, "Certainly, there can be doubt whatsoever that You are the Son of God—even the Messiah!" They recognized their Master as God, ruler of wind and wave.[22]

And in addition to all this, as soon as Jesus entered the boat, it miraculously reached shore at exactly the place where they were originally headed![23]

It had been a day and night of amazing events. But, being caught up in all these things, the disciples still did not comprehend the true meaning of the miracle of the dividing of the loaves and fish. Why is that? Because their emotions were focused upon their own disappointment that Jesus had not allowed Himself to be declared King by the people. Their minds were closed to the true purpose of the miracle of the feeding of the 5,000.[24]

> The miracle of the Lord's walking on the water was to teach the disciples a vital lesson. But they were so disappointed that Jesus had refused to allow them to make Him King that it eluded them. They were hurting, and doubts and perplexities were rising within them. This miracle was to teach them that no matter how difficult things might appear to them, they were fully to trust in Jesus as their Master. They were to understand that faith and trust in the Lord was to remain paramount in their lives. They had to learn that though they might not at any given moment understand just why Jesus did what He did—as in this case—they still needed to trust in Him. Even though He had refused to allow the crowd pronounce Him King, the disciples were, nevertheless, to continue to have total, unwavering faith in Him.

## The "Bread of Life" Teaching[(e)]
## < Spring, A.D. 30 (5/7) >
## (Matthew 14:34-36; Mark 6:53-56; John 6:22-7:1)

Jesus and the disciples arrived on land at place called Gennesaret. As soon they disembarked, the people of the area immediately recognized that it was Jesus arriving in their midst. Obviously excited at the sight of the Lord, they sent word to their surrounding neighborhoods that the Miracle Worker was among them. People swarmed to the location, especially those who desired to have Jesus heal them. Some of the sick were carried on beds, so that the Lord would cure

22 Matthew 14:32, 33; Mark 6:51; John 6:21

23 John 6:21

24 Mark 6:52

them. As Jesus moved through the market places and streets of their towns and cities—and in some cases, even in the fields outside of the towns—the ailing ones were brought to Him. They begged of the Savior to allow them to just touch the hem of His garment so that they might be healed. And those who did touch His clothes were, indeed, completely cured![(f) 25]

Meanwhile, some of the crowd from the previous day or so—those who had witnessed the miracle of the loaves and fish [*Harmony* 9:12]—came back looking for Jesus at the same location where the miracle had taken place. They expected to find Him nearby, for they knew that the disciples, traveling without the Lord, had taken the only little boat. But Jesus was nowhere to be found. All this was puzzling to the people searching for the Lord. They did not know that Jesus had indeed left the area, walking on water! [*Harmony* 9:14-16][26]

Determined to find the Lord, they began to look for Him in earnest. Even after a thorough search Jesus was still nowhere to be found. [*Harmony* 9:14] Boarding a few small boats that had beached nearby from Lake Tiberius—that is, Galilee—as the result of the previous night's storm [*Harmony* 9:15; 11:133/], they sailed across the lake, a few miles to the west to the town of Capernaum. They went there, for it was known that this town was the headquarters of the Lord's ministry. Perhaps Jesus had somehow gone to that city, they thought. And, indeed, by the time they landed there, Jesus and His disciples had already arrived at the place. In fact, Jesus was teaching in the local synagogue, and there the people finally found him. At that point, they heard from the disciples about the amazing events involving the storm and the Lord's walking on the surface of the sea.[(g) 27]

Coming up to Jesus, these people sought to find out more details regarding this incredible event. They hinted at the miracle by asking Him, "Teacher, when was it that You arrived here? And how did You get here?" Maybe, they reasoned, He would give them a stirring account of the walking-on-the-water miracle![(h) 28]

But, rather, what followed that day was a dialogue between Jesus and the people—a group composed of the Jewish leaders and many of His

---

[25] Matthew 14:34-36; Mark 6:53-56
[26] John 6:22
[27] John 6:23-25, 59
[28] John 6:25

Galilean followers. This discussion would have a far-reaching impact upon the future ministry of Jesus as well as His relationship with the people who lived in Galilee. In this dialogue—a two-sided discussion between the Master and the people—Jesus emphasized the *true* nature of His miracles. He wanted His listeners to understand that the primary purpose of His miracles was the teaching of *spiritual* truths [*Harmony* 4:62/2-7; 9:12/; 11:80/], rather than the immediate *physical* impact of the miracles upon those who either experienced them or observed them. Understandably, the people were much more interested in the physical aspects of the miracles—such as the demon-possessed who were freed [*Harmony* 4:23-26], the paralyzed who could walk [*Harmony* 4:42-48], plentiful food provided [*Harmony* 9:7-12], and so forth. Their spiritual meaning—that is, that the power of the devil could be broken in people's lives—was not as apparent to them. [*Harmony* 4:62/3] For example, the Lord wanted the people to note that the spiritually crippled could now "walk" in victorious living [*Harmony* 4:62/5], the spiritually blind could now "see" the truth of the Gospel [*Harmony* 6:10-14], and the Gospel could be spread dramatically to the world. [*Harmony* 9:12/] To make His point as powerfully as he could, the Lord, through His dialogue with the people that day, made it clear that the miracle that was *most important* for the people to experience was the miracle of personal conversion. [*Harmony* 9:30] The Savior further indicated that the only physical miracle that actually counted, in the long run, was the resurrection of the dead at the end the world—a *physical* miracle that would involve those who had previously experienced the *spiritual* miracle of conversion. [*Harmony* 9:37] Jesus strongly emphasized the need for His followers to maintain a personal relationship with Him in order that His spiritual miracle-working powers would continue to dwell within them, transforming their characters into His likeness. [*Harmony* 9:41, 42] But, shamefully, the reaction of most of those who listened to the Lord's teaching that day was a sad mixture of misunderstanding, hostility, and even blatant sarcasm. [*Harmony* 9:43]

Ignoring their implied request for details regarding the miracle of His walking on water, Jesus began to answer the people by declaring, "It is an absolute fact that you seek Me, not because you saw confirming miracles—which are actually signs of My divine power to heal your souls from sin—but because you have stuffed your stomachs with this so-called 'miracle' bread. And you have come back to Me for more *physical* bread of this sort to eat!"[29]

> Here, the Lord made it clear that the recent miracle of the feeding of the 5,000 was to have served mainly as an *illustration* of how He was able to satisfy the *spiritual* needs of the people through the power of the Gospel which He was able to distribute to all those willing to receive it.

The Lord added, "So then, instead of toiling for food which is fresh one day, and is stale the next—such as the bread and fish I fed you the other day—put your effort in laboring for the 'bread' of eternal life—that is, the power of the Gospel—which will satisfy your souls for all eternity! This is the bread that I, the Son of Man, will give to you, for God, the Father, has anointed the Son of Man to fulfill that exact purpose." [*Harmony* 2:34/2, 4:62/1-7; 9:28/][30]

> Here, Jesus challenged the thinking of the people. They saw in Jesus merely the power to work *miracles of the flesh*. Again, they figured that this kind of power could be used by the nation of Israel to conquer its political foes, such as Rome. [*Harmony* 9:13/] They did not realize that Jesus had worked the miracle of the feeding of the thousands primarily to teach them that He wished to heal their souls from sin and satisfy their spiritual hunger, and that, through them, He would also be able to heal the souls of many around the world. [*Harmony* 9:12/] Again, they focused upon the physical miracle itself, rather than upon its spiritual meaning: that is, the Messiah, the Healer of the soul, was able miraculously to change their lives, and, through them, change the lives of many others. By the Lord's strong declaration, He tried to get the people to switch their emphasis away from the physical miracles which He had performed, and to seek rather the transformation of the heart of which the physical miracle was only an illustration.

After hearing the Lord's statement that they needed to labor for a different kind of food, the people thought for a moment. They were used to being instructed in the details of living rather legalistic lives—to do this, or to not do that. Perhaps, they thought, there was some new thing they had to do in order to be saved. So, changing the subject for a just a moment, they asked, "What thing

29 John 6:26
30 John 6:27

is it that we need to do in order that we might more effectively work the works of God?"[31]

Jesus answered, "*This* is the 'work' of God: Believe on the One whom God has sent!" Of course, the "One" in whom they should believe was Him.[32]

> In effect, Jesus was saying: "Instead of working to be good—following some prescribed system of laws and restrictions—you should 'work' at believing in Me. If you put the same amount of effort into trusting in Me as you do in trying to be good—as you have been taught in your synagogues to do—your belief in Me would enable you to *be* good . . . and to *do* good!"[1]
>
> The Lord's main point was that the people needed to have faith in *Him* as a Person and a Savior to be able to change their spiritual lives miraculously, as opposed to being excited about His physical miracles, as dramatic as they might be. Of course, belief in His physical miracles was fine, but faith in the deeply spiritual aspects of His ministry was truly vital to their souls.[2]

But ignoring these pointed words of Jesus, the people returned to the subject of physical miracle-working by responding, "All right, if you would have us believe in *You*, what dramatic physical miracle can You perform that would convince us to do so? What miracles do You perform that show that You have really come from God, as You claim? [*Harmony* 9:32] For example, our fathers, while in the wilderness, ate manna—the miraculous food which Moses provided for them. As it is written, 'He gave them bread to eat out of the heavens.' [Loosely based on Psalm 78:24 and Nehemiah 9:15] In other words, can You do better than what Moses did? Are You a more powerful miracle worker than he?" [*Harmony* 12:150/4][33]

> Tragically, the people misapplied the Lord's statement regarding His working of spiritual miracles. They still clung tenaciously to the belief that the Lord was talking about His ability to work miracles of the flesh. They simply ignored the obvious fact that the Lord was talking about miracles of the *heart*, and not of the flesh![1]

---

31 John 6:28
32 John 6:29
33 John 6:30, 31

> Yes, it was nothing short of incredible to hear what the people were saying. They had already seen Jesus work mighty miracles! Why would they demand even more miracles? In their twisted thinking, it was as though the Lord was to be in competition with Moses. In effect, they were saying: "Can You work greater miracles than Moses in order to prove Your supposed calling that You have come from God? Don't forget, Moses fed hundreds of thousands of people with manna, six days a week, for 40 years. You fed just a few thousand . . . and that was only once. Can You really do better than our father, Moses? If You really want us to believe in You as You desire, You must perform *more* impressive miracles for us than You did the other day. And You must perform them repeatedly!" In short, they still did not grasp the meaning of the Lord's words. They saw only the physical miracles themselves and not their spiritual purpose and meaning. Their faith in Jesus was based solely on His ability constantly to work more and greater physical miracles in their presence. They put their faith and interest in the miracle of multiplying of a few pieces of bread and fish [*Harmony* 9:12], rather than in the *Miracle Worker* as a Person and a Savior who sought to save them from their sins.[2]

Jesus answered, "What are you talking about? Listen to this truth: First of all, it was not really Moses who provided literal manna for our fathers—it was God! You should know that! Just as surely, it is also God the Father, who in a like manner, has provided the true 'Spiritual Bread' who has come down from heaven."[34]

> Here, of course, by "Spiritual Bread" Jesus was speaking of Himself. The Lord's point was that the literal manna given by God—and not Moses—was merely *symbolic* of the spiritual bread—the life and ministry of Jesus—which the Father had provided for the salvation of the world. Again, it was God who performed the daily miracle of the manna. And it was the *same* God who provided the spiritual bread of life—that is, the work and ministry of Jesus—which the manna only symbolized. And, once more, the Lord sought to transfer the people's thinking from the mere physical miracle to the spiritual one, and encourage them to experience the power and transformation available through His own work and ministry.

---

[34] John 6:32, 33

But most of the people, in the dullness of their minds, still did not understand that Jesus was indeed speaking of Himself and the miracle of His spiritual ministry. They still thought that He was talking about literal bread—the kind baked in ovens! This would explain their short-sighted comment when they answered, "Master, forever give us this bread to eat. This way, we will not ever get hungry again!"[35]

> This response was similar to the reaction of the woman at Jacob's well when she thought Jesus was speaking about literal water as opposed to the "spiritual water" of the Gospel. [*Harmony* 3:39] So once again, the focus of the people in the synagogue in Capernaum was upon the miracle of the multiplication of *literal* bread as opposed to character-altering *spiritual* bread—that is, the power of the life and ministry of Jesus.

Frustrated by their misunderstanding, Jesus declared, "I am that Bread of Life! Don't you get it? If you eat physical bread—even bread that has been miraculously provided, as I gave you the other day—you will get hungry again. But those who come to *Me* for salvation and its miracle-working power within their souls, will never be hungry again . . . within their souls, that is. [*Harmony* 2:31] Neither will they thirst for salvation anymore! [*Harmony* 5:6] But even though you have *seen* Me and have had the opportunity to listen to Me, yet you continue to refuse to *trust* in Me and My words! No, I am not rejecting you. It is you who are rejecting Me! But, on the other hand, there have been those who *have* accepted Me," the Lord explained. "These are those who are truly My followers because they trust in Me. These are the ones whom the Father has given to Me to teach and to protect. Therefore, I can tell you, I will never reject those who come to Me with humility and faith, accepting the miracle of salvation within their lives."[36]

> Here Jesus made a clear distinction between those who trusted in Him and those who doubted Him. Those who trusted in Him—such as His disciples—had, most of the time, their primary focus on the spiritual nature of the Lord's work. But those who doubted Him continued to emphasize the physical miracles of the Lord as though they were the main—even sole—focus of His ministry. Of course it is true that even His disciples misunderstood much of what the Lord taught of the true spiritual nature of His ministry. [*Harmony* 9:24] Nevertheless, in spite

---

[35] John 6:34
[36] John 6:35-37

of their misconceptions, they were usually willing to place their trust in Him. In short, they had faith in Jesus, even though they did not always fully understand His words or His mission.

The Lord continued, "For remember, I have come down from heaven, as the 'Bread of Life,' to do the will My Father, not My own will. And this is the will of the Father: That, of those who have responded to God's call to follow Me, I will make sure that every one of them will be saved. Indeed, every single one of them I will resurrect at the end of the world. To state it again, this is the will of the Father: That all who truly listen to the Son, and accept Him as their Savior—that is, as the true 'Bread of Life'—will receive eternal life. And again, I will, *Myself*, resurrect them at the end of the world. This way, not a single one of them will be lost. Neither will anything else, I might add, be lost that the Father has given Me to be under My authority." [*Harmony* 9:28/][37]

Here, the Lord referred to the *only* real physical miracle that truly counts: the resurrection at the end of the world. *But* those who participate in that physical miracle must have *first* participated in the spiritual miracle—that is, a relationship of faith with the true Bread of Life, Jesus, who had changed their lives and given them the hope of eternal life. Indeed, the spiritual Bread—the ministry of Jesus which results in the conversion of the heart through a thorough knowledge of Him—leads to the physical "miracle bread," as it were—that is, the resurrection at the end of the world that ushers in eternity. [1 Corinthians 15:51-58; 1 Thessalonians 4:13-18; Revelation 1:18]

The Jews began to grumble among themselves regarding these powerful words of Jesus, when He said, "I am the Bread of Life who has come to you out of heaven." [*Harmony* 9:37] They complained, "Is this not a mere mortal, the son of Joseph? Don't we know both His mother and father? Then how can this Man say, 'I have come down from heaven'?" [*Harmony* 11:44/][38]

Obviously, these complainers focused solely on the Lord's humanity. They failed to grasp the reality of His divinity. [*Harmony* 1:1, 2] They ignored what they had every opportunity to know and understand, that Jesus was the true Son of God. Also, they persistently failed to comprehend the primary miraculous aspect of the Lord's work: that He

---

37 John 6:38-40

38 John 6:41, 42

> was the spiritual Bread of Life, and, that His physical miracles—such as the multiplying of the bread and fish—only symbolized His spiritual power.

Jesus responded to their complaint by saying, "Stop your grumbling among yourselves! It seems that there is not a single person listening to Me now who truly understands these things which I've been explaining to you! For, if you did, you would certainly believe in Me. But the truth is, you have not accepted Me because you have refused to respond to the Father's call. He is the One who has sent Me, and He is the One who is calling you through the voice of the Holy Spirit within your consciences. And yet, you persistently refuse to listen to Him. And," Jesus added, "those who accept Me are the ones whom I will resurrect at the end the world. Of them, it is written in the Scriptures, 'And they shall all be taught by God.' [Isaiah 54:13] Thus, because they have listened to Me, I have been able to teach them. But you have not listened to Me. And that is why I have not been able to teach you. That is also why I tell you that you must allow God, through the Spirit, to speak to you so that your preconceived opinions may be changed. Yes, you must listen to Him, and learn the real truth of the Gospel from Him. Only then can you approach Me as a true follower of Mine. But alas, you continue to refuse to do so!"[39]

> Once more, Jesus referred to the resurrection at the end of the world—the only physical miracle that truly counts. And this miracle would affect only those who, through the Holy Spirit, had truly listened to the Lord, and were willing to be changed through the power of the Gospel within their lives.

The Lord continued, "Of course, don't forget, none of you has actually seen the Father. So, then, you do not know on a firsthand basis what He wants to teach you. Nevertheless, you think you do, but you don't! Now, there is only One who has actually seen the Father. And He's the One who knows the true teaching. Yes, because He is the only One who has come directly from the presence of the Father, He is the only One who knows what the true teaching should be. Obviously then, if you would be truly wise, you would listen to Him and trust Him as opposed to your own patently false pet ideas and opinions." Of course, the One of whom Jesus was speaking—the One who had been with God—was none other than Himself![40]

---

[39] John 6:43-45

[40] John 6:46

> This part of the discussion—no doubt especially directed at the Jewish leaders in the crowd that day—is similar to the dialogue Jesus had had with Nicodemus a few years before. [*Harmony* 3:20] In that case, as in this one, Jesus made it clear that no mere human being had the knowledge or wisdom to challenge His statements, because *only* He had been in the heavens with the Father. This meant that *He* knew what He was talking about, not anyone who was, at any given moment, debating with Him.

"Therefore," Jesus went on, "it is only those who are completely willing to place their trust in what I have to teach who will receive eternal life. That is the absolute truth! Again, I am the 'Bread of Life!' Remember, your fathers who ate the manna in the wilderness [*Harmony* 9:33]—the literal bread that you consider so miraculous—well . . . they're all dead, aren't they? They did not listen to God back then, just as you are not willing to listen to Me today. And the eating of that so-called miracle manna did not impart eternal life to them, did it? Thus, the Bread that really counts is the truth of the Gospel as contained in Me and My ministry. Yes, that is the Bread that truly imparts eternal life. Indeed, that is the real Bread that came down from heaven, as opposed to the manna, which was there one day and filled with worms the next. [Exodus 16:20] Yes, it is only by trusting in Me that you can be assured of eternal life, as opposed to placing your trust in the eating of some stale crust of bread." [*Harmony* 9:28/; 16:23/2][41]

> To drive home His point, Jesus referred to the obvious fact that the ancient Jews, who had eaten the "miracle bread"—that is, the manna—were all dead. Not only were they dead, but the larger portion of them were lost for eternity. Therefore, the so-called "miracle bread" of manna did not, and could not, impart eternal life! And this was same kind of physical bread which the people of the Lord's day were clamoring to have the Savior provide for them. "So then," Jesus, in effect, argued, "why do you want more bread, as the result of physical miracles, that cannot, ever, impart eternal life? Why don't you, instead, strive for the miraculous spiritual Bread—that is, a relationship of faith with Me—which truly gives eternal life to those who seek it?"

The Lord continued, "Once again, I am the Living Bread who has come down from the Father out of heaven. If anyone 'eats' of this Bread—that is, fully accepts, by faith, My teachings—he or she will live forever. The Bread which

[41] John 6:47-50

I will give for the salvation of the world is My Flesh"—that is, the sacrifice of the Lord's life for the world on the cross. "Focus on this Bread," the Lord re-emphasized, "and not on the bread that merely fills your stomachs for a few hours. Do you see that?"[42]

The Jewish leaders debated among themselves as to what Jesus was saying. Their shocked response was, "How can this man give us His flesh to eat? Does He think we're human flesh-eaters? What foolishness!" [*Harmony* 9:28/; 11:50][43]

> Obviously Jesus wasn't talking about His *actual* flesh—or body—which they should eat! Clearly, though, He was talking about His death on the cross which would serve as a payment for the sins of all those who accepted that death by faith. Thus, this incredulous statement of the Jewish leaders regarding the eating of the Lord's *actual* flesh revealed one of two things. Either they were still totally and inexplicably ignorant of what Jesus had been saying to them, or they understood what His point was, but were trying, by ridiculing Him, to divert the attention of the common people away from the truthfulness of the Lord's words. Most likely it was the latter. In any case, they ridiculed Him, using no little sarcasm. In short, they did not want the masses to continue to follow Jesus with a renewed, spiritual understanding. Indeed, they wanted the people to reject Him just as they had done.

Jesus, ignoring their inability or outright refusal to understand the spiritual nature of His message, reiterated His point, this time making it even stronger, "It is an absolute fact when I tell you again, that unless you eat the flesh and drink the blood of the Son of Man, you shall never possess eternal life. No! Never! In other words, anyone who eats My flesh and drinks My blood now possesses eternal life, for I will resurrect that person at the end of the world. This is true because My flesh and My blood are the real food and drink that you need for your souls, not the bread that is baked in ovens—the kind which you are seeking. This means that those who eat My flesh and drink My blood are those who have an abiding relationship with Me, based upon their faith in My sacrifice for the sins of the world. Consequently, I will dwell within them and them with Me."[44]

---

42 John 6:51
43 John 6:52
44 John 6:53-56

This declaration served as a summary of everything that the Lord had been telling the people that day. First, by the use of the phrase, to "eat the flesh and drink the blood" of Jesus, the Lord, in symbol, indicated the need for all His listeners to experience a complete acceptance of and reliance upon the words and ministry of Jesus as a basis of their salvation. It also symbolized the reality of having by faith a close, personal relationship with the Savior through the power of the Holy Spirit. [Revelation 3:20] Second, Jesus referred to the only physical miracle that truly counts for eternity: the resurrection at the end of the world, which would be the result of experiencing the *true spiritual* miracle of conversion. Third, the Lord clearly stated that a reliance upon physical miracles—such as the eating of the bread and fish of recent days—was worthless, unless one had a personal relationship of faith in Him.

The Lord did not back off but said, "I am sent here to the earth by My Father, and am alive because of Him. So it will be with those who 'eat' Me—that is, have a personal, one-on-one relationship with Me. They will live the true Gospel life because of Me. This is what I meant when I said that I am the true Bread come down out of heaven, as opposed to literal bread—the manna—that our, now dead—and, by and large, lost—fathers, ate in the wilderness. As you clearly know, and as I've just said, that bread—the manna—was not able to give them eternal life. [*Harmony* 9:41] On the contrary, those who eat of this other Bread—Me—of which I've been speaking will live forever, for I will resurrect them! Miracles of the flesh—such as the eating of manna—cannot save anyone. Rather, it is the miracle of the soul—eating and assimilating the true 'Bread of Life'—that imparts eternal life. Do you get it now?"[45]

Here, once again, Jesus compared the experience of those who accepted Him as their Savior with the experience of their ancient fathers who ate the miracle manna in the wilderness. To those who trusted in Him He promised eternal life, which would be given to them at the resurrection at the end of the world. [1 Thessalonians 4:13-18] However, Jesus clearly implied that many of those who ate the miracle manna in the wilderness, and had died, would not be resurrected to eternal life at the end of the world. The Lord's point was clear: To trust in Him as the spiritual "Bread of Life" would impart eternal life to the people. But to trust, as it were, in mere physical bread—in either the manna of years

---

[45] John 6:57. 58

gone by or the bread and fish of His recent miracle—would not impart eternal life at all. Trust in the Lord, which results in a spiritual miracle of the conversion and transformation of the soul, was the issue, not trust in any physical miracle, however amazing it might be.[1]

For all those who were listening to Jesus that day—the Jewish leaders and the common people—a time for decision had arrived.[2]

These were the things which Jesus discussed in the synagogue in Capernaum. Unfortunately, as a result of this discussion, many of the Lord's disciples—besides the Twelve—said among themselves, "What He has said is very puzzling to us! How are any of us able to figure it out?"[46]

So, then, why did so many disciples of Jesus reject the Lord's teaching regarding the true Bread of Life? And why was the teaching so confusing to them? It was either because they were so dull in their understanding—that the Lord found it literally impossible to get through to them—or because they believed in their own leaders, who, in order to drive the people away from following Him, had declared, by ridicule and sarcasm, that it was impossible to understand Him. If the leaders of Israel could not understand Jesus, then, the common people reasoned, how could they? Most likely both factors played a role in what happened, but, no doubt the latter was by far the main reason for their rejection of the Lord and His teaching that day.[1]

It should be added that many people rejected Jesus on that occasion because they were obsessed with the Lord's power to work physical miracles and with using those miracles for their own selfish purposes. [*Harmony* 9:13/] They had little or no interest in understanding and experiencing the spiritual aspects of the Lord's miracle-working ministry. They chose to trust their leaders—no matter how sinful and insolent they were—rather than put their faith in the Son of God. They were so steeped in sin that they refused to give their hearts to the Lord and develop a relationship of faith and trust in Him as their personal Savior. The sin of pride—the pride of opinion—controlled them. Sadly, in their refusal to accept the spiritual meaning of His miracles and ministry, they unfitted themselves to participate in the only physical miracle that truly counts: the resurrection of the body at the end of the world.[2]

---

46 John 6:59, 60

But Jesus, quite aware of what these now *former* disciples were complaining about, declared to them, "Do the things which have I been saying to you cause you to stumble? So you can't believe that I've come down from heaven? [*Harmony* 9:40, 42] Well then, what would you say if you were to actually see the Son of Man *ascending into heaven* from where He originally came? [*Harmony* 18:91-98] What would you say then? Well, I'm sure that you still would not believe! For, in the final analysis, it is the Holy Spirit who convicts the soul, as opposed to the things you actually see with your eyes and experience with your feelings. Indeed, it is He who provides life for you. There are so many of you who simply refuse to listen to the Holy Spirit as He speaks to you. That is why you seem to be so puzzled by the fact that I claim to have come from the Father out of heaven. [*Harmony* 11:44/][47]

"You have failed to understand," Jesus concluded, "that the things of this world, even physical miracles—the 'flesh,' so to speak—provide no life whatsoever. No, indeed! Instead, it is having an attitude of acceptance of the words which I've been explaining to you, that will truly impart to you eternal life through the Holy Spirit. Yes, that's what really counts! But alas! Some of you simply will not accept what I have to say to you, no matter what! You have continued to possess a rock-solid attitude of total, unrelenting unbelief against Me!"[48]

Of course Jesus was always aware of who it was who would believe in Him, as well as who would not. The latter included Judas, who would be His betrayer. [*Harmony* 17:17, 18] That is why the Lord said, "This is the reason why it is that no one will come unto Me unless it is the Father who is leading him, and, accordingly, will persistently follow as the Father has led."[49]

> Here Jesus referred to Judas as well as to many of the people who had been listening to His Bread of Life teaching that day. In effect, He was saying, "My Father, by the Spirit, is trying to get through to you, but you are either not listening, or are refusing to respond to the Spirit's call. And because you are not listening, or are refusing to respond, you will not be saved."

Sadly, because of the words which Jesus spoke that day in the synagogue regarding the Bread of Life, a significant number of those who had been following

---

47 John 6:61-63
48 John 6:63, 64
49 John 6:64, 65

Him, at that point completely withdrew their support from Him and no longer considered the Lord to be the Messiah.[50]

> Indeed, a large portion of His followers walked away from Him, never more to follow Him as the Savior of the world. In effect, the Lord had called for a decision, and many of them had firmly said, "No!"

So at that moment Jesus asked the twelve disciples, "You are not planning on leaving Me as these others have done . . . are you?"[51]

Simon Peter responded spontaneously, "Lord, where would we go? Who would we follow? It is You who have the words of eternal life! We have trusted in You, and have come to know personally that You are the Holy One of Israel—the Christ, the Messiah, the Son of God!"[52]

> There can be no doubt that, even though the disciples did not completely understand all that Jesus was saying, they were willing to trust Him. [*Harmony* 9:24/] They knew of no one else to whom they might turn. They were willing to trust Him and follow His leading. That's genuine faith!

The Lord answered ruefully, "Yes! I chose you, did I not? But, even at that, one of you is a devil!" Of course Jesus was speaking about Judas Iscariot, the son of Simon, one of the Twelve who would betray Him.[(i)] [53]

Now, because so many had maliciously rejected Him, Jesus continued to live primarily in the province of Galilee away from the main group of Jewish leaders in Judea. It was this same group of Jewish leaders who were passionately seeking to kill him. Of course, the Lord's rejection by these *Judean* leaders was the main reason for His rejection by the common people in Capernaum during His Bread of Life teaching. Therefore, He would rarely be found in the province of Judea, except during the times of the Jewish festivals.[54]

> The largely negative reaction to the Lord's "Bread of Life" teaching had, for all practical purposes, ended His concentrated ministry in Galilee. For roughly a year, Jesus had had a ministry in that province which

---

50 John 6:66
51 John 6:67
52 John 6:68, 69
53 John 6:70, 71
54 John 7:1

was noted for its large, enthusiastic crowds. During that time, Jesus had conducted three major evangelistic campaigns in Galilee [*Harmony* 4:32-34; 6:18, 19; 8:37-39], with the third one involving His disciples going out on their own, two by two. Jesus had accomplished some additional significant goals. He had given His "Sermon on the Mount" wherein He had outlined the major teachings of the Gospel message. His disciples, now officially called and ordained, had received solid training in the Gospel ministry which would affect them positively for the rest of their lives. Many, many miracles of healing were performed by both Jesus and His disciples. A good number of people began to follow the Lord and His message. A fair number of them would follow Him for the rest of their lives.[1]

However, because many people had followed Jesus for the wrong reasons—to seek only the miracles of the flesh, or to pronounce Him King—Jesus had to confront them regarding this grave misunderstanding. The Lord had to make a decision as to what was the best option: To have many people follow Him for the *wrong* reasons, or to have fewer people follow Him for the *right* reasons. The Lord clearly preferred the latter option. Nevertheless, when a significant portion of His followers actually left Jesus after His Bread of Life teaching, it was a rather sad ending to what had appeared to be, earlier on, a spectacular success. Of course, many people still continued to follow Jesus, but the overall excitement in the Lord's work in Galilee was dampened. With a little over a year left in His ministry, Jesus would soon change the emphasis of His work.[2]

Further, it is of interest to note that even though many did not understand the spiritual meaning of the Lord's miracles and had been seeking Him for the wrong reasons, He continued to perform physical miracles among the people. Why did He do this, despite knowing that the people were largely following Him for the wrong reasons? Apparently, the Lord knew that it was better to work miracles among the people, even if they were misunderstood. He knew that if He ceased to perform miracles, greater harm would be done. Doubt in His power would ensue. Further unnecessary questioning of His Messiahship would result. So then, the dismay at such a refusal to work miracles would be more damaging than the confusion caused by performing them. Besides all this, Jesus, always the loving and compassionate Savior, still greatly desired to ease the pain of human suffering. How could He, the Master Healer, bypass those who were suffering in anguish?[3]

**Supplementary Notes:**

**(a) [9:5]** The record says that the actual amount of money needed to purchase food was 200 denarii. The daily pay for a commoner laborer was one denarius. Thus 200 denarii would equal 200 days of labor—which is about nine months of labor (allowing labor for six days each week).

**(b) [9:15]** The text reads that the disciples rowed for about 20-30 furlongs. This distance is about three to three and half miles. That is the way I recorded it in the *Harmony*.

**(c) [9:15]** The "fourth watch" of the night was between 3-6 a.m.

**(d) [9:21]** See **Note "ee"** in Chapter 5, for more about the meaning of the phrase, "little-faith" as a nickname.

**(e) [9:24/+]** The message of the Lord's "Bread of Life" teaching is one the most important chapters in the entire ministry of Jesus. So much about the ultimate outcome of His work can be understood in the light of what happened during this famous teaching experience in Capernaum. That is why, in order to explain what can often be deep, profound statements of Jesus, I have taken much more space to explain, define, preview, and *often* review what He said on this subject. Here repetition is I think, very useful!

**(f) [9:25]** The timing of the Lord's "Bread of Life" teaching, as it relates to the "walking on water" miracle, is unclear. Was it the next day, or later than that? We don't know for sure. I suspect it was not more than a day or two after the miracle.

**(g) [9:27]** We are not informed in the record that the disciples told the people of the Lord's miracle of walking on the water. However, the fact that the people questioned Jesus regarding *how* He arrived in Capernaum (*Harmony* 9:28) indicates that they must have had some information that had piqued their curiosity. Additionally, it is inconceivable to me that the disciples would have remained silent regarding such an amazing miracle! They were still hoping that Jesus would proclaim Himself King. From their perspective, any encouragement from the crowd was sure to help in this regard. So, why not tell the people of the miracle? Accordingly, I included this reasonable assumption in the *Harmony.*

**(h) [9:28]** (See above.)

**(i) [9:53]** For more on the fact that Jesus most likely did not choose Judas to be one of His twelve disciples, see *Harmony* 4:79/1; 16:21-23, 21/, 23/.

# Part III

*Instruction:*

*The Respite From*

*Ministry Among Jews*

*And the Ministry*

*To the Gentiles*

*(Passover, Spring, A.D. 30 -*

*Passover, Spring, A.D. 31)*

# CHAPTER TEN

## WORKING AMONG GENTILES—

**From the Contention About Tradition and Ceremonial Washings, to the Lord's Teaching on Humility and Forgiveness**

**(Just Before Passover, Spring, A.D. 30 - Autumn, A.D. 30)**

—

### The Timeline of the Ministry of Jesus, Segment Six: Spring, A.D. 30—Autumn, A.D. 30[a]

Two and a half years had passed since the Lord began His ministry in the Autumn of A.D. 27. During the first six months—A.D. 27 through Spring, A.D. 28—Jesus was baptized, called His first disciples, and worked His first miracle. It was a "getting started" time for Jesus.[1]

During the next six months—Spring, A.D. 28 through Autumn, A.D. 28—Christ worked in the southern province of Judea. This time period began when He cleansed the Temple of the moneychangers. This event caused a great deal of animosity with the Jewish leaders that would continue to increase and plague Him throughout His entire ministry. Though Jesus worked in Judea for a while after that, His labor there was relatively short and details limited.[2]

The next six months—Autumn, A.D. 28 through Spring, A.D. 29—the Lord spent in the northern province of Galilee. Events recorded during that time are very few in number. No doubt He spent most of this time privately instructing His disciples.[3]

However, the next six-month time period—Spring, A.D. 29 through Autumn, A.D. 29—was very busy, with many events recorded in the Gospel story. During this time, the Lord firmly established His ministry in that province. This included the official call of His disciples and their ordination, followed by His "Sermon on the Mount." Also, during this time the number of miracles that Jesus performed greatly increased. His popularity, as a result, reached an all-time high. This time period represented the zenith of His ministry.[4]

The next six-month period of the Lord's first two and half years of ministry—Autumn, A.D. 29 through Spring, A.D. 30—ultimately led to the unofficial conclusion of His work in Galilee. Before that, the Lord had met with what appeared to be great success in in that province. During the time of His extensive work there, Jesus worked many significant miracles. There were two of special note: the resurrections of both the son of the widow of Nain, and the daughter of Jairus. In addition, there were a couple of events involving storms on the Sea of Galilee. In the first situation, Jesus calmed the storm. In the second, He actually walked on the water! The Lord also introduced a method of teaching that would strongly characterize His ministry from that time onward: the telling of parables to illustrate the Gospel truth. However, during this time period, Jesus continued to have confrontations with the Jewish leaders. In fact, on one occasion, Jesus actually declared that the Hebrew leaders were on the verge of committing the unpardonable sin! To make matters worse, the Lord ran into trouble with many of the common people who were following Him. This was because so many of these people were seeking Jesus solely to reap the benefits of His miracle-working power. So, to make the true purpose of His ministry clear to the people, Jesus fed the 5,000, and then gave them His "Bread of Life" teaching in the synagogue in Capernaum. The purpose of both of these events was to teach the people the true spiritual meaning of His miracles. As a result of this, though, a large number of His followers no longer considered Him to be the Messiah. Sadly, it was a significant, negative turning point in His overall ministry.[5]

The next six-month segment of the Lord's ministry (6/7)—from Spring, A.D. 30 through Autumn, A.D. 30—was primarily focused on working with non-Jews—that is, Gentiles.(b) [6]

During this time, Jesus visited such Gentile strongholds as Phoenicia, Decapolis, and Caesarea Philippi. He also fed 4,000 people with just a small amount of food—a miracle similar to the feeding of the 5,000. But the 4,000 people who were fed that day were primarily Gentiles.[7]

Also during this time period, the Lord was transfigured. In addition, He discussed with His disciples the tragic future of His ministry—that He was to die at the hands of the Jewish leaders.[8]

Overall, Jesus spent this segment of time primarily working with Gentiles, and in personally instructing His disciples to prepare them for the issues and troubles they would face in their future work. Among the things the Lord discussed with His disciples was how to work with one another, effectively and happily, even under trying circumstances.[9]

—

## Contention Regarding Human Tradition and Ceremonial Washings
## < Spring, A.D. 30 6/7) >
## (Matthew 15:1-20; Mark 7:1-23)

In spite of the loss of many disciples over the Lord's "Bread of Life" teaching [*Harmony* 9:50], a number of scribes and Pharisees, hearing of the dramatic extent of His ministry, traveled all the way from Jerusalem to Galilee to observe what Jesus was doing, carefully listening to what He was preaching. They gathered closely around Him to watch every movement of the Lord and His disciples. They were obviously seeking to find something that they were doing—or not doing for that matter—that they might use as an issue of contention between themselves and Jesus.[1]

In the course of the Jewish leaders' observations, they noticed that, before the Lord and His disciples ate food, they did not wash their hands according to the usual Jewish rituals. [*Harmony* 12:20] From the perspective of the Pharisees and scribes, the hands of the Lord and His disciples were considered unclean, thus making them unfit for handling food. This ritualistic cleansing was, surprisingly, *not* for sanitary purposes. Rather, it was an elaborate system of *ceremonial* washings, involving the pouring of water from one hand to the other, as well as the rubbing of the water around the hands in a specific, regimented way. To be sure, this system of washings had no foundation whatsoever in Scripture, but was merely an invention of the elders of the church. Again, its purpose was to *ceremonially* cleanse the hands—that is, to have the effect of publicly showing off to others just how morally holy they were, in contrast with the people around them! This ritual was especially required when eating in public areas—such as the market place—where a person might come into contact with all types of ritualistically unclean situations and people. This cleansing also involved special ceremonial washings of various cups, pitchers, and copper pots . . . and even beds!

1 Matthew 15:1; Mark 7:1

Of course, Jesus had no use for such silliness. Consequently, neither He nor His disciples bothered themselves with such tedious procedures.[(c) 2]

But instead of directly attacking the personal actions of Jesus, the scribes sought, rather, to challenge the Lord by criticizing the actions of His disciples when they ate food. Accordingly the scribes and Pharisees questioned Jesus, asking, "Why is it that Your disciples do not follow the traditions of the church? They are eating food without going through the proper hand-washing system set up by the elders." [*Harmony* 14:121-124, 150/2][(d) 3]

In response, Jesus shot back at them, "Answer me this: Why is it that *you* break the law of *God* for the sake of your traditions? Isaiah was right about you hypocrite actors when he wrote, 'These people pay honor to Me with their lips, while their heart is far from Me! Thus it is that in vain they attempt to worship Me by teaching doctrines that they require all to perform. But these so-called doctrines are merely the traditions of men,'—and nothing more." [Isaiah 29:13] [(e) 4]

Jesus continued His rebuttal, saying, "In doing this, you neglect the direct commandments of God, while at the same time you strictly follow your own foolish traditions of the washing of pots, cups, and many other such things." The Lord added, "Yes, you are certainly experts at setting aside the commandments of God![5]

"For instance," Jesus explained, "remember that God, through Moses, said, 'Pay due honor to your father and your mother [Exodus 20:12],'"—the Fifth Commandment—"and 'He who speaks evil regarding his father or mother shall be killed.' [Exodus 21:17] Isn't that right? But to get around such a direct commandment of God, you say, 'If a man who is morally obligated to support his aging parents financially wills his resources to God or the Temple by pronouncing them as "Corban"'"—that is, a gift reserved for God—"'he is exempted from using that money to support his parents'! In effect, you are giving permission for a man to say to his parents, 'It pains me to tell you this, but the money which I had set aside to help you has been dedicated to the church instead.' Thus his parents greatly suffer. To make matters worse, until his death, this man can

2 Mark 7:3, 4
3 Matthew 15:1, 2; Mark 7:2, 5
4 Matthew 15:3, 7-9; Mark 7:6, 7
5 Mark 7:8, 9

use this supposedly dedicated money for his own personal use, while brazenly ignoring his parents. In fact, you even refuse to allow this money to be used in support of his parents. It is all despicable!" [*Harmony* 14:121][6]

Jesus concluded, "By this procedure, you invalidate the direct will of God—even the Fifth Commandment of the moral Law—by this man-made tradition which you have handed down. And, sadly, this is just one of the many ways that you have used human traditions to abrogate the will of God. And the worst part is that you have done so for your own evil and avaricious purposes!"[7]

The scribes and Pharisees, frustrated and humiliated by the Lord's incisive response, with no little embarrassment, left the presence of Jesus. After they were gone, Jesus went outside the house and called the crowds to come closer to Him. Based upon what had transpired between the Jewish leaders and Him, the Lord explained some additional things to the people. He said, "Allow me to make something clear to all of you. Please comprehend what I'm saying: These foolish hand-washings of the Jewish leaders do not, as they think, make people more pure in their hearts and souls than other individuals. Now, of course, it's fine to eat and drink from clean utensils, and too, with clean hands. But it is not the dirt on a man's hands that can be cleansed by these elaborate hand-washings and the scrubbing of cups and the like, that would pollute his *soul or heart,* should such dirt enter his body through his mouth. Rather, it is those things that are already in the heart of a man which defile his soul—such as a perverse and rebellious character. Yes, it is that which is already in the soul that leads to the evil words which a man speaks. In short, a man's soul is polluted by what comes out of the mouth rather than by what goes in through the mouth. Now, I hope you are listening carefully to what I'm telling you so that you will understand its true meaning. In short, a man is made morally pure by having a pure heart, not by merely washing his hands. Do you see that?" [*Harmony* 12:21][(f)] [8]

After the crowds left His presence, He went into the house. His disciples began to question Him regarding the point He had been making in His little illustration. "Don't you know," they told Him, "that the Pharisees were stymied by what you told them? They must be really upset with you!"[9]

---

6 Matthew 15:4-6; Mark 7:10-12
7 Matthew 15:6; Mark 7:13
8 Matthew 15:10, 11; Mark 7:14-16
9 Matthew 15:12; Mark 7:17

"Well," the Lord remarked, "every plant which the heavenly Father has not planted will be pulled up! So then, let them alone! Those people are nothing more than blind leaders of others who are, themselves, just as blind! And what can you expect? If someone who is blind tries to lead someone just as blind as himself, they will both fall into a pit! Isn't that true?" [*Harmony* 5:59][10]

But the disciples, led by Peter, pursued the matter further, "Please explain what You meant by Your illustration when You said that it is not what a man eats that defiles him. That's a bit confusing to us."[11]

"Can't you figure out what I'm telling you?" Jesus responded, with some surprise. "Are you just like the many people who struggle with the meaning of My words? Don't you get it when I tell you that it is not what enters the body through the mouth that pollutes the heart and soul? Figure it out! Things enter the stomach, and after some time, are eliminated from the body into the latrine, right? It bypasses the heart altogether—even the soul of man. Do you get it now?"[12]

Jesus was saying, in part, that the food people ate was not materially affected—or improved—by all the *ritual* washings of the Jews. Jesus continued to amplify His point by adding, "The things that leave the body—the words a man speaks and the actions he performs—that is what defiles the soul of man! Evil words come from their source: an evil heart. For, from within the heart and mind of man proceed wicked ideas, such as sexual impurities, thieveries, murders, adulteries, covetousness, and all other types of wicked things. I should add to this list such things as deceit, uncontrolled passions, greed, vicious accusations against others, lying under oath, arrogant attitudes, foolish actions, as well as all other types of wicked behavior. Ah yes, these *are* the evil things which leave the body, and defile the man from whom they have come! But there is no way that eating with unwashed hands will pervert the morals of an individual—that's all such foolishness!"[(g)] [13]

> Of course, it is fine to eat food with hands that are washed—it is more sanitary. But ingesting sanitary food does not make a person *morally*

---

10 Matthew 15:13, 14
11 Matthew 15:15; Mark 7:17
12 Matthew 15:16, 17; Mark 7:18, 19
13 Matthew 15:18-20; Mar 7:19-23

better than eating unsanitary food. A *ritualistic* cleansing does not make one *morally* cleaner or better. That was the Lord's point.[1]

## The Lord Among the Gentiles
## < Spring and Summer, A.D. 30 (6/7) >
## (Matthew 15:21-39; Mark 7:24-8:10)

### — The Lord's Withdrawal to Phoenicia; the Healing of a Gentile Woman's Daughter
### < Spring, A.D. 30 (6/7) >
### {Matthew 15:21-28; Mark 7:24-30}

The ministry of Jesus had reached a crisis point. The previous year, because of the extreme resentment of the Jewish leaders, Jesus had had to leave the southern province of Judea. [*Harmony* 4:1] During the ensuing year, His ministry had flourished in the northern province of Galilee. But of late, even in Galilee, things had taken a significant turn for the worse. Many of those who had eagerly been following Him there were turned off by what Jesus had said to them regarding the "Bread of Life." [*Harmony* 9:50] In addition, the Jewish leaders, alarmed by what they had been hearing about the success of the Lord's work in Galilee, had sent some of their own to spy on Him there. Christ's refusal to accept their chiding over the issue of ritual cleansings had made the matter even worse. [*Harmony* 10:8] There was no doubt that these representatives from Judea would return home with an evil report of the Lord's ministry. Most likely even more of the Jewish religious leaders would soon be seeking actively and persistently to disrupt and even stop His ministry in Galilee.[2]

Also, Jesus would normally have attended the impending Passover celebration in Jerusalem. It was His custom to do so. [*Harmony* 3:1; 3:72] But because of what had just transpired, Jesus skipped the Passover of that year.[h] [3]

To take the heat off Him and His ministry for a while, Jesus withdrew from Galilee and moved toward the north, even further from Judea. Jesus ended up in an area known as Phoenicia, which was located about 35 miles to northwest of Galilee. There, He secluded Himself in the house of someone whom He could trust. This was a region populated mainly by non-Jews, whose prejudice against Him was negligible. Jesus ultimately traveled into the area where the cities of

Tyre and Sidon which were located on the Mediterranean Sea. These cities were about 20 miles apart from each other.[14]

> A sojourn in this vicinity would also provide Jesus with the opportunity to instruct His disciples in the principles of working with non-Jews. Such instruction would be of great assistance to them in the future. For the largest part of His ministry thus far, Jesus had worked mainly among Hebrews. Only on rare occasions—such as with the Samaritan woman at Jacob's Well [*Harmony* 3:34-61], the centurion at Capernaum [*Harmony* 6:1-9], and the demon-possessed men of Gergesa [*Harmony* 7:65-74]—did the Lord work significantly with Gentiles. But mingling among the non-Jews of Phoenicia would be of great value to the disciples as their work of ministry would ultimately expand deep within the Gentile community. One such opportunity for teaching the disciples soon arose during the Lord's stay in Phoenicia.

A Syro-Phoenecian woman of Canaanite ancestry in that coastal area suddenly approached Jesus. She was a Gentile—a non-Jew. She had heard of the healing power of Jesus and recognized Him to be the famous Miracle-Worker. Even though Jesus sought to escape the notice of most of the people for a while, this woman, nevertheless, discovered His whereabouts and sought Him out.[15]

Upon finding the Lord, she cried out to Jesus unceasingly, pleading, "Please have mercy upon me, Lord, Son of David!"—which was a common designation for the Messiah. But for a Gentile to use this phrase clearly indicated that such a person had an advanced understanding of the Jewish faith. "My little daughter," the woman continued to plead, "is viciously possessed of a demon!" However, Jesus appeared to ignore her obviously implied request to have Him heal her child.[16]

> As will be seen, the Lord gave a seemingly callous response to the woman because He wanted to teach His disciples some vital lessons about ministering to people of a non-Jewish background. Now the Jews, simply put, despised almost anyone who was not of their nationality. They considered such people for the most part to be unworthy of either

---

14 Matthew 15:21; Mark 7:24

15 Matthew 15:22; Mark 7:24-26

16 Matthew 15:22, 23; Mark 7:25, 26

their time or of their religion. The disciples, steeped in their nation's traditions, naturally had the same prejudices.[1]

The Lord's plan in the way He treated this woman was twofold: First, He would treat her as any Jew might relate to such a non-Jew. Second, the Lord would then treat her as *He*, the Savior of the whole world, would relate to her. This way, the disciples would clearly discern the contrast between the *two* methods. In the final analysis, they would learn the correct way to treat anyone who was a sincere seeker of the Gospel, whether he or she was a Jew or Gentile. In the process, they would also learn how *not* to treat a Gentile as they had been used to doing. It would take a long time for the disciples to grasp this subtle concept fully, but a seed would be sown, bearing good fruit much later on in their experience. [Acts 10:34, 35; 13:46](i) [2]

Jesus initially responded to the woman in the typical Jewish fashion by completely ignoring her request. The disciples were not at all surprised by the Lord's reaction to the woman—in fact, that was the way they would have reacted. Indeed, they begged Jesus to free Himself of this woman. "Lord! Send her away!" they implored. "Get rid of her—she's making such a loud commotion behind us with her shouting! Have her stop bothering us!"[17]

Jesus continued to play along with this typical reaction a Jew might manifest in relating to a non-Jew. That is why He explained to the woman, "I have been sent to minister only to those of the Jewish nation who are lost in their sins." By making this surprising statement, Jesus was not only showing the disciples the callousness of their own attitudes, but also testing the faith of the woman. How would she respond to such an apparently strong rebuff?[18]

But instead of leaving His presence, the woman immediately came closer to Him, even bowing down before Him. She cried out, "Lord! Nevertheless, I beg of You, help me!"(j) [19]

Yet Jesus still did not change His behavior toward the woman. He continued to play the part of a typical Jew, declaring, "It is not proper to take the children's

17 Matthew 15:23

18 Matthew 15:24

19 Matthew 15:25; Mark 7:25

food set aside for their satisfaction and throw it to little dogs! Let the children eat first!"[20]

> This truly amazing statement by Jesus—the Master of compassion—demonstrated just how nasty Jews could be to Gentiles! The "children," in this illustration, represented the people of Israel, and the "dogs" represented the Gentiles. The "children's food" represented the Gospel message and its power. It is sad but very true that most Jews considered the majority of Gentiles to be worth nothing more than pesky, barking dogs, running wild in the streets of the cities![1]
>
> By this time, the disciples must have begun to see just how terrible their attitude toward Gentiles really was. Jesus was acting in a way and to a degree that they had never previously observed in Him.[2]
>
> Also, as stated before, the faith of the woman was being tested to the limit. But this time she caught the significance of Jesus' subtle use of the phrase "little dogs"—meaning puppies, such cute, lovable creatures. How would she respond to this latest statement of the Lord that contained this hint of hope for the woman?[3]

She came up with a good rejoinder, "Yes that is true, Lord! But it is also true that even little dogs"—that is, puppies—"can eat the crumbs of the children's food that fall from their masters' tables. I'll take whatever You have to give me, knowing that it is sufficient for my needs!"[21]

The woman had passed the test! And the Lord had gone far enough with His object lesson for the disciples. Thus Jesus informed her, "O woman! You have such great faith! Your answer is excellent! Therefore it will done as you have wished of Me: your daughter is healed of the demon!" And instantly her daughter was healed. Sure enough, when the woman returned home, she discovered her daughter resting on her bed, free from the evil spirit that had tormented her for so long![22]

> But beyond this miracle, the disciples had much to ponder. First, they had observed how despicably the Jews had been treating Gentiles. Second, they had seen how even Gentiles could show a great measure of

---

20 Matthew 15:26; Mark 7:27

21 Matthew 15:27; Mark 7:28

22 Matthew 15:28; Mark 7:29, 30

faith—just like Jews, and perhaps even more so! In time, this and other experiences would wean them away from the old, narrow attitudes they had toward non-Jews. In time, the *real* attitude of Jesus, that of showing love and compassion to everyone—Jew or Gentile—would replace the old intolerant thinking of the past. It would take considerable time to accomplish this purpose, but Jesus had dramatically and effectively planted the seed!

**— The Healing of a Deaf-mute and Other Miracles in Decapolis**
**< Spring and Summer, A.D. 30 (6/7) >**
**{Matthew 15:29-31; Mark 7:31-37}**

After some time of respite in the northern region of Phoenicia—traveling through the area of Tyre and then Sidon—Jesus headed south again toward Galilee and beyond. On the way, He passed through Decapolis, southeast of the Sea of Galilee.[23]

Jesus had been in this same general region about 10 months before [*Harmony* 7:65-74], when He had cast a legion of devils out of two demoniacs. On that occasion, the stunned people of that region had asked Him to leave. The two formerly demon-possessed men had wanted to accompany Him, but Jesus sent them to share their faith among the people of that region. So now, when Jesus returned to the area, many, many people came out to welcome Him. What a change of attitude—all the result of the sharing of their faith by the two men Jesus had healed!

Some of the inhabitants brought to Him a man who was deaf and mute. They begged the Lord to heal the man by laying His hand on him. Jesus took the man away from the people surrounding Him, and privately handled the situation. First the Lord placed His fingers in the man's ears, and then after putting His own finger in His own mouth, He touched the man's tongue with the saliva. Why did Jesus heal this man using these unusual procedures? It was so that the man, who was unable to hear the act of his own healing, would be able to see and feel it. And, being a Gentile, his understanding of faith was limited. Therefore, this "hands on" approach to healing would have the effect of strengthening his faith. Then, looking into heaven, and with a heavy sigh of sympathy for the man's plight, the Lord declared, "Ephphatha!"—the Aramaic words for "Be

---

[23] Mark 7:31

opened!" [*Harmony* 2:58] At that very moment, the man's ears were opened, and his inability to speak was cured. Now, he was able to both hear and speak freely. And everyone could hear his words plainly! [*Harmony* 10:44][(k)][24]

As Jesus had done so often before, He commanded the people to tell no one about what they had just witnessed. The Savior made this command because He did not want the people of this mainly Gentile region to have the false hope that He would work many miracles in their area at this time. He was, after all, just passing through their land. Nevertheless, it seemed that the more the Savior made such a command, the more the people spread the news of His miracle-working ability. The completely amazed people of that region kept saying, "He does everything well! He is even able to make the deaf to hear, and the mute to speak!"[25]

Continuing His journey—now back toward Galilee—the Lord traveled near the edge of the Sea of Galilee. On its eastern bank, Jesus sat down on a large hillside. Huge crowds of people—mainly composed of Gentiles—came to Him, bringing many who were sick. There were those who were lame, crippled, blind, and mute, as well as many who were suffering from various other types of illnesses. When they laid these people at His feet, He healed them all. Of course, the masses continued to be astonished as they watched the mute talking, the crippled dancing, the lame walking, and the blind gazing with rapture at the world around them! They all praised the God of the nation of Israel.[26]

> Here, Gentiles were praising the God of the Jews! The influence of the ministry of Jesus was changing, in a very positive way, the attitude of Gentiles toward the Jews, their God, and their religion.

### — The Feeding of the Four Thousand
**< Summer, A.D. 30 (6/7) >**
**{Matthew 15:32-39; Mark 8:1-10}**

The interest in the Lord's healing ability and His teachings was so outstanding that the people came to the hillside in droves. The crowds, made up mainly of non-Jews, were prepared to stay for days if need be. Accordingly, many brought their own food with them. After the people had stayed in His presence for some days, Jesus commented to His disciples, "I feel badly for the crowds around Me.

---

24 Mark 7:32-35
25 Mark 7:36, 37
26 Matthew 15:29-31

They have been here with Me for the better part of three days, and have run out of food. I really don't want to send them away hungry, lest they faint with hunger on their way home. Many of them have come from long distances."[27]

"But," the Lord's disciples wondered, "in this deserted place, where would we get enough food to feed so many people?"[28]

> Now it had been just three or four months since the miracle-feeding of the 5,000 several miles to the north [*Harmony* 9:1-13], so it was surprising that the disciples would react this way. However, in that earlier situation, those who were fed were primarily *Jews*. In this case, the people needing to be fed were mainly *Gentiles*. The fact that the disciples had doubts about how so many could be fed indicated that they were still filled with prejudicial feelings toward Gentiles. Obviously they did not believe that these non-Jews were worthy of participating in a dramatic miracle like the earlier feeding of the 5,000 Jews!

Nevertheless, Jesus responded to the disciples, asking, "How many loaves of bread do you suppose we have left among this vast crowd?"[29]

After a little research, they reported back, saying, "There are only seven loaves of bread, and also a few fish."[30]

After, having directed the crowd to sit down on the ground, Jesus took the bread and fish, blessed the food, and He broke it into pieces. Next, He gave the morsels to the disciples. They, in turn, distributed the food among the people. The entire crowd ate the food and was filled to satisfaction! There was so much food that there were enough pieces left over to fill seven large baskets! The number of people who ate the miracle bread and fish that day was 4,000 men, besides women and children—perhaps up to 12,000 in all. [*Harmony* 10:41][31]

> As in the miracle of the feeding of the 5,000 [*Harmony* 9:1-13], here Jesus taught a vital spiritual lesson. The bread represented the Gospel message. Feeding the multitude represented the spreading of the Gospel to the people. In this case—the feeding of the 4,000—Jesus taught that

---

27 Matthew 15:32; Mark 8:1-3
28 Matthew 15:33; Mark 8:4
29 Matthew 15:34; Mark 8:5
30 Matthew 15:34; Mark 8:5
31 Matthew 15:35-38; Mark 8:6-9

> the Gospel was to be spread also among the Gentiles, just as the previous miracle—the feeding of the 5,000—had taught that the Gospel was to be spread among the Jews. [*Harmony* 9:12/]

At this point, Jesus sent the people home. He entered a boat and set sail toward the town of Magadan—also known as Dalmanutha—several miles directly across the lake to the west.[32]

> Thus Jesus concluded a couple months of ministry primarily among Gentiles. This was the longest period of time thus far that He had spent working almost exclusively with non-Jews. What was remarkable, and certainly would be remembered by His disciples, was the fact that the same kind of things the Lord had done for Jews—preaching and miracle-working—He had done for Gentiles. Over time it would become clear to them that their ministry was not to be limited to Jews, but was to include ministering to the Gentiles of the region, and ultimately to all the peoples of the entire earth. Again, the seed had been planted. In time it would bear great fruit. [Acts 1:7, 8]

### The Lord's Critics Demand a Sign
### < Summer, A.D. 30 (6/7) >
### (Matthew 16:1-12; Mark 8:11-21)

Upon the Lord's arrival at Magadan, the Pharisees and Sadducees—both the conservative and liberal Jewish leaders—approached Jesus to start an argument with Him. They demanded that He perform some kind of sign—or miracle—from heaven to prove that He had the authority to do and say the things that He did. They hoped to trick Him into some embarrassing debate with them. The Lord was very disappointed by this demand, sighing deeply within His being. [*Harmony* 7:13][33]

Then, responding indirectly to their demand, the Lord answered, "Why, oh why is it that this generation is constantly demanding a miraculous sign from Me to prove the veracity of My ministry? Signs of the authority of My ministry"—such as healings and Spirit-filled preaching—"are all around you. But you don't discern them! However, you are quite adept at recognizing the signs which indicate changes in the weather. For example, when nighttime is approaching, you say, 'It will be fair weather tomorrow, because the sunset sky

32 Matthew 15:39; Mark 8:9, 10

33 Matthew 16:1; Mark 8:11, 12

was red.' Or some morning you will say, 'It will rain today, because the sky is red and ominous.' Yes, isn't it amazing that you hypocrite actors have the ability to forecast the weather by looking at the color of the sky, but are quite unable to figure out the signs of the times in which you are living! Yes, it is an evil and faithless generation of people—such as you—that keeps seeking from Me yet another miraculous sign of My authority. Yet, if I did give you a miracle, you wouldn't believe in Me anyway! So therefore I tell you with certainty that I will give you no such sign as you demand . . . that is, except this one sign: the sign of the prophet Jonah!" At that point, Jesus turned and left the Jewish leaders standing alone, without explaining the meaning of His brief reference to the prophet Jonah as a sign![34]

> What, then, did Jesus mean by giving this cryptic statement regarding Jonah? Only later would the disciples and perhaps some of the Jewish leaders understand its meaning. In the Old Testament book of Jonah, the story is told of the prophet Jonah, who preached to Nineveh. This led to the conversion of many people of that heathen city. [Jonah 3:1-10] In a like manner, as the Lord had already pointed out [*Harmony* 7:15], His preaching had led, and would continue to lead, to the conversion of many in His day. And, as Jonah preached to Nineveh—a city composed all of Gentiles—so Jesus would preach to many Gentiles, and they would also be converted. These many miraculous conversions would be as was in the case of Jonah, a "sign"—evidence or proof—of His power and authority. Also, as Jesus had earlier pointed out [*Harmony* 7:14], just as Jonah spent three days in the stomach of the fish, the Lord would spend three days in the grave following His crucifixion. Indeed, His death and burial, followed by His glorious and incredible resurrection, would be an indisputable "sign" of His divine power and authority!

Entering the boat, Jesus and His disciples set sail for the opposite side of the lake, toward the town of Bethsaida, about eight miles to the northeast. Because they had left Magadan in haste, the disciples had forgotten to bring along with them a sufficient amount of bread to eat. They had only one loaf left. This could present a problem because Bethsaida was primarily a non-Jewish town and the disciples, following the usual Jewish custom of refusing to buy food from any Gentile [*Harmony* 10:16/1], would not want to purchase bread there. So, when

---

[34] Matthew 16:2-4; Mark 8:12, 13

they reached Bethsaida and discovered that they had not enough bread with them, they openly expressed some concern over the matter.[35]

Seemingly in line with their conversation, Jesus commented, "You had better watch out for the yeast of the Pharisees and the Sadducees! Beware of it! While you'll at it, you had better be careful about the yeast of Herod, the tetrarch." [*Harmony* 12:33][36]

After hearing these words, the disciples discussed among themselves what the Lord could have meant by such an apparently strange statement. They said, "He is probably talking about the yeast of the Jewish bread bakers because we forgot to bring a sufficient amount of bread with us. He must be saying that we should be careful not to buy bread from any Pharisee or Sadducee baker in this town, because the quality of the yeast in their bread is probably poor. So," they concluded, "because we don't want to buy bread from a Gentile, nor should we buy bread from a Pharisee or Sadducee, we will have a hard time getting any bread in this town! What will we do then?" However, they had no idea about what Jesus meant when He told them to beware of the "yeast of Herod." "What could that mean?" they wondered.[37]

Overhearing this conversation, Jesus chided them, "Why are you discussing the fact that we don't have enough bread? Don't you get what I'm trying to say? Are your hearts as insensible as the Jewish leaders' hearts in understanding the meaning of My words? Do not the Scriptures say, 'Having eyes, but refusing to see. And having ears, but refusing to hear'? [Jeremiah 5:21] Does this apply also to you? I hope not![38]

"Why are you men of such little faith that you are discussing this lack of bread among yourselves? Do you not remember that I was able to feed 5,000 with just five loaves of bread which I broke? [*Harmony* 9:1-13] And that, afterward, you collected how many baskets of leftovers?"[39]

"Twelve!" the disciples chorused.[40]

---

35 Matthew 16:5; Mark 8:14
36 Matthew 16:6; Mark 8:15
37 Matthew 16:7; Mark 8:16
38 Mark 8:17, 18
39 Matthew 16:8, 9; Mark 8:18, 19
40 Mark 8:19

"Or have you forgotten that I just very recently did the same thing with seven loaves, making them sufficient to feed 4,000? [*Harmony* 10:27-31] And, how many large baskets of leftovers did you collect that time?"[41]

"Seven!" was their reply.[42]

"All right then, you don't need to worry about the lack of bread!" the Lord flatly declared. "Can't you figure out that I'm not really talking about the kind of bread you eat when I mentioned the poor quality of the yeast of the Jewish leaders?" It was only then that it dawned on the disciples that Jesus was talking about the *doctrinal* "yeast" of the Jewish leaders, rather than the kind of yeast one might put into oven-baked bread.[43]

> The Lord wanted the disciples to remember that the false doctrines as well as the sins of the Pharisees and Sadducees, left unchallenged, could have a subtle but deadly effect upon the disciples themselves as well as the common people in general. That is why He said to watch out for the Jewish leaders' yeast! And, when the Lord mentioned the "yeast of Herod," He was talking about the wickedness of that tyrant, especially his compromising lifestyle. His was a lifestyle [*Harmony* 3:71] that especially the liberal Sadducees often endorsed and emulated.

## Jesus Heals a Blind Man Near Bethsaida
**< Summer, A.D. 30 (6/7) >**
**(Mark 8:22-26)**

As Jesus and His disciples were entering Bethsaida, some people brought a blind man out to Him. They begged the Lord to touch him and heal him of his blindness. So the Lord took the man by his hand and led him a distance out of the town. The Lord placed some of His own saliva on his eyes. He also laid His hands on him. The Master asked the blind man, "Do you see anything yet?" [*Harmony* 10:24][44]

Looking around him, the blind man answered, "I can see men—they look like walking trees!"[45]

---

41 Matthew 16:10; Mark 8:20
42 Mark 8:20
43 Matthew 16:11, 12; Mark 8:21
44 Mark 8:22, 23
45 Mark 8:24

Then the Lord laid His hands on the man's eyes. The man looked around, carefully trying to see clearly. Indeed, he could! His sight was completely restored—he could see everything perfectly. Jesus sent the man back to his home, instructing him, "Don't go back into the village! Don't tell anyone, no matter where you might go, about your sight being restored."[46]

> This story is a very unusual. First, this is the only recorded example of Jesus healing someone in stages! Why did He do so? Perhaps because the blind man was a heathen, his faith might have been weak. By healing him in two steps, the Lord might have been strengthening the man's faith, one step at a time. Second, why did the Lord put saliva in the man's eye as part of the healing process? Perhaps this procedure would be more dramatic for a man who was blind, and also a heathen. It is likely that the man had very little knowledge of Jesus and His ministry—quite possibly, none at all. And too, in the ancient world, saliva was believed to have curative properties. There is no real question, however, as to why Jesus healed the man outside the town and also forbade him to re-enter it. The Lord did not want large crowds of people coming to Him for healing. Ever since the "Bread of Life" teaching about three months previously [*Harmony* 9:25-54], the Lord was winding down His public ministry. Accordingly, He wanted less and less attention to be focused on His healing ministry. From now on, His primary emphasis was to instruct and to teach His disciples, to prepare them for the coming trials that they would be facing. He only rarely deliberately ministered to large crowds any more.

### Withdrawal to Caesarea Philippi — The Great Confession
### < Summer, A.D. 30 (6/7) >
### (Matthew 16:13-28; Mark 8:27-9:1; Luke 9:18-27)

To avoid any further confrontation with spies sent by the Jewish leaders, Jesus decided to move due north from the Sea of Galilee, to dwell in an area where He was not so well known. There He could live in relative peace and security. Ultimately, Jesus stopped in the district of Caesarea Philippi, which was about 20 miles northeast of Capernaum.[47]

---

46 Mark 8:25, 26

47 Matthew 16:13; Mark 8:27

As Jesus visited the various villages of the region, He took some time to pray alone with His disciples. Then the Master asked the disciples a question, "The crowds of the people have given their opinions as to who the Son of Man might be. So, based upon what you've been hearing, who do people say I am?"[48]

The disciples gave various answers: "Some say that You are John the Baptist, raised from the dead." [*Harmony* 8:72-74] "Others say that You are Elijah, the prophet." "Still others say You are Jeremiah, or one of the other prophets of the old days who has been resurrected from the dead."[49]

"But," Jesus questioned them more closely, "who is it that *you* say I am?"[50]

Without hesitation, Peter responded, "You are the Christ—even the Messiah—of our God! Indeed, You are the Son of the living God!"[51]

"Ah! God bless you, Simon, the son of John! You are blessed because no human being has revealed this fact to you. Rather, it was the heavenly Father who told you this!" was the Lord's triumphant reply.[52]

Christ continued, "I must say to you that your name is Peter—that is, a 'stone.'" Then, pointing to Himself, Jesus added, "And upon this 'Bedrock' will I build My church. And the gates of wickedness—even of death and the grave, will not overcome it!" Here, the Lord contrasted the humanity of Peter—that is, as a little *"stone"*—with Himself and His divine message—that is, a huge *"Rock"*! "Nevertheless," Jesus went on, "I will give to you, My disciples, the 'keys' which will unlock the door to My kingdom so that those to whom you witness will be able to enter in. But whatever you 'lock' must already have been locked in heaven, and whatever you 'unlock' on earth must have already been unlocked in heaven. You will, in short, be given authority to function in My behalf, provided, of course, that you seek only to fulfill My will on the earth as outlined in Scripture and through the inspiration of the Holy Spirit." This meant that the disciples' authority on earth would be broad, provided their actions were based upon the principles which He had given them.[(l) 53]

---

48 Matthew 16:13; Mark 8:27; Luke 9:18
49 Matthew 16:14; Mark 8:28; Luke 9:19
50 Matthew 16:15; Mark 8:29; Luke 9:20
51 Matthew 16:16; Mark 8:29; Luke 9:20
52 Matthew 16:17
53 Matthew 16:18, 19

> The disciples were not, it should be noted, to have authority, *on their own,* to "lock" or "unlock" the things of heaven. Rather, their authority was to be based upon what the Lord had already Himself "locked" or "unlocked." They only had authority to permit or deny things based upon what the Lord had previously declared to be permitted or denied. In short, their authority was restricted by what Jesus had already determined.

At that point, Jesus strictly warned and instructed the disciples that they should not announce to the world that He was the Messiah. To do so at that time would only antagonize His sworn enemies, causing them to seek to kill Him before the appointed time.[54]

> Why did Jesus prohibit His disciples from declaring Him to be the Messiah—the Christ? And further, why did He Himself not openly declare that He was, in fact, the Messiah? [*Harmony* 10:69/] Now there was a wide variety of opinion among the Hebrew people as to who the Christ was and what He would accomplish during His ministry. If Jesus Himself declared categorically that He was the Messiah, then people would judge Him based upon their *pre-conceived* views as to who and what the Christ was to be, and what He would do. Rather, Jesus preferred that people should judge His ministry based upon what He actually taught and accomplished. This way, their view of the Messiah would be founded and molded upon what they observed in Him and what He taught, as opposed to what their pre-conceived ideas might have been. But there can be no doubt that Jesus did, in fact—albeit indirectly—claim to be the Christ. The evidence for this is abundant. [*Harmony* 3:82-99]

From that time on, Jesus began to emphasize to His disciples what He would soon be facing. He described that He would, at some point, go to Jerusalem. "While there," Jesus explained, "I will be rejected and persecuted by the elders, chief priests, and scribes. So severe will this persecution be that they will actually kill Me! However, I will be resurrected three days later." He continued to describe the whole matter to the disciples in some detail and with great clarity. [*Harmony* 7:14; 10:55, 84, 85; 13:46, 99, 100; 15:59][55]

---

54 Matthew 16:20; Mark 8:30; Luke 9:21

55 Matthew 16:21; Mark 8:31, 32; Luke 9:22

> Even though He had hinted at it before [*Harmony* 7:14], this was the first time in His ministry—just nine or ten months before the actual events—that the Lord clearly and emphatically detailed His sufferings, death, and resurrection. The disciples were shocked by what Jesus told them.

Peter, in particular was very distressed by what Jesus had explained to them regarding His death. So he took the Lord aside and began to question the veracity of His predictions. Peter challenged Jesus, saying, "No! No! God must be merciful to You, Lord! No! This must never happen to You as You have just described!"[56]

But Jesus turned and looked toward the disciples, and perceiving the real power behind Peter's words, said, "Get out of My sight, Satan! Peter, you are allowing the devil to speak through you! Your suggestion is actually a hindrance to the ultimate completion of My ministry. I must die as I have said I will. You are thinking, Peter, as a man thinks. You need to reason as God reasons." [*Harmony* 10:85; 17:3/, 4][57]

> It may seem quite surprising that Jesus would answer Peter with such words—insinuating that Satan was talking through His own disciple! But these strong words indicate just how important this issue was. If Jesus, for even one moment, should give serious thought to backing away from what He was about to face, the entire plan of salvation could be derailed. In fact, this was the basis of the devil's third temptation of Jesus in the wilderness. [*Harmony* 2:34] Of course, it should be noted Satan wasn't really speaking directly through Peter. Rather, Peter was thinking in such a way that the devil could use the disciple's concern for Jesus and subsequent words to his own evil advantage. [*Harmony* 17:4]

Then, openly addressing all the disciples as well as the crowd that was beginning to surround Him, Jesus added, "If you really wish to follow Me and remain faithful disciples of Mine, you must be willing to renounce your own will and desires. You must take up your cross"—that is, bear full sacrificial responsibility for what it means to be the Lord's true followers, no matter what the price or cost might be—"and walk in the way that I have set before you. For anyone who thinks that he or she will be able, on one hand, to follow Me, and,

---

56 Matthew 16:22; Mark 8:32

57 Matthew 16:32; Mark 8:33

on the other hand, maintain a life of ease, will in the end lose his or her life in the final judgment. Of course, the opposite is also true: Anyone who determines to remain faithful to Me and the Gospel message—even at the risk of losing one's life—will, in the end, gain eternal life. [*Harmony* 12:106][58]

"Tell Me, what profit is there in it for a man or woman to gain all that the world has to offer, while at the same time lose the gift of eternal life? And also tell Me, what is it that a man or a woman would really give in exchange for losing the greatest of all treasures: even eternal life itself? But I must tell you that when the Son of Man comes in the brightness of His Father, with all His angels with Him to establish His eternal kingdom, He will, at that time, generously recompense every person for his or her works of faithfulness to Him.[59]

"But," the Lord added, "whoever, in this unfaithful and sinful world, is ashamed of Me and the words which I have spoken, the Son of Man will also be ashamed of him or her when He comes in His own brightness, combined with the brightness of His Father, and the brightness of the angels, to establish His everlasting kingdom." [*Harmony* 10:64/][60]

Then, looking directly at His disciples, the Lord added, "It is a fact that there are some of you who are standing here with Me who will not die until you actually see that kingdom—yes, to see the Son of Man coming in His own powerful kingdom, as well as the kingdom of His Father." [*Harmony* 10:65][61]

> By these words, Jesus referred to His Transfiguration that would take place within a week. [*Harmony* 10:62-68] Of course, Jesus wasn't referring to the His *actual* glorious Second Coming, but to the Transfiguration that would serve as a *foretaste*, or microcosm, of that future event.

## An Amazing Couple of Days: The Transfiguration and the Healing of a Demon-possessed Boy
**< Late Summer, A.D. 30 (6/7) >**
**(Matthew 17:1-21; Mark 9:2-29; Luke 9:28-43)**

---

58 Matthew 16:24, 25; Mark 8:34, 35; Luke 9:23, 24
59 Matthew 16:26, 27; Mark 8:36, 37; Luke 9:25
60 Mark 8:38; Luke 9:26
61 Matthew 16:28; Mark 9:1; Luke 9:27

## — The Transfiguration
## < Late Summer, A.D. 30 (6/7) >
## {Matthew 17:1-13; Mark 9:2-13; Luke 9:28-36}

After Peter's confession of the Lord's Messiahship, Jesus and His disciples returned to the province of Galilee, about 20 miles southeast of Caesarea Philippi. It was about a week later—six days, to be exact—since Peter had made his confession. The Lord arrived with the disciples at the base of a relatively high mountain. At that place, the Savior took with Him just three of His disciples—Peter, and the brothers, James and John—and climbed the mountain to pray, leaving the remaining nine disciples behind. [*Harmony* 10:94][(m)] [62]

These three of the Lord's closest followers would be given the special privilege of seeing for themselves the transfiguration of the Master—wherein His human body was temporarily changed into a divine likeness![63]

> Peter, James, and John—to the exclusion of the other nine disciples—on this and at least two other occasions [*Harmony* 8:18; 17:2], were given the honor of being alone with Jesus. This indicated that these three had a superior understanding of the work and mission of the Lord. While Jesus wasn't "playing favorites," He nevertheless had a closer relationship with these three men.

While Jesus was praying on the mountain, the three disciples grew drowsy, and soon fell asleep. Then, in the middle of His prayer, the Lord's face changed. It began to glow like the sun, and His clothes glistened with a bright white light. The brightness was like snow reflecting the rays of the sun! Indeed, His clothes were much brighter than any launderer could ever make them, even with the strongest bleach! And then, even more dramatically, both Moses and Elijah—of Old Testament times—appeared in glorious splendor before the now, partially awakened disciples! The three disciples actually observed these two famous prophets of God talking with their Master. They even heard what the three of them were discussing among themselves. They were talking about what Jesus would ultimately face in Jerusalem, including His impending death. Hardly surprisingly, these amazing events completely shook the disciples' tiredness from them. [*Harmony* 7:14; 10:55-61, 84, 85; 13:99, 100; 15:59][64]

---

62 Matthew 17:1; Mark 9:2; Luke 9:28

63 Matthew 17:2; Mark 9:2

64 Matthew 17:2, 3; Mark 9:3, 4; Luke 9:29-32

> The Transfiguration was intended to encourage both Jesus and His three closest disciples. Within months, the Savior would face the greatest tests of His ministry. Certainly, the memory of the Transfiguration would lift His spirits during the time of His severest trials. And of course, these trials would also dramatically affect the disciples. Their faith would be pushed to the limit, as it would appear to them that the Lord's ministry was crashing down in utter failure. The Transfiguration was a foretaste of the glorious return of Jesus at the end of the world when He will establish His eternal kingdom. Its memory would encourage the disciples—as it would Jesus—to have confidence that better times were coming to those who patiently waited for them. That is why the Lord's face and clothes shone—as they would at the Second Coming. [*Harmony* 10:60] For, when the Lord was transfigured, His hidden divinity [Philippians 2:5-8] flashed through His humanity. [*Harmony* 1:1, 4] At the Second Coming, His divinity will shine forth in its full, unaltered brightness. The presence of Moses on the mountain represented those who would be resurrected [Deuteronomy 34:5, 6; Jude 9] when the Lord comes, while Elijah's presence represented those who would be saved without dying—that is, be translated—at the Lord's coming. [2 Kings 2:11] At that moment, though, the disciples did not understand any of this.[(n)]

Peter, unsure of what was happening, thought that perhaps Moses and Elijah were officially uniting with Jesus to establish His kingdom on that mountain at that very moment. After all, Jesus had predicted less than a week previously that some of the disciples would see the Son of Man coming into His kingdom. [*Harmony* 10:61] So, as Peter reasoned, here they were, and the Lord's kingdom was on the verge of being established![65]

Even though all three disciples were terrified by the sight, Peter thought that they should do something to memorialize the event permanently. That's why he, responding without completely thinking it through, called out to Jesus, saying, "Teacher! Lord, it is good for us to be here with You. If you desire, we can make three tents: one for You, and one each for Moses and Elijah—!"[66]

Then suddenly, a loud, thundering voice interrupted Peter right in the middle of his suggestion. The voice came from a glowing cloud that had quickly formed over their heads. As the disciples looked up, the cloud cast a dark shadow

---

65 Luke 9:33

66 Matthew 17:4; Mark 9:5, 6; Luke 9:33

over them all, causing even more intense fear to grip them! Next, they heard a loud voice coming from the cloud. And the powerful voice they heard was that of God, the Father, declaring, "This is My dear, beloved Son—the Chosen One! I am very pleased with Him. Never stop listening to what He has to say!" [*Harmony* 2:27] Seeing the cloud, and hearing the actual voice of God, the three disciples fell on their faces in sheer terror. At that very moment, both Moses and Elijah entered into the cloud above them.[67]

Shortly, Jesus came over to the three frightened disciples. He bent over and touched them, saying, "Please get up! There is no reason for you to be afraid!" Looking up, the three could see that Jesus was now alone with them, for Moses and Elijah, along with the cloud had instantly and completely vanished![68]

After they had risen to their feet, Jesus led them back down the mountain to rejoin the other nine disciples. On the way, the Lord commanded them, "Let Me be perfectly clear: Do not tell a single soul about the glorious things that you saw on the mountain. Keep it only among yourselves until the Son of Man is resurrected from the dead." Accordingly, they obeyed the command of their Lord, and told no one—not even the other disciples—what the three of them had seen on the mountain.[69]

> To have shared this incredible event with the other nine disciples at this time would have caused more harm than good. It would only have led to confusion in their minds. They were not sufficiently prepared to deal with what had happened on the mountain. [*Harmony* 10:54/][1]
>
> Ultimately, it would become clear to the three disciples with Jesus that day that, instead of this event marking the establishment of the Lord's eternal kingdom, the Transfiguration would serve as a foretaste—or promise—of what would happen in the far distant future when the Lord's glorious kingdom would actually be established at His Second Coming. [*Harmony* 10:60] The memory of the Transfiguration would give them courage when circumstances in their lives and ministry would appear bleak.[2]

At the time, the three disciples continued to be confused about all that had happened and the words that Jesus had said to them—especially the part about

---

67 Matthew 17:5, 6; Mark 9:7; Luke 9:34, 35
68 Matthew 17:7, 8; Mark 9:8; Luke 9:36
69 Matthew 17:9; Mark 9:9; Luke 9:36

His upcoming resurrection from the dead. They discussed it among themselves, wondering what the Lord meant by such a strange statement. This was because, in spite of the Lord's insistence that He would soon die and be resurrected [*Harmony* 10:55], the disciples tenaciously clung to the traditional belief of the Jews that the Messiah's ministry would be marked only by glory . . . and certainly not by death![70]

The three disciples were further confused by what they had always been taught as compared with what they had actually seen on the mountain. This confusion led them to question the Lord by asking, "Why is it, then, that the Jewish scribes say that Elijah must first come—before the Messiah arrives—to announce the Christ's coming? That's what we've always been taught to believe. Then why did Elijah appear with You on the mountain *after* You arrived, and not *before* Your arrival, as we've been taught? You see, Elijah has never announced Your coming as we had supposed he would do." [*Harmony* 11:16][71]

> The issue that the disciples discussed with Jesus here was based upon the prophecy of Malachi 4:5, 6. This last Old Testament prophet had predicted that Elijah's coming would *precede* the arrival of the Messiah, to announce and confirm His coming. Of course, the disciples believed that Jesus was the Christ. But when had Elijah come to announce the arrival of the Messiah? Once again, they had just seen Elijah on the mountain, but that was *after* the Lord had arrived as the Messiah—not before. Further, they believed that when both Elijah and the Christ had arrived, then the Messiah would establish His eternal kingdom and reign in glory. So the gist of the disciples' multiple questions to Jesus was: "What do the scribes—and Malachi—mean by saying that Elijah would come before the Messiah's appearance? Because You—as the Christ—are already here, when was it that Elijah arrived to announce Your coming? When did that happen? And, too, if that has already happened, then why do You—the Messiah—have to suffer? That's not what we've been taught. We are all terribly confused!" Certainly the time had come for the establishment of the Lord's eternal kingdom, they reasoned! Therefore, compared with what they had been taught all their lives, the way things were actually transpiring made no sense to them whatsoever.

---

70 Mark 9:10

71 Matthew 17:10; Mark 9:11

Jesus answered them, saying, "Yes, in this case the scribes are right: Elijah would come to restore all things and announce the Messiah's coming—just as Malachi prophesied. [Malachi 4:5, 6; *Harmony* 2:4] In fact, Elijah has already come! And, too, I know what you are thinking: Why do the Scriptures say that the Son of Man will need to suffer many things and be treated with such contempt, if, indeed, Elijah has already come to restore all things? It is because, I tell you, that even though Elijah has already come, these same scribes did not recognize nor accept him. In fact, they treated him just as their evil hearts led them to do. Because they rejected Elijah, they have *also* rejected the Son of Man—the actual Messiah. Therefore, their rejection of the Messiah and His ministry will lead to His suffering, just as has been in the case of Elijah, for they have hated him too." [*Harmony* 2:47] It was then that it dawned on the three disciples that Jesus equated the ministry of *John the Baptist* with the Malachi prophecy regarding the coming of Elijah, the prophet. [Malachi 4:5, 6][(o)] [72]

> First of all, it was now very clear to the disciples that Jesus, in talking about Elijah, referred directly to the ministry of John the Baptist. [*Harmony* 2:45, 47, 49] Of course, John was not actually the person Elijah. Rather, John's ministry was in the spirit and power of Elijah, thus fulfilling the prophecy. And second, it was just beginning to become clear to the disciples that because the Jewish leaders had rejected John, they would reject Jesus also. That is, in rejecting the forerunner of the Messiah—John, as "Elijah"—it was logical, then, that they would likewise reject the One who followed after him—the Messiah Himself. But it would be much more than a mere rejection. They would actually kill Him! In fact, just as John was killed by Herod [*Harmony* 8:63-71], so Jesus would be killed by the Jews and the Romans. [*Harmony* 17:111] The establishment of the Lord's glorious kingdom in the disciples' day pre-supposed that the Jewish leadership would first accept Jesus. So, sadly, because the Jews rejected Jesus, such an establishment of His glorious kingdom would have to come much later on at His Second Coming. All this the disciples would better understand in the future.[(p)]

---

72 Matthew 17:11-13; Mark 9:12, 13

## — The Healing of a Demon-Possessed Boy[(q)]
## < Late Summer, A.D. 30 (6/7) >
## {Matthew 17:14-18; Mark 9:14-27; Luke 9:37-43}

The next day—after the Transfiguration [*Harmony* 10:62-68]—Jesus, and the three disciples who were with Him on the mountain during the time of the Transfiguration—Peter, James, and John—made their way down the hill to rejoin the other nine disciples. As they arrived at the base of the mountain, they noticed a large crowd surrounding the remaining disciples. There were also some scribes heckling them. Seeing the Lord approaching, the crowd ran up to Him. They were amazed when they saw those who had been on the mountain, for their faces were still glowing from the brightness of the event that had transpired on the mountain![73]

The Lord asked the scribes, "What have you been debating with My disciples?"[74]

Before the scribes could answer this question, a man within the crowd immediately came forward. "Teacher," he begged loudly, as he fell on his knees before the Lord, "have mercy on my son! He throws fits and is very, very ill. I brought my only child to You to be healed. Please look at him. He is possessed of a demon that has rendered him unable to speak. And whenever the demon takes hold of him, the devil screams, tears him, and causes him to foam at the mouth and to grind his teeth. His whole body, then, becomes as stiff as board. It is only after much anguish that the demon finally leaves him, terribly wounding him on the way out.[75]

"Then, before long," the man continued his agonizing story, "the demon comes back, and it starts all over again! Often, too, the demon throws my son into the fire so as to burn him. Also he casts my son into water so as to drown him. As I have said, I came here to have You heal my son. Because You were not here, I begged Your disciples to heal him . . . but they were quite unable to do so. Now, can You help me? I beg of You to look at my son!" [*Harmony* 10:104/3][76]

In His response, Jesus addressed not only the boy's father but also the scribes, the crowd, and the baffled nine disciples. "Oh unfaithful and perverse generation!"

---

[73] Matthew 17:14; Mark 9:14, 15; Luke 9:37
[74] Mark 9:16
[75] Matthew 17:14, 15; Mark 9:17, 18; Luke 9:38, 39
[76] Matthew 17:15, 16; Mark 9:18; Luke 9:39, 40

He declared. "How long must I plead with you to understand what I've been saying? How long must I put up with your lack of faith?" Then speaking directly to the father, He added, "Bring the boy to Me!" They brought the man's son to Jesus, and as soon as the boy saw the Lord, the demon within him instantly threw the youngster into a convulsion. The demon knocked him to the ground, causing him once more to roll around and foam at the mouth. [*Harmony* 104/3][77]

"How long has the boy been suffering this way?" Jesus questioned the father.[78]

"From childhood," was the father's answer. "As I have been telling You, the demon has often thrown him into the fire and the water, trying to kill him. But, Lord, if You can do anything to help, do so. Please take pity on us and help!"[79]

"'*If* You can'?" Jesus answered, repeating the doubting words of the father. This indicated that the Lord recognized that the father was only a partial believer. "Ah! All things are possible to those who *truly* believe!" Jesus firmly concluded.[80]

Sensing that his partial unbelief might prevent his son from being healed, the father cried out, "Lord, I do believe—please help me with the part of me that does not yet believe!"[81]

Jesus saw that the crowd was growing larger by the second. So, in front of them all, He commanded the devil with a rebuke, declaring, "You deaf and mute demon, I, Myself, demand that you come out of this boy, and I command you never to enter him again!"[82]

After once more screaming and throwing the boy into one last convulsion, the demon came out of him, causing the child to lie still as though he were dead. In fact, most in the crowd declared, "He's dead!" But Jesus took him by the hand and raised him up . . . and the boy stood up by himself, quite alive! He returned the boy, completely healed, to his father. Everyone in the crowd was amazed at

---

77 Matthew 17:17; Mark 9:19, 20; Luke 9:41, 42
78 Mark 9:21
79 Mark 9:21, 22
80 Mark 9:23
81 Mark 9:24
82 Matthew 17:18; Mark 9:25; Luke 9:42

the majestic thing which they had just seen as the result of the power of God. (r) 83

## Jesus Makes a Secret Journey Through Galilee
## < Late Summer, A.D. 30 (6/7) >
## (Matthew 17:22, 23; Mark 9:30-32; Luke 9:43-45)

The people continued to marvel at the miracle of the healing the demon-possessed boy. [*Harmony* 10:73-85] But Jesus, leaving the mountain area where the miracle had occurred, traveled incognito around the province so that no one except His disciples knew where He was. He continued to teach and instruct the disciples regarding His prediction about His upcoming sufferings and death. The disciples were wondering about all that Jesus was telling them regarding His future agony. He repeated, "You must listen carefully to this. Don't miss a single word I'm saying. The Son of Man will be delivered by a betrayer into the complete control of evil men . . . and they will definitely kill Him! But don't be afraid, for, after He is killed, He will rise again after three days." [*Harmony* 7:14; 10:55-61, 13:46, 99, 100; 15:59; 16:1, 11][84]

Even though the Lord re-emphasized these facts over and over again to the disciples, they did not understand what He was telling them, for they were greatly pained by such a suggestion. Remembering the Lord's negative reaction to Peter's previous challenge of His assertion that He would die [*Harmony* 10:56, 57], they were afraid to question Him further on the matter! Obviously, they did not like what He was telling them, neither were His words consistent with what they had been taught regarding the future glories of the Messiah. So, they refused to accept what He was saying. They, in effect, rejected His prediction. And, as a result, they did not comprehend the gravity of what He had told them. It remained completely beyond them. [*Harmony* 10:94, 104/3[(s) 85]

## The Tribute Money Incident; and the Lord Teaches About Humility and Forgiveness
## < Late Summer, A.D. 30 (6/7) >
## (Matthew 17:19-21, 24-18:35; Mark 9:33-50; Luke 9:46-50)

---

83 Matthew 17:18; Mark 9:26, 27; Luke 9:42, 43

84 Matthew 17:22, 23; Mark 9:30, 31; Luke 9:43, 44

85 Matthew 17:23; Mark 9:32; Luke 9:45

## — The Confused Disciples and the Tribute Money Incident < Late Summer, A.D. 30 (6/7) > {Matthew 17:19-21, 24-27; Mark 9:28, 29}

After the Lord's semi-secret travels around the province of Galilee [*Harmony* 11:2], He, with His disciples, arrived back in Capernaum. When Jesus and the disciples had entered Peter's home, they secretly asked Him, "Why was it that we could not drive the evil demon out of the boy?" [*Harmony* 10:73-83, 94][86]

Jesus said, "It was because of the smallness of your faith, that's why! I declare with certainty that if your faith were just the size of a tiny mustard seed, you would be able to say to a problem, even the size of a mountain, 'Move from here to there,' and it would move accordingly. Yes, nothing of great significance would be impossible for you! But, this kind of miracle—to cast out a demon—can only happen to those who are constantly living, by prayer and fasting, in a close relationship with God." [*Harmony* 2:34/2; 10:104/3, 105][(t) (u) 87]

> While Jesus was on the mountain with the three disciples [*Harmony* 10:62-72], the remaining nine were whining about their problems, and thus were losing their close contact with God. In the past they had, indeed, been able to work miracles such as this. [*Harmony* 8:58] But on this occasion, they were very upset that they had not been invited to be with Jesus and the other three on the mountain. This evil attitude had prevented them from receiving the power of God to work through them in the performance of this particular miracle.

While Jesus and His disciples were sojourning in Capernaum for a while, some tax-collectors saw Peter on the street one day. These were not the regular tax-collectors who worked for the Roman government. Rather, these tax-collectors assisted the Jewish church by collecting taxes for the upkeep of the Temple in Jerusalem. They asked Peter, "Does your Teacher pay the Temple tax of two drachmas?" The amount of this tax was equivalent to two days' wages of a common laborer.[88]

> This assessment was a non-compulsory tax. Nevertheless, it was considered a religious duty for people to pay it. [Exodus 30:12-16] Whether Jesus paid this tax or not was irrelevant. This was because

---

86 Matthew 17:19, 24; Mark 9:28

87 Matthew 17:20, 21; Mark 9:29

88 Matthew 17:24

> Jesus could claim a valid exemption from paying the tax, for prophets and teachers of the law were free from this requirement. Besides, this was not the normal time of the year when the tax was due. Thus it was apparent that this question was prompted by a sinister motive. That is, the tax-collectors were trying to trick Jesus—or any of His disciples—into doing or saying something that could be used to injure the Lord's positive reputation with the people. If, for example, He or His disciples claimed He was exempt from paying the tax, it could be said that He was stingy toward the work of the church, thus showing disrespect for the hallowed Temple. On the other hand, should Jesus have paid the tax, it could be said that His willingness to pay it meant that He did not believe that He was either a prophet or a true teacher of the law. Either way, the tax-collectors thought they would have accomplished their evil purpose!

Peter, partially recognizing the evil motives of the questioners, impulsively answered, "Why yes! Of course, my Master pays the tax!" Peter thought, considering the circumstances, that this was the best course to pursue in answering this tricky question.[89]

Peter returned to his home where Jesus was staying. There the Lord already miraculously knew about the conversation between Peter and the tax-collectors, for even before Peter had a chance to tell Him what had happened, Jesus questioned him regarding the incident. "What do you think, Simon?" Jesus began. "From whom do the kings of this world collect their taxes or customs: from their own sons or from strangers?"[90]

"From strangers," was Peter's obvious answer.[91]

"Well, then," Jesus responded, "the sons are free from paying the tax. Isn't that right?"[92]

> As the Son of God, Jesus was, of course, exempt from financially supporting the Temple which represented Him! In addition, as a prophet and a teacher, He was also exempt as far as the law of the land was concerned.

---

89 Matthew 17:25
90 Matthew 17:25
91 Matthew 17:26
92 Matthew 17:26

"However," the Lord concluded, "so that we not give a reason for these tax-collectors to stumble and have cause to accuse Me, I want you to go down to the sea. There, throw in a hook, and take up the first fish that you catch. When you open its mouth, you will find a shekel there! Take it and pay the tax for both you and Me." The worth of a shekel was the exact amount for the Temple tax for two people: Peter and Jesus.[93]

> By this incident, the Lord showed that He was not willing to allow such a minor issue as paying a small tax to create an unnecessary crisis between Him and His enemies. Furthermore, by paying the tax, Jesus would completely disarm His critics. First of all, by paying it Jesus would prove that He was a loyal citizen and a clear supporter of the Temple. And second, when paying the tax, no doubt Peter would tell the tax-collectors of the miraculous source of the coin. So, when he did, this would prove that Jesus was a miracle-working prophet, and therefore exempt from paying the tax in the first place! In either case, His critics could have no basis for challenging Him. Jesus was both a loyal supporter of the Temple . . . and a prophet. In short, Jesus had completely foiled His enemies' plan![1]

So Peter went and did as the Lord had directed him.(v) [2]

**— The Lord's Teaching on Humility and Forgiveness(w)**
**< Late Summer, A.D. 30 (6/7) >**
**{Matthew 18:1-35; Mark 9:33-50; Luke 9:46-50}**

While Peter was busy hooking the fish that had the coin in its mouth [*Harmony* 10:93], Jesus remained in Peter's home in Capernaum with the eleven other disciples. The Lord questioned them, "On our way back to Capernaum, I noticed that you were talking among yourselves. Tell Me, what were you discussing? I could tell that it was more than a conversation. In fact, it appeared to Me to be an argument!" Apparently startled by the question, the disciples hesitated to give an answer. They were embarrassed to answer, for they had been debating among themselves, with some passion, regarding which of them was the greatest of the twelve. No doubt this debate was the result of the frustration nine of the disciples felt over their exclusion from being on the mount with Jesus when He was transfigured [*Harmony* 10:62], as well as their dismay over not being able to heal the demon-possessed boy. [*Harmony* 10:86] Also, the Lord's

---

93 Matthew 17:27

distressing statements regarding His future sufferings [*Harmony* 10:84, 85], had no doubt set them on edge. In any case, they obviously knew that Jesus would disapprove of such a debate. [*Harmony* 10:104/3, 105][94]

For the moment, Jesus did not press the issue. A short time later, Peter returned from paying the Temple tax with the coin he found in the fish's mouth. Peter told the Lord and the other disciples of his grand adventure.

With Peter, their usual spokesman, back with them, the disciples finally had enough courage to respond to the questions Jesus had earlier asked of the eleven. [*Harmony* 10:94] Coming to Jesus, they asked Him, "Who, then, is the greatest in the kingdom of heaven?" They were hoping that, maybe, the Lord would indicate which of the Twelve was the greatest of His disciples.[95]

Sitting in their midst, the Lord called the twelve disciples to come closer to Him. Jesus knew their thoughts. Accordingly, He began to give an answer to their question by saying, "If anyone of you really wants to be great, let him view himself as being the least among those around him, even as the servant of the others." [*Harmony* 16:8] To illustrate His point, the Lord took a little child who was running around in the house and placed him in their midst. Holding the child in His arms, He further explained, "It is certain fact that, unless you repent from your superior-like attitudes toward one another, and become like this child, you will not be saved! What do I mean? Notice the child-like trust and simple faith little ones have toward one another and toward people in general. That is what you need to have toward each other. And, too, whoever has the accepting spirit and submissive attitude of a child—such as this little one here—will be considered great in the kingdom of heaven. [*Harmony* 10:107, 13:73][96]

"Furthermore, notice how I am holding this child in My arms. Well, whoever reaches out to one of my humble followers in a similar way, has, in reality, accepted Me. He or she has accepted not only Me, but also the Father who has sent Me. That's the kind of accepting spirit you should have toward one another. These, then, are the true signs of greatness: to be least among the others, as a child, and to treat one another as you would a little child!" [*Harmony* 12:152][97]

---

94 Mark 9:33, 34; Luke 9:46, 47

95 Matthew 18:1

96 Matthew 18:2-4; Mark 9:35, 36; Luke 9:47

97 Matthew 18:5; Mark 9:36, 37; Luke 9:48

Here, Jesus compared His disciples' relationship with each to that of children in a family. In doing so, He made three points: First, His disciples were to act as though they were the least—like younger children might act among older children. This means, in part, being submissive to one another, as children would be. Second, they were to relate to the others with a trusting spirit—also as children would normally act. And third, they were to treat one another with the same kind of compassion and tenderness that a parent would show to his or her own child.

Still thinking about the Lord's illustration of the child, John asked Him, "Teacher, some time ago, we saw someone casting out demons in Your name. However, we rebuked him for what he was doing, because he was not one of our group. Based upon what You've just told us, did we do the right or wrong thing by this action?"[98]

Jesus relied, "You did the wrong thing! Indeed, do not stop him! No one will, at one moment, truly work a miracle in My name, and then the next moment say something evil about Me. Remember, he who is not against us is really on our side. You are not to be that person's judge."[99]

Here, Jesus did not address the existence of false prophets, or, as He did elsewhere, those who work miracles in the power of Satan. [*Harmony* 15:18] Rather, He was talking about those who have genuinely worked miracles in His name. The Lord was saying that people who, one minute, genuinely work under the power of God, will not, the next minute, turn on the Lord and become critical of Him. More importantly, it was not the prerogative or responsibility of the disciples, who could not read the hearts of others, to judge their motives or ministries. That is the prerogative of God alone. [*Harmony* 5:68, 69]

"Also," Jesus continued, "should one of My servants, give you—a fellow servant—a cup of cold water to drink, just because you are another one of My followers, I declare to you that he or she will be rewarded by God for such an act of kindness. On the other hand, should anyone cause one of My humble followers to stumble, it would have been better for that person to have had a large millstone"—used for grinding wheat into flour—"tied around his neck, and be thrown into the deep sea and drowned! You see, to offend one of My followers

98 Mark 9:38; Luke 9:49
99 Mark 9:39, 40; Luke 9:50

would be just as awful as doing something evil to this child sitting here in My arms! So then, treat one another with great kindness and compassion. [*Harmony* 12:152][100]

"Of course, it is true that while we live in this sinful world, unavoidable things will happen which will cause people to be offended and hurt. That's life, and in the judgment, God will take care of it appropriately. However, just think how bad it will be in the judgment for those who, *deliberately*, cause others to stumble and fall! Indeed, woe to them in the judgment![101]

"As I have said on a previous occasion [*Harmony* 5:29]," Jesus continued, "if your hand should cause you to do evil things to one another, I say: cut off that hand! In that case, it would be far better to enter into eternal life with only one hand, so to speak, than to be sent to hell with both hands to suffer in its fires. In that day, so complete will be your destruction that you will be like a dead body utterly consumed by worms. Yes, I tell you, those fires of hell will not be put out until they have finished their work of complete destruction![(x)] [102]

"In a like manner, I might add, should your foot cause you to do evil against another, I say again, cut it off! It would be much better to enter eternal life lame, so to speak, with only one good leg, than for your entire body to be thrown into hell fire! Once again, your total destruction can be compared to a dead body that has been completely consumed by worms. The fires that destroy you in hell will never go out until they have completely consumed you.[(y)] [103]

"And, once more, if your eye causes you to do something evil against another person, I say, pop it out of its socket and cast it away! It would be better for you to enter eternal life with only one eye—again, so to speak—than to have both eyes and see and feel the fires of hell! As the Scripture says, 'In hell their worm will not die, neither will the fire be quenched until it destructive work is completed.'" [Isaiah 66:24] Here, the "worm" in this illustration is not literal but refers symbolically to a destruction that cannot be reversed, just as worms continue to live until they have totally consumed the flesh of a dead body. [*Harmony* 10:107][104]

---

100 Matthew 18:6; Mark 9:41, 42
101 Matthew 18:7
102 Matthew 18:8; Mark 9:43, 44
103 Matthew 18:8; Mark 9:45, 46
104 Matthew 18:9; Mark 9:47, 48

In effect, Jesus was saying, "Of course, I'm not suggesting that you mutilate your body in order to be saved! What I'm saying is this: Being kind to others is not always easy. On occasion, it might feel like cutting off a foot or hand, or plucking out an eye! But it is always the best thing to do. The struggle to always be kind to one another—which sometimes may feel like a fiery trial to you—is far less painful than hell-fire! Yes, while it is often difficult, in the end, it is well worth it!"[1]

It should be noted that the Lord's three illustrations of the hand, foot, and eye were very powerful. The punishment the Lord will mete out to those who unnecessarily offend someone else is dire: complete destruction . . . in hell-fire![2]

Next, Jesus wanted to illustrate to His disciples the importance of maintaining a positive attitude toward the struggles they were at that time facing in their lives. Indeed, they were at that moment distraught about a number of things. First, He was talking about His impending death, which was contrary to what they had been taught throughout their lives. [*Harmony* 10:84, 85] The thought that their Master was going to die was more than they could bear. Second, they were trying to determine which one of them was the greatest, causing no little jealousy to arise among them. [*Harmony* 10:94, 95] And third, nine of the disciples were especially upset about a couple of things. They were distressed that they were not on the mountain with the other three during the Transfiguration, and further, they had no clue as to what had happened on the mountain! [*Harmony* 10:87/] This, not surprisingly, really upset them! Furthermore, they were embarrassed by that fact that they could not heal the demon-possessed boy [*Harmony* 10:76], and they were hurt that Jesus had publically called them down for their lack of faith. [*Harmony* 10:77] At this point, Jesus really needed to give His disciples instruction in how to cope with such distresses that might arise during their ministries as they attempted to work with each other.[3]

The Lord continued with His explanations, saying, "Let Me give you an illustration. As you know, during the Temple services, all sacrifices which you might bring to the Lord—whether they are animals or otherwise—represent, in part, the total commitment of your life to the cause of God. That's right, isn't it? And, as you further know, all such sacrifices are to be presented with fire and salt. [Leviticus 2:13] That's also true, isn't it? But what do this 'fire' and 'salt' represent? First of all, the 'fire' involved in your sacrifices represents the 'fiery' struggles—doubts, perplexities, persecutions, and so forth—that you've had in your lives—especially the kind you've have been experiencing lately. [*Harmony* 10:85-87, 94] That makes sense, doesn't it? However, having a *positive attitude* toward those fiery struggles and difficulties that happen in your lives is represented by the 'salt' that has also been added to these same sacrifices. And further, this positive attitude—again, represented by the 'salt'—*should and will* produce a spirit of kindness and gentleness in your lives toward one other. In summary, therefore, when you have the right attitude toward difficult things—the 'fiery' trials of your life—you will be able to treat with compassion those who are going through the same kind of difficult experiences. Certainly, you can see that![(z)] [105]

"Yes, as I just indicated," Jesus continued, "a positive attitude toward the 'fiery' trials in your lives is the 'salt' of the righteousness of God that is being produced within you. But I must ask, if you have a *negative attitude* toward the 'fiery' trials of your life, what happens then? The 'salt' of kindness and gentleness, which should be strong in your lives, has lost its savor! And if that 'salt' loses its so-called 'saltiness,' then can anyone really make it salty again? So here's the bottom line: When you *continue* to debate and argue among yourselves as to who is the greatest among you—as all of you have been doing lately—you will start to lose the 'saltiness' of the 'salt' of God's righteousness in your lives. [*Harmony* 5:16, 17] And if you *still continue* to debate among each other, you will lose altogether the 'salt' of God's righteousness within you. This happens because your constant arguing will ultimately destroy the patience and compassion of your heart toward one another that a positive attitude toward the 'fiery' trials should have produced in you. So I say, have plenty of life's good 'salt' in your heart so that you will be able to continue to live at peace with each another. Then the question of who is the greatest among you will no longer be an important issue to you. Do you see that?[(aa)] [106]

"What, then, do you think would happen to you," the Lord asked, continuing to make His point, "if you were to treat in a despicable manner this child I've been holding in My arms? [*Harmony* 10:96] Indeed, what would happen if you were, in general, to treat children in an evil way? Of course, you would be in deep trouble in the final judgment because their guardian angels, who are constantly in the presence of My Father in heaven, will tell Him of your evil deed! Isn't that right? In the same way, should you treat one another—that is, *any* of God's

105 Mark 9:49
106 Mark 9:50

children, so to speak—in a despicable manner, their guardian angels will also tell My Father what you have done. And, in the final judgment, you will dearly pay for it! [*Harmony* 10:102-104] Remember that I, the Son of Man, came to this world to save those who were lost. Thus, be very careful how you treat those whom I have come to save. Most assuredly, I will hold you, as My followers, personally accountable. [*Harmony* 12:110][107]

"What do you think of this other illustration?" Jesus added. "If a good shepherd has a 100 sheep and one of them ends up missing, will he not leave the remaining 99 alone on the hillside and go and search for the single missing one? Of course he will! And should it happen that the shepherd finds that missing sheep, I can declare to you that he will rejoice over that one lone sheep more than over the 99 who had not strayed. Isn't that right? So, it is not the will of your Father in heaven that a single one of My followers who is weak and needs His help should be lost!" [*Harmony* 8:4; 12:112, 113][108]

At this point, the Lord, to clarify His statements, began to discuss the principles of dealing with people who need discipline within the structure of the church. He said, "Yes, even though you are to treat one another with kindness and dignity, there are times when you may need to discipline one another. But, even in that case, you must still treat one another in a kind and loving way. For example, if someone within the church should do some sinful thing against you or the church, go to him in private and discuss the issue with him. If he responds positively to your effort, you will have won him back to you, and no one will have known that you have discussed the issue with him. This way you will preserve both his privacy and dignity.[(bb)] [(cc)] [109]

"However, if he should be unwilling to respond to you in private, then take one or two other people with you so that in this second discussion these two or three witnesses will be able to confirm what you have discussed with him. And should he repent, then only a few will have known what has taken place. But, if he still refuses to respond to you and the witnesses, then, in that case—and only in that case—tell the issue to the leaders of the church. And should he still continue to refuse to respond, even to the leaders of the church, then you are

---

107 Matthew 18:10, 11

108 Matthew 18:12-14

109 Matthew 18:15

justified in openly severing him from the fellowship of the church as though he were a heathen, even a wicked man of the world." [*Harmony* 18:51][(dd)] [110]

> Here the Lord made it clear that under the circumstances just outlined, it was *appropriate* to sever someone from the fellowship of the church. On the other hand, He did not suggest that such an individual should not, afterwards, be worked with, leading to his or her reuniting with the church at some reasonable time in the future. In fact, all that is known about Jesus would clearly indicate that such an effort should be attempted. [*Harmony* 10:108; 11:33-41]

"I tell you the truth," Jesus concluded, "if you follow this procedure, then God will ratify your decisions. In that case, the things which you think best not to do on the earth will be ratified in heaven. Likewise, the things which you agree to do on the earth will also be ratified in heaven. Yes, what you, together, have properly agreed upon in the work of the church while you are in this world, God will ratify in heaven. But please note, that if it is necessary to separate one from the church, you are not to do it on your own. You must agree and work together as a body of believers. When two or three agree on something which you have properly decided, and you ask the Father in heaven to bless your decision and effort, He will do so. In fact, when you work together as a team in My name, two or three or more people at a time, in all types of problem-solving, I will, in effect, be there in your midst!"[(ee)] [111]

Then Peter came forward and asked Jesus, "Lord, you've been talking about accepting one another. Such acceptance requires on many occasions a willingness to forgive others. So then, how often should we be willing to forgive others when they sin against us? We've been told by the scribes that we should forgive people up to three times. Are you suggesting that we should extend the forgiveness to others up to . . . let's say, seven times?" [*Harmony* 5:53; 12:153][(ff)] [112]

Jesus answered, "No! Not up to seven times. I say, rather, up to seventy times seven! Actually, the number of times is not the issue. The issue is that we must have, and continue to have, a forgiving spirit and attitude toward one another,

---

110 Matthew 18:16, 17

111 Matthew 18:18-20

112 Matthew 18:21

especially when they want us to forgive them. Let me tell you a story to illustrate this concept of generous forgiveness: [*Harmony* 12:8, 8/][113]

"The kingdom of heaven can be compared to a king who wished to settle accounts with various servants who owed him different sums of money. In the process of this account-settling, one servant was brought in who owed him 10,000 talents of money. This amount was so large"—millions of dollars—"that he would never be able to pay it back, not even over many lifetimes! Thus, the king ordered that the man, his wife, and children, be sold into slavery. In addition, all the man's possessions were to be seized and sold so that as much of the debt as possible could be paid. But the servant fell down before the king, begging him, 'Please be patient with me. I will pay back everything I owe you.' In response, the king felt compassion for the servant, and not only did he not sell both him and his family into slavery, but he also forgave his entire debt! In fact, he allowed the servant to go back to his home totally free of all debt.[114]

"However, the forgiven servant, when he left the king, saw a fellow servant who owed him 100 denarii—just four months' wages. He grabbed hold of that servant by the neck and began to choke him, demanding, 'Pay back what you owe me!'[115]

The fellow servant fell before him and begged, 'Please have patience with me. Over time, I will pay back what I owe you.' But that wicked servant—who had been so generously forgiven by the king—refused this reasonable offer. Instead, he had the man thrown into debtors' prison until he paid his debt to him in full![116]

"Well, when the circumstances of this shameful incident became public knowledge, the other servants of the king were extremely upset. Accordingly, they reported the sad situation to the king himself. As a result, the king demanded that the servant whom he had forgiven his awesome debt be brought before him again. The king confronted him, saying, 'You ungrateful servant! I forgave all your debt, just because you pleaded with me to be patient. So then, should you not have shown mercy and forgiveness to your fellow servants, just as I have shown mercy and forgiveness to you?' Not surprisingly, the king was so enraged

113 Matthew 18:22, 23
114 Matthew 18:23-27
115 Matthew 18:28
116 Matthew 18:29, 30

that he handed the servant over to the torturers until he should have paid back every penny that he owed the king![117]

"So then," Jesus concluded, "My heavenly Father will do the same to you if are not willing, from the depth of your heart, to forgive your brothers for the things which they have done against you!" [*Harmony* 5:53; 12:153][118]

> In this powerful parable the king represents God. The man who owed the huge, virtually *infinite* debt, represents every sinner—for, indeed, every sinner owes God an *infinite* debt of sin. The other debtor—the one who owed just 100 denarii—represents a sinner who owes a fellow sinner a *finite* debt of sin. The forgiven debtor in the story—the one who owed 10,000 talents—represents the sinner who has had his *infinite* debt forgiven by God, but refuses to forgive a fellow sinner who owes him only a *finite* debt. The bottom line of the parable is this: If God is willing to forgive the *infinite* debt of sin the sinner owes Him, then logically, that sinner must be willing to forgive the *finite* debt of sin a fellow sinner owes him. If, conversely, a sinner is unwilling to forgive a *finite* debt a fellow sinner owes him, then God will not be willing to forgive the *infinite* debt the sinner owes Him! It's just that simple.[1]
>
> The message of this dramatic parable clearly underscores the necessity of exhibiting a forgiving spirit and attitude toward others. And Jesus has required all His followers to possess such a forgiving spirit.[2]

**Supplementary Notes:**

**(a) [10:0+]** This is the sixth of eight insertions in the *Harmony* that places the events of the three-and-a-half-year ministry of Jesus on a "timeline," divided into seven six-month segments. (The eighth insertion is at the end of the seventh segment.) The other segment insertions can be found in the following locations: Segment One, *Harmony* 2:21/; Two, *Harmony* 3:0; Three, *Harmony* 3:33/2; Four, *Harmony* 3:71/; Five, *Harmony* 6:17/; Seven, *Harmony* 11:0; and Eight, *Harmony* 18:99/1-21.

**(b) [10:0/6]** This segment has the designation 6/7 for its "Segmental Placement" number. (See "Segmental Placement" in the "Features for Using the

---

117 Matthew 18:31-34

118 Matthew 18:35

*Harmony* as a Reference Book" section near the back of this book for more information.)

**(c) [10:2]** The record indicates that the Jewish leaders were concerned that the Lord's disciples, rather than Jesus Himself, were not participating in the handwashing rituals. However, it is clear to me that Jesus was not ritualistically washing His hands either. In reality, the fact that the Jews picked on the disciples only and not Jesus was, I think, because they didn't have the nerve to challenge Him personally and openly on the issue. However, to clarify the whole situation for the *Harmony,* I included the Lord's non-participation in the handwashings as though it were part of the record.

**(d) [10:3]** (See above.)

**(e) [10:4]** Matthew's order of events in this story is different from Mark's. I followed Mark's sequence, considering it more plausible.

**(f) [10:8]** The record does not say that Jesus left the house; however, Mark says (*Harmony* 10:9) that Jesus went *into* the house later on. So then it appears that when the Pharisees left the house in a huff, Jesus went out to see them leave. It was then that He called the people outside the house to come closer to Him. After His conversation with them, He went back into the house to be with His disciples. Accordingly, that is the way I put it in the *Harmony.*

**(g) [10:13]** Mark, in his account (as written in the KJV), ends verse 19 with the phrase, "purging all meats." What does this phrase mean? Many have interpreted this phrase to mean that Jesus cleansed all *flesh foods* which had previously been declared unclean by God in Leviticus 11. That being the case, did Jesus, by making His statements in this text, really cleanse all foods, including those God had earlier declared unclean? In an attempt to understand the true meaning of this phrase, please consider the following points: *First,* the Lord was condemning a false teaching of the Jews, not seeking to cleanse foods that He already pronounced unclean (such as in Leviticus 11). Remember, the Jewish leaders taught that food eaten by people who had not gone through the *ritualistic* handwashing, polluted their *souls.* All such people were now *ceremonially* unclean. *Second,* the context seems to make it clear that it was *Mark,* as a commentator—not Jesus—who made the statement, "purging all meats," of the KJV. It appears that Mark was trying to clarify the Lord's statement. But, ironically, in his effort to clarify the statement, Mark may have actually "muddied the waters" more! *Third*, the word "meats" refers to all types of food, not just flesh food.

So then, what did Mark mean by this confusing phrase? In essence, Mark was saying: *The ingestion of food eaten with unwashed hands does not pollute the* ***soul****. The food itself is fine.* This interpretation is consistent with the point Jesus was making. Again, Jesus was not making all flesh foods clean, as some say, thus eliminating the clean and unclean flesh food laws of Leviticus 11. That wasn't the Lord's point at all! Anyone carefully reading the text can clearly see that. He was merely saying that eating food with unwashed hands does not *innately* affect the *ceremonial* cleanliness or uncleanliness of any food, even flesh food.

Remember, the Jews in this story believed that eating food with unwashed hands *ceremonially* polluted the food itself, and thus *ceremonially* polluted the persons eating such food—thus making them *less morally worthy* than those who went through the rituals. In other words, beyond the physical elements of the food, they taught that, when eaten with unwashed hands, the food became *spiritually* unclean, making one eating it also *spiritually* unclean! This meant that one became a sinner by what came from *outside the* ***body***, rather than by what came from *within the* ***soul****.* To the contrary, Jesus dramatically indicated that such *spiritual pollution* came from *within* the person, *not* from *without.* The utter foolishness of this false teaching of ritualistic handwashings of the Jews is what Jesus condemned.

In summary, by the Lord's protest against this practice of the Jews, He was "purging all foods"—that is, the Lord declared that all food, fit to eat of itself, was clean of itself, and *could not pollute the soul,* even though the one eating it had not washed his hands, using the elders' meaningless ritual cleansings. Clearly, the issue at stake was the handwashings, not the food!

Nevertheless, the text—and the Lord's main point—are still a bit confusing. Not surprisingly, perhaps, that is why the disciples themselves were confused by the Lord's overall statement (Mark 7:17, 18)! (See *Harmony* 12:21 for more on this handwashing issue.)

**(h) [10:13/3]** I suggested that Jesus skipped the Passover on this particular year, A.D. 30. In truth, we really don't know if Jesus did so. The fact is that there are four Passovers mentioned in the Gospel record during the course of the Lord's ministry—A.D. 28, 29, 30, and 31. However, during only three of these Passovers does the record state that Jesus actually went to Jerusalem (*Harmony* 3:1; 3:72; 16:1)—most likely A.D. 28, 29, and 31 However, we are told that another—a fourth—Passover was *soon* to take place (*Harmony* 9:1). Either there is no record of the Lord's attendance in Jerusalem during this Passover, or He actually *did* skip it, as I suggest. Based upon the severe troubles the Lord was having with the Jewish leaders at this time in His ministry, it seems very plausible that He did, indeed, skip this Passover. Accordingly, I stated so in the *Harmony*.

**(i) [10:16/2]** The way that Jesus treated this woman was very unusual—even shocking—to say the least! I suppose there could be other ways of interpreting this story, but I am comfortable with the way I explained it, and think it adequately explains the reasons for the way the Lord treated this woman.

**(j) [10:19]** It is not clear when the woman actually bowed down before Jesus: when she first came to Him (as Matthews indicates), or after He first spoke to her (as Mark indicates). I followed Mark's account, considering it more likely.

**(k) [10:24]** See *Harmony* 2:58, for more about the Aramaic language.

**(l) [10:53]** Against the belief of many, I do not accept that Jesus actually called Peter the "Rock" in this story. That would be contrary to everything we know about Peter, or Jesus, for that matter. *Jesus was the huge "Rock!"* (the Greek, *"petra"*). Peter (the Greek, *"petros"*) was only a "stone"—or smaller stone, or pebble. It is plausible that Jesus was contrasting the meaning of words "stone" and "rock," thus comparing Peter's well-documented unstable character with that of His (the Lord's) own rock-solid character.

Therefore, in the *Harmony*, after Jesus' reference to Peter ("petros"), *I have Jesus pointing to Himself*, declaring that He was the true Rock ("petra"), thus contrasting Himself with Peter. This makes sense to me. I think this is quite consistent with the entire Gospel and New Testament record of the Lord and Peter's position and influence within the church. While Peter was certainly influential among the disciples and the Christian church, there is no evidence that Peter ever had such a *rock-like* status in the early church. However, I must admit, the way the event is recorded in the Gospel story, it is easy to see that confusion could arise as to the exact meaning of the account.

**(m) [10:62]** Matthew and Mark say the Transfiguration took place six days later, while Luke says it was eight days later. Six days is the exact accounting of time, while eight days—based on Jewish inclusive reckoning—means "about a week later." That is why I interpreted the text the way I did in the *Harmony*.

**(n) [10:64/]** The text in Jude 9 (which reads cryptically in the KJV: "Yet Michael [another name for Jesus] the archangel, when contending with the devil he disputed about the body of Moses, durst not bring against him railing accusation, but said, The Lord rebuke thee"), has been regularly and usually interpreted to refer to the time in history when Jesus, some indeterminate time before His incarnation (*Harmony* 1:1), debated with Satan over the body of Moses when the Savior was about to resurrect Moses from the dead! That being the case, then, Moses was indeed resurrected, and therefore, could, in his resurrected flesh, be with Elijah on the mountain when Jesus was transfigured many years later. This means that Moses is now in heaven with Elijah.

**(o) [10:72]** There are a number of prophecies in the Old Testament that dealt directly with various aspects of the suffering and humiliation that Jesus would experience as He died for the sins of the world. The following are some such examples (with the *Harmony* references confirming their fulfillment)—the Lord's betrayal: Psalm 41:9 (*Harmony* 14:23); the price paid to the traitor: Zechariah 11:12 (*Harmony 14:24*); the beating and abuse of the Savior: Isaiah 50:6 (*Harmony* 17:33, 49, 80, 95, 96, 111); the Lord's pierced hands and feet (indicating His crucifixion): Psalm 22:16 (*Harmony* 18:47); condemned with transgressors: Isaiah 53:12 (*Harmony* 17:116); lots cast for Jesus' clothes: Psalm 22:18 (*Harmony* 17:119); and Christ's words spoken on the cross: Psalm 22:1 (*Harmony* 17:129).

**(p) [10:72/]** It is very likely that if the Jewish leaders had accepted Jesus, many more of the common people would also have accepted Him. If that had happened, then it is conceivable that the entire nation would have accepted Jesus as the Messiah. And should that have happened, it is possible that the entire course of history could have been changed! Indeed, what *would* have happened had the Jewish nation accepted Jesus as the Messiah? In truth, we really don't know for sure, but it is interesting to think about! But such a discussion is only academic, for obviously the Jews as a people did not accept the Lord as the Messiah.

**(q) [10:72/+]** The reality of devil-possession during the days of Jesus is very dramatically illustrated by the story of the boy who was so afflicted. For more information on devil-possession in the Gospel record, see *Harmony* 4:24/; 7:65/, as well as the individual listing of Jesus casting out devils, under "Miracles of Jesus," in the *Alphabetical Index* in the back of the *Harmony.*

**(r) [10:83]** See *Harmony* 10:86, 87 for a continuation of this event.

**(s) [10:85]** Luke indicates that the disciples' failure to understand the Lord's future suffering was because it was "hidden" from them. On the surface, then, it appears that Jesus did not want them to understand the future! However, such an interpretation makes no sense whatsoever. Why else would Jesus repeatedly share these details with them? Rather, it was hidden from them in the sense that they *refused to believe what He declared would happen to Him.* It short, it was hidden from them, *not* because God willed it so, but because they *deliberately closed their minds to the truth.* This interpretation makes sense to me, even though the actual words of the text seem to say otherwise. Nevertheless, I am very comfortable with my interpretation.

**(t) [10:87]** Is it really possible to move mountains by faith? Of all His many statements in the Gospel record, this declaration of Jesus is, in my estimation, the *most difficult to understand and explain!* And, He made such a statement not only here, but also, in a similar way, several times elsewhere (*Harmony* 12:155; 14:54). It seems to me Jesus did not mean it literally! Perhaps He was referring to problems as though they were "mountains." But maybe it *is* possible that because we have such a lack of faith, we cannot move mountains—just as He said! In any case, I must honestly confess, I am quite at a loss to explain this most profound statement of the Lord adequately and satisfactorily.

**(u) [10:87]** Matthew's record mentions both *prayer and fasting* as what the Lord required for the disciples to do, in order to successfully cast the demon out of the boy. Mark mentions *only prayer.* While I included Matthew's reference to *fasting* in the *Harmony,* I was not completely comfortable in doing so. And why is this? There are two reasons: (1) Matthew 17:21 is *not* found in most of the older manuscripts; and (2) fasting, as a requirement for a relationship with God and the authority to work miracles, is not an emphasis of Scripture. Nevertheless, in an effort to be faithful the entire written record, I included Matthew's reference to fasting, for whatever it may be worth.

**(v) [10:93/2]** There is no specific record of Peter actually securing the money from the mouth of the fish, but it is obviously assumed that he did so in response to the Lord's injunction. Accordingly, I included such in the *Harmony* to preserve the proper flow of events.

**(w) [10:93/2+]** In the story listed here, Jesus compares the way we would normally treat children with the way we would treat our fellow workers in our ministry for Jesus. Sometimes the examples Jesus gave about children in the story recorded here are used by Bible teachers to show how we should relate to children. While such a use of the Lord's illustrations might be appropriate, His *real* purpose was to tell us how we should treat our fellow disciples. The context of these illustrations makes this abundantly clear. To treat children appropriately—that is with kindness and tenderness—is considered by Jesus to be an established and obvious fact that needed no further explanation.

Further, to compare the way that the Lord's followers should treat one another to the way that children should be treated is an incredibly powerful comparison. The majesty of this concept should not be underestimated by all who claim to follow the Lord faithfully as His disciples!

**(x) [10:102]** Matthew, in his account, combines the hand and foot illustration as one. Mark separates them. I followed Mark's account.

**(y) [10:103]** (See above.)

**(z) [10:105]** The illustration of "salt in the fire sacrifices" is hard to understand and even harder to interpret in a short amount of space. Consequently, I took a lot of space to interpret just a few words! I felt it necessary to do so as to explain this powerful illustration adequately.

**(aa) [10:106]** (See above.)

**(bb) [10:109]** To provide a smooth transition from one thought to another, and based upon the context of the Lord's overall discussion, I added some words to what the Lord said in this text. I am sure that this fits the thrust of the Lord's statements here.

**(cc) [10:109]** It is clear from the context that the methodology Jesus gave to deal adequately with disagreements among one another *also includes* disagreements within the church body. That is why I added the word "church" to the description the Lord gave.

**(dd) [10:110]** (See above.)

**(ee) [10:111]** See **Note "bb"** above.

**(ff) [10:112]** The Jewish scribes taught that people should forgive one another up to three times. To give Peter's statement more clarity and force, I included this teaching of the Jews as part of what Peter might have said.

# CHAPTER ELEVEN

## CONTENTIONS WITH JEWS AND SUCCESS AMONG GENTILES—

**From Jesus Visits the Feast of Tabernacles, to Jesus at the Feast of Dedication**

**(Autumn, A.D. 30 - Early Winter, A.D. 30)**

—

***The Timeline of the Ministry of Jesus, Segment Seven: Autumn, A.D. 30-Spring, A.D. 31***[a]

Three years had passed since the Lord began His ministry in the Autumn of A.D. 27. During the first six months—Autumn, A.D. 27 through Spring, A.D. 28—Jesus was baptized, was tempted in the wilderness, called His first disciples, and worked His first miracle.[1]

During the next six months—Spring, A.D. 28 through Autumn, A.D. 28—He ministered in Israel's southern province of Judea. It all started when He cleansed the Temple of the moneychangers, which led to the beginning of a great struggle between the Jewish leaders and Him. The Lord labored in Judea for only a relatively short period of time.[2]

The next six months—Autumn, A.D. 28 through Spring, A.D. 29—the Lord spent in the northern province of Galilee. The record of that entire time period is sketchy.[3]

The next six-month period—Spring, A.D. 29 through Autumn, A.D. 29—was a very busy time for the Lord. There are many events of this span of time that are a part of the Gospel record. During His ministry in Galilee, the Lord officially called His disciples and ordained them. This was followed by His famous "Sermon on the Mount." And, this time period is distinguished by many miracles that are a part of the Gospel story. The level of the Lord's influence with many people was very positive.[4]

The next six-month period of the Lord's work—Autumn, A.D. 29 through Spring, A.D. 30—marked a turning-point in His ministry. Because so many people were following Him primarily as a result of His miracles, Jesus gave His "Bread of Life" teaching in the synagogue in Capernaum, which emphasized the spiritual aspects of His ministry. After that, many of His former disciples no longer continued to follow Him as the Messiah.[5]

The next six-month segment of the Lord's ministry—from Spring, A.D. 30 through Autumn, A.D. 30—was primarily focused on ministering to Gentiles. Accordingly, the Lord labored in areas where the population was more Gentile. Also, Jesus began to emphasize to His disciples the fact that He would soon suffer and die at the hands of the Jewish leaders. And too, Jesus started to give strong counsel to His disciples as to how they should relate to one another as fellow workers in the Gospel ministry.[6]

The next six-month segment of Christ's life (7/7)—from Autumn, A.D. 30 through Spring, A.D. 31, the final half-year portion of the Lord's ministry—was spent primarily in giving a wide range of counsel and advice to the closest of His followers. This was the kind of advice that would be invaluable to them as they would begin to learn how to minister to the church and the world without Jesus being present with them. In His teachings, there was a large emphasis upon faithfulness to duty, and the gravity of that faithfulness.(b) [7]

During this time, also, Jesus sent the "Seventy" out, two by two, to do their work of ministry, mainly among Gentiles.[8]

And of course, it was during this time period that Jesus would, as the Savior and Sin Bearer of the world, be arrested, tried, crucified, and resurrected from the dead. The Lord, too, during His last days on the earth, following the resurrection, gave His disciples final instructions, and then ascended into heaven. The events of the concluding week of the Lord's ministry—often called the "Passion Week"—and the weeks that led up to His ascension, comprise well over one fourth of the entire Gospel record.[9]

—

## Jesus Visits the Feast of Tabernacles
## < Autumn, A.D. 30 (7/7) >
## (John 7:2-10:21)

### — Jesus Debates With His Brothers Regarding a Visit to the Feast of Tabernacles
### < Autumn, A.D. 30 (7/7) >
### {John 7:2-13}

A yearly festival of the Jews was soon to begin. It was called the Feast of Tabernacles—or Booths. [Leviticus 23:33-36][1]

> This festival was a grand celebration that lasted for eight days, commemorating Israel's experiences during their wilderness wanderings after the Exodus from Egypt. It also served as a time of rejoicing over a bountiful harvest at the conclusion of their summer farming season. It was celebrated in the fall of the year, beginning on the 15th day of the month of Tishri. It was one of the Jewish festivals that all the nation's men were required to attend.

The Lord's brothers, James, Joses, Simon, and Judas—sons of Joseph from a previous marriage [*Harmony* 7:1]—strongly suggested to Jesus that He should go with them to Jerusalem to celebrate the feast. They explained, "Leave Galilee with us, and go to the feast in Judea. This way, many of Your disciples and followers in that province will be able to observe Your miracles there. It's been nearly two years since You've done any serious work in that province. Besides, if You really want to be well-known, You can't accomplish anything significant by living in virtual secrecy as You've been doing lately! [*Harmony* 10:86] We think that if You go to Jerusalem for the feast, and present Yourself in some dramatic, public way, soon the whole world will discover who You really are."[(c) 2]

Now, Christ's brothers did not fully believe that Jesus was the Messiah. [*Harmony* 2:34/2; 7:1; 8:61][3]

> They, of course, knew that He was a miracle-worker. That was clear. They suspected that He *might* be the Messiah, but because Jesus did not act as they expected the Messiah would function, they had their doubts

---

1 John 7:2
2 John 7:3, 4
3 John 7:5

about His authenticity. They thought Jesus was not assertive enough in proclaiming Himself as the Christ. He was too reserved for their pre-conceived concept of what the Messiah should be and do. Thus they thought that if Jesus was truly the Messiah, then a big, public swing through Judea at the time of a popular festival might bring out the best in Him. They figured that, perhaps, a dramatic show of miracles in Israel's most populous province would make a big splash, forcing the Lord to be more open about His ministry. If He truly was the Christ, this would be the best thing to do to make His Messiahship obvious to as many people as possible. At least, that was their reasoning, well-intentioned or not.

But Jesus declined His brothers' suggestion, explaining, "My time to make a public display has not arrived yet." That time was still some six months in the future, when He would be arrested and crucified. [*Harmony* 17:23, 116] "On the other hand," Jesus continued, "it's fine for you to go to the feast just as the law prescribes for you to do. [Exodus 23:16; Leviticus 23:33-36] If you go to the feast, nothing evil will happen to you, for the world has nothing against you. But in my case, because I've been preaching against the sins of the world, the world hates Me. So then, all of you should go up to the feast. I will not go at this time—certainly not in the dramatic manner that you wish for Me to go. As I have said, My time for such a public exposure has not arrived yet." So accordingly, and no doubt disappointed in the Lord, His brothers went to the feast, leaving Jesus behind in Galilee.[4]

However, some time after the brothers had left for the Feast of Tabernacles, Jesus did leave for the festival Himself. But instead of traveling in some kind of public manner—as His brothers wished He would—He used a more private, less traveled road to Jerusalem. In addition, because most of the regular attendees to the festival were already at the feast, there would be very few, if any, people on the road heading toward the province of Judea. This way Jesus could travel without the usual large crowds of followers tagging along. Thus Jesus was able to arrive in Jerusalem relatively unseen. This is the way that He had wanted it to be: to draw as little attention to Himself as possible.[5]

This was a wise course of action because many of the Jewish leaders who were seeking to kill Him were going around among the crowds at the feast, inquiring,

---

4 John 7:6-9
5 John 7:10

"Do you know where Jesus of Nazareth is?" Of course they were unsuccessful in their efforts to find Him within the crowds.[6]

Besides the leadership of Israel who were seeking to find Him, the crowds of common people conjectured about who Jesus was, and who He claimed to be. Many in the multitudes had personally observed Jesus, especially in Galilee. Others were curious regarding Him, after hearing so much about what the Lord was doing. Indeed, there was strong division of opinion among the people regarding the ministry of the Lord. Some in the crowd were saying, "He's a good Man!" while others were saying, "No! He's leading the people in the wrong direction." But of course, none who were in any way supportive of Jesus were willing to have their comments heard too loudly, lest this reach the Jewish leaders. They were fearful that anything they said could be construed as loyalty to Jesus and lead to their expulsion from the church. Sadly, they were clearly afraid of their own spiritual leaders! [*Harmony* 11:95][7]

### — The Lord's Teaching in the Temple During the Feast of Tabernacles < Autumn, A.D. 30 (7/7) > {John 7:14-8:1}

On about the fourth day of the feast, Jesus appeared unexpectedly in the Temple area. There, taking the Jewish leaders by surprise, and leaving no time for His enemies to stop Him, Jesus began to teach the people assembled there. Even though violently opposed to Jesus, the religious leaders of Israel could not help but be deeply impressed by the high quality of His teaching. They said among themselves, "How is it that this Man has so much Scriptural knowledge and wisdom without ever having been taught in one of our religious schools? It makes no sense!"[(d)] [8]

Overhearing their comments regarding Him, Jesus interrupted them by saying, "My teaching is not Mine, but is rather from Him who sent Me." What Jesus meant was that His message was powerful because it was not of human origin. Instead it had come directly from God, His Father! [*Harmony* 3:86] The Lord continued, "Yes, if anyone desires to follow the will of God, he will make sure that the teaching is from God, as opposed to being the result of mere human wisdom. A person who speaks solely for himself seeks personal praise. But," now

---

6 John 7:11

7 John 7:12, 13

8 John 7:14, 15

speaking of Himself in the third person, Jesus added, "He who is seeking only the praise of the One who has sent Him, He it is who is teaching the truth! And, too, there is no unrighteousness in Him or in what He is teaching."[9]

> Here Jesus compared His own motivations for the things He taught with those of the Jewish leaders, who were amazed at His teachings. While it was God who had sent Jesus, the Jewish leaders had sent themselves, so to speak. Thus Jesus sought the praise of His Father, while the Jewish leadership wanted praise only for themselves, and from themselves. Because of that, the Lord's teachings were reliable while those of the Jewish leaders were not.

Changing the subject, and coming directly to the point with the Jewish leaders, Jesus added, "Is it not true that Moses gave you the Law—the Law that you supposedly teach? Yet none of you really follows that Law. And why do I say that? Because I know that you are trying to figure out a way to kill Me! Clearly, Moses would never have done that, nor sanctioned such evil intentions!" [*Harmony* 3:85][10]

Many of the leaders in the crowd, taken aback by these strong, revealing words, tried to cover up their intentions by giving a mocking answer to the Lord. "You must be crazy!" they declared. "A demon is in you! Who is it that is trying to kill You? That's ridiculous!"[11]

Jesus was quick to answer, declaring, "About eighteen months ago, I healed a crippled man at the pool of Bethesda. [*Harmony* 3:72-81] I did one good deed—a deed which caused you, I must add, to marvel at My authoritative power to work miracles. Yet, nevertheless, because I did it on the Sabbath, you have ever since wanted to kill Me. This makes no sense at all. Listen! Moses gave you the law of circumcision, which requires a baby boy to be circumcised on the eighth day of life. [Leviticus 12:3] Well, actually circumcision predates Moses—it goes all the way back to our father, Abraham. But nevertheless, you circumcise a baby on the Sabbath, if the eighth day of a baby's life falls on the Sabbath, isn't that right? And, why do you circumcise someone on the Sabbath, which is a technical violation of the Sabbath commandment which requires one to rest from labor? [Exodus 20:8-11] It is because you consider strict adherence to the circumcision

---

9 John 7:16-18

10 John 7:19

11 John 7:20

law of Moses to be more important than a small, technical violation of the Sabbath law. Now isn't that right?[(e)] [12]

"That makes sense. But why then were you upset with Me when I made a whole man well on the Sabbath? Now that doesn't make sense at all! Stop passing judgment on what I do! Rather, use some practical logic and wisdom. Think with a righteous, enlightened mind and not with an evil, fault-finding one. Simply put: If you are willing to excuse the breaking of the Sabbath commandment for the purpose of performing the rite of circumcision, then stop condemning Me for the Sabbath-day healing of a whole person! You treat My actions as though they were heinous sins. Yes, use some sanctified reasoning for a change!" The Jewish leaders had nothing to say in response to the irresistible logic of the Lord's powerful argument. [*Harmony* 11:15][13]

Many of the people of Jerusalem, after hearing this confrontation between Jesus and the Jewish leaders, began to wonder what was happening here.[14]

> Now, most of these people had only limited first-hand knowledge of Jesus and His work. Of course they had heard a great deal about the Lord's labor, but with most of Christ's ministry having taken place in regions north of Judea and Jerusalem, they had not had the opportunity to observe His work personally. Instead, most of the information they had was what they had heard from the Jewish leaders. And, to be sure, this information was loaded with personal hatred toward and prejudice against the Lord. Thus most of the discussion among the people regarding Jesus was in the form of gossip based upon incomplete or prejudicial rumor. In short, most of what was previously said about Jesus was distorted and negative. Therefore, for many of them, this was their first direct exposure to Jesus and His teachings.

Now that the people actually had the opportunity to see the Lord themselves, their discussion regarding the struggle that was taking place between the Jewish leaders and Jesus became confused. Some said, "So is this the Man of whom the Jewish leaders have been talking? Is this the Man that they are actually trying to kill? They've been boldly criticizing His work and ministry, suggesting that He should die. And yet, now that He is here in their presence, speaking in public,

---

12 John 7:21-23

13 John 7:23, 24

14 John 7:25

they seem to be afraid to challenge Him openly—or even say a word! Do you suppose that, after actually observing Him in person, they have come to the conclusion that He must indeed be the Messiah? Yes, that must be the reason that they have been silenced in His presence." [*Harmony* 11:13][15]

> Surely, though, these people were mistaken in their conclusion! The Jewish leaders had not accepted Jesus as the Messiah—they still, in fact, were privately seeking to kill Him. They were just afraid to do their dirty work in public.

However, there were others in Jerusalem who were still heavily under the negative influence of the Jewish leadership. These people were very doubtful that Jesus was the Messiah, for they reasoned among themselves, saying, "It has been generally accepted in Israel that when the Messiah comes both the people and the Messiah Himself will not know that He is the Messiah until He is officially anointed by Elijah the prophet. [*Harmony* 10:71, 72] This does not appear to be the case with this Man, for we know who this Man is and where He has come from. And certainly, this Man has never been anointed by Elijah. So as to whether He really is the Messiah or not, it's difficult to say. In reality, though, considering all the facts, it appears to us that He isn't the Messiah."[16]

> But unknown to them, Jesus *had* in fact, been anointed by Elijah. That is, based upon Bible prophecy, John the Baptist was Elijah the prophet. [*Harmony* 2:41; 10:72] His "anointing" had taken place when John baptized Jesus in the Jordan River. [*Harmony* 2:25, 26] But all this really wasn't the main issue. This was because the concept that the Messiah would not know who He was or where He came from until He was anointed, was a false teaching with no basis in Scripture.

Hearing such comments, Jesus began explaining the truth about Himself as He continued to teach in the Temple. He declared in loud words, "The fact that you know My earthly name and where I have been raised does not disprove that I am the Messiah. In fact, it means nothing, because that is a false teaching. But what is important to know is that I did not come by My own will. Rather, My calling is from God, the Father. He is the One who has sent Me. This is more important than any calling by a mere human being. The heavenly Father is the true source of My calling! But sadly, you do not know Him as you ought. On the

---

15 John 7:25, 26

16 John 7:27

other hand, I know Him intimately. I came from where He dwells. Yes indeed, it was He who sent Me here." [*Harmony* 3:86][17]

These plain words really upset the Jewish leaders. While they were still hesitant to say much in public at the time, they continued in earnest to scheme secretly as to how they might capture Jesus and kill Him. But for the moment they took no direct action to seize Jesus. In part, this was because it wasn't yet the prophetically prescribed time for His death. That was still another six months in the future. [*Harmony* 13:98-100] Besides, they were genuinely afraid of what the people would say—or do—should they seize Jesus in public.[18]

Even though most of the religious leaders of Israel had rejected Jesus as the Messiah, the power of the Lord's statements and ministry greatly influenced a large segment of the people of Jerusalem in a positive way. In fact, many people came to believe that Jesus was, indeed, the Messiah. A good number of them said, "There is no way that the Messiah, when He does come, would work any more miracles than this Man has worked. Certainly that is the truth! Therefore, this Man must be the Christ—even the Messiah!"[19]

When the top echelon of the Jewish leaders, the Pharisees, along with the chief priests, heard these words whispered around—words that were affirming Jesus as the Messiah—they were incensed. Their previous fear of seizing Jesus was effectively overwhelmed by uncontrollable anger. They had had enough! Accordingly, they sent some of the Temple police to have the Lord arrested on the spot. [*Harmony* 11:26][20]

But before the police could make such an arrest, they overheard Jesus speaking to the crowds. His words came in the form of a riddle-like message. He declared, "For only a little while longer, I will be with you. Then, I will go to be with the One who has sent Me. Even though you will try to find Me, you will not succeed, for where I have gone, you will not be able to follow." [*Harmony* 11:49; 16:36][21]

> The Lord deliberately spoke these words in cryptic fashion. He wanted to confound His listeners. What Jesus meant by these words is this: "I

---

17 John 7:28, 29
18 John 7:30
19 John 7:31
20 John 7:32
21 John 7:33, 34

will be with you for yet another six months. Then, you will kill Me. But I will be resurrected and go and dwell once more with My Father in heaven. He is the One who sent me. When I'm in heaven, you will not be able to harm Me anymore. At the end of the world, you will think that you will be worthy of eternal life, and dwell in heaven yourselves. But, because of your evil ways, you will never be allowed to enter the heavens where I dwell."

But totally dumbfounded by the Lord's riddle-like statement, the Jewish leaders made fools of themselves by trying to figure out what He meant by this cryptic message! They questioned one another regarding its meaning. They said, "Where is it that this Man is going that we will not be able to find Him? He is not going to preach to the Dispersion among the Greeks, is He? But on the other hand, maybe He is going to leave us and teach the Greeks. In any case, we can't figure out what He is trying to say!"[22]

The "Dispersion" was a word used to describe those Jews who had been scattered throughout the world outside of Israel. Their use of the word "Greeks" here referred to those Jews who had become worldly in their religion, accepting the customs and practices of Greek philosophy. Apparently, the Jews thought Jesus might give up on them in greater Palestine and flee to other nations to preach to the Jews living there.

Still baffled by the words of the Lord, the Jewish leaders concluded, "But even if He were to flee to some foreign country, what could He possibly mean by saying, 'You will try to find Me. But where I am, you cannot come'? Certainly we have no desire to follow Him there, but we would easily be able to find Him if we were to look for Him. It wouldn't be that hard." Accordingly, the Jewish leaders remained confused as to the true meaning of the Lord's riddle. [*Harmony* 11:33/][23]

Several days later, on the seventh—and greatest—day of the Feast of Tabernacles, Jesus stood in front of the crowd of people. A priest, at the blowing of three trumpet blasts, ascended the steps of the Temple before the crowd. He then poured a large pitcher of water into a silver bowl that, as it emptied, mingled with wine flowing from another bowl. Together, the water and the wine flowed into an underground passageway that drained into the base of the

22 John 7:35
23 John 7:36

Altar of Burnt Offering. The flowing water and wine represented the water that flowed from the Rock that quenched the thirst of God's people while they were in the wilderness [Exodus 17:1-7; Numbers 20:8-11], and also the flowing of the gift of salvation into the lives of all of God's people. Watching this dramatic ceremony taking place, Jesus stepped forward and cried out for all to hear, "If there are any of you who are thirsty, come to Me and drink! If you choose to place your trust in Me, it will be as various Scriptures indicate when they declare, 'From the depths of his soul, will flow rivers of water which give life!'" [Proverbs 18:4; Isaiah 44:3; 55:1; *Harmony* 3:38] Here, Jesus spoke about the power of the Gospel as it was manifested through the work of the Holy Spirit within His ministry. Some months later, this same gift of the Spirit would be given to all those who believed in Him. [Acts 2:1-4] But this special outpouring of the Holy Spirit would come to His followers only after the Lord was glorified—that is, after He had ascended into heaven, following His death and resurrection. [*Harmony* 11:28; 18:94, 95][24]

After listening to all these events and the Lord's declaration, the overall response of the people still remained mixed. Basically, there were three kinds of reaction. First, some said, "There is no doubt that this is the Prophet spoken of by Moses!" [Deuteronomy 18:15; *Harmony* 2:42] (Now, in the time of Jesus, there was a division of opinion as to who this "Prophet" mentioned by Moses would be. Some thought He was the Messiah. Others believed He would be Moses himself, raised from the dead.) And second, there were some in the crowd who did believe the words of Jesus, for they declared, "He is the Messiah—the Christ!" But third, there were many others who remained unconvinced, saying, "It is a fact that the Messiah will not come from Galilee, isn't that right? Haven't the Scriptures made it plain that the Messiah will come from the royal family of King David? [2 Samuel 7:12, 13] He is to come from Bethlehem of Judea, which is David's home town. [Micah 5:2; *Harmony* 1:64] All this does not apply to this Man. He's from Nazareth, not Bethlehem. Also, He's worked in Galilee, not Judea, as we would have expected."[25]

> Those taking this position were certainly confused in their thinking. First of all, Jesus was born in Bethlehem. [*Harmony* 1:61-66] Second, He was of the royal bloodline of David. [*Harmony* 1:60] And third, the Scriptures did predict that the Messiah would spend time in Galilee.

---

[24] John 7:37-39
[25] John 7:40-42

[Isaiah 9:1, 2] Again, of these facts these people were either confused, ignorant . . . or perhaps, willfully ignorant.

Because of this diversity of opinion regarding who Jesus was, a significant dispute arose among the crowds of people. Because of this division of ideas, there was also no clear unity of opinion among the Jewish leadership—who had personally listened to the words of the Lord that day—about what should be done with Jesus. Even those who wanted to arrest Him, were, at that moment, afraid to do so. They were afraid that the people who trusted in Jesus to be the Messiah might riot if He was arrested. Thus, not one of the Temple police who had been sent to arrest the Master several days before [*Harmony* 11:20] made any attempt to lay a hand on Him.[26]

Accordingly, the Temple police returned, empty-handed, to the chief priests and Pharisees of the Sanhedrin. These particular Jewish leaders had not heard the words that Jesus had spoken to the people that day. Neither had they heard the discussion of the people regarding who they thought Jesus was. Instead, they remained in seclusion, waiting for the Temple police to bring the arrested Jesus back to them. "Why was it that you did not arrest Jesus and bring Him here as we instructed you?" the Jewish leaders challenged the police on their arrival back in the Temple.[27]

The police, who were overwhelmed by the wise words of the Lord which they had heard, answered, "We have never heard any Man speak as this Man speaks!" [*Harmony* 11:24][28]

The Pharisees, upset by the police's admiration of Jesus, further challenged them, declaring, "Have you, like the ignorant crowds, been led astray by this Man? We hope not! Don't you know that not one the chief rulers and Pharisees of Israel believes that this Man is the Messiah? Not one! Doesn't that mean anything to you? Certainly you must know that the ignorant group of people, who supposedly believe in Him—those who know nothing about the Law, we must add—are, with justification, being cursed by God for their trust in that Man!"[29]

---

26 John 7:43, 44
27 John 7:45
28 John 7:46
29 John 7:47-49

But then, Nicodemus—the one who had visited Jesus by night [*Harmony* 3:10-24] two and a half years previously—stepped forward to try to defend Jesus. As he was a fellow Pharisee and a member of the highest Jewish court, the Sanhedrin, his opinion would have weight with the other Jewish leaders. He reasoned with them, saying, "Please don't forget that our law does not condemn a man unless we give him an opportunity to speak directly to us, so that we can be exactly sure what he has done and what he actually believes. [Deuteronomy 1:16, 17] Isn't that true? It's only fair! So, let's be cautious here." While Jesus had spoken to the Sanhedrin previously [*Harmony* 3:82-99], that had been 18 months earlier. So much had happened since then. Nicodemus obviously thought it reasonable that Jesus should have another hearing in front of the Sanhedrin before He was condemned. [*Harmony* 18:8][(f)] [30]

Unconvinced, the other Jewish leaders questioned Nicodemus. "Aren't you also from Galilee?" they said. Here, they implied that Nicodemus was showing undue favoritism toward Jesus, who was from the same province as himself. "Check it out for yourself." they added. "It as a historical fact that no prophet has arisen, or ever will arise from within the province of Galilee!"[31]

> Quite interestingly, so blinded were these religious leaders toward the ministry of Jesus that they did not know, or had forgotten, that one of Israel's prophets, Jonah, had been raised in Galilee, for Gath-hepher, Jonah's home town, was in southern Galilee. [2 Kings 14:25]

Even though the Jews disputed the counsel of Nicodemus, they nevertheless did nothing further in an effort to arrest Jesus at that time. Instead, they all went back to their homes. But Jesus went to the Mount of Olives. [*Harmony* 11:48][32]

### — The Lord Defends the Woman Caught in Adultery[(g)] [(h)]
### < Autumn, A.D. 30 (7/7) >
### {John 8:2-11}

The next morning—the eighth day of the Feast of Tabernacles—Jesus returned from the Mount of Olives to the Temple area in Jerusalem. Many people noticed His arrival in the city and followed Him to see what might happen next. The Master sat down and began to teach the people.[33]

---

30 John 7:50, 51
31 John 7:52
32 John 7:53; 8:1
33 John 8:2

Meanwhile, the Jewish religious leaders, who, the previous day, had been humiliated by Jesus [*Harmony* 11:21-23], had been frantically scheming as to how they might entrap Him in some other manner. They hoped that they might successfully trick and embarrass Him. So they carefully devised a sinister plan. Now they ruthlessly put the plan into action.

The scribes and Pharisees brought to Jesus a certain woman who had been caught in the act of adultery. And they had her stand in front of Jesus where He was sitting, teaching the people. They did this so He might judge her case.[34]

However, this was wholly inappropriate for them to do this. First of all, no doubt this woman had been unfairly set up. Also, such a woman, caught in adultery, was to be tried in a court of law, not in the public square before a mass of people. And too, the woman's husband, or husband-to-be, should have brought the charges against her, not the Jewish leaders. The purpose, then, of the Jewish leaders in this whole affair was to test Jesus so that they might find just cause to accuse Him of some impropriety. And, while the woman certainly was a sinner, she was being cruelly and unjustifiably used by the Jewish leaders for their own selfish and evil purposes.

Interrupting the Lord's teaching, the Jews questioned Him. "Teacher," they began, "this woman has been caught in adultery—indeed, in the very act. Now, Moses, in his law, prescribes that such a woman should be stoned to death. [Deuteronomy 22:23, 24] That's what Moses says. Now what do You say?"[35]

The Jews' purpose was clear: However Jesus responded, He would be in trouble. If He said that the woman should be stoned, the common people might lose confidence in Him as a compassionate, forgiving Person. Furthermore, in that case, it would appear that He was taking over the role of an executioner, thus angering Roman authorities who might be watching. But, on the other hand, if Jesus declared that the woman should not be stoned, they could charge Him with attempting to set aside one of the laws of their revered ancient leader, Moses. They figured they had Jesus trapped no matter which way He might answer their question.

---

34 John 8:3
35 John 8:4, 5

Of course, the Lord knew that they were testing Him so as to find a reason to unfairly accuse Him of some evil action. So, instead of answering their question, Jesus stooped over and began to write with His finger in the dust on the ground, as though He had not even heard them at all.(i) [36]

> While it is uncertain as to what Jesus wrote in the dust, it is probable that He wrote the various secret sins of the Jewish leaders who had brought the woman to Him. In doing so, the Lord make it clear to them that He knew the private thoughts of their hearts.(j)

Distressed by the Lord's refusal to give them an immediate answer to their challenge, the Jews persisted in urging Him to respond to their question. After they went on for a while longer, Jesus straightened up, looked at them, and said, "All right then! He that is without any sin, let him be the first one to throw a stone at her!" Stooping over again, He continued to write on the ground.[37]

> No doubt, the Jewish leaders looked down to see what Jesus was writing on the dirt. They were shocked when they saw their secret sins so openly revealed!(k)

At the Lord's challenge that those sinless among them cast the first stone, they began to leave the scene, one by one, starting with the older ones, and ending up with those who were younger. The voice of their guilty consciences was too loud in them for them to remain there. Out of respect, the younger accusers left only after the older ones had gone. This was because the older ones would normally take the lead in such an affair. Before too long, though, all of them were gone, leaving the woman standing alone with Jesus, in the center of the crowd. (l) [38]

Straightening up yet again, Jesus noticed that everyone who had accused the woman had slunk away, leaving her alone with Him. He then asked her, "Woman, where have all your accusers gone? Tell Me, is there no man left here to condemn you?"[39]

"No man, my Lord!" was the woman's simple reply.[40]

---

36 John 8:6
37 John 8:7, 8
38 John 8:9
39 John 8:10
40 John 8:11

Jesus answered back with assurance, saying, "Well then, in that case, neither do I condemn you!" Then He added, very gently chiding her, "Go home then . . . and from this moment forward, never sin like this again!"[(m)] [41]

> Once more, Jesus had ingeniously foiled the evil plans of His enemies who were seeking to destroy Him and His ministry! And, He had accomplished such a thing by humiliating His enemies, albeit discreetly, as well as encouraging those—especially the woman—who trusted in Him![1]

**— Jesus Declares Himself to be the "Light of the World"**[(n)]
**< Autumn, A.D. 30 (7/7) >**
**{John 8:12-30}**

> During the night ceremonies of the Feast of Tabernacles, giant, torch-like candlesticks, 75 feet high, were lighted in the Temple area. A great fanfare of music and religious dancing accompanied this lighting. The massive fire on the candlesticks illumined the entire Temple area and much of Jerusalem. The fire could be seen for miles. This grand celebration served as a reminder of the pillar of fire that had led the children of Israel throughout their wilderness journeys over a century earlier. [Exodus 13:21, 22] It also looked forward to the coming of the Messiah, who would be the "Light of Truth" to the entire world. The people, with the remembrance of this ceremony fresh in their minds from the various nights during the week before, were in the same Temple area in the morning hours as the sunlight gloriously reflected its rays off the Temple walls. The panorama of light—the memory of the torches at night, and the present bright sunlight of the day—was vividly impressed on their eyes and minds.[2]

On this particular morning, Jesus once more cried out dramatically for all to hear, "I am the Light of the World! And whoever chooses to follow Me will no longer walk in the darkness of untruth and evil. Rather, he will be led by the Light which gives life to all who follow it." [*Harmony* 1:2; 2:18; 5:18; 3:24; 11:80][42]

---

41 John 8:11
42 John 8:12

> Even though Jesus did not specifically declare that He was the Messiah, by His declaration that He was the "Light of the World," the Lord was, in fact, making clear to all the people that He was indeed the Messiah!

The Pharisees who were still in the crowd after Jesus had humiliated their fellow leaders during the-woman-caught-in-adultery episode [*Harmony* 11:33-41], retorted, "Who do You think You are? You are the only one who bears testimony regarding Yourself. Because You have no one else to bear witness of You—that is, to stand with You—we can say for certain that Your testimony is false. Thus, we will not accept You as the so-called, 'Light of the World' as You claim—a designation that belongs exclusively to the coming Messiah!" [*Harmony* 12:123/7][43]

Jesus shot back at them, "Even if it were true, as you say, that I alone bear testimony of Myself, My testimony would still be valid. And why? For I know where I have come from, and where I am going. And, apparently you have no idea where I have come from, or where I am going!"[44]

> Here Jesus was subtly claiming that He had originally come from heaven, where God dwelt. That being the case, there was no human standing there worthy to challenge His implied contention that He was the Messiah. Neither was it necessary for some human to certify His ministry. Rather, Jesus claimed that God the Father had certified His ministry by sending Him to the earth in the first place. [*Harmony* 9:38, 47] And that was quite enough! Further, He declared that at some point He would go back to heaven to be with His Father again. Jesus further stated that the Jews, because of their obstinate attitude, refused to understand this and probably never would. [*Harmony* 11:21] Of course, for the Jews to accept the Lord's claims would mean that they would have to also accept Him as the Messiah—One whom, as Jesus claimed, had come from heaven, and would later return there. This, they would not do, and, indeed, never would.

Jesus added, "The way you judge things is the way that sinful, wicked men judge. For Me, it is not My present responsibility to judge anyone. But, make no mistake: If I were to judge you, you can be sure that My judgment would be fair. That is because both My Father, who sent Me, and I, work together as a team.

---

43 John 8:13
44 John 8:14

Now, it is written in your Law that the testimony of two people is considered enough to confirm the truth on a particular issue. [Deuteronomy 17:6] Isn't that right? Well, in My case, not only is what I claim regarding Myself definitely true, My Father *also* claims that it is a fact. Thus, this is the clear, powerful, indisputable witness of two: My Father and I! Do you understand that?" [*Harmony* 3:89][45]

"Where is Your Father?" the Jews sarcastically responded, insinuating the questionable circumstances of His human birth. [*Harmony* 1:18-23, 38-42][46]

> Here, instead of accepting the miraculous nature of the Lord's conception and birth, these Jewish leaders cast the worse possible aspersions upon that those events. In short, they clearly implied that Jesus was illegitimate.

The Lord answered, "You don't know Me. Neither do you know My Father. Because you refuse to accept who I am, you refuse to accept who My Father is." Here, of course, Jesus was talking, not about His earthly father, Joseph, but His heavenly Father—God Himself![47]

Now, this debate with the Jewish leaders took place in the Court of the Women, where worshippers brought their gifts of money to give to the work of God. [*Harmony* 14:134] This was the place where He had been teaching the people. Even though there was a strong desire on behalf of those who were seeking to kill Jesus, to have Him arrested on the spot, they still, as the day before [*Harmony* 11:32], did not have the nerve to make a serious attempt to seize Him then. In part, this was because the time of His death was yet several months away—that is, His prescribed time to die was yet in the future. This meant that God would not allow them to arrest Jesus at this time.[48]

Jesus continued to repeat His basic theme to the Jewish religious leaders by exclaiming, "I will go away, and you will try to go where I am. But you will be condemned, and die for your sins. And why is that? Because where I am going, you will not be permitted to come." [*Harmony* 11:21; 16:36][49]

---

45 John 8:15-18
46 John 8:19
47 John 8:19
48 John 8:20
49 John 8:21

> Once again [*Harmony* 11:21], Jesus was saying that He would go back to heaven to be with the Father. In the future, these same critics would desire to go to heaven themselves. But because of their wicked ways, they would not be allowed to experience this privilege. Instead, they would be condemned to eternal death.

When Jesus had discussed this issue with the Jews a short time before [*Harmony* 11:21], they foolishly suggested that He might be leaving the nation of Israel to preach to the Jews scattered among the nations of the world. This time they suggested an even more ridiculous reason for the Lord's declaration on this occasion. They said, "Surely, He must be planning to kill Himself and thus end up in the grave—a place where we certainly have no desire to follow Him!" Thinking for a moment, they added, "Certainly this cannot be what He means when He says, 'Where I am going, you will not be able to follow after Me,' can it? Well, maybe it is . . . in any case, we just don't know. Obviously, this Man is too confusing for us to understand. He speaks in too many foolish riddles! He must have gone mad!" [*Harmony* 9:43][50]

The Lord, ignoring their preposterous suggestion, became even more direct with them regarding their evil intentions, by replying, "You are from below—from the depths of wickedness. I, on the other hand, have come from above—from the place where God dwells. In short, you are from this world and its sinfulness and I am from heaven and its righteousness. That is why I said you will be condemned in the judgment because of your persistence in clinging to your sins. Yes, if you continue to refuse to believe that I AM, you will, most assuredly, die in your sins!" [*Harmony* 9:17; 11:76, 77; 16:22][51]

> When the Lord used the phrase "I AM," in referring to Himself, He was unequivocally claiming to be God. [Exodus 3:13, 14] And, in doing so, Jesus was, in effect, claiming to be the Messiah.

The Jews, shocked by this strong claim that Jesus made regarding Himself, demanded of Him, saying, "You! Who are You?" [*Harmony* 11:166, 167][52]

> That is to say: "Tell us once more who You claim to be!" They wanted Jesus to declare *directly* that He was, in fact, the Messiah. If He did so, they could accuse Him of blasphemy—that is, the sin of a mere mortal

---

50 John 8:22

51 John 8:23, 24

52 John 8:25

being claiming to be God—a religious crime worthy of death. [Leviticus 24:15, 16]

Instead, Jesus answered them indirectly, by saying, "Of course, it is what I have been telling you all along about whom I am." [*Harmony* 11:168][53]

Here, Jesus cleverly reiterated His position, without specifically telling them what His position was! At the same time, He placed the onus upon the Jews to give an answer to their own question. [*Harmony* 11:168/]

The Lord continued, saying, "I certainly have many more things that I could say to you. I could also judge your actions. But why should I waste My time? My main responsibility has been to simply teach the truth which I have heard from the One who has sent Me. This I will continue to do as I present the truth to the world. I am tired of arguing with you." Again, in the dullness or obstinacy of their minds, they did not realize or refused to accept that when Jesus talked about the One who sent Him, He was talking about the heavenly Father.[54]

Nevertheless, Jesus added, "When you lift up the Son of Man"—which referred to His upcoming crucifixion, some months in the future—"then, you will finally figure out that I AM! And only then will you comprehend that I have never spoken on My own initiative but have taught only those things that the Father has instructed Me to say. Yes, He who has sent Me remains by My side to be with Me. Because I have always done that which has pleased Him, He has not left Me to struggle alone nor has He abandoned Me."[55]

Once more Jesus claimed to be the I AM—even God. [Exodus 3:13, 14; *Harmony* 11:51] These, along with many other things that Jesus spoke, caused a large number of the people to believe in Him as the Messiah. Unfortunately, this did not include most of the Jewish leadership. [*Harmony* 9:17, 17/, 76, 77; 16:22]

---

53 John 8:25

54 John 8:26, 27

55 John 8:28-30

## — An Argument Regarding Who Has Descended from Abraham[(o)]
## < Autumn, A.D. 30 (7/7) >
## {John 8:31-59}

Now, there were three groups of Jewish people who had listened to Jesus that day. First, there were those—which included most of the Jewish leaders—who completely rejected Him. These were the ones who were planning to kill Jesus. Second, there were those who accepted Jesus, not only as the Messiah of Israel, but also as their personal Savior. Third, there were many others—including a number of the Jewish leaders—whose faith in Him was limited, for they had come to accept *intellectually* that Jesus was the Messiah of Israel, but they did not receive Him *personally* as their Savior. These people were in particular trouble. They had a false sense of security. True, they believed in Jesus, but not with a faith that was sufficient to secure salvation for them on a permanent basis. Again, their belief was only intellectual in nature. It was not based upon a conviction rooted deeply within their hearts. These people, especially, were in grave danger, for, while thinking that their head knowledge had saved them, they were quite unaware that their lack of heart experience was condemning them. If they were not careful, they could easily slip back into the other category of those of total unbelief and outright rejection. Jesus needed to give some strong counsel to this last group of people.[56]

Thus it was that to this group of halfhearted believers Jesus said, "I must explain something to you: If you are to continue to grow in your understanding of My words, and ultimately accept Me as your personal Savior, only then will you truly become wholehearted disciples of Mine. And then, and only then, you will learn the real truth of the Gospel . . . and that truth will set you free from your slavery! But if you do not grow as I have said, you will be in deep trouble. Before long, you will reject Me as have the others who are seeking to kill Me. As they have planned My death, so also will you."[57]

> By the word "truth" in this statement, Jesus meant the reality of knowing Him as a personal Savior, as well as the reception God's life-changing power in their lives. In talking about being "free," Jesus meant freedom from sin and its control in the life.[1]

---

[56] John 8:31

[57] John 8:31, 32

> These words offended the Lord's listeners. Instead of waiting until Jesus could explain Himself to them, they interrupted His discourse to challenge His statement about slavery. They misunderstood what Jesus was saying to them, repudiating His suggestion that they had ever been in slavery of any kind. Also, perhaps thinking that a mere belief in Jesus as the Messiah was sufficient, they were upset that He would suggest that there was a shortcoming in their lives that they needed to correct, or some weak area that they needed to strengthen. While these people had accepted Jesus as the Messiah, they were already slipping back into outright rejection of His ministry.[2]

These people challenged His words by saying, "Abraham was our father! We are *his* children! Therefore, we have never been slaves under the control of anyone. So, what do You mean by saying, 'You will become free'?"[58]

> On the surface, such a declaration might have appeared foolish, for Israel had been, indeed, slaves in Egypt. [Exodus 20:2] Later, they were under the dominance of Babylon. [2 Chronicles 36:5-7] And presently, they were under the control of Rome. [*Harmony* 1:8/] But their refusal to accept the words of Jesus was based upon the assumption of what they as a people had always maintained: While they might be dominated by another nation, in their hearts they were still free, and would always remain so!

But Jesus wasn't talking about political slavery or domination. He had something much more important in mind. That is why He continued, "It is a fact, when I tell you: Everyone who continues to commit sin is a slave to sin. It's just that simple! You see, that's the kind of slavery I'm talking about.[59]

"Let Me illustrate," the Lord continued. "A slave does not stay in his master's house forever—he may be either expelled by the owner for insolence, or perhaps, because he is nothing more than a slave, he might escape. On the other hand, the son of the master stays in his father's house forever. And why? Because he is not a slave in any respect at all. Rather, he belongs to the family of the master, for he is the son! Isn't that right? So it is with you and Me. Unless you have a close, personal relationship with Me, you will end up feeling like a slave, and thus, act like a slave. That is, sooner or later, you will escape . . . or perhaps, be thrown out

---

58 John 8:33
59 John 8:34

for insubordination. But if you have a close personal relationship with Me—like the son in My story—you will consider yourselves to be no longer slaves but sons and daughters of God. Thus you will truly be a part of the family and remain faithful to the Master. Therefore, in summary, if you are in a relationship with Me—the Son of God—I make you free from sin and its burdens, and then you will be truly free and be joint-heirs with Me in our Father's kingdom. Do you see that?"[60]

Jesus continued, addressing this time all the people in the crowd, especially those who were trying to figure out a way to kill Him. He said, "Yes, I know that you are literally the sons and daughters of Abraham, as some of you have just claimed. But that's just of the flesh. In reality, this technical fact really means nothing! [*Harmony* 2:10] To prove My point, I know that some of you have been part of a scheme to kill Me. In short, because you have flatly rejected My words, you have been actively seeking to kill Me! So now, let Me ask you: Would a true son of Abraham really do that? Certainly not! But I know who My Father is, and I do the things that I have seen My Father do. And you are also seeking to do the things that you have learned from *your* 'father.' You are doing what he has always done." By this, of course, Jesus meant that their "father" was none other than the devil![61]

"But, wait a minute!" they challenged Him. "We insist, in spite of what You say, that Abraham is, indeed, our father! We have no other father!" [*Harmony* 11:75][62]

"Well, all right then," Jesus replied, "if you are truly the children of Abraham—as you claim to be the case—then do the deeds that Abraham was accustomed to doing! Nothing could be more logical and simple. But, as I have said, you have been trying to kill Me—a Man who has spoken only the truth to you, the truth which I received directly from God. Now admit it, there is no way that Abraham would have ever done such a horrendous thing as you are planning to do! Now would he? So it is as I have just said, and I repeat: You are doing the deeds of your father—and he's *not* Abraham, if you get My point!"[63]

By now, these people were growing extremely angry. They cried out, "We are not the children of spiritual adultery as you suggest! We have remained faithful

---

60 John 8:35, 36
61 John 8:37, 38
62 John 8:39
63 John 8:39, 40

to our one and only Father—God Himself! We would never serve the devil!" [*Harmony* 11:74][64]

Jesus responded, "I don't follow your logic at all. Listen to this: If God were really your Father, then you would love and accept Me, because I have come from where He dwells. In fact, God sent Me here! Again, I didn't come on My own initiative. I was sent by God! So then, why is it that you can't figure out what I'm trying to tell you, and accordingly, accept My words? I'll tell you why. It is because you have closed your ears to the words which I have been teaching you, that's why! You have refused to listen to Me.[65]

"And again, that's why I continue to maintain that you are all like your father, the devil! And because of that, you have the evil desires and passions of your father. He never listened to anyone! Neither do you listen to Me. Furthermore, you are planning My murder. That is just what the devil would do. Indeed, your father, the devil, is a murderer, even from the beginning of this world. Obviously, you can't stand to hear the truth! Neither can your father stand the truth, for there is absolutely no truth in him whatsoever! Whenever he opens his mouth, he lies, for it's his nature to lie! Yes, he is a liar, and the father of all lies . . . including all your lies!"[66]

> First, Jesus compared *His* declaration that the devil was the Jewish leaders' "father" with *their* claim that God was their "Father." The Lord made it clear that such a determination should be made, based upon which "father" they were in the habit of obeying. Because they were planning to kill Jesus and openly lying about their intention to so, made it clear that their father was also a murderer and a liar—that is, the devil.[1]
>
> Second, what did Jesus mean by calling the devil a "murderer" and a "liar"? When Jesus spoke of the devil being a murderer, He referred to the fact that all the murders in the world are ultimately the result of his original instigation of sin in the beginning, when he lied to Adam and Eve. [Genesis 3:4] Thus, the first murder—Cain killing Abel—came relatively quickly on the heels of that first lie. [Genesis 4:8] His success

64 John 8:41
65 John 8:42, 43
66 John 8:44

in tempting first Eve and then Adam to sin, resulted in cutting off their access to the Tree of Life. It was, in effect, a death sentence for them.[2]

The Lord continued with His point, contrasting His own passion for the truth with the slander which they were spreading regarding Him. He declared, "As for Myself, I speak only the truth. And for that, you refuse to believe Me! You have all closely watched Me during the entire span of My ministry. So let Me ask you: Which one of you can name even one thing that I have done that is morally wrong? Tell Me, what is it? You know that I am telling you the truth, right? Then, why do you still refuse to believe Me? Tell Me that! Why do you keep lying about Me? The bottom line is this: He who is of God, believes the words of God—the words which I have been saying to you. But you don't believe them. This is true because you are not of God! Instead you would rather believe the lies of the devil, your father, and spread those lies to others. It's just that simple and logical!"[67]

Here Jesus contrasted His passion for the truth with the Jewish leaders' penchant for dishonesty. Such a contrast could not be starker!

Angered and frustrated, the Jewish leaders retorted, "Aren't we correct in saying that You have a demon living in You and that You are as wicked as a Samaritan?" [*Harmony* 7:3, 5; 11:120] The Jews considered Samaritans to be wicked people, and thus, virtually worthless. Accordingly, they treated the Samaritans with great contempt. [*Harmony* 3:34/1, 2][68]

Jesus simply declared, "I do not have a demon!" He did not, however, respond to the Samaritan criticism, considering it irrelevant.[69]

The Lord added, "While I always honor"—that is, to obey—"My Father, you always dishonor"—or disobey—"Me! Throughout My life, I have never sought My own glory. Rather, it is My Father who is the One who has given glory to Me, just as it has been His will to do so. And why will He give Me glory and honor? Because I have always glorified and honored Him! [*Harmony* 16:105] Furthermore, I can always count on Him to do the right thing. He makes no mistakes! So then, He is the One who will ultimately pass judgment upon your

67 John 8:45-47
68 John 8:48
69 John 8:49

actions . . . and words which you have spoken here today. No, He will not let Me down.[70]

"In summary, I can say with certainty that when anyone obeys My words—the words that My Father has given to Me to say—that person will never die." Here, Jesus was promising His followers that they would receive eternal life at the resurrection at the end of the world.[71]

> Of course, Jesus clearly implied that the Jewish leaders, because they did not believe in Him—that is, to "honor" Him [*Harmony* 11:70]—they would not receive eternal life. Such an implication really agitated them.

The Jews responded angrily, "Now we are sure that You have a demon dwelling within You. Abraham, our great father, is dead. All the famous prophets are also dead. And yet, You say, 'If anyone obeys My words, he will never die!' Ridiculous!" Of course, again, Jesus was referring to eternal life that will be given to those in the world to come—as a result of the resurrection [1 Thessalonians 4:16, 17]—not to the transitory life of this present world. But the Jews were too upset to understand this.[72]

"There is no way," the Jews continued, "that You are greater than our father Abraham. But Abraham is dead, right? The prophets, too, are dead, right? Then, who do You claim to be? How can you offer eternal life to anyone, if our father Abraham couldn't—even to himself? Do you really claim to be better than he?"[73]

Christ, ignoring at the moment their reference to Abraham, answered, "How many times must I tell you? It's not what I claim, but what My Father claims for Me. If I sought My own glory, that would be wrong! Again, it is the Father—not I—who has given Me honor and glory. And, I remind you, this is the same Father, of whom you say, 'He is our God!' [*Harmony* 11:64] It's simple logic: If He really were your God and Father, then you would believe what He has said regarding Me. But, quite obviously, He's not your God because you don't know Him as you claim . . . but *I know Him!* In fact, if I were to say that I don't know

---

70 John 8:49, 50
71 John 8:51
72 John 8:52
73 John 8:53

Him, then I would be a liar—just like you! Yes, I know Him, and have faithfully kept His word."[74]

Here, Jesus did not make any personal claim about His own greatness. Rather, He talked about His relationship with His Father who was the ultimate source of His power and the gift of eternal life that He promised His followers.

Jesus added still more, this time returning to the subject of Abraham. [*Harmony* 11:73, 74] He said, "Now, according to your traditions, Abraham—the one whom you call your father [*Harmony* 11:62]—had a vision, in which he saw the time of the Messiah. [Genesis 15:9-21] Yes indeed, he did in fact have such a vision! And in that vision, he, with great joy, saw Me and the day in which we are now living. And when he saw it, I can tell you, he was so happy that he actually jumped for joy!"[75]

Here, the Savior pointed out the fact that if the Jews truly believed in Abraham, as they claimed, they also had to believe in Him. And why? Because Abraham saw the Lord in vision, and was happy about the Lord's upcoming ministry. In a real sense then, Jesus argued, if Abraham accepted Jesus as the Messiah, Abraham's children had no real choice but to also accept Jesus as the Messiah!

"Wait a minute! You are not even 50 years old!" the Jews shot back. "How, then, have you seen Abraham?"[76]

But Jesus did not claim that He had seen Abraham, rather that Abraham had seen His day in a vision. Perhaps the Jews misunderstood what Jesus had said. But it is more likely that they understood very clearly what Jesus was claiming: That Abraham, seeing Jesus in His vision, was, in fact, viewing the Messiah, who pre-dated Abraham, as Jesus claimed regarding Himself. And, in reality, that is exactly what Jesus meant!

But to erase all ambiguity and uncertainty regarding Himself [*Harmony* 9:17, 17/; 11:51-55, 76; 16:22], Jesus emphatically declared, "It is the truth, when I tell you, before Abraham was born, I AM!" In other words, with the declaration that He was the "I AM," Jesus claimed that He had always existed—indeed, that

---

74 John 8:54, 55

75 John 8:56

76 John 8:57

He was God! When Jesus made this strong statement, the Jews picked up stones to throw at Him! There can be no doubt whatsoever that the Jews attempted to stone the Lord because He claimed to be divine! That is why they wanted to kill Him, for this crime of supposed blasphemy was punishable by death by stoning. [Leviticus 24:15, 16; *Harmony* 4:10, 11; 11:171, 175; 12:27, 31][77]

> The phrase, "I AM!"—the words Jesus used to describe Himself—was reminiscent of the words used by God to describe Himself and His pre-existent nature when He spoke to Moses at the burning bush. [Exodus 3:13, 14] In short, this was the same nature Jesus claimed for Himself. That is why the Jews sought to stone Him for blasphemy.

But the Lord quickly and miraculously hid Himself from the Jews, and escaped out of their sight. Indeed, as He left the Temple area, He mysteriously disappeared! [*Harmony* 11:175][78]

### — The Healing of a Man, Blind from Birth
### < Autumn, A.D. 30 (7/7) >
### {John 9:1-41}

On the seventh-day Sabbath—the first Sabbath after the conclusion of the Feast of Tabernacles—Jesus was walking along and saw a man who had been blind from the day of his birth. According to the false religious teachings of the day, God sometimes punished people for their sins by inflicting them with some type of disease. For that reason, the Lord's disciples asked Jesus, "Teacher, who was the sinner in this case that this man would be born blind? The man himself, or his parents?"[79]

> In part, this was a foolish question. While, theoretically, it was true that God could punish the man's parents for some sin *they* might have committed—that is, by allowing their child to be born blind—it made no sense that God would punish this man for some sin he had committed. After all, he hadn't been born yet!

Christ's answer to the disciples' questions was clear and direct. He firmly declared, "This man's blindness was not the result of any particular sin this man committed . . . nor his parents, for that matter. His blindness, rather, is the result

---

77 John 8:58, 59

78 John 8:59

79 John 9:1, 2, 14

of living in a sinful world." Then Jesus added, "But the good news is, as a result of his blindness, the works of God will be performed within him. And as long as I am in this world, I must perform the works of the Father who has sent Me. Indeed I say to you, My disciples, that both your works and Mine are like the shedding of the Gospel light into the sinful darkness of this world, just as the sun shines in the morning to dispel the darkness of the night. But when our work is finished, it will be as though the darkness of nighttime has returned again. So for Myself, while I remain in this world, I will be the Light of the world—to give light to the physically blind, and more importantly, to the spiritually blind!" [*Harmony* 1:2; 4:62/2; 9:28/; 11:42] Of course, when Jesus left this earth, His disciples continued to spread the majestic Light of their Master to the entire world.[80]

> Here Jesus compared the blindness of this man's eyes to the darkness of the thinking of the people who had not yet been saved. Just as He was able to heal this man and restore light to his eyes and his life, He would be able to do the same for those who were in spiritual darkness, blind to the reality of the light of the truth of the Gospel. In fact, this was a primary purpose of all His miracles: to teach spiritual lessons regarding the conversion of the human heart. In reality, this statement by Jesus was the clearest declaration—along with His "Bread of Life" teaching [*Harmony* 9:25-54]—that Jesus ever made regarding the true purpose and meaning of His miracles. [*Harmony* 4:62/2-7]

After explaining Himself, the Lord spat on the ground. He then made a paste of clay from the moistened earth. Next He placed the mudpack on the blind man's eyes. Then Jesus said to him, "Go now! Wash your eyes in the pool of Siloam." This pool—its name meaning "Sent"—was located in the southern part of Jerusalem. There was no miracle-working power in the water of this pool. Rather, by asking the blind man to participate in his healing, Jesus knew his faith would be strengthened. The blind man went and washed in the pool as the Lord had directed. And, he came back from the pool with his full sight given to him![81]

> Why did Jesus put mud on the blind man's eyes and ask him to wash in the pool? As already said, by his participation in the process of his own healing, his faith would be increased. Further, the healing of the blind

---

[80] John 9:3-5
[81] John 9:6, 7

man illustrated the way the plan of salvation works in one's life. That being the case, Jesus taught that in the plan of salvation, it is important that the convert participate in the process. It is as the sinner reaches out and responds by faith to the power of the Gospel that salvation's wonderful energy is experienced. If one does not participate by faith, salvation is impossible. In short, salvation is a cooperative experience between the sinner and God. [*Harmony* 16:73] This is proven by the fact that the Jewish leaders, because of their lack of faith, never received the Gospel's salvation in their lives, even though Jesus strongly desired to provide saving grace for them.

After the blind man had been healed, many of the man's neighbors as well as his friends who knew him as a blind beggar said, "Look! Isn't this the blind man who used to sit and beg?" Others answered confidently, "I think you're right. It is he!" But some others were unconvinced, for they said, "No! He only looks like the blind man."[82]

The man himself, however, cleared up any doubts about who he was by firmly declaring, "I am indeed the one who was blind!"[83]

So they all asked him, "But how is it that your eyes were opened to see? What happened to you?"[84]

The healed man replied, "The Man who is named Jesus made some clay, and anointed my eyes. Then He commanded me, 'Go wash in the pool of Siloam.' So I went and washed in the pool just as He said. And look! Now I am able to see!"[85]

"Where did this Man named Jesus go?" they asked him.[86]

"I really don't know," he responded.[87]

Because this miracle was performed on the seventh-day Sabbath, there were some of the Jewish leaders who were concerned that this was in violation of one or more of their own man-made Sabbath regulations. Therefore, they

---

82 John 9:8, 9
83 John 9:9
84 John 9:10
85 John 9:11
86 John 9:12
87 John 9:12

brought the man before the Pharisees in a court of law—the Sanhedrin—to explain the healing process. This way, the Jewish leaders could determine if any of the man-made Sabbath regulations had indeed been broken or not. Indeed, there was a high probability that the Lord's making of clay on the Sabbath day was a clear violation of a Sabbath commandment that they themselves had crafted. Accordingly, the Pharisees questioned the man in regard to the method Jesus had used to heal him. He explained to them, saying, "This Man made clay, and applied it to my eyes. I washed in the pool as He instructed. And now I see!"(p) [88]

This simple explanation really upset some of the Pharisees. They stated, with conviction, "This Man Jesus cannot be of God, because He has clearly broken several of the Sabbath day commandments!" [*Harmony* 12:73][89]

> In truth, the Lord's miracle did violate a couple of *man-made* Sabbath laws. First, according to Jewish law, it was illegal to knead anything on the Sabbath. In making the clay, Jesus had to knead it. Second, any technical violation of a Sabbath commandment—such as kneading—was not considered permissible if it did not involve a matter of life or death. Because the man had been blind from birth—many years before—to heal him on that particular Sabbath was not necessary. [*Harmony* 12:91] Certainly, they reasoned, Jesus could have waited at least another day to perform the healing. Therefore, kneading the clay on the Sabbath was deemed by them to be, without doubt, a clear violation of one their Sabbath laws. Thus, according to the Pharisees, Jesus was obviously a Sabbath-breaker. However, Jesus did not violate any Scriptural commandments regarding the Sabbath. [*Harmony* 4:51/1, 2; 12:73]

Some of the less strict Jewish leaders were not so convinced that Jesus had broken the law. They reasoned, "How can a sinner, as you think Him to be, perform such an amazing miracle? It doesn't make sense." In short, the court was divided. Some said Jesus was guilty. Others had determined that He was not.[90]

> Trying to hide their division of opinion from the man, and attempting to break the impasse, the members of the court asked the man what he thought of Jesus. Perhaps he might be willing to condemn the Lord,

88 John 9:13-15
89 John 9:16
90 John 9:16

> thus freeing them from having to make the decision themselves. But why would a man who had been healed of blindness condemn the Man who had healed him? However, the man knew that Sabbath-breaking was a serious offense. If declared guilty of the crime, he could be thrown out of the church. Maybe, some of those on the court reasoned, that, in order to save his own neck, the man might be willing to blame Jesus for the whole affair so that he would not himself be condemned. This way, when they ultimately passed judgment upon the Lord, the divided court could say they were only following the conclusion of the man who had been led into wrongdoing by Jesus.

The court questioned the man, "What is your opinion of the Man who healed you of the blindness? Indeed, what do you think of Him?"[91]

"He must be a prophet!" was the man's opinion. That didn't help at all! Instead of condemning Jesus, the man actually endorsed Jesus as being a prophet. This, the most legalistic of the Jewish leaders could not believe nor accept. Perhaps, they thought, the man had not been healed at all. Maybe it was all a set-up to make them look bad. They decided that they needed to get to the bottom of story.[92]

So they brought the man's parents before the court to find out their opinion of the event. Maybe they could be of help to them. They asked the parents, "Is this really your son? Was he actually born blind? And, how is it that he is now able to see?"[93]

The parents gave answers to each of these questions, by saying, "Yes, he is our son. And yes, he was born blind. But as to how he is now able to see, we do not know. Who it was that opened his eyes, we do not know. Why not ask him? He's old enough. He is quite able to speak for himself."[94]

The man's parents were deliberately sidestepping the issue. They knew that it was Jesus who had healed their son. But they were afraid to admit this fact to the Jews. They, as common Jewish people, knew that the Jewish leaders had declared that those who confessed their faith in Jesus as being the Messiah, would be at least temporarily, disfellowshipped from the church. [*Harmony* 11:7] Not

---

91 John 9:17
92 John 9:17, 18
93 John 9:18, 19
94 John 9:20, 21

wanting this to happen to them, the parents dumped the full responsibility for the episode on their son. That's why they said, "Ask him! He's old enough!"[95]

For a second time, the formerly blind man was brought before the court. They demanded of him, "Give God the glory. Now admit it, this Man, Jesus, is a sinner. That is what we have determined. So, why don't you admit it too? It is clear: He has broken the Sabbath commandments. Certainly you can see that, can't you?"[96]

With noble courage, the man replied, "As to whether He is a sinner or not, I am not as sure as you seem to be. But there is one thing I know for certain: I used to be blind, but now I can see! He healed me!"[97]

Nevertheless, the Jews still wanted to pin a Sabbath-breaking charge against the Lord. They tried to get the man to describe the healing process. In doing so he might reveal an indisputable violation of one or more of their Sabbath laws. Once again, they demanded of him, "What was it that He did to you? How is it that He opened your eyes? Give us the details!"[98]

A bit frustrated now, the man answered with even greater courage than before, "I have already told you what he did, and how it happened, but you did not listen to me before. So why do you want me to tell you again? You are not planning to become His disciples, are you? So then, what value is there in telling you again what He did to me. It seems to me that you do not want to know what really happened."[99]

They answered with great disdain, "You can choose to be His disciple if you wish—and pay the consequences if you desire—but we are the disciples of Moses! We know that God spoke to Moses. However, as far as this Man Jesus is concerned, we don't know where He has come from, or the source of His actions. Therefore we cannot trust His words or the things He has done." [*Harmony* 11:172][100]

---

95 John 9:22, 23
96 John 9:24
97 John 9:25
98 John 9:26
99 John 9:27
100 John 9:28, 29

Shocked at their answer, the man responded, "That is certainly an amazing answer you have just given me. You say that you don't know the source of this Man's actions, and yet, He had the power to give me my sight! Isn't it obvious? Certainly, we all know that this kind of power to heal a blind man is not given by God to sinners, right? On the other hand, we know that God listens to those who trust Him and do His will. Listen! Why don't you admit it? There has never been a single person in history who has healed a man who was born blind! Name one other such example, if you can! I know you can't! Logically then, I must conclude that if this Man did not come from God, He would not be able to do such an amazing thing to me! As far as I'm concerned, it's just that simple."[101]

Stung by these strong words from this courageous man, the Jews retaliated, declaring, "Who are you to teach us? You were born as a sinner—that's why you were blind! So, how dare you try to lecture us! Just who do you think you are?" Then, the Jewish leaders had the man thrown out of the fellowship of the church.[102]

When the Lord found out that the man had been disfellowshipped from the synagogue—the Jewish church—He searched him out, and asked him, "Do you have faith in the Son of Man?" The Lord's use of the phrase "Son of Man" was a clear reference to Himself as the Messiah.[103]

The man answered back, "But who is He, Sir, that I might believe in Him?"[104]

With a touch of drama, the Lord responded, "You have both seen Him and heard His words . . . in fact, He is the One who is speaking to you right now!" [*Harmony* 3:50][105]

Overwhelmed, the man fell down at the Lord's feet to worship Him, declaring, "Oh, Lord, I do believe in You!"[106]

Jesus added, "My coming into the world has had the effect of separating those who reject me from those who accept Me. This is true so that those who

---

101 John 9:30-33
102 John 9:34
103 John 9:35
104 John 9:36
105 John 9:37
106 John 9:38

have been 'blind'"—that is, steeped in sin—"may be able to 'see,' by experiencing the power of the Gospel through a transformation of their lives. On the other hand, those who self-righteously think that they 'see' all the truth—that is, those who reject Me—have made themselves truly 'blind' by their rejection of Me as well as My ministry."[107]

There were some Pharisees standing by when Jesus spoke these words. Hearing this accusation, they asked Him, "What? You are not really telling us that we have made ourselves 'blind' to the truth, are You? We are not in that group, are we?"[108]

Jesus answered, "If you were really 'blind'—that is, truly ignorant of the truth of the Gospel—I would not hold you responsible for your actions. But, because you claim, 'We see'—that is, you falsely think that you understand all the things of the Gospel—then there is no way to deny it: You are stuck in your sins, unable to free yourself from them! And consequently, you are fully responsible for them. Yes, you have, on your own volition, made your own selves blind!"[109]

**— The "Good Shepherd" Teaching**
**< Autumn, A.D. 30 (7/7) >**
**{John 10:1-21}**

Jesus continued to teach the people by telling a parable: "It is a fact, when I tell you, the one who does not enter into the sheep pen by the gate is the one who seeks to enter by climbing over the fence. And I can assure you, that person is nothing more than a thief and a robber! But the one who enters by the gate of the sheep pen is the legitimate shepherd. He is the one who truly cares for the sheep." [*Harmony* 11:169, 170][110]

> Because a significant number of the Hebrews were shepherds [*Harmony* 1:46], many of His listeners would be familiar with the points Jesus made in this parable regarding the shepherd and his sheep.

"And when the true shepherd arrives at the sheep pen," the Lord went on, "the gatekeeper recognizes who he is, and opens the gate so that he may enter in and be with his sheep. And the sheep in the pen know the sound of the shepherd's

---

107 John 9:39
108 John 9:40
109 John 9:41
110 John 10:1, 2

voice. He calls them all by name. They trust him. And he is able to lead them out of the pen because they are quite willing to follow him wherever he directs them. The sheep willingly leave the safety of the pen, for the shepherd goes out in front of them. He is able to lead them effectively, for they continually follow his voice. For certainly, his is a voice which they easily recognize and trust.[111]

"But the voice of a stranger the sheep will simply refuse to follow! Instead, they run away from the stranger whose voice they do not know nor recognize."[112]

This was a parable illustrating the comparison between the Lord and the Jewish leaders in their relationship with the people. However, some who heard these words did not understand the point He was making. So Jesus had to explain what He meant. He began, "It is a certainty that I am the Gate of the sheep pen. Those who were here before My arrival"—that is, many of the Jewish leaders—"have treated the sheep badly, no better than if they were thieves and robbers! The good news is that the sheep"—the Lord's humble followers—"did not completely follow these wicked leaders. And because of that, they were prepared to listen to the voice of the Good Shepherd when He finally arrived. Yes, I am also the Door of the sheep pen. That is, My words are the Way of entrance into eternal life, and a full understanding of the Gospel.[113]

"If anyone seeks to enter eternal life through Me and My words, he will, indeed, receive eternal life. Sheep, under the leadership of a good shepherd, will live a life of freedom, being able to move safely in and out of the pen, to enjoy the fresh grass of the pasture. That will also be true of the one who places his or her trust in Me, for he or she will enjoy the privileges of salvation: forgiveness, assurance, and victory." [*Harmony* 11:169, 170][114]

Jesus continued with His explanation: "But the thieves"—again, representing the Jewish leaders—"seek only to control the sheep, to use them for their own benefit. Whatever suits the purposes of sheep thieves—to steal, kill, or destroy the sheep—is all that is important to them. In like manner, that is the way it is with those who seek to control My people, to use them for their own glory and purpose. But as for Me, I have come to give My people life—and the life that I

---

[111] John 10:3, 4
[112] John 10:5
[113] John 10:6-9
[114] John 10:9

give them will be more productive and fulfilling, indeed, greater than they have ever imagined![115]

"As I have said in my parable [*Harmony* 11:113], the gate of the sheep pen represents Me and My words. In addition to that, I am also the Good Shepherd who tenderly cares for His sheep. In sheep herding, a good shepherd is willing to forfeit his life for his sheep. And so, as the Good Shepherd of My people, I am willing to give My life for them." Jesus went on, "As everyone knows, someone who is merely hired to care for sheep does not care for them as efficiently as does the shepherd. Because the hired hand is not the owner of the sheep, when he sees a wolf approaching, he runs away to protect himself. He leaves the sheep defenseless! That way, the wolf is able catch some of them, which in turn, causes the other sheep to run around in terror. Why does the hired hand run away? Because he doesn't truly care about the sheep as does the owner. But I am not at all like a hired hand!"[116]

> Perhaps, the "hired hand" in this parable represented those Jewish leaders who were not as devious in their motives as were many of the other leaders whom Jesus had compared to "thieves" earlier in His parable. However, even these "hired hand" types did not lead the people with compassion and understanding—the way that Jesus did.

Jesus concluded, "But because I am the Good Shepherd, I know My sheep, and My sheep know Me! We know each other, just as the Father and I know each other. And, accordingly, I am willing to lay down My life for My sheep." Of course, Jesus did just that some months later when He died on the cross for all the sinners of the world. [*Harmony* 11:169][117]

"Now, I have other sheep—or followers—who are not yet a part of My flock in the sheep pen," the Lord added. Here Jesus referred to the Gentiles who in time would become His followers—that is, His sheep. "These other sheep," Jesus continued, "I will bring and they will become a part of My flock. Indeed, they will hear My voice, obey it, and come to Me to be a part of My total flock of followers. Then there will be one large flock and one Shepherd." Here, the

---

115 John 10:10
116 John 10:11-13
117 John 10:14, 15

Lord referred to the influx of Gentiles into the Christian Church, all under the leadership of Jesus, the Good Shepherd.[118]

Moving away from the Good Shepherd parable, Jesus spoke literally, saying, "Because I am willing to die for My people, the Father loves Me. And after I die for My people, I will live again." Of course, here Jesus referred to His death and resurrection. "No one has the power, on their own, to kill Me," the Lord added. "But, of My own accord, I shall willingly give Myself to die for the sinners of the world, to pay for their sins. No one can touch Me unless I say so. Yes, I have both the full authority to lay down My life"—to be willing to die—"and to take it up again"—to be resurrected. "And the Father has ordained that I have such authority."[119]

These powerful words caused quite a stir among the people who heard them. The opinions of many of them were divided. A good number of the Jewish leaders said, "See! We told you! He has a devil in Him. At the very least, He's crazy! No doubt He has lost His mind! So why waste your time listening to Him?" [*Harmony* 7:5; 11:68] But others said, "No! These are not the kind of words that a devil-possessed person would speak. And besides, a devil has no power to make a blind man see, has he? This is especially true if that man were blind from birth." Here, these Jewish leaders referred to the Lord's recent miracle of healing a man who had been born blind. [*Harmony* 11:79-109] This division of opinion among the Jewish leadership prevented them from being sufficiently unified in their efforts to arrest Jesus. Accordingly, they were quite unable to dispose of the Lord at that time. [*Harmony* 17:22][120]

## The Lord's Ministry Continues Among the Gentiles
## < Autumn and Early Winter, A.D. 30 (7/7) >
## (Matthew 19:1, 2; Mark 10:1; Luke 9:51-10:42)

### —Jesus Wraps Up His Galilean Ministry, and Begins His Samaritan-Peraean Ministry
### < Autumn, A.D. 30 (7/7) >
### {Matthew 19:1, 2, Mark 10:1; Luke 9:51-56}

At the conclusion of the events surrounding the Feast of Tabernacles, Jesus returned to Galilee for a while. [*Harmony* 11:133] After a relatively brief stay in

118 John 10:16
119 John 10:17, 18
120 John 10:19-21

that northern province of Israel, the Lord officially ended His ministry in Galilee. Next, Jesus started a slow movement south toward to the province of Judea. On the way, He planned to minister to the people living on both the eastern and western banks of the Jordan River. It was less than six months away from the Passover of A.D. 31—the Passover when He would be crucified and resurrected. And, He would soon after that, ascend into heaven. [*Harmony* 17:116; 18:14, 14/, 95] Even though He was facing death there, the Lord was determined to go on to Jerusalem.[121]

While traveling, the Master and His disciples entered the land of the Samaritans which was located between Galilee and Judea. [*Harmony* 3:34/1, 2] Just as they began their trip, they arrived at a certain unnamed city of the Samaritans. Jesus sent several of the disciples into town to make arrangements to stay there overnight. But the people of that town refused to allow them to stay there because of the bitter hatred that existed between the Jews and Samaritans. Besides the usual disdain that Samaritans had toward Jews, there was another reason why they rejected Jesus on this occasion. Because He was heading toward Jerusalem to worship there, they were offended that He did not appear to want to worship with them. They felt that Jesus was disrespecting their own Samaritan religion.[122]

When the town refused admittance to them, James and John—two of the Twelve—were extremely angry. They asked Jesus, "Master, do You want us to command fire to streak down from Heaven to destroy these evil people as Elijah did in the old days?" This was reminiscent of an event that took place near that same region some 700 years previously, when Elijah called fire to fall upon the enemies of God. [2 Kings 1:10; *Harmony* 4:70, 71][123]

But the Lord, looking at them, rebuked them, "No, My friends! You have no idea what a dangerous spirit you are demonstrating by making such a request! Remember, the Son of Man did not come to this world to kill people, but to save them! Let's just go on to another village—one that will accept us!" And they did just that.[124]

---

121 Matthew 19:1; Mark 10:1; Luke 9:51
122 Luke 9:52, 53
123 Luke 9:54
124 Luke 9:55, 56

While some of the Samaritans of that area rejected Jesus, the Lord was not unduly distressed with them. The Savior took into account that they did not fully realize just what they were doing. Accordingly, Jesus did not judge them harshly, neither did He allow His disciples to do so.

But in spite of that initial rejection in Samaria, most of the people of that region as well as those who lived near both banks of the Jordan River in Judea were very receptive to the Lord's ministry. In fact, large crowds of people came out to hear Him, providing Him the opportunity once more to preach and to teach the Gospel among the people there. Jesus also healed a number of them from various diseases.[125]

### — The Test of Discipleship
### < Autumn, A.D. 30 (7/7) >
### {Luke 9:57-62}

As Jesus and His disciples were traveling through that region, someone approached the Lord. Obviously very impressed by what the Master was teaching, he declared to the Savior, "Lord, I am willing to follow You wherever You lead!" But Jesus wanted him to know that such a desire to follow Him would call for a level of sacrifice and commitment that the man had not truly considered.[(q)][126]

So, the Lord said to the man, "Foxes have holes in which to live and sleep. Even the birds of the sky have a place to roost in their nests. However, the Son of Man has no place to lay His head that He can call His own. Are you sure that you are ready to live such a life as that?" (This is the second time an event such as this took place, the first being about a year previous to this particular one. [*Harmony* 7:57, 58])[127]

Also along the way, the Lord met another man. Jesus really wanted this individual to follow Him on a permanent basis. Accordingly, Jesus invited him with the simple words, "Follow Me!"[128]

---

125 Matthew 19:2; Mark 10:1

126 Luke 9:57

127 Luke 9:58

128 Luke 9:59

But the man hesitated, explaining, "Lord, my father is old. I don't know how much longer he will live. Please let me return to my home, and wait for him to die. Then, after I bury him, I will be glad to follow You!"(r) [129]

The Lord, disappointed by the man's answer, responded, "Allow the 'spiritually dead'"—that is, others in the man's family who did not appreciate the power of the Gospel as he did—"to take care of waiting for your father to die, so that they can be responsible for burying him. But as for you, I want you to give of yourself now to preach the Gospel of the kingdom of God everywhere you can. I need you now—not later on!" (This is the second time an event such as this took place, the first being about a year previous to this particular incident. [*Harmony* 7:59, 60])[130]

There was another man whom the Lord met along the way. Jesus wanted this one to follow Him, too. But this person answered the Lord's invitation by saying, "I really want to follow You, Lord. But I need to return to my home and say good-bye to my family."[131]

But Jesus, knowing that the man was just making an excuse for not responding to His call, challenged the depth of his commitment. The Lord said to him, "It could take years for you to say good-bye! You are hesitating! No! You must respond now, or you may never do it. No one, after putting his hand to a plow to make a furrow in a field, should look back, or the furrow will be crooked! In a like manner, if you look back after I have called you, I am fearful that you will never follow Me as you should. Your ministry for Me will careen off course, just like a crooked furrow. I'm sorry to say, if you hesitate to follow Me now, you are unfit for the work of the kingdom of God!"[132]

> These three stories illustrate three types of individuals who have a desire to follow the Lord, but are unprepared to do so. The first—the man whom the Lord hesitated to accept his desire to follow Him [*Harmony* 11:126, 127]—represented those who quickly make a decision on the spur of the moment to follow the Lord and His will, but have not counted the cost of that decision. It is easy to say "yes," but not so easy to follow through with the decision, to remain faithful to the Lord forever, especially when

129 Luke 9:59
130 Luke 9:60
131 Luke 9:61
132 Luke 9:62

> things get difficult, as they always do. The second man—the one who was waiting for his father to die [*Harmony* 11:128-130]—represented those who want to decide for the Lord, but are waiting for some big problem to be resolved first. They fail to appreciate the fact that the Lord helps them to overcome the problems of their lives. The third man—the one who wanted to go home and say goodbye to his family [*Harmony* 11:131, 132]—represented those who are always making some excuse as to why they can't follow the Lord. It doesn't make any difference if the excuse is based on some big item, or just some little thing, they always seem to put off that decision.

**— The Mission of the "Seventy"**
**< Autumn and Early Winter, A.D. 30 (7/7) >**
**{Luke 10:1-24}**

Jesus, of course, had His twelve disciples surrounding Him. He had previously sent them to do personal work in the villages and towns of Galilee. [*Harmony* 8:37-58] But now, with less than six months left before His crucifixion, the Lord appointed seventy other workers to work house-to-house, and village-to-village. These Seventy were selected from among the followers He had accumulated while working in Galilee. This group probably included others who either had come to Him, or whom He had called, after He had left the Feast of Tabernacles, some days or weeks earlier. [*Harmony* 11:121][(s)] [133]

> But instead of working the province of Galilee, as had the Twelve, the Seventy were to work the area of Samaria and Peraea—the block of land sandwiched in between Galilee to the north and Judea to the south. [*Harmony* 3:34/1, 2] While a number of Jews lived in this region, it was populated primarily by Gentiles. It could be said, then, that the Twelve, during their time of personal ministry, worked mainly with Jews, while the Seventy worked largely with Gentiles. In fact, ever since the Lord's "Bread of Life" teaching [*Harmony* 9:26-54], Jesus had worked primarily among non-Jews.

The Savior sent the Seventy to do their work in pairs—that is, two-by-two. He sent them to lead the way before Him, preparing the people of the various cities of the region for His arrival. Before He actually sent them out to do their work, however, He gave them instructions. He began with these words, "The

---

133 Luke 10:1

harvest of souls is potentially abundant! However, there are so few people to do the work of the harvesting of souls. That is why you need to plead with the Lord of this 'harvest,' to cast, as it were, more workers into the fields to gather the fruit of souls." [*Harmony* 3:57; 8:37][134]

> These words were, in part, similar to the words He used when He first worked with the Samaritans almost exactly two years before. [*Harmony* 3:57-59] As in this case, Jesus had used the symbol of the harvest to make His point. But in both cases, the Lord referred to the success of the work among Gentiles, not Jews.

Jesus continued His instructions by saying, "Go! Do your work, but look out: I am sending you as lambs, as it were, in the middle of a pack of wolves! Make no mistake: The enemies of the Gospel will try to destroy you. [*Harmony* 8:45][135]

"Now here's some specific advice: Take no extra money with you on your mission—people who appreciate what you are doing will provide adequately for your needs. The same goes for your belongings: Don't take extra clothes or shoes with you. Again, these physical needs will be provided for you by others when you faithfully do spiritual work for them. [*Harmony* 8:42][136]

"Also, don't spend too much time talking to people along the way. Save your energy for those you will greet in their homes. There is not enough time left for you to spend it just chatting around with people. [*Harmony* 8:43][137]

"Whenever you do enter someone's home, first say, 'May the peace of the Gospel settle upon the people of this house!' If those in that house accept what you have to say and allow the message of the Gospel to settle upon them, they will be blessed accordingly. But if they reject your words, well then, your blessing of peace will not remain with them. In a sense, it will come back to you so that you will be able to share it with someone else who is willing to accept it. [*Harmony* 8:44][138]

"Now," Jesus continued, "once you find a place where people are willing to give you food and lodging, do most of your eating, drinking, and resting in that

---

134 Luke 10:1, 2
135 Luke 10:3
136 Luke 10:4
137 Luke 10:4
138 Luke 10:5, 6

house. They will provide for you, for indeed, as I have said, a faithful worker is worthy of fair payment for his work. But My main point is: As I've also said before [*Harmony* 8:43], don't spend time running from house to house, merely socializing with people. You have much work to do in a short period of time—so spend that time wisely![139]

"And, whenever you are accepted in a place, eat the food they give to you. Please don't offend them by complaining or refusing to eat it! Because you are Jews and they are Gentiles, you may not be used to their food. But eat it anyway! In addition, while you may heal those who are sick, your main work is to preach the Gospel. In that regard, you are to tell the people, 'The time has come for you to accept the message of the Gospel—indeed, the kingdom of God is close to you. Now is the time to accept it!' On occasion, you will enter certain areas where the people will reject your teaching. In those cases, you are to go into the streets of that place, and declare, 'We are going to shake from our feet the dust which has clung to us from your city streets! Mark our words! This will show that you have rejected the Gospel message that has been personally presented to you!' These strong words will make it clear to these people just how serious has been their rejection of the Gospel and its messengers—to say nothing of its Messiah!" [*Harmony* 8:44][(t)] [140]

> These last words, which seem harsh, were intended to indicate that the time for decision had come. For three years, off and on, Jesus had labored among the people. Now they needed to make a decision. To decide for or against the Gospel message was very serious business. Time was getting short for them.

"For I tell you," Jesus continued—repeating words He had said on another occasion [*Harmony* 8:44]—"during the time of the final judgment, the city of Sodom [Genesis 19:1-29] will have an easier time than that city which rejects you now! It will be like the cities of Galilee that have previously rejected Me during My ministry among them. Yes, woe to Chorazin!"—a town near Capernaum in Galilee which had rejected the Lord. "Woe to you, Bethsaida!"—another village in Galilee which had, for the most part, rejected Him. "If I had done the things in Tyre and Sidon"—two heathen cities in Phoenicia to the northwest—"that I have done within your confines, they would have repented long ago, sitting in sackcloth and ashes"—a symbol of extreme sorrow and repentance! "Yes, Tyre

139 Luke 10:7
140 Luke 10:8-11

and Sidon will have an easier time in the day of judgment than these two cities. [*Harmony* 8:32-34][(u)][141]

"And while I'm at it, oh, Capernaum, you are not as exalted to the heavens as you think, are you? No! Instead you will be cast into the grave! Remember, it was within your own town's limits that I centered My ministry in Galilee. Why then did you reject Me? How could you be so foolish?" [*Harmony* 8:32-34][(v)][142]

In conclusion, Jesus gave parting words to the Seventy before they began their mission. He said to them, "Remember, the one who accepts what you tell them, will, in effect, be accepting Me! On the other hand, the one who rejects you will be rejecting Me! And too, the one who rejects Me will have rejected the Father who sent Me! So, if someone rejects you, don't take it personally, for they, in reality, will be rejecting both My Father and Me. Therefore, allow us—the Father and the Son—to deal with that rejection. Don't you worry about it!" [*Harmony* 8:48][143]

After their time of ministry was completed, the Seventy returned to Jesus, overflowing with excitement and joy. "Even demons are subject to the authority of Your Name, Lord!" they declared. [*Harmony* 11:148][144]

Commenting on the Seventy's positive report, Jesus added, "Yes! And because of that authority, I have seen Satan fall from heaven, as it were, like a flash of lightning that quickly fades, fizzling out into nothingness. Indeed, he will be a conquered foe. What you observed is just the beginning. I tell you, through My death the devil and his power will be totally crushed. [Revelation 12:7-9][145]

"Yes, I have given to you the authority to step upon, as it were, the snakes and scorpions of sin and wickedness. The power of Satan"—the real Serpent [Revelation 12:9]—"will be crushed, and ultimately you will be victorious over him. He will not be able to hurt you. Nevertheless, your greatest joy will not be in your miraculous victory over Satan and his demons as you have just experienced. No! That is insignificant compared to the joy you will experience when you

141 Luke 10:12-14
142 Luke 10:15
143 Luke 10:16
144 Luke 10:17
145 Luke 10:18

discover that your names are written in the Book of Life in heaven!" [Exodus 32:31-33; Daniel 7:9, 10; 12:1; Revelation 20:11, 12][146]

> The Book of Life contains the names of those who will be saved at the end of the world. Obviously it is very important to have one's name recorded in that book. Again, as Jesus indicated, it will be the ultimate honor to have one's name found there.

At that moment, the excitement that the Seventy expressed regarding the success of their combined ministries provided intense happiness for the Lord. Filled with the Holy Spirit, and with great passion, Jesus cried out to God, declaring, "My Father, I give You praise—You who are the Lord of both heaven and earth! I am so happy that You have hidden the good things of the Gospel from the self-righteous snobs who think they know everything, as though they were all-wise"—such as the Jewish leaders. "Instead, You have revealed these good things to the so-called infants of this world, who, with child-like faith, have given their full trust to You. Yes, You are well-pleased to bless these children of faith."[147]

Jesus concluded by adding, "Full authority to bless My followers has been given to Me by the Father. This makes logical sense because no one really understands the Son as does the Father, and no one really knows the Father better than the Son. We work as a team! That is why I have the authority to give the knowledge of the Gospel, and the power to overcome Satan and his demons, to whomever I desire should receive it." [*Harmony* 11:144][148]

Taking the twelve disciples aside from the Seventy, Jesus, in secret said to them, "You are so blessed to have seen the things that you have been permitted to see—that is, to view the success of My ministry firsthand. I must tell you that many of the prophets and kings of the old days of Hebrew history greatly desired to view the things that you have been privileged to see. But no, they never saw these things. Neither did they hear the things that your ears have heard." [*Harmony* 7:47][149]

> The level of the Lord's excitement and optimism at this time seemed to be quite high. Why was this? In a sense, the mission of the Seventy had

---

146 Luke 10:19, 20
147 Luke 10:21
148 Luke 10:22
149 Luke 10:23, 24

> been the culmination of the work of His ministry that had been going on for some months. Early in the Lord's ministry, Jesus had worked just among the Jews. He had some success with them, especially in Galilee. Now Jesus had equal success among Gentiles, which had been the primary mission of the Seventy. The seeds of the entire ministry of the Christian church had been planted. Now they were beginning to bear fruit. For indeed, the Gospel was to go to the whole world—to both Jews and Gentiles [*Harmony* 18:94], and the results were to be dramatic. [Revelation 7:9-17] Jesus could see that, in spite of the many disappointments He had experienced, things were shaping up just as He had planned. His work of training a group of vibrant workers, who in turn, would also train others, was almost complete! [*Harmony* 16:113]

### — Who Is Our Neighbor? The Story of the "Good Samaritan"
### ‹ Early Winter, A.D. 30 (7/7) ›
### {Luke 10:25-37}

Sometime later, as Jesus was nearing Jerusalem, he passed through Jericho, 17 miles northeast of that city. There, an expert in the laws of Moses suddenly stood up among the crowd of listeners to try to trick Jesus in to saying something that might be used to embarrass Him. Interrupting the Lord's teaching, the lawyer asked, "Master, what shall I do that I might inherit eternal life? To be sure, what action can I perform that will ensure me of everlasting life?"[150]

> The Jews had always debated among themselves the answer to this question. Yet there never seemed to be an answer upon which they could all unite. In fact, great disputes arose among them, sometimes bitterly dividing them. The Jews believed that if Jesus could be brought into the controversy, it would cause Him to be confused and unsure of Himself. Should this happen, then their persistent purpose to embarrass the Lord might succeed.

But instead of answering the question, Jesus challenged the lawyer to give his best response to his own question. "Well, what is written in the Law?" the Lord asked. "How do you read the Law? After all, you're the expert in the Law!"[151]

The lawyer quoted, "Well, the Law says, 'You shall love the Lord your God with your entire heart, with your complete soul, as well as with your total strength

150 Luke 10:25

151 Luke 10:26

and mind. And you are also to love your neighbor as you would love yourself.'" [Deuteronomy 6:5; Leviticus 19:18; *Harmony* 14:100-106][152]

"You have given the correct answer, My friend!" Jesus returned. "I tell you that if you do as you have just declared, you shall inherit eternal life! As you have just said, the principle of love—not just the mere obedience of the words of the Law—is the essential issue involved here. This is what *you* must do: love both God and your neighbor in your everyday life. This is the true meaning of the Law!"[153]

Theoretically, the lawyer agreed that, based upon the Scripture, people should love their neighbors as themselves. But when Jesus demanded that he, the lawyer, must, *himself*, love his neighbors—especially those whom he might dislike—he was offended. He had exempted himself from doing what he admitted the Law said a person should do! After all, it was common practice among the Jewish hierarchy to consider themselves too good to really love others whom they considered less pious or worthy than themselves. To the lawyer, mere intellectual assent to the teaching was sufficient. Therefore, to justify his guilt feelings regarding his personal non-compliance with the principles of the Law, he challenged the Lord's statement by asking, "But who is my neighbor? Are you saying that everyone I meet—even the heathen or Samaritans—is my neighbors? Must I love them as I love myself?"[154]

As Jesus often did, He responded by telling a parable. He said, "Let me tell you a story. A certain man was traveling the 17 miles from Jerusalem to Jericho. Of course, as you know, he had to travel through the lonely and sometimes dangerous wilderness between these two cities. Well, on the way, a group of robbers accosted him. They stripped him of his clothes, severely beat him, and left him for dead.[155]

"Coincidentally, a priest"—one who ministered before the Lord in the Temple—"was traveling the same road, and came upon the beaten man. Seeing him, the priest passed by on the other side of the road, totally ignoring the injured man. A bit later, a Levite"—one who worked in the Temple, assisting the priests—"also passed by. The Levite did the same thing as the priest by moving

---

152 Luke 10:27
153 Luke 10:28
154 Luke 10:29
155 Luke 10:30

over to the other side of the road, pretending he had not seen the poor, beaten man.[156]

"But," the Lord continued with His story, "a Samaritan—a man who you feel is unworthy of your respect, honor, or love—traveled by the same place. [*Harmony* 3:34/1, 2] Seeing the injured man lying beside the road, the Samaritan felt deep compassion for him. He went over to him and, after soothing the man's wounds with oil and wine, he bandaged them. He tenderly placed the injured man on his donkey and brought him to an inn near town. There the Samaritan further cared for the injured man.[157]

"The next day, he took two denarii"—the equivalent of two days' wages—"and gave the money to the innkeeper, saying, 'Please continue to take care of the injured man for me. And should it cost more than this to care for him, when I come by on my way back home, just bill me, and I will gladly pay you in full.'" [*Harmony* 2:37][158]

With the story finished, the Lord pointedly asked, "Which of these three—the priest, the Levite, or the Samaritan—was a good neighbor to the man who was robbed?"[159]

"Why, of course, the one who showed mercy to the injured man!" the lawyer quickly but evasively gave the obvious answer.[160]

"Then in that case," Jesus declared, "*you* should go and do likewise! Being a good neighbor is doing to others as you would wish they would do to you—no matter who they are. So, if you wish to be treated well as a neighbor, then you, yourself, must be a good neighbor to others."[161]

> In order for this parable to have the impact the Lord wanted it to have, it would have had to have been a true story. For, if the Lord had simply made it up, the lawyer could have argued that there was no way that a Samaritan would show such kindness as the one in the parable. Because the lawyer did not make this argument, it is very likely, then, that the

---

156 Luke 10:31, 32
157 Luke 10:33, 34
158 Luke 10:35
159 Luke 10:36
160 Luke 10:37
161 Luke 10:37

story was true. Accordingly, one of the points that the Lord made by telling this story is that what counts in life is not what a person merely professes, but what one actually does! And, the Samaritan, who was thought to be a sinner, was, in fact, the real neighbor, because he lived as a good neighbor! Thus by this story Jesus was teaching that a mere profession of faith—such as in the case of the priest and the Levite . . . and even the lawyer himself—was not enough. A profession of faith must be demonstrated by action.[1]

By this parable the Lord drove home at least three powerful points. First, as already stated, one must live his or her profession of faith in a practical, loving way. And second, the Lord indicated that the Samaritan—one whom the lawyer would have considered a great sinner—was a better neighbor than was the lawyer! Thus, the Lord made it clear that the judgmental and prejudicial attitude of the lawyer—and of most Jews—toward non-Jews was totally inappropriate. Third, in the final judgment, people will be judged by what they've actually done and not by what they've merely professed. Neither will they be judged solely by their nationality or religion.[2]

**—Jesus In the Home of Mary and Martha**
**< Early Winter, A.D. 30 (7/7) >**
**{Luke 10:38-42}**

Jesus and His disciples continued on their way to Jerusalem to attend the Feast of Dedication. [*Harmony* 11:165] Just outside the city, the Lord stopped at the town of Bethany a couple of miles to the east. There He stayed in the home of Martha, who invited Him to rest there. Martha had a brother named Lazarus [*Harmony* 13:1] and a sister named Mary. This family knew Jesus as a close, personal friend. Mary had previously worked with Jesus in Galilee during His ministry there. She was more commonly known as Mary Magdalene. The Savior had previously healed her of demon-possession. [*Harmony* 6:19][(w)][162]

While Martha was busying herself by preparing a meal for the Lord, Mary was sitting at the feet of Jesus, listening carefully to every word He spoke. Upset that Mary was not helping her in the kitchen, Martha came out to Jesus and complained, "Lord, why is it that You don't seem to care that Mary has left me

162 Luke 10:38, 39

to do all the work of cooking alone? Tell her to get up and help me!" [*Harmony* 14:2, 3][163]

Jesus tactfully said, "Martha! Martha! You are so worried and distressed about many things. There are but a few things that are essential . . . in fact, when all is said and done, only *one* thing is really necessary: to sit at My feet and listen to the words of truth. And Mary has chosen that one thing! Neither you nor I must take that from her!"(x) [164]

> By this event the Lord taught that having a calm devotional life—that is, "sitting at the feet of Jesus," so to speak—is the most important thing in one's life. Everything else, no matter how important it might appear to be, is only secondary.[1]

> Martha, in spite of the Lord's gentle rebuke, had done a good thing for Jesus by preparing a meal for Him. It is easy sometimes to criticize Martha. However, such should not be done. Rather, the Lord emphasized that the important thing for Mary to be doing at that time was to sit at the feet of Jesus. While Martha should have learned from Mary's pious act, nevertheless, Martha was a woman of great virtue herself. Preparing a meal for the Messiah was a noble task! And, too, Martha would later show a significant knowledge of Biblical truth as well as great faith in the Lord as a miracle worker. [*Harmony* 13:14-18] Martha was, indeed, a virtuous woman with very few peers![2]

## Jesus at the Feast of Dedication
## < Early Winter, A.D. 30 (7/7) >
## (John 10:22-40)

At last, Jesus arrived in Jerusalem for the Feast of Dedication—commonly known by its Hebrew name, Hanukkah. This particular festival, not commanded in Scripture, was set up by the Jews to celebrate a time in their history—about 160 years before the birth of Jesus, and 300 years after the last book of the Old Testament was written—when the Temple was cleansed after it had been defiled by a Greek king. This festival, celebrated in the winter of the year, was sometimes known as the "Festival of Lights." [*Harmony* 11:162][165]

---

163 Luke 10:39, 40
164 Luke 10:41, 42
165 John 10:22

Jesus was walking near the porch of Solomon, a portion of the Temple area that remained from the original building constructed by King Solomon a thousand years earlier. The Jewish leaders, tipped off that the Lord might be in town for the festival, spied Him there. They had determined that they were going to place pressure on Him to declare Himself the Messiah, even the Son of God, so that they might accuse Him of blasphemy—that is, the sin of a mere human being claiming to be God. [Leviticus 24:15, 16][166]

That is why, after crowding around the Savior, they demanded of him, "How long will You keep us in nervous suspense? If You are really the Christ—even the Messiah—tell us now! Make it clear to us!" [*Harmony* 11:52][167]

> Of course Jesus was the Messiah. However, the Jews' concept of what the Messiah would be or do was quite different from what the Messiah actually was. For one thing, the Jews were looking for the Messiah to come as a conquering king to overthrow the dominion of the Roman government. For the Lord's part, however, His ministry did not include such a thing. To publicly declare Himself as the long-awaited Messiah would cause great distress among the nation if He refused to live up to their perception of what the Messiah was to be. For this and other good reasons, Jesus always refrained from directly declaring Himself to be the Messiah. He wanted people to decide for themselves whether He was the Christ or not, based upon their own observation of the things that He said and did. He also wanted them to compare His words and actions with what the Scriptures had to say about them. To be sure, the Lord wanted His followers to be students of the Word.

In His answer to their demand, Jesus was somewhat indirect. He said, "I have told you before, yet you refuse to believe what I have said. Look at the works that I have done throughout My ministry under the power of My Father—the miracles, the teachings, and the like. These clearly show to you who I am! Yet, even with all this evidence, you still do not believe." [*Harmony* 11:53][168]

> By this answer, Jesus brilliantly claimed to be the Messiah without actually saying, in so many words, that He was the Messiah! This way, the Jews could not say that Jesus claimed to be the Messiah, thus having

---

166 John 10:23, 24
167 John 10:24
168 John 10:25, 26

a reason, from their perspective, to kill Him. Yet, on the other hand, those who honestly and sincerely observed the details of His ministry which He had just outlined for them could clearly see that He was, indeed, the promised Messiah. [*Harmony* 11:53/]

Jesus further added, "Let Me tell you why you do not accept My words and actions as being valid. It is because you are not truly My sheep"—that is, genuine followers of His. "Yes, My sheep recognize My voice—the voice of the Shepherd. I know who My sheep are, and they willingly follow Me wherever I lead them, because they know Me. And, in the end, I will grant them eternal life. At that point, they will never die again! And no one, not even you, will be able to snatch them from My protecting grip!" Here, Jesus picked up the theme of the parable of the Good Shepherd He had mentioned some weeks earlier. [*Harmony* 11:110-118] Here, too, He made it clear that in eternity the Jewish leaders would no longer have any negative influence on the Lord's true followers.[169]

"Furthermore," Jesus continued, "My Father, who is greater than anyone, is the One who has given these sheep to Me. For that reason, not only do I hold them in My protecting hand, but the Father likewise holds them in His hand. And clearly, no one will be able to snatch My followers from the strong protecting grip of the Father! In truth, the Father and I work together as one, to protect My sheep. So then, there is no way that you will be able to overcome Us as We work together in the protection of My sheep!"[170]

The Jews, correctly interpreting the Lord's words as an indirect claim to be the Messiah, took stones in their hands to throw at Him. Jesus calmly challenged them by asking, "I have performed many good works that the Father has given Me to do. Now, tell Me, for which of these noble works are you going to stone Me?" [*Harmony* 2:34/2; 4:10, 11; 11:77, 78][171]

Indignant, the Jews shot back, "We are not going to stone You for any so-called good work You have done. No! Instead, we are going to stone You for blasphemy! [Leviticus 24:15, 16] For You have claimed to be God when You are, in fact, only a mere mortal human being." [*Harmony* 13:5; 17:100][172]

---

[169] John 10:26-28
[170] John 10:29, 30
[171] John 10:31, 32
[172] John 10:33

Jesus, seeking to get them off track from their evil intentions, referred to a Bible verse the Jewish leaders liked to quote regarding themselves when they taught the Law to the common people. He questioned them, saying, "Let Me ask you a question: Isn't it written in your own Law—the Scriptures—these words, 'I said, you are gods.' [Psalm 82:6] Now, according to your own tradition and your interpretation of this text, you as teachers of the Law—when you teach the Law—are very willing to accept God's declaration that you can legitimately be called 'gods.' And when those whom you teach consider you 'gods' as such, you are well pleased. That is the truth, isn't it? Well then, if you, who have received the Word of God to teach to others, can be called 'gods'—and the words of Scripture cannot be changed, for that's what it says—then why is it that you have threatened Me? Why do you say of Me, whom the Father has *personally set apart* to be sent to this world, 'You are a blasphemer,' because I said, 'I am the Son of God'?"[173]

> The Lord's argument was clear: If the Jewish leaders—mere human beings—were willing to be called "gods" when they taught the Law to the people, then why did they accuse Jesus of blasphemy when He claimed to be God's Son when He did the work of His Father who had sent Him?

"Now," Jesus concluded, "if I did not faithfully do both the will and works of My Father, then you would be quite justified in refusing to believe in Me. But, because I have faithfully done both the will and works of My Father, then believe in Me based upon what I have done and taught. Both My words and My actions clearly testify of Me. While you may not believe the words of My claim, then at least be willing to know the truth and believe in Me, based upon the mighty works—even miracles—that I have performed. Because of My miracles, you may be sure that the Father dwells in Me, and I in the Father." By this statement Jesus implied, too, that just as clearly as He did the will of God, they did not do the will of God. [*Harmony* 2:31/2][174]

The Jews' reaction to the Lord's declaration was very negative, for they still sought to grab Him for the purpose of killing Him. However, Jesus miraculously eluded their grasp and escaped from their presence. From there, He went into

---

[173] John 10:34-36

[174] John 10:37, 38

the wilderness beyond the Jordan River. [*Harmony* 3:9/; 4:10, 11; 11:77, 78, 171; 12:1, 27][175]

**Supplementary Notes:**

**(a) [11:0+]** This is the seventh of eight insertions in the *Harmony* that places the events of the three-and-a-half-year ministry of Jesus on a "timeline," divided into seven six-month segments. (The eighth insertion is at the end of the seventh segment.) The other segment insertions can be found in the following locations: Segment One, *Harmony* 2:21/; Two, *Harmony* 3:0; Three, *Harmony* 3:33/2; Four, *Harmony* 3:71/; Five, *Harmony* 6:17/; Six, *Harmony* 10:0; and Eight, *Harmony* 18:99/1-21.

**(b) [11:0/7]** This segment has the designation 7/7 for its "Segmental Placement" number. (See "Segmental Placement" in the "Features for Using the *Harmony* as a Reference Book" section near the back of this book for more information.)

**(c) [11:2]** See **Note "a"** in Chapter 7, to learn more about the brothers of Jesus.

**(d) [11:8]** The "midst of the feast" would be about the *fourth day* of the feast, considering the fact that the feast lasted eight days. Accordingly, that is the way I recorded it in the *Harmony.*

**(e) [11:12]** In the record, Jesus did not mention that it had been 18 months since He had healed the paralytic. But because, according to my reckoning, it had been 18 months, I included Jesus making such a declaration. This gives a good flow to the narrative.

**(f) [11:30]** I included in the record the fact that it had been 30 months (two and a half years) since Nicodemus had visited Jesus by night. Such a time frame is not in the Gospel record, but, based upon the best evidence I have, it was about 30 months. So, to give a smooth flow to the record, I mentioned that fact in as part of the *Harmony.*

**(g) [11:32+]** The marvelous story of how Jesus related to the woman caught in adultery is not found in the older manuscripts of the Gospel record of John. This means that the story may not have actually taken place, but was added to give flavor to the record. However, it is just as possible that the story is

---

[175] John 10:39, 40

true, and that it was added later to the record to accurately complete the message of John's Gospel. I must admit, considering the power and majesty of this story, I want to believe the latter possibility! In any case, I do include the event in the record of the *Harmony,* considering it so much like the way Jesus would have acted in such a situation.

**(h) [11:32+]** A few have suggested that the woman in this story was Mary Magdalene. However, considering the timing of the story during the overall ministry of Jesus, it is very unlikely that this woman was Mary.

**(i) [11:36]** This is the only record we have in the Gospel story of Jesus writing something!

**(j) [11:36/]** What was it that Jesus wrote in the dirt? The record does not tell us. It is often suggested that the Lord wrote the secret sins of those who brought the woman to Jesus. I think that this is a very strong possibility. Accordingly, that is the way I recorded it in the *Harmony.* Taking into consideration an important fact of the story (that Jesus suggested that those "without sin" should "cast the first stone," *Harmony* 11:37), and the strong reaction of the Jewish leaders who saw what Jesus wrote, it is likely that He was openly exposing their sins in the dirt. Such a possibility indicates why the Jewish leaders reacted the way they did—that is, to flee from the scene, knowing that they were certainly not without sin. Thus, they were effectively silenced.

**(k) [11:37/]** (See above.)

**(l) [11:38]** (See **Note "j"** above.)

**(m) [11:41]** I cannot resist dwelling for a moment on the impact of the Lord's message to the woman. First, He told her that He did not condemn her, for she certainly felt guilty enough on her own. Next, He told her to go on her way. And then—only then—did Jesus tell her to stop this kind of sinning. In short, the Lord accepted her before He told her to leave her life of sin. Such is the love of the Savior for the sinner!

**(n) [11:41/+]** The severity of the dialogue that took place between Jesus and the Jewish leaders in this event (and the one following) is quite striking. (In fact, it was a bit depressing to me just to record them!) Not only were the leaders of Israel relentless in their attacks on the Lord, but He was just as persistent with them. The overall impact of this exchange can be shocking, considering the high level of compassion Jesus showed to people elsewhere throughout His ministry. It should be remembered that, not only were these Jewish leaders seeking to kill the Lord, but they were, even more importantly, swaying many of the common people away from fully accepting Him as the Messiah. In fact, it could be said that, had these leaders not been so obstinate in their attitude toward Jesus, the vast majority of the people of their nation would have quite willingly accepted Jesus as the true Messiah, not only of Israel, but of the world. Indeed, the Jewish leaders openly opposing Jesus were probably very few in number compared with the total population of the nation. In truth, then, a very small minority was responsible for the fact that so many of the common people rejected the work and ministry of Jesus.

The reality is that the responsibility of leadership is awesome. Many of the common people in the Lord's day naively looked to their spiritual leaders for guidance and direction. And unfortunately—to an extreme—their leaders miserably failed them. Therefore, in part, the reason the Lord leveled such strong words at the Jewish leaders was that they as leaders had failed to be the kind of guides that they should have been. The fact remains that God has always held a very high standard for those who lead His people. He has always expected much of them, for, in a sense, they represent Him on this earth. When these leaders have failed, He has always held them ultimately responsible. Eternal destinies were at stake!

It could be said, then, that the Lord's debates with the Jewish leaders, detailed here and elsewhere, were not petty arguments over various theological points between Jesus and a few people. Rather, it was the Lord God challenging those who should have known better. They were directly responsible for the fact that so many of those who were less educated and informed did not accept Jesus as they could have. Again, such is the grave responsibility of leadership in the cause of the God of the universe.

Furthermore, it should be noted that all we have in the Gospel record is the *words* that Jesus spoke to the Jewish leaders. We have no record as to *how* they were spoken—indeed, no "body language" is noted. Accordingly, some have suggested that when Jesus said these really tough things to the Jews, He actually spoke them in a very compassionate way, as though he had "tears in His voice." It seems to me that such a real possibility needs to be kept in mind when one studies this dialogue between Jesus and the Jewish leaders—as well as all such conversations Jesus had, I might add.

However, it is clear to *me* that the tough words Jesus spoke to the Jewish leaders were, in a large part, the result of His frustration—and even His anger—over the fact the *spiritual leaders* of Israel had rejected Him as the Messiah, and further, that, as a result, many of the common people of the nation would also reject Him. It was a really a sad state of affairs!

**(o) [11:55+]** (See above.)

**(p) [11:88]** The record does not say that the formerly blind man was arraigned before the Sanhedrin, but the likelihood was that he was so arraigned. Actually, first of all, there was the Great Sanhedrin, in front of which Jesus was later tried (*Harmony* 17:36, etc.). Then, second, there were the lesser Sanhedrins where others on lesser charges might be tried. No doubt this was one of these lesser courts before which the healed blind man was questioned and condemned.

**(q) [11:126]** This story, or one like it, is found twice in the Gospel record. It is possible that this event took place just once, and that is was misplaced by either one (Matthew or Luke) of the Gospel recorders. It is possible, though, considering that many people might have approached Jesus with a similar type of an issue, that this story was repeated. Unsure of which situation is the reality, I have chosen to treat it as two different events.

**(r) [11:129]** (See above.)

**(s) [11:133]** It would be interesting to know the names and circumstances of the people who made up this group of Gospel missionaries, but of course we don't know who they were, or even whether the Twelve disciples were a part of this group. In any case, it is of some importance to note that the true followers of Jesus who worked directly for His cause comprised a group significantly larger than just the Twelve.

**(t) [11:140]** I am intrigued by the concept that the Lord told His Gospel workers to "eat such things as are set before you" (Luke 10:8, KJV). When the Lord had earlier sent His twelve disciples on a similar mission (*Harmony* 8:37-58), He gave no such advice. This may not mean anything. However, I suggest that such is not the case. In the earlier mission, the Twelve were sent to minister among *Jews*, while in the later situation, the Seventy worked among *Gentiles*. Now, in the case of Jews, the Twelve's hosts would have followed more strict dietary rules—ones that they were familiar with. In the case of Gentiles, their hosts would have not followed such rules. In short, the Seventy would have faced the prospect of eating food that was strange—even unpalatable—to them, perhaps even unclean or not Kosher. Therefore, the Lord's counsel to eat what was put before them was apropos. The gist of Christ's point was that the Seventy were not to offend the Gentiles by refusing to eat their food. This meant that to offend someone who has provided food for them to eat—food that might undesirable to the one eating it—was worse than the personal unpleasantness of eating such food! To me, this is an interesting principle for the Lord's workers to consider and follow!

**(u) [11:141]** Jesus had made a similar statement earlier in His ministry (*Harmony* 8:32-34). Some might think that this was only a repetition of the same event. Perhaps this is so. However, I take the position that the Lord repeated Himself here. In the first instance in *Harmony,* chapter 8, it was right after the Twelve had come back from witnessing. In this case, it was after the Seventy had returned from their mission. It seems reasonable to me that the Lord simply repeated Himself in this situation, reminiscent of what He had said during the earlier situation.

**(v) [11:142]** (See above.)

**(w) [11:162]** See **Note "e"** in Chapter 14 for fuller explanation of who Mary Magdalene was.

**(x) [11:164]** There is a variant reading in the Greek for this text that expresses the thoughts that I have included in this portion of the *Harmony.* This variant reading indicates that Jesus first said there were *several things* that were important. Then He added that there is *really only one thing* that is essential. I consider this variant reading so fascinating that I could not resist recording it that way in the *Harmony.*

# CHAPTER TWELVE

## CONTROVERSY AND INSTRUCTION—

**From Jesus Goes Into the Wilderness, to the Teaching on Forgiveness, Faith, and Service**

**(Winter, A.D. 30 - Later Winter, A.D. 31)**

**The Peraean Ministry of Jesus:**
**The Lord's Various Experiences and Teachings While Sojourning in Peraea**
**< Winter, A.D. 30-31 (7/7) >**
**(Luke 11:1-13, 33-54; 12:1-17:10; John 10:40-42)**

### —Jesus Goes Into the Wilderness
**< Winter, A.D. 30 (7/7) >**
**{John 10:40-42}**

After escaping from the Jews in Jerusalem during the Feast of Dedication [*Harmony* 11:175], Jesus hid Himself in the wilderness area of Peraea on the eastern bank of the Jordan River 25 miles or so northeast of the city. It was the same region where John the Baptist had begun his ministry of teaching and baptizing over three years before. The people living in that area fondly remembered the ministry of John. Of course, they had heard much about the work of Jesus, but had not, up until then, had the opportunity to observe the Lord's accomplishments for themselves.[1]

While Jesus ministered in that same place for some time, the people came to listen to the Master's words, and to experience His healing powers . . . and they were impressed! Many said, "While it is true that John worked no miracles among us when he ministered here, as Jesus is doing, it certainly is a fact that John was correct in everything he said regarding the majesty of this Man's

1 John 10:40

ministry." [*Harmony* 2:19, 20] Accordingly, many of them believed that Jesus was the Messiah.[2]

> Even though John the Baptist performed no miracles involving the healing of the body, he, as a preacher, saw many people converted through his ministry—individuals who were transformed by the power of the Holy Spirit. In that sense, then, John was a great miracle worker!

**— The Lord's Instruction on Prayer**
**< Winter, A.D. 30 (7/7) >**
**{Luke 11:1-13}**

A bit later, the Lord's disciples discovered Jesus praying in a secluded place. When He had completed His prayer, one of the disciples requested of him, "Lord, please teach us to pray the same way that John the Baptist taught his disciples to pray." [*Harmony* 5:44-52][(a) 3]

"Well then," Jesus said, "this is what you should say when you pray:[4]

"'Our Father, may Your name be made holy in the hearts of all people.'"[5]

> All prayer should begin with a person's recognition of the holiness of God as well as the need for it to be experienced by all, thus resulting in the giving of praise to Him.

"'May Your kingdom of the Gospel appear in the lives of everyone.'"[6]

> This concept expressed the desire that the power of the Gospel should permanently change the lives of everyone everywhere.

"'Please provide for us the food and basic sustenance that we need for each day.'"[7]

> Obviously, it is important to ask God to provide for the common necessities of life.

---

2 John 10:41, 42
3 Luke 11:1
4 Luke 11:2
5 Luke 11:2
6 Luke 11:2
7 Luke 11:3

"'And, of course, forgive us our sins—but only in the same way that we are willing to forgive those who have wronged us.'"[8]

> The longing to be forgiven of one's sins and cleansed from all unrighteousness [1 John 1:9] is a primary desire on the part of any true follower of Christ. And, as Jesus reminded His disciples, such forgiveness is based upon people's willingness likewise to forgive others. This was a recurring theme throughout the teachings of Jesus. [*Harmony* 5:53; 10:112-117]

"'And lastly, lead us in such a way that we will not be overcome by temptations—rather, give us victory over them.'"[9]

> While forgiveness is important to the Christian life, victory over sin is the ultimate goal.[1]
>
> The Lord did not intend that this prayer should necessarily be repeated, word-for-word, when His disciples prayed. Rather, the various points listed in the prayer are to serve as an *outline* of the kind of things one might include in a prayer. Jesus had done a similar thing, when, in the Sermon on the Mount, He first gave what is commonly called "The Lord's Prayer." [*Harmony* 5:46-52][(b)] [2]

As Jesus often did, He told a parable—this time, to illustrate the impact of prayer in one's life. He began by saying, "Just suppose that one of you has a friend to whom you go at midnight to beg of him, saying, 'My friend, please lend me three loaves of bread. Another friend of mine, who has journeyed from some distance, is visiting me. I have nothing in the house to feed him! Could you help me out?'[10]

"But your friend calls from within his house, saying, 'Leave me alone! My door is locked for the night. My children are in bed, fast asleep. I'm also in bed—in fact, you have just awakened me! I cannot get up and help you now. Come back in the morning.'[(c)] [11]

---

8 Luke 11:4
9 Luke 11:4
10 Luke 11:5, 6
11 Luke 11:7

"However, instead of returning to your own home empty-handed, you persist in asking your friend for help. Now I tell you, your friend will not get up and help you because he is your friend. No! Instead, he will get up and give you the three loaves of bread because of your shameless begging! He will help you in order to get rid of you, so that he may go back to sleep! Isn't that right?[12]

> "Now, asking your heavenly Father through your prayers to help you is *not* like this story which I have just told you. On the contrary, you do not need to beg Him for help. While, as in this story, a friend might help you because you beg him, your heavenly Father will help you, not because you beg Him, but because He is your Friend. It is just the opposite as in this parable. [*Harmony* 13:56][(d)]

"Instead of begging your heavenly Father to help you," the Lord added, "just ask Him! That is why I say to you: Ask your Father for something, and He will give it to you. Seek Him for help, and He will help you. Knock, as it were, on heaven's door, and the Father will open it for you. I promise you, when you ask, you will receive. When you seek, you will find. And when you knock, it will be opened for you." [*Harmony* 5:73][(e)] [13]

"Let me illustrate further," Jesus added. "Now suppose one of you who is a father that is asked by your son for a fish to eat. Now, you would not give him a snake instead of a fish, would you? Or, if your son asks you for an egg, you would not give him a scorpion, would you? Of course not!" [*Harmony* 5:74][(f)] [14]

"Now here's the point: If you then, being sinners, know how to give good things to your children, how much more will your sinless heavenly Father give good things—such as the Holy Spirit—to those who ask Him. That makes sense, doesn't it?"[15]

### — The Inner Light Illustration
### < Winter, A.D. 31 (7/7) >
### {Luke 11:33-36}

During this time, Jesus discussed the value of having the "Light of the Gospel Message" shining within one's heart. He said, "There is no one who, after

---

12 Luke 11:8
13 Luke 11:9, 10
14 Luke 11:11, 12
15 Luke 11:13

taking the time to light a lamp, would hide it from sight in a basement or under a basket. That would be foolish! Rather, one obviously puts the lamp on a lamp stand so that all who enter the house will benefit from its light. So it is with the Gospel: Once you experience it, you must not hide it. You must share it with others who are in the darkness of sin! [*Harmony* 5:18][16]

"And once the light of the Gospel comes into your life," the Lord continued, "it will change the way you relate to everything that happens to you. To illustrate, your eye is like a lamp to your body. If you have good eyesight, then your life is full of light and of the beauty your eyes can see. If, however, your eyesight is poor, you cannot see clearly, for everything appears in a shadowy darkness. So it is with the Gospel truth. If the light of the Gospel shines in your life, it will affect the way you view everything. And it will change your life for the better. But if the light of the Gospel does not shine into your life, then the darkness of evil will surround you, making everything in your life to appear dark and dreary. Obviously then, make sure that the light of the Gospel shines in your life so that the darkness of sin does not overwhelm you![17]

"This way," the Savior concluded, "your entire life will be filled with the brightness of the truth of the Gospel's salvation. All the darkness of sin will be dispelled. Yes, your life will be enriched by the Gospel's great brightness—just as a lamp provides light by its fire to everyone in the house where you live." [*Harmony* 5:18, 58; 12:16][18]

**— Jesus Dines With a Pharisee**[(g)]
**< Winter, A.D. 31 (7/7) >**
**{Luke 11:37-54}**

A short time later, a Pharisee invited Jesus to have a meal with him. Jesus accepted the invitation and reclined at the dinner table. In those days, people reclined on couches around the table instead of sitting on chairs. In doing so, they would rest on one arm and eat with the other hand. Also reclining at this dinner table were other Pharisees. Present too were lawyers—also known as scribes. But the purpose of this meal was not at all social in nature. Rather, the Lord's enemies were trying to discover some way of finding fault with Jesus so as to

---

16 Luke 11:33
17 Luke 11:34, 35
18 Luke 11:36

create a controversy with Him. Jesus was aware of this evil motive, nevertheless He accepted the invitation to the meal. [*Harmony* 12:90][19]

So, true to form, as they began to eat, the Pharisee—who had invited Jesus—verbally expressed shock that the Lord did not go through the usual meticulous ceremonial washings of the hands which the Jews were accustomed to performing. These washings were expected of any conservative Jew eating a meal in public. Now these washings were not for sanitary purposes. Instead, this detailed and complicated procedure was to show that those participating in such washings were better than others who did not—that is, they were of a higher moral worth than others. Of course, Jesus did not participate in such a farcical activity. [*Harmony* 10:1-13][20]

Unwilling to allow this condemnatory comment of the Pharisee to pass without a challenge, Jesus responded, "It's hard to figure out why you Pharisees do the things you do." Then, using a parable, Jesus explained what He meant. He said, "You go to great pains to clean your hands, as you would the outside of a cup or dish. Yet, the thing that really counts—the soul of a man—you are content to leave completely filthy with evil, robbery, and all sorts of wickedness. It is just like leaving the inside of a cup or dish filthy while the outside is washed. You foolish Pharisees! Is it not true that God made not only the outside of things but also the inside? So then, why are you obsessed with the outside, but ignore the inside? If your spiritual heart—which is inside you—is righteous, then automatically that which shows on the outside—such as acts of kindness and gifts to the poor—would be equally righteous. In that case, your life would be truly clean and you would not need to waste your time with all those silly ceremonial washings and cleansings that amount to nothing. Indeed, cleansing and re-cleansing the outside of your body, such as your hands, does nothing to cleanse your heart, which is what really needs the cleansing. Can't you see that?" [*Harmony* 10:8-13; 14:127][21]

Jesus continued with His explanation, expanding on this theme. He next questioned the Pharisees' hypocritical way of paying their tithes to the church. Now the tithe which the Lord required them to return consisted of the tenth part of their income. [Genesis 28:22; Leviticus 27:30, where tithe means, "tenth" and vice versa] "But shame on you, you Pharisees!" Jesus declared. "On one hand,

---

19 Luke 11:37

20 Luke 11:38

21 Luke 11:39-41

you are so exacting in the faithful payment of your tithes that you actually count out the tenth part of the leaves of both the mint and bitter rue plant you might grow. You do the same with all sorts of herbs from your gardens. Yet at the same time you totally ignore what is really important, which is to show justice to others and to imitate the love of God in your life. These are the essential things that you should be doing, while not neglecting the less important other things that you do. [*Harmony* 14:125][22]

"Again, shame on you, you Pharisees!" the Lord continued, "Yes, you love to sit in the best seats in church so that everyone can see you. Also, you crave the greetings of honor you receive when you walk through the marketplace.[23]

"Yes! Shame on you! You are just like graves filled with dead people—graves that are hidden underground, so that people are unaware that they are walking over decaying dead bodies when they pass on the beautiful green grass overhead! Likewise, people who see your so-called piousness think that you are indeed righteous when they see you sitting so smugly in the seats in the church, or walking pompously around in the marketplace showing off your so-called goodness. But what they don't know is that you are evil within—rotten to the core!"[24]

Also at the dinner table was a lawyer. Such a lawyer—or scribe—was a Pharisee who specialized in the copying and study of Biblical Law. This lawyer was upset with what Jesus was saying. Very agitated, he said to the Lord, "Master, I know that You are leveling Your critical comments at the Pharisees. While I am technically a lawyer, I'm also a Pharisee. So when You criticize the Pharisees, You are also insulting the lawyers—such as me—who are here today."[25]

But instead of backing off, Jesus became even more pointed in His criticism. He said, "In that case, let Me directly address you, too: Shame on you, you *lawyers*! Through your false interpretations of the Law, you weigh down under great burdens the lives of those whom you instruct. You have written so many rules and restrictions—'do's and don'ts'—that the people are being crushed under a heavy load of utter foolishness. And no! Not for one second do you with a single finger of yours help lift the tiniest one of these poor people's burdens.

---

22 Luke 11:42
23 Luke 11:43
24 Luke 11:44
25 Luke 11:45

No indeed! Instead you continue to pile on even more rules and restrictions!" [*Harmony* 12:30; 14:150/2][26]

Then addressing everyone in the room, Jesus continued, declaring, "And again, shame on all of you! You have built up the tombs of the prophets, while it was your fathers, whom you reverence, who killed them in the first place! You have worked as partners with your fathers. First, your fathers killed the prophets. And second, to cover up the crime, so to speak, you built tombs to honor those murdered prophets, as though your fathers had no part in killing them. Such hypocrisy! You don't fool Me. You not only agree within your hearts with the evil your fathers did, but you also, by your attitude and actions toward Me, have shown that you have endorsed it! And how is this? Even though you supposedly honor these prophets whom your fathers have killed, I tell you, if these prophets were alive today, you would be trying to kill them too . . . just as you are trying to kill Me! [*Harmony* 11:78, 175][27]

"For this reason, God in His infinite wisdom and foreknowledge has declared, 'I will send them prophets and apostles. They will kill some, and treat others as outcasts.'"[(h) 28]

> To be sure, the prophets of the old days were killed by the fathers of the Jews who were at that moment sitting at the table with Jesus. And some of the apostles would be killed by the same people—or ones like them—sitting that very day at the table with the Lord! [Acts 12:1-3]

The Savior added, "I say that you of this generation will be held responsible for all the blood of all the prophets that has been shed since the foundation of the world! This includes first of all the shedding of the blood of Abel [Genesis 4:1-8] as well as every other shameful murder, ending with the death of Zechariah who was despicably slaughtered between the altar of burnt offering and the Temple. [2 Chronicles 24:20-22] Yes! I tell you again, this generation will be held responsible for all of this murder! As the fathers have done, so will the sons do also!" [*Harmony* 14:130][29]

> In the book of Genesis is the story of Abel, the first recorded martyr of the Bible. Genesis was the *first* book of the Hebrew Bible of Christ's day.

---

26 Luke 11:46
27 Luke 11:47, 48
28 Luke 11:49
29 Luke 11:50, 51

> The *last* book of that same Hebrew Bible was 2 Chronicles, where, in its last chapter, is described the death of Zechariah—the person whom Jesus mentioned here. Thus, Jesus claimed that the attitude of the Jews of His day was the same evil attitude that that led to the martyrdom of *all* those murdered throughout the entire recorded history, as contained in the Hebrew Scriptures!

"Shame upon you once more, you scribes!" [*Harmony* 12:25, 26] Jesus continued. "You have hidden the key of the good news of the Gospel from the very people you have been commissioned by God to serve. Shameful! You have refused to allow them to enter through the gate of knowledge that leads to eternal life. I say to you, that because of your actions, neither will you enter in!" [*Harmony* 12:26][30]

Quite understandably, the meal broke up! As Jesus began to leave, the Jewish leaders started to heckle Him with great hostility. They tried to challenge the Lord on many other questions of theology as well as various issues regarding His ministry. But the Master, in silence, disappeared from their sight. So from that moment on the Jews re-doubled their efforts to catch Him in some slip of the tongue or to twist some of His words so as to have just cause—from their wicked perspective—to have Him killed. [*Harmony* 4:62; 11:78, 175; 12:104/][31]

> In all that the Lord shared with the Jewish leaders during the meal, He emphasized the importance of having a heart religion in contrast with mere outward actions. This was a recurring theme with the Lord. [*Harmony* 5:19]

### — Jesus Warns His Followers Regarding the Pharisees
### < Winter, A.D. 31 (7/7) >
### {Luke 12:1-12}

The reputation of Jesus began to expand greatly in that area of the country. His determination to stand up to the Jewish leaders really excited the masses. Large crowds started to follow Him again, reminiscent of the glory days of His ministry in Galilee. [*Harmony* 4:63-66] In fact, so many people came to hear the Master teach that they were literally stepping on one another![32]

---

30 Luke 11:52

31 Luke 11:53, 54

32 Luke 12:1

Jesus continued His assault upon the Pharisees. Speaking to the crowds—and especially to the twelve disciples—Jesus began by exclaiming, "Beware of the leaven of the Pharisees [*Harmony* 10:35-43], which is their shameless hypocrisy. Just as yeast permeates the bread dough, so do their hypocritical teachings pervade and thus ruin the good news of the Gospel message which they should be teaching the people. Because of them, the good news has actually become so much bad news!" This was a recurring theme of Jesus.[33]

"However," Jesus continued, "in spite of the negative influence of the Jewish leaders' teachings, the real truth of the Gospel will shine through. They may try to hide it from the masses, but through your ministry"—that is, the ministry of His twelve disciples—"the glorious truth will ultimately be told. Yes, the people will be able to learn the truth. This means that the good things of the Gospel which we first talked about in our many private sessions in the moonlight will be trumpeted in the sunshine. And the things regarding the Gospel that we've had to whisper to each other in the secret places will be shouted from the housetops, so to speak, for all to hear. [*Harmony* 8:50][34]

"I must tell you, My friends, please don't be afraid of those who are seeking to kill you. For, after you are dead, there's nothing more that they will be able to do to you. On the other hand, I must warn you to fear the One—that is, God—who can, with full authority, totally and forever destroy you in hell-fire . . . if you are unfaithful to Him, that is. Yes! I tell you, fear God!"[35]

> Here Jesus used the phrase, "fear God." What does that mean? A careful study of the Scriptures reveals, perhaps surprisingly, that to "fear God" means to have a personal relationship of trust with God where His will is carefully followed, including the eradication of sin from the life. Obviously, in the final judgment, the wicked Jewish leaders would receive the punishment of eternal death, for they did not "fear" the Lord—that is, they refused to have a personal relationship of faith with Him. However, in the case of the genuine followers of the Lord, the promise of eternal life will be their reward. This is because they have learned to "fear" the Lord—that is, again, to have a personal relationship of faith and trust with Him.

---

33 Luke 12:1

34 Luke 12:2, 3

35 Luke 12:4, 5

To show that this concept of "fear" meant a good thing, Jesus explained to the disciples just how much God loved them. For, He said, "Are not five sparrows sold for two cents—the least valuable of all coins? Yet, God does not forget even one of those birds! To be sure, God has numbered all the hairs of your head—that's how much He cares for you! So don't be afraid to place your confidence and trust in your heavenly Father—to 'fear' God, so to speak. You are worth much, much more than many, many sparrows! [*Harmony* 5:65; 12:48][36]

"Yes, indeed, I tell you, everyone who publicly confesses their trust in Me can be certain that I will confess My confidence in them before all the many angels of God who dwell in heaven. [Revelation 5:11] But I must also tell you, the one who denies Me before others I will also deny before God's angels.[37]

It is serious business to deny the Son of Man," Jesus continued. "But even at that, such a sin can be forgiven. But to refuse to listen to the words of conviction from the Holy Spirit, as He speaks to the heart, is a sin that simply cannot be forgiven. That sin cannot be forgiven because a refusal to hear the Spirit cuts off the communication link between heaven and earth. And that link is the only way that one can experience complete forgiveness of sins, which is so absolutely necessary for eternal life. Thus, should that communication link be broken, there can be no more forgiveness of your sins. So be careful how you treat the Holy Spirit. [*Harmony* 7:9-17][(i)] [38]

"But don't misunderstand Me: the Holy Spirit is not your enemy. Don't be afraid of Him either. For, in addition to convicting your hearts of sin, He will be sent to empower you in the work of your ministries. For example, when your enemies present you in trial before the Jewish church, its rulers, and authorities, do not be concerned about what you are to say in your defense. I repeat: Don't worry about what you are to say. And why? Because the same Holy Spirit—your Friend—will instruct you, at that very moment, what you are to say and how you are to say it. Yes, you can trust the Holy Spirit if you listen to Him!" [*Harmony* 8:46; 15:8][39]

---

36 Luke 12:6, 7

37 Luke 12:8, 9

38 Luke 12:9, 10

39 Luke 12:11, 12

### — The Folly of Riches is Condemned
### < Winter, A.D. 31 (7/7) >
### {Luke 12:13-34}

One day a man in the crowd approached Jesus, asking of Him, "Master, make my brother split our family's inheritance with me!"[40]

Without hesitating, the Lord answered, "Man! Who has appointed Me to be a judge or problem-solver between you and your brother? Go to the civil authorities who have been set apart and trained for that purpose."[41]

> No doubt this man's brother was taking for himself a share of the family inheritance that this man considered unfair or wrong. The Savior's stern response to the man's request may seem harsh. But Jesus wasn't sent to the world to solve the petty disputes that arise between people. He came to save the world from sin. The task of being an arbitrator Jesus left to the civil authorities of Israel's government. They were well equipped to handle these types of disputes. If Jesus had begun to settle such petty disputes, there would be no end to the number of people who would come to Him in like situations. He would have no time left to pursue the real purpose of His ministry. And too, how could anyone challenge the judgment of One whom the people considered to be the Messiah? This would turn the nation's appeal system upside down. And further, Jesus had enough problems with the leaders of Israel without creating more trouble over issues that were not directly pertinent to His work. To make sure that no one else would come to Him with a similar problem, the Lord's response was of necessity as strong as it was.

After Jesus turned the man away, He continued to talk with the crowd. He said, "What you have just seen should serve as a lesson to you. So then, beware! Guard against all types of greed. It can destroy you! Remember, even those who have many possessions should know that the true meaning of life is not found in the amount of things one has.[42]

"To illustrate My point, here's a parable: A certain rich man had land that produced an extraordinary amount of crops. He had everything he could possibly want, but he wanted even more! He began to reason with himself, saying, 'What

---

40 Luke 12:13
41 Luke 12:14
42 Luke 12:15

will I do? I don't have enough room to store all the crops that I have! Indeed, what will I do?'[43]

"Still thinking, the man said to himself, 'I know what I'll do! I will demolish all my barns, and in their place I'll build even bigger ones. Then I'll have enough space to store all my crops. Yes, that's what I'll do! And then I'll be able to say to myself, "Self, you have so many things laid up in your barns that you won't need to work again for years! Instead you'll be able to spend your time in the lap of luxury, eating and drinking in merriment."'[44]

"But the man never considered what God might think of what he was planning. And you can be sure that God strongly disapproved of this man's plans, for He told him, 'What a fool you are! Indeed, this very night you will die for the despicable way you are acting. And once you are dead, who will take over all your possessions as their own? It certainly won't be you!'[45]

"Ah! This is the way it is for the greedy man: He is rich in the possessions of this world, but very poor in the wisdom and ways of God. Instead of hoarding things to himself, how much better would it have been for him to give of the abundance of his things to those who are truly in need! That would have been the best way in the sight of God to truly *add* to his 'riches.'"[46]

To drive home His point even further, Jesus repeated some concepts that He had previously presented in the "Sermon on the Mount" a year and half before. [*Harmony* 5:56, 57, 61-67] He said to His disciples, "That is why I tell you to stop worrying so much about your life as it relates to what you will eat. Neither be overly concerned about your body as to what you will wear. The true meaning of life is much more than food. And too, your body is much more precious than what you wear on it. This means that you can be sure that a loving God will help you to take care of your person. Also, He will help provide for your clothing. And how can you be so sure of this? Let Me explain.[47]

"For a moment, think about the ravens. Notice that they don't plant seeds, nor do they reap crops. In fact, they have no storehouses or barns! Yet they survive.

---

43 Luke 12:16, 17
44 Luke 12:18, 19
45 Luke 12:20
46 Luke 12:21
47 Luke 12:22, 23

And why? Because God feeds them! And think! You are infinitely more valuable than birds! Isn't that right? [*Harmony* 5:63, 65; 12:36][48]

"And besides, with all your worrying, can you add a foot to your height? Of course not! It is God who makes you grow taller. That's nothing for Him! Indeed, without you even thinking about it, it is God who makes you grow up during your natural course of living. So then, if God—the Creator—who, by a natural miracle, makes you grow taller year by year, don't you think that He is quite capable of helping you provide for your regular, day-to-day needs? So stop worrying so much![(j)] [(k)] [49]

"Think about the lilies, and how it is that they grow. They do not work. They do not make clothes for themselves. But even in the case of the flamboyant King Solomon [1 Kings 10:1-13, 21] arrayed in all his glory, he was not nearly as beautiful as a single lily! Was he? [*Harmony* 5:65][50]

"So then, if God makes the fields look beautiful with grass that is alive one day and is dead the next day—so dead that it is burned as fuel—don't you think that he will provide clothing for you? Oh my, sometimes you are such 'little faith' people! [*Harmony* 5:65; 7:61-66; 9:21][(l)] [51]

"In conclusion, then, do not spend so much of your life struggling to provide food and drink for yourself. Stop the constant worrying about these things! Of course, you know that the primary emphasis of the world is to passionately seek after these things. [*Harmony* 5:66][52]

"But," Jesus continued, "remember that God knows that you need all of these things. So then, if you spend the majority of your time seeking to belong to the kingdom of God, He will provide you with these needed things in addition to giving you salvation. Please don't be afraid, My little flock. My Father is very excited and happy to give you His kingdom . . . as well as the material things that you need!" [*Harmony* 5:66][53]

---

48 Luke 12:24
49 Luke 12:25, 26
50 Luke 12:27
51 Luke 12:28
52 Luke 12:29, 30
53 Luke 12:30-32

> Here, the Lord was not suggesting that people should not work to provide for themselves. No! His point was that people should not be *obsessed* with providing for themselves. In the world, many spend all their time trying to provide for their physical needs so that they have little or no time left to take care of the salvation of their souls. The Lord wanted His listeners to have more balance than this in their lives.

"Rather than following the foolish passions of the world as it seeks after things," Jesus concluded, "you would be better off selling your possessions and giving them to charitable causes. In doing so, it will be like making wallets and purses for yourselves that will never wear out. That is because your treasure is in heaven, so to speak. Yes, it is a treasure that will never run out. Neither will any thief be able to steal it. No moth can eat it. Furthermore, it is a principle of life: Where your treasure is, there will your heart be lodged also. For, if your money is in heaven—that is, given to help others—then, your heart—your passions and desires—will also be in heaven. Do you see that?" [*Harmony* 5:56, 57][54]

**— Being Ready for the Master's Return**
**< Winter, A.D. 31 (7/7) >**
**{Luke 12:35-59}**

> The Lord's ministry was fast coming to a conclusion with just a few months remaining. For that reason, Jesus began to set His sights on the future. Looking beyond His present stay on the earth, He started to talk about His Second Coming when He would establish His eternal kingdom. Jesus warned His listeners that they needed to be ready for that Coming.

The Master cautioned, "You need to be dressed for a wedding feast, as it were, in order to be ready for the coming of the Son of Man. Also, your lamps need to be burning in effective witnessing. [*Harmony* 5:18] Yes, you need to be like servants ready for their master when he returns home from the wedding feast. You need to be watching for the Son of Man, with your lamps all aglow, so that as soon as He knocks on the door, you will immediately open the door for Him to enter, to provide light for Him within the darkness of the house." [*Harmony* 16:9] Spiritually speaking, Jesus meant that His followers needed to be "dressed" in the righteousness of the Gospel. Their "lamps need to be burning"

---

54 Luke 12:33, 34

with the power of the Holy Spirit in their lives. And the "darkness of the house" represents the sinfulness of this world. [*Harmony* 15:32-41][55]

"Indeed," the Lord added, "happy are those servants who are ready and alert when the Master comes home! It's a fact that He will honor their faithfulness to Him by being their servant for a change. This time, to show His pleasure in them, He will let them recline at the feasting table, and *He* will serve *them* the meal . . . just as they used to do for Him! It doesn't make any difference if the Master comes between 9 o'clock in the evening, up through midnight, or if He comes between midnight and 3 o'clock in the early morning . . . His faithful servants will be ready for His arrival. I say again, those servants will have good cause to be happy, for the Master will reward them handsomely." [*Harmony* 15:26, 27; 16:9][56]

> Here Jesus referred to His Second Coming. Because His servants have been faithful to Him in His absence, and are ready for Him when He does appear, the Lord will have a special reward for them: He will serve them in the same way that they have been used to serving Him! The reward which the saints receive at the Lord's coming will be a rich repayment of the faithfulness that they have shown toward Him.

"To use another illustration," the Lord said, "consider a man who was the head of the household. To be sure, he is careful to protect his family and property. Of course, if he knew the hour in which a thief would break into his house, he would certainly be ready for him. There's no way that he would allow his house to be broken into and robbed! That's why he must be constantly prepared for such a break-in. In a similar way, you are to be constantly ready for the coming of the Son of Man, because you do not know the exact hour when He is coming. If you are not prepared, the Lord will come when you are not expecting Him to appear."[57]

> In this parable, Jesus compared His Second Coming to a thief breaking into someone's house. And, as the owner of the house must be prepared for such a break in, the disciple of Jesus must also be prepared for the coming of Jesus. Now, to compare His coming to the breaking in of a

---

55 Luke 12:35, 36

56 Luke 12:37, 38

57 Luke 12:39, 40

robber may seem strange, but, nevertheless, that is exactly what Jesus did in this parable.

Peter interrupted to ask the Lord, "Have you told this parable for us, the Twelve, or is it also for the crowds who have been listening to You?"[58]

Jesus answered, "Well, who is that faithful and wise steward whom the Lord has placed in charge of the other servants, to provide food for them at the right time? Of course, you, the Twelve are the leaders! It is primarily you whom I've been addressing. And truly happy will be that steward—even you—whom the Lord will find faithfully performing his prescribed duties when He comes! Yes, indeed, as a reward for his faithfulness, the Master will place that steward in charge of all His possessions.[59]

"But, on the other hand, should that steward say to himself, 'My Master is delaying His coming,' he will get himself into serious trouble with the Master. Especially is this true if that steward begins to treat harshly the other servants—both men and women—the Master had placed under his supervision. That steward will also get into trouble, should he spend his time eating and drinking to excess. And when the Master returns unexpectedly on a certain day or hour, the Master will have that steward cut in pieces"—that is, punished severely—"and be treated as a great sinner. [*Harmony* 15:28][60]

"The servant who fully knew the will of the Master and yet did not get ready, or perform his duties in accordance with the Master's will, shall, indeed, be beaten with many lashes of the whip. But the servant who did not fully understand his responsibilities, and yet acted in a way worthy of a beating, will receive but few lashes of the whip. In short, of everyone who has received a more complete understanding of God's will for them, much more will be required. Indeed, the more that has been entrusted to them, the more that will be asked of them."[61]

By this parable, Jesus illustrated the heavy responsibilities *leaders* have in the work of the Gospel. God will hold these leaders responsible to a high degree for their actions, whether they are good or bad. Those who follow the leaders will not be held nearly as responsible as those who were the leaders. Again, being a leader in the cause of the Lord

---

58 Luke 12:41
59 Luke 12:42-44
60 Luke 12:45, 46
61 Luke 12:47, 48

> carries with it a huge and solemn responsibility that cannot be ignored. The comparison of the punishments of slothful servants in this parable—"many lashes" for the leaders, and "few lashes" for those under the leaders—is puzzling. It is not at all clear how, in the final judgment, such punishments will actually be administered. Nevertheless, Jesus gave the warning for all to be aware of the consequences of not being faithful to their responsibilities. Apparently, the way the rewards are given in the judgment will be based upon one's faithfulness . . . and unfaithfulness, as the case may be! [*Harmony* 15:27, 28][(m)]

Jesus concluded, "I know that what I'm telling you sounds tough! Well . . . it is tough! I have come, as it were, to start a fire on the earth, to be compared to the refining process of fine gold. I am going to separate, as it were, the purity of My true follower who wishes to lead others, from the dross of the false leader who is slothful in his duty. Yes, it will be a time of judgment. Oh, how I wish that it were already started so as to be completed soon! But, before that happens, I must first go through My own baptism of suffering which will overwhelm Me. And how agitated I will be until the entire plan of salvation is brought to completion!" Here, Jesus referred to His own sufferings and death, soon to take place.[(n) 62]

"Do you really think," the Lord continued, "that My ministry is one that will bring unity and peace on earth among all peoples? No, I tell you, it will bring division among people. Things will only get tougher. For example, the members of one household will be divided against each other, two against Me and three for Me, or three against Me, and two for Me. Yes, they will be divided: father against the son, and the son against the father; mother against the daughter, and the daughter against the mother; mother-in-law against the daughter-in-law and the daughter-in-law against the mother-in-law, and so on. Truly, on occasion it will be traumatic!"[63]

> While the Lord promised peace in the hearts of all His followers [*Harmony* 16:55], He did not promise peace in the world when it comes to the effects of the preaching of the Gospel message. [*Harmony* 16:104] Those who reject the Gospel will often be aligned against those who accept it. Thus it has been throughout almost all of the history of Christianity. The impressions of the Holy Spirit will call for great changes in the lives of those who respond to those impressions. Distress

---

62 Luke 12:49, 50

63 Luke 12:51-53

comes when others—often in the same family—do not understand nor appreciate what is happening in the lives of those who accept the Gospel.[1]

Next, Jesus discussed with the people the importance of responding positively to the Gospel message, even though it might cause distress in the lives of those who accept it.[2]

Realizing that the people did not fully comprehend the utter seriousness of His message, Jesus turned to the crowds, and explained, "When you notice a dark cloud arising in the western sky from off the Mediterranean Sea, instantly you say, 'Ah, a rain storm is coming!' And indeed, you are right, for the rains do come from that direction. And likewise, when you feel a wind blowing from the south, from off the desert, you say, 'It will be hot today.' And, of course, that is what happens.[64]

"Such hypocrites—actors! You have the ability to figure out the things of the weather by observing nature in both heaven and earth. Yet, why is it that you are unable to discern the times in which we are living, especially considering the fact that I have told you what to look for?[65]

"Why is it that you are so unable, on your own, to figure out how to live your own lives? Why is your judgment so faulty and off track in your relationship with your God? Let Me give you an illustration: It is obvious that when you are on your way to court to be sued for a debt which you know you owe a creditor, you should first try to settle with him before you arrive in the courtroom. Isn't that right? If you don't do this, your creditor will drag you before the judge. Next, the judge, after passing sentence on you, will turn you over to the officer of the court. And finally, the officer will throw you into the debtors' jail. You know that it's true when I tell you that you will stay in jail until you have paid the last cent to your creditor! Clearly, then, it would have been far better to settle the account outside of court without facing the judge and doing serious jail time, isn't that right? In like manner, you had better make peace with God before it's too late! For, when He comes, I tell you, it will certainly *be* too late!" [*Harmony* 5:27][66]

64 Luke 12:54, 55
65 Luke 12:56
66 Luke 12:57-59

## — Divine Mercy and Justice
## < Winter, A.D. 31 (7/7) >
## {Luke 13:1-9}

As Jesus was talking to the people, some individuals came to tell Him that the Roman governor, Pontius Pilate, had just had a number of Galilean Jews massacred in Jerusalem. In fact, he had them killed during the very moment that they were offering sacrifices to the Lord. So brutal was their death that their blood was actually mixed with the blood of the sacrifices they were offering! [*Harmony* 12:69; 17:60/][(o)] [67]

> Quite surprising was the belief, implied by the tellers of this event, that these victims were actually being punished for some hidden evil in their lives—that is, the result of divine justice being leveled against these poor people! To be sure, many believed that when this wicked act was performed by the cruel tyrant of a governor, the victims must have deserved what was done to them, and that, the governor was actually doing the will of God by killing them! They figured that because these were *Galilean* Jews—whom they considered less worthy than Jews from *elsewhere in Israel*—they deserved their punishment. Thus was the warped religious philosophy of that day. Jesus knew that this was the twisted thinking of some of His listeners. He also knew that the people wanted Him to comment on this terrible event, to give His own opinion about why this had happened to these people.[1]
>
> Besides correcting the twisted thinking of the people who came to Him in this situation, Jesus took advantage of this situation to discuss the certainty of the upcoming judgment. In effect, the Lord argued that instead of judging others in *this life,* the people needed to be concerned about their own future as *they* would face the final judgment. That was much more important for the people to consider![2]

So Jesus asked them, "Do you think these Galileans who had this horrible act perpetrated against them were worse sinners than other Galileans?" Before anyone could reply, Jesus answered His own question, "I tell you no! God doesn't work that way—not in this lifetime. But, unless you repent of your sins, you will all die in a similar way in the time of judgment at the end of the world! In this life, terrible things will happen—such as happened to these poor souls. But God

---

[67] Luke 13:1

is not punishing them. As long as we live in a sinful world unfair things will take place inexplicably."[68]

> Here, Jesus made it clear that God does not necessarily punish people in this life for their sins. On the other hand, He wanted to make it clear that God would indeed in the final judgment punish evildoers—even His professed people—for their wicked ways. Then, there will be no escape!

"Or," Jesus continued, "do you think that the 18 people who died when the tower of Siloam fell on them some time back were greater sinners than the other people of Jerusalem?" Jesus referred to an act-of-fate event that had happened in Jerusalem near the pool of Siloam, of which there is no historical record outside the Biblical account. In this case, these victims were *Judean* Jews, not the supposedly less righteous *Galilean* Jews of the previous story. [*Harmony* 12:67] "Again I tell you, no!" Jesus commented. "God doesn't punish people this way in this lifetime. But if you refuse to be repentant, in the final judgment you will be punished in like manner! That will be the time when God takes charge to punish people fairly and justly for their evil lives.[69]

"Let Me give you a parable," Jesus continued. "There was a certain farmer who had a fig tree that he planted in his vineyard. One day, he came looking to see if it had borne fruit, but it had not. Turning to the one who cared for the vineyard, he said, 'Look, for the last three years I've been coming and looking for figs on that tree. But I have yet to find any. So, cut it down! Why let it waste the ground where it stands?'[70]

"But the one who cared for the vineyard answered, 'Please, sir, let it alone for the rest of this year also. I'll dig around it, and even mulch it. If it bears fruit within the next year, that would be great! But if not . . . well, I say, then cut it down! Let's give it another chance to bear fruit.'" [*Harmony* 14:77][71]

> In this parable the owner represented God the Father. The one who cared for the vineyard was Jesus. The fig tree was the nation of Israel—especially its leaders. For the three years of the Lord's ministry to date, the Father had looked for the nation of Israel to bear fruit—that is, to accept Jesus

---

68 Luke 13:2, 3
69 Luke 13:4, 5
70 Luke 13:6, 7
71 Luke 13:8, 9

as the Messiah. His patience was wearing thin. The cutting down of the tree represented the time when God would no longer consider Israel as His special people. The one who cared for the vineyard, who asked for more time, represented Jesus asking for the Father to give Israel more time for them to accept Him. He would do His best to lead them to full repentance during the remaining time of His ministry—about six more months. If, however, they still refused to accept His ministry, then they would no longer be His special people. And, in the final judgment, they would pay a heavy price for their insolence. [*Harmony* 14:67-78]

### — The Healing of a Crippled Woman on the Sabbath[(p)]
### < Winter, A.D. 31 (7/7) >
### {Luke 13:10-17}

One Sabbath—the seventh day of the week—Jesus was teaching in a synagogue—a Jewish church. Standing out among the congregation was a woman who for 18 years had had a sickness caused by a demon. The disease's symptom was that she was bent over, almost double. There was no way that she could straighten herself up. Jesus noticed the unusual condition of this woman. Calling her over to Him, He said to her, "Ma'am, you are forthwith freed from your debilitating illness!" And so it was, as Jesus laid His hands on her, she instantly was able to stand up straight. The woman, overwhelmed by her recovery, naturally began to praise God.[72]

But the man in charge of the synagogue—called a synagogue officer—was extremely upset that Jesus had healed the woman on the Sabbath day. Trying to embarrass the Lord, the officer chastised the crowd who sought additional blessings from His healing powers. The officer said, "Why, there are six days in a week in which God commands that work be done. If you want to be healed, come on one of those days for that purpose. But the seventh-day Sabbath is not to be used for a healing such as this!" [*Harmony* 11:89/][73]

Jesus said to the synagogue officer—and to the others there who thought like him, "You are all hypocrite actors! Doesn't each one of you, on the Sabbath, untie your ox or donkey and lead it from its stall so that it can drink water? Why, of course you do!" Then, motioning in the direction of the woman, Jesus explained, "Now, here we have a woman who for 18 long years has been bound by the power

72 Luke 13:10-13
73 Luke 13:14

of the devil. As a daughter of Abraham"—a Jew—"is it not appropriate for her to be loosed from her bondage on a Sabbath day—a day set up to be a blessing for people?" [*Harmony* 4:60; 12:92][74]

Instead of Jesus being embarrassed, by the Lord's impeccable logic He was able to turn the tables on His critics and embarrass them! And the congregation, whom the synagogue officer had hoped would turn on Jesus, was, in fact, so excited by what they had seen and heard that they started to rejoice out loud. Indeed, the entire crowd was deeply impressed by both the great works and the irresistible logic of the Master![75]

**— Growing Within the Kingdom of Heaven**
**< Winter, A.D. 31 (7/7) >**
**{Luke 13:18-21}**

> Jesus was teaching the people about the rudiments of salvation. Often He repeated concepts that He had mentioned previously. Two such examples are the parables of the Mustard Seed and the Yeast in the Bread which he had initially given over a year before. [*Harmony* 7:30, 31]

The Lord said, "What is the kingdom of God like? And to what can I compare it? Well, it's like a mustard seed that a farmer cast on the ground of his garden. This seed, though very small, germinated, and when the mustard plant grew, it became as large as a small tree. It was so big that birds from the sky were able to build their nests in its branches." [*Harmony* 7:30; 12:76, 155][76]

> This means that the Gospel experience, though perhaps small at first, has the potential to grow into a large, life-changing experience. It can become so large that it is able to help support the growth of the spiritual lives of others who are likewise seeking the truth of the Gospel.

"Also, to what else can I compare the kingdom of God? It's like yeast that is placed in over 34 quarts of bread dough. Ultimately, the entire amount of dough will be permeated by the yeast, which causes it to rise and expand. From the dough, a huge amount of bread can be baked." [*Harmony* 7:31][77]

---

74 Luke 13:15, 16
75 Luke 13:17
76 Luke 13:18, 19
77 Luke 13:20, 21

This meant that the Gospel experience, when permeating the life, will in time cause one's experience to greatly expand and produce much fruit in character development.

## — What It Takes to be Saved
## < Winter, A.D. 31 (7/7) >
## {Luke 13:22-30}

The Master passed through one city and village after another throughout the land of Peraea while on His way toward Jerusalem to the south. Along the way, a Jewish man asked Him, "Lord, we've been listening to You for some time. And we need to know something: Are there just a few people who will be saved?"[78]

Jesus replied to the Jewish people standing by, saying, "It's a matter of your choice! You must be willing to put forth the effort to walk through the right door to eternal life. The entrance is narrow—that is, you cannot be saved just because you have a half-hearted desire to be saved. Instead, you must be willing to follow the prescribed way. There are many who really desire to be saved. But to date, there are very few who are truly willing to follow the way that leads to eternal life. And what is the prescribed way? The reality is, I am the Way! Yes, you must follow My teachings and words . . . and you must do it now, I should add! Everyone who decides for the truth—whether the number is large or small—will be saved. But you must decide! [*Harmony* 5:76][79]

"It's like the innkeeper," the Lord went on, telling a parable, "who has locked the door of the inn for the night. You may stand outside and knock on the door all you want, but he will not let you in. You can even say, 'Lord! Lord! Please open the door for us!' But he will say back to you, 'I don't know who you are or where you have come from!' Thus it will be in the judgment. Again, you must decide now, and follow Me as the only true way. You must do it now, while the door is open. For when the judgment begins, the door will be shut—and it will be too late—because you did not listen to and follow the truth when you had the opportunity to do so. And now is clearly that time to do it. [*Harmony* 5:80, 81; 15:32-41][80]

"Nevertheless, in the final judgment of this world, as it were, out of frustration you won't take 'No' for an answer. You will continue to argue with the divine

---

78 Luke 13:22, 23

79 Luke 13:23, 24

80 Luke 13:25

Innkeeper of the house, saying, 'But we ate and drank at Your table. You even taught in the streets of our villages.'[81]

"But," Jesus continued with His parable, "the Innkeeper will call back to you, 'No! As I have told you before, I don't know who you are and where you have come from! Get away from the door, you wicked people! You had your chance earlier on and you wasted it.'[82]

"I can tell you, in that place there will be much weeping and lamenting. Why? For you will see Abraham, Isaac, and Jacob, and all the prophets, already in the kingdom of God. But you, the children of the patriarchs, will not be allowed to enter in. No, instead you will be thrown out![83]

"In fact," the Lord added, "the really sad part is that there will be many Gentiles who will be saved while you will be lost. The Gentiles—those who you consider to be unworthy of eternal life—will come from the east and west, from the north and south. And they will recline at the banquet table, celebrating the blessings of eternity in the kingdom of God. They will be there . . . but you won't![84]

"At that time," the Master concluded, "it will be said that those of you"—the Jews—"who thought yourselves to be first, will, instead, be last! And those whom you considered to be last,"—the Gentiles—"will, in fact, be first!" [*Harmony* 13:88, 97][85]

### — A Warning of Divine Justice
### < Winter, A.D. 31 (7/7) >
### {Luke 13:31-35}

About that same time, some Pharisees approached Jesus, saying, "Quick! You need to leave this area! Go now! For we have heard that Herod Antipas is seeking to kill You, now that You are teaching in a province where he has authority!"[86]

---

81 Luke 13:26
82 Luke 13:27
83 Luke 13:28
84 Luke 13:29
85 Luke 13:30
86 Luke 13:31

> It was quite unlikely that this charge was true. All evidence indicates that Herod actually had positive thoughts regarding the Lord. [*Harmony* 8:72; 17:79] But even if it was really true that Herod was trying to kill Jesus, it was also unlikely that the Pharisees would actually attempt to save the Lord's life. After all, they themselves were trying to kill Him! Why not have Herod do their dirty work for them? The reality was that the Jews were probably trying to scare the Lord out of Peraea toward the south where Judea was located, where it would easier for them to seize Him. In any case, Jesus played along with their warning, ultimately using it against them.

The Lord said to the Pharisees, "In that case, go and tell that sly fox, Herod, these words: 'Look! I have cast out demons and healed people today. Tomorrow, I will do the same. The day after tomorrow, I will have finished My work!"[87]

> Jesus was not speaking literally here. The words, "today," "tomorrow," and the "day after tomorrow," are to be understood as figurative language, which means, in effect, "I still have work to do. While My ministry will end relatively soon—in a few months—it is not finished yet. That is, until I am finished with My work, neither Herod—nor you—can touch Me!"[1]

> When Jesus used the phrase, "sly fox," to describe Herod, He referred to the tetrarch's crafty, even evil, nature. All the kings of that day were noted for such a nature as this. Herod was hardly a noble man! [*Harmony* 3:71][2]

Jesus continued, "Therefore, I will go about My ministry, journeying until I am finished. Indeed, I will go on for a bit longer: today"—as it were—"and also tomorrow, and the day after tomorrow. My ministry will yet continue for a while longer. Indeed, I have nothing and no one to fear in this place, not even Herod. He cannot touch Me! It is in Jerusalem where I will die! History reveals that it is only in Jerusalem where the prophets of old have been killed!" This was true because that is where the murderous leaders of Israel were located. Of course it would in Jerusalem where Jesus would be tried, and it was just outside the city where He would be crucified.[88]

> Here, Jesus made it abundantly clear that He would not die in any place other than Jerusalem. He also made it clear that He would not die—even

---

87 Luke 13:32

88 Luke 13:33

in Jerusalem—until the prophetic time of His death had arrived. [Daniel 9:24-27] In short, He was never afraid to go to Jerusalem. However, the Lord sometimes avoided going to Jerusalem. And why was this? Because He knew that going to Jerusalem on certain occasions would cause such a stir with the Jewish leaders that it would negatively affect His overall ministry, as well as those who were sincerely listening to Him. Thus the Savior's occasional refusal to go to Jerusalem was to protect His ministry and His followers, rather than to save His own life.

Jesus added, with deep sorrow in His voice, "O Jerusalem! O Jerusalem! You are that city which has killed the prophets, and has stoned those that God has sent to minister to you! For Myself, how often have I passionately desired to gather all your children"—that is, its inhabitants—"together, just as a mother hen would gather her flock of chicks under her wings in a time of trouble . . . but you would not allow Me to do so! Thus, consider this: Your house—your Temple—is left empty and desolate for you, for I will be gone from it forever. And after I leave it, the next time you see Me is when you will declare, 'Blessed is the One who is coming in the name of the Lord!'" Of course, here Jesus was referring to His Second Coming. Jesus would repeat these words when He actually left the Temple for the last time [*Harmony* 14:132], several months later.[89]

**—Jesus Heals on the Sabbath While Eating in the Home of a Pharisee**
**< Winter, A.D. 31 (7/7) >**
**{Luke 14:1-24}**

Sometime after this, Jesus was invited to have a Sabbath dinner in the home a certain distinguished Pharisee who was a member of the Jewish court, the Sanhedrin. The motive for this invitation was neither social nor innocent but sinister. For the guests were looking at Jesus like hawks, to see if he would do or say something wrong that they could use against Him. [*Harmony* 12:19-31][90]

Their chance to condemn the Lord soon arose as they had hoped, because there appeared before Jesus a man who was suffering from a certain illness. This man had an excess amount of fluid in his body, which caused him to be in a grossly swollen condition. Looking at the man, and then at the guests at the table, Jesus responded to their evil thoughts by asking them, "What do you think?

89 Luke 13:34, 35
90 Luke 14:1

Is it consistent with the Sabbath Commandment in the Law of God [Exodus 20:8-11] to heal someone on the Sabbath day, or not?" [*Harmony* 11:89/][91]

Probably embarrassed that their secret thoughts were so openly revealed, they kept their mouths shut. So Jesus took hold of the swollen man, healed him, and sent him away normal-sized! Turning to the speechless guests, Jesus asked, "Tell Me! Which one of you who has an ox, or a donkey that has fallen into a well, would not immediately pull it out of that well on the Sabbath day? Tell Me!" Seeing His obvious point—that healing a man in misery on the Sabbath was even more a sign of compassion than saving an ox or donkey from a well—they remained speechless. Indeed, no one endeavored to respond to His piercing question. [*Harmony* 4:60; 12:74][92]

After dealing with the issue of healing on the Sabbath, the Lord began to address another matter that had been a source of concern to Him regarding the Pharisees. There was a strong tendency for these Jewish leaders, when invited to a dinner, to choose for themselves the seats of highest honor, closest to the host of the feast. On these seats they would recline while they ate. This showed a terribly arrogant and selfish attitude. It was their way of showing off how important they thought they were! So the Lord, noticing that this very thing had happened on this occasion, decided to address this issue by telling the dinner guests a parable. [*Harmony* 12:100][93]

But before He actually told them the parable, Jesus began directly and openly to address the issue. He said, "Please! When you are invited to someone's wedding feast, don't rush to recline at the most honored position close to the bridegroom! If you do, you might end up making a fool out of yourself. And how? Should someone more important than yourself show up later on, you may be asked to move to a lesser place. Indeed, the bridegroom—the one who had invited you in the first place—will come up to you and say, 'Uh! You have to give up your couch to this other person! Please move!' Then, in front of everyone, you, with a red face, will have to move down to the least desirable position.[94]

"But let Me tell you what you should do. Instead of seeking out the best place when invited, choose a lesser place to sit—perhaps even the least desirable

91 Luke 14:2, 3
92 Luke 14:4-6
93 Luke 14:7
94 Luke 14:7-9

one. This way, should the bridegroom—who had invited you—see you sitting far away from him, might come over to you and say, 'Hey, my friend! Come on over and recline next to me!' Can you imagine how proud you will feel when everyone else reclining and eating at the table watches as you move higher up to a seat of honor, closest to the bridegroom![95]

"Ah yes!" the Savior concluded. "Everyone who seeks to exalt himself in front of others shall be humiliated! And everyone who humbles himself in front of others will be treated with honor. Think about it!"[96]

The Lord, talking directly to the Pharisee who had invited Him to the feast, said, "My friend, let Me give you some advice: The next time you have a luncheon, or a feast, don't invite all your friends, brothers, relatives, or rich neighbors. Yes, of course, they will repay you by inviting you to one of their feasts. But that's the *only* payment you will get![97]

"No! Instead, when you have banquet, invite the poor, the crippled, the lame, and the blind. No, they won't be able to repay you by inviting you to a similar feast, but nevertheless, you will be blessed by a much greater invitation. That is, you will hear the voice of God at the resurrection of the righteous! [1 Thessalonians 4:13-18] And then, you will be invited to sit down with God at His banquet table! How about that?" [*Harmony* 5:40][98]

Hearing these words of subtle rebuke, one of the Pharisees reclining at the table with Jesus was made uneasy by the Lord's words. This Jewish leader interrupted Jesus by saying, "Indeed, everyone who eats food at the table of God in His kingdom will be happy!" By making this statement, the man hoped that Jesus would change the subject to a more pleasant, less soul-searching one.[99]

But Jesus would not be deterred. Now the time had come for Him to tell the parable He had been planning to recite. [*Harmony* 12:93] Accordingly, He said, "Listen to this! A certain man was throwing a big party. He invited many, many guests. When the time for the feast had arrived, the man sent his

95 Luke 14:10
96 Luke 14:11
97 Luke 14:12
98 Luke 14:13, 14
99 Luke 14:15

servant personally to remind the invited guests. 'Come!' he was to say to them all. 'Everything is ready! Let's eat!'[100]

"But all the invited guests began to make excuses as to why they could not attend the feast. Some of the excuses sounded good. Others were quite flimsy. But they all made excuses of one sort or another. The first one said, 'I have just purchased a new field. I need to go and carefully inspect it. So, please, allow me to be excused.' Now, don't you agree that's really a silly excuse! Another one explained, 'Oh no! I have just bought five yoke of oxen. I really need to try them and see if they can plow a field. I beg of you, excuse me from your master's feast.' This excuse was a bit better, but not much. Still another gave excuse, saying, 'I have just been married! Certainly you can understand that I can't come to the feast!' Now, that on the surface seems to be a great excuse![101]

"So the servant," the Lord continued, "returned to his master, and reported to him all the excuses—good and bad—the invited guests had made. Not surprisingly, the host was furious and commanded his servant, 'Well then, if they won't come to my feast, go immediately into the streets and roads of the city and bring back the poor, the crippled, the blind, and the lame. And let them eat at my feast!'[102]

"So the servant did as he was told. After completing his assignment, he reported back to his master, and said, 'Master! I did exactly what you commanded me to do. But there is still room at your feasting table for even more people.'[103]

"'All right, then,' the master answered, 'I want you to go out into the highways outside the city limits. There, I want you to beat the bushes, as it were, along the highway, and find everyone you can. Plead with them to come to the feast! This way, my banquet hall will be filled, and no food will go to waste. But I want to make it clear to you,' the master added to his servant, 'none of those whom I originally invited to the feast will ever taste of my food—no, never!'"[104]

> By this stinging parable, Jesus was pronouncing condemnation upon the Jewish leaders. They had been invited by God to feast at the table of salvation, so to speak. But, because they were more interested in

---

[100] Luke 14:16, 17
[101] Luke 14:18-20
[102] Luke 14:21
[103] Luke 14:22
[104] Luke 14:23, 24

acquiring the things of this world—buying land, oxen, and even getting married—they missed out on the one thing that counted the most: eternal life. They gave excuses to God's servant, Jesus. Some excuses were poor, while others were more plausible. But all were just that: excuses! So, because of their refusal to accept God's invitation, His servant, Jesus, ministered to the publicans and the so-called sinners—the lame, the blind, and the crippled of the parable. When there was still room left for others, God sent Jesus—and ultimately His disciples—to minister to the Gentiles of the world—those who lived in the "bushes" along the highways in the story. All these will eat at God's table in eternity, while the leaders of God's people—such as the Pharisees—will not, in any way, be a part of that festive occasion, or share in that feast. Even though the record does not state it, following these tense discussions, this luncheon with the Pharisee must have broken up as it had on another occasion. [*Harmony* 12:31]

**— The Cost of Discipleship**
**< Winter, A. D. 31 (7/7) >**
**{Luke 14:25-35}**

From time to time huge crowds followed after Jesus. Seeing one such crowd coming up behind Him, the Lord turned and looked back at them. He offered them a challenge, by declaring, "If there is anyone who truly wishes to follow Me, and yet does not 'hate,' in comparison to his love for Me, his own father, mother, wife, children, brothers, and sisters—even his own life—simply cannot be My disciple! Of course family is important. Loyalty to, and love of, family is also important. But loyalty to Me and My calling is even more important."[105]

Obviously Jesus was not literally suggesting that one should actually "hate" his or her family in order to love Him. Instead Jesus was making a comparison between one's *natural* love for family, and one's *cultivated* love of Him. So, to make His point, He expressed it in very extreme terms for His listeners to grasp the power of His message. The Lord was saying, in effect, "If your love for Me is not strong enough, the pressure from your family members who do not trust Me may drive you away from Me altogether. So, in a sense, you need to 'hate' them in order to be sure that you truly love Me."

---

105 Luke 14:25, 26

"Indeed," the Lord continued, "whoever refuses to carry his own cross of sacrifice for Me, and also refuses to follow Me by obeying My words, cannot become a disciple of Mine. Yes, to follow Me is a high calling. It must not be entered into lightly. [*Harmony* 10:58][106]

"For example, which one of you, wanting to build a watchtower for your vineyard, does not first sit down and calculate the total cost of the project to determine if you have enough money on hand to finish the project? None of you would! You would make yourself a laughingstock, if you laid the foundation for the tower but were not able to build the tower itself. People would say, 'Look at this idiot! This man started to build a tower, but wasn't able to finish it because he ran out of money.'[107]

"Take another example," the Master added. "What king is there who desires to defeat another king in battle, who doesn't first sit down and figure out whether he is strong enough with 10,000 soldiers to compete with his enemy who has 20,000 warriors? If he doesn't plan wisely, he will be forced to send emissaries under a flag of truce to sue for peace, while his enemy is still some distance away. And after doing that, he will certainly return home in total humiliation.[108]

"To interpret, this means that if you do not count the total cost of following Me, and in the end, be willing to give up everything you possess to follow Me, well, you simply cannot be a disciple worthy of Me! And why? There will be all sorts of pressures upon you to give up your faith in Me. If you are not truly and totally committed to Me, you will end up, in the final analysis, forsaking Me.[109]

"It's like salt. When salt is good, it is valuable for seasoning or preserving food. Isn't that right? But if salt has lost its power to season things, what good is it anymore? What will you be able to season with it? Nothing! It isn't good to even season the ground, or even to be used for rubbish! It's just thrown away! So then don't be like worthless salt. If you wish to follow Me, then plan on giving up your passions for the things of this life in order to be My disciples. For if you do, you will be like good 'salt.' If not, don't even try to follow Me. Don't waste your time! If you have ears to really understand what I'm saying to you, then you had better listen to Me!" [*Harmony* 5:16, 17; 10:105, 106][110]

---

106 Luke 14:27
107 Luke 14:28-30
108 Luke 14:31, 32
109 Luke 14:33
110 Luke 14:34, 35

### — The Lost Sheep, Coin, and Son Parables
### < Winter, A.D. 31 (7/7) >
### {Luke 15:1-32}

During the entire course of the Lord's ministry, a number of tax collectors and others, considered by most Jews to be little more than worthless sinners, followed after Him. They lingered close to the Lord, and listened intently to what He was teaching. His words filled them with hope and courage. This caused the Pharisees and the teachers of the law to complain. They whined, "This Man allows sinners to follow Him. He even eats with them! It's disgusting!" [*Harmony* 8:1-4, 30][111]

Hearing their complaint, Jesus told them a parable—one which He had told before. [*Harmony* 10:108] He said, "Tell Me, which one of the many shepherds of Israel, who has 100 sheep, and has lost one of them, will not leave the remaining 99 in the field, and search for the solitary missing one? He will search until he finds it. That's right, isn't it? Yes, and further, when he finds the missing sheep, that shepherd will with great joy lay it on his shoulders, and bring it back to be with the other 99. In fact, when he comes back to his home, he will call out to his friends and neighbors, saying, 'Celebrate with me! I have found my sheep which was lost! Rejoice with me, I say!' [*Harmony* 12:123/2][112]

"I tell you, in like manner, there will be more rejoicing in heaven over the repentance of one of these so-called 'sinners' whom you consider to be so unworthy, than over the remaining 99 of you who think you are so righteous that you have no need to repent. Think about it!"[113]

Then Jesus told them a second story. He said, "Is it not true that a poor woman, having ten coins"—worth ten days' wages—"would, if she should lose one of those coins, search diligently for it? Of course she would! Won't she take a lamp and sweep the floor, carefully looking for the coin until she finds it? Indeed, when she does find that coin, she will call together her neighbors and friends, saying to them, 'Rejoice with me! I have found the coin that I've lost!'[114]

"Again, in a similar way, I declare to you that in heaven there is the same kind of rejoicing among the angels of God when even one sinner has repented! That

---

111 Luke 15:1, 2
112 Luke 15:3-6
113 Luke 15:7
114 Luke 15:8, 9

sinner may be quite unimportant or insignificant to you, but to those in heaven, that sinner is most precious." [*Harmony* 12:123/2][115]

Jesus gave a third parable. He said, "A certain man had two sons. The younger of the two came to his father and demanded, 'Father, give me my portion of the family inheritance that rightly belongs to me. I want it now, not later after you've died.' So, the father, sick at heart, nevertheless gave in to his son's demand and handed over his portion of the inheritance to the son.[116]

"Well, not too many days later, that son, converting his inheritance into cash, took all his belongings and left his father's home. To be independent, he traveled to a far distant country, where he foolishly squandered his entire inheritance on a reckless, care-free lifestyle. And then, when everything that he had was gone, a terrible famine afflicted that country, making matters even worse for him. So, in order to make some kind of living—as poor as it might be—the wayward son took a job with one of the residents of that country, working in the fields as a feeder of hogs! With no other help from anyone, he became so hungry that he actually fantasized about eating the carob pods that he was feeding to the swine![117]

"In the depths of despair, he began to face the reality of his situation. He said to himself, 'How many of my father's employees have an abundance to eat? All of them! Why is it, then, that I am literally starving to death? I will get up from this despicable job and go back to my father and say to him, "Father, I have sinned against heaven and also against you. Indeed, I am not worthy to be called your son anymore. But I will be satisfied to be just one of your servants. Just please let me stay around home!"'[118]

"So accordingly, the son quit his job and came back to his own father's house. But even before he was close to the house, his father, still looking for him to return, saw his wayward son coming toward home. Touched with great compassion for his son, the father ran out to meet him. The father wrapped his arms around his younger son's neck in a firm embrace, and kissed him. According to his plan, the son confessed to his father, saying, 'Father, I am such a sinner! I

115 Luke 15:10
116 Luke 15:11, 12
117 Luke 15:13-16
118 Luke 15:17-19

have disgraced both God in heaven and you! Father, I am no longer worthy to be called your son—!'[119]

"But before the son could say anything more, his father interrupted him in mid-sentence, commanding his servants, 'Go quickly and get the best suit of clothes and shoes you can find. Bring them back to my son and dress him, head to toe. Also, place on his finger my ring that symbolizes that he truly is my son. I also want you to find the healthiest looking, plump calf you can. Kill it, and let's eat in great celebration! For my son, who for all practical purposes was dead, has been resurrected! He was lost . . . but now he is found! Go, and quickly do what I've commanded you!' And so they started the celebration in honor of the wayward son as the father had directed.[120]

"In the meantime, the older son who was working in the fields was not aware that his younger brother had returned home. But on his way back to the house after work, he heard the sound of music and dancing coming from the house as he approached the front door. Seeing one of his father's servants, he asked him to come over to him and demanded of him as to why there was a celebration going on in the house. The servant answered, 'Why, didn't you hear? Your brother has come back home! That's why your father has roasted a fat calf. Your father is so happy that your brother is back home safely, not much the worse for wear.'[121]

"Well," Jesus went on with His story, "the older brother was incensed, and seethed with anger. He refused to even enter the house. His father had to come out to him to try to persuade him to come in. But the older son would not be convinced. He protested to his father, complaining, 'There is no way that I will ever be a part of any such celebration! Look here! For many years—even my whole life—I've served you faithfully. On not one occasion did I ever disobey one of your commands, even the least of them. And yet, after all that, you have never, ever, even roasted an inexpensive young goat for me, let alone an expensive calf! You have never even provided an opportunity for me to celebrate anything with any of my friends. Never! But, then, when this worthless son of yours comes home—your son who has squandered all your money on whores, I might add—well, for him you have slaughtered a fat calf to eat! Unbelievable!'[122]

119 Luke 15:20, 21
120 Luke 15:22-24
121 Luke 15:25-27
122 Luke 15:28-30

"The father tried to explain to him, 'My son, yes, you have always been with me. And for that reason, everything I have is yours. But, we just had to celebrate and make merry! For after all, your brother, who was as good as dead, as it were, has been found alive. He was lost, but now he is found! Don't you get it?'" [*Harmony* 12:123/2][123]

By this parable, Jesus was telling the Pharisees, in effect, "In My story, you are represented by the older brother. The publicans and sinners are represented by the younger one. Yes, just as that son squandered his inheritance, so it has been with sinners: They have wasted the message of the Gospel by living wicked lives. But the point of this story was that the younger son—that is, the sinner—repented of his evil ways. The father—representing the heavenly Father—was excited and eager to welcome the wayward son back home. That is the way our heavenly Father is. What is disappointing in this story is that the older son—that is, you—refused to welcome a sinner back home. Why is that? You should have rejoiced as does the heavenly Father! That's what your so-called profession of faith should be about."[(q)] [[1]]

By these three parables, Jesus taught the essential truth that repentance—the returning of the sinner to God—is an act that should excite all the true followers of Jesus. They should rejoice at the repentance of any and all sinners. By the lost sheep [*Harmony* 12:112, 113], Jesus illustrated those who are lost and know it, but are unable to find their way back to the Lord. The good news is that the shepherd—the Savior—carried the lost sheep back home. By the lost coin [*Harmony* 12:114, 115], the Master illustrated those who are lost and do not know they are lost. Fortunately, someone searches for them and takes them back. By the story of the son who squandered his inheritance [*Harmony* 12:116-123] is illustrated those who are lost, and know it, and finally are able to find their way back home. In the Gospel experience, these stories illustrate three kinds of sinners who ultimately find the Lord.[[2]]

---

123 Luke 15:31, 32

## — The Dishonest Steward, and the Rich Man and Lazarus Parables[r] < Winter, A.D. 31 (7/7) > {Luke 16:1-31}

Jesus was approaching the end of His ministry. The time had come for Him to explain firmly and clearly to the Jewish leaders just where they were in their relationship with both the Father and Him. They also needed to understand exactly where they had failed as His "stewards" of the truth that God had committed to them, beginning way back at Mount Sinai. [Exodus 19:3-6] To accomplish this task, the Lord would connect together a couple of parables—the parable of the Dishonest Steward and the Rich Man and Lazarus. The Savior would add to those parables several specific counsels and advice. These discussions would include a brief description of His own ministry along with that of John the Baptist, a reference to the doctrine of marriage and divorce, the need for His followers to serve only one Master, and finally—*and most importantly*—the need for His servants to be faithful, humble students of the Scriptures. All this, then, Jesus would ultimately tie together along with His greatest and most important miracle, the resurrection of His dear friend, Lazarus. [*Harmony* 13:1-30] The final result of this endeavor would be the crowning achievement of the Lord's entire teaching and miracle-working ministry, all brilliantly combined. When He finished, there could be no doubt as to where He stood, and where the Jewish leaders were in their relationship with Him.[3]

God had entrusted the Jewish nation—and especially its leaders—with great privileges *and* responsibilities. This included the fact that they had been given the Holy Scriptures as a guide, carefully instructing them in the way of salvation. [Romans 3:2] But beyond their personal salvation, the Scriptures directed the Jews to share the entire Gospel message with the Gentile—or non-Jewish—world. [Genesis 12:2, 3] In a sense, then, the people of the Jewish nation were to be "stewards" of the truth of the Gospel, to spread it ultimately to the entire planet. This meant that, in theory, when Jesus arrived as the Messiah, there was to be a large group of people—composed of both of Jews *and* Gentiles—who would be ready to receive enthusiastically both the Messiah and His heart-penetrating message. This was to be *the* mission of Israel. [Isaiah 56:6, 7] Of course, such was clearly *not* the case! Instead, because of years of neglect and apostasy, not only were they as a people quite ill prepared personally to accept the Messiah, they certainly did not have others ready to receive Him either! [*Harmony* 1:3] Nevertheless, in spite of their past failures, God gave them another, last minute chance, as it were, to accept the Lord's ministry. This was to be accomplished through the labor of John the Baptist who was to prepare the *immediate* way for the coming of the Messiah. [*Harmony* 2:4] Even though it would come late in their history, the Jews still had the chance to be ready for the Messiah's appearance, should they, as a nation, accept the message of John's preaching. But, even though John had *some* success, many of the people—and most of the nation's spiritual leaders—failed to receive the true message of John. [*Harmony* 3:95] In summary, then, the Jewish people did not accept Jesus when He actually arrived. In short, they had squandered their last opportunity to be ready for His appearing. They, most assuredly, could have and should have been prepared! They had the Scriptures to guide their way. They had the prophets—including, especially, John the Baptist—to preach the truth to them. To a great extent, of course, such a preparation was a failure. However, even though the Jews for the most part had rejected John the Baptist's "last-call" message of repentance, they still had the chance to accept the Messiah Himself when He actually arrived. No, it still wasn't too late! But they—and especially their leaders—wasted even this *additional* second chance.[4]

A bit surprisingly, though, in spite of the aforementioned failures of the Jews and their leaders to be prepared adequately for the coming of the Messiah, they were, nevertheless, students of the Scriptures which were to be their guide. [*Harmony* 3:97] *But most unfortunately,* however, they, with pre-conceived opinions, constantly searched and studied the Scriptures for only those things that appealed to their wicked, selfish desires. In a very real sense, then, the message of the Gospel, as contained in the Scriptures, instead of being a blessing to them, turned out to be a curse, for they used the various verses of Scripture to prove their own false concepts and philosophies. Because this was so, they were most ill-equipped to recognize the real, unvarnished truth of the Messiah and His ministry when He arrived. So then, instead of enthusiastically accepting the good news of the *true* Gospel of the grace of God that Jesus taught, they tenaciously clung to their works-oriented religion—in reality, a *false* Gospel. They also hoarded the truth of the Scriptures to themselves, stubbornly refusing to share it graciously with others. Furthermore, when the Lord arrived on this earth, He acted in a way that was contrary to their errant thinking and theology. [*Harmony* 11:43] Therefore, many of the Jews and most of their leaders refused to submit their will to Jesus as the Messiah when He lived and taught the real truth of the Scriptures among them.[5]

So, to drive home the point of their dire failure to be faithful stewards of the knowledge that God had shed upon them through the Scriptures, Jesus told them a parable about an equally unfaithful and evil steward. In this parable, though, Jesus told the story of a certain steward of the *world*, not of the church. This unfaithful steward in the parable, when he was confronted with the reality of losing his job, used sly worldly wisdom safely to secure his financial security. By telling this story, Jesus showed how this very worldly man was actually wiser than were His own failed stewards of the church—the Jewish people, and their leaders! To be sure, the Jews who heard Jesus tell this story were shockingly ignorant of how desperately serious their shortcomings were. Indeed, they had acted as though everything was perfect in their relationship with God. Because they were Jews by natural birth, they felt totally secure in their salvation. In fact, they felt so secure in salvation—albeit misguided—that they were not afraid to actually plot the death of Jesus, the One who was to be their true leader and Messiah![6]

Jesus, in explaining a parable to His disciples as well as the Jewish leaders and the people who were listening to Him, said, "Now, there was a certain rich man who had a steward who had been assigned to care for all the rich man's possessions. Word had reached the rich man, however, accusing this particular steward of squandering his master's wealth.[124]

"Distressed, the owner called his steward to appear before him. He demanded of him, 'What is this that I hear about you? Explain yourself to me! Give an account of your actions! If what I hear about you is true, I can no longer trust you to be my steward. I will, however, give you some time to prepare yourself to defend your actions.'[125]

"Knowing that he had no real justification for his evil actions, the steward said to himself, 'Oh no! What am I going to do? Once he finds out the facts, my lord is going to remove me from being his steward. Then, what will I do? I have

124 Luke 16:1
125 Luke 16:2

not the physical strength to be a common laborer. And, I have too much pride to beg for a living.' After thinking it over for a moment, he said to himself, 'I know what I'll do! When I'm fired as my master's steward, I will have a plan already in place that will provide enough friends for me who will welcome me into their homes and their employ. And they will take good care of me!'[126]

"So, he called each of the rich man's debtors—those who owed his master significant amounts of money—to appear before him. He questioned the first debtor, 'How much is it that you owe my master?'[127]

"The first debtor answered, 'About 580 gallons of olive oil.'[128]

"The steward responded, 'Forget that debt! Instead, quickly sit down and rewrite your bill to read 290 gallons of oil—half the original amount.'[129]

"Asking another debtor, he said, 'And how much is it that you owe my master?'[130]

"That debtor replied, 'About 624 bushels of wheat.'[131]

"'No you don't!' the steward shot back. 'Take your bill and change it to 498 bushels—which is just 80% of the original debt.'[132]

"When the actions of the unfaithful steward were made known to his lord, he was brought to appear before him. Surprisingly, the lord actually praised the steward for his shrewdness in providing for his future." Then, pausing for a second, Jesus added the punch line to the parable, saying, "Ah yes! The *children of this world* are shrewder as it relates to their own evil kind, than are the supposed *children of the light* of this generation, who claim to know the Gospel truth. Yes, the people of the world have figured out how to take care of themselves. They know what it takes. But, My own people haven't figured it out yet! They don't have a clue!"[133]

---

126 Luke 16:3, 4
127 Luke 16:5
128 Luke 16:6
129 Luke 16:6
130 Luke 16:7
131 Luke 16:7
132 Luke 16:7
133 Luke 16:8

Directly addressing the Pharisees in the crowd, Jesus added, with a bit of sarcasm, "I must warn you, you had better make friends of the people of this world, for when God throws you out as His stewards of the truth, you will have no place to go! The people of the world will have to provide a place for you in eternity, for God certainly won't!" [*Harmony* 12:136] Obviously that would be quite impossible, for in eternity no other human being could either save them or provide for them! [*Harmony* 14:67-78] "On the other hand," Jesus continued, "if you repent, then you had better resolve to be faithful to your stewardship of the Gospel . . . and do it quickly! Yes, you need to repent immediately if you are to be privileged to live with God in eternity as part of His kingdom. Time is running out for you! [*Harmony* 2:9][134]

"God has called you to be faithful stewards," the Lord continued. "If while in this life you are faithful in the little things of the Gospel—that is, to receive the power of the *true* Gospel message into your lives through a proper study and understanding of the Scriptures, and next, share it with enthusiasm with others—then God will accordingly trust you to be faithful in the really big things which are a part of eternity. On the other hand, if you continue to be unfaithful in the little things, so to speak, of the Gospel message that have been committed to you in this world, then you would be just as unfaithful with the really big things of eternity. Thus God cannot and will not trust you . . . unless you repent *now!* Once again, if God can't trust you with the spiritual responsibilities He has given to you in this life, how can He possibly trust you to care for the things that make up the riches of eternity? How? If you have failed to teach God's children properly who have been committed to your care, do you expect that in eternity God will shower you with honor, praise, and added responsibility? Never!"[135]

> Because of the Jewish leaders' failure to submit fully to the will of God, and their determination to cling to their selfish pride and opinions, their ability to interpret accurately the words of Scripture—especially as it related to the Lord's own ministry—was quite flawed—and even downright false. But, beyond their inability to understand the Scriptures properly as they related directly to the ministry of Jesus, their ineptitude with the Scriptures also included their poor understanding of the basic rudiments of the Gospel, as well as most other things. In short, then, as faithful stewards of the Scriptures, they were utter failures. The importance of this failure cannot be overemphasized! But, not only

134 Luke 16:9

135 Luke 16:10-12

had the Jewish leaders failed to be faithful stewards of the spiritual responsibilities the Lord had given them, but they were, accordingly, for the most part, caught up in the concerns and riches of this life. [*Harmony* 12:137, 150/4] *Indeed, when selfish desires and beliefs are cherished in the soul, the passion for the material things and praise of this world is the natural result.* And so it was that, just like the people of the world, the acquiring of wealth and worldly praise had become the primary passion of most of the Jewish leaders. Shockingly, seeking a close personal relationship with God and depending upon Him for their salvation held little or no place in their lives. This meant, in practice, they hardly ever cared for the poor among them. Instead, the acquisition of *personal* possessions became paramount to them. In truth, the material riches the Lord had given them, they failed to use for the care of others less fortunate than themselves. Rather, they hoarded the things of this world for themselves. In fact, on occasion they even tried to seize the meager possessions of others, including widows! But, beyond that, their desire for such worldly things and possessions had effectively robbed them of any additional fervor they should have had for *accurately and humbly* interpreting the Word of God and sharing its glorious message of the Gospel with others. To be sure, they were caught in a vicious, downward spiraling cycle of greed *as well as* constant and deliberate misapplication of Scriptural truth. Such is the power of sin and the selfish pride of opinion! Thus, the Lord needed to address these failures of the Jews: *first, their failure to care adequately for others less fortunate than themselves, and second, their failure to accurately interpret the Word of God and the Gospel message.*

"Therefore," Jesus concluded, "as I have told you before [*Harmony* 5:60], no servant can serve two different masters. He will either hate one of them and love the other. Or, he will be faithful to one of them, and treat the other with contempt. You cannot ultimately serve both God and the things of this world at the same time. This includes your own pet theories and ideas. You must choose: Either be faithful to the things of God—that is, to diligently study the Scriptures and to share the truth of God's Word and your material possessions with others—or be faithful to the possessions of this world. If you choose God, then you had better be faithful to Him now! If you choose the world, well, you had better hope the world takes good care of you, for God won't!" [*Harmony* 12:134][136]

[136] Luke 16:13

The Pharisees were angered by these words of Jesus, for they were caught up in the glories of the things of this world and in its riches and honors. Accordingly, as they listened to the Lord, their response was one of outright anger and ridicule![137]

Jesus responded directly to their ridicule by saying, "Quit your scoffing! As might be expected, you are the kind of people who seek to justify yourselves before men, to be honored by the world. But God is able to read the thoughts of your heart. And don't forget, the things that are laudable in the sight of men, God usually treats with disdain.[138]

"Sadly, for years you have inaccurately preached the Scriptures—even the Law and the Prophets. Of course I know that you consider yourselves to be experts in the teaching of the Scriptures, and the Law contained in it. But, as I have just said, your teaching of the Law has been greatly flawed. Then, John the Baptist came along and began to teach the real truth of the Scriptures—such as, accepting the true Gospel message [*Harmony* 2:3] and caring for others. [*Harmony* 2:11, 12] And the good news is that ever since John began his ministry, a new, more complete understanding of the truth of the kingdom of God has been preached. He taught a more complete understanding of repentance, forgiveness, and character transformation—a message greatly superior to the legalistic way to salvation you presently understand or teach. Yes, John preached it. And I continue to preach it. And when the people who have been used to listening to you in the past, have heard what John and I have preached, well . . . many of them have stopped listening to you, and instead, have joyfully listened to what we have taught. First of all, they followed John. And now, they've been following Me. They have come in droves, almost as it were, forcing their way into the Gospel's realm so that they might fully experience its power and joy. You should learn from them. Oh that you had the same kind of passion for the things of the Gospel and the Messiah's kingdom that they do! [*Harmony* 8:27; 12:150/4][139]

> In summary, Jesus emphasized the difference of His teachings and those of John the Baptist, when compared with those of the Jewish leaders. What Jesus and John taught led the people to a happy, more victorious walk with God, while the things the Jewish leaders taught resulted in a lifestyle that was unable to provide victory for its adherents. And what

---

[137] Luke 16:14
[138] Luke 16:15
[139] Luke 16:16

> was the cause of this stark difference? In the case of Jesus and John, their teachings were based upon sound Biblical truth, which led the people to share of themselves *and* their possessions with others. [*Harmony* 2:11, 12] In the case of the Jewish leaders, their teachings were based upon self—a false understanding of the Scriptures—which led people to seek to acquire personal wealth and material possessions, as well as to hoard the truth of the Scriptures for themselves. Of course, the Jewish leaders claimed that their teachings were Biblical, but, in reality, their teachings were quite selfish and humanistic—indeed, far from the truth of the Scriptures and the Gospel.

"Thus," the Lord continued, "because your pride has been dreadfully wounded—when people followed John and Me instead of you—you have, accordingly, unceasingly criticized My teachings, saying that they are contrary to the Law. But My teachings are not contrary to the Law as you claim! In fact, as I have said on another occasion [*Harmony* 5:20], it would be more likely that both heaven and earth would disintegrate to nothingness than for even a single stroke of a word of the Law to fail. Now that's what I teach! Stop criticizing Me! The true purpose of My ministry, rather, is to give new meaning and power to the Law—even beyond the mere words themselves. I have not come to destroy it! You must understand that both John and I have taught the truth which really empowers people to keep the *whole* law with joy and excitement." [*Harmony* 12:150/4[140]

> The Jewish leaders' false teachings and interpretations of the Gospel message were shallow and empty. This increasingly led both them, and the people who followed them, to a style of religion that appealed to the weaknesses of humanity. So then, instead of gaining victory over sin, they actually fell deeper into wickedness! But not only were the Jewish leaders' interpretations of the Gospel message mostly inaccurate, but accordingly, their interpretations of most other things in the *general line of theology* were just as inaccurate and shallow. For example, the Jewish leaders had quite an irreverent attitude toward marriage and divorce. This irreverent attitude toward this issue was very upsetting to Jesus. So, to drive this point home to the Jewish leaders, the Lord decided to address directly the specific and seriously sacred concept of marriage and divorce.

---

[140] Luke 16:17

"You are so wrong about so many issues," Jesus started to explain. "In one such example—and a major one, too—you have a dangerous, cavalier attitude toward divorce and remarriage. You have sanctioned divorces for the most ridiculous reasons. But the Gospel that I have preached has given a much deeper meaning to the seriousness of marriage than what you have taught the people. That is why I say, anyone who divorces his wife, except for adultery, and then marries another woman, has, in fact, committed adultery with that woman. And anyone who marries a woman who has been divorced from her husband—except, of course, for adultery—has committed adultery himself. The Gospel I've been preaching changes the life in such a way that couples, empowered by the Gospel, will remain married, happily living with each other." [*Harmony* 5:30, 31; 13:62-67][(s)] [141]

> In effect the Lord was saying, "Yes, you brag about your supposed profound and deep interpretations of various aspects of the Law. You try to give them deep meaning. But, in reality, your interpretations are shallow, even dangerously empty. For example, you often treat marriage laws with virtual contempt. However, My teachings are the ones—as opposed to yours—that truly give deep meaning to the Law. My teachings treat marriage and its laws with honor and respect. On the contrary, your teachings give the people nothing to help solve their marital problems. To many, then, divorce is the only option. On the other hand, My teachings have strengthened the marriage vow."[1]
>
> Next, Jesus came to the point in His discussion with the Jewish leaders where He needed to drive home dramatically the entire issue in unmistakable terms so that they could clearly see that their misinterpretations of the Scripture—and their resultant errors—had obviously placed them in grave danger, even to the extent of affecting their eternal destiny. To accomplish this, Jesus told another parable. In this parable, Jesus contrasted the situation of *two groups of people*. The first group was composed the Jewish leaders who considered themselves superior to nearly everyone else around them. In the parable, the Jewish leaders are compared to a certain Rich Man. The second group was made up of the common people as well as many others—the so-called "sinners" and most of the Gentiles. In the parable, this group of people—whom the leaders of Israel treated with distain—are compared to a certain Beggar named Lazarus. Sadly, the first group—the Jewish

[141] Luke 16:18

leaders—considered the second group—the common people, the sinners, and the Gentiles—to be almost unworthy of eternal life. Now, as the parable unfolds, in this life, the Jewish leaders—that is, the Rich Man—seemed to have it all—power, influence, and the hope of eternal life. At the same time the common people, the sinners, and the Gentiles—the Beggar Lazarus in the parable—appeared to have nothing—no power, no influence, and no real hope of eternal life.[2]

Jesus told a parable, saying, "Here's another story to illustrate your condition: I want you to suppose that there was a certain Rich Man. He was always dressed in rich clothes, even in royal purple. He even had fine linen undergarments—obviously the clothes of the very rich. Indeed, he was happy in his lifestyle. And he basked in the joy of living such a splendid life each and every day.(t) 142

"In this story, I would also like you to picture that there was a certain sickly Beggar whose body was covered with open wounds. His name was Lazarus. He often lay at the gate of the Rich Man's house so that he might beg for food and money. Lazarus was so famished that he was obsessed with the fantasy that he just might be able to eat some of the crumbs that fell from the Rich Man's feasting table. But alas, the Rich Man gave him nothing—not even crumbs from off his table. To make matters worse, vagabond dogs would come and lick Lazarus's wounds, making them even more infected."[143]

Thus far in the Lord's parable, Jesus contrasted, *in this life,* the situation of both groups of people whom he wanted to illustrate. Again, the "Rich Man" represented the Jewish leaders, and their pompous self-righteous lives. They had it all: possessions, power, and influence, and accordingly, a self-imposed security of eternal life. In the parable, such things are illustrated by the Rich Man's clothes, food, and joyful lifestyle. And, without question, this is how the Jewish leaders pictured themselves. Please note, though, that the elegant lifestyle of the Jewish leaders was just an illusion. That is, to those around them, they *appeared* to be rich and well-placed in society. But in *reality* they were far from how they *seemed* to appear. Indeed, because of their failure to assimilate into their lives true Biblical principles of living the Gospel, they were actually quite *spiritually* destitute. [Revelation 3:14-22] On the other

---

142 Luke 16:19

143 Luke 16:20, 21

hand, from the perspective of the Jewish leaders, the people they despised—the common people who followed Jesus, the sinners, and the Gentiles, who had also reached out to the Lord—had nothing: no possessions, power, or influence, and accordingly, they had little or no hope of eternal life. In the parable, these things are symbolized by Lazarus's poverty, hunger, and the sickly infected wounds that were licked by the dogs.[1]

Again, it must be noted that the condition of both groups of people as described by Jesus in the parable was from the *perspective of the Jewish leaders.* That is, *the Jewish leaders* considered *themselves* to be rich, while *they* looked upon the others around them as being *poor and sickly*, not even worthy of their care or concern—in either *spiritual* or *material* things. Of course, because the Jewish leaders constantly looked down upon those whom they considered of less value than themselves, it was natural for these people to lose confidence in ever being truly worthy of eternal life. However, when Jesus came and preached to them, hope began to spring up and blossom in their hearts. Nevertheless, because the Jewish leaders still relentlessly criticized these people, their hope in salvation continued to lag. That is why, as the parable indicated, Lazarus longed to eat of the crumbs that fell from the Rich Man's table—that is, the people who were despised by the Jewish leaders just hoped that something good, no matter how little, would happen to them. Additionally, the fact that the Rich Man never gave Lazarus anything from off his table—not even crumbs—indicated that the Jewish leaders never really provided any real, lasting hope to these poor individuals.[2]

"Now, in this story," Jesus continued with His parable, "Lazarus died. I want you to suppose that this poor man was carried by the angels to Paradise—sometimes symbolically called 'Abraham's bosom.' Now, imagine too, that the Rich Man died and was buried. He ended up in Hades—the place of fiery torment—where he was suffering in anguish, struggling with the guilt of having wasted his life in self-indulgence. As the Rich Man looked up, he saw Lazarus sitting in Paradise—that is again, in Abraham's bosom."[144]

Here, *in death,* the situation of both groups was obviously *completely switched.* The Rich Man—that is, the Jewish leaders—would be lost,

[144] Luke 16:22, 23

while Lazarus—the common people and the Gentiles who had reached out to Jesus—would be saved. The false teachings of the Jewish leaders ultimately led to their dismal end, while the true Gospel message taught by Jesus, joyfully accepted by the common people, led to their salvation.[1]

Please note, though, that the death of both individuals in the story does *not* represent death as we know it. No! Rather, in the parable, the situation in death of the Rich Man—in "Hades"—and Lazarus—in "Paradise"—represents what will happen to both groups of people during the *time of judgment at the end of the world.* That is, in the final judgment, the Jewish leaders would be lost, and the common people, and the Gentiles—who followed Jesus—would be saved, to enjoy the blessings of Paradise. In other words, what *appeared* to be true in *this* life—the Jewish leaders being rich and saved, and the common people and the Gentiles being poor and lost—was actually the *opposite* of what will happen when the God of heaven takes charge during the *final judgment.* It must be noted, then, that the reason both situations were reversed in "death" is because of the various attitudes each group had toward Jesus and His message. That is, in the first case, the Rich Man—the Jewish leaders—will be lost because they rejected Jesus and His Scripturally-based teachings. And, in the second case, Lazarus—the common people and the Gentiles who reached out to Jesus—would be saved because they had accepted the mercy of the Savior, as He taught it from the Scriptures. Yes, while in this life the Jewish leaders considered the common people and the Gentiles to be usually unworthy of eternal life, Jesus knew otherwise. And while the Jewish leaders in this life considered *themselves* to be worthy of everlasting life, Jesus, of course, knew otherwise!(u) [2]

"Well," Jesus went on, "the Rich Man called out, 'Father Abraham! Please have mercy on me! Send Lazarus to help me. Have him dip the tip of his finger in water, and with it, have him cool my tongue. As you can see, I am in dreadful agony in this fire!'"[145]

In *symbol,* the Rich Man, filled with remorse for his sinful life, now asks for mercy. However, it is of interest to note that the Rich Man did not call out for God to save him while he was in torment, but rather he

[145] Luke 16:24

> called out to "Father Abraham." This means that, in the final judgment, the Jewish leaders' confidence and faith will *still* be placed, not in a relationship with God, but in the fact that they were born as Jews—that is, the children of "Abraham." [*Harmony* 11:61] And the "agony in the fire" in the story *symbolically represents* the "torment" of the *realization the sinner will feel when he knows that he is lost* as the result of the final judgment of God. This is very similar to the "weeping and gnashing of teeth" anguish that is mentioned in other parables by Jesus. [*Harmony* 6:7; 7:35, 55; 14:84; 15:28, 50] Accordingly, then, the Rich Man's impassioned request to have Lazarus cool his tongue with water from the tip of his finger, *symbolizes* the great desire on behalf of those who are lost to have a second chance to repent during the judgment.

"But," the Lord continued, "Abraham answered the Rich Man, saying, 'My child, do remember that during your lifetime, you received all the good things that life had to offer. Isn't that right? But you failed to share these blessings'"—that is, the Jewish leaders failed to share their possessions *and* the truth of the Gospel with others. "'In the case of Lazarus, he received nothing good from life. Now the tables are turned'"—that is, the Jewish leaders are lost, and the common people and the Gentiles who reached out to Jesus are saved. "'The blessings you had in this life, he now has in eternity. Yes, he is now at peace, while you are suffering with the realization that you are lost! And besides, there is a huge gulf fixed between you and us. It is so large that no one is able to bridge the gap. You cannot come here. And, no one on this side can go over to where you are.'" Yes, in the final judgment, it will be too late to change reality—that is, those who are saved will stay saved, and those that are lost will stay lost.[146]

> Here, Jesus made it clear that how people relate to the things of this world will determine what will happen to them in the world to come. In this life, the Rich Man—the Jewish leaders—had every opportunity to accurately study the Scriptures which would result in their acceptance of the true message of the Gospel *as well as* a belief in the ministry of Jesus as the Messiah. But because of their failure to do so, they would be lost. In this life, Lazarus—the common people and the Gentiles—never were taught by the Jewish leaders the real truth regarding either the Gospel or the ministry of Jesus. However, before these people gave up in total despair, John the Baptist and Jesus came along to teach them the truth

[146] Luke 16:25, 26

and to give them hope that they could possess eternal life. And, in the final judgment, when the reward of everlasting life is given out, those who reached out to Jesus in faith will be saved! Also, in this part of the parable Jesus made it abundantly clear that there will no second chance during the time of the judgment. That is the meaning of the phrase, "a huge gulf fixed between you and us." People have only this lifetime in which to get ready for the Lord's coming and the final judgment.

Jesus went on with His story, describing what happened next. He said, "Well, the Rich Man responded to Abraham, saying, 'In that case, I beg of you, Father, that you send Lazarus to my father's house. You see, I have five brothers who are still alive. That way, Lazarus can warn them regarding their lifestyle, which is similar to the kind which I lived. Please have Lazarus tell them that if they don't change, they will end up where I am in this place of torment. They must be warned!'"[147]

This part of the parable—the Rich Man's urgent request that his brothers be warned—*symbolically* represents the Jewish leaders' continued insistence that they be given a second chance to repent in the final judgment. They will not take "No!" for an answer! Indeed, just as Jesus had made it clear in other parables and sayings [*Harmony* 5:81; 12:80-83], when people are lost in the judgment, some of them will cry out in grave protest and utter frustration, almost demanding another chance! As the Rich Man did, so will the Jewish leaders do the same! Knowing one is lost is certainly a devastating thought!

"But Abraham refused the Rich Man's request, saying, 'They have the Scriptures to read—Moses and the Prophets, as they are called. That will have to be sufficient for them.'"[148]

The crux of this part of the parable is this: *A correct understanding and acceptance of the Scriptures will prevent anyone from being lost!* That was what Jesus had always taught. [*Harmony* 3:97] Conversely, because the Jewish leaders had refused to study and teach accurately the Scriptures regarding the true Gospel message and the ministry of Jesus, they would be lost! Their woeful misapplications of the Word of God and its Gospel message—which led ultimately to their obsession with material

---

147 Luke 16:27, 28

148 Luke 16:29

things—was the cause of their condemnation in the judgment. But, on the opposite side, because many of the common people and the Gentiles believed and followed the words of John and Jesus, they, unlike many of the Jewish leaders, would be saved.

"Jesus continued with the parable, saying, 'No, Father Abraham!' the Rich Man protested, 'If someone coming back from the dead were to explain things to them, they would repent. I just know it!'"[149]

Two points are being made here. First, in the final judgment, the Rich Man—the Jewish leaders—will *unceasingly continue* to protest the fact that they are lost. [*Harmony* 5:80] But, of course, they will not be given a "second chance." It will be too late for them. Second, the Jewish leaders indicated that another miracle—such as someone being resurrected from the dead—would make a world of difference for them. Throughout the ministry of Jesus, the Jewish leaders had constantly demanded that the Lord perform a miracle to prove His authority. Indeed, the miracles He did perform never were quite able to satisfy them. "Just one more miracle—something big!" they demanded.

"Once more Abraham refused, saying, 'To be sure, if they are determined not to listen to the words of the Scriptures, they will not be convinced of the truth even if someone resurrected from the dead were to tell them!'" [*Harmony* 12:150/4][150]

Here, the Lord made it clear to the Jewish leaders, that because of their failure to accurately study the Scriptures, another miracle—no matter how big—would not be sufficient to help them to secure their salvation. Rather, Jesus emphasized that a correct understanding of the Scriptures—especially as it relates to the Gospel and the ministry of Jesus—forms the very foundation of what is necessary for salvation. In summary, no miracle—not even one as dramatic as a resurrection—will make up for the failure to study *and* follow the Scriptures correctly! Miracles, as such, do not save the soul! Salvation is the result of faith in the ministry of Jesus as has been described in the Scriptures. And it was, with no little irony, that soon after telling this parable, Jesus did actually raise someone from the dead—in fact, a man named Lazarus—and they

[149] Luke 16:30
[150] Luke 16:31

still did not believe in Jesus as the Messiah! [*Harmony* 13:24, 24/] It was just as Jesus had said: *If they could not believe in Him based upon the word of Scripture, they would not believe in Him even if someone did, indeed, come back from the dead!*[1]

This last exchange between the Rich Man and Abraham contains the thrust of the whole parable. By it, the Lord made it clear that people will be saved or lost by what they do in this life. As said before, there will be no second chance. They have only this lifetime in which to prepare for the world to come. It is a correct understanding of, and adherence to, the words of Scripture, and its Messiah, that makes eternal life possible for the believer. The Jewish leaders constantly besought Jesus to perform miracles for them so that they might believe in Him as the Messiah. But, while doing so, they ignored the clear statements of Scripture that pointed to the obvious fact that the Lord was, indeed, the Christ.[2]

Here is a summary of the entire parable: First, the Jewish leaders—like the Rich Man in the story—had lived a privileged life. They had had the opportunity to share the complete good news of the Scriptures with the common people and the Gentiles—that is, the Beggar Lazarus—in the story. But they—like the Rich Man—refused to do so. And what they actually taught from the Scriptures were things that only worsened the lives of their hearers. Indeed, they hardly ever presented truths that would strengthen and enrich the experiences of the people. Consequently, the common people, as well as the Gentiles whom the Jews ignored, lived in despair—just as in the case of the Beggar. And at the end of their lives, the Jewish leaders would be lost—as was the Rich Man—and the common people and the Gentiles, *now changed by the power of the Lord's teaching*, would be saved—as was the Beggar Lazarus. Simply put, because of the ministry of Jesus, everything will be reversed in the world to come, when compared to this world![3]

Second, instead of studying the Scriptures to learn the real truth regarding the ministry of Jesus [*Harmony* 3:97], the Jewish leaders constantly demanded that the Lord prove the veracity of His ministry by working miracles that would impress them. [*Harmony* 3:4; 7:14/; 9:33] Of course He did just that! Yet, instead of accepting the miracles as clear evidences of His authority, they constantly asked for even more miracles. So, in effect, Jesus was also saying through this story, "Miracles can never change the heart that has refused to accept the plain truth of the Word of God . . . and, it is foolish to even expect so. You must believe who I am based on the Scriptures as opposed to some miracle, or miracles, I might perform." Even though the Jewish leaders studied the Scriptures, they interpreted them in a legalistic and shallow way. [*Harmony* 12:137-141] They prided themselves on their interpretations of Scripture but never seemed to find the truth about Jesus or His powerful, transforming Gospel message in them. [*Harmony* 3:97] In short, Jesus condemned the Jewish leaders for the deeply flawed way that they studied and taught the Scriptures. Instead of demanding more and greater miracles from the Savior, they needed to more faithfully, diligently—and humbly—study the Scriptures to understand the real truths contained therein and accordingly follow them.[4]

Third, it is amazing that no more than several weeks after Jesus told this parable, a man named Lazarus was actually raised from the dead by Jesus [*Harmony* 13:1-30] . . . and the Jews still did not believe—just as Jesus had predicted![5]

(It should be noted that this unusual, even rather strange story Jesus told in this parable is fictitious. It should not be used as a description of what happens to people—both righteous and evil—when they die.)(v) [6]

An overall summary of the Lord's entire present discussion with the Jewish leaders is as follows: First, the Lord illustrated the Jews' faulty relationship with God by telling the parable of the Unfaithful Steward. [*Harmony* 12:124-135] Jesus, in this story drove home the point that the Jews had failed to fulfill their duty to be faithful stewards of the vital truths of Scripture and the Gospel message, by sharing them accurately with the Hebrew nation as well as with the Gentiles. Second, the Master emphasized the concept that the Jewish leaders had foolishly placed their passion upon acquiring the things of this world, rather than passionately, faithfully, and accurately interpreting—and living by—the truth of God. And in doing so they fatally rejected the Gospel—the teaching of both John the Baptist and Jesus. [*Harmony* 12:136-140] Third, the Savior *illustrated* His point that the Jewish leaders were really very poor and shallow interpreters of the Scriptures by showing how they had grossly and shamefully misinterpreted the true meaning of marriage and divorce. [*Harmony* 12:141] And fourth, Christ told the parable of the Rich Man and Lazarus to show how the Jews' failure to interpret the Scriptures accurately had caused those who depended upon them for understanding the truth to live desperate lives of despair. [*Harmony* 12:142-150] Further, by this parable Jesus demonstrated that because of their failure to be faithful to the Lord, the Jewish leaders had falsely placed their security both upon the acquisition of the things of this life and upon miracles—which they never really accepted anyway, especially the one involving the resurrection of Lazarus. In doing so, they failed to accurately interpret, believe, and follow the dictates of Scripture. *Indeed, the truth of Scripture must be the foundation of one's faith, not miracles, no matter how exciting they might be.* The final result of all of this was that the Jewish leaders were in eminent danger of losing their souls. Such was the sad condition of the people who should have understood the Gospel message the best, and then present it with great clarity to the world![7]

**— Forgiveness, Faith, and Duty**
**< Winter, A.D. 31(7/7) >**
**{Luke 17:1-10}**

When Jesus was alone with His disciples, He gave them counsel that He had previously given. [*Harmony* 10:100, 101] On this particular occasion, the Master said, "From time to time terrible things will happen to people that could cause them to become discouraged or perhaps even lose their faith. Maybe it will be some tragedy or severe illness that results in extreme distress in a person's life. These kinds of things, however, are usually unavoidable. But nevertheless, as a result of these difficult situations, people may be tempted, in despair, to fall back into sin. But, while this may happen, there is something I must tell you: Be careful that you, by evil word or action, are not the cause of someone's temptation or discouragement! You are to lift people up, and not knock them down. In fact, I will hold you responsible for causing someone to stumble needlessly or become discouraged. Yes, if you should cause someone to stumble needlessly, shame on you![151]

"In truth, you would be better off to have a large stone used for grinding wheat tied around your neck and be thrown into the sea than needlessly and selfishly cause one of My followers to stumble and fall. They are to be treated

151 Luke 17:1

with the type of tenderness that you would show to helpless little children. Yes, you are to gently lead people—not oppress them." [*Harmony* 10:97, 100][152]

Adding more counsel which He had discussed with His disciples on a previous occasion [*Harmony* 10:109-113], Jesus said, "Watch out! If your brother in the Gospel should sin against you, privately point out his mistake to him. And should he say, 'I'm sorry,' fully forgive him! In fact, even if he should sin against you seven times in a single day and should say, 'I repent,' each of those seven times, forgive him! Yes, forgiveness must be the rule that motivates your life." [*Harmony* 5:53; 10:112-118][153]

The disciples—the apostles—overwhelmed with the force of the Lord's counsel to them, realized that they were falling far short of the faith it took to comply with this powerful instruction. Therefore they pleaded with Him, saying, "Show us how to have more faith!"[154]

Jesus answered with an illustration, similar to one He had used before [*Harmony* 7:30; 12:76], saying, "If you had the faith of the size of a tiny mustard seed, you would be able to say to a black mulberry tree, 'Be ripped up from your roots and be thrown into the sea,' and it would do as you have commanded it. Of course, I don't want you to spend your time casting mulberry trees into the sea! I'm speaking about being able to grasp the power of faith to forgive others—the kind of forgiveness and compassion the world does not comprehend. To the world, to demonstrate such a forgiving faith is just as impossible—and ridiculous—as it would be by the mere force of words to uproot a tree and cast it into the sea. Do you understand that? [(w)] [155]

"Yes, what the world considers to be impossible you are to do as a natural course of action. That is the way it is with the Gospel. Let me tell you a story that makes My point: Which one of you, when hiring a servant to plow your field or tend your sheep, would say to him after only one day of work, 'Come right now, and recline on a couch and eat supper with me'?[156]

"No! Instead, you would say to him, 'Fix something for me to eat! Then, after putting on suitable clothes, serve me the meal of both food and drink. Only

---

152 Luke 17:2
153 Luke 17:3, 4
154 Luke 17:5
155 Luke 17:6
156 Luke 17:7

when I am finished with my meal, can you eat and drink something yourself.' Of course, neither would you go out of your way to thank that servant effusively for simply doing his duty as he was commanded, would you? That's the way it is with servants.[157]

"In a similar way when you as My servants, do the things that I have commanded you to do, don't constantly expect some special word of thanks from Me. You have simply done your duty as servants. Instead, you are to say, 'We deserve no special treatment! We have done only what we should have done.' Yes, again, that which the world considers *extraordinary*—such as forgiving others, and treating people with tender kindness—you are to treat as *ordinary*. That is the impact and power of the Gospel. Again, do you understand what I'm telling you?"[(x)] [158]

**Supplementary Notes:**

**(a) [12:3]** Even though the incident of John the Baptist teaching his disciples how to pray is not a part of the Gospel record, it is clear that whenever it happened, his disciples were deeply impressed. From the record, then, it is also clear that both John and Jesus were distinguished by their prayer life.

**(b) [12:9/2]** This is a shorter, less complete version of the so-called "Lord's Prayer." The longer version is found in *Harmony* 5:47-52.

**(c) [12:11]** To personalize the parable and give it more force, I changed the individual seeking help from a neighbor to "you"—that is, the listener, or reader—as opposed to just anyone asking for help.

**(d) [12:12/]** In this paragraph, I gave the explanation as though it was Jesus who was speaking. This, of course, was not in the original text. However, I believe that this paragraph fairly represents what might have been said, should He have given such an explanation.

**(e) [12:13]** The concept expressed in this paragraph could give the impression that all one needs to do is ask God for something, and He will comply with your request by giving it to you. However, life reveals that things do not happen so easily! It is clear, I would think, that it is implied in the text, that such requests and how they are answered are contingent upon the will of

---

157 Luke 17:8, 9
158 Luke 17:10

God. Nevertheless, I left the message of the text just as it was recorded. (See also **Note "w"** below, and **Note "s"** in Chapter 14, for more on this general subject.)

**(f) [12:14]** To make these verses more meaningful, I changed the illustration to read from "*a* father" to "*you,*" as a father.

**(g) [12:18+]** The general tenor of this section, as it relates to the discussion that took place between Jesus and the Jewish leaders is quite severe. This is not the first time such strong words were exchanged between the Lord and those who were seeking to do Him great harm (*Harmony* 11:8-32, 56-78). Neither would this be the last such time (*Harmony* 14:111-132). When one considers the meekness of Jesus during His trials (*Harmony* 17:45) and crucifixion (*Harmony* 17:116), such strong words may seem surprising—perhaps even shocking! Yet one must remember that during the time of the Lord's great sufferings, He was suffering and dying as the Sin Bearer. As the Scripture says (Isaiah 53:7), He died in silence. However, it should be noted that during the other portions of His ministry, He as the Messiah was clearly in charge and spoke to His enemies accordingly. In fact, it must be noted that even when He was quiet during the time of His sufferings and death, the Lord was still very much in charge. (Also see **Note "n"** at the end of Chapter 11.)

**(h) [12:28]** There is no known record of God saying such a thing. Perhaps Jesus was just speaking on behalf of God as though He was actually saying this. Or perhaps there was some such quote of which we are not presently aware. In any case, we don't know.

**(i) [12:38]** For more on the unpardonable sin, see *Harmony* 7:9-12, 17. The exact meaning of this concept has proved to be confusing to many people.

**(j) [12:49]** There is confusion as to whether Jesus was talking about one's height or the length of one's days or life. For the *Harmony,* I chose one's height as the Lord's topic of discussion.

**(k) [12:49]** The main concept found in these two verses (Luke 12:25, 26) was a bit hard for me to discover and interpret. In short, trying to relate clearly the meaning of both verses in the *Harmony* presented quite a challenge for me. I did the best I could, and am reasonably satisfied with my interpretation.

**(l) [12:51]** In this verse, Jesus used the word "little faith" as a nickname. That is, He called His listeners "little-faiths," rather than "people of little faith." (See also *Harmony* 5:65; 7:61-64.)

**(m) [12:61/]** As indicated, the precise meaning of the concepts "many lashes" and "few lashes" is quite puzzling to me. The way this is expressed in the parable leaves one at a loss to explain its meaning adequately. Could it be that there will be some kind of punishment in eternity actually meted out to those who are saved? To many that would seem to be unthinkable! Perhaps, though, the Lord was talking about degrees of joy in heaven. But how would such a thing be meted out by the Lord? I would suppose that this is one of the things that Jesus said that for now must remain a mystery.

**(n) [12:62]** The Lord places an awesome responsibility on those who are His leaders in the cause of the Gospel. (See **Note "g"** above, and **Note "n"** in Chapter 11 for more on this subject.)

**(o) [12:67]** To learn more about Pilate, see *Harmony* 17:60/1, 2.

**(p) [12:71/+]** In this case, the woman's demon possession resulted in a physical illness. I still maintain, though, that the woman's problem was demon possession, not the physical malady demonstrated through it. (See also **Note "f"** in Chapter 4.)

**(q) [12:123/]** Actually Jesus was somewhat easy on the Jewish leaders when He compared them to the brother who stayed home! While their attitude toward converted sinners was accurately described in the parable, when their attitude is compared to that of the older brother, they were not nearly as obedient to God as the older brother was to his father!

**(r) [12:123/2+]** This section of the *Harmony* contains roughly four parts: (1) The parable of the unjust steward (12:124-137); (2) A discussion about the veracity of John the Baptist and the Lord's own ministry (12:138-140); (3) A discussion of divorce and re-marriage (12:141); and (4) The parable of the Rich Man and Lazarus (12:142-150). Usually, these stories and events are studied and discussed separately. But, in truth, I believe the real thrust of this entire section is best understood when all four of the above parts are studied as a *group, and in order*. This is what I attempted to do in the *Harmony*, and I would suggest that the reader do the same. The basic message of the two parables (especially that of the Rich Man and Lazarus) are difficult enough to understand when studied together, let alone separately! That is why I have, of necessity, included within this section a number of additional paragraphs to clarify, as I see it, the overall message the Lord sought to teach.

**(s) [12:141]** For more on divorce and re-marriage, see *Harmony* 5:30, 31; 13:62-71. Also, especially see **Note "h"** in Chapter 13.

**(t) [12:142]** Some have suggested that this story is not a parable, but, rather, a true description of the state of men in death—both those who are righteous or evil. I do not agree. While I must admit, this is a *most unusual parable*, it is, nevertheless a parable. The story begins with the phrase: "There was a certain rich man . . ." This is the kind of introduction one would expect Jesus might use when beginning a parable. For this and other reasons, I am convinced this story *is* a parable, and accordingly, not given by Jesus to teach His listeners the truth regarding the state of men in death, but rather other truths discussed in the *Harmony* both within and at the end of the parable. Further, the description in the story—of Paradise and hell—is not at all consistent with the overall Biblical teaching on these subjects. Again, the main purpose of this story, rather, was to teach the fact that people need to decide for the truth based upon the weight of Biblical evidence, not on some miracle they might see or experience. Specifically, the people were to believe that Jesus was the Messiah, based upon their diligent study of the evidence of the prophecies of Scripture, as they were compared to the actual details of the Lord's life. The Jewish demand for more and more powerful miracles was not a basis for a valid belief. In fact, Jesus would actually bring a man named Lazarus back from the dead (*Harmony* 13:1-30), and the people still would not believe in Him!

So then, why did the Lord use this story if it was fictitious and inaccurate in its description of the true condition of those who have died? Why did He do it? The answer to these questions is a bit uncertain. However, there is evidence that the belief in Paradise and hell, as graphically described in the story, was, indeed, a part of the philosophical thought regarding the afterlife as taught by *some liberal* Jews in the days of Jesus. In truth, there were many things taught by some Jews that were quite contrary to true Scriptural teachings. Some of these things, including the philosophies of death as depicted in this parable, were, in reality, clearly based upon pagan thought. So it appears, then, that Jesus used one of the Jews' own *false* teachings of His day to instruct the people in the way of *truth!* It is interesting to note that in a portion of ancient writings, often ascribed to the noted Jewish historian of the first century, Flavius Josephus, is described a *Jewish* belief of Hades (hell) and Paradise that reads strikingly similarly to the concept Jesus gave in His parable. This gives credence to the idea that Jesus borrowed a *false* teaching of the Jews of His day as a vehicle to instruct them regarding the *truths* He presented within His parable. Here are some of the words and/or concepts found in the writings of Josephus that *directly parallel* the words of the parable of Lazarus and the Rich Man, as contained in Luke 16:19-31: (1) Hades (or hell), as the place of punishment and torment for the wicked dead (verses 23-25); (2) Paradise (also Abraham's bosom), as the place of comfort for the righteous dead (verse 22 and 25); (3) The angels carry the righteous dead to Paradise (verse 22); and (4) A great gulf (or chaos) is fixed between the two places, obviously preventing an individual from moving from one place to the other (verse 26). Again, all four of the above are found *both* in the writings of Josephus and the Biblical account of the parable of Lazarus and the Rich Man. It must be noted that nowhere else in Scripture are such concepts found to describe these details regarding those who have died. Yes, there will be a place called hell (the Greek word "gehenna," not "hades"), where the wicked will be burned. But this takes place *after* the Second Coming of Jesus, *not before*. (*Harmony* 15:55) Also, the reward of the righteous—that is, to live forever with Jesus—is given at the Second Coming, and not before. (*Harmony* 10:59)

I must conclude, then, that this story is a parable, based upon a *false* teaching of the Jews—a false teaching, no doubt, that the Jewish leaders who heard Jesus tell this parable would have been familiar with. It is a story that was used by Jesus to teach a *truth*—that is, in part, one must accept Jesus based upon the study of the Word of God, not by demanding or depending upon miracles, as the Jews of the Lord's day did. Yes, indeed, it is a most unusual parable . . . but nevertheless, a parable!

Indeed, there are some aspects of this story (of Luke 16:19-31) that indicate that Jesus intended it to be understood as a parable, and is not to be taken as a literal story of an actual event—that is, one that teaches various doctrinal truths regarding death and/or hell. Here are some things that indicate that this story is a *fictitious* parable: (1) The basic sense of the phrase "There was a certain rich man . . . ," was commonly used by Jesus to begin a parable (verse 19); (2) As a contradiction, the rich man was "buried" and yet he is in "hell" (verses 22 and 23); (3) That Abraham's bosom was large enough to hold all the righteous (verse 22) is foolish; and (4) For the rich man to believe that a mere drop of water from the tip of Lazarus's finger would really cool him off (verse 24) is ridiculous, and can hardly be taken literally. In summary, it is clear to me that this story is not to be taken literally, but should be understood as a parable teaching truths other than the condition of men in death.

And finally, why did I suggest that the death of Lazarus and the Rich Man in the parable, represent the *final judgment,* as opposed to death, as we know it? (See *Harmony* 12:144/.) I did so for two reasons: (1) Nowhere else in the Bible is death in this world explained or described the way it is in this parable—no burning hell, and so forth. In short, such a description does not fit the regular pattern of the Bible in this regard. And (2), applying it to the final judgment fits rather nicely the various other descriptions Jesus gives about the final judgment elsewhere in His other parables and teachings, as it relates to those who are lost, complaining that they deserved a second chance (*Harmony* 5:80, 81; 12:80-82; 15:37-41).

**(u) [12:144/]** (See above.)

**(v) [12:150/5]** (See **Note "t"** above.)

**(w) [12:155]** This concept of having the faith the size of a mustard seed which would give one the power to cast a tree into the sea, is, in my opinion, tough to interpret and explain adequately. For more on this, see **Note "e"** above, and **Note "s"** in Chapter 14.

**(x) [12:158]** The Lord expressed an unusual concept here: *that we are not to expect thanks for what we do for the Lord.* While I think we should thank people for their faithfulness in the cause of God, we should not expect it, or become unduly upset if it doesn't happen. Besides, the Lord's main point here was to teach that doing what the world might consider *extraordinary* in the work of the Lord—such as treating one another with compassion and forgiveness—is to be *ordinary* with us. And, too, in eternity the Lord will *more than adequately* give us thanks for what we have faithfully done for Him.

# CHAPTER THIRTEEN

## THE FINAL, SLOW TRIP TO JERUSALEM —
**From the Raising of Lazarus, to the Parable of the Nobleman and His Money**

**(Late Winter, A.D. 31 — Just Before Passover, Spring, A.D. 31)**

### The Raising of Lazarus; the Jewish Leaders Plot the Death of Jesus; the Lord Relocates to Ephraim
**< Late Winter, A.D. 31 (7/7) >**
**(John 11:1-57)**

### — The Raising of Lazarus
**< Late Winter, A.D. 31 (7/7) >**
**{John 11:1-46}**

About two miles southeast of Jerusalem was the village of Bethany. In that town lived Lazarus, along with his sisters, Martha and Mary. This was the same Martha and Mary in whose home Jesus visited some weeks previously when Mary sat at His feet. [*Harmony* 11:162-164] And, this was the same Mary who would later anoint the feet of Jesus with precious perfume—pure nard—while she wiped His feet with her hair. [*Harmony* 14:1-4] Jesus had a very close relationship with these three siblings. In fact, it was commonly known that Jesus especially loved them.[(a)] [1]

But Lazarus was gravely ill. Deeply concerned, Martha and Mary sent someone to find where Jesus was ministering, to inform Him of Lazarus's sickness. The messenger found the Lord as He was preaching and teaching in the nearby region of Peraea, about some 25 miles to the northeast beyond the Jordan River. The messenger said to Jesus, "Lord, You need to know: Lazarus, whom You dearly love, is gravely ill!"[(b)] [2]

---

1 John 11:1, 2, 5

2 John 11:1-3

As soon the Savior heard this urgent message, He responded, saying, "Don't worry! This is not an illness that will end in the death of My friend. Rather, his sickness will result in great praise for God. And, by it, the Son of God"—referring to Himself—"will also be honored." But, instead of going quickly to be with Lazarus, Jesus, a bit surprisingly, remained two days longer in the area where He was laboring.[3]

After the two days had passed, Jesus told the disciples, "Let's go to Judea again!"[4]

But the disciples protested, "Teacher! Remember that the Jews tried to stone you the last time you went to Judea. [*Harmony* 11:165-175] That was just a few months ago. You are not really thinking about going back to that province again so soon, are You?" [*Harmony* 13:107/][5]

Jesus answered cryptically, "There are twelve hours of daylight in each day, aren't there? This means that if anyone walks while it is daylight, he will not trip over anything, for he is able to see where he is going. The sunlight in the daytime will certainly shine on the path on which he walks. On the other hand, at nighttime, when everything is dark, a person might trip over something that is in his path. Of course this is true because there is not enough light to illuminate his way." [*Harmony* 13:11][6]

> In effect, Jesus was saying, "Don't be concerned. My time to die has not yet arrived. There are twelve hours of light in a day, is that not so? Well, as long as I continue to be the Light of world, there will be people who will appreciate My work and follow My words, and the Jews cannot touch Me. Yes, there is still daylight in which I can work! But, when night comes—that is, when My work is finished—then they will totally reject Me and murder Me! But until then, it will be quite safe for Me to go to Judea."

After saying these things, Jesus paused briefly. Then He added, "Our good friend, Lazarus, is just asleep. I will go now and awaken him out of his sleep!"[7]

---

3 John 11:4, 6
4 John 11:6, 7
5 John 11:8
6 John 11:9, 10
7 John 11:11

The disciples, relieved concerning the condition of Lazarus, answered, "Well, that's good then! If Lazarus is just sleeping, he certainly will be getting better soon."[8]

Of course, what the disciples did not understand is that when Jesus spoke of Lazarus being "asleep," He meant that Lazarus was dead—that is, Jesus was comparing death to a sleep. The disciples obviously thought that Jesus was referring to literal sleep.[9]

> Why is it that Jesus referred to death as only being asleep? From the perspective of the Lord, it would just as easy for Jesus to resurrect someone from the dead as it would be for a person to awaken someone who is sleeping in a normal way! That is why Jesus compared death to a sleep. [*Harmony* 8:17, 17/]

But to make sure that the disciples did not misunderstand the intent of His words, Jesus stated unequivocally, "Lazarus is dead!" That removed all doubt for the disciples. Jesus concluded, "I am very happy for you that I was not there before Lazarus died. This way, you will be blessed by what I am planning to do. As a result, your faith will be greatly strengthened. So now, let's go to him!"[10]

As Jesus and the disciples headed off toward Bethany, the disciples' concern for Lazarus was replaced by a concern for both Jesus and themselves. They either had not understood the Lord's explanation that nothing of danger would happen to them on this particular trip to Judea [*Harmony* 13:6], or they did not accept His confidence in His safety as being valid. For, whatever the case might have been, one of the disciples, Thomas—also known as Didymus, the "Twin"—commented, rather fatalistically, to the other eleven, "Well, let us go on to Bethany, so that we may die with Him!" [*Harmony* 13:107/][11]

After traveling the 25 some miles from Peraea to Judea, Jesus and the disciples arrived near Bethany. Upon His arrival at the outskirts of the village, the Lord was informed that Lazarus was already dead. In fact, he had been in the tomb for four days.[(c)] [12]

---

8 John 11:12
9 John 11:13
10 John 11:14, 15
11 John 11:16
12 John 11:17

Lazarus was well known, not only in Bethany, but also in Jerusalem, just two miles away. The news of his death had spread to the largest city of Israel. Many of the family's Jewish friends—including some of the leadership of Israel—had come from Jerusalem to comfort Martha and Mary for the loss of their brother.[13]

When Martha heard that Jesus was in the vicinity, she went out to greet Him somewhere outside of the town. However, Mary, overwhelmed with grief, remained at home, sitting by herself. When Martha met the Savior, she exclaimed, "Lord! If You had only been here, I know that Lazarus would not have died! I know that, even now, whatever You ask of God, He will do for You." [*Harmony* 13:26] No doubt Martha was hinting that she had the confidence that Jesus could resurrect Lazarus if He chose to do so. She surely knew that at least on two other occasions [*Harmony* 8:15-18; 6:20, 21], Jesus had, indeed, resurrected individuals.[14]

Jesus answered, "Your brother will indeed rise again!"[15]

Martha was unsure as to what Jesus meant by this statement. It was not clear from His words whether He intended to resurrect Lazarus at that time or at the resurrection at the end of the world. So she replied, "Of course, I know that he will rise again in the resurrection at the end of the world." [1 Thessalonians 4:16-18] Perhaps with this response Martha thought that Jesus might be more specific as to what His intentions were.[(d)] [16]

Still, Jesus did not tell Martha what His plans were. However, He sought to build more confidence in her. Jesus declared, "I, Myself, am the resurrection and the life! He who trusts in Me will live again, even after he has died. And everyone who lives for Me, and also believes in Me, shall not die the eternal death." That is to say, everyone who places their trust in the Lord during their lifetime, will never suffer eternal death, for they shall be resurrected at the end of time, to live forever. "Martha," Jesus asked, "do you believe this?"[17]

---

13 John 11:18, 19
14 John 11:20-22
15 John 11:23
16 John 11:24
17 John 11:25, 26

"Of course I believe!" Martha confirmed. "Yes, Lord, I have always believed that You are the Christ—the Messiah, even the Son of God—and that You are the One who has come into this world to save it!"[18]

Jesus then asked where Mary was. At that point Martha left Jesus and returned to her home to inform Mary about Jesus' arrival, saying, "The Teacher is here and He is asking that you come to Him." Martha had secretly given Mary this message, for she did not want the many mourners that were trying to console her in the house to follow along when Mary went to see the Lord. She hoped that Mary could have a private meeting with Jesus where He was outside the town. Nevertheless, when Mary left at Martha's request to find the Lord, the crowd did in fact follow her. But they mistakenly said, "She is going back to the tomb to weep for her brother there."[19]

Soon Mary found Jesus where He was waiting for her. Seeing the Lord, Mary fell down at His feet, lamenting, "Oh Lord! If only You had been here earlier, my brother would have not died!"[20]

As she bowed low at His feet, Jesus saw her weeping. This deeply touched His heart, causing Him great pain, for He knew that her heart was breaking. Then the Lord looked around and saw many of the Jewish mourners also weeping. His reaction to their sorrow was very different from His reaction to Mary's crying. Instead, He felt great anguish and distress, even indignation![21]

> Why did Jesus react the way He did when He saw the weeping crowd? It was because He knew that many of them where hypocritical. Some, perhaps, were even then plotting His death. They did not accept Him as the Messiah, as did Martha and Mary. Obviously, they did not accept the things which He did as being genuine either. In fact, most of them would never accept Him or His work.

After meditating for a bit, Jesus asked them, "Where is it that you have laid Lazarus?"[22]

---

18 John 11:27
19 John 11:28-31
20 John 11:32
21 John 11:33
22 John 11:34

"Lord, come and see for Yourself," they all answered.[23]

They could see that Jesus was openly crying. Some of the Jews said among themselves, "My, He must have really loved that man!" While it is true that Jesus loved Lazarus, that is not the reason why He was weeping, for, after all, He was planning on resurrecting Lazarus in a few moments! His weeping was rather the result of His sadness over the fact that most of the people in the crowd that day did not accept Him as the Messiah. Some in the crowd declared, "Why hadn't this Man, who supposedly is able to make a blind man see, been able to keep Lazarus from dying? He can't be genuine!" Indeed, their lack of trust in Him caused great grief within the Lord's heart, for such a lack of faith would lead them to be eternally lost. Thus, Jesus was overwhelmed with emotion. While He sympathized with real sorrow for His beloved friends, Martha and Mary, He was deeply wounded by the lack of faith of many of the Jews who were there that day. Overall, it was a very emotional time for the Lord! [*Harmony* 12:150/][24]

> No doubt, Jesus was particularly sad, because, after over three years of ministry, so very few people had truly accepted Him as the Messiah. Most of Israel—especially the Jewish leadership—had rejected Him. And the reaction of the leaders had had a very negative effect upon many of the people who had been listening to Him. A short time before, the Lord had spoken directly to the Jewish leaders about their dire spiritual condition. To drive home His point, Jesus had told two dramatic parables: the Dishonest Steward and the Rich Man and Lazarus. Besides these parables, Jesus gave strong counsel to the Jewish leaders regarding their clear failure as the Lord's representatives on earth. At that time, the Savior indicated that even the miracle of a resurrection—even a man named Lazarus—would not be enough to rouse the Jews from their evil ways. [*Harmony* 12:123/3-150/7] Now Jesus was on the verge of performing this miracle of the resurrection of a man named Lazarus. And sadly, He knew that the Jewish leaders would still remain defiant and unbelieving even after seeing this mighty miracle. The eternal destiny of the Jewish leaders was headed for disaster!

---

23 John 11:34

24 John 11:35-37

Still overcome with emotion, Jesus arrived at the tomb. The tomb itself was actually a cave with a large stone rolled in front of its entrance. Jesus commanded, "Remove the rock away from the entrance!"[25]

Martha, who had been hoping that Jesus might resurrect Lazarus, seemed to weaken in her confidence [*Harmony* 13:14], for she answered, "But, Lord, the odor must be overwhelming! It's been four days since his death!"[26]

Jesus gently chided her, "Martha, did I not say that if you believe, you would see the glory of God? Roll away the stone!"[27]

Accordingly, the people rolled the rock away from the opening of the tomb where they had laid Lazarus. Then Jesus, lifting His eyes toward heaven, prayed openly to God, saying, "My Father, I do thank You that You have heard My voice. I know that You will always hear Me. But because there are so many here who do not believe that We are one, I have said these things in front of them so that they might believe that it is You who have sent Me to this world." [*Harmony* 3:89] Then after pausing for a second, Jesus gave a loud, clarion call, "Lazarus, come out of there!" [*Harmony* 14:2][28]

> So determined was the Lord to see even the Jewish leaders repent of their wicked ways that He openly prayed to His Father that the resurrection of Lazarus, soon to take place, would encourage them to change their sinful ways of thinking.

Presently, Lazarus—who, of course, had been dead—staggered out of the tomb, with his hands and feet wrapped with burial clothes! His face was also covered with a face cloth. "Unbind him and allow him to go free!" Jesus told the crowd. So some in the multitude unbound Lazarus.[29]

Not surprisingly, many of the Jews—including some of the leaders—who had come to comfort Mary, when seeing this incredible miracle, believed that Jesus was the Messiah. Also not surprisingly, there were some of the Jews in the

---

25 John 11:38, 39
26 John 11:39
27 John 11:40
28 John 11:41-43
29 John 11:44

crowd, filled with disdain, who went to tell the Pharisees in Jerusalem what Jesus had just done. [*Harmony* 13:37; 14:25, 35][(e) 30]

While Jesus had previously resurrected two other individuals—Jairus's daughter and the son of the widow of Nain—this resurrection of Lazarus was special. Why was that? In the case of Jairus's daughter, just a few were in the room at the time. It was really a private resurrection. [*Harmony* 8:15-18] In the case of the son of the widow of Nain, even though this resurrection was performed in public, the town of Nain was small and far away from the larger groups of people. [*Harmony* 6:20, 21][[1]]

The resurrection of Lazarus, though, was performed, not only in public but also before a large crowd of people—including many of the Jewish leaders. And, it was performed just two miles from the main city of Israel. In addition, Lazarus was a well-known member of his community. No doubt, there were many of society's important people watching when Jesus resurrected Lazarus. And finally, Lazarus's resurrection took place at a time in the Lord's ministry when interest in His work was at a high point—when many were wondering and deciding if He was truly the Messiah. That being the case, the resurrection of the Lord's special friend served as a foretaste of the drama and interest that will take place when the Lord resurrects all his dead followers at the end of the world. [1 Thessalonians 4:16] In a certain sense, then, the resurrection of Lazarus was the crowning achievement of His entire ministry, as it related to His miracles. This was particularly true because this resurrection took place four days after Lazarus had died, providing incontrovertible evidence of the authenticity of Jesus' ability to bring to life those who had died.[[2]]

### — The Jewish Leaders Plot the Death of Jesus
### < Late Winter, A.D. 31 (7/7) >
### {John 11:47-57}

Reports of the resurrection of Lazarus were borne by the Jewish leaders, who had witnessed the miracle, to their fellow leaders back in nearby Jerusalem. It was felt that a meeting of the Jewish Council, the Sanhedrin, needed to be convened. [*Harmony* 16:85][31]

---

30 John 11:45, 46

31 John 11:47

The Sanhedrin was composed of the most powerful and influential leaders of Israel. There were, of course, the religious conservatives, the Pharisees, who, for some time, had been trying to find a way to kill Jesus. But on this occasion, many of the chief priests—the Sadducees—were also enraged at this particular action of Jesus. The Sadducees were much more liberal in their beliefs than were the Pharisees. Among their beliefs was a denial of the resurrection of the dead. Of course, with the actual resurrection of Lazarus, one of their pet theories was effectively debunked. This caused great anguish among this class of Jewish leaders. Normally, there was a great deal of dispute between these two groups of rulers. But, in this case, they were united in their animosity against the Savior. [*Harmony* 14:93-106]

Once they were gathered together, there was a lot of hand-wringing among them. Some moaned and said, "What are we going to do? This Man is working so many miracles! If we allow Him to continue to do this, all the people will follow after Him! Then there will be an uprising, and once the Romans find out, they will take away our power as leaders over the people. They will also take away the little national independence that we now possess. Indeed, what will we do? On the other hand, if we arrest Him, there's no telling what the people who passionately love Him will do to us. It is such a tough choice for us to make." [*Harmony* 14:51][32]

Because Israel was under the control of the Roman Empire, the Jewish leaders were limited in their authority. Nevertheless, except in capital offenses—involving the death penalty—the Jews were allowed to exercise considerable authority in their own affairs as a nation. However, their fear that the actions of the people who followed Jesus would lead to some kind of a national uprising, bringing the wrath of the Romans down on the entire nation, was clearly unfounded. There never was anything that Jesus had ever done that would have caused the Roman authorities any genuine concern. To blame Jesus for a potential conflict with Rome's authority was very unfair. Nevertheless, in their personal, blind rage against the Lord, they tried to blame Him for any future problems they *might* have with Rome!

As the Jewish leaders were lamenting the situation, Caiaphas the High Priest at that time [*Harmony* 17:25], interrupted them and declared, "What's

---

[32] John 11:47, 48

the matter with you? You're allowing your worries to dull your thinking. There is a solution here, if we just think it through. Think now! It is better for one Man to die on behalf of all the people than for the whole nation to be destroyed. Isn't that right?" Caiaphas implied that it would be better for Jesus to die than for the entire nation to be further persecuted by the Romans. He suggested that Jesus should be offered as a "sacrificial lamb," so to speak, so as to save the nation. But while Caiaphas spoke these words from the depths of his evil motivations, there was also a spiritual, prophetic tone to them, well beyond what the High Priest had realized. And what was that? Indeed, Jesus would die for all the people of Israel—that is, He would die for their sins, substituting His life for the lives of His people! [Isaiah 53:4-7] But not only would Jesus die for the sins of the people of the nation of Israel, He would also die for the sins of all the peoples of the whole world. The result of His sacrifice—as the *sacrificial* "Lamb of God" [*Harmony* 2:49]—would lead to the gathering together of all of God's children scattered around the world. Truly, Jesus would be the real "sacrificial lamb" who would die for the sins of the whole world. Yes, Caiaphas, the High Priest during that fateful year of the Lord's death, did not realize just how prophetic his wickedly motivated remarks truly were![33]

From that moment on, all the Jewish leaders were both unified and determined in figuring out a way to kill Jesus. Indeed, up until now, *some* of the Jewish leaders had been determined to kill Jesus. But from now on, virtually *all* of Israel's leaders—both Pharisees and Sadducees alike—were bent on seeing Jesus killed. [*Harmony* 16:85][34]

### —Jesus Relocates to Ephraim
### < Late Winter, A.D. 31 (7/7) >
### {John 11:54-57}

The place of the resurrection of Lazarus, Bethany, was just two miles from where the Sanhedrin was plotting the Savior's death. Jesus knew that He would die at the upcoming Passover in Jerusalem just a few weeks away. So, in the interim, Jesus relocated to a town named Ephraim. This village, near a wilderness, was about 15 miles or so north of Jerusalem. There the Jewish leaders would have a hard time finding Him. During the Lord's sojourn there, He no longer mingled among the Jewish people. Instead, He was primarily alone with His disciples.[35]

---

33 John 11:49-52
34 John 11:53
35 John 11:54

With the Jewish Passover soon to take place, many of the Jews of the entire region were making their way to Jerusalem to prepare themselves for this particular spring festival. This preparation involved a ceremonial cleansing of themselves. [Numbers 9:10; 2 Chronicles 30:17-20; *Harmony* 17:60][36]

As many people began to gather in the Temple area of Jerusalem, they were looking around to see if Jesus might be there. Not surprisingly, then, the discussion in the Temple area centered on Jesus as to where He might be as well as to what He might do. Everything had been building to a fever pitch brought on in no small way by the miracle of Lazarus's resurrection. [*Harmony* 13:1-30] The people said to one another, "What do you think? Jesus won't show up around here for the feast, will He? Certainly He knows better than that!"[37]

By now, too, it was common knowledge that the Sanhedrin, composed of the chief priests and Pharisees, had issued a decree regarding Jesus and His whereabouts. They had declared that if anyone knew where He was staying, such an individual was required to inform the leaders so that they might gives orders to have Him promptly arrested. To be sure, Jesus was a "marked Man"![38]

## The Lord's Roundabout Journey to Jerusalem for His Final Passover < Early Spring, A.D. 31 (7/7) > (Matthew 19:3-20:34; Mark 10:2-52; Luke 17:11-19:28)

### —Jesus Heals Ten Lepers < Early Spring, A.D. 31 (7/7) > {Luke 17:11-19}

After staying briefly in Ephraim, Jesus traveled one last time through the central part of Israel. He was walking along the border that separates Samaria to the south from Galilee to the north. This was about 40 miles north of Jerusalem. After spending a short time there, He planned on heading south and then slowly make His way back to Jerusalem, to arrive there less than a week before the annual Passover Festival.[39]

While still on the border between Samaria and Galilee, the Lord was about to enter a certain village. There He met 10 men who were suffering from leprosy,

---

[36] John 11:55
[37] John 11:56
[38] John 11:57
[39] Luke 17:11

the most dreaded disease of the ancient world. [*Harmony* 4:35] This disease was extremely horrid and known to be highly contagious. Lepers would congregate together, being total outcasts from regular society. Standing some distance from Him—as was required by the law [Leviticus 13:45, 46]—these 10 lepers loudly called out to Him, saying, "Jesus! Master! Please show us some mercy!" This was their way of asking the Lord if He would be willing to heal them of their dreaded disease.[(f)] [40]

Christ saw the lepers. He also heard their plea. So He said to them, "Go now, and show yourselves to the priests." Accordingly to Jewish law [Leviticus 13], anyone who thought himself to be cured of leprosy needed to present himself before a priest to be certified that he or she was truly healed of the disease. As soon as Jesus commanded that they comply with the law's requirement regarding leprosy, they immediately started out to find a priest for such an inspection. And at that same instant, they were all healed of their leprosy![41]

One of the 10 lepers, when he realized that he had been healed, turned around and headed back to Jesus. On the way he loudly praised God for his healing. Once again in the presence of the Lord, the former leper fell on his face before the Savior, personally thanking Him for His act of kindness in healing him. This man was a Samaritan. The other nine former lepers were Jews.[42]

Jesus took note of the thankfulness of the Samaritan leper. He commented, "Were there not 10 of you whom I healed? But the other nine . . . where are they? Was there no one else, except this non-Jew, to give thanks? Why did not the others return and give praise to God?" To the Samaritan, Jesus added, "Stand up! Go to the priest. Your faith has made you clean from this disease."[43]

### — The Lord Explains the Meaning of the Words, "The Kingdom of God"
### < Early Spring, A.D. 31 (7/7) >
### {Luke 17:20-37}

> Throughout His entire ministry, Jesus often referred to the kingdom of God, or the kingdom of heaven. It was a recurring theme of His teaching and preaching. What did the Lord mean by this phrase? It

---

40 Luke 17:11-13
41 Luke 17:14
42 Luke 17:15, 16
43 Luke 17:16-19

> referred to two things. First, it described the thrust of His ministry while He was here on the earth, which included the preaching of the Gospel message. When someone accepted the truths which the Lord taught, within his or her life, that person became a part of the kingdom of God, or heaven. This could be called the "kingdom of grace"—that is, one's personal acceptance of the power of the Gospel into the life, resulting in a transformation of one's entire being and character. Second, the phrase could also refer to the time when the Lord would establish His eternal kingdom at His Second Coming. Thus, this phase of the kingdom can be called the "kingdom of glory." [*Harmony* 4:4/; 7:23/]

For many of the Lord's listeners, there was some confusion in their understanding as to what Jesus meant by the words, "kingdom of heaven." So it was, during His journey on His way to Jerusalem for the last time, that some Pharisees questioned Jesus regarding His understanding of this phrase, as to what it meant and when such a kingdom would arrive. Christ answered the question by explaining, "The kingdom of God is not something that comes in a way that can be easily discerned or observed. It is not something of which one can say, 'Look! Here it is,' or 'There it is.' No! Rather, the kingdom of God is within you. It is in your heart and mind."(g) [44]

> Here, the Lord was talking about a heart religion as opposed to some earthly political kingdom. No doubt the Jewish leaders were curious as to the meaning Jesus attached to this phrase—and the similar one, the "kingdom of heaven"—which He often used in His preaching and parables. They wanted to know if He intended to establish some type of *literal* kingdom as they had figured the Messiah would do. Here, instead, Jesus was clearly referring to the "kingdom of grace" that is established in an individual's heart at conversion. [*Harmony* 13:43/]

After the Pharisees left, Jesus continued to talk about this issue with His disciples. In this discussion Jesus emphasized the establishment of the kingdom of *glory* that would take place when He returned to this earth many years later at His Second Coming. Some days later, Jesus would repeat a number of these same concepts to His disciples. [*Harmony* 15:4-31] On this occasion, He explained, "The time will come when you will greatly desire to see the day when the Son of Man establishes His glorious kingdom at the end of the world. However, it will not happen nearly as quickly as you wish! Some, growing impatient, will say,

---

44 Luke 17:20, 21

'Look here!' or 'Look there!' But I say, do not listen to them nor follow after them. And why is that? My coming will not be secret, or in one place as opposed to another. In fact, when I actually do come, everyone, everywhere, will know it. It will be like lightning. You know that when lightning flashes, its light shines from one end of the heavens to the other. Isn't that right? That's the way it will be in the day when the Son of man comes—His Coming will be seen from one end of the heavens to the other.[45]

"But until then, for now, the Son of Man must be rejected by the people of this generation. And He will suffer much at their hands." [*Harmony* 7:14; 10:55-61, 84; 13:99, 100; 15:59] Here, of course, Jesus referred to His impending sufferings and death.[46]

"But let's return again to the subject of the end of the world when the Son of Man comes," Jesus continued. "That time in history will be like the time when Noah lived on this earth. [Genesis 6:1-5] Back then, as you know, the people were spending all their time and passion in eating and drinking, marrying and being given in marriage . . . that is, until the day that Noah entered his big boat. Then soon after that, the flood waters came and drowned them all. [Genesis 7:13-23; *Harmony* 15:23][47]

"The day of the coming of the Son of Man will also be similar to the days of Lot of old times. The people of those days were obsessed with eating and drinking, buying and selling, planting crops, and building houses. That was their whole life. They had no time left for God. So of course they were not prepared. For on the day that Lot escaped from Sodom, fiery sulfur rained down from the heavens and burned all of them to nothingness. [Genesis 18:16-19:29] Yes, it will be the same as that in the day when the Son of Man comes to this earth again. People will be unprepared, for they will have been totally involved in the things of this life. [*Harmony* 15:13][48]

"When the Son of Man comes," Jesus continued, "the one who is resting on his housetop must not waste time to get his possessions in his house. The one who might be working in his field should not come back to his home to gather

---

45 Luke 17:22-24
46 Luke 17:25
47 Luke 17:26, 27
48 Luke 17:28-30

his belongings. All his things will be worthless on that day, for all of them will be destroyed. His focus, rather, must be only on the things of heaven and eternity.[49]

"Yes! Remember Lot's wife! [Genesis 19:26] She was more interested in the things of this life than in the saving of own her soul for eternity. Yes, those who give all of themselves, just to preserve the things of this life, will, in the final analysis, lose all these things . . . and eternal life as well. On the other hand, those who give their lives, so to speak, for the things of eternity, will live forever, possessing the great things that eternity has to offer.[50]

"It will be tough choice," Jesus continued, "but all must make it. The day of the Lord's coming will separate those who have made the right choice from those who have made the wrong choice. This division may take place among the members of the same family, and among workers in the same field. I tell you, therefore, two will be sleeping in the same bed the night of the Lord's coming . . . one will be saved, and the other one lost. Two women will be working together, grinding wheat at the mill . . . one will be saved, and the other will be lost. Again, two will be laboring in the same field . . . one will be saved, the other will be lost." [*Harmony* 15:13, 24][51]

The disciples, shocked at the seriousness of the Lord's message, asked Him, "When and where will all this happen, Lord?"[52]

Jesus answered, "You've heard the saying, 'Where a dead body is lying, there the vultures will gather.' [*Harmony* 15:20] Of course, this means that when you see vultures circling above, you know a dead body is lying below them, isn't that right? When you see all these things that I've been describing to you taking place—like the circling of the vultures, as it were—then you will know that the coming of the Son of Man is upon you. It may not be clear to you now, but it will be clear to you then." Some days later Jesus would reiterate some of these concepts with many additional details. [*Harmony* 15:4-31][53]

---

49 Luke 17:31
50 Luke 17:32, 33
51 Luke 17:34-36
52 Luke 17:37
53 Luke 17:37

## — The Parable of the Unjust Judge
## < Early Spring, A.D. 31 (7/7) >
## {Luke 18:1-8}

Jesus knew that His disciples needed encouragement as they anxiously looked ahead to the difficult events preceding His Second Coming. The Lord did not want them to lose heart, but rather, never to cease in their prayers, asking for courage. To illustrate, Jesus told them a parable, saying, "Now, in a certain city there was a judge who did not honor God or care about people. In that same city there was a widow who persistently came before this judge, pleading, 'Give me justice! Protect me from the one who has been oppressing me.'[54]

"Now the judge was quite unwilling to come to her assistance. But after the widow persisted in begging him for help, the judge said to himself in exasperation, 'Even though I don't honor God, nor care about people, I'm so sick and tired of this widow pestering me that I am going to do something for her. I will provide the legal protection she demands so that she will finally leave me alone. I can't take her constant begging and pleas anymore!'"[55]

Jesus paused for a moment and then asked, "Do you notice what this unjust judge said? He was willing to help the widow just because she continued to beg him, if for no other reason. Do you expect that God, who loves you, will ignore your pleas when you cry to Him both day and night? Will He, a compassionate and just God, delay His assistance to you? I say, no! On the contrary I declare to you, He will provide justice—and quickly—to those who call out to Him. To be sure, God is not at all like the evil judge in My story. No, indeed! Please understand: God's faithfulness is not the question. That's a given! The question is rather, when the Son of Man comes back again, will He find people who are faithful? Indeed, will they still be calling upon Him, placing their trust in Him? [*Harmony* 12:10-12] Now that's the question!"[56]

## — The Parable of the Pharisee and the Publican
## < Early Spring, A.D. 31 (7/7) >
## {Luke 18:9-14}

Throughout the Lord's ministry He encountered many people who were confused about the way of salvation. This confusion was not surprising,

---

[54] Luke 18:1-3
[55] Luke 18:4, 5
[56] Luke 18:6-8

considering the false concepts of salvation that were being taught by most of the Jewish leaders in the synagogues around Israel. It was especially the teachings of the Pharisees that were the problem. [*Harmony* 2:7/1, 2] By both their teaching and example, they instructed the common people in a "works-oriented" religion, as opposed to a faith-based confidence in the power of the Gospel within their lives. A works-oriented religion tended to emphasize a dependence on one's merits as a basis for salvation. In short, the people were taught to trust in their own works. Such a teaching also had a strong tendency to make people critical of others, even to the point of treating them with contempt.[57]

Jesus addressed this false concept of religion by telling another parable. He said, "There were two men who went to the Temple in Jerusalem to pray. One of them was a Pharisee. The other was a tax-collector, or publican. Of course, in the sight of most people, the Pharisee was considered to be a very righteous man, while the tax-collector was thought to be a great sinner.[58]

"Now, the Pharisee stood in front of everyone and prayed. He thought he was praying to God, but, in fact, he was praying just to himself. This is what he said in his prayer: 'God, I do thank You that I am not a sinner like other people—cheaters, the unjust, adulterers . . . just like that tax-collector over there! You know of my righteous acts: I fast twice a week, depriving myself of food. [*Harmony* 5:54, 55; 8:5-8] I pay a faithful tithe of everything I own and of what I earn.' [*Harmony* 12:22; 14:125, 126] And so, on and on he went.[59]

"But the tax-collector, who was standing some distance away, felt so unworthy that he was unwilling even to lift up his eyes toward heaven. Instead he beat his chest as an expression of sorrow for his sins. He softly spoke to God, pleading, 'My God, please show mercy to me, the sinner!' [*Harmony* 4:49/2][60]

"I declare to you," Jesus concluded, "that this man—the tax-collector, that is—went back to his house forgiven, as though he had never sinned. The other one—the Pharisee—left the Temple unforgiven and unsaved. In short, everyone who seeks to build himself up by comparing himself to others, will be brought down by God in condemnation. But everyone who, without either making excuse or comparing himself to others, humbly presents his sins to the Lord, asking

57 Luke 18:9
58 Luke 18:9, 10
59 Luke 18:11, 12
60 Luke 18:13

for forgiveness, will be lifted up by God through the gift of His forgiveness." [*Harmony* 5:4][61]

## —Jesus Discusses Marriage and Divorce[(h)]
## < Early Spring, A.D. 31 (7/7) >
## {Matthew 19:3-12; Mark 10:2-12}

Along His journeys, during those last weeks before His death, Jesus was approached by some Pharisees with questions which were calculated to find some cause to accuse Him of impropriety. They began by asking the Master, "Is it consistent with the Law of Moses for a man to divorce his wife for any reason at all? Is it lawful to do so?" Just short of two years previously, in His famous "Sermon on the Mount," the Lord had addressed this subject. [*Harmony* 5:30, 31] In that sermon, Christ had commanded a course of action that, on the surface, seemed to the Pharisees to contradict the words of Moses. [Deuteronomy 24:1-4] Of course, this apparent discrepancy might be used by the Lord's enemies as a way of finding some fault with the words of Jesus that consequently could be used to secure a charge of heresy against Him. And just recently, Jesus had reiterated these same concepts. [*Harmony* 12:141] Indeed, it would be considered a serious charge, should Jesus be found to be teaching something contrary to the laws that Moses, Israel's acclaimed leader, had commanded.[62]

> Obviously, Jesus knew the Pharisees' evil purpose. But beyond this, the way the Lord answered this question would affect not only His own future but also His credibility with His followers. Moreover, He must give an answer that could be used effectively by the Christian Church from that point onward. So then, He must be prepared to give an answer that would end up confounding the Pharisees' purpose as well as providing a sound theological basis for the Christian doctrine of marriage and divorce.

Putting some of the pressure back on them, the Lord first asked them a question, saying, "Tell Me, what it was that Moses commanded you?"[63]

---

61 Luke 18:14

62 Matthew 19:3; Mark 10:2

63 Mark 10:3

Quoting from the Old Testament, they answered, "Well, Moses allowed a man 'to prepare a certificate of divorce and send his wife away.'" [Deuteronomy 24:1-4][64]

Jesus replied, "Yes, that is what Moses said. But it's only because of the hardness of your hearts that he introduced this law of divorce. You see, you were determined to get divorces anyway, so the Lord, through Moses, tried, at least, to regulate them. In part, this divorce law was set up to protect the women who were being abused by your divorces. But beyond that, the text you quoted is what Moses said in *just one* part of the Scriptures. In fact, have you also read what Moses said elsewhere in the same Scriptures? Remember that Moses declared that God, in the beginning—at Creation—'made them male and female.' [Genesis 1:27; 5:2] That's right, isn't it? Then, speaking of marriage, Moses added, 'For this reason a man should leave both his father and mother and be joined together with his wife. And the two of them should be as one flesh.' [Genesis 2:24] Are you aware that this declaration of Moses I just quoted was made many, many years before any divorce law was given? So then, as you can see, Moses's statement here was clearly the *original* purpose of God when He *first* instituted marriage. Don't you agree? Again, Moses says that a husband and wife are no longer two different people, but they are, in effect, one person or flesh. Strong words indeed! So then, I declare, what God has joined together in marriage, do not let any man break apart!"[65]

These powerful words shocked the Pharisees. Their simple response was, "If what you say is true, then why did Moses later on, command that a husband *could* give his 'wife a certificate of divorce and send her away'?" [Deuteronomy 24:1][66]

"Again [*Harmony* 13:65], let Me tell you why," Jesus replied. "It was because of the hardness and perverseness of your hearts that God allowed you to divorce your wives. You were determined to divorce your wives anyway, so He sought to regulate it by giving you reasonable divorce laws. But, as I have already shown you from the Scriptures, this was not the original will of God from the beginning of the earth. So then, as I have said to you before [*Harmony* 5:30, 31; 12:141], whoever divorces his wife—except in the case that she has committed adultery against him—and marries another woman, he has committed adultery. And, whoever marries one who has been put away by divorce has also committed

---

64 Mark 10:4

65 Matthew 19:4-6; Mark 10:5-9

66 Matthew 19:7

adultery. That standard is consistent with the original purpose of God. Therefore, I say: That which God may have allowed at one time, I declare He no longer allows."[67]

> The Pharisees themselves had been used to debating the fine points of the law. In their own interpretations, they had often taken into account the times and circumstances of the enacting of a particular law. Therefore, using their own method of argument, Jesus had quite effectively silenced the Pharisees. Thus they left His presence, completely defeated in their purpose to trick Jesus!

After the Pharisees had gone, the disciples were alone with Jesus in the house. They were amazed by the strong words of the Lord. Accordingly, they questioned Him regarding what He had said to the Pharisees. They ventured, "If the marriage relationship of a husband and wife is as you have just described, it would be better if some people were never married in the first place! Isn't that right?"[68]

Without backing down a bit, Jesus declared, "In some situations you may be right. Indeed, not everyone can take on the seriousness of the marriage vow. On the other hand, there are certainly others, who, through the power of the Gospel, can be happily married for the rest of their lives.[69]

"People must choose what is best for them. There are some who have been born with birth defects that have made it impossible for them to be married in a normal way. There have been others who have been maimed"—or castrated—"by people, thus making it impossible for them to experience a normal marriage relationship. And then, there are some people who willingly choose to remain unmarried, for they are not able, for whatever reason, to live up to the marriage vow. There may even be those who are divorced for reasons other than adultery that cannot marry again. In any case, each person must live consistently with the principle of marriage that I have outlined. That's essential and I require it!"[70]

The disciples, just to make sure that they understood correctly the strong words of Jesus in this matter, continued to question Him on this issue. The Lord answered, "Let Me say it once more so that there can be no doubt in your minds:

---

67 Matthew 19:8, 9
68 Matthew 19:10; Mark 10:10
69 Matthew 19:11
70 Matthew 19:12

Whoever divorces his wife, except for adultery, and then marries another woman, has committed adultery with her. It's just as true for a wife: If she divorces her husband, except for adultery, and then marries another man, she is committing adultery. Is that clear?"[71]

**—Jesus Blesses the Children**
**< Early Spring, A.D. 31 (7/7) >**
**{Matthew 19:13-15; Mark 10:13-16; Luke 18:15-17}**

On one occasion, as the Lord was teaching the people, some mothers brought their little children—some being babes—to Him so that He might bless them by laying His hands on them and praying for them. When the mothers surrounded Jesus, the disciples tried to send them away openly criticizing the mothers' desire to have Jesus bless their little ones. The disciples wanted to protect Him from what they viewed as an unnecessary intrusion.[72]

When the Lord saw what His disciples were trying to do, He was very upset. Jesus interrupted their efforts to send the children and their mothers away. He chided the disciples by saying, "No! No! Let the little children alone. Do not prevent them from coming to Me. Remember, the kingdom of heaven belongs to them too. And in certainty, those who do not receive the kingdom of heaven with the child-like simplicity of these little ones, shall not enter that kingdom themselves." [*Harmony* 10:96][73]

Then the Master took the children into His arms, and laid His hands on them, blessing each one of them. He completed the blessing of the children, and, considering this to be the most important thing He had done that day, He left the place and moved on to another location.[74]

**—Jesus Converses with the Rich Young Ruler, and the Parable of the Workers in the Vineyard**
**< Early Spring, A.D. 31 (7/7) >**
**{Matthew 19:16-20:16; Mark 10:17-31; Luke 18:18-30}**

Along the way on one of Jesus' journeys, a certain ruler of the Jewish leadership suddenly approached Him on the highway. He came running to the

71 Mark 10:10-12
72 Matthew 19:13; Mark 10:13; Luke 18:15
73 Matthew 19:14; Mark 10:14, 15; Luke 18:16, 17
74 Matthew 19:15; Mark 10:16

Lord, knelt before Him, and asked, "Good Teacher, what one good thing must I do so that I can be assured of eternal life?"[75]

The Lord instantly noticed the use of the word "good" that the man used to address Him. Jesus knew that the man did not use such a designation lightly. It was a common and proper practice among Jewish leaders to use the word "good" only when referring to God or to some act that God had performed. For the most part, the Jews did not recognize the Master as being divine. Thus, for this man—a Jewish-trained ruler no less—to use the word "good" in describing Jesus indicated that he was of the opinion that Jesus was, indeed, divine in nature—even the promised Messiah! [Isaiah 9:6, 7] And further, the fact that the man knelt before Jesus also indicated that he believed that the Lord was God. Accordingly, Jesus wanted to strengthen the man's faith in the reality of His divinity. That is why the Savior answered, "Why is it that you call Me good? You well know that there is no mere human being who can truly be called good—only God can rightly be called good. You know that's true." In effect, it was if Jesus were asking the man, "If you call Me good, is it because you recognize Me as being the Son of God—even the Messiah?"[76]

Then, not waiting for the man to give an answer to His implied question, the Lord addressed the ruler's original inquiry. He said, "If you truly desire to enter into eternal life, then I would say, keep the commandments."[77]

> Of course, Jesus taught that people were saved by faith in the power of divine forgiveness and grace. [*Harmony* 3:22] Nevertheless, the Lord also knew that the power of grace, when in force in one's life, ultimately results in obedience of the Law of God. [*Harmony* 16:47] It was to this *end result* that Jesus referred when He declared that if one desires eternal life, one needs to keep the commandments of God. [Romans 3:31]

"But which ones?" the man asked.[78]

"You know them:" Jesus responded, "'You shall not commit murder,' 'You shall not commit adultery,' 'You shall not steal,' 'You shall not bear a false witness against your neighbor,' 'Honor you father and your mother,' and 'You shall love

---

75 Matthew 19:16; Mark 10:17; Luke 18:18

76 Matthew 19:17; Mark 10:18; Luke 18:19

77 Matthew 19:17

78 Matthew 19:18

your neighbor as you would yourself.' You know them well. They are the laws that you might read as part of the Ten Commandments." [Exodus 20:2-17][79]

The man seemed a bit puzzled as he answered the Lord, "Well, Teacher, I've been keeping all of these things which you have mentioned—even from the time that I was a youngster. Is there still something I lack?"[80]

Looking upon the man, Jesus felt a strong love for him. Jesus wanted this man to become a part of His closer circle of disciples. Thus He added, "Well then, if you really want to be perfect, then go from here and sell everything you own, and give the proceeds to the poor. At that point, you will have deposited your treasure in heaven. And then, free from encumbrances, come back and follow Me. That is, take up your cross, so to speak, of sacrifice and commitment!"[(i) (j) 81]

Shocked, dismayed, and filled with gloom when he heard this command, the young man left Jesus. He, being very rich, felt that he had too many possessions to part with.[82]

> There are at least two reasons for the Lord's strong response to this rich ruler:[1]
>
> First, while the words Jesus spoke to the young rich man may seem harsh, in truth, they fitted his particular situation perfectly. He was a man who truly desired to follow the Lord, even on a full-time basis, as one of His extended group of disciples. But his love for his many possessions was hindering him from making this vital commitment. Jesus knew that if this man refused to sell his possessions and give the proceeds to the poor, he would never make that final decision to become a follower of the Master. For, all the Lord's followers in every age must be willing to give up everything to follow Him. The Lord may not require it, but they must still be willing. However, in the case of this man, at that moment in his life, the Lord did require such a sacrifice. Without it, he would lose his way. Unfortunately, that is what happened. Again, while the Lord may not require all His followers to sell all their possessions and give the proceeds to the poor, He always requires those who follow Him to live a life of sacrifice. This principle always applies. Exactly what the Lord

---

79 Matthew 19:18, 19; Mark 10:19; Luke 18:20
80 Matthew 19:20; Mark 10:20; Luke 18:21
81 Matthew 19:21; Mark 10:21; Luke 18:22
82 Matthew 19:22; Mark 10:22; Luke 18:23

requires each person to do may be different. But in the case of this man, a commitment to follow the Lord required that the rich young man to do exactly what the Lord had asked of him.[2]

Second, the man claimed that he had always kept the Law of God. In reality, he had kept only the "letter" of the law, but not the "spirit" of love that permeates true obedience to the law. For example, he had not killed anyone. Thus, he assumed that he had kept that portion of the law. But did he really love people, as the law implies? [*Harmony* 11:150-161] To show that he really loved his neighbor, he needed to demonstrate that love by giving of his wealth to the poor. In this specific case, this is clearly what the Lord required of him. And that was something the man was not willing to do.(k) [3]

The rich young man left in great despair, and Jesus looked around at the amazed faces of the disciples. He explained the situation of the young man to them, saying, "I must tell you, it is hard for a truly rich man to enter the kingdom of heaven and be saved." The disciples looked even more overwhelmed by the force of His words. Jesus repeated His statement, "My children, I must tell you how hard it is to be rich . . . and also to be saved! Yes, the wealthy will find it hard to be saved. And why? It is because their possessions will often take control of them. They will be more attached to the things of this world than to Me. It is in their riches that they have placed their security. For this reason, they will be in grave danger. In fact, it is easier for a camel to be crammed through the eye of a needle than it is for a rich man to make the critical decisions necessary for his salvation! Alas, it is true as I have just said, riches have such a control over the human heart. While this man has kept the letter of the law, he has been far from its spirit. My requirement that he sell everything and give the proceeds to the poor, clearly indicated to him his dire shortcomings."(l) 83

After hearing these strong words, the disciples responded in astonished amazement, for they had always been taught that wealth was evidence of divine favor. That is why they questioned both themselves and the Lord, saying, "If that's the case, Lord, then who it is that can be saved? It looks impossible!"84

83 Matthew 19:23, 24; Mark 10:23-25; Luke 18:24, 25

84 Matthew 19:25; Mark 10:26; Luke 18:26

Looking intently at them, the Lord gave a straight answer, "Well, with men it *is* quite impossible . . . but not with God—for all things that seem impossible with man, are, in fact, possible with God! Indeed, God can save the rich!"[85]

Peter, thinking about all that he, personally, had given up to follow the Lord on a full-time basis, asked, "Look, Lord! We gave up everything for You when we left our earlier lives of fishing to follow You. [*Harmony* 4:14-22] What is it that we will get in return? What is left for us?"[86]

Jesus, reassuring the twelve disciples, answered, "I can declare to you that all of you who have left everything to follow Me will, in God's eternal kingdom, receive a greater reward. Indeed, when the Son of Man sits on His throne of glory in eternity, you will also sit with Him on twelve other thrones, serving as judges of the twelve tribes of Israel! How about that! And, everyone who has left houses, wives, brothers or sisters, father or mother, or children, or even farms, for the sake of My name—or for that of the Gospel—will receive back many fold—even a hundred times as much. And this is to say nothing of the gift of eternal life itself! That's not bad, is it?[87]

"In truth though," Jesus went on, "even in this present age, you will receive a hundred times more blessings, so to speak, of houses, wives, brothers, sisters, mothers, children and farms. And how is this possible? It is because you now belong to the family of God! You may have lost members of your own family of blood relatives. But you have gained a whole new family of fellow believers. You may have lost your possessions in this world. But the possession of eternal life, which you now have, is of much greater worth to you than anything you've given up. But that's not all! Along the way, in this life, there will be persecutions, but after all this has passed, there will be everlasting life for you. So then, many that are now first—in terms of earthly possessions and family—will be last, ending up with nothing. And those who are now last—who have given up all to follow Me—will be first in My kingdom in possessions and responsibility." [*Harmony* 12:85; 13:97][88]

However, the Lord was concerned that His disciples might think that because they had given up so much to follow Him as the Messiah, they

---

85 Matthew 19:26; Mark 10:27; Luke 18:27

86 Matthew 19:27; Mark 10:28; Luke 18:28

87 Matthew 19:28, 29; Mark 10:29; Luke 18:29, 30

88 Matthew 19:30; Mark 10:31, 31; Luke 18:30

deserved some special treatment in eternity. While they would be blessed by such a sacrifice, they needed to know that there would be others in eternity who had not sacrificed as much as they had, yet would be there too. True, even though there would be various degrees of responsibility and privilege given out in God's glorious kingdom [*Harmony* 15:42-50], the gift of eternal life would be given out equally to everyone there. After all, how could there be one heaven for those who had sacrificed much, and another, lesser heaven, for those who had sacrificed less? That would make no sense at all. To clarify this point, Jesus told a parable that illustrated this particular concept.

The Lord said, "The kingdom of heaven can be compared to a certain landowner who went out to the marketplace as the sun was rising, to hire workers to labor in his vineyard. As the potential workers came forward to be hired, he agreed to pay each a denarius—a normal day's wages. Once hired, the workers were sent to labor in his vineyard. [*Harmony* 13:133/2][89]

"A few hours later, about 9 a.m., the landowner went again to the marketplace and noticed that there were other potential workers standing around with nothing to do. So he said to them, 'You can work for me in my vineyard, if you wish, and I will pay you what your labor is worth to me. Alright?' They agreed to the arrangement, and went to work in his vineyard.[90]

"The landowner repeated this method of hiring workers at 12 noon, and also at 3 p.m. He even went once more at 5 p.m., and found others still standing around with nothing to do. He said to them, 'Why have you been standing around all day with nothing to do?'[91]

"They answered, by explaining, 'Because no one has offered to hire us to work for them.'[92]

"The landowner replied, 'In that case, you can work for me in my vineyard. And I'll pay you what is fair. Is that all right with you?' And they went to work for him at that late hour.[93]

---

89 Matthew 20:1, 2
90 Matthew 20:3, 4
91 Matthew 20:5, 6
92 Matthew 20:7
93 Matthew 20:7

"Well, when nightfall came, the landowner returned to the vineyard and summoned the foreman in charge of the workers, and told him, 'Call all the laborers and pay them their just wages. First, pay those who started to work for me during the late part of the day.'[94]

"Those who started to work a 5 p.m., came forward and received a denarius for their short time of labor. When the other workers, especially those who had worked from sunup, saw that those who had worked such a short time received the same pay that they received, they made quite a fuss. When they saw the one-hour laborers getting a denarius, they expected that the landowner would pay them more money, even though they had originally agreed to work for a single denarius. They complained, 'Hey! What's going on here? These, who have worked just one hour, are receiving the same pay that we are receiving. And yet, we have worked hard for you out under the hot sun all day long. It just isn't fair!'[95]

"But the landowner was not to be dissuaded from his plan of payment of his workers. He challenged their complaint by saying, 'Now friends, did you not agree to work for me for the wage of one denarius? Well, that's what I am paying you. I have done you no wrong! Take what is yours. Be happy with that and go home! I have decided to pay those who worked for just one hour the same that I have paid the rest of you. That's my privilege. Isn't it allowable for me to pay my workers what I choose to pay them? It is my money, right? Is it not true that your mindset is wicked, not respecting my authority to pay such a generous wage to anyone I choose?'"[96]

Jesus concluded the parable by using the same principle He mentioned before, saying, "The last will be first, and the first will be last. This means those who have been faithful in their work for Me, even though they came on later, will receive a payment equal to those who went to work for Me at the beginning. And, those who think that they are first in privilege because they began working for Me before the others, will end up receiving what they think is unfair treatment. And thus, a bad attitude will result. So don't have such an attitude. Rejoice, rather, that there are those who choose to follow Me at the last minute, and that they will be with you in eternity. You are not to labor for Me to receive special privileges. The gift of salvation—eternal life—is given equally to everyone who accepts it . . .

---

94 Matthew 20:8

95 Matthew 20:9-12

96 Matthew 20:13-15

no matter when they accept it, or who they are. Unfortunately, there are so few who are willing to follow the way of eternal life that I've prescribed for them." [*Harmony* 13:86-88][97]

> In this parable, Jesus taught that the gift of eternal life would be given equally to everyone who is to receive it, *no matter when* they accepted the Lord as their personal Savior. In later parables [*Harmony* 13:120-133; 15:42-50], the Lord illustrated the various gifts of *responsibility* His followers would receive in eternity. These responsibilities would be given out, based upon the level and duration of faithfulness each follower demonstrated during his or her lifetime.

### —Jesus Foretells His Own Death
### < Early Spring, A.D. 31 (7/7) >
### {Matthew 20:17-19; Mark 10:32-34; Luke 18:31-34}

The time for the Passover was fast approaching. Jesus was determined to go to Jerusalem. The Savior, His disciples, and many others who were following along made their way toward the city on the highway. On this occasion, the Lord walked a good bit ahead of them all, as though He wished to be alone. It was most unusual for Him to do so. This rare situation amazed the disciples, and distressed the other followers. So, to explain His actions, and to help prepare the twelve disciples for what they and He were facing, Jesus took them aside and explained to them what would happen in Jerusalem.[98]

He said, "Listen to this! We are going up to Jerusalem. When we get there, all the things the prophets of old have written about the Son of Man will be fulfilled. [Isaiah 53:3-12] Yes, the Son of Man will be betrayed. And through this betrayal, He will be delivered up to the chief priests and scribes. And by them He will be condemned to death! Then, they will turn the Son of Man over to the Gentiles"—the Romans—"to be mocked, spat upon, severely mistreated, scourged [*Harmony* 17:64], and finally, crucified! But, don't worry, on the third day, He will be resurrected from the dead!" [*Harmony* 7:14; 10:55-61, 84, 85; 11:18; 13:46; 15:59; 18:17, 18, 21, 50/][99]

Nevertheless, in spite of the Lord's direct and clear explanations as to what precisely would happen to Him in Jerusalem, the disciples, quite amazingly, still

---

97 Matthew 20:16

98 Matthew 20:17; Mark 10:32; Luke 18:31

99 Matthew 20:18, 19; Mark 10:33, 34; Luke 18:31-33

did not comprehend. In short, because of their determined refusal to believe the Lord's dire predictions, they did not understand a single thing He explained to them. Their partial and distorted concept of who the Messiah was and what He would do prevented them from believing or understanding His words as to what He would soon face in Jerusalem.[100]

## —James and John Make a Special Request[(m)] < Early Spring, A.D. 31 (7/7) > {Matthew 20:20-28; Mark 10:35-45}

It is truly astonishing that the Lord's disciples did not comprehend the gravity of the situation regarding His impending death. He had made it clear as to what was going to happen. Nevertheless, the apostles' dullness of understanding was readily apparent. [*Harmony* 10:55-57] This fact was underscored when the mother of the sons of Zebedee—James and John—approached Jesus. She came along with her two sons while they were traveling on toward Jerusalem. Her name was Salome. She had been closely involved with the Lord's ministry in Galilee. [*Harmony* 4:15; 17:136] Because of this close association with the Lord's work, she thought that she would be able to receive a special favor from the Master. So, in anticipation that Jesus would pronounce Himself King of the Jews in Jerusalem within a short time, publicly declaring His position as the Messiah, James and John conspired with their mother on a secret plan to ask the Lord for a special favor. In the immediate presence of the Lord, Salome bowed to the ground before Jesus, and begged of Him, "Lord, please do for my sons exactly what I ask." [*Harmony* 14:21/3][(n)] [101]

"What is it that you want Me to do for you?" Christ responded.[102]

With unusual boldness she requested, "Promise me that when You soon establish Your glorious eternal kingdom, my two sons shall sit, one on Your right side and the other on the left side, of Your throne." [*Harmony* 13:107/][103]

Responding to the woman, Jesus answered, "You have no idea what you are asking of Me!" She had no clue as to what her sons were to face in the future. And then looking at the woman's two sons, He questioned them, saying, "Are you sure that you are able to drink of the cup of woe of which I'm going to drink?

---

100 Luke 18:34

101 Matthew 20:20; Mark 10:35

102 Matthew 20:21; Mark 10:36

103 Matthew 20:21; Mark 10:37

Can you really drink it along with Me? And too, are you sure that you are able to experience the baptism of anguish with which I am going to be baptized?" Of course, the "cup" and the "baptism" that Jesus referred to represented His impending sufferings and death! But the two disciples seemed to be quite oblivious of that fact.[104]

So James and John, without hesitation, replied in unison, "Yes, we are able!"[105]

> No doubt James and John thought that Jesus was going to establish His glorious kingdom very soon! They certainly did not comprehend that the establishment of the Lord's kingdom was yet in the far distant future. Neither did they perceive that any place of honor in that kingdom which they might receive was not going to materialize any time soon. For them, there must be a great deal of suffering first!

In a matter-of-fact way, Jesus calmly responded, "Well then, in that case, of My cup you will drink! And the baptism which I experience, you will also be baptized with!" Here the Lord predicted the agonies they would suffer throughout their lives for their commitment to Him. [Acts 12:1, 2; Revelation 1:9] Then the Lord added, "However, as to whether you can sit on My right hand or My left hand is not up to Me. That privilege will be determined by My Father. And those for whom that privilege has been reserved will receive it in due course."[106]

When the remaining ten disciples heard of this conversation, they were, not surprisingly, indignant toward James and John. Taking the disciples aside, the Lord strongly counseled them. "Listen!" He said. "You all know that the recognized rulers of this world lord over their subjects, and that the supposedly great men of earth exercise complete control over the masses. But I want to make it abundantly clear: That is not the way it should be among you. In fact, he who truly desires to be considered great among you must be the servant of the others. And whoever wishes to be first among you must be the slave of the others. I use Myself as an example: When the Son of Man came to this world, He came not to be served but to serve, even to the extent of giving His life for the full payment for the sins of many." [*Harmony* 16:8][107]

---

104 Matthew 20:22; Mark 10:38

105 Matthew 20:22; Mark 10:39

106 Matthew 20:23; Mark 10:39, 40

107 Matthew 20:24-28; Mark 10:41-45

A strange and inexplicable paradox was taking place among the Lord's disciples. On one hand, Jesus made it clear that He was going to face death in Jerusalem. And to some extent the disciples comprehended the reality of the Lord's prediction. [*Harmony* 13:5, 11] Yet, on the other hand—such as in the case of James and John [*Harmony* 13:104, 105]—the disciples still persistently clung to the belief that the Master would soon establish His glorious kingdom. So then, there was a great contrast between what the Lord said and what the disciples actually believed would happen. And, too, there was a contrast among the various disciples as to what they believed. Perhaps, also, the disciples believed different things at different times. All of this is quite puzzling, even mysterious. It is clear, then, that the disciples remained very confused as to what was going to happen. Would Jesus die as He predicted, or would He establish His glorious kingdom?

## — The Lord Talks With Zaccheus, Heals Two Blind Men, and The Parable of the Nobleman and His Money(o)
## < Early Spring, A.D. 31 (7/7) >
## {Matthew 20:29-34; Mark 10:46-52; Luke 18:35-19:28}

The Lord was fast approaching Jerusalem. The Passover was just days away. On His way out of Peraea, He crossed the Jordan River and headed toward the city of Jericho, less than ten miles away. Jesus passed through that city and was beginning to go on toward Jerusalem, some 17 miles beyond there to the west. A rich tax-collector named Zaccheus lived in Jericho. He desperately wanted to see the Savior. He had heard much about Him, and wanted to get a good glimpse of the One whom many thought was the Messiah. But because Zaccheus was short in stature, and the number of people surrounding Jesus was huge, he was unable to get close enough to Jesus to get even a glimpse of Him. Knowing the opportunity to view the Master would soon pass by when Jesus traveled out of Jericho, Zaccheus ran on ahead of the crowd. A bit down the road, he climbed into a sycamore tree that was beside the road. This species of tree was noted for its large, over-hanging branches. There, he waited until the Lord would pass by right under him.[108]

Before long, Jesus passed under the branches of the tree where Zaccheus had perched himself. To Zaccheus's surprise, the Lord looked up into the tree overhead and, seeing the tax-collector, urged, "Zaccheus, hurry and come down

[108] Matthew 20:29; Mark 10:46; Luke 19:1-4

out that tree! For today, I must stay at your house!" Miraculously, Jesus knew who Zaccheus was! He also knew that the tax-collector's desire to see Him was based upon more than mere curiosity. The Spirit of God had been working mightily in Zaccheus's heart to encourage him to change his lifestyle. Before Jesus would go on to Jerusalem to die, He must help this man—a sinner rejected of society—to turn his life around. So, without hesitating a second, Zaccheus climbed down out of the tree and gladly accepted the Lord's request to visit with him in his own home! [*Harmony* 5:39][109]

> However, many in the crowd were greatly displeased with what Jesus said to Zaccheus. Tax-collectors were hated among the Jews, for they collected taxes for the despised Romans. In a real sense, then, any Jew who had this occupation was considered to be a traitor to the Hebrew nation. And too, tax-collectors were notoriously dishonest with those from whom they collected the taxes. In fact, the name "tax-collector"—or publican—was a byword used to describe any despicable or evil person! And Zaccheus himself was looked upon as being one of the worst of those wicked tax-collectors. To many in the crowd, the thought that Jesus, who was presumed by many to be the Messiah, would actually enter a home of a tax-collector—especially Zaccheus—was downright repulsive. [*Harmony* 4:49/2]

When the people saw Jesus actually returning to Jericho to visit with Zaccheus in his home, they began to grumble loudly, saying, "Is He actually going to lodge in the home of that man who is such an awful sinner—a tax-collector no less? How can this be?"[110]

Zaccheus heard these insults. He was amazed that Jesus, in spite of what many were saying about him, was still willing to visit with him in his home. Thus, quite overwhelmed with the Lord's kindness and generosity, Zaccheus felt an even greater conviction of heart. Any doubts he might have had about Jesus were erased. Stopping in his tracks, in front of the entire crowd, Zaccheus declared to the Savior, "Look, Lord! I will give half of all my possessions to the poor. In addition, if I have ever defrauded anyone of a single thing, I will repay it back fourfold!"[111]

---

109 Luke 19:5, 6
110 Luke 19:7
111 Luke 19:8

Jesus responded, making sure the crowd could hear. He declared, "Ah yes! Salvation today has come to this man's house, because he, too, is a son of Abraham"—that is, Zaccheus was a Jew. And, as such Zaccheus was as worthy to be called a "son of Abraham" as was any Jew who *wasn't* a tax-collector. Jesus concluded, "The Son of Man has come to seek those who are lost. And when He has found them, indeed, He will save them."[112]

But before Jesus and His disciples, in the midst of the large crowd, were able to reach the city of Jericho on the way to Zaccheus's home, they were interrupted by two blind men sitting by the side of the road, begging. One of the blind men was named Bartimaeus, the son of Timaeus. Sensing by the noise of the crowd that something was happening in front of the two of them, they asked what the commotion was about. Once told that Jesus of Nazareth was passing by, they cried out to Him, "Lord, Jesus! Please have mercy on us, You Son of David!" By using the title, "Son of David," the blind men showed that they recognized Jesus as the Messiah.[(p) (q) (r) 113]

Even though the two blind men were sternly hushed by bystanders, they cried out even more loudly, "Oh, Lord! Son of David! Have mercy on us!"[114]

Jesus abruptly stopped where He was and asked that the two men be brought up to Him. "Have them come over here!" He said.[115]

"Be of courage! Stand up! Jesus is calling for you to come over to Him," some in the crowd instructed the blind men. Throwing aside their cloaks, the men jumped up and were led over to where Jesus was standing.[116]

When they were brought into the Lord's presence, He asked them, "What is it that You want Me to do for you?"[117]

"Lord, our Master, we want to see again!" was their impassioned reply.[118]

Jesus, moved with great compassion, touched their eyes, and said, "Receive your sight again! Go on your way! Your faith has made both of you whole!"

---

112 Luke 19:9, 10
113 Matthew 20:29, 30; Mark 10:46, 47; Luke 18:35-38
114 Matthew 20:31; Mark 10:48; Luke 18:39
115 Matthew 20:32; Mark 10:49; Luke 18:40
116 Mark 10:49, 50
117 Matthew 20:32; Mark 10:50, 51; Luke 18:40, 41
118 Matthew 20:33; Mark 10:51; Luke 18:41

Instantly, they received back their sight. They, with praise on their lips, followed the Lord as part of His extended group of disciples. The miracle also influenced many in the crowd in a positive way, for they, too, praised God for what they had seen.[119]

Presently Jesus arrived in Jericho at the home of Zaccheus. He visited there for a while. Jesus could tell that the people within His hearing were living under the false belief that because He was nearing Jerusalem, He would soon establish His glorious kingdom and rule from that city as the Messiah of Israel. But the idea that He was, in fact, going to die, rise from the dead, and return to heaven—all without establishing that glorious kingdom—was completely foreign to their thinking. Therefore, Jesus decided to tell them a parable to help rectify their twisted mindset. [*Harmony* 13:97/][120]

The Lord began: "There was a certain nobleman who went away into a distant country to receive a kingdom. After receiving the kingdom, he planned on returning home."[121]

> In this parable, Jesus illustrated Himself. He was the nobleman going into a distant country—that is, to heaven—to receive a kingdom. That kingdom, of course, was the kingdom of glory that all the people were hoping He was going establish in Jerusalem in just a few short days. The nobleman returning from the distant country represented Jesus returning to this earth *after* receiving the kingdom of glory. This, obviously, referred to His Second Coming, an event yet very far in the future.

Jesus continued with His parable: "But before he left for the distant country, the nobleman called ten of his servants to appear before him. He gave them a total of ten minas"—which was equal to about three years' wages. "That was one mina per servant. Then he instructed them, 'Take care of my business until I come back.'" [*Harmony* 15:42-50][122]

> These ten servants represented the Lord's followers—His disciples of the entire Christian age. Instead of receiving the benefits of the Lord's kingdom of glory within a few days—as was the hope of the disciples hearing this parable that day—they first had to prove their faithfulness

---

119 Matthew 20:34; Mark 10:52; Luke 18:42, 43
120 Luke 19:11
121 Luke 19:12
122 Luke 19:13

> by working for the Lord until He returned the second time. This would include the Lord's disciples throughout the entire Christian age. Only then, when He came the second time, would they receive the honor of being a direct part of that glorious kingdom. But the question the Lord, in effect, was asking through the parable was, "How many of you in this crowd today will be willing to work for Me, the Lord, patiently awaiting the establishment of the kingdom of glory sometime in the yet far distant future?"

Jesus continued with the parable, saying, "However, the citizens of the nobleman's country despised him. They even sent a contingent of representatives after him, declaring, 'There is no way that we will accept this man as our ruler . . . now or in the future!'"[123]

> The "citizens" in the parable represented the Jews—specifically its leaders—who had rejected Jesus as the Messiah. They would make it quite clear during His upcoming trial, to take place just a few days later, that they had no desire to serve Him as their Leader, then or at any time in the future! [*Harmony* 17:105-110]

Moving on in the parable, Jesus said, "Well, the nobleman, after receiving his kingdom, returned to see how his servants had performed their duty. Each servant to whom he had given the mina, was ordered to appear before him to give account of how he had handled the money that had been entrusted to him.[124]

"The first servant appeared and reported, 'Master! The mina you gave me I have increased ten-fold to a total of eleven minas!'[125]

"'Well done, my servant!' the master praised him. 'Because you have been faithful with the little things that I have given you, I will give you authority over ten cities of my kingdom.'[126]

"The second servant appeared before the nobleman. This servant reported, 'Your mina I have increased by five, to a total of six.'[127]

---

123 Luke 19:14
124 Luke 19:15
125 Luke 19:16
126 Luke 19:17
127 Luke 19:18

"'In your case,' the nobleman exclaimed, 'you will be in charge of five cities in my kingdom.' Then, one servant after another made his report.[128]

"At last, the tenth servant appeared to make his report. He explained, 'Master, here is your mina. I kept it tucked away in a napkin. I was afraid of you, for I know you to be a harsh master. You would only take what I had earned, and would not give me any reward for my faithfulness. So I thought, what was the use to even try?'[129]

"Angered, the nobleman replied, 'I will use your own words to condemn you, you worthless servant! You say I'm tough. Well then, tough I will be! So you really think that I am such a harsh master, that I not only want what is mine but will not fairly reward my servant's faithfulness? If that were the case, then at least you could have put the mina in the bank and earned a little interest on it to present to me. Why didn't you do even that?' Turning to others standing by, the nobleman commanded, 'Take that mina from him and give it to the servant who increased his mina ten-fold.'"[130]

Those who were listening to Jesus tell the parable interrupted Him and asked, "But, Lord, he already has ten minas. Why should he get any more?"[131]

"It is because I will reward faithfulness! That's why!" the Lord replied. "Yes, I tell you, everyone who is faithful in increasing that what has been given to him will receive even more. And those who are slothful in increasing that which has been given to them will lose even that what they received initially. In short, they will end up with nothing![132]

"Now, back to the story," Jesus continued. "Regarding the enemies of the nobleman who did not want him to rule over them, this is what the nobleman said to his servants, 'Bring them here, and slay them in my presence!'"[133]

> The intent of the Lord's parable was clear. First, the kingdom of glory was an event yet in the distant future. Second, until that kingdom would be officially established, the Lord's disciples must faithfully work for

---

128 Luke 19:19
129 Luke 19:20, 21
130 Luke 19:22-24
131 Luke 19:25
132 Luke 19:26
133 Luke 19:27

Him. They must use the gifts of the Gospel He has given them to increase and expand the church. Third, if found faithful in the end, they will receive as a reward a generous part of the glorious kingdom. The larger the work accomplished, the larger will be the reward. But until then, they must patiently work for the Lord. The Lord will accept no excuses for laziness. Fourth, if the servants are not found faithful, there will be a high price to pay. Thus, to receive a part of the kingdom of glory requires faithfulness of duty. And, fifth, those who rejected the Lord as the Messiah—in the parable, the nobleman's enemies—will tragically pay with their lives. In real life, this represented the Jewish leaders. This parable was similar to another one Jesus would tell some of His closest disciples some days later. [*Harmony* 15:42-50][1]

This parable, though, is different from the one He had told earlier about the workers in the vineyard. [*Harmony* 13:89-97] In that parable, each worker, no matter how long he worked for the master, received the same pay. In the present parable, though, each received a reward based upon the level of his or her involvement in the work. Why is the meaning of these two parables so different? It is because they deal with different concepts. By the former parable—the one of the workers in the vineyard—is represented the *basic gift* of eternal life as it is given by the Lord. In that case, eternal life is given to each one equally. By the latter parable—the one of the servants with the minas—is represented the kinds of responsibilities each one of God's faithful servants will receive in eternity. And that is based upon the level of performance each has given to the cause of the Lord. In the final analysis, the Lord is eminently fair: Eternal life is given to everyone equally, while *responsibilities* in eternity are given based upon performance. However, just what those responsibilities may be is not clear. God's faithful servants will have to wait and see![2]

Once He had completed the narration the parable of the minas, and His visit in the home of Zaccheus, the Lord left the city of Jericho and began to travel the remaining 17 miles to Jerusalem, a steady climb of some 3,000 feet.[134]

134 Luke 19:28

## Supplementary Notes:

**(a) [13:1]** I take the position that the Mary of this story was commonly known as Mary Magdalene. For more information on this, see **Notes "a"** and **"e"** in Chapter 14 of the *Harmony.*

**(b) [13:2]** The text does not say that Jesus was in Peraea, but based upon the information found in Chapter 12 of the *Harmony*, it is reasonable to assume that Peraea was where Jesus was ministering at the time.

**(c) [13:12]** (See above.)

**(d) [13:16]** Martha's knowledge of events as they relate to the resurrection at the end of the world, is, it seems to me, quite advanced for her day. This shows just how in tune with the truth of the Gospel this woman truly was. Sometimes Martha gets criticized (*Harmony* 11:162-164), but, in reality, she had a great understanding of the overall mission and ministry of Jesus as the Messiah.

**(e) [13:30]** There is an interesting connection between the resurrection of Lazarus and the parable of Lazarus and the Rich Man (*Harmony* 12:142-150). Read that parable, including the **Explanatory Notes 12:150/1-6** (especially **Note** 4) for more information.

**(f) [13:40]** For more on the disease of leprosy, see *Harmony* 4:35-39.

**(g) [13:44]** There is dispute over whether Jesus was talking about the Gospel being *within you*, or just being *among you*—or, that is, just in your *presence.* There is room for argument on both sides of the issue. I took the former position, thinking it the more reasonable.

**(h) [13:61+]** Of the several times that the Lord addressed the subject of divorce (*Harmony* 5:30, 31; 12:141), this particular presentation was the strongest and most detailed. The seriousness of this subject, as far as the Lord was concerned, cannot be over-emphasized.

However, it is not within the scope of this book to discuss the finer application of this law as it relates to various circumstances that might take place at any given time. Indeed, dealing with the wide-ranging application of the divorce and remarriage issue can be quite complicated and extremely difficult to administrate. I decided, for the purpose of the *Harmony,* to state the message as strongly as Jesus seems to have presented it, and let the reader decide how to relate it to any particular situation one might face.

**(i) [13:81]** I really struggled over the story of the rich young ruler. The question is: Did the Lord *actually require* that he sell his possessions, or that he just be *willing* to sell his possessions? And also, was the demand made of him (that is to actually sell his possessions) *unique* to him, or does it apply to everyone? Finally, I came to the conclusion that Jesus did, in fact, require that the ruler of this story actually sell his possessions. I also think that the Lord's requirement of him was *unique*—that is, in the specific case of rich man, the Lord required *him* to sell his possessions in order for him to be among His followers. However, I further believe that even though Jesus does *not* necessarily expect everyone to sell his or her possessions, should Jesus make this demand of any of us, we must be willing to do so. Overall, I am comfortable with my various interpretations of this story as it is recorded in the *Harmony.*

**(j) [13:81]** It seems to me that based upon the Lord's command for this man to sell all his possessions and give the proceeds to the poor, He was asking him to become a part of the closer circle of disciples and not just a regular follower of Jesus. Because I think this is the case, I stated it as such in the *Harmony,* even though the Gospel record does not actually say so.

**(k) [13:82/3]** (See **Notes "i"** and **"j"** above.)

**(l) [13:83]** Some have suggested that Lord's description of a camel going through the eye of a needle refers to a particular small gate in the wall of Jerusalem which made it difficult for a camel carrying a load of goods to pass through. While this may be true, I still think that Jesus referred to the *literal* camel and needle. The impossibility of the literal camel going through the eye of a literal needle far better describes the impossibility of a rich man being saved, I think, than the relatively minor difficulty of a camel hauling goods crawling through a gate in the wall. Accordingly, I reflected thus in the *Harmony.*

**(m) [13:100+]** Matthew records that it was the mother of John and James who brought this request to Jesus; Mark says that it was John and James themselves. I went with Matthew's account, considering it much more likely.

**(n) [13:101]** How do we know that James and John's mother's name was Salome? Comparing a few texts, we can come to that conclusion. Mark 15:40 tells us that Salome (along with Mary Magdalene and Mary, the mother of James and Joses) were at the crucifixion of Jesus. In the parallel account of Matthew 27:56, we are told that (along with the same two Marys), the mother of Zebedee's children were there. Then, in Matthew 4:21, we are told that James and John's father was Zebedee. Putting these three texts together, then, we can safely conclude that the mother of James and John was Salome, the wife of Zebedee, the one who was also at the crucifixion.

**(o) [13:107/+]** The exact sequence of events surrounding the Lord's encounter with Zaccheus and the healing of the two blind men is a bit confusing. I think that, in the *Harmony,* I have followed a sequence that makes the most sense.

**(p) [13:113]** Were there two blind men (as Matthew records), or one blind man (as Mark and Luke record)? I chose two for the *Harmony,* considering it the more logical possibility.

**(q) [13:113]** Matthew 20:29 and Mark 10:46 say that the blind men (see above) were healed as Jesus *left* Jericho, while Luke 18:35 says they were healed while Jesus was *entering* Jericho. Which one was true? Of course, it is a small point, but there is a reasonable explanation that *both* accounts are true. How can this be? Consider this logic: Jesus visited Jericho for a while. But while Jesus was in the *process of leaving* Jericho, He met up with Zaccheus. Then, the Lord went back into the city to visit with the tax collector. It was while He *entered* the city the *second* time, that He healed the blind men. But even in that case, then, He was still in the *general process of leaving the city*—that is, His visit with Zaccheus and His healing of the blind men were really *only a detour* on His way *out* of Jericho! Do you get it?

**(r) [13:113]** It has been suggested that one of the blind men, Bartimaeus, the son of Timaeus, ultimately became a well-known follower of Jesus. If that is so, that explains why the specific name of one the blind men was given, something that was quite unusual in the Gospel recording of the Lord's miracles.

# Part IV

*The End . . . And the Beginning!*

*(Passover, Spring, A.D. 31 -*

*Just Before Pentecost, A.D. 31)*

# CHAPTER FOURTEEN

## THE PASSION WEEK: FRIDAY THROUGH TUESDAY AFTERNOON—

**From Simon's Feast, to the Final Rejection by the Jewish Leaders**

**(Just Before Passover, Spring, A.D. 31)**

**Celebration and Betrayal**
**< Friday (The Preparation) Nisan 7 Through Saturday Night, Nisan 9, Spring, A.D. 31 (7/7) >**
**(Matthew 26:3-16; Mark 14:1-11; Luke 7:36-50, 22:1-6; John 12:1-11)**

**— Simon's Feast[a]**
**< Saturday Night, Nisan 9, Spring, A.D. 31 (7/7) >**
**{Matthew 26:6-13; Mark 14:3-9; Luke 7:36-50; John 12:1-9}**

The last week of the Lord's life is often called the "Passion Week." It was the time when Jesus brought His ministry to a dramatic conclusion. The events of this week—beginning with Friday, the week before His crucifixion, and ending with His death on the cross, the next Friday—contain, by far, the most detailed record of any week in the Savior's life. It was the time, not only for the Lord to wrap up His ministry, but also for the Jewish nation—and especially its leaders—to make a final decision to either accept or reject Jesus as the Messiah. In fact, during the sequence of the events of this week, Jesus, while still in their presence, gave all His listeners one last chance to open their hearts to Him as the true Savior of their souls as well as the Savior of the whole world. During this week, in all His actions and words, the Lord pleaded, as it were, for everyone He met to accept His ministry as a genuine fulfillment of Old Testament prophecy regarding the coming of the promised Messiah. Time was very quickly running out for many of them. Indeed, it could well be said, the "Passion Week" was a time for decision.[(b)]

It was on Friday, the Jewish "Day of Preparation" for the weekly Sabbath, the seventh day of Nisan, that Jesus arrived in Bethany, a small town two miles to the southeast of Jerusalem. Almost exactly one week later, He would be crucified. The Lord had been invited to attend a feast to be given in His honor. The feast was scheduled for Saturday night, Nisan 9, at the home of a Pharisee named Simon. Jesus had previously healed Simon of the dreaded disease of leprosy. Simon, ignobly known as "Simon the leper," wanted to show off Jesus as the One who had cured him of that horrible illness.[(c) 1]

The invitees to the feast arrived some time after sundown after the seventh-day Sabbath rest of Nisan 8. It was just six days before the Jews would celebrate the annual Passover Festival the following Friday. The guests reclined at the feasting table and began to eat. Among the guests was one of Bethany's most famous citizens, Lazarus, whom Jesus had resurrected from the dead some weeks previously. [*Harmony* 13:1-30] There were also many people from among the Jewish religious leadership. They not only wanted to see Jesus, the Miracle Worker, but also Lazarus, the man raised from the dead! In addition, Lazarus's sister, Martha, served the meal at the feasting table. [*Harmony* 11:162-64][(d) 2]

During the feast, someone else who knew that Jesus was to be there that evening, entered the banquet hall, uninvited. It was Mary Magdalene, Lazarus and Martha's sister, who, at that time, was living with them in Bethany. Mary was notoriously known as a "sinner." She was a former prostitute who had been possessed of seven devils. But, sometime during His ministry in Galilee, Jesus had forgiven her and cast the devils out of her. After that, Mary assisted the Lord in His ministry while He continued to labor in that province. [*Harmony* 6:18, 19; 17:136] At that time, she had been living in the Galilean town of Magdala. Thus she was commonly known by the name Mary Magdalene—that is, Mary of Magdala. All this happened about a year and half before this feast at Simon's house. At some point, however, Mary had returned to her home town of Bethany where she now lived with her siblings. In fact, several months before Simon's feast, Jesus had visited in the family's home. This was when Martha had been

1 Matthew 26:6; Mark 14:3; Luke 9:36; John 12:1, 2
2 Luke 7:36; John 12:1, 2, 9

upset that Mary did not help her prepare a meal for the Savior, but sat at the Lord's feet. [*Harmony* 11:162-164][(e)] [3]

When Mary entered Simon's feasting hall, she slipped inconspicuously across the room. She carried an alabaster stone box containing twelve ounces of pure nard, a very costly perfume. Standing behind the reclining Jesus, near His feet, she broke the box to expose the perfume. Mary then began to pour the entire contents of the nard upon the Master's head and feet as He was eating. While weeping, mixing her tears with the thick ointment, she began to wipe the feet of Jesus with her hair. All the while, she repeatedly kissed His feet. The strong, sweet, yet musty aroma of the pure nard, permeated the entire banquet hall.[(f)] [4]

> Nard was extracted from a plant that grew high in the Himalaya Mountains, many, many miles to the east of Israel. The risk involved in securing the nard, the time consumed in obtaining it, and the miles of travel required to deliver nard to a place such as Israel, contributed to its high price. It was, in fact, among the most costly of all perfumes of the ancient world.

The Lord's disciples—led by Judas Iscariot, the son of Simon, who had been thinking for some time about betraying Jesus for money—were very distressed at the apparent waste of money that Mary had spent on the perfume. "Why was so much money wasted on this?" Judas exclaimed. "This perfume could have been sold for a very high price—even 300 denarii—and the proceeds given to the poor!" Indeed, 300 denarii was the equivalent of nearly a year's wages of a common laborer! The other disciples, discussing Mary's action among themselves, also severely chided her for what she had done. Of course, in the case of Judas, he was not really concerned about helping the poor at all. In fact, as treasurer of the disciples, he regularly took money for himself from the common purse. So then, an additional 300 denarii would have been a handsome sum from which to secure even more funds for himself![5]

Now Jesus, noticing the disciples' criticism of Mary, chided Judas and the other disciples, saying, "Why are you bothering this woman? Let her be! She has done a good thing for Me. You will always have poor people living among you to help whenever you desire. However, you will not always have Me living in your

---

3 Matthew 26:7; Mark 14:3; Luke 7:37

4 Matthew 26:7; Mark 14:3; Luke 7:37, 38; John 12:3

5 Matthew 26:8, 9; Mark 14:4, 5; John 12:4-6

midst! This woman is to be allowed to use this perfume to anoint Me as she has just done. In truth, she has done everything she could to show her love for Me.[6]

"As I have said, she has performed a good deed for Me, for when she poured this perfume on My body, she was, in reality, preparing My body for My burial. In fact, I must tell you with certainty, that wherever the message of the Gospel is preached throughout the entire world, what this woman has done for Me here in this room will be included as part of the Gospel story. Thus, she will always receive honor for what she had done for Me today. Yes, her memory will be preserved forever!" To be sure, it would be less than a week later that Jesus would be lying dead in the tomb, anointed with this and other burial spices. [*Harmony* 18:8][7]

> Mary's sinful life was common knowledge in the community of Bethany. However, what the residents of that town did not know was that Simon, the former leper, was the one who had originally seduced Mary into having an adulterous affair with him. And, it was this illicit affair that had led Mary to fall deeper into sin, which ultimately influenced her decision to become a full-time prostitute. Furthermore, it was Mary's sinful life which ultimately resulted in her demon possession. Thus, in shame, Mary for a time relocated to the town of Magdala in Galilee, many miles away from her family and the people who knew her.[(g)]

When Mary anointed Jesus with the pure nard perfume, Simon, in his heart, hypocritically condemned Mary for what she had done, choosing to ignore his part in the sinful affair which he had had with her! Even in spite of the Lord's rebuke of His disciples, Simon was still upset by what Mary had done. He thought to himself, "If Jesus were the true Prophet of Scriptural prophecy [Deuteronomy 18:15], He would have known just how evil a person this woman really is! Surely, the Prophet would not have allowed such a vile, immoral sinner to touch Him in the way she has done. So, He must not be that Prophet!" he concluded to himself.[(h) 8]

> The mindset of the Pharisees was such that Simon, even though he was just as sinful as Mary—and even more sinful—he was able to exonerate himself of the extreme wickedness that dwelt in his own life!

---

6 Matthew 26:10, 11; Mark 14:6-8; John 12:7, 8

7 Matthew 26:12, 13; Mark 14:8, 9; John 12:7

8 Luke 7:39

Jesus, reading the Pharisee's secret thoughts, openly said to him, "Simon, I have something I need to tell you."[9]

Simon answered, "Tell me what it is, Master."[10]

The Lord began to relate to the Pharisee a parable, saying, "A certain banker had two people who owed him large sums of money. One of them owed the banker 500 denarii—over a year's wages. The other one owed him 50 denarii—less than two month's wages. Both debtors were unable to make payment on what they owed, so the banker graciously forgave both their debts. Now, which one of the two debtors do you suppose would appreciate the banker's forgiveness more?"[11]

"Well, I would suppose," Simon responded, "the one who had owed him the most money!"[12]

"Right you are!" Jesus answered. "Your judgment is correct!"[13]

> Through this story, Jesus sought to impress upon Simon his dire need to repent and receive forgiveness for the tragic part he had played in Mary's sinful life. He had clearly taken shameful advantage of the woman. Jesus could have announced to the guests at the feast that it was Simon who had caused Mary to sin in the first place, thus exposing the Pharisee's terrible hypocrisy. But Christ did not do that. Instead, through the parable, Jesus subtly communicated with Simon. While the guests at the feast, no doubt, assumed that the debtor in the parable who owed the larger debt referred to Mary, Simon knew better. Instead, it was made clear to him that the debtor with the larger debt referred to himself, not Mary. By leading Mary into sin, Simon was the greater sinner of the two. By this parable, Jesus was, in effect saying to Simon, "You need to seek forgiveness for the part you played in this woman's sinful life. I have already forgiven her for *her* involvement. So, instead of condemning her, you need, yourself, to repent and seek forgiveness for the despicable part *you* played in destroying her life."[(i)]

---

9 Luke 7:40
10 Luke 7:40
11 Luke 7:41, 42
12 Luke 7:43
13 Luke 7:43

Pointing toward Mary, Jesus continued His conversation with Simon. He explained, "Do you see this woman and what she has done for Me? Well, when I came into your home tonight, you did not bother to wash My feet with water. On the other hand, she has washed My feet with her tears, and has dried them with her hair. Neither did you give Me a kiss when I entered your house. But this woman has not ceased, since I came into your home, to kiss My feet. Also, you did not anoint My head with oil as an indication of special honor, but she has anointed My feet with a most precious and costly perfume. That is why I must tell you that her sins—which are indeed many—have all been forgiven. It is clear that is why she loves Me so much!"[14]

Then Jesus added, "But the one who senses only a little forgiveness, loves only a little." Here Jesus referred to Simon. The Pharisee clearly understood what Jesus was saying to him.[(j)] [15]

Then, speaking directly to Mary, Jesus, reassured her, "Yes! All your sins have been completely forgiven!"[16]

Hearing this, the Lord's critics who were reclining at the feasting table whispered among themselves, "Who does this Man think He is, that He imagines He is able to forgive sins? Shameful! It's blasphemous!"[17]

Jesus, ignoring these accusations, concluded His words of comfort to Mary by adding, "Your faith has saved you from your sins! Go, now, in complete peace of mind and soul!"[18]

> During His discussion with Simon, Judas, and the others at the feast, Jesus appealed to their hearts, encouraging them to experience the true meaning of repentance and forgiveness—the type that Mary had received. Any viable relationship with Jesus as one's personal Savior includes both repentance and forgiveness. And, especially in the case of Judas, such a necessity was at a crisis point!

---

14 Luke 7:44-47
15 Luke 7:47
16 Luke 7:48
17 Luke 7:49
18 Luke 7:50

## —Judas's Betrayal Plot[k]
## < Saturday Night, Nisan 9, Spring, A.D. 31 (7/7) >
## {Matthew 26:3-5, 14-16; Mark 14:1, 2, 10, 11; Luke 22:1-6; John 12:10, 11}

At about the same time that Jesus was at the feast at Simon's house, a number of the chief priests, scribes, and the elders of the nation were in a secret council meeting in the court of Caiaphas, the high priest. This was in Jerusalem, about two miles away. It was just days before the beginning of the spring Festival of the Passover and Unleavened Bread, and they were in the process of scheming how they might be able to capture Jesus secretly and have Him killed.[19]

Even though they were determined to do just that, they were deeply concerned about many of the people who revered Jesus. The Jewish leaders knew that these people would be very upset, should any serious attempt be made to kill their Lord. The specter of angry, rioting people truly terrified them. This was especially true considering the fact that the city of Jerusalem would be packed with people from all over the country and surrounding nations during the yearly celebration of the Passover Festival. [*Harmony* 14:36][20]

> Their only hope, they figured, was to capture Jesus in secret. But, because of the Passover, Jesus would be surrounded constantly by many admirers—so many that the Jewish leaders knew it would be very difficult, if not impossible, to capture Him unobtrusively. But, in spite of such a difficulty, they knew that if Jesus *could* be captured in some out-of-the-way place and quickly condemned by the corrupt Roman government, it would be too late for the people to protest, even though there would be a public execution. After all, the Romans would squelch any such protest. So then the Jewish leaders had just one seemingly insurmountable problem to solve: Where could they capture Jesus in secret? They did not know where Jesus spent His time when He wasn't in public, ministering to the people. In reality, then, they probably needed someone on the "inside"—a traitor, that is—to help them out with their plan. But who, among His disciples, would actually betray his Lord? At this point, they did not know what to do. Surely no such betrayer existed! The Jewish leaders were, therefore, tending toward delaying the capture and execution of Jesus.

---

19 Matthew 26:3, 4; Mark 14:1; Luke 22:1, 2

20 Luke 22:2

They concluded, "We can't do it during the Passover, else there could be a riot among the people who love this Man! We'll wait until the people leave town and there are fewer individuals around to cause trouble. Then it will be easier to arrest Him in private."[21]

About that time, Judas Iscariot, left the feast at Simon's house and began to walk the two miles toward Jerusalem. No doubt he had been thinking for some time about betraying his Lord. However, from the Gospel record it is not clear just when this plan began to grow within his heart. It is probable, though, that the Lord's open rebuke of his criticism regarding Mary's anointing of Jesus with the pure nard [*Harmony* 14:6], truly upset Judas. It is very likely that it was an angry Judas who traveled to Jerusalem that Saturday night.[1]

But what was the specific thinking of this dissident disciple that led him to actually betray his Lord? Quite surprisingly, very little is said directly in the Gospel record regarding his motivations. However, there are *indications* as to what his thinking might have been. [*Harmony* 17:17/][2]

As a disciple, Judas no doubt harbored the hope—as did the rest of the eleven disciples—that Jesus would soon establish a Messianic kingdom. [*Harmony* 13:101-107] And certainly Judas wished to play an important and authoritative role in that kingdom. And most assuredly, he, along with the other disciples, must have been irate when the mother of James and John had recently asked that her sons have special rank in the Lord's establishment of His upcoming kingdom.[3]

What was it, then, that drove him to actually betray his Lord? Judas had noticed throughout the ministry of Jesus that the Lord showed a certain toughness and determination—especially when He dealt with the Jewish leaders. Judas knew that this toughness would serve Him well when He ultimately established His *earthly* Messianic kingdom. But the problem, from Judas's perspective, was that the Savior did not seem to have the gumption to actually establish this kingdom! It appeared to Judas—as well as to the other disciples—that whenever the Lord had had a perfect opportunity to establish the kingdom, He always seemed to back down—at least that was the way Judas saw it. The classic example was when Jesus refused to allow the people to proclaim Him

21 Matthew 26:5; Mark 14:2

King after the miracle of the feeding of the 5,000. [*Harmony* 9:13] This would have been particularly galling to Judas. Judas must have thought that Jesus really wanted to assert Himself, but *just lacked the courage* to take that final step.[4]

Added to that, Judas certainly must have been very upset when Jesus talked about His impending death. How could He die, Judas reasoned, when He had such power and authority? After all, Jesus had escaped from a number of attempts on His life before. [*Harmony* 4:10; 11:77, 78, 171, 175] Why couldn't He do it again? Furthermore, Judas—even more than the other disciples—had a very hard time understanding the spiritual aspects of the Lord's ministry, such as the Lord's emphasis on character growth, victory over sin, and the like. [*Harmony* 5:3-84] In fact, he cared little for those things. Rather, Judas focused only on the temporal power of the Messiah, hoping that Jesus would overthrow the Romans. Judas was in it for the power and prestige. He had no concept that, in dying, Jesus would be securing the salvation of all those who placed their trust in Him as the "Lamb of God." [*Harmony* 2:49] Ironically, Judas did not understand that the Lord's death, once received by faith, could actually guarantee for *him* his own salvation![5]

Finally Judas asked himself: "What if Jesus were placed in such a position that He had either to assert His awesome power or lose His life?" Judas was certain that if this happened, in the final analysis, Jesus would exercise His power and declare Himself King. Thus the disciple devised a really simple plan: He would set Jesus up to be arrested in private. Next, once the Lord faced the very real prospect of death, He would assert His authority, and pronounce Himself King. And finally, when Jesus—who, Judas believed, really wanted to declare Himself to be the Messiah—realized that it was Judas who had worked out this scheme, the Lord would honor the brilliance of his plan by appointing him as His chief assistant. Added to this, as part of the scheme, Judas would end up getting money from the Jewish leaders for betraying Jesus. Judas figured that he couldn't lose, no matter what might happen. Unfortunately, though, added to his natural tendency toward greed and a thirst for power, Judas had allowed his anger toward the Lord over the incident with Mary Magdalene at Simon's feast to cloud his mind, destroying whatever little spiritual reason he had left within him.(1) [6]

So it was, at that very moment that the Jewish leaders were meeting together, Judas—one of the Lord's closest twelve disciples—appeared in Jerusalem, seeking an audience with them. Judas's heart was filled with the spirit of Satan. The potential betrayer found the Jewish priests and leaders huddled together in the council room in the process of plotting the death of Jesus. He wanted to work out a deal with them to betray Jesus into their control.[22]

Brought into their presence, Judas made a proposal to the priests. "What would you pay for me to betray Jesus, and hand Him over to you?" he asked them. "I know where He spends His time in seclusion away from the people. For the right amount of money, I will take you to the place where He can be found. There, you may seize Him in private, and no one will know! So, how much will you give me?" [*Harmony* 16:58][23]

With gloating excitement, they agreed to pay Judas 30 silver shekels for him to betray his Lord. [*Harmony* 17:56] Judas consented to the deal. They counted out the money on the spot and promised to give it to him when he delivered on his part of the bargain. He promised to contact them again very soon, when the best opportunity for them to seize the Lord secretly would arise. [*Harmony* 16:35/] He would know the exact moment! Thus the plot was set in motion! The chief priests and elders were both relieved and elated that they, because of the great fortune of having the Lord's betrayer actually come to them, would at last silence their nemesis, the Savior. [*Harmony* 14:41/3, 67, 78; 15:60/; 16:7; 17:33][24]

So emboldened were these Jewish leaders that they began to plot a way that they might also kill Lazarus, who had recently been raised from the dead by Jesus. [*Harmony* 13:1-30] His resurrection had inspired many of the Jews to become more dedicated in their allegiance to Jesus. Thus, as Israel's leaders, they were losing control over these new followers of the Lord. And too, a significant number of these leaders—specifically the Sadducees—did not believe in the resurrection. Having Lazarus as living proof that their belief was false was more than they could stand. Both Jesus and Lazarus had to go![25]

---

22 Matthew 26:14; Mark 14:10; Luke 22:3, 4
23 Matthew 26:15
24 Matthew 26:15, 16; Mark 14:11; Luke 22:5, 6
25 John 12:10, 11

There is no Biblical reference as to whether the Jewish leaders ever succeeded in their efforts to have Lazarus killed along with Jesus. They probably didn't.

## Triumph and Sadness
## < Sunday Afternoon and Early Evening, Nisan 9, Spring, A.D. 31 (7/7) >
## (Matthew 21:1-11; Mark 11:1-11; Luke 19:29-44; John 12:12-19)

Meanwhile, Jesus and His remaining disciples spent the rest of Saturday night in Bethany. Sometime on Sunday—the next day—they made their way to Jerusalem, about two miles to the northwest. It was just days before the Feast of the Passover. A short distance out of Bethany, they were about to pass through the village of Bethphage, which was on the eastern side of the Mount of Olives. This mount was about half a mile east of Jerusalem, and about 300 feet higher in elevation than the large hill upon which the Temple was built. The Kidron valley lay in between these two mounts.[26]

As they came close to Bethphage, Jesus gave instructions to two of the disciples, saying, "Go into Bethphage, opposite from where we are standing. As soon as you enter the village, you will see a donkey and its colt tied to a pole there. No one has ever ridden on the colt. Untie both animals and bring them back to Me. Should anyone ask you what you are doing, you are to say, 'The Lord has need of them!' and you will immediately be allowed to return here with the two animals."[27]

The two disciples went into Bethphage and, just as the Lord had told them, a donkey and its colt were tied near a doorway at a street corner beside a courtyard. The disciples did exactly what the Lord had instructed them to do and untied both animals. Some people standing nearby—the animals' owners—noticed the disciples taking the creatures. They challenged the disciples, exclaiming, "Hey! What are you doing? Why are you untying these animals?" They answered the questioners as Jesus had instructed them to do, and, just as the Lord had predicted, they were allowed to continue on with the donkey and its colt. It is not clear just how this whole arrangement regarding the securing of these two animals had originally been set up, if at all.[(m)] [28]

---

26 Matthew 21:1; Mark 11:1; Luke 19:29; John 12:12

27 Matthew 21:1-3; Mark 11:1-3; Luke 19:29-31

28 Matthew 21:6; Mark 11:4-6; Luke 19:32-34; John 12:14

After bringing the donkey and its colt to Jesus, the disciples laid their coats on the animals, and Jesus sat upon the colt. It was a Hebrew custom for their kings, before their inaugurations to ride on a colt which had never before been ridden. It was then, astride the colt alongside the donkey, that the potential king was to be led into the city amidst a crowd of cheering people. On this occasion a large crowd of people had formed along the roadway where Jesus was sitting on the colt. Many of them were traveling to Jerusalem for the Passover Festival just a few days away. They were very excited to find Jesus sitting on the animal, and began to follow along with Him, fully anticipating that the Lord was about to proclaim Himself the King of Israel—the Messiah—during the Passover festivities in Jerusalem! Many of them, as a sign of respect and honor, placed their coats on the roadway over which the animals walked. Others in the crowd cut leafy palm branches from trees and nearby fields to cast on the roadway before Jesus.[29]

The entire mass of people, sensing what was happening, surrounded the Lord. They could not restrain their joy. They shouted together, "Hosanna!"—an Aramaic expression that means, "Save now!" or, "Save, I ask of You!' It was a word used to praise God for His power to save His people. "Hosanna to the Son of David—the King of Israel!" [*Harmony* 2:58; 14:109/] the people in the swelling crowd continued to cry out. "Blessed is the One who comes in the name of the Lord!" "Blessed is the coming kingdom of our father, King David—even the Messiah King of Israel!" "Hosanna in the highest!" In their minds, there was no doubt whatsoever that Jesus was the promised Messiah, and that He was about to proclaim Himself King![(n)] [30]

Before long, the entourage reached the top of the Mount of Olives, overlooking the city of Jerusalem, across the valley below. Just before they began their descent toward the city, the crowd of extended disciples shouted even louder, praising God with great joy for all the miracles they had seen throughout the ministry of Jesus. "Blessed is the King!" they continued their various words of praise. "Blessed is the King, who has come in the name of the Lord!" "Peace in heaven!" And, "Glory in the highest!"[31]

---

29 Matthew 21:7, 8; Mark 11:7, 8; Luke 19:35, 36; John 12:12-14

30 Matthew 21:9; Mark 11:9, 10; John 12:12, 13

31 Luke 19:37, 38

However, there were some Pharisees in the crowd who were, quite understandably, very unhappy about what was taking place. "Tell Your disciples to stop all this noise, Teacher," they demanded. "Rebuke them!"[32]

But Jesus refused. Instead, the Lord declared, "I must tell you: If they stop their shouting, then the stones you see scattered on the ground around Me will cry out in praise! Yes, one way or another, I will be praised!"[33]

As the procession began to descend the mount, Jesus stopped and looked for a long time at the city on the hill beyond them . . . and then He began to weep! With tears on His face, and a certain trembling in His voice, He addressed the city as if it were actually a person: "Oh Jerusalem! If you only knew, even you, what it would really take for you to find for yourself true and lasting peace! But, unfortunately, you will never know. It has been hidden from you because of your blindness, and your refusal to see the truth! Ah! The days will come when your enemies will build a wall completely around you, to hem you in so that you cannot escape. Then they will flatten you right down to the ground! And your children—your citizens—will be trapped within your walls. And they all will be slaughtered! Your enemies will not allow one stone of your Temple to remain upon another. All will be destroyed! And why? Because you never realized that your rejection of the truth that I've been teaching will lead to such devastation. Indeed, such destruction will be visited upon you, just as I have declared!" [*Harmony* 12:89; 14:132] The Lord's prediction of that day was fulfilled, in horrible detail, some 39 years later when the city of Jerusalem and the Temple were razed by Roman armies in A.D. 70. [*Harmony* 15:1, 15/][34]

The procession then descended the western slope of the Mount of Olives, crossed the brook Kidron, and ascended the hill leading up into the city. The sounds of those praising the Lord grew louder as they came closer and closer to the gates of the city. Hearing the noise, curious people within the city came out to see what all the commotion was about. In addition to this new crowd, there were other people who were coming toward the city from all directions. This group included those from various parts of Israel and other surrounding countries who were arriving to celebrate the Passover. Now there were some in the crowd, who, weeks before, had been eyewitnesses to the resurrection of Lazarus in Bethany. [*Harmony* 13:30] These eyewitnesses excitedly shared the details of the miracle

---

32 Luke 19:39

33 Luke 19:40

34 Luke 19:41-44

with those who were coming out of the city, as well as with those who were going into the city. After hearing the facts of the Lord's ability to even raise the dead, both crowds—those coming out of the city, and those going in—wanted to see Jesus, up close, for themselves. Accordingly, they joined in with those already praising the Lord, to form one grand multitude of joyful people. Indeed, a great sense of excitement and anticipation was building. Perhaps this Man *was* the Messiah, they all thought. And, maybe He was about to pronounce Himself the King and Messiah of Israel![35]

The Pharisees, who wanted to kill Jesus [*Harmony* 14:19, 20], murmured among themselves, "Do you see that all our efforts to destroy Him have been in vain? Look! The whole world is following after Him! All is lost! All is lost!" they moaned.[36]

The whole community there seemed to be in an uproar, asking, "Who is this Man?"[37]

Some in the crowd shouted back, "This is the Prophet, Jesus. He is from Nazareth in Galilee." Even though these people were willing to recognize the Lord as a prophet, they were not yet certain that Jesus was the Messiah. But they were certainly hoping that He was![38]

Jesus made His way to the Temple area. But instead of proclaiming Himself as King, as most hoped and even expected that He would, Jesus looked around for awhile. Beyond that, the Lord did nothing further to indicate that He had any intention of pronouncing Himself King. Accordingly, the crowd slowly began to disperse. And quite anticlimactically, as the day came to a close, Jesus, with His disciples with Him, without any fanfare, walked the two miles back to Bethany to spend the night there. [*Harmony* 14:44][39]

> The people—as well as the disciples—must have been confused and severely disappointed. What had gone wrong? They wondered why the Lord did not proclaim Himself King.

---

[35] John 12:17, 18
[36] John 12:19
[37] Matthew 21:10; Mark 11:11
[38] Matthew 21:11
[39] Mark 11:11, 12

However, the so-called "Triumphal Entry" took place just as God described it should in fulfillment of an Old Testament prophecy which reads, "Say this to the daughters—the inhabitants—of Zion: 'Fear not! Behold, your King is coming to you! He is gentle, and mounted on a donkey—even on a colt, the offspring of a beast of burden." [Zechariah 9:9][40]

> Following the custom of the old days when a king was inaugurated, Jesus wanted the people of Israel to recognize Him as the true King of the nation. While it is true that His *earthly* kingship did not come to fruition that day, He, nevertheless, wanted the people to recognize Him as the "King" of their *hearts*. Much later on, after His ascension into heaven, He would return again—at the Second Coming—as the glorious, eternal King of both heaven *and* earth. That's when the real, literal Triumphal Entry will take place! Thus, the Lord's Triumphal Entry into Jerusalem two thousand years ago served only as a symbol. First, it symbolized the fact that Jesus is the true King of converted human hearts—that is, the Savior of all those who would follow Him. And second, it symbolized the Lord's glorious Second Coming, when He would truly be "King of Kings and Lord of Lords" of the entire universe! [Revelation 19:11-16][(o)]

But at the time it happened, the disciples did not understand the meaning of the Lord's Triumphal Entry into Jerusalem. To them, it was a bitter disappointment. But after His resurrection and ascension into heaven, they would remember that all these things had been prophesied regarding Him in the Old Testament, even the part about the people praising His name.[41]

> It was after the ascension of Jesus that they would begin to appreciate its true meaning and purpose. As time went by, they—as well as all of the Lord's followers—would be reminded of the fact that the Lord must be, first of all, the King of their hearts. Also, they would be reminded to look forward with courage and faith to the day when Jesus would return to this earth at His Second Coming as the true conquering King.[1]

> There can be no doubt that Jesus was appealing to the hearts of all those that day—the crowd, His disciples, and even the Jewish leaders—to accept Him as the Messiah of prophecy. He strongly desired that each

---

40 Matthew 21:4, 5; John 12:14, 15

41 John 12:16

one of them would develop a strong personal relationship of faith with Him.[2]

How devastated the crowd—including the disciples—must have been that day when Jesus did not pronounce Himself King! From their perspective, He had come oh, so close to doing so! This must have been especially distressing for Judas. He must have concluded that he now had no real choice but to go ahead with his plan to betray his Lord. [*Harmony* 14:19-25] In this way, Jesus would be forced, at the risk of death, to declare His Kingship. Thus Judas was resolved to follow through with his plan of betraying the Savior.[3]

## A Curse and a Cleansing
## < Monday, Nisan 10, Spring, A.D. 31 (7/7) >
## (Matthew 21:12-19; Mark 11:12-19; Luke 19:45-48)

### —Jesus Curses the Fruitless Fig Tree
### < Monday, Nisan 10, Spring, A.D. 31 (7/7) >
### {Matthew 21:18, 19; Mark 11:12-14}

The next day—Monday—Jesus and His disciples returned to Jerusalem from Bethany where they had spent the night. Jesus was hungry. In the distance along the road the Lord noticed a fig tree covered with leaves. The other trees in the area had no leaves yet, so Jesus thought that the tree with leaves might have fruit on it. While it was yet early in the season—perhaps too early to expect figs to be present—the fact that there were so many leaves on the tree indicated some early figs might be there, albeit unripe. To many people, unripe figs were especially appetizing.[42]

However, approaching the tree, Jesus discovered that it had only leaves and no fruit at all. Quite surprisingly, in the hearing of the disciples, Jesus cursed the fig tree. "May it be a fact that no one will ever eat another fig from you! No! Never!" the Lord declared. A bit shocked, the disciples wondered why Jesus had placed such a strange curse on an innocent fig tree. But they said nothing to Him about the incident at the time. The next day and beyond, the reason for the Lord's curse of the fig tree would become clearer to them. [*Harmony* 14:52-54][43]

---

[42] Matthew 21:18; Mark 11:12, 13

[43] Matthew 21:18, 19; Mark 11:13, 14

## —Jesus Cleanses the Temple for the Second Time[(p)] [(q)]
## < Monday, Nisan 10, Spring, A.D. 31 (7/7) >
## {Matthew 21:12-17; Mark 11:15-19; Luke 19:45-48}

Continuing on into Jerusalem, Jesus entered the outer court of the Temple area. It was the same place where He had been the day before. [*Harmony* 14:39] On this occasion, He spent some time looking around. There, the Lord noticed that once again there were many people who were buying and selling sacrificial animals in the area. Almost exactly three years before, Jesus had witnessed a similar sight and had driven the buyers and sellers out of the Temple court. [*Harmony* 3:1-9; 14:150/2][44]

> The Jews provided these animals for the visitors of the Passover to be used for their sacrifices. This way, such visitors would not need to bring animals along with them on their trip to Jerusalem. Instead, they could be purchased at the Temple. However, the animals could be bought only by a special "Temple coin," which could be secured only by exchanging regular money for the higher priced "coin." This meant that these moneychangers made a stiff profit at the expense of the people who were in town for the purpose of worshipping God! Also, the animals were themselves overpriced. The motive of the Jewish leaders behind this practice was very upsetting to Jesus. And, no doubt, such a procedure greatly detracted from the holy atmosphere of the entire Temple area. That is why, three years before, Jesus had driven out the moneychangers and their animals.

On this day, Jesus did the same thing. He overturned the moneychangers' tables as well as the chairs on which the sellers of doves were sitting. He threw out both those who were buying and those who were selling. He refused to allow anyone to continue carrying any more merchandise into the Temple area. Raising His voice for all to hear, He taught the people the true meaning of the Temple, declaring, "It is written in the Scriptures, 'My house will be called a house of prayer for all nations!' [Isaiah 56:7] However, by your despicable actions, you have made it like a dark cave where thieves hang out!" [Jeremiah 7:11][45]

Once the buying and selling in the Temple court was terminated, many diseased people—including the lame and the blind—were brought in and filled

44 Matthew 21:12: Mark 11:15; Luke 19:45

45 Matthew 21:12, 13; Mark 11:15-17; Luke 19:45, 46

the space that had shortly before been used for trading. There, Jesus healed them.[46]

After some time had passed, a number of the chief priests and the scribes who had recently been driven by the Lord from the Temple area began to filter back in to see what was happening. In place of the selling of animals, they now saw the marvelous miracles of healing which the Savior performed. Instead of the noise of animals and commerce, they heard sounds of children praising God in the Temple area. The little ones were crying out, "Hosanna!"—an Aramaic expression of divine praise which honored God for His power to save. "Hosanna to the Son of David—the King!" [*Harmony* 2:58][(q)] [47]

Seeing and hearing this praise that was directed toward the Lord really made the Jewish leaders furious! "Do You hear all the noise these children are making in the Temple?" they demanded of Jesus. "Make them be quiet! It's all quite irreverent! Stop it!"[48]

But the Lord answered, "Yes, there is a lot of noise! But have you never read in the Scriptures where it says, 'Out of the mouth of infants and nursing babies You will inspire praise for Yourself'"? [Psalm 8:2][49]

> From the Lord's perspective, noise in the Temple wasn't the issue. Rather, it was the *kind* of noise. The noise of genuine praise to God was very appropriate. The noise of the selling of animals was not.[1]
>
> But beyond the mere act of cleansing the Temple, the Lord was appealing to the Jewish leaders to understand the extreme danger of their rebellion against Him. He so much wanted them to repent of their sin and accept Him as the Messiah. Even yet, it wasn't too late for them to find the true way of salvation.[2]

The Lord spent the major part of the day in the Temple ministering to the people. Because evening was approaching, Jesus left the Temple area and returned once more to Bethany to spend the night there.[50]

---

46 Matthew 21:14
47 Matthew 21:15
48 Matthew 21:15, 16
49 Matthew 21:16
50 Matthew 21:17; Mark 11:19

Meanwhile the Jewish leaders—both the chief priests and the scribes, as well as other of Israel's leaders—continued to plot the death of Jesus out of indignation for when the Lord cast out the moneychangers. [*Harmony* 13:32] Nevertheless, they were frustrated in their planning, quite unsure of what action they should take. True, they had made a deal with Judas [*Harmony* 13:31-34], but they couldn't be absolutely sure that he'd follow through with his part of the bargain. In addition, the Jewish leaders were increasingly concerned about the Lord's influence with the people, for the masses were amazed at the power of His words of truth. In fact, the people, starving for the truth of the Gospel, were hanging on to every word that the Master spoke as they intently listened to Him. For it was on a day-by-day basis, that Jesus had been teaching the Gospel in the Temple area. They were also fixated with His ability to heal the sick.[51]

## The Day of Judgment for Israel
## < Tuesday, Nisan 11, Spring, A.D. 31 (7/7) >
## (Matthew 21:19-24:1; Mark 11:20-12:40; Luke 20:1-47)

### — The Fruitless Fig Tree Is Withered
### < Tuesday, Nisan 11, Spring, A.D. 31 (7/7) >
### {Matthew 21:19-22; Mark 11:20-26}

The next morning—Tuesday—Jesus returned once more to Jerusalem and the Temple area. On the way, the Lord and His disciples passed by the place where He had cursed the fruitless fig tree the day before. [*Harmony* 14:42, 43] Much to the disciples' surprise, the cursed fig tree had completely withered and died from the roots up! In fact, it had begun to wither at the very moment that the Lord had cursed it.[52]

With Peter taking the lead, the shocked disciples commented to Jesus with amazement, "Teacher, look! The fig tree which You cursed has withered! How is it that the tree withered and died so quickly?"[53]

The Lord answered them, "Have faith in God! It is very true when I tell you that if you possessed an undoubting faith, you would able to do much more that what was done to the fig tree." Jesus pointed toward the Mount of Olives nearby and added, "You would be able to say to this mountain, 'Be lifted up and be thrown into the sea'—and it would happen just as you have so declared! In

---

51 Mark 11:18; Luke 19:47, 48

52 Matthew 21:19; Mark 11:20

53 Matthew 21:20; Mark 11:21

fact, all the things that you shall ask in prayer, if you believe with an unwavering heart, you will be granted those things for which you have asked. Therefore, I tell you again, whatever things for which you pray—fully believing that you will receive them—your desire will be granted you. On the other hand, when you stand in prayer, asking God to forgive your sins, you must first forgive those against whom, for some reason, you may hold a grudge. This is the only way that the heavenly Father will be willing to forgive your sins. However, if you are not willing to forgive others, well, then, your heavenly Father will not forgive your shortcomings either!"[54]

The story of the withered fig tree is one of the most unusual in the Scriptures. Why did Jesus do what He did? What can it mean? And further, is it really possible to move mountains by faith? And still further, does God really grant *all* our requests, if we ask for them in faith?[1]

First of all, the cursing of the fig tree had a spiritual meaning. The fig tree represented the nation of Israel. Jesus had been searching for the "fruit" of salvation that the nation should have borne for Him. But of course, they had failed to bear such fruit. Just as the fig tree was cursed, Israel would also be cursed. And, as the tree withered, so Israel would wither way as God's special people. [*Harmony* 12:70, 71] At the moment of the withering of the literal tree, though, the disciples were interested only in the miracle itself, rather than its spiritual meaning. Thus Jesus, at that time, addressed only the power demonstrated through the miracle, ignoring its spiritual meaning altogether.[2]

Second, in regard to the moving of mountains, it is not realistic to really think that Jesus was being literal in this case. Jesus was discussing the "mountains" of difficulty and of sins Christians can face in their lives—especially, as was indicated in the story, the load of guilt a sinner might bear in his or her heart. With faith, these obstacles, which appear as massive as mountains, can be removed! And often, indeed, a person's guilt for the sins committed may look like "mountains" to the sinner. By a willingness to forgive others, and by faith in God's power to forgive sins, such "mountains" can be cast into the sea, so to speak, as the Lord had mightily declared.[3]

---

54 Matthew 21:21, 22; Mark 11:22-26

In this case, the Lord appealed to His disciples—and especially to Judas—to recognize the power of repentance and subsequent forgiveness. Indeed, there was no sin—not even the transgression of betrayal—that, once given to the Lord, could not be forgiven and be victoriously expelled from the heart![4]

And third, Jesus could not possibly have meant that all our requests will be answered if we ask for them with faith. Clearly, reality tells us otherwise! Jesus must have been talking about something else. Perhaps He was talking about having our prayers answered—maybe even with a "no!"—rather than about actually *getting* everything we want. In that case, the Lord's point was that God will always listen to us and respond if we ask in faith. Perhaps, too, the Lord was talking about *spiritual issues*—such as forgiveness of sins—as opposed to getting the *material things* we want. In fact, Jesus openly mentioned the forgiveness of sins in His discussion with the disciples. In any case, it remains somewhat a mystery as to what Jesus precisely had in mind when He made this strong statement. It should not be forgotten, too, that in other places the Lord indicated clearly that prayer requests need to be made in the His Name [*Harmony* 16:47] and that God's will should be done. [*Harmony* 5:48] Such conditions in prayer would appear to preclude selfish and unwise requests.(s) [5]

In the final analysis, the literal and more specific meaning of the miracle—the part Jesus did not at the time address—relating to Israel's future, would become more obvious to the disciples as the week wore on. [*Harmony* 14:67-77][6]

### — The Jewish Leaders Challenge the Lord's Ministry < Tuesday, Nisan 11, Spring, A.D. 31 (7/7) > {Matthew 21:23-32; Mark 11:27-33; Luke 20:1-8}

A short time later, Jesus entered the city of Jerusalem and went straight to the Temple. Upon His arrival there, He walked around and began to teach the people who were surrounding Him. In doing so, He appealed strongly to their souls. He preached the message of the Gospel to them. Soon, however, the chief priests, scribes, and elders interrupted His preaching and teaching to challenge

Him. They demanded, "By what authority are You able to do the things that You do? And, who is it who gave to You this supposed authority?"[55]

The Lord replied, "I'll tell you what: First, I'll also ask you a question. If you answer that question, then I'll tell you by what authority I do these things. If, however, you are not able to give an answer to My question, then I will not tell you by what authority I do these things. All right? Here's my question for you: Was the baptism of John the Baptist from heaven or just an invention of a man? [*Harmony* 2:3] Indeed, where did it come from? Answer me that!"[56]

This question placed the Jewish leaders in an awkward situation. They began to debate among themselves as to how they should answer this question. "If we say," they reasoned, "that John's baptism was 'from heaven,' He will say, 'Then why didn't you believe in him as you should have?' If, on the other hand, we say that John's baptism was 'a mere invention of a man,' then we are afraid that the people will be upset with us, for they consider John to have been a true prophet. They might even stone us to death!" So accordingly, the Jewish leaders came back to Jesus, saying, "We really cannot say for certain what the source of John's ministry was!"[57]

"Ah then," the Master responded, "neither I will not tell you by what authority I do the things I do!"[58]

> By having this conversation with the Jewish leaders, the Lord sought, once more, to appeal to their hearts to accept John the Baptist as the true forerunner of the Messiah. [*Harmony* 2:4] And in doing so, they would accordingly indicate their acceptance of Jesus as that Messiah. Once again, time was running out for them!

"I do have a story for you, though," Jesus continued. "What do you think it means? A certain man had two sons. He approached the first son, saying, 'My child, please go and work for me today in my vineyard.'[59]

---

55 Matthew 21:23; Mark 11:27, 28; Luke 20:1, 2

56 Matthew 21:24, 25; Mark 11:29, 30; Luke 20:3, 4

57 Matthew 21:25-27; Mark 11:31-33; Luke 20:5-7

58 Matthew 21:27; Mark 11:33; Luke 20:8

59 Matthew 21:28

"But the son answered the father, saying, 'No, I won't!' However, a little later on he regretted that he had answered his father that way, and went to work in the vineyard, just as his father had originally requested.[60]

"Now, the father approached his second son and asked him to do the same thing. Well, this son answered, 'Of course, sir, I will go and work in your vineyard.' However, he did not go as he had promised.[61]

"Now, let Me ask you, which one of these two sons ended up actually doing the will of his father: the first or the second son?"[62]

"The first son—the one who finally went to work in the vineyard—that's obvious!" the Jewish leaders answered.[63]

"Ah, yes! You have just confirmed that I can safely declare to you that the tax-collectors and the prostitutes will be saved in the kingdom of heaven before all of you will!" [*Harmony* 8:1-4] Jesus said. "This is what I mean: John the Baptist came preaching righteousness—the things that you should have agreed with—yet, you refused to believe him. [*Harmony* 2:7-16] You are like the second son. You say you believe, but you don't, not really.[64]

"On the other hand, many of the tax-collectors and the prostitutes—the so-called sinners who you would think would reject the message of righteous living—have ended up, in the final analysis, believing in John and accepting his message. That's just like the first son, who ended up obeying, even after first refusing to do so. Do you get the point I'm making? But, to make matters worse for you," Jesus added, "even after understanding all this, you still do not feel guilty about your rejection of John's message. Instead, you have continually refused to believe in him and in Me . . . then and now!"[65]

> By this powerful story, Jesus appealed yet once more to the hearts of the Jewish leaders to accept Him as the Messiah, through appealing to them to believe in the obviously deeply spiritual ministry of John the Baptist.

---

60 Matthew 21:29
61 Matthew 21:30
62 Matthew 21:31
63 Matthew 21:31
64 Matthew 21:31, 32
65 Matthew 21:32

## — The Story of the Evil Vine-growers[(t)]
## < Tuesday, Nisan 11, Spring, A.D. 31 (7/7) >
## {Matthew 21:33-46; Mark 12:1-12; Luke 20:9-19}

The Lord followed this illustration with yet another story. By this parable, Jesus sought to send a powerful message to the nation of Israel and its leaders as to where they were heading if they did not immediately cease their rebellion against Him as the Messiah—including their plans to kill Him. [*Harmony* 14:22-24] In this story, the Master compared the Hebrew nation to tenant farmers who had been left in charge of a vast vineyard owned by a rich landowner. The landowner represented God, the Father. As the landowner sent various individuals to check on how the tenant farmers were progressing with their responsibilities, the tenant farmers treated these representatives very badly. The individuals sent by the landowner represented the various prophets of Old Testament days. Finally, the landowner sent his own son, his heir. This son, of course, represented Jesus. How the tenant farmers would treat him would determine their eternal fate. [*Harmony* 12:134][66]

Jesus began to relate this parable to the Jewish leaders by saying, "Let Me tell you yet another story to illustrate a point: There was a certain wealthy landowner who planted a fine vineyard. He had a wall constructed around the vineyard to protect it from thieves. As part of the wall, he had a tower built so that any oncoming enemies might be spotted well in advance. Then, inside the vineyard itself, he had a winepress built to make and hold a large amount of wine from all the grapes he was sure would be produced by the vines. Because he was going to travel to a foreign country for a long time, the landowner appointed tenant farmers to care for the vineyard. They were to protect its environs and produce a large quantity of superior quality wine."[67]

> Thus far in His parable, the Lord laid out the basic story. In symbol, it told of God's establishment of the Jewish church, represented by the fine vineyard which the landowner planted. The wall around the vineyard symbolized the Law which, when obeyed, protected God's people from evil. [Exodus 20:2-17] The tower represented the Hebrew's understanding of Scriptural prophecy, which gave them a clear view of what was going to happen in the future. The wine press symbolized the message of the Gospel. The filling up the wine press with wine,

66 Matthew 21:33-37; Mark 12:1-6; Luke 20:9-13

67 Matthew 21:33; Mark 12:1; Luke 20:9

represented the influx of converts to the Jewish church as the result of the Jews effectively sharing the Gospel with the world. God's official establishment of the Jewish nation—or church—and its mission at Mount Sinai, and the time given them to fulfill their mission, was illustrated by the landowner's going away to a foreign country, leaving the vineyard under the care of the tenant farmers. Thus the tenant farmers represented the Jewish leaders, who, throughout the years, had been placed in charge of the church.

Jesus continued with the parable: "Now, when the time arrived for a huge harvest of grapes and wine, the landowner sent some of his representatives to visit the vineyard and receive of its produce. But the tenant farmers whom he had placed in charge of the vineyard in his absence seized the landowner's representatives. They beat one and sent him away with nothing. They killed a second, and stoned a third! Undeterred, the landowner sent a second group of representatives, larger than the first. And what did the tenant farmers do to these men? They treated them just as badly as they had done to the first group. They wounded one of them, brutally hitting him on the head, treating him awfully. Another one of them they murdered. Yet still others were sent by the landowner. But they, like the first ones, were treated badly—either beaten and cast out . . . or even killed."[(u)] [68]

In the parable, the various representatives sent by the landowner symbolized the many prophets and spiritual leaders whom God had sent during Old Testament days to warn Israel's leaders of their pitfalls and to try to persuade them to focus their lives and mission in the right direction. But, as the history of Israel clearly reveals, the nation, for the most part, refused to listen to these prophets and other spiritual leaders sent to them by God. In fact, these messengers from God were treated brutally. Many were simply ignored. Others were persecuted. Still others were killed. Wave after wave of these representatives from God were treated very badly by the Jewish people and their leaders.

The Lord continued, "But still undeterred, the landowner said, 'What shall I do? I have yet one more representative to send to them: my beloved son! Yes, as a final effort, I will send my son to see how things are going. Surely, they will respect my son! At least, I will give them an opportunity to do so.'[69]

---

68 Matthew 21:34-36; Mark 12:2-5; Luke 20:10-12

69 Matthew 21:37; Mark 12:6; Luke 20:13

However, when these farmers saw the son approaching the vineyard, they, talking among themselves, said to one another, 'Look! The landowner's son—the heir to the vineyard—is approaching us! Let's kill him! And because he is the heir of the vineyard, we will be able to seize all of his inheritance and make it our own!' So accordingly, they seized the son, killed him, and threw him out of the vineyard!"[70]

> Obviously, the son in this story is none other than Jesus Christ! The tenant farmers' despicable attitude toward the landowner's son represented the equally despicable attitude of the Jewish leaders toward Jesus and His ministry. The killing of the son in the story symbolized the crucifixion of Jesus that would take place just a few days after Jesus told this story. When Jesus was killed, the Jewish leaders thought that they could claim the nation of Israel as their own. This was symbolized by the farmers in the parable saying that, after killing him, they would seize the son's inheritance from him. By predicting His own death, Jesus was giving the Jewish leaders one last chance to change their minds and turn them from the self-destructive direction they were going in. And, by describing the death of the son in the story, Jesus was letting the leaders know that He, indeed, had full—and supernatural—knowledge of their evil plans to kill Him.

Then, in concluding this parable, Jesus asked this pointed question, "Now I have a bottom-line question for you: What do you suppose the landowner will do to these tenant farmers to whom he had entrusted his vineyard and its produce, especially considering how brutal they were to his representatives, and ultimately, even to his own son? Indeed, what should he do to them when he comes back?"[71]

The Jewish leaders, caught up in the story Jesus had been telling, quickly answered, "They were terrible men! Why, of course, he will bring those despicable people to a dire end—the kind of end that they surely deserve! Then, he will rent the place out to other farmers who will treat the vineyard and the landowner's representatives with proper respect. Then, these new farmers will produce the right kind of harvest at the appropriate time!" Quite amazingly, without thinking

70 Matthew 21:38, 39; Mark 12:7, 8; Luke 20:14, 15

71 Matthew 21:40; Luke 20:15

it through, the Jewish leaders had actually pronounced, unwittingly, an accurate, yet damning judgment, directly upon themselves![72]

"Yes!" the Lord said in agreement with their verdict. "Indeed, what will the landowner do? He will do just what you have declared he should: He will come and kill those worthless tenant farmers, and give the vineyard over to others who will take proper care of it!" [*Harmony* 12:71/][73]

> Jesus totally agreed with the Jews' own judgment upon themselves. God would, indeed, do two things. First, He would destroy them for their evil ways. This happened, in part, when Jerusalem was destroyed 39 years later in A.D. 70. And second, God would give the responsibility of sharing the Gospel with the world to another group of people who would successfully fulfill the task. This happened, of course, through establishment of the Christian Church, ultimately much of it Gentile—or non-Jewish—in composition. [*Harmony* 14:55/6]

Finally figuring out that Jesus was, in reality, talking directly about them, the Jewish leaders cried out, "May that never happen to us as You declare! No!"[(v)] [74]

> The truth was that the nation of Israel was on the verge of losing its special status of being the Lord's chosen people, commissioned to share the Gospel message with the whole world. This was mainly because of its leaders. Should they fail to quickly repent, God would have no choice but to give this special responsibility to another group of people—both of Jews and Gentiles in a newly formed "Christian" church. In the final analysis, this is exactly what happened!

Despite the fact that the Jewish leaders objected that Jesus was implying that they would be removed from their privileged status as His special people, Jesus continued His assault upon the leaders by relating to them yet another story. He said, "Well then, have you ever read what the Scriptures have said, 'The stone which the builders rejected as being worthless, this same stone has become the chief cornerstone of the building. All of this was the will of God, and we were amazed to see how He worked things out for us'?" [Psalm 118:22, 23; *Harmony* 14:77][75]

---

72 Matthew 21:41

73 Mark 12:9; Luke 20:15, 16

74 Luke 20:16

75 Matthew 21:42; Mark 12:10, 11; Luke 20:17

> Jesus referred to a story that was well known among the Jews. When the original Temple was built some 1,000 years earlier, an odd sized stone was delivered—apparently mistakenly—to the building site. Because it wouldn't fit anywhere, the builders rejected it, considering it worthless. It just lay there at the building site, getting into the builders' way! In the meantime, a suitable foundation cornerstone for the Temple could not be found anywhere. One after another, each crumbled under the load. At last, in frustration, the builders tried the stone which they had previously rejected. Surprisingly, it fit perfectly! Not only that, it held up well under the weight of the entire Temple wall. Indeed, the stone that the builders had rejected as worthless, became the chief cornerstone! So it would be with Jesus: Even though these Jewish leaders would reject Him as the Messiah, in time, He would become the very foundation cornerstone upon which the church of the true Gospel message would be based! This was because Jesus was, without any doubt, the promised Messiah!

Next, Jesus reiterated the punch line of the parable of the landowner: "I must further tell you, therefore, oh leaders of Israel, because of what you have failed to do, and what you are now planning to do, God's kingdom will be snatched away from you and given to another nation of people. And they will produce the anticipated fruit from the vineyard. This will be the same fruit that the Father had originally asked you to produce!"[76]

> Again, the inescapable message of the Lord's parable was that, should the Jewish leaders continue with their scheme to kill the Savior, they would lose their special blessing of being God's chosen people. This privilege would be "snatched" from them and given to another "nation"—that is, the people of the Christian faith—who would bear the fruit which the Lord required of them.

"And yes," the Lord continued, returning to the illustration of the cornerstone [*Harmony* 14:75], "anyone who falls on that stone will be broken. But, should that stone fall on someone, that person will be shattered and pulverized, and scattered by the wind. This means that you must choose between *either* being broken and converted by the power of the Gospel"—symbolized by the falling upon the stone—"*or* to have the wrath of God fall upon you and destroy you"—symbolized

[76] Matthew 21:43

by the falling of the stone upon someone in the final judgment! [*Harmony* 12:70, 71][77]

> Here, by these two illustrations—the parable of the evil vine-growers and the story of the chief cornerstone—the Lord sought, unequivocally, to appeal to the hearts of the Jewish leaders to quickly and thoroughly repent of their evil intention to kill Him. For them, there remained little time. Not only could their repentance save their own souls, but it could also change the dangerous direction the entire nation of Israel was heading. Indeed, the Hebrews were on the verge of losing their special status of being the Lord's chosen people. The seemingly harsh message of these two illustrations was actually calculated to penetrate the extremely hard-hearted attitudes of Israel's leaders, so that they could be saved as individuals, and, consequently, save their entire nation.

Clearly, all the chief priests and Pharisees knew that Jesus was talking directly about them when He told these parables. Understandably angered, they were ready to seize Jesus and kill Him on the spot. But with so many people watching them, they were afraid to do so, for the crowds considered Jesus to be a prophet. And should the Jewish leaders kill the Lord, a riot might ensue, leading, perhaps, to their own deaths. Out of complete frustration, they walked away from Jesus, leaving Him alone with the people. Thus, in secret, they began to plot yet another scheme to entrap and kill Jesus. They were still unsure if Judas would follow through with his agreement to betray the Lord into their hands [*Harmony* 14:19-25], so they decided that they needed to keep trying, on their own, to entrap the Lord in some manner. Later on, they would certainly make several attempts. [*Harmony* 14:85-106][78]

### — Jesus Tells the Parable About a Man Without a Wedding Garment[(w)]
### < Tuesday, Nisan 11, Spring, A.D. 31 (7/7) >
### {Matthew 22:1-14}

Jesus, now alone with the people, continued to explain the Gospel's kingdom to them through yet another parable. He said, "The kingdom of heaven can be compared to a certain king who gave a wedding feast to honor his son. He had previously sent invitations to many guests to come to the feast. He sent out some

---

77 Matthew 21:44; Luke 20:18

78 Matthew 21:45, 46; Mark 12:12; Luke 20:19

of his servants to remind those who had been invited to attend that the time was nearing for the feast to begin. But the invited guests refused to come![79]

"So, the king sent for more servants, declaring to them, 'Please, for a second time, tell those whom I have invited, "Behold! I have prepared the wedding feast: My oxen and my plump cows have all been butchered and roasted, and are now ready to be served. So, please come to the feast!"' But these invited guests still continued to pay no attention to the king's servants. Some went about their own business: one to work the fields of his farm, another to his place of business, and so forth. And then, some of the remaining invited guests actually took hold of the king's servants, and treated them badly, even to the extent of killing them!"[80]

In this parable, the Lord explained just how patient God had been with the Jewish nation. He had given them opportunity after opportunity to accept the Gospel message personally, as well as to accept their mission to take that message to the world. In the story, the king represented God, the Father. The son symbolized Jesus. The wedding feast illustrated the privileges of accepting the Gospel and its call to serve others. The ministry of the Old Testament prophets was symbolized by the sending of the original invitation to the wedding feast. [1]

On two separate occasions, God sought to remind the Hebrew people of this invitation to participate in the Gospel experience. The first was through the ministry of John the Baptist and his disciples. This was illustrated by the king's first effort to send servants to remind the invitees. In the parable, when they rejected that reminder, the king, instead of giving up on them, sent even more servants to remind them.[2]

This second wave of servants represented the combined ministry of Jesus and His disciples. This ministry included, not only the three and one half years of the Lord's ministry, but also the ministry of the early Christian church after Jesus would return back to heaven. But on this second occasion, most of the Jews refused yet again to come to an understanding of the Gospel. But they did more than refuse to accept the Gospel message. They persecuted those of the early church! [Acts 5:17, 18, etc.] They even killed some of the apostles and early Christians! [Acts 7:59, 60; 12:2] This was symbolized by the rude way the invitees

79 Matthew 22:1-3
80 Matthew 22:4-6

in the parable treated the second set of servants the king sent to remind the people to come to the feast.[3]

Continuing with the parable, Jesus said, "Quite understandably, the king was furious. So he sent his armies to kill these ingrates, and to burn their city with fire."[81]

This would find its fulfillment in the destruction of Israel's main city of Jerusalem by the Roman armies in A.D. 70.

Jesus went on with His parable, "Then the king said to his remaining servants, 'The wedding feast is still ready, and as you can see, the ones that I have originally invited are not worthy to attend. So then, go to the main highways, and invite everyone you see to come to the feast.' The servants did exactly what the king had instructed them to do. They went into the streets and invited everyone they could find. So many of these newly invited guests came that the wedding hall was filled to capacity with people reclining at the tables."[82]

This part of the parable symbolized the taking of the Gospel message to the Gentiles of the world. If the Jews would not accept the message, then the rest of the peoples of the world would be given the opportunity to do so. And, for the most part, it worked. Many people from all around the world accepted the truth of the Gospel. The Christian church dramatically grew and expanded.

Then Jesus moved on to another part of the story. He said, "The king entered the feasting hall to inspect his new wedding guests who were seated at the feasting table. In the process of inspection, he noticed a man who was not dressed in the special wedding garment which he had provided for each one of the invitees. Looking directly at the man, the king asked, 'My friend, how is it that you are sitting in here without the wedding garment which I have provided for you?' The man had nothing to say in explanation! He had no excuse whatsoever![83]

"Turning to his servants, the king commanded, 'Tie up this man's hands and feet, and throw him into the outer darkness, where there will be great sorrow and grinding of teeth in despair of squandered opportunities!' Many have been

---

81 Matthew 22:7
82 Matthew 22:8-10
83 Matthew 22:11, 12

called to be saved, but only comparatively few will ultimately agree to live by the requirements of salvation."[84]

> This final part of the parable represented the time of judgment at the end of the world. [Ecclesiastes 12:13, 14; Revelation 14:7] Even though many Gentiles apparently accepted the Gospel message, there must be a judgment to determine which of those who had accepted the Gospel were truly sincere. In the parable, the man who was not wearing the special wedding garment, symbolized those—no doubt many in number—who rely on their own righteousness and do not accept the righteousness of Christ—symbolized by the special wedding garment.[1]
>
> It is true that, for the most part, the Jews rejected the Gospel message. It is also true that many of the non-Jews who seemed to accept the Gospel were, themselves, insincere in their commitment. By the same criteria by which the Jews were to be judged, the Gentiles would also be judged. By this part of the parable, Jesus was giving a sober warning to all—Jews and Gentile alike—to be truly prepared for the coming of the Lord and His kingdom. Salvation would be given only to those who were truly worthy. It was not to be given by special rite or privilege.[2]
>
> By this parable, Jesus appealed to the hearts, not of the Jewish leaders, but of the people who had been listening to Him for some time. He so much wanted to make clear to them that, just as their leaders had failed to appropriately follow Him, they, if not careful, would make the same mistakes as their leaders had made. Furthermore, through the parable Jesus appealed to all Christians throughout history—Jews and Gentiles alike—to warn them that a mere intellectual acceptance of the Lord was not sufficient. Instead, they must all have a deep, heart-felt experience with the Lord. Whatever the cost, they must possess the true righteousness of Christ as a covering for their sins—symbolized, again, by the special wedding garment.[3]

[84] Matthew 22:13, 14

### — The Lord Is Tested: Should a Jew Pay Tribute to Caesar? < Tuesday, Nisan 11, Spring, A.D. 31 (7/7) > {Matthew 22:15-22; Mark 12:13-17; Luke 20:20-26}

The Pharisees [*Harmony* 2:7/1, 2] were still trying to figure out a way to ensnare the Savior by the words He might use. After consulting with one another for some time, they decided to send some of their followers, along with a number of Herodians, to ask Jesus a question that would accomplish their designs. The Herodians were a Jewish political party that favored the reign of Herod Antipas. [*Harmony* 4:62] Normally, the Pharisees, strong opponents of Herod's reign, were bitter enemies of the Herodians. However, in their obsessive determination to destroy Jesus, the Pharisees were willing, on this occasion, to form an alliance with the Herodians to secure the Lord's condemnation. Thus they sent spies, both Pharisees and Herodians, to ask Jesus a tricky question. They acted piously, but their intentions were evil. They wanted to catch Jesus saying something wrong against the secular government. If He did, they would be able to use even a tiny misstatement of His against Him when they brought Him before the Roman governor after His arrest. In that case, in order to secure His death, they could accuse the Lord of violating of one of the Roman Empire's rules. [*Harmony* 17:30][85]

This unlikely alliance of devious Jews approached Jesus. Seeking to put Him at a disadvantage by using some grossly insincere flattery, they said to Him, "Teacher, we know that You truthfully teach the correct way of God, and that You do not worry about what people say about You, because you do not take political sides on any issue. Rather, You teach what you believe to be the truth no matter what others might think."[86]

Then they arrived at the main point of their question: "In that case, then, would You tell us what You think on an important issue of our time? Should we Jews be lawfully obligated to pay the poll tax that the Roman Caesar has levied on us? Or should we be free from that tax?" No matter how Jesus answered the question, they figured He would be in trouble. If He answered "No" to the question, then He would incur the wrath of the Herodians, and more importantly, the Romans. If, however, He answered "Yes," then the Pharisees and many of the Hebrew people would be equally upset with Him, considering Him to be a virtual traitor to His own nation, remembering how much the Jews despised

---

85 Matthew 22:15, 16; Mark 12:13; Luke 20:20

86 Matthew 22:16; Mark 12:14; Luke 20:21

paying taxes to the hated Romans. The Jewish leaders felt that they had Jesus in a major fix no matter which way He answered their question![87]

But the Lord could read their evil motives and sly intentions. So He responded, "Why are you trying to trick Me, you hypocrite actors? You really don't care to know My answer for you are just attempting to test Me. You just want to trap Me![(x)] [88]

"Nevertheless," he added, "show Me a Roman denarius coin used to pay the tax." Accordingly, they showed Him a denarius—a coin worth about a regular day's wages. Holding the coin up for all of them to see, He asked them, "Whose face and title do you see on this coin?"[89]

"Why, Caesar's, of course!" they chorused with the obvious answer.[90]

"Then, in that case, give to Caesar the things that belong to Caesar . . . while, at the same time, give to God the things that are His!" was the Lord's definitive reply. [*Harmony* 17:65][91]

The Jewish contingent knew that Jesus had defeated their evil purpose. With the power of His words, Jesus had tricked and silenced them, instead of the other way around! Nevertheless they marveled at His wisdom, and went away shaking their heads. Indeed, they had utterly failed to get Him to say some embarrassing thing in front of the people that might be used against Him in a Roman court of law.[92]

> Here Jesus had made it clear that, as followers of the Lord, and also citizens of the Roman Empire, the Israelites had responsibilities to *both* powers. They must pay taxes to Rome as well as remain faithful to God. It was obvious that it was possible to do both. Also, by the Lord's response to this question, He appealed to the hearts of the Herodians, who had placed so much confidence in their friendly relationship with the things and powers of this world. He made it clear that a strong

---

87 Matthew 22:17; Mark 12:14, 15; Luke 20:22
88 Matthew 22:18; Mark 12:15; Luke 20:23
89 Matthew 22:19, 20; Mark 12:15, 16; Luke 20:24
90 Matthew 22:21; Mark 12:16; Luke 20:24
91 Matthew 22:21; Mark 12:17; Luke 20:25
92 Matthew 22:22; Mark 12:17; Luke 20:26

relationship with God was even more important. They would have much to consider.

### — The Lord Is Tested a Second Time: Is There a Resurrection? < Tuesday, Nisan 11, Spring, A.D. 31 (7/7) > {Matthew 22:23-33; Mark 12:18-27; Luke 20:27-38}

The Pharisees were still undeterred in their determination to trick Jesus. They had yet another plan up their sleeve. This time they aligned themselves with another political party, a bitter rival of theirs: the Sadducees, who did not believe in the doctrine of the resurrection. [*Harmony* 2:7/1, 2] The Sadducees believed only in the writings of Moses: the first five books of the Scriptures. The rest of the Scriptures they did not accept as reliable. And because Moses did not make specific mention of the resurrection in any of his books, they, therefore, did not accept the resurrection as a valid teaching of Scripture. So, after consorting with the Pharisees, some of the Sadducees came that same day to ask Jesus a question which they thought would place the Lord in some kind of embarrassing situation. They, of course, chose the subject of the resurrection as an issue upon which to challenge Him. [*Harmony* 13:31/][93]

They approached Jesus, saying, "Now, Teacher, Moses clearly directed us, saying, 'If a man should die, having no children, his brother—as next of kin—must marry his dead brother's wife, for the purpose of raising children in behalf of his brother's name.' [Deuteronomy 25:5] Considering this command, now suppose there were seven brothers from one family. The oldest one married a wife. Then he died, having no children. Under the law, the second oldest brother would be required to marry his older brother's wife, which he did. However, this brother also died, still leaving no children. And so on it went from the third brother all the way down to the seventh! All died childless. Then finally, the woman died.[94]

"Now, here's the question we have for You: In the resurrection, when all seven brothers and the woman are raised, whose wife would she be? The first? The second? The third? The seventh? Remember, she had been the wife of them all!" This was the question that the Sadducees had used for years to stump the Pharisees who believed in the resurrection. The Pharisees were quite unable to

93 Matthew 22:23; Mark 12:18; Luke 20:27

94 Matthew 22:23-27; Mark 12:18-22; Luke 20:27-32

answer this riddle. The Sadducees were quite sure that Jesus would be unable to do so too.[95]

But the Master answered the Sadducees, "Do you not realize that you are quite mistaken with your supposed tricky story? You see, your problem is twofold: First of all, you do not know the Scriptures as you think and claim that you do. And second, you do not understand the power of God. Can't you figure that out?[96]

"Before I explain what I just said, let Me make one thing clear—something that you have never heard before: At the time of the resurrection at the end of the world, there will exist a different order of things. In this world, people get married and are given in marriage. But in the world to come, people who are found worthy of eternal life and the resurrection will not marry nor will they be given in marriage. Instead, they will live like the angels of heaven—that is, in an unmarried state. They will be sons and daughters of God, children of a perfect and immortal resurrection. Now, that's the truth![(y)] [97]

"Now, let me address both your ignorance of the Scriptures and of the power of God as it relates to the resurrection. Yes, I want to say something regarding the resurrection—the existence of which, of course, you deny that the writings of Moses teach. But listen! Have you never read, how, in his book, Moses directly quotes God's words while at the burning bush? In that very text, Moses actually taught the resurrection. Did you know that? Allow Me to explain. Do you remember that God said in that Scripture, 'I am the God of Abraham, and the God of Isaac, his son, and also the God of Jacob, Isaac's son'? [Exodus 3:6] Well, don't you agree that God was trying to impress Moses with the majesty of His own divine power when He made this declaration? But how could He do that if all His followers to whom He referred—in this case, Abraham, Isaac, and Jacob—were to remain dead for all eternity? That would not make sense! Yes of course, Abraham, Isaac, and Jacob had all died when God made this declaration. But even though these great men were dead, in order for our God to be a real, powerful God, He must, at some point in the future, resurrect them. Can't you see the logic of that? Indeed, tell Me, what kind of God would He be if He were only a God of dead people? So then, I ask, do you, as Sadducees, really think our God is just a God of dead people? Of course not! So in summary, I say that

95 Matthew 22:28; Mark 12:23; Luke 20:33

96 Matthew 22:29; Mark 12:24

97 Matthew 22:30; Mark 12:25; Luke 20:34-36

if you believe in God—that is, in the all-powerful Creator of both heaven and earth—then you must also believe in the resurrection—that the saints will be alive with God for eternity . . . even if Moses never directly mentioned it. Yes, in this issue of the resurrection, you are greatly mistaken about what the Scriptures actually teach, as well as about how truly great is the power of our God!"[(z) 98]

> The Lord's point was simple and marvelously profound: Could the God of heaven, the Creator of the universe, truly be God if He was only a God of dead people? What kind of God would He be if that were so? Therefore, if He is truly God, then He must resurrect His people. They cannot stay dead forever. Indeed, heaven will be filled with living, functioning people . . . not cemeteries!

Thus the Sadducees were effectively silenced by the words of Jesus. He had clearly shown that they did not know the Scriptures, nor understand the true power of God, as they had thought they did. And the crowds, listening to the debate, were amazed at the depth of the Lord's wisdom and knowledge.[99]

> In this case, the Lord appealed to the Sadducees to rethink their false concept of refusing to accept the resurrection of the dead as a valid teaching of Scripture. How could the Sadducees be faithful followers of God, as they claimed, while at the same time, not believe in the resurrection—the doctrine that so clearly defines the ultimate power of God as the Creator?

### —Jesus Is Tested a Third Time: Which Is the Greatest Commandment?
### < Tuesday, Nisan 11, Spring, A.D. 31 (7/7) >
### {Matthew 22:34-40; Mark 12:28-34; Luke 20:39, 40}

When the Pharisees found out that Jesus had confounded both the Herodians and the Sadducees, effectively silencing them, they themselves gathered together to scheme their own plan of attack against the Savior. They chose from among themselves a certain lawyer who was considered to be an expert in the Law of Moses. Together they formulated a question that they were certain would confuse the Lord, and embarrass Him in front of the people. This learned scribe approached Jesus, having observed how that the Lord had completely baffled His other opponents.[100]

---

98 Matthew 22:31, 32; Mark 12:26, 27; Luke 20:37, 38
99 Matthew 22:33
100 Matthew 22:34, 35; Mark 12:28

The lawyer questioned Jesus, saying, "Teacher, which is the first, greatest, and most important commandment of all the Law?" The Jews had listed what they considered to be the commandments in order of importance. This meant that the ones listed higher were more significant than those which followed further down the list. He hoped that Jesus would mention one the laws that the Jews considered of lesser importance, thus creating a point of contention between them and Him. The argument that they envisioned would ensue would make Him appear weak in front of the people.[101]

The Lord said with confidence, "The foremost commandment begins with these words of Scripture, 'Listen, O Israel! The Lord your God is One'"—that is, the members of the Godhead are totally unified as one. [Deuteronomy 6:4] "Then the text continues, 'You shall love the Lord your God with all your heart, with all your soul, and with your entire mind, as well as with all your strength'—that is, your whole being. [Deuteronomy 6:5] Yes, this is the first and primary commandment. But the second most important commandment is just like it, which says, 'You shall love your neighbor as you would love yourself.' [Leviticus 19:18; *Harmony* 5:75/2; 11:152][102]

"Now, upon these two commandments are based all the rest of the Law and the Scriptures. There are no laws greater than these! This means that the essence of all good Law, then, is love: to love God and to love your fellow man. As you can readily see, the operative word in both of these laws is *love!* This means that all good law is more than a list of rules or restrictions, but rather, a principle—the principle of love that motivates and activates the human heart." [*Harmony* 5:40/2, 75][(aa)] [103]

"Right You are, Teacher!" the amazed and obviously impressed scribe exclaimed. "It is certainly true what You have said: God is One, and there is no god but Him! And to love Him with the entire heart, understanding, passion, and strength . . . and to love one's neighbor as one would love oneself, is certainly much more important that all the burnt offerings and sacrifices one might bring to God!"[104]

101 Matthew 22:35, 36; Mark 12:28

102 Matthew 22:37-39; Mark 12:29-31

103 Matthew 22:40; Mark 12:31

104 Mark 12:32, 33

The Jewish religious system of the day was based on the bringing of sacrifices and offerings. However, these offerings and sacrifices merely symbolized the rudiments of the plan of salvation. They were quite unimportant in and of themselves. The lawyer could see that the true motive of obedience—beyond its rituals—was love. This included both a love for God and for mankind. Apparently, with all his learning, such a simple, yet profound understanding of true religion had escaped him thus far in his life. But, when Jesus gave His powerful answer, its reality clearly dawned on him. The lawyer was truly overwhelmed by the Lord's response, and readily and openly admitted so in front of all the people.

When Jesus realized that the lawyer had given a very intelligent response to His answer, the Lord said to him, "My friend, your understanding of the Law is one that has led you very close to the correct knowledge of what it takes to be saved!" Seeing that both Jesus and His questioner were in virtual agreement with each other, the Pharisees and their cohorts realized that there was nothing they could say that would entrap the Lord! Three times they had tried, and three times they had totally failed.[105]

In this situation, the Master powerfully demonstrated the importance of love as the true motivating factor in all genuine obedience to any and all divine laws. By doing so, He appealed to His strongest opponents, the Pharisees, to understand and experience more perfectly the power of true love in their personal lives. This truth was especially brought to the forefront by the fact that even one of their own—the lawyer in this story—had admitted the same!

"Teacher," some of the scribes said to Him, "it is clear that You know what You are talking about! Well done!" They did not know how to challenge Him any further with similar questions or riddles. They were speechless, deeply impressed by the Lord's wisdom. But nevertheless—and quite sadly—they were totally undeterred in their clearly focused determination to kill Him! [*Harmony* 14:78][106]

---

105 Mark 12:34

106 Mark 12:34; Luke 20:39, 40

## — Finally, Jesus Silences His Critics < Tuesday, Nisan 11, Spring, A.D. 31 (7/7) > {Matthew 22:41-46; Mark 12:35-37; Luke 20:41-44}

But before all the Pharisees and their associates left the Lord's presence, He turned to them from His teaching in the Temple, and said, "You've been asking Me a few tough questions. All right, now let Me ask you a question and see what answer you are able to give to it. You know that the scribes say that the Christ is the Son of David. So, here's My question for you: What do you have to say about the Christ—the Messiah? Whose Son is He?"[107]

"That's easy," they quickly responded. "Of course, He's the Son of David." Here, the Jews gave the usual and standard answer to this question of the Lord.[108]

"All right then," Jesus responded, "why is it, then, that David, in the book of Psalms, under the inspiration of the Holy Spirit, calls the Messiah his 'Lord'? Indeed, remember what David actually said in the Psalms—and I quote—'The Lord'—that is, God—'said to my Lord'—that is, the Messiah—'sit at My right hand, until I put all Your enemies under Your complete control, as though they were Your footstool'? [Psalm 110:1] Now, to be specific, My question is: Why is it that David calls the Messiah his Lord—as David clearly does here—when the Messiah is only David's son—as you say? So then, I ask, in what sense is the Messiah David's son, while, at the same time, He is also his Lord? Yes, how can He be *both* David's Lord *and* son at the same time? Answer Me that!"[109]

> By this question, Jesus was challenging the Pharisees' concept of who He was as well as who they thought the Messiah was. The truth was that Jesus, as the Messiah, was at the same time both David's *Lord* and his *Son!* How is that? Before Jesus came to this earth, He was the eternal God—even David's Creator and *Lord!* But, in His incarnate state, He was born as a man, as a *son* of David's lineage, through Mary. If the Jews recognized this concept as a fact, then they would be forced to recognize Jesus as the Messiah, for this was exactly what He had claimed of Himself. However, the Jewish leaders consistently refused to accept the Lord's divinity, claiming that, born as a human, He was nothing

---

107 Matthew 22:41, 42; Mark 12:35

108 Matthew 22:42

109 Matthew 22:43-45; Mark 12:35-37; Luke 20:41-44

> more than a human being. From their perspective, He might be a *son* of David, but certainly not David's *Lord!* But, more importantly, most Jews did not think that the Messiah would be divine in nature—they believed that He would be merely human. By using this text, Jesus showed the Jews that they were wrong in their teachings and Biblical interpretations. This really upset the Jewish leaders for they were very proud of their supposed ability to interpret the Scriptures correctly. [*Harmony* 14:30]

Realizing the Lord's intent, they refused to give an answer to the question. In fact, they were completely speechless! In reality, they were so silenced, that, from that day on, they never again asked Him another question. With glee, the large crowd relished the words of Jesus and was pleased by the way He had effectively handled—and defeated—His critics![110]

> In the Lord's pointed challenge to the Jewish leaders, He appealed one last time, based upon the powerful proof of Scripture, for them to accept Him as the *divine* Messiah. There was not much time left for them to do so before it would be, tragically, too late for them and their nation.

**—Jesus Pronounces His Woes on the Pharisees**[(bb)]
**< Tuesday, Nisan 11, Spring, A.D. 31 (7/7) >**
**{Matthew 23:1-24:1; Mark 12:38-40; Luke 20:45-47}**

Obviously the crowd that surrounded Jesus in the Temple was quite large. Besides His own close disciples, it was composed of many of the common people—those who had been excited by the Lord's ministry during the past three and a half years. Also in the crowd were a number of His sharpest critics and antagonists: the Pharisees, scribes, and Jewish leaders of every stripe. This would be the Savior's last public statement to the masses before His crucifixion. Jesus began by addressing the common people in the crowd, sharing with them some of His teachings.[111]

He declared, "Beware of the scribes and Pharisees who walk around in long, fancy robes. They have taken it upon themselves to sit in the seat of authority of Moses. They think that they are the last word in the correct interpretation of the Scriptures. Well, even though I have disputed much of their theology, for the most part, I must tell you, obey what they tell you to do. That is, if what they tell you to do is consistent with the Scriptures, then do it. On the other hand,

---

110 Matthew 22:46; Mark 12:37

111 Matthew 23:1; Mark 12:38; Luke 20:45

in no way should you act the way they act! For what they tell you to do, they refuse to do themselves. They have one standard for you, and yet another for themselves.[112]

"They make up all kinds of tedious things that they want you to perform in order to receive their brand of salvation. They place these burdens on all the people of this nation. And these foolish burdens are like a huge weight on your shoulders. And how oppressive these burdens are! To make matters worse, they do not lift even one finger to help any of you carry the burdens which they have placed upon you. Neither do they remove even the tiniest restriction and law which they have conjured up. For example, they, in effect, steal the homes of widows from under them—by trying to take their possessions for themselves—while at the same time making long public prayers to show off their so-called righteousness. But don't be concerned. They will dearly pay for such injustices in the final judgment!"[113]

> The Jewish leaders were notorious for figuring out ways of getting their hands on the few remaining possessions of defenseless widows who were dependent upon those possessions to provide necessary income for themselves. It was all quite shameful![1]

> Next, Jesus attacked the Pharisees' obsession with showing off their so-called righteousness. One of the most outlandish ways that the Pharisees used to demonstrate to others just how good they were was their use of phylacteries. Phylacteries were small but often wide strips of parchment on which were written portions of the Law. These strips were placed in small leather receptacles and worn on the left forearm, or even the forehead. They were worn on weekdays, at the time of morning prayer. The use of phylacteries was based on a literal—but highly twisted—interpretation of several Old Testament texts. [Exodus 13:1-16; Deuteronomy 6:4-9; 11:13-21] Jesus condemned the use of these phylacteries. He directly addressed their use. Also, it was traditional for Jews to have tassels on the end of their garments. The Pharisees, however, to show their supposed religious superiority over the common people, made their tassels longer than usual! Jesus addressed this procedure, too.[2]

112 Matthew 23:2, 3; Mark 12:38; Luke 20:46

113 Matthew 23:4; Mark 12:40; Luke 20:47

"But the things that they are willing to do," Jesus continued, "they do only to be noticed and praised by others. For example, they have made their phylacteries larger and larger. How impressive! For yet another example, they have made the tassels on the bottom of their robes larger than normal to show off their supposed inner piety. Such nonsense! While I'm at it, they also relish the most honored seats when at a feast. And they must sit on the front seats reserved for them in the synagogue so that everyone can see them when they walk in and are seated. Such show-offs![114]

"But I'm just getting started," Jesus continued, not letting up a bit. "They enjoy going to the market place, where the people of a city are gathered for conversation, so that you will greet them with honor and respect. Yes, they really love it when you call them, 'Rabbi! Rabbi!'"—that is, "My great teacher and lord!" "Fostering pride in this way is wrong. So stop doing it! When you call these people 'Rabbi,' they think that you recognize their words as being virtually infallible. So then, don't call anyone 'Rabbi.' Neither, do not let anyone call you 'Rabbi!' as though you were actually better than anyone else. There is only One who is really your infallible Teacher—that is, of course, the Christ! Remember, in reality, you are all just brothers and sisters in your relationship with one other.[115]

"Neither should you go around calling your religious leaders, 'Father!' They are not your religious father—the heavenly Father is the only One who is your religious Father. In the same sense, don't be calling other people professor or teacher—you have only one true Leader: the Christ, the Messiah!"[116]

> The Lord was not opposing the use of a technical title—such as teacher, or birth father—but rather the use of such titles that would imply spiritual honor and rights beyond that which humans should receive. In the days of Jesus, these titles did imply great but unjustified and inappropriate honor—almost that of infallibility.

"Instead of the use of such titles of ill-placed honor," the Lord went on, "you should know that true greatness is demonstrated by one becoming the servant of the others. Indeed, the greatest of you needs to be the servant of the others. To summarize, he who exalts himself before other humans, shall in the judgment be

---

114 Matthew 23:5, 6; Mark 12:39

115 Matthew 23:7, 8; Mark 12:38; Luke 20:46

116 Matthew 23:9, 10

justly humbled. On the other hand, he who humbles himself before his fellow human beings, will, in the judgment, be exalted by God Himself."[117]

Looking at the Pharisees and scribes in the crowd, Jesus began to address them directly with very strong words. He started by exclaiming, "Doom is coming upon you, scribes and Pharisees, hypocrite actors! And why? Because you have slammed the door of salvation in the face of the people! And because of your sanctimonious lifestyle, you shall not be allowed to enter in yourselves. But the really sad part is that you have tried to block the way of salvation for everyone else who truly desires to enter in![(cc) 118]

"Doom is coming upon you, scribes and Pharisees, hypocrite actors! Why? Because you swindle widows out of their houses, leaving them destitute, while living sumptuously on their money. Then, you show off your fake piety by making long public prayers. [*Harmony* 5:44] But I must warn you, the condemnation you will receive in the judgment will be in proportion to your dastardly deeds.[(dd) 119]

"Doom is coming upon you, scribes and Pharisees! Why? Because, in your efforts to win a single convert to your foolish way of thinking, you are willing to travel over both land and sea. But sadly, when converted to your false teachings, such a convert is twice as evil as you are. In the end, you will be responsible for bringing upon that person the wrath of hell-fire![(ee) 120]

"Doom is coming upon you—you who are like blind people trying to lead the blind! And why? Because you say that if anyone makes a promise upon the Temple, he is not under obligation to keep it. But . . . if he makes a promise upon the gold of the Temple, well then, you say he must keep that promise. Now, how foolish is that!" [*Harmony* 10:4-7][121]

> Here, Jesus began to detail a number of items that the Jewish leaders listed as sufficient to make a promise or religious vow binding. Some of these items were strong enough to obligate the one making the vow to fulfill it. Others were weak, thus allowing the people leeway to break their commitment. The purpose of this list was to provide an "out" for Jews in their vow-making. So, while looking pious when making such

117 Matthew 23:11, 12
118 Matthew 23:13
119 Matthew 23:14
120 Matthew 23:15
121 Matthew 23:16

a vow—such as by swearing upon some sacred object—they could, in reality, be freed from fulfilling the vow. Thus this would allow them to look good in public, while, at the same time, giving them the freedom to back out of the commitment at a later date. This system had the effect, if used shrewdly, of providing a person a way to slither out of any commitment made to another person, or to God! But the Lord had consistently argued that if one made a vow to God, one should not swear to the vow upon any particular object or thing. Rather, one should undertake to keep the vow . . . or not make it in the first place! [*Harmony* 5:32-35]

Jesus continued, "You are fools and spiritually blind! Tell me, as a basis for making promises, which is more sacred: the gold of the Temple, or the Temple itself that made the gold holy? The fact that you would make such a distinction is ridiculous![122]

"Further, you say that if anyone makes a vow based on the altar of burnt offering, that person does not need to fulfill his promise. However, if a person swears upon the gift offered on the altar, he must fulfill it! What inconsistent foolishness! Are you so blind that you cannot see that there is no real difference in greatness between the altar itself and the gift which is placed upon it?[123]

"The truth is—and I declare it—if anyone swears upon the altar, he is, in reality, swearing, not only upon the altar, but upon any gift that is placed upon that altar. And, if anyone swears upon the Temple, he is swearing not only on the Temple, but upon God, who dwells in it! In fact, if anyone swears upon heaven, he is swearing upon God's throne which is in heaven . . . as well as on God who is sitting on that throne, I might add! Bluntly put, if you make a promise to any man or to God, plan on keeping it! God will not allow you to find some flimsy, man-made way to get out of it.[124]

"Doom is coming upon you, scribes and Pharisees—you hypocrite actors! And why? When you pay your tithes, you are so exacting that you actually count out ten percent of mint leaves—even dill and caraway seeds—so that you will pay an accurate tithe as the Scripture requires. [Malachi 3:10, etc.] Okay, that's fine! But, at the same time, in spite of your zealousness in tithing, you totally ignore

---

[122] Matthew 23:17

[123] Matthew 23:18, 19

[124] Matthew 23:20-22

the other parts of the Law which are much more important. These include: One: Justice—that is, being honest and fair with people. Two: Mercy—that is, showing compassion and forgiveness to those around you. And three: Faithfulness—that is, putting trust in God as opposed to your own pet ideas. Keep counting out leaves and seeds if you must, but, don't neglect the more important things!" [*Harmony* 12:22][(ff)] [125]

"You are certainly blind leaders!" Christ went on. "Your blind leadership is made obvious when you use a sieve to strain out a gnat from your drinking water so you will not drink some unclean insect. [Leviticus 11:23] In a spiritual sense, you 'strain out the gnats'—such as counting seeds when tithing—and yet, you end up swallowing a whole camel—by ignoring the more essential parts of the Law I've just listed! Yes, both are unclean—the camel and the gnat [Leviticus 11:4, 23]—but which one is more dangerously unclean? In like manner, then, which part of the Law is most important: counting seeds in tithing, or showing justice, mercy, and faith?[(gg)] [126]

"Doom," Jesus continued, "is coming upon you, scribes and Pharisees, hypocrite actors! It's amazing! You clean the outside of cups and dishes, so that it looks as though you eat and drink from only clean things. That's fine! But, in doing so, you think yourselves morally better than others. Yet, your lives and hearts are filled with thieving, and self-indulgent ideas and practices! Oh blind Pharisees! Please clean the inside of the 'cup' and 'dish' of your life—your heart and mind—so that the things you do in life, which others can observe, are really and honestly clean and pure! [*Harmony* 12:21][(hh)] [127]

"Doom is coming upon you, scribes and Pharisees, hypocrite actors! Ah yes, you are like crypts that have been whitewashed on the outside, so as to appear all clean and bright. Yet, these sepulchers are filled with dead people—bones and rotting flesh! That's just the way you are: You look righteous on the outside—the part of your life people can see—but you are, in fact, filled with gross hypocrisy and rotting evil within your hearts—the part that no one, except God, can see![(ii)] [128]

[125] Matthew 23:23
[126] Matthew 23:24
[127] Matthew 23:25, 26
[128] Matthew 23:27, 28

"Doom is coming upon you, scribes and Pharisees, hypocrite actors! While I'm mentioning the tombs of the dead, you have the practice of building fancy crypts for the prophets and adorning such tombs with great monuments. And further, you say, 'If we had lived in the times of our fathers, we would have not joined with them in the persecution and slaughter of these holy prophets!' Such a lie! For, by your actions you have shown that you truly are the sons of your fathers who did all those terrible things to the prophets. Indeed, just as your fathers began to fill the cup of this nation's evil with their wickedness, you continue to fill the cup to the brim with your own transgressions! You snakes! You hole full of vipers! Tell me, just how do you plan on escaping hell-fire at the time of judgment? How?[(jj)] [129]

"And let me tell you why you will suffer hell-fire. It is because I will send prophets, wise men, and teachers to minister to you. And what will you do to them? You will kill some, crucify others, and beat still others with whips right in your own churches! In short, you will relentlessly persecute My servants, chasing them from one city to another, so as to keep them from escaping. And what will be the result for you when you do these horrible things? I tell you, you will be held responsible for all the blood that has been shed, beginning at the martyrdom of Abel, right up through the death of Zechariah, the son of Jehoiada, whom you slaughtered between the Temple and the altar." [2 Chronicles 24:20-22; *Harmony* 12:29][(kk)] [130]

> In the Old Testament—the Bible of Christ's day—the first book was Genesis and the last book was 2 Chronicles—not Malachi like that of the present Old Testament. And it was in 2 Chronicles—the last book of the Bible of Christ's day—that the story of the death of Zechariah was recorded. Thus, in effect, Jesus was saying that the Jews were responsible for the deaths of all the martyrs, from the beginning of time, all the way through to the end of their written record!

"It is a fact—and I predict it—" Jesus continued, "all these things will happen to you just as I have declared them. They will take place to this very generation of wicked people who are listening to My voice at this very moment!"[131]

---

129 Matthew 23:29-33
130 Matthew 23:34, 35
131 Matthew 23:36

Then, Jesus, with great emotion and compassion, declared, "But . . . Jerusalem, oh Jerusalem, you who have killed the prophets and stoned those whom I have sent to you: Oh! How often I have wanted to cuddle your children"—or, inhabitants—"together in My arms, the same way that a mother hen gathers her chicks under her wings in time of danger . . . but, you refused Me! I can't say anything else, therefore, but that your house—this Temple—I will leave to you, empty of My presence. It will be desolate! I declare to you, in a few days from now"—after the Lord's death and resurrection—"you will not see Me again, until you say of Me, 'Blessed is He who is coming in the name of God!'" [Psalm 118:26] Of course, Jesus was speaking here of His glorious Second Coming. [*Harmony* 3:99/4; 12:89; 14:34][132]

And accordingly, Jesus left the Temple . . . for the last time! Forever! He was gone![133]

> While there can be no debate that the Lord's condemnation on the Jewish leaders was severe, He did it with the hope that they might still respond to His pleas. With His final statement regarding the city of Jerusalem's future [*Harmony* 14:132], Jesus appealed to the leaders to repent and quickly turn to Him. But it was all for naught!

### The Lord's Final Contact with the People in the Temple Court
### < Tuesday, Nisan 11, A.D. 31 (7/7) >
### (Mark 12:41-44; Luke 21:1-4; John 12:20-50)

#### — The Widow's Two Tiny Copper Coins
#### < Tuesday, Nisan 11, A.D. 31 (7/7) >
#### {Mark 12:41-44; Luke 21:1-4}

On His way out of the temple area, Jesus paused to look at the worshippers who were coming to bring their offerings to God in the Women's Court. He sat down right across from the place where the offering chests were placed, so that He could get a good look at the people who were dropping their offerings into these chests. Jesus saw a number of rich people with great fanfare bringing their huge gifts and placing them in the money box. Then, He spied an obviously poor widow approaching the chest, and hurriedly dropping in two lepta coins—the smallest, and least valuable of all Jewish money. Two such coins equaled a

---

[132] Matthew 23:37-39

[133] Matthew 24:1

kodrantes, which was worth about 1/64 of a Roman denarius. In the wages of the day, that would represent only about 10 minutes of common labor![134]

Calling the disciples to His side, the Lord commented to them, "Look! With certainty, I tell you, this woman has given more in the sight of God than all the other contributors, combined, who have placed money into the treasury! And why is that? They have given from their abundance—they gave and still had much, much more left. But this woman, rather, has given from her abject poverty. In fact, she put everything she possessed in the money chest, even what she needed to live on. Yes, she has nothing left for her own needs!"[135]

> On this occasion, Jesus made it clear that the amount of money one gives to the cause of God is of less importance than the spirit and attitude by which it is given. Also, the Lord addressed the essential nature of sacrificial giving. Of course, this concept applies not only to money but also to the giving of one's person, time, and talents to the work of God.[1]

> While it is true that only His disciples heard the Lord's comment regarding the woman who gave the two lepta coins, His statement would serve throughout the years as an appeal to all—both rich and poor—that one's attitude in giving, found deep within the soul, is the thing that really counts. Indeed, the *amount* one gives is to be determined, in large part, by the depth of one's relationship with God, not the other way around.[2]

### — The Lord's Conversation with Greek Visitors, and Comments on the Encounter
### < Tuesday, Nisan 11, A.D. 31 (7/7) >
### {John 12:20-36, 44-50}

On the day that Jesus was leaving the Temple for the last time, two of the Lord's disciples, Andrew and Philip, came to Him, bearing a special message. A short time before, a number of Greeks had entered the outer court of the Gentiles. They were in the process of becoming converts to the Hebrew religion, and were coming to the Temple to worship during the Passover Festival. Hearing of the ministry of Jesus, they sought to meet with Him personally to learn more about what He was teaching. Accordingly, they contacted the Lord's disciple, Philip,

---

134 Mark 12:41, 42; Luke 21:1, 2

135 Mark 12:43, 44; Luke 21:3, 4

who was from Bethsaida of the northern province of Galilee. They probably contacted Philip, for his name was from the Greek language. "Sir, we would like to see Jesus," was their simple request. Philip was unsure as to how to proceed with the request. Even though the Lord's ministry had touched the lives of many Gentiles, it was still somewhat rare for Him to spend private time with them. So Philip asked Andrew, another disciple with a Greek name, what he should do. They decided, as a twosome, to approach Jesus with the Greeks' request. Jesus granted their request, and went out to meet them.[136]

During the course of His conversation with the Greeks, Jesus explained His ministry to them, by saying, "The time has arrived for Me, the Son of Man, to be glorified"—that is, to be crucified. "It is certainly true," the Master continued, "that when a kernel of wheat falls on the ground, it dies—so to speak—and is buried all alone—as it were. But because it dies, it will germinate, and grow into a wheat plant, which will ultimately bear fruit in the form of many other kernels of wheat." Jesus was speaking in symbol of His death and burial, which, after His resurrection, would bear much fruit, including the salvation of a great multitude of both Jews and especially Gentiles—including Greeks—from all around the world.[137]

The Lord's death, burial, and resurrection would lead to many conversions of people to the Christian faith. Each convert would be challenged to follow on the path that He, their Lord, had walked. That is why the Savior added these words, "He who loves to live in this world, to do the things of this world, will end up losing his life in the world to come. But he who hates living in this world, so to speak, will end up living forever in the world to come. Thus anyone who wishes to truly serve me must follow Me on the path which I have walked. That means we must walk that road together, that where I am, there My followers will be also. And the good news is, if anyone truly serves Me, the heavenly Father will honor him by bestowing eternal life upon him."[138]

> The Lord's statement to the Greeks can to be taken as an appeal to all—both Gentiles and Jews—to be faithful to the Lord, not only by shunning the world, but also by pursuing, with vigor and excitement, a vibrant and close relationship with God.

---

136 John 12:20-22
137 John 12:23, 24
138 John 12:25, 26

Jesus, then remembering the personal sacrifice He must pay to secure the salvation of the world—of both Jews and Gentiles—added these words, "At this moment, My soul is distressed. But can I say, 'Father, save Me from anguish during the time of My sufferings—even of the crucifixion'? No! For it is but for this grand purpose that I am about to suffer. Indeed, the time has come for Me to suffer for the sins of the world, to secure salvation for all those who would seek to be My disciples, whether they are Jews or Gentiles."[139]

Appealing directly to God, Jesus added, "Father, glorify Your name!" By these words, Jesus was, in effect, saying, "Father, I will honor You and Your name by fulfilling My mission for the world, including any suffering that I must endure." [*Harmony* 16:105, 107][140]

At that very instant, the voice of God sounded from heaven with clarity, declaring, "I have both glorified it, and will glorify it again!" Here, God the Father was saying, "I have honored Your name and Your mission by blessing Your ministry. And I will continue to bless it, even through Your death and resurrection."[141]

The crowd standing around Jesus heard the voice from heaven. Some were positive that the voice sounded like thunder. Others testified, saying, "No, it was an angel who spoke to Him!"[142]

But the Lord explained, "The voice that you heard was not for My benefit, but for yours! The time has come for those who have observed these things to make a choice. The time has come for the power of Satan to be broken—that the intense evil of his wickedness might be fully exposed for what it is. Yes, it will happen, for, when I am lifted up from off the earth, I will draw all mankind to Me." By these words, Jesus was speaking of His crucifixion—the manner of His impending death—as well as its dramatic impact upon the peoples of the whole world.[143]

But these words confused the crowd, composed significantly of Jewish leaders. Accordingly, they challenged Him, asking, "But we have been taught from the Scriptures that the Messiah—the Christ—will live forever. There are

---

139 John 12:27
140 John 12:28
141 John 12:28
142 John 12:29
143 John 12:30-33

a number of such examples. [Psalm 89:36, etc.] So why do you say, 'The Son of Man must be lifted up'—even to be crucified? Who is this 'Son of Man'—the so-called Messiah—that You are describing?"[144]

Perhaps surprisingly, Jesus did not answer their questions. Instead, He directed them to remain faithful to Him, even though they might not yet understand all the aspects of His ministry. He told them, "What is important for you to understand now is that for yet a little longer you will have the true Light living among you. I say, walk in that Light while you still have that Light! That way, you can be assured that the Darkness of sin and ignorance will not overwhelm you. Do remember that he who walks in the Darkness cannot see where he is going. So then, once more I say, while you have the Light among you, trust in the Light. That way, you will become the sons or daughters of Light!" Of course, when Jesus spoke of the "Light," he was referring directly to Himself. And by the word, "Darkness," Jesus meant the devil and his false teachings that had blinded so many of them. [*Harmony* 5:58; 7:37][145]

> Had Jesus directly answered the people's questions [*Harmony* 14:144], He might have said the following: "The 'Son of Man'—the Messiah—will live forever. But that is after He dies for the sins of the world. After He is raised from the dead, He will ascend into heaven to be the Father. And then, the Son of Man's eternal kingdom will be established when He descends from heaven in the distant future. That is the Son of Man—the Messiah—I'm describing." While Jesus, at different times, mentioned one or more of these concepts, on this occasion, He chose not to review these details. Instead He emphasized the need for the people to live by faith.

Sensing that He should not say anything further, Jesus quickly left the Temple complex, and hid Himself from the Jewish leaders. He would never again return to the Temple![146]

As He made His hasty departure from the Temple area, the Master cried out to His disciples, "He who believes in Me, trusts not only in Me, but also in the Father who sent Me. Those, therefore, who seek to comprehend the things which I have taught them, will also comprehend the Father's will for their lives.

---

144 John 12:34

145 John 12:25, 36

146 John 12:36

As I have just said, I have come as the Light of the world so that everyone who trusts Me will escape the Darkness of evil that now pervades the earth.[147]

"But, let Me make it clear," the Lord cautioned, "if anyone hears My words, and refuses to follow them, I will not be their Judge! For as I have always said, I did not come into the world to judge it but rather to save it. [*Harmony* 3:22] But make no mistake: they, nevertheless, will be judged—not by Me personally, but rather, by their own rejection of My words. Yes, those who hear My words, and yet reject them, will be condemned. The mere rejection of My words will, in the final judgment at the end of the world, be sufficient to condemn everyone who rejects Me. In a very real sense, then, they will have condemned themselves!"[148]

> By this statement, Jesus meant that the sin that would condemn people in the judgment was not so much any particular thing they did or did not do. Rather, people would be condemned by their attitude—that is, by a mindset of rejection of the Lord's words and ministry. This means that the Jewish leaders of the Lord's day would be condemned in the judgment, not merely because they actually did something wrong, but rather, because of their *attitude* of rejection and rebellion. This rejection and rebellion was the sin of the heart as opposed to the some specific thing that they did or did not do.

"And also remember," the Lord concluded, "I never spoke My own words to the people. I spoke only as the Father directed Me to speak. Yes, it was He who instructed Me as to what to preach, and what to teach. In the same way as I have trusted in the word of the Father as to what to say, you are to place your trust in what I have said, and then you will have eternal life. That's why I spoke just as He directed Me, for My words will provide eternal life to all of you who believe in them."[149]

> Here, Jesus indicated that those who would ultimately be saved would be saved, not because they had done some particular thing, but rather because they had possessed an attitude of belief and acceptance of the Lord and His ministry. And they accepted it because, as Jesus said, it came from the Father.[1]

---

147 John 12:44-46
148 John 12:47, 48
149 John 12:49, 50

> Throughout the "Passion Week," Jesus had strongly appealed to many people to have a closer, more vibrant walk of faith with Him. He had appealed to Jew and Gentile, rich and poor, critic and disciple, leader and follower. No one was left out. His appeal was for all those who had heard what He said that week, and for all those who would hear *of* Him throughout the years that followed. [*Harmony* 16:113][2]

## — The Reasons Behind the Jewish Leaders' Rejection of Jesus
**< Tuesday, Nisan 11, A.D. 31 (7/7) >**
**{John 12:37-43}**

But why did the Jewish leadership end up rejecting the ministry of Jesus? It is hard to comprehend that they truly rejected the Messiah—the One whom they had so desperately wanted to come and dwell among them! Why would they do such a thing? Of course, even though the Lord had performed many miracles in their presence, most of them still refused to believe in Him. These miracles—such as many healings, large distributions of small amounts of food . . . even resurrections—should have clearly indicated to them that the Lord's power and authority were unusual—even miraculous. While these miracles certainly piqued the Jewish leaders' curiosity, they, nevertheless, ended up rejecting His overall ministry, considering it to be a fraud. [*Harmony* 1:3; 3:7/4; 8:31/][150]

> While it is true that Jesus had some theological differences with the Jewish leaders, that was just the beginning of why they rejected Him as the true Messiah. There are at least five other reasons why the Jewish leaders rejected Jesus, His teachings, and overall ministry.(ll) [1]

> First, they rejected Jesus because He refused to endorse their philosophies and teachings. For example, He stood up to them over the way they used the Temple. [*Harmony* 3:1-3; 14:44-51] He refused to support their ridiculous system of handwashings. [*Harmony* 10:1-8] He constantly challenged their cold, uncaring attitude toward the sinners whom He had come to save. [*Harmony* 12:26, etc.] The list could go on and on. But indeed, had Jesus supported the mindset of the Jewish leaders, it is quite conceivable that some of the theological differences He had with them would have been minor points which they could have ignored. Therefore there had to be other reasons why they rejected Him.(mm) [2]

---

[150] John 12:37

Second, without doubt jealousy played a large role in the Jewish leadership's rejection of Jesus. Simply put, they were jealous of the huge following Jesus had from the common people. They had craved such a following for themselves, but they had never achieved it. And because the Lord did have such a following, they couldn't stand it. They hated it! They hated Him! They wanted Him dead![(nn)] [3]

Third, the Jewish leaders never were willing to accept the reality of the full divinity of Jesus. Theologically, many of them did not believe that the coming Messiah would be divine in nature, and accordingly, they were not willing to follow One who so clearly claimed divinity for Himself. For in part if they did, they would have to subordinate their own opinions on theology and other matters to what Jesus declared to be true and right. To be sure, they would never be willing to do that. [(oo)] [4]

Fourth, the Lord's ministry did not match the preconceived ideas of the leaders of the Jews as to what the Messiah was to be or to do. To give just one example, they wanted a conquering Messiah King to overthrow the cruel Roman government. Not only did the Lord refuse to do this, He even told the Jews to love their neighbors . . . including the Romans! How could they accept One as the Messiah, they reasoned, who made such an offensive demand of them?[(pp)] [5]

Fifth, the Jewish religion, falsely taught, was based upon the concept that a man could save himself by the performance of various rituals, and by conformity to certain rules and restrictions. The fact that Jesus indicated that salvation was a gift of God, received by faith through reliance upon Him as their personal Savior, was something totally foreign to the thinking of many Jews, especially the leadership of Israel. They were too self-centered to depend upon Him for their salvation.[(qq)] [6]

For these—and other reasons—the Jewish leadership could not—and would not—accept Jesus as the true Messiah of Bible prophecy. And unfortunately, because of this negative attitude toward Jesus, they lost out on the most precious things the Lord had in mind for them: *true* national greatness, and their personal salvation![7]

Actually, the Jews' rejection of Jesus did fulfill a couple of prophecies given by Isaiah the prophet in regard to this very issue. The first said, "Lord, who is it that has been willing to believe our report regarding the ministry of the Messiah? And to whom has the strong arm of the Lord been revealed through the ministry of the Messiah, so that His ministry will be recognized as the true demonstration of the power of God?" [Isaiah 53:1] The implied answer to these two questions is: very few! Yes, the work of the Messiah had been revealed, even demonstrated for the world to see. And the ministry of Jesus was clearly both a revelation and demonstration of the power of God. But comparatively few chose to accept it. And of the leadership of Israel, even fewer chose to believe and trust in it.[151]

Isaiah further predicted that the people would refuse to believe in the Messiah. The Old Testament prophet said, "God has blinded their eyes—so that they could not understand. He has hardened their hearts, so that they cannot see with their eyes, nor comprehend with their minds. Thus, they have been prevented from repenting and allowing the Lord to heal their wickedness." [Isaiah 6:10; *Harmony* 7:45][152]

> This meant that people had their minds set against accepting the Lord in the first place. So when the Lord spoke to them, their rejection became even stronger. The more the Lord sought to convert them by impressing their minds and hearts, the more determined they were to rebel against Him. In fact, their situation continued to get increasingly worse the more the Lord tried to reason with them. In the end, they were worse off than if He had never spoken to them in the first place! This is the meaning of the phrases "God blinded their eyes" and "hardened their hearts." In summary, then, their rejection was based upon their *own* choice, not upon God actually wanting them to rebel, as the text might *seem* to imply.

Isaiah's understanding of those who would reject God and His Messiah was based upon a vision he had when he saw God—even Jesus—in all His glory. Isaiah then wrote about what he had seen. [Isaiah 6:1-10][(rr)] [153]

> In this story found in Isaiah 6:1-10, the prophet saw the incredible glory of Jesus—the glory He had had in heaven before His incarnation. [*Harmony* 16:107] On the surface, it might appear that the "Lord" of this story found in Isaiah was the Father. However, John clearly indicated

---

151 John 12:38, 39

152 John 12:39, 40

153 John 12:41

that the glory of Jesus was included as part of Isaiah's description of heaven, God, and His glory. All these things Isaiah had seen in vision! To be sure, in Isaiah 6, the prophet was powerfully changed—even transformed—by his awesome experience of seeing God in His glory. However, on this earth, the Jewish leaders were not at all changed when they saw this *same* glory—the character of God—so clearly and dramatically demonstrated in the life and ministry of Jesus. Indeed, because of their hard-headedness, they absolutely refused to be changed by what they observed in Him! [*Harmony* 14:152, 152/][(ss)]

But, even though most of the Jewish leaders rejected Jesus, there were many of them who actually did believe in the Lord, even being convinced that He was the Messiah. But because of the oppressive, dictatorial attitudes of the Pharisees, they were afraid to come out publicly in support of the Lord's ministry. Also, they were fearful that their acceptance of Jesus might lead to their excommunication from the church. Sadly, they desired the approval of men rather than the honor of God! And, in the end, most of these individuals lost their way.[154]

## Supplementary Notes:

**(a) [14:0++]** There are four different accounts of the Lord being anointed with perfume by one of His followers (Matthew 26:6-13; Mark 14:3-9; Luke 7:36-50; John 12:1-9). Considering the various details of this event by the four Gospel writers, as well as its placement in the Gospel record, some have taught that there are *two* such anointings. I believe, however, that there was only *one* such anointing, and accordingly, I recorded the story in the *Harmony* that way.

The question as to whether there are two such stories primarily arises because Matthew, Mark, and John place the event, at the same time, *late* in the life of Jesus, *while* Luke places it *much earlier* in the Lord's ministry. This has led some to think that there were two such stories. But, after analyzing all the details of the various accounts, I am convinced that there was only one such event. The reason why Luke placed the event earlier in the ministry of Jesus as compared to the other Gospel writers is unknown. However, such a placement need not be too disconcerting. Perhaps Luke listed it earlier, unaware of its proper location. Perhaps he had other reasons unclear to us. And most importantly, it should be noted, that, except for John's record,

154 John 12:42, 43

there are a fair number of events in the entire Gospel account that are not listed in strict chronological order. So then, Luke's placement of the story out of its proper sequence is not surprising. Therefore, in the *Harmony*, I feel very comfortable in merging all the details of the entire story as found in all four Gospel records as though it were a single event.

**(b) [14:0/++]** The following is a listing of where the evaluation of the various appeals the Lord made during the "Passion Week" can be quickly found: *Harmony* 14:18/, 41/2, 54/3, 58/, 66/, 77/, 84/3, 92/, 99/, 105/, 110/, 135/2, 138/, 149/2.

**(c) [14:1]** The actual sequence of days, relating to Simon's feast and the events that follow, is a bit of intelligent guesswork. However, John tells us that the feast took place *"six days"* before the Passover—which clearly took place the following Friday. Therefore I feel quite comfortable with the placement of the event of Simon's feast on Saturday night. Furthermore, my choice for the overall sequence of events which took place after the feast, I consider to be the most likely timeline.

**(d) [14:2]** (See above.)

**(e) [14:3]** Who was Mary Magdalene? This question has been disputed for years, and is still the source of great debate, even today! Traditionally, Mary has been declared a *"sinner"*— no doubt a word indicating that she was a prostitute. Logically, what else could it mean? She has often been tied to a family in Bethany comprised of her sister Martha and brother Lazarus. But, some people have argued that this individual is Mary *of Bethany*, not *Mary Magdalene*—that is, one from the city of Magdala in Galilee. (It should be noted that this Mary of Bethany is never actually called "Mary of Bethany;" rather this is a designation some, outside of the Bible record, have given to this woman to distinguish her from Mary Magdalene.) In short, some have actually said that there is not a shred of evidence that Mary Magdalene was a prostitute and that she was the one who anointed the Lord with ointment. But such, I firmly believe, is not the case! From my perspective, there is a great deal of evidence, to the contrary, in support of the so-called traditional position. Allow me to explain:

For the time being, *let's just assume* that Mary Magdalene *and* Mary of Bethany *are* the same person, and that the anointing of Jesus—contained in the four Gospel records—was performed by the same person (see **Note "a"** above). What then, are the *possible* facts? Here they are as I suggest them:

Jesus cast seven devils out of Mary Magdalene (Luke 8:2). These devils could be the cause of her being a prostitute—that is, a "sinner" (Luke 7:39). After her healing and conversion, Mary ministered with Jesus in Galilee for a time (Luke 8:1, 2). To show her appreciation to the Lord for her marvelous healing (Luke 8:2) and the resurrection of her brother Lazarus (John 11:1-44), she later on anointed the Lord with precious perfume. And because of the Lord's gracious healing of her, she earlier sat at Jesus' feet while Martha cooked a meal for the Lord (Luke 10:38-42). Finally, it makes perfect sense that it was this same Mary who went to the tomb early Sunday morning (John 20:1 2) and was the first person to meet with Jesus after His resurrection (John 20:11-18).

But then, some would ask, why would Mary, who lived in Bethany with her brother and sister, be called Mary *Magdalene*—one from the city of Magdala, which was many miles to the north? Follow this logic of a suggested scenario: Mary, who originally lived in Bethany, is seduced by Simon, the Pharisee—also of Bethany. Burdened by the guilt of this secret sin, she ultimately becomes a full-fledged prostitute, ending up possessed of devils. This is a great embarrassment to her and her family in the small town of Bethany. Because of this embarrassment and her desire to get away from Simon, she moves away to a town up north: Magdala of Galilee. When living there, plying her shameful trade, she meets Jesus and is forgiven and healed. She then travels with Jesus for a time, assisting Him in His ministry. After a while, now converted, she returns to Bethany, and lives again with her brother and sister. While there, she sits at the feet of Jesus, sees her brother resurrected, and ultimately anoints Jesus with perfume at Simon's feast—the Pharisee who had seduced her and who had been healed by Jesus from leprosy. And finally, she is at the tomb of Jesus on the resurrection day. Indeed, it would not be surprising that a woman filled with such courage and passion at Simon's feast on Saturday night—the woman whom Jesus said was anointing His body for burial—would be the *same* woman, less than a week later, who would be at the tomb to watch the Lord's burial, be among the first at the tomb on Sunday morning, and then be favored to be the first to personally meet with Jesus after His resurrection. Following this scenario, it is easy—and even logical—to see that Mary of Bethany and

Mary Magdalene can be the same person. Accordingly, this is the position I confidently take in the *Harmony.*

It is possible, too, that the identity of Mary Magdalene could have been concealed. What do I mean by that? It has been suggested that when the Gospel story was written Mary was still alive. And to preserve some privacy for her—considering the fact that she was once a prostitute—the Gospel writers could have written her story in such a way to include some ambiguity. Well, it is something to think about.

**(f) [14:4]** Spikenard really means "pure nard."

**(g) [14:7/]** (See **Note "e"** above.)

**(h) [14:8]** (See **Note "e"** above.)

**(i) [14:13/]** (See **Note "e"** above.)

**(j) [14:15]** (See **Note "e"** above.)

**(k) [14:18/+]** Properly meshing together all the events of the last week of the Lord's ministry is not easy. Sometimes the events are not listed in strict chronological order—especially by Matthew and Mark. But I have tried to do the best I can to list them in a logical sequence.

**(l) [14:21/6]** Consideration of the reasons Judas had in betraying Jesus is, because of the lack of Biblical evidence, somewhat speculative. However, I think what I said of his motivations is both reasonable and logical.

**(m) [14:28]** Why did the Lord go through such an elaborate process to secure the animals for the Triumphal Entry? Perhaps it was to emphasize the powerful meaning of the Entry itself. Also, had the Lord made prior arrangements with the owners of the animals? We don't know, but it is interesting to think about.

**(n) [14:30]** See *Harmony* 2:58/ to understand more about the Aramaic language.

**(o) [14:40/]** Why did the Lord go through the entire Triumphal Entry process when He had no intention of following it through to its logical conclusion? Why did He seemingly "lead the people on" with the false hope that He would actually allow them to officially proclaim Him Messiah and King? I tried to give a reasonable response to these questions in my interpretations found throughout the recording of this event in the *Harmony*. I am fairly comfortable with my effort in that regard.

**(p) [14:43+]** There is a question as to whether there were two cleansings of the Temple—as the Gospel record would seem to indicate—or just one. I take the position that there were, indeed, two such cleansings. Such a possibility makes sense to me. If that is the case, the Lord *began* His ministry with a cleansing, and *ended* it with the second cleansing. It was as if the Lord gave the Jews a chance to "clean up their act" after the first cleansing. But after more than three years, the same old problem existed, necessitating the second cleansing.

**(q) [14:43+]** To better understand the Lord's purpose in cleansing the Temple, it would be useful to compare the first cleansing with the second one. To do so, refer to *Harmony* 3:1-9, including all **Explanatory Notes**.

**(r) [14:47]** See **Note "n"** above.

**(s) [14:54/5]** Without doubt, the greatest struggle I had in the putting together the *Harmony* is trying to explain such teachings as Jesus implied here. That is: *Just ask for something, and if you have the faith, it will happen as you request!* Of course, such a concept would be nice *if* that is what happens! But, considering the reality of life, we know that such is not the case. To be sure, I have not come up with a completely satisfying answer to this dilemma. Perhaps nobody has ever done so! And besides, life is best lived by accepting the will of God in one's life no matter what might happen.

**(t) [14:66/+]** The severity of the Lord's encounter with the Jewish leaders in this event is quite strong. This was not the first time this happened, neither would it be the last. When we consider the mild nature of Jesus when He faced His accusers during His trials and crucifixion, such a negative exchange can appear shocking. However, once the circumstances that led up to such a heavy exchange are properly understood, the severity of the dialogue is easier to comprehend. Please note that the leaders of God's people—the ones whom the Lord addressed on this occasion—had utterly failed as God's leaders. Also, because they were actually, at that moment, in the process of plotting the death of Jesus, He gave them one last chance to change their terrible course of action. He had to warn them—even quite strongly—for the time for decision which would affect their eternal destiny had arrived. The

Lord could not be silent any longer; He could no longer treat them gently. (For more information on this issue, refer to **Note "n"** in Chapter 11.)

**(u) [14:68]** There are a few details of this parable that are stated differently by the Gospel recorders—the kind of small details that are *impossible* to reconcile. I did my best. However, the differences are of minor significance, I think.

**(v) [14:74]** This is one of the very few times that the Jewish leaders seemed to accept the Lord's authority over them. Here they expressed concern and worry that the dire consequences explained by the Lord in the parable would actually apply to them. And further, they actually seem to recognize that Jesus had the power to bring about that which He had declared would happen to them! I consider their reaction in this case to be most unusual, to say the least, especially considering the fact that *they* had earlier pronounced the same judgment on the wicked vine-growers! (*Harmony* 14:72) Of course, though, that was before they fully realized that Jesus was talking about them!

**(w) [14:78+]** (See **Note "t"** above.)

**(x) [14:88]** The word "hypocrite" is the Greek word for "actor." So, accordingly, I stated it as such throughout the *Harmony.*

**(y) [14:97]** The condition of humanity in eternity—relating to marriage—as described by Jesus here, is an interesting concept—that is, it is new to the Bible and its theology. When we consider its ramifications, it is fascinating to think about.

**(z) [14:98]** The true meaning of the Lord's response to the Sadducees' riddle is incredibly profound. In truth, I found His answer difficult to express in clear, distinct words. Nevertheless, I tried my best.

**(aa) [14:103]** Giving consideration to the true impact of love in commandment-keeping, as was implied by Jesus here, took a great number of extra words to describe it adequately. I am confident, though, that I did no injustice to the words or intent of Jesus.

**(bb) [14:110/+]** (See **Note "t"** above.)

**(cc) [14:118]** (See **Note "x"** above.)

**(dd) [14:119]** (See **Note "x"** above.)

**(ee) [14:120]** The power of the Lord's indictment of the Pharisees in this verse is quite shocking! It shows that false teachings—especially legalistic ones—are particularly insidious, even dangerous.

**(ff) [14:125]** (See **Note "x"** above.)

**(gg) [14:126]** I wanted to comment especially on the fact that the Lord's strong emphasis on justice, mercy, and faithfulness—as opposed to legalistic tithing—is quite striking to me. Accordingly, I have done so in the *Harmony*.

**(hh) [14:127]** (See **Note "x"** above.)

**(ii) [14:128]** (See **Note "x"** above.)

**(jj) [14:129]** (See **Note "x"** above.)

**(kk) [14:130]** In the Greek manuscript of the text, the name Barachias (or Berechiah) is written rather than Jehoiada, the father of the slaughtered Zechariah (of 2 Chronicles 24:20-22). There is no record that the real Zecharias, the son of Berechiah (the *other* Zechariah, found in Zechariah 1:1) was ever martyred. The obvious answer to this discrepancy is that when one of the earlier transcriptions of Matthew's Gospel took place, a scribe, confused over which one of the *two* Zechariahs he was writing about at the time, mistakenly wrote in the wrong name of Zechariah's father.

**(ll) [14:150/1]** I took the liberty to add significantly to what John stated as to the reason why the Jewish leaders rejected Jesus. Based upon the overall evidence, I consider my reasons sensible and logical.

**(mm) [14:150/2]** (See above.)

**(nn) [14:150/3]** (See **Note "ll"** above.)

**(oo) [14:150/4] (See Note "ll"** above.)

**(pp) [14:150/5] (See Note "ll"** above.)

**(qq) [14:150/6]** (See **Note "ll"** above.)

**(rr) [14:153]** I am particularly intrigued by John's reference to Isaiah in John 12:41, which reads in the KJV: "These things said Esaias (Isaiah), when he saw his glory, and spake of him." Clearly, John was referencing the story found in Isaiah 6:1-10. After studying this story and its background (as it relates to the Jewish leaders rejection of Jesus), I am very excited by its meaning and how it dramatically affects this portion of the message of the Gospel of John. Accordingly, I have taken a good deal of space to expand upon this whole concept as John uses it.

Briefly told, this is the story of Isaiah 6:1-10:

Isaiah is taken into God's throneroom, where God is seated majestically upon His throne. There is he sees the glory of God as He is surrounded by the angels (seraphim). The angels praise God by declaring, "Holy, holy, holy, is the Lord of hosts: the whole earth is full of his *glory*." Then the whole place shakes and is filled with smoke. Not surprisingly, Isaiah is so overwhelmed with the sights and sounds of it all that he cries out, "Woe is me! For I am undone." He further describes the sinful condition of both himself and the Hebrew people. He particularly mentions that he and his people have "unclean lips." He, as a sinful man with "unclean lips," has seen, with his own eyes the greatness of God—indeed, the *"glory"* of God that filled the whole earth. Accordingly, Isaiah feels terribly unworthy—even lost! But then, the angel takes a burning coal from the altar and touches his lips to purge them of sin. Then the angel declares that his "iniquity is taken away." Next, Isaiah hears God ask who will go to work for Him. Isaiah volunteers, declaring that he is willing to speak for God. Then, finally, God explains that even though Isaiah will share the truth with the people, they will not listen to him. In summary, Isaiah's apparent conversion experience was brought about by the fact that he saw the glory of God, and what follows is also a direct result of seeing God's glory.

How does this relate to John's present discussion as to why the Jewish leaders rejected Jesus? Consider this:

I am reminded of the text in John 1:14, in the KJV, which reads: "And the Word [Jesus] was made flesh, and dwelt among us, (and we beheld his glory, the glory as of the only begotten of the Father,) full of grace and truth." In part, this text tells us that the disciples viewed the "glory" of Jesus—which, I am convinced, is His *character*. And further, it is clear that by viewing on a firsthand basis the character of Jesus, the disciples were transformed by its power and greatness (John 1:12, 13). In other words, the disciples were transformed by viewing—and of course, by accepting—the character of Jesus. Now, here's the main point: Even though the Jewish leaders had ample opportunity to personally view the character of Jesus—that is, again, His "glory"—they refused to be changed by its power. The Jews of Isaiah's day (as the passage in Isaiah says), and the Jewish leaders of Jesus' day (as John paraphrases Isaiah's words in John 12:40), all refused to be changed by seeing the glory—or character—of God. Isaiah's actual words in the KJV are: "Make the heart of this people fat, and make their ears heavy, and shut their eyes; lest they see with their eyes, and hear with their ears, and understand with their heart, and be converted, and be healed." (See *Harmony* 14:152 ***and*** *Harmony* 14:152/.) In short, then, when the Jewish leaders refused to be changed by the power of Christ's glory—His character—they were, in effect, rejecting Jesus, just as the Jews of Isaiah's day rejected God. *Thus, in a very real sense, they all—both in Old and New Testament days—rejected both God the Father and Jesus, because they refused to be changed either by them or their characters—that is, their glory.*

There is one more point that might be stated. In the Isaiah 6 story, the prophet sees God on His throne. It is the "glory" of God that ultimately, in a step-by-step process, that changes him. But, based on John 1:14, Jesus possesses, as the "only begotten of the Father," the same "glory" of that of the Father. (See also Hebrew 1:1-3.) So then, John can accurately declare that when Isaiah saw the glory of the Father, *he was also viewing the glory of Jesus—a glory that, once accepted by faith, can change people!*

**(ss) [14:153/] (See above.)**

# CHAPTER FIFTEEN

## THE PASSION WEEK: TUESDAY AFTERNOON THROUGH WEDNESDAY

**From the Signs of the Lord's Second Coming, to the Parable of the Sheep and the Goats**

**(Just Before Passover, Spring, A.D. 31)**

### Jesus Gives Signs of His Glorious Second Coming, And Illustrates the Preparation Needed for this Climatic Event[a]

**< Tuesday Early Evening and Night, Nisan 12, Spring, A.D. 31 (7/7) >**
**(Matthew 24:1-25:46; Mark 13:1-37; Luke 21:5-36)**

### — Signs of the Lord's Second Coming

**< Tuesday Early Evening and Night, Nisan 12, Spring, A.D. 31 (7/7) >**
**{Matthew 24:1-51; Mark 13:1-37; Luke 21:5-36}**

The Lord and His disciples left the Temple area for the last time. As they were making their way around the Temple along the path that led down the hill from Jerusalem, the disciples pointed back toward the majestic Temple structure just behind them. They drew to the attention of Jesus just how well built the building truly was. One of them commented, "Teacher, notice how large these stones are. And see, too, how magnificent these buildings are!" He also pointed out the various items that had been installed to adorn the face of the Temple. Now, Jesus had already told them, two days earlier—on Sunday—that the entire Temple would be destroyed. [*Harmony* 14:34] No doubt the disciples, seeing the massive structure of the edifice, were having a hard time understanding how this prediction of the Lord could possibly come to pass. Therefore, they made these comments to encourage Jesus to elaborate on His prediction which seemed so surprising, even shocking.[1]

1 Matthew 24:1; Mark 13:1; Luke 21:5

Their plan worked, for the Lord once more discussed with them the future of the Temple. As if to emphasize what He would say next, the Lord reiterated what had just been described to Him: "Yes, do you see how majestic these things are? Just look at them!" Then pausing for a second, Jesus added sadly, "Well . . . nevertheless, I tell you again, the time is coming when not one stone of the Temple will left upon another. In fact, the entire building will be torn down!" But He added nothing further to these cryptic words.[2]

They continued their way from the Temple area down the road toward the brook Kidron. From there they climbed the hill that led to the Mount of Olives. While resting there directly opposite the Temple, four of the disciples—James, John, Peter, and Andrew—came to Him in private and inquired, "Lord, earlier You told us that the Temple would be destroyed. Teacher, tell us when this will happen! Certainly it must happen at the end of this present world, when the Messiah's kingdom will begin. So then, what is the sign that indicates when the end of the world *and* the destruction of the Temple will take place?" [*Harmony* 15:15/][3]

> Of course, the destruction of the Temple—and Jerusalem, the city surrounding it—would take place many years earlier than the end the world, but the disciples had no concept of that. However, instead of explaining this fact to them, Jesus answered their questions by *blending* together the events surrounding the destruction of the Temple *with those* of the end of the world. Later on the disciples would begin to distinguish more clearly the difference between these two events. But at the present moment, such an understanding would be too much for them to comprehend or cope with.

The Lord began His explanation by saying, "Be careful that nobody misleads you. Yes, many will come in My name, saying, 'I am the Messiah!' or, 'The time of the end is near!' But don't follow after them. They will trick many people, but not you . . . if you are prepared. You will first hear of wars, and there will also be many additional rumors of war . . . and of other disturbances, for that matter. But don't let that frighten you. You see, all these things must take place just as they're supposed to, but, no, the end will not come as quickly as that."[4]

---

2 Matthew 24:2; Mark 13:2; Luke 21:5, 6

3 Matthew 24:3; Mark 13:3, 4; Luke 21:7

4 Matthew 24:4-6; Mark 13:5-7; Luke 21:8, 9

Next Jesus made a general statement regarding events that would begin to take place during the days of the disciples—events that would continue right until the last days, just before His actual Second Coming. The Lord said, "Nation will fight against nation, and kingdom against kingdom. And in many places there will be famines, plagues, and earthquakes. In addition, terrible things will transpire, even awesome signs in the heavens. But these things will be only the beginning of earth's horrors. They will be like the beginning of labor pains when a woman is about to give birth to a child. By that I mean that even more horrific things—like progressive labor pains—must yet follow."[5]

Then the Lord began to discuss the events that would apply more specifically to the disciples themselves and the things they would face personally during their lifetime. He explained, "Your enemies will persecute you. They will even kill you. And why? Because all nations will hate you. And why is that? Because they have hated Me and My name, and what I have stood for. And because of the anguish of this distress and persecution, many of your friends will apostatize. As a result, they will turn against you and hand you over to the authorities to be arrested. Indeed, extreme hatred toward one another—and toward you—will greatly abound."[6]

> When He made this statement, Jesus had mainly His disciples in mind, as well as the ones who would immediately follow after them. However, the concepts of distress and persecution which He mentioned here would apply, in principle, to all His followers in every age throughout the entire history of Christianity.

"Yes, beware!" the Lord continued. "Your enemies will grab hold of you and force you to stand before the Sanhedrin"—the church court. "They will beat you with whips in the synagogues"—or churches. "They will throw you into prison. But because of this, some of you will be privileged to bear testimony in My behalf in front of kings and governors. And the good news is that your witness will be the reason that many sinful people shall change their attitudes, in a positive way, toward the Gospel. Yes, its message must be preached to the entire world. Indeed, your persecution will provide a great opportunity for you to share the news of the Gospel with those who have never heard it before.[7]

---

5 Matthew 24:7, 8; Mark 13:8; Luke 21:10, 11

6 Matthew 24:9, 10

7 Mark 13:9, 10: Luke 21:12, 13

"Make up your mind right now," the Lord counseled, "that when they arrest you, you need not be concerned as to what you will say in your defense when you are brought before a court of law. Indeed, don't worry about it! For the Holy Spirit will speak through you at that time. Say whatever He impresses you to say! It won't be your words, anyway, but His. In verity, I will, through the Holy Spirit, give all of you the wisdom you need in order to speak the types of things that your enemies will not be able to refute. [*Harmony* 8:46; 12:39][8]

"Yes, people will treat you very badly. Brother will turn against brother, even to the extent of having him killed. A father will have his own child slain. Even children will rise up to condemn their own parents to death. Parents, brothers, friends, and relatives may turn on you—they will even put some of you to death. It will be, as I have just said, that you will be hated by many because of Me. But . . . be of good courage. I assure you, the one who endures to the end shall be saved![9]

"Yes, to be sure," Jesus continued with His point, "they may even kill you, but in eternity, not a single hair of your head will be lost or destroyed. By enduring to the end—even if it costs your life in this world—you will live forever with Me in eternity! So be of good courage.[10]

"To make things even more difficult for you," the Lord went on, discussing additional woes His disciples would face, "a number of false prophets will come along, deceiving many. Because wickedness will increase, many will lose their capacity to love one another. However, as I have just said [*Harmony* 15:9, 10], the one who remains faithful to the end will be saved! And finally, when this Gospel which I've been teaching these past several years will be preached in the whole world, as a witness to all nations, then the end will come!"[11]

> The "end" to which Jesus referred in this prediction was the destruction of the city of Jerusalem, as well as the Temple, in A.D. 70, some 39 years into the future. The Gospel would be successfully preached to a large part of the then-known world. [Colossians 1:23; Romans 1:8] When this happened, based upon the Lord's prediction, the disciples could be sure that the destruction of Jerusalem and the Temple was at hand.

---

8 Mark 13:11; Luke 21:14, 15

9 Mark 13:12, 13; Luke 21:16, 17

10 Luke 21:18, 19

11 Matthew 24:11-14

> This was the *primary* meaning of all that Jesus had said thus far in His discussion with His disciples.(b) [1]
>
> However, these same words can also be used to apply to the times of the end of the whole world. That is, the predictions of war, famines, earthquakes, persecutions, and things such as that, can, in a *secondary* sense, apply to events of the last days of this earth. But it should be noted that the Lord's original, *primary* intent of His predictions, thus far, was to apply all these things to the days of the disciples, from the time that He first gave the predictions in A.D. 31 up until A.D. 70 when the city of Jerusalem was destroyed—a total of 39 years. Again, *only* in a secondary sense do they apply to the time of the last days of this earth. (c) [2]

Jesus continued with His warning regarding the destruction of the Temple, saying, "Carefully note this: You will see the 'abomination of desolation' which Daniel the prophet mentioned [Daniel 9:27]. This abomination of desolation will stand in the holy place where it should not be. This prophecy in Daniel refers to the surrounding of the city of Jerusalem—and consequently, the holy place of the Temple—by Roman armies. When you actually see this happen, then you will know that this 'desolation' is upon you. This will be a warning—or sign—for you. This means that those who are living in Judea need to flee immediately to the mountains. Those who are in Jerusalem must escape quickly out of the city, and those who are living in the countryside must not enter the city again. Now listen to this: Whenever you read the book of Daniel, I want you to understand all this, because, just as he, God's prophet, predicted, those days will be filled with vengeance against Israel. Indeed, everything that has been written about those horrible days must take place just as it has been predicted. To be sure, there will be no escape for the city of Jerusalem. [Deuteronomy 27:11-26; 28:15-68, etc.](d) [12]

"And when this happens," Jesus continued, "should someone be resting on a housetop, he must not risk his life to go into his house to get his belongings. No! Instead, he must flee immediately for his life. Likewise, if someone is working in a field, he must not go back home to even get his cloak. He also must escape right away. [*Harmony* 13:48, 51][13]

---

12 Matthew 24:15, 16; Mark 13:14; Luke 21:20-22

13 Matthew 24:17, 18; Mark 13:15,16

"In fact, in that day, it will really be tough on those who are pregnant, as well as on those who have nursing babies. For that reason you should be praying now, that when you have to flee, it will not be in the winter, because it will be too cold. Also pray that your flight will not take place on the seventh-day Sabbath, for it will be impossible to keep the Sabbath as a day of rest if you are fleeing for your life!"[14]

The Lord added even more, saying, "There will be incredible anguish in all the land of Israel, because of the great anger shown against its inhabitants. Indeed, many will be slaughtered with swords. Others will be led captive into foreign nations. Jerusalem itself will be totally crushed by the Gentiles. In fact, it will be under the control of Gentiles until the Lord sees fit to remove the non-Jewish control of the city."[(e)] [15]

> As outlined in the Lord's discussion with His disciples [*Harmony* 15:4-15], all the various predictions of Jesus were strikingly fulfilled within the next 39 years—up until A.D. 70—when the city of Jerusalem was surrounded by Roman armies—the "abomination of desolation," as described in the book of Daniel. [Daniel 9:27] Preceding that particular event, there were wars, rumors of wars, persecutions, and executions . . . just as the Lord had predicted. Finally, the city of Jerusalem, many of its inhabitants, and its Temple were destroyed. Not a stone of the Temple was left upon another. The disciples had thought that such a terrible destruction would signal the end of the whole world. [*Harmony* 15:3] But they were wrong, for the time of the end had not yet arrived. There would be much, much more that would happen over a very long period of time. [*Harmony* 14:34]

Jesus continued, saying, "After the destruction of the Temple, there will be a time of grave tribulation and distress, greater than at any time since the beginning of the world, and even greater than any time yet to take place. In fact, so severe will this tribulation be that unless those days should be shortened, none of My people would survive! But because God cares for His people—the ones whom He has chosen—those days *will* be shortened."[(f)] [16]

---

14 Matthew 24:19, 20; Mark 13:17, 18; Luke 21:23

15 Luke 21:23, 24

16 Matthew 24:21, 22; Mark 13:19, 20

Within this brief statement Jesus encompassed the history of the world and His people, from the destruction of Jerusalem in A.D. 70, up until a time just before the end of the world—a period of roughly 2,000 years or more! At times, the level of persecution of God's people would be horrific. On occasion, Christians would even persecute fellow Christians! While the persecution of Christians, by both the Jews and the Roman Empire of the first and second centuries, was terrible, the persecutions during the time in history often called the Dark (or Middle) Ages would be even worse. Further, when Jesus said that this particular time of distress would be worse than at any time in recorded history, He probably referred primarily to the *length* of the time of persecution—that is, about 2,000 years. In fact, when one totals up the number of people killed for the name of Jesus—no doubt a total in the very high millions—during that 2,000-year period, this figure would certainly dwarf that of any other in the history of all the persecutions of God's people!(g) [1]

The Lord indicated that this time of persecution would be "shortened." What does that mean? Note that Jesus did not say that the time would be *short*, but that it would be "shortened." This means that *ultimately* the time of severe persecution *would cease*, before all of God's people were killed. Yes, the time of persecution was indeed long, but it would finally come to an end, sparing the majority of God's people. When persecution is taking place, the duration of the persecution seems—to those being persecuted—to never end. It *would*, nevertheless, come to an end. Thus it was, as Jesus said, the days of the persecution would be "shortened."[2]

Note further that Jesus did not give any real clue as to how long this time of persecution would actually last. For, had the disciples known at the time when Jesus spoke to them, that so many years would pass before the Lord's actual return to the earth—much of it filled with unceasing persecution—it certainly would have overwhelmed them with despair. That is why Jesus gave the disciples no indication of how long this time period of persecution would last.[3]

Next, the Lord described events that would occur at the end of this long period of severe distress and persecution. He said, "Very soon after the tribulation of those days of which I have just spoken [*Harmony* 15:16] there will be signs in the sun, moon, and stars. Specifically, 'the sun will be made dark, and the moon will not give its normal light, and even the stars will fall' from the heavens. [Isaiah 34:4] Also, there will be on the earth distress among the many nations. People will be upset when the waves of the sea roar with extreme intensity against the shore." Without question, the severity of the times depicted by Jesus was quite dramatically illustrated by the strength of the words He chose! However, the specific events the Lord had in mind when He made this powerful declaration, remain a subject of debate.[(h)] [(i)] [17]

Jesus admonished, "Then, if anyone says to you, 'Look! Here is the Messiah!' or 'There He is!' don't you believe it! For, there will be many false Christs and fake prophets who will come upon the scene. They will even perform many signs and miracles. So amazing will these miracles be that many will be deceived. In fact, only the most informed of My followers will be able to pick out the fakes. So then, be careful! Don't forget that I am telling you these things now so that, when they actually happen, you will be amply prepared. [*Harmony* 7:6/; 10:99, 99/][(j)] [18]

"Take note," the Lord continued, "if they tell you, 'Look, the Lord is in the wilderness, away from large groups of people,' I say: don't go to the wilderness to look for Him, for He will not be found there. Or maybe they will say to you, 'Don't look for the Lord to come literally, but only within the inner part of your heart.' This, also, will not be true. On the other hand, this is the way the coming of the Son of Man will actually be: it will be like the lightning which comes from the east and shines all the way across the sky toward the west. That is, His coming will be literal and it will fill the entire heavens . . . for all to see."[(k)] [19]

> Here, the Lord went to great lengths to describe, not only how His coming would take place—"as lightning comes from the east"—but also how it will *not* happen—such as the deceptive declaration that "the Lord is in the wilderness," and so forth. Apparently there will be a great deal of deception surrounding the actual coming of Jesus, and the Lord wanted His people to be properly prepared. Certainly He did not want them to be deceived.

"You know the proverb that I've used before [*Harmony* 13:53], which states, 'Wherever there is something dead, you will see vultures circling overhead'? Well,

---

17 Matthew 24:29; Mark 13:24, 25; Luke 21:25

18 Matthew 24:23-25; Mark 13:21-23

19 Matthew 24:26, 27

when you see the sky filled with brightness, as I have just described to you, then you will know that the Son of Man has returned!"(l) [20]

Jesus continued, "After that, the entire powers of the heavens will be shaken. Next, the sign of the Son of Man shall appear in the sky. When these things begin to happen, you will know with certainty that He is actually returning to this earth! To be sure, His appearing will cause the unconverted and unprepared people of the earth to be overwhelmed with stifling fear when they see all these things taking place around them. They will faint within their hearts for the uncertainty of what will happen to them. Yes, those on this earth who are not ready for His coming will surely weep when they see the 'Son of Man coming in the clouds of heaven' [Daniel 7:13] with power and great brightness! That is when the Son of Man will direct His angels, with a clarion trumpet blast, to gather together His chosen people from the four corners of the earth—from one distant end of the sky and the earth to the other. Yes, while the wicked will tremble at the sight, you are to rejoice! In fact, you are to stand tall with courage. Indeed, you are to lift up your heads in triumph because your Redeemer has come to save you!"(m) [21]

To explain Himself more fully, the Lord added an illustration, "I want you to learn the parable of the fig tree—as well as any tree, for that matter: As you know, when a tree's branches become tender with moisture, and begin to sprout leaves, you know that summer is fast approaching. So then, when you see happening around you all these things which I have just described to you, then you will know that the arrival of the kingdom of God and the Son of Man, is very close—even at the door! It is a fact that, in spite of the distress that will take place on this earth and in the heavens, My followers will survive. They will witness the complete fulfillment of all these things. I assure you, heaven and earth may pass away, but My words will never be proven false."(n) [22]

Then Jesus added a word of caution, "Now, as to the actual day and hour of the Son of Man's coming, no one knows this except the heavenly Father. Not even the angels in heaven know. In fact, even I, the Son of God, don't know. It will take the inhabitants of this earth by surprise. To give an example, the coming of the Son of Man will be like it was in the days of Noah. [Genesis 6-9] The people of that day, as you remember history, saw the ark being built. They heard

---

[20] Matthew 24:28

[21] Matthew 24:29-31; Mark 13:25-27; Luke 21:26-28

[22] Matthew 24:32-35; Mark 13:28-31; Luke 21:29-33

Noah's preaching, but when the flood came, they were totally unprepared. And why? Because, in those days, they were eating and drinking, marrying and being given in marriage . . . that was their whole life. They continued to do these things until the very day that Noah entered the ark. They seemingly could not figure out what was happening . . . that is, until the flooding rains came and swept them all away! The preaching of Noah and the building of the ark should have created a sense of urgency within them. But unfortunately, it didn't. And, again, that's the way it will be at the coming of the Son of Man. In the last days, people will see events taking place which should shake them from their lethargy. However, such will not be the case. Many will ignore the events and go on living like nothing special is going to happen. [*Harmony* 13:47][23]

"Some people, however, will be ready for that day. Nevertheless, as I just indicated [*Harmony* 15:23], many others will not. It will like two men who will be working in a field. One of them will be saved, the other one will be lost. Two women will be grinding wheat at a hand mill. One will be saved, the other one lost. [*Harmony* 13:51][24]

"As you can see," the Lord added, "the only way to be safe, is to be ready at all times for the coming of the Son of Man. That is why I warn you to be always in a state of alertness, for you do not know the exact day of your Lord's coming. [*Harmony* 15:29] But you can be sure of this—to use a parable—that had the man of the house known the exact time of the night when a thief was going to break into his home, he would have been ready and waiting. Isn't that right? This way, the thief would have not been able to break into the house. In a similar way, you must be always carefully prepared—stay awake, so to speak, and pray—for the Son of Man will come at time when you do not expect Him to do so."[(o)] [25]

To explain further the need for His people to be ready for His coming, the Lord added, "I would like to illustrate My coming with yet another parable. Isn't it wise for a servant to do faithful work for his master when he has put him in charge of his entire household, even serving the meals at their proper time? Of course, it is! The end of the world, then, is to be likened to the return of the master—illustrative of the Son of Man—who was traveling to a far country. Upon leaving the house, he placed his servants in charge of everything, giving

---

23 Matthew 24:36-39; Mark 13:32

24 Matthew 24:40, 41

25 Matthew 24:42-44; Mark 13:33

each one a specific duty to perform. He also warned the doorkeeper to continue to watch diligently for his return, whenever that might be. [*Harmony* 12:55](p) [26]

"Indeed, I am sure you will agree that those servants whom the master finds faithfully performing their duties when he eventually returns to his home will certainly be happy! Isn't that right? Yes, it is clear, in that case, that the master will put those faithful servants in charge of all his possessions as a reward for their constant faithfulness! And that is what the Lord will do for you when He returns to this earth, if you are likewise found faithful in the performance of the duties that the Son of Man has assigned to you. [*Harmony* 12:55, 61/](q) [27]

"On the other hand, consider the case of unfaithful, wicked servants," the Lord continued with His parable. "They will say in their hearts, 'My master is not coming for quite a while.' So, as a result, some will begin to beat their fellow servants"—that is, be critical of others in the church. "Others will begin to eat and drink with drunkards"—that is, become worldly in their lifestyle. "Now, what do you suppose will happen to these two kinds of servants when the master unexpectedly comes home? Indeed, the master will show up one day, much to the servants' dismay and alarm! And yes, you can be sure the master will cut him in two!"—that is, punish them severely. "Those unfaithful servants will be treated as hypocrites, and they will weep and grind their teeth in despair, realizing how they have wasted their opportunities. Indeed, how unfaithful those servants will be, for they were to have served their master, but obviously, they utterly failed! [*Harmony* 12:60](r) [28]

"In conclusion, then," the Lord went on, "as I have just said: Be on the alert! [*Harmony* 15:25] You do not know when the Master of the house—the Son of Man—is coming home. It may be at sunset! It may be at midnight! It may be in the predawn hours, when the rooster crows! It may even be during the morning hours when the work day has well begun! Yes, He may come suddenly, even when you are fast asleep in the middle of the night! So then, what else can I say to you but what I've said several times before, 'Be on the alert!'"[29]

The Lord drove home the point, "So, My friends, once again I say, be on guard. [*Harmony* 15:25, 29] Do not allow your hearts to become distracted with

---

26 Matthew 24:45; Mark 13:34

27 Matthew 24:46, 47

28 Matthew 24:48-51

29 Mark 13:35-37

riotous living or drunkenness. Do not allow even the normal worries of this life to control you. If you do, then that day will come upon you suddenly and unexpectedly. It will be like getting caught in a trap that someone has hidden in the ground—the kind of trap that one might use to catch a wild animal! Yes, getting caught in such a trap is certainly a fit illustration of how that day will come unexpectedly upon those who dwell on the earth, who are not alert and ready for the Lord's coming.[30]

"So, once more, I say, be on the alert at all times! And do keep on praying that you will have the strength to escape the terrible things which will come upon this world just as the Son of Man returns to this earth. Not only that, you will need to pray for the strength to be able to stand before the Son of Man at the time of the judgment which will take place after He comes."[31]

> The number of times that the Lord warned His disciples to be "alert" in watching for His Second Coming is quite striking. [*Harmony* 15:25, 29, 30, 41] Such repetition indicates that Jesus knew His followers would easily become careless, losing a sense of the need to be constantly vigilant. The main point He made was this: No matter what people think or believe, at some point Jesus will come again! And, therefore, His people must ever be ready![1]
>
> Concluding His discussion of the signs of His Second Coming as well as the preparation for it, Jesus told three parables that would serve as additional illustrations of how people should prepare effectively for that coming.[2]

**— Parable One: The Ten Maidens**
**< Tuesday Night, Nisan 12, Spring, A.D. 31 (7/7) >**
**{Matthew 25:1-13}**

Jesus began by saying, "The kingdom of heaven can be compared to ten maidens who had been invited to a wedding feast. As part of their participation in the festivities, each was to bring a small lamp with her to help illuminate the wedding feast when the bridegroom and the rest of the bridal party arrived. This responsibility was required of all ten in order for them to attend the feast. [*Harmony* 15:58/][32]

---

30 Luke 21:34, 35
31 Luke 21:36
32 Matthew 25:1

"In this story, five of the maidens were foolish and five were wise. But, what made the difference? The five foolish virgins had only a limited supply of oil with them, so that their lamps would burn for just a short period of time. The five wise maidens brought along an extra supply of oil. This meant that they would be able to keep their lamps burning for a very long time.[33]

In this parable, the ten maidens represented all those who profess a belief in the Second Coming of the Lord. The bridegroom represented Jesus, the Son of Man. The lamps the maidens carried with them represented the power of the Scriptures in their lives. The oil represented the Holy Spirit's influence in them, both to convict their hearts of sin and to empower them to share their faith with others. The wedding feast represented the Second Coming of the Son of Man. The fact that five of the maidens were foolish meant that some of these maidens were not *completely* prepared. They had only a theoretical knowledge of the Messiah in their hearts. They did not allow the Holy Spirit to completely refine and empower their lives as they should have. Yes, they knew about the truth of the Scriptures, but the truth had been assimilated only partially into the life. On the other hand, the five wise maidens obviously represented those who were fully ready for the Lord's coming. The Holy Spirit, who had begun a good work in them, would carry it on to completion. He was a living, active power, constantly working within their lives. [1]

"Now, all ten maidens went to the place where the wedding party was to arrive for the feast. When the maidens arrived at the feasting hall, the wedding party, including the bridegroom, had not yet arrived. So the maidens had to wait for a while.(s) [2]

"Well," Jesus continued, "because the bridegroom had not yet arrived at the feast, from the maidens' perspective, he was late. So, all ten maidens became drowsy and soon fell asleep. Yes, it will appear to the Lord's followers that the coming of the Son of Man has been delayed. In fact, it will be difficult for the Lord's people to remain alert all the time, ready for the Lord's appearing—even as it was for the wise maidens in our story.[34]

---

33 Matthew 25:2-4

34 Matthew 25:5

"But then . . . finally . . . at midnight, there was a shout that awakened all ten maidens. A voice declared, 'Wake up! The bridegroom has arrived! Go out to greet him!' Of course, this represents the coming of the Son of Man at the darkest time in the history of this world, when corruption will so dramatically abound. [*Harmony* 12:55][35]

"All ten maidens, now fully awake, worked to get their lamps burning brightly so that they would be admitted to the feast. However, the five foolish maidens had not enough oil left to get their lamps burning sufficiently—indeed, their flames were flickering. Of course, the five wise maidens had plenty of oil, so their lamps began to burn brightly.[36]

"'Please give us some of your oil,' the five foolish maidens begged of the five wise ones. 'Our lamps are ready to go out!'[37]

"'No! No!' the wise maidens answered back. 'If we were to give you some of our oil, there would not be enough left for ourselves. Go and purchase some at the oil supply store.'"[38]

> This meant that people must be responsible for their own spiritual growth. It cannot be gained from others. Of course, because this is just a story, it was possible for the foolish virgins to go and purchase extra oil—even when the bridegroom was about to arrive. In real life, however, the power and work of the Holy Spirit *cannot* be secured after the Lord comes again. But the point is, in either case, it was too late for those who were not ready—both for the foolish virgins in the parable, and for those in real life who are not prepared for the Lord to come.

"Immediately," Jesus continued, "the five foolish maidens went to purchase the extra oil. While they were gone, the bridegroom arrived at the feasting hall. All those who were ready—including the five wise maidens—were allowed to enter the feast. These maidens had their lamps brightly burning. Once every one was in the feasting hall, the door to the hall was firmly shut![39]

---

35 Matthew 25:6
36 Matthew 25:7
37 Matthew 25:8
38 Matthew 25:9
39 Matthew 25:10

"Well, soon after this, the five foolish maidens arrived back at the hall. They desperately banged on the door, and anxiously cried out, 'Lord! Lord! Please open the door and allow us to come in!'[40]

"However, the bridegroom reluctantly replied, 'I must confess to you, I really do not know who you are!' So, here's the point," Jesus concluded. "You must always be alert! You must always be ready! For you do not know the day nor the hour of the Lord's appearing." [*Harmony* 5:81; 12:80, 147/][41]

> In effect the Lord was saying, "You must have a generous supply of the power of the Holy Spirit now at work in your life. If you do not, a theoretical knowledge of the Word of God will not be sufficient. When the Lord comes, it will be too late. For, when the door is shut, so to speak, your opportunity to be saved will be over. In short, probation will have closed for you. So then, you must prepare now! You must be ready now! The Spirit of God must now be constantly at work in your life. If not, no amount of begging will get you into the kingdom of heaven then. So beware!"

**— Parable Two: The Talents**
**< Tuesday Night, Nisan 12, Spring, A.D. 31 (7/7) >**
**{Matthew 25:14-30}**

Jesus continued with another story. This one was similar to one He had told just days before. [*Harmony* 13:120-133] Jesus began by saying, "I'll give you another parable. The coming of the Son of Man can be compared to a certain man who was about to go on a trip to a foreign country. So he called his servants to appear before him. He entrusted to them all his possessions to take care of while he was gone. To one servant, the man gave five talents of money. In this case, that was worth the total earnings of about 75 years. To another servant he gave two talents—worth about 30 years of salary. And, to a third servant, he gave just one talent, or the income of 15 years of salary. Now, the man gave to his servants the varying amounts I've mentioned in accordance with their individual ability. Finally, the man left on his trip." [*Harmony* 13:88/, 133/; 15:58/][42]

> In this story, the talents represented the gifts of the Holy Spirit which the Lord had left with His disciples—the disciples of His day, as well

40 Matthew 25:11
41 Matthew 25:12, 13
42 Matthew 25:14, 15

as His disciples of every age of history. These gifts He expected them to use to improve and expand the church so that when He came back again, they would have many others ready to enter His kingdom with them. The Lord gave those gifts to each of His disciples based upon his or her ability to use them effectively. Some would have more, while some would have less. But the Lord expected each to use wisely what was given to him or her. [*Harmony* 13:97/]

"So," the Lord continued with His story, "the servant who was given five talents went out quickly and invested them—that is, effectively used his talents—and increased their number to ten. The servant that was given two talents did the same and accordingly increased their number to four. However, the servant who was given the single talent dug a hole in the ground and buried his lord's money in it.[43]

"After a very long time, the master of the three servants returned from his trip. He called them to appear before him, each to give an account of how he had used the talents his lord had entrusted to him. That is the way it will be when the Son of Man comes back again. He will summon you, His servants, to see how faithful you have been with the gifts of the Holy Spirit which He had given to you to use for His cause.[44]

"Then," the Lord continued with His story, "the servant who had received the five talents appeared before his master, proudly presenting his five additional talents. He declared, 'Master, you gave me five talents. Look! I've gained yet another five talents, for a total of ten!'[45]

"His master congratulated him by saying, 'Good job! You are a good and faithful servant to me. Indeed, you were faithful in the small things which I gave to you to do. Therefore I can trust you with something even greater. Yes, I will be put you in charge of much more. It is with great joy that I bestow this privilege on you!'[46]

---

43 Matthew 25:16-18
44 Matthew 25:19
45 Matthew 25:20
46 Matthew 25:21

"Next, the servant who had been given two talents appeared before the master. He said, 'Look, Master, you gave me two talents to improve. I did so. See, I have gained two additional talents, for a total of four.'[47]

"Just as the master had praised the first servant, so did he also the second. He said, 'You've done a good job! You have proven yourself to be a good and faithful servant. Yes, you were faithful in the few things which I have given you to do. Therefore I will put you in charge of many other things. It is with great joy that I bestow this honor upon you.'[48]

"Finally, the servant, who had been entrusted with the one talent, came before his master. But in his case, he gave excuse, 'Master, I know you to be a hard man to deal with. You take to yourself the things that others have produced with their own labor. You do not care about the one who works for you . . . just as long as you can get what you want. So I was scared! I hid the talent in the ground. Here it is, just as you gave it to me.'[49]

"The master was indignant, saying to this servant, 'You are an evil and lazy servant! So you really think that I would only take from your labors and give you nothing valuable in return? Well then, in that case, you should have at least put the talent in the bank. That way, upon my arrival, you could have given the talent back to me with some earned interest.' Then, turning to other servants standing by, the master commanded, 'Take the single talent from this wicked servant and give it to the one who has ten talents. Everyone who has worked with what I have given him, will receive even more. But the one who has not used and improved what I've given him, will have it taken from him. So then, throw that worthless servant into the darkness of the night. There, he will weep and grind his teeth in despair.'"[50]

> What does this parable mean? The Lord has given His disciples the gifts of the Holy Spirit to be used for the work of the Gospel to improve and enlarge the church. To some disciples He has given a larger number of gifts than to others. But each disciple has received at least one gift. If His disciples are faithful in the use of the gift or gifts given to them, the Lord will honor them by making them a part of His eternal kingdom.

---

47 Matthew 25:22
48 Matthew 25:23
49 Matthew 25:24, 25
50 Matthew 25:26-30

In addition, the talents or gifts one uses to enhance the growth of the church will actually expand into even greater talents and gifts, enriching the one who uses them. And more than that, each faithful servant will be given greater privileges and responsibilities in that upcoming kingdom. The Lord will reward faithful work, diligently performed in His behalf! If, on the other hand, they should fail to use what He has given them to expand the work of the Gospel, then during the judgment, they will lose out on eternity altogether. The message and intent of this parable was extremely serious and powerfully sobering.[1]

The servant who had been given just one talent apparently was upset that he had but one talent. He even foolishly blamed the master when he returned to see how faithful he had been in using his talent! But, instead of using it as he should have, he hid it in the ground—meaning that he foolishly declined to use his talent to expand the work of his master. This means that people within the church who think that they don't have much of anything to give to the cause of God should, nevertheless, use what they have to advance the work of the Gospel. There is absolutely no excuse for being lazy or non-productive, even if one has little to give![2]

**— Parable Three: The Sheep and the Goats**
**< Tuesday Night, Nisan 12, Spring, A.D. 31 (7/7) >**
**{Matthew 25:31-46}**

Jesus told yet a third parable to illustrate one's eligibility for citizenship of His kingdom. He said, "When the Son of Man comes in His glory at the Second Coming, He will bring all His angels with Him. He will also sit on His throne of glory as a King to judge the world. Indeed, all the nations of the earth will be gathered before Him to be so judged. Then He will separate the wicked from the righteous the same way that a shepherd might separate his goats from his sheep. He will put the sheep—the righteous ones—on His right side, and the goats—the wicked ones—He will place on His left side. [*Harmony* 3:27/, 88; 15:58/][51]

Here, the Lord clearly taught that there will be a judgment when *all* must give an account of how effectively they have served the Lord in

[51] Matthew 25:31-33

ministry for Him. Clearly, this judgment will take place at the end of the world.

"Then," the Lord continued, "to the sheep on His right side, the King will say, 'Come! You are the ones who have been blessed by My father. You shall inherit the kingdom which has been prepared for you, even from the very beginning of this world. And why? You will inherit the kingdom because, when I was hungry, you gave Me something to eat. When I was thirsty, you gave Me a drink. I was a stranger and you took Me into your own home. I was naked, and you gave Me clothes to wear. When I was sick, you visited Me. I was in prison, and you came to see Me.' [*Harmony* 5:43][52]

"Then the righteous, obviously surprised—even shocked—by these words, will answer, 'Lord! When was it that we saw You hungry and fed You? Or thirsty, and gave You drink? And when was it that we saw You a stranger and took You into our own home? Or naked, and clothed You? When did we see You sick, or in prison, and came to visit You? When, Lord?'[53]

"Then the King will gladly reply, 'Truly I say to you, when you did these things to one of these brothers of Mine—even the least important of your fellow human beings—it was as if you had done it directly to Me!'[54]

"Then turning to the wicked ones on His left side—the goats—the King will command, 'Leave My presence! You are condemned! You will end up in hell-fire which shall destroy you utterly and completely. This is the fire that has been prepared for the destruction of the devil and all his angels. And why will you end up in this fire? Because I was hungry, and you gave Me nothing to eat. I was thirsty, and you allowed Me to remain thirsty. I was a stranger, and you left Me to sleep on the streets. I was naked, and you refused to give Me any clothes. I was sick, and in prison, and you took no time to visit Me.'[55]

"The wicked, shocked at these strong words from the King, will question Him, 'But Lord! When was it that we saw You hungry, or thirsty, or a stranger, or naked, or sick, or in prison, and did not take proper care of You? When was that?'[56]

---

52 Matthew 25:34-36
53 Matthew 25:37-39
54 Matthew 25:40
55 Matthew 25:41-43
56 Matthew 25:44

"Then the King—the Judge—will answer, 'It is a fact when I tell you that when you did nothing to help even the least important of My people—your fellow human beings—you neglected to do it for Me!'[57]

"I tell you," Jesus concluded, "these wicked people will be cast into hell-fire that will not go out until it has finished its destruction. But the righteous will be given eternal life. Thus it is that the main issue of the judgment will be whether you cared for people or not. That is what counts!" The message and intent of this parable was obvious.[58]

Thus Jesus finished His three parables dealing with His disciples' fitness for eternal life. The first—the Ten Maidens [*Harmony* 15:32-41]—dealt with having the refining power of the Holy Spirit in their lives. The second—the Talents [*Harmony* 15:42-50]—dealt with whether the Lord's followers would use to advantage the talents and gifts of the Spirit which the Lord gave them to finish the Gospel work. The third—the Sheep and the Goats [*Harmony* 15:51-58]—dealt with the attitude of God's people relating to their caring spirit toward others, even those who might seem unworthy. All three teach the Messiah's disciples what they need to be and to do, to prepare for the commencement of His glorious kingdom. All three teach what wonderful privileges His faithful servants will receive in eternity. However, all three parables teach the dire consequences of not being faithful to duty.

## Jesus Predicts His Death Again
## < Tuesday Night, Nisan 12, Spring, A.D. 31 (7/7) >
## (Matthew 26:1, 2; Mark 14:1)

It was Tuesday night, Nisan 12, when Jesus shared the signs of His coming with His disciples. As He finished His discussion with them, the Lord added, "You should know by now that the Son of Man will be handed over to the Roman authorities to be crucified on the Passover, when the Feast of Unleavened Bread begins. That's just two days from now." [Harmony 7:14; 10:55-61, 84, 85; 13:46, 99, 100][(t)] [59]

---

57 Matthew 25:45

58 Matthew 25:46

59 Matthew 26:1, 2; Mark 14:1

## A Summary of the Lord's Activities of the Past Couple of Days
## < Monday and Tuesday, Nisan 11 and12, Spring, A.D. 31 (7/7) >
## (Luke 21:37, 38)

A large portion of the daylight hours of both Monday and Tuesday Jesus had spent in the Temple area. The people would get up early each day to hear what Jesus had to say as He taught them. On both Sunday and Monday, Jesus spent the night in Bethany. But on both Tuesday and Wednesday, He spent the night on the Mount of Olives. During the day, both Wednesday and Thursday, the Lord spent time in retirement, preparing Himself for the most challenging few days of His entire life.[(u) 60]

> No doubt it was during this same time period [*Harmony* 15:59] that Judas returned to the Jewish leaders to confirm his original betrayal plot with them—the one he had proposed some days before. [*Harmony* 14:19-24] It was then that Judas informed the Jews that he would soon come back to them to tell them when and where Jesus could be arrested in secret. Both Judas and the Jewish leaders—who each played a crucial role in the betrayal plot—were all determined to follow through with their evil plans. Unfortunately for them, their eternal destiny was about to be sealed.

### Supplementary Notes:

**(a) [15:0+]** More than any chapter in the *Harmony,* Chapter 15—dealing with the signs and/or prophecies of the Lord's Second Coming—presented me with my greatest challenge in the writing of this book. Without doubt, Bible scholars have debated for years over how to interpret most effectively and accurately this portion of the Gospel record as it relates to what each item mentioned by Jesus means, as well as where to place each of them on some kind of time line. That being the case, this *Harmony* will hardly be the definitive solution to all questions as to the meaning of the various parts of the Lord's message to the disciples regarding the end of the world! Nevertheless, I had to decide upon which principles of interpretation *I would pursue,* and then try to follow them consistently through to completion. However, even when I would decide how to interpret parts of the chapter, I would run into a problem that would seem to contradict what I was doing! In the final analysis, though, I am reasonably comfortable with the finished product. Of

60 Luke 21:37, 38

course, I would have wished—and originally hoped—that I could have been much more certain about the way I interpreted the various sections of this chapter. But there are certain things in the Gospel record that still remain mysterious to us. The subject of this chapter, certainly, is one of them.

What follows is a list of the various principles I used in the interpretation of this portion of the *Harmony:*

**(1)** In general, the interpretation of this or any other Bible prophecy presents certain challenges. Not the least of these is the fact that the prophecy might have meant one thing to the people who *first* heard or read it, and something quite different to those who read it—as in the case of the prophecies found in this chapter—*nearly 2,000 years later*. To resolve this issue, many serious students of prophecy have come up with a very workable principle of prophetic interpretation, often called *primary and secondary application of Bible prophecy*. Let me state this principle simply and succinctly: The *primary application* is what the prophecy meant to those who *first* heard it; while the *secondary application* is what the prophecy means to those living *much later* on in history—such as today. In short, such prophecies have a *dual* application or interpretation.

Here is a good example of how this principle works, as applied to this chapter: Matthew 24:14 KJV [the last sentence of *Harmony* 15:11] reads, "And this gospel of the kingdom shall be preached into the entire world for a witness unto all nations; and then shall the *end* come." [Italics supplied] Now, considering the context of this declaration, it is clear that the "end" the Lord mentioned in this verse referred to the *end of (or destruction of) Jerusalem* in A.D. 70. So then, those who first heard this statement, understood it that way. That is its *primary application.* However, to those living *today*, the "end" of this verse refers to the *end of the world*—not of Jerusalem! This is its *secondary application.* The net effect of this method of interpretation is that this verse accurately applies to *both* applications. That is, the Gospel went to the whole then-known world before the destruction of Jerusalem in A.D. 70, *and* the Gospel will go to the whole world before the end of time. In this case, then, the events surrounding the destruction of Jerusalem in A.D. 70 are similar to the events that will attend the Second Coming of Jesus. Thus, in a certain sense, the destruction of Jerusalem serves—on a limited scale—as an illustration of the event of the Second Coming—on a much broader scale.

It should be noted, however, that not all Bible prophecies have this so-called dual application. For this reason, it must be used with considerable caution!

I apply the *primary and secondary application of Bible prophecy rule* throughout some portions of this chapter of the *Harmony.*

**(2)** The timing of certain events in this chapter is not always easy to determine. In truth, though, the Lord's main emphasis during His discussion contained in this chapter is *not* on the specific timing of events, but rather, on the *necessity of being ready* for the Lord's coming, no matter when that might occur. (Remember, too, Jesus claimed that even He did not know the exact time of the Second Coming!) The only event that is clearly linked to a certain time is the destruction of Jerusalem in A.D. 70 (*Harmony* 15:11-15). Again, the timing of most other events—even the actual Second Coming—is much more uncertain. Accordingly, in the *Harmony,* I emphasized the events themselves, attaching *less* significance to their actual timing. *The importance of this principle in the writing of this chapter cannot be over-emphasized!*

**(3)** There are different approaches to interpreting the events contained in this chapter. The one I favor is the *historical* progression of events. This means that there is a general, sequential progression of events throughout the chapter that *begins* in the days of the Lord, and will *end* at the Second Coming. One example of how this principle works is the correct placement of the "tribulation" of *Harmony* 15:16. I believe that the most logical *historical* placement of this tribulation would be the great persecution of Christians which began after the destruction of Jerusalem and extended up through the Dark Ages (when millions were killed)—a time period of many hundreds of years. Accordingly, that is the way I describe it in the *Harmony.* I assume that there may be those who may view this "tribulation" as a much shorter time period taking place near the end of time. I will allow the reader, though, for the most part, to determine for himself or herself what method of interpretation to follow.

**In conclusion,** I am satisfied with the various approaches *I used* in interpreting the events of this chapter. In the process, I believe that I have preserved the "flavor" and general thrust found in the Lord's message and His emphasis contained therein.

**(b) [15:11/]** (See above.)

**(c) [15:11/2]** (See **Note "a"** above.)

**(d) [15:12]** There is a question as to whether it was Jesus who told the reader to study the book of Daniel, or if it was Matthew, the Gospel recorder. I think it was Jesus Himself who said it, and reflected this in the *Harmony.*

**(e) [15:15]** What is the "time of the Gentiles" in the KJV? That is unclear to me. It probably refers to the time that Israel was under the domination of non-Jews. Perhaps this domination ceased when the nation of Israel was formed in 1948. (See also **Note "n"** below.)

**(f) [15:16]** The phrase "for then" (in Matthew 24:21, KJV), I take to mean that the tribulation will take place after the destruction of Jerusalem. Accordingly, that is the way I expressed it in the *Harmony.*

**(g) [15:16/]** In Daniel 12:1, we read that there will be time of trouble worse than any that arose before. However, I believe that this is NOT the same of time of trouble referred to in *Harmony* 15:16. Rather, the time of trouble of Daniel 12:1 takes place just before Jesus comes, not during the Dark Ages many years before. Then, how can Jesus say in Matthew 24, that the time of trouble is worse than any before or since, and Daniel say almost the same thing about a time of trouble later on in history? Here's my suggested answer: The time of trouble in Matthew 24 (the persecution of the Dark Ages), was worse in terms of its *overall length* of many hundreds of years, while the time trouble in Daniel 12 is worse for the *overall intensity* of its severity. Thus, the one in Matthew 24 was *unique in its duration,* while the one in Daniel is very short, but *unique in terms of its intensity!*

**(h) [15:17]** There are at least two viewpoints regarding the meaning of these words. First, some believe that the sun turning "dark" and the moon not giving its "normal light" took place on May 19, 1780. The time when the "stars will fall" refers to the great meteoric shower of November 13, 1833. Both of these events were *signs* to mark the beginning of the time when all should note that the time of the end was at hand. Many who lived in those days did actually believe that such events were a direct fulfillment of this prophecy. And these events did, in fact, take place very soon after the end of the great persecutions of the Dark Ages, as Jesus indicated that they would. I greatly favor this view. According to the second viewpoint, though, some believe these descriptions refer to events that will yet take place just before the Lord returns. Here we may have another example of a *dual prophecy* (see

**Note "a," point (1)** above). In any case, I will allow readers to decide for themselves as to the exact meaning of this portion of the Lord's prophecy.

**(i) [15:17]** I removed the last part of Matthew 24:29, and applied it to events immediately prior to the Lord's coming. (For more information of this, see **Note "j"** below.)

**(j) [15:18]** Only very rarely in the *Harmony* did I change the order of verses. In this particular case, I did. Why? As I see it, Jesus, in Matthew 24:21, 22, talked about the tribulation time; then He immediately, in Matthew 24:23-28, *jumped ahead* and discussed deceptions regarding the end of the world, concluding with a brief description of the actual end of the earth. Next, in Matthew 24:29, first part, Jesus *returned* to events just after the tribulation. Finally, in the last half of Matthew 24:29, Jesus discussed a sign that would take place immediately before His coming which is mentioned in Matthew 24:30, 31. So accordingly, to make the events read smoother, in the *Harmony,* I followed this sequence of verses: Matthew 24:21, 22, 29 (first part), 23-28, 29 (last part)-31. I believe that in doing so, that I've done no injustice to the words of Jesus and their intent.

**(k) [15:19]** (See above.)

**(l) [15:20]** (See **Note "j"** above.)

**(m) [15:21]** (See **Note "j"** above.)

**(n) [15:22]** In Matthew 24:34 is found one of the most difficult verses in the entire Gospel record to interpret. What does this mean, as recorded in the KJV: "This generation shall not pass, until all these things are fulfilled"? To make matters more difficult, Jesus preceded these words with the assurance that His declaration is absolutely true (by adding, "Verily I say unto you"), and follows it, declaring with great certainty, the utter reliability of His words (verse 35). Obviously, then, He was quite serious when He used such strong words!

But what did He mean? On the surface it would appear that the present generation of people living—when He spoke these words 2,000 years ago—would not pass away until He came the second time! Clearly, this *cannot* be what He meant—for all these people have been long gone! Also, it has been suggested by some modern scholars that Jesus was speaking about the generation of those who were alive when the nation of Israel was founded in 1948. This is based, I assume, on a particular interpretation of Luke 21:24 (which is a parallel account of Matthew 24), which says when the "time of the Gentiles" is fulfilled, the Jews will establish their nation again. Of course, this happened in 1948. I am quite skeptical of this interpretation. First of all, there is no clear evidence that the supposed fulfillment of this prophecy marks the beginning of the generation He is talking about. Second, the generation of 1948 is quickly passing away! Before long, they, too, will all be gone!

So then, what did Jesus mean? In short, I really don't know for sure! I *do suggest*, however, that the Lord *may* have been talking about His "generation" *of believers*—who would survive. What do I mean by this? With all the persecution Jesus talked about in the Gospel record—including great tribulation, earthquakes, etc.—one could get the impression that all God's people might be killed or completely scattered. Instead, the Lord gives hope that His "generation" of followers would survive. This means that the *time* is not the issue that Jesus discussed here, rather it is the ultimate *survival* of His disciples. That is why, in the *Harmony*, I interpreted the concept as: "And, it is a fact, that, in spite of the distress that will take place on this earth and in the heavens, My followers will survive." While I am hardly certain that this is actually the true meaning of these words of the Lord, I am *reasonably* comfortable with it.

**(o) [15:25]** Perhaps strangely, the Lord compares His coming to a *thief* who comes in the night to rob someone! Nevertheless, that is exactly what the Lord does in this case. Of course, the Lord's meaning for this illustration is to show the His coming will take the unsuspecting and unprepared by surprise, much as the unannounced arrival of a thief coming in the night would do.

**(p) [15:26]** The account in Matthew mentions a "servant" (singular); while the account in Mark mentions "servants" (plural). In the *Harmony* I went with Mark.

**(q) [15:27]** (See above.)

**(r) [15:28]** (See **Note "p"** above.)

**(s) [15:33/2]** I wrote this **Explanatory Note** as though it was Jesus who had spoken it.

**(t) [15:59]** Even though in Mark 14:1, 2, it says that "after two days was the feast of Passover," there is, nevertheless, confusion as to when all the events mentioned in the verses which follow (Mark 14:3-5) actually took place. In the final analysis, I chose to tie a portion of these verses with events that took place on Saturday night (*Harmony* 14:19-21), and a portion with what Jesus said, as I have determined, on Tuesday night, as recorded in Matthew 26:1, 2 (*Harmony* 15:59; also see *Harmony* 15:60/). I think that this represents the most logical sequence of events as they *probably* happened.

**(u) [15:60]** The sequence of events, as I've listed them in the *Harmony,* is my best estimation as to when these particular things happened.

# CHAPTER SIXTEEN

## THE PASSION WEEK: THURSDAY AFTERNOON AND NIGHT—

**From the Preparation for the Celebration of the Passover, to the Lord's Intercessory Prayer**

### (Just Before Passover, Spring, A.D. 31)

### The Lord's Final Passover[a]
### < Thursday Afternoon and Evening, Nisan 13 and 14, Spring, A.D. 31 (7/7) >
### (Matthew 26:17-30; Mark 14:12-26; Luke 22:7-30, 39; John 13:1-37; 14:1-31)

### — Preparation for the Celebration of the Passover Feast < Thursday Afternoon, Nisan 13, Spring, A.D. 31 (7/7) > {Matthew 26:17-19; Mark 14:12-16; Luke 22:7-13; John 13:1}

As the Passover Feast was about to begin, Jesus knew that the time had finally arrived when He would be killed. But, He also knew that He would be resurrected on the third day. [*Harmony* 7:14; 10:55-61, 84, 85; 13:46, 99, 100; 14:46; 15:59] The Lord further knew that soon after, He would leave this world and return to heaven to be with the Father. However, while here on this earth, Jesus had loved His disciples dearly. And, to be sure, He would love them forever![1]

And so it was that the first day of the feast of the Unleavened Bread—the Passover—arrived, the time for the killing of the Passover Lamb. As the disciples came to Jesus, He said to two of them, Peter and John, "Go! Prepare the place for the Passover so that I may eat it together with you."[b] [c] [2]

---

1 John 13:1

2 Matthew 26:17; Mark 14:12; Luke 22:7, 8

And they asked Him, "But where is the place that You want us to prepare for You to eat the Passover with us?"[3]

Jesus answered, "Listen carefully! Go into the city of Jerusalem. There you will see a man carrying an earthenware pitcher of water. Follow him! When he enters a house, say to the man of the house, 'The Teacher says, "My time has come. I want to celebrate the Passover with My disciples at your house tonight. Where is the guest chamber? It's there that I wish to eat the Passover with My disciples."' Then, he will show you a large upstairs room that has been set up for such a purpose. Prepare the supper there."(d) [4]

Peter and John did as Jesus instructed them. Indeed, they saw the man carrying a pitcher of water, just as Jesus had said. They entered the place where he went, and asked the man of the house for the use of his upper chamber. He consented. Then, they prepared the upper room for the Passover celebration. Everything turned out just as the Lord had predicted it would! But it is not clear as to how the arrangements for the use of the upper room, if any, were originally made.(e) [5]

> The Passover feast had been celebrated by the Hebrew people since its inception over 1,000 before. It was to commemorate the Exodus of the Jews from Egypt. [Exodus 12:1-28] While looking back into history, it also looked forward to the coming of the Messiah, who was to be the Savior, not only of the Hebrew people, but also of the whole world. The heart of the celebration was the eating of the Passover lamb. When, three and half years before, John the Baptist declared that Jesus was the "Lamb of God" [*Harmony* 2:49], he specifically indicated that Jesus was the real Passover Lamb—the one symbolized by the animal which was eaten by each family during the annual Passover festival. [1 Corinthians 5:7][1]

**—The Lord's Final Passover Celebration Begins**
**< Thursday Evening, Nisan 14, Spring, A.D. 31(7/7) >**
**{Matthew 26:20; Mark 14:17; Luke 22:14-16; John 13:2}**

> God had originally decreed that the Passover supper was to be eaten by individual families gathered together. They were to eat while standing, as

---

3 Matthew 26:17; Mark 14:12; Luke 22:9

4 Matthew 26:18; Mark 14:13-15; Luke 22:10-12

5 Matthew 26:19; Mark 14:16; Luke 22:13

> though they were ready to go on a journey. [Exodus 12:11] However, now that the nation of Israel was well settled in their land, this procedure was changed. Therefore, instead of standing, they reclined around the table on couches. This should not be surprising, for this was the customary way of eating most festive meals at that time in history.[2]

When the evening hour arrived for the celebration of the Passover to begin, Jesus reclined at the table with His twelve apostles. He said to them, "For some time I have strongly desired to eat this Passover with you before I suffer." Regarding His suffering, Jesus, of course, was speaking of His crucifixion. The Lord added, "I say to you, never more will I celebrate the Passover like this again, until we can celebrate it together in the eternal kingdom." Here Jesus referred to the so-called "Marriage Supper of the Lamb" in heaven. [Revelation 19:7-9; *Harmony* 16:26][6]

It was during the early part of the Supper, and the devil had already entered into the heart of Judas Iscariot, the son of Simon. This meant that Judas was determined to go ahead with his plan to betray his Lord—the plan he had made with the Jewish leaders earlier that week. [*Harmony* 14:22-25][7]

### —Jesus Washes His Disciples' Feet
### < Thursday Evening, Nisan 14, Spring, A.D. 31 (7/7) >
### {Luke 22:24-30; John 13:1-20}

Even as the Lord and His disciples were about to celebrate the Passover together, there was a great deal of ill feeling among all the disciples. They had been debating among themselves as to which one of them was the greatest—the one who would be ranked first behind Jesus when He set up His glorious kingdom. When, some weeks earlier, the mother of James and John had boldly requested that her two sons receive the highest rank in that kingdom [*Harmony* 13:101-107], the anger of the other disciples toward them, and jealousy among all of them, had reached a high pitch. Previously, Jesus had addressed the disciples regarding this issue. [*Harmony* 10:96] But sensing that this problem still existed among His disciples, Jesus reasoned with them, saying, "The kings of this world lord over the subjects of their nations. Yes, those with political authority wield control over the common people. And when this happens, these political authorities are called benefactors—that is, so-called 'doers of good' to

---

6 Matthew 26:20; Mark 14:17; Luke 22:14-16

7 John 13:2

those who, supposedly, are under them. But this is not what you, My disciples, should be! Instead, let the ones who are truly great in your group show their greatness by being as though they were the younger ones among you." (In Jewish culture, the younger members in a group acquiesced to those who were older.) "And," the Lord continued, "this means that those who are in charge of others should show true leadership by serving one another. Now let Me ask you—using worldly reasoning—who is considered the greater, the one serving food at a feasting table, or the one reclining at the table, ready to be served the food? Of course, you will say the one reclining! Isn't that right? But if that's your answer . . . you would be wrong! You see, I, as Your Master, came to you as One who served, not the One being served! That is what indicates true greatness. Yes, the real 'doers of good' are those who serve and not those who are being served, as it is in the political world! [*Harmony* 13:107; 16:10/][8]

"Nevertheless, in spite of your shortcomings," Jesus added, moderating His tone, "you have shown your loyalty to Me by continuing to stay with Me even during times of trial and stress. So, in the future, I will appoint you a kingdom to rule, just as My Father has appointed one for Me. Then you will be able to relax, eating and drinking at My table. Yes, it is then that you will be served! [*Harmony* 12:55, 56] In addition, you will sit on thrones, judging the twelve tribes of Israel. Again, at that time, you will be served by someone else. But until then, I want you to serve others!" Even though the Lord used these strong words of counsel, the disciples did not seem to respond to Him as He desired. Therefore Jesus needed to use a more drastic measure to fully get their attention.[9]

Jesus knew that the Father had given Him the authority and responsibility to carry to its completion and ultimate fulfillment the Gospel plan. The Savior further knew that He had come from the Father and that soon He would return to be with Him. In short, Jesus completely understood His divinity. Yet, even though He was God, Jesus would show His true greatness by serving others rather than being served. Because He had complete confidence in His past and in His future—and in His position with the Father—the Lord was not afraid. He did not hesitate—neither was He embarrassed—to humble Himself before His disciples by serving them.[10]

---

8 Luke 22:24-27

9 Luke 22:28-30

10 John 13:3

> It was the custom of the times for a servant to wash the dusty feet of those who were in attendance at a feast such as the Passover. However, on this occasion, no such servant was present. And certainly none of the disciples would humble themselves to do such a menial task! [*Harmony* 16:8] With their twisted thinking, if any one of them should have done so, the others would have considered him unworthy of a place of true honor and leadership among them.

Thus it was that Jesus arose from the supper table and removed His outer dining garment. After wrapping a towel around His waist, the Lord filled a basin with water, and began the process of washing His disciples' feet, including those of His betrayer! And with the towel, He wiped them dry.[(f)] [11]

When the Master arrived at Simon Peter's place to wash his feet, the disciple challenged Jesus, questioning Him, "Lord, are you really going to wash my feet?"[12]

Jesus answered indirectly by saying, "What I'm going to do now, you won't, at first, understand. But later on you will."[13]

But Peter, humiliated by the fact that the Messiah was about to wash his dirty feet, strongly protested, declaring "There is no way, Lord, that You will ever wash my feet. No! Never!"[14]

Jesus responded, "But Peter, unless I wash your feet, you will have no part with Me!"[15]

Simon Peter, completely overwhelmed by the Lord's surprising, even shocking, response, cried out, "In that case, Lord, wash not only my feet, but also my hands and my head!"[16]

However, Jesus said to him, "That won't be necessary. The one who has been bathed this way, has no need but to have his feet washed. Then he is completely clean."[17]

---

11 John 13:4, 5
12 John 13:6
13 John 13:7
14 John 13:8
15 John 13:8
16 John 13:9
17 John 13:10

> Here Jesus was initiating a ritual sometimes called the "Ordinance of Humility." Obviously, the Lord did not refer here to a mere physical cleansing but rather to a spiritual cleansing. In this case, the washing of the feet was symbolic of an entire cleansing of the soul from sin—a miniature baptism, so to speak. [*Harmony* 2:3] That is why Jesus told Peter that unless He washed Peter's feet, he would have no part with his Lord. Again, the Lord was being not literal but symbolic. So then, when people's feet are washed during this ritual, it symbolizes the washing away of their sins, something obviously necessary for one's eternal life. And, in a like manner, when people, as part of this particular ritual, wash the feet of others, it symbolizes their desire to serve others in the overall ministry of salvation, just as Jesus had served others for the purpose of providing salvation for them.

After completing the foot-washing of all the disciples, Jesus commented sadly, "You are all now made clean, and yet not all of you." Of course, here He referred to Judas, the one whom He knew would betray Him. That is why Jesus said, "Not all of you are clean." Then the Savior put His outer garments back on Himself and reclined once more at the supper table.[18]

Then Jesus asked them, "Do you have any idea why I washed your feet the way that I just did? Well, let me explain. You call Me your Lord and Teacher. And in doing so, you have spoken correctly, for so I am! Now listen carefully. If I, your Lord and Teacher, have stooped down to wash your feet, you should also wash one another's feet. You see, I have given you an example, that as I have done to you, you should do to one another. For it is certainly a true statement when I say to you that a slave is not better than his master. Neither is a messenger more important than the one who has sent him." [*Harmony* 1:50/; 16:82][19]

> Here Jesus was not only initiating the ritual of foot-washing but He was also describing its meaning. For, as He, the Lord and Master, served others, then His disciples and followers—His servants—should be willing to do the same: that is, be willing to serve others.

Jesus continued, "If you truly understand these things, you certainly will be happy if you do them! You will discover that true happiness is found in serving

---

18 John 13:10-12
19 John 13:12-16

others just as I have done throughout My ministry among you and all the people." [*Harmony* 1:50][20]

## — The Lord Celebrates the Passover With His Disciples < Thursday Night, Nisan 14, Spring, A.D. 31 (7/7) > {Matthew 26:26-29; Mark 14:22-25; Luke 22:17-20; John 13:18-20}

Jesus continued, "Of course, I am not speaking about all of you. I know the ones whom I have chosen, but as the Scripture has predicted, 'There is one who is eating bread with Me, who has lifted up his heel to trample upon Me, and to destroy Me.'" [Psalm 41:9] Jesus, of course, spoke of Judas Iscariot.[21]

> This was a somewhat curious statement of Jesus! What did He mean when He said, "I know the ones whom I have chosen"? The process by which Jesus selected His closest disciples—the "Twelve"—was quite elaborate. [*Harmony* 4:67-79] By saying that He knew the ones He had chosen, Jesus implied that He had not really chosen Judas, just the other eleven! Because of this, it would appear that Judas was not chosen by the Lord, but rather, he was probably selected by the other eleven, who asked the Lord to include him in their group. It seems, then, that Jesus consented to the disciples' request to ordain Judas in order to teach them that mere outward appearances are not sufficient to determine the true worth of anyone's character. [1 Samuel 16:7]

Jesus continued with His prediction regarding Judas's betrayal, saying, "At this moment, while we are sitting here, I'm telling you what will happen, so that, when it does happens, you can be assured that I AM!" [*Harmony* 9:17; 11:51-55, 76, 77][22]

> By using the unusual designation, "I AM," in describing Himself—a phrase indicating His divinity—Jesus was making it clear that He was able, as the Son of God, to accurately predict the future. [Exodus 3:13, 14] Thus, Jesus was claiming divinity for Himself. The words, "I AM," indicate the pre-existent nature of God. That is, the past, the present, and the future are all the same to God. To God, then, the past and the future are just as real as the present is real to human beings. By His use of these words at this time, the Lord's remaining disciples would realize that

---

20 John 13:17

21 John 13:18

22 John 13;19

> He was not deceived, nor would He be surprised when Judas ultimately betrayed Him. In other words, He already knew what Judas was going to do—something one might expect a divine Person to know.

Jesus concluded His statement by adding, "It is absolutely true that the one who accepts any individual whom I have sent in My behalf, has, in fact, accepted Me. And the one who has accepted Me has also accepted the Father—the One who originally sent Me."[23]

> Here, Jesus referred to His disciples. When, during their ministry, the eleven faithful disciples would be accepted by people, Jesus would consider this acceptance as an acceptance of both the Father and Him. This meant, though, that in the case of Judas, the betrayer would be rejected, because, obviously, Jesus had really never sent him in the first place![1]

> Now the time had come to eat the Passover Supper. The meal, of course, included the Passover lamb. Also, there was the eating of bread made without yeast—often called unleavened bread. The unleavened bread represented the word of God, without the taint of sin or wickedness. In a sense, too, it represented the Messiah and His message. [*Harmony* 9:41] In Jewish thought, yeast—or leaven—in the ceremonial bread represented sin. As part of the meal, they dipped the bread in a fruit and nut relish, called charoseth. [*Harmony* 16:31] Also included in the meal were bitter herbs. These herbs were symbolic of the hard times the Jews had had while they were slaves in Egypt. There were also other vegetables that were eaten. Another very significant part of the Supper was the drinking of four cups of wine—or grape juice—interspersed throughout the Supper. The drinking of each cup had a special, individual meaning. [*Harmony* 16:24-26][(g)] [2]

They started to eat the Passover Supper together. The Lord took one of the several cups of wine—grape juice—and after offering a prayer of thanks over it, He passed the cup around to the disciples, saying, "Each of you, take a sip of wine from this cup. I must tell you that I will not drink anymore of the juice from a grapevine until My eternal kingdom is finally established." [*Harmony* 16:26][(h)] [24]

---

23 John 13:20

24 Luke 22:17, 18

Then, as they were eating the meal, Jesus, took a loaf of unleavened bread, blessed it with prayer, broke it into pieces, and gave the various pieces to the disciples. As He did so, the Lord said, "Take this and eat. This represents My sinless broken body, which I will give in your behalf and for your benefit. Do this so that you will never forget what I have done for you." [1 Corinthians 11:24] [(i) 25]

> Here the Lord was instituting the first part of "The Lord's Supper" ritual—the eating of the unleavened bread. The eating of this bread symbolizes a person's acceptance of the Lord's death on the cross as a complete payment for his or her sins. When Jesus died on the cross—as "the Lamb of God which takes away the sin of the world" [*Harmony* 2:49]—the total debt of sin of each believing sinner was completely paid.

After they had eaten a while longer, Jesus took a second cup of wine—grape juice—[*Harmony* 16:24] and pronounced another blessing upon it. After taking a sip of juice, He said, "I want all of you to drink from the cup. This wine represents My blood which I will shed in abundance in your behalf. This provides forgiveness of the sins of all those throughout the whole world who accept Me as their Savior. This blood further represents the power of the New Covenant [Jeremiah 31:31-34] in the hearts and lives of all those who follow Me. As often as you drink this cup in this manner, you will show that you remember what I have done for you in providing salvation for the world . . . and, of course, for each of you." [1 Corinthians 11:25] Repeating Himself [*Harmony* 16:6], the Lord added, "But I declare to you that I will not drink of the fruit of the vine from this time forward, until I drink it with you in the renewed kingdom of God, My Father." And all the disciples took a drink from the cup as He commanded.[(j) (k) 26]

> Here, Jesus instituted the second part of "The Lord's Supper" ritual—the drinking of the grape juice. When people drink the juice during a communion service, they bear public testimony that they accept the blood of Jesus as a covering for their sins. The juice, here, represents, not only the death of Jesus, but also the perfect righteousness of His life. Jesus not only died for sinners, but He also lived a perfect life for them, the kind of life that they could never have lived on their own. And, it is this perfect righteousness that covers the sinful life of each

---

[25] Matthew 26:26; Mark 14:22; Luke 22:19
[26] Matthew 26:27-29; Mark 14:23-25; Luke 22:20

follower of the Lord. Through the power of the indwelling Spirit, all can be transformed and empowered to live a righteous life. When Jesus mentioned the "New Covenant," He referred to this power of the Holy Spirit to change the minds and thinking of His followers from evil to that of righteousness. [Jeremiah 31:31-34][(l)]

**—Jesus Reveals His Betrayer**
**< Thursday Night, Nisan 14, Spring, A.D. 31 (7/7) >**
**{Matthew 26:21-25; Mark 14:18-21; Luke 22:21-23; John 13:21-30}**

Saying these things caused Jesus to be deeply troubled in His heart. All the events that had happened, and would happen, weighed heavily upon His mind. As the group, reclining at the table, continued eating the Passover meal, Jesus added, "I must declare with certainty that one of you will betray Me! It will be one of you who is eating with Me—right here and now—at this very table!" In response to this shocking declaration, the disciples looked at each other, questioning as to whom the Lord was speaking about. Who would do such a despicable thing to their beloved Lord and Master? It made no sense to them whatsoever.[27]

Extremely upset by the Lord's statement, the disciples began to examine their own hearts as to whether any of them would be able to actually do such a terrible thing to Jesus. Then, one by one, the disciples personally questioned the Lord, "I'm not the one, am I?" or, "Master, is it I?"[28]

One of the disciples, John—whom Jesus especially loved—was reclining on the couch next to Jesus. Because he was reclining next to the Master, when he leaned back, his head was actually resting against the Lord's chest. This, obviously, put him into a position to be very close to Jesus, to be able to whisper a question to the Lord without the others being able to hear either the question or Christ's response. That being the case, Simon Peter whispered to John to have him secretly ask the Lord who it was that would betray Him.[29]

So, leaning back upon the Lord's chest, John quietly asked the Lord, "Lord, who is it that will betray You?" [*Harmony* 18:83][30]

27 Matthew 26:21; Mark 14:18; Luke 22:23; John 13:21, 22
28 Matthew 26:22; Mark 14:19
29 John 13:23, 24
30 John 13:25

Jesus answered back, "It is he to whom I will give a piece of bread, dipped in charoseth."Then, dipping the bread into the charoseth relish [*Harmony* 16:23/2], Jesus gave it to Judas Iscariot, the son of Simon. (The charoseth relish was composed of a mixture of almonds, dates, raisins, spices, and vinegar. It was used to give flavor to the bland-tasting unleavened bread.) [*Harmony* 16:34, 35][31]

> John's question and the Lord's answer and response were given so quietly that the other disciples either did not hear or understand what was being said or done. And, perhaps shocked by the Lord's reply to his question, John did not tell Peter or the others what Jesus had just told him.

Jesus continued to explain, "It is sad but true that he, one of the twelve, who has dipped his hand into the same dish with Me will betray Me! Consider this: My betrayer has blatantly placed his hand on the same table as Mine! The Son of Man will die, as has been both written and determined regarding Him. [Isaiah 53:3-11] But nevertheless, woe unto that man who would actually betray the Son of Man! Indeed, it would have been far better for him had he never been born!"[32]

Then, Judas, the betrayer, not wanting to appear too conspicuous by remaining silent—sheepishly asked Jesus, "Lord, I'm not the one, am I?"[33]

Jesus answered, "You have said it!" Now, Judas was twice exposed as the betrayer: by the Lord's statement to John [*Harmony* 16:31], and by His clear affirmation to Judas himself that he was in fact the betrayer. At that moment Satan—the devil—entered with special power into the heart of Judas. This means that Judas's time of probation had effectively closed, and accordingly, his fate was sealed! After taking the morsel of bread Jesus had given him, Judas rose to leave. And, as he was leaving, Jesus said to him, "Whatever you are planning to do, please do it quickly!"[34]

Even though Jesus had exposed Judas as the betrayer [*Harmony* 16:31], the other disciples, except for John, clearly did not grasp the reality of the situation. Preoccupied by the Lord's startling statement regarding the fact that one of them would betray Him, they did not understand the Lord's affirmative answer to Judas's question, "Lord, I'm not the one, am I?" Neither did they comprehend the

---

31 John 13:26

32 Matthew 26:23, 24; Mark 14:20, 21; Luke 22:21, 22

33 Matthew 26:25

34 Matthew 26:25; John 13:27, 30

Lord's message to Judas to do his work of betrayal quickly. Rather, some of them thought that because Judas was the carrier of the moneybag, Jesus was telling him to purchase something for the feast, or to give some money to the poor! But in any case, into the darkness of the night, Judas quickly left the upper room, determined to betray his Lord.[(m)] [35]

> Very soon after that, Judas went and met with the Jewish leaders to finalize his evil plan to betray His Lord. Indeed, for him, there would be no turning back! [*Harmony* 16:58][(n)]

### —Jesus Gives Counsel to the Remaining Eleven Disciples < Thursday Night, Nisan 14, Spring, A.D. 31 (7/7) > {Matthew 26:30; Mark 14:26; Luke 22:39; John 13:31-37; 14:1-31}

As Judas left, Jesus knew that His former disciple was going to go through with the betrayal. Thus the progression of the Lord's arrest, trial, and crucifixion was firmly set in motion. Therefore Jesus said, "Now the Son of Man is going to be greatly honored in fulfilling His mission of giving Himself as a sacrifice for the sins of the world. And, because the Son is going through with the plan of salvation, the Father will also be honored. And once the Father is honored by the sacrifice of the Son, the Father will heap even more honor upon Him, the Son, even to the extent of soon restoring to Him the glorious privileges of heaven He originally had with the Father before He came to this earth. Thus, My little children, for just a short time longer will I be with you. Then, you will try to find Me, but alas, I'll be gone! It will be just as I have previously said to the Jews, 'Where I am going, you will not be able to follow Me.' [*Harmony* 11:21, 49; 16:38, 55] Indeed, I must use these same words in describing to you what will happen to Me. To be sure, you will not be able to go where I am going! [*Harmony* 14:24; 16:50][36]

"I have this additional advice, though," Jesus added. "Because I am leaving you, it is doubly important that you obey a new commandment I wish to give to you. Actually, it is not really a new commandment, but it is one that most people in the world have ignored . . . but I don't want you to forget it. Indeed, it is new in the sense that I have demonstrated it for you. And what is this so-called 'new' commandment? That you love one another! And what is the standard for this love? You shall love one another in the same way that I have loved you! In fact,

[35] John 13:28-30
[36] John 13:31-33

this quality of love will be the standard by which all the world will know for certain that you are My followers—that is, by the quality of love you have for one another."[37]

Simon Peter began to think about the words Jesus had spoken about going away to a place where they could not follow after Him. [*Harmony* 16:36] Therefore, Peter asked Jesus, "But where is it that You are going that we cannot follow after You?" [*Harmony* 16:89][38]

Jesus answered him, "Where I am going, you will not be able to follow Me *now*. However, after some time, you will be able to follow after Me!"[39]

> Jesus was speaking of when He would go back to heaven. Of course, the disciples would not be able to follow Him there at that time. However, at the Second Coming of Jesus, they would be able to go to heaven themselves to be with the Lord there!

But Peter, unsatisfied and confused by the Lord's answer, responded, "But, Lord, why can I not go with You now?"[(o) 40]

Jesus answered, "Do not allow yourselves to be distressed. You say you believe in God—well, that's the way it should be! Because you believe in God, the Father, I say, believe also in Me. Let Me tell you, where My Father lives, there are many places where you will be able to dwell with Him. If this were not an absolute fact, you can be sure that I would have told you so. Listen! I am going make ready a place in which you will be able to dwell with Me! And if I do that, you can be assured that I will come back here again, and take you with Me, so that where I live, there you will live also. I know where that place is, and, by now, you should know the way to get there."[41]

> The place Jesus referred to was heaven, and the way to get there was, of course, the plan of salvation which Jesus had carefully outlined for them throughout His entire ministry. And they would be able to go to heaven to be with Jesus at His Second Coming.

---

37 John 13:34, 35
38 John 13:36
39 John 13:36
40 John 13:37
41 John 14:1-4

But Thomas, totally bewildered by the Lord's explanations, said to Him, "Lord, we don't even know where You are going, so how can we possibly know the way to get there?" [*Harmony* 16:44][42]

Thomas's confusion in this matter is a bit surprising. Obviously, he hadn't been listening closely enough to the Lord.

Jesus spoke patiently, "Don't you get it? I am the Way! I am also the Truth and the Life. In fact, no one can come and dwell with the Father, unless I lead the way. This means that if you have really come to know Me, then you will also end up knowing the Father, for I will lead the way before you. In fact, you already have come to know Him, because you have had the privilege of seeing Him in Me. Finally, you will dwell with Me in heaven, because you have accepted Me as the Messiah." Jesus clearly indicated that the way to eternal life—and heaven—was to obediently follow His words, and, in doing so, they would know the Father, for Jesus and the Father were one in mind, purpose, and character.[43]

Then Philip, just confused as Thomas [*Harmony* 16:42], said to Jesus, "Lord! What you've been telling us is so confusing. Just show us the Father so that we can know Him now. That will satisfy us." Clearly, Philip did not comprehend the words of Jesus either.[44]

Jesus answered back, "Oh, Philip! Anyone who has had a good look at Me has also seen the Father! We've been together for years—don't you know Me yet? So then, why would you ask Me, 'Show us the Father'? Can't you get it? Can't you see that I am in the Father, and the Father is in Me? We work together as a team. We are one in both character and purpose. And, not only that, the words that I have been speaking to you are not My words, but they are the words of the Father who dwells in Me. In fact, in addition to these words, the works that I have done are also His, not Mine! Trust Me, the Father and I have this close relationship—He's in Me, and I'm in Him, so to speak. If you have a hard time accepting this simple statement of Mine, then at least believe My claim because you have seen the great works which I have done. Indeed, they testify to the fact that the Father dwells in Me. To be sure, there is no way that anyone would be able to do the things that I've done unless he has been led of God.[45]

---

42 John 14:5
43 John 14:6, 7
44 John 14:8
45 John 14:9-11

"But there is more," the Lord went on, as He began a rather lengthy discussion with His disciples regarding the Holy Spirit. [*Harmony* 16:86-104] "If you can accept this fact, and trust in Me, then the works that I have done in the Father you will be able to do too. That's right! Indeed, even *greater* works you will be able to do, simply because I go back to the Father. Not greater, of course, in the sense that your works will be of higher quality than Mine. No! But greater in the sense that you will be able to do more things"—including the winning of souls—"through your combined ministries than I have been able to do during the three plus years of My ministry, with you standing by watching Me. Yes, you will be able to accomplish more without Me than with Me!" [*Harmony* 16:56/; Acts 2] Here, Jesus referred to the ministry of the Holy Spirit—the Spirit that He would send when He went back to the Father. And, it would the Holy Spirit who would empower and greatly expand their combined ministries.[46]

"In other words," Jesus continued, "just as the Father has blessed Me as an individual, He will bless all of you as a group! In fact, I will ask Him to bless your works—and you can be sure that He will do it! So then, anything that you ask—for the cause of the Gospel—that will I do for you. This way, the Father will be honored by the Son's disciples when they do great work for Him. Again, you will find out. Just ask Me and I'll do it for you! You'll see! In addition, if you really love Me, as you claim, than you will cherish all the commands that I have given you. Yes, I know that you will obey Me if you truly love Me and cherish My will for you. [*Harmony* 13:77/][(p) 47]

"This is the way it will actually work," Jesus further explained. "I will ask the Father [*Harmony* 16:86], and then He will send the Holy Spirit—the One who will stand by your side. And He—the Holy Spirit—will be there to provide comfort for you forever! He is the Spirit of Truth. Now, He is called the Spirit of Truth because He will reveal the truth to you and bless your ministries. [*Harmony* 16:50][48]

"However," Jesus continued, "the people of this world, who don't care one whit about the truth of the Gospel, will never receive the ministry of the Holy Spirit within their lives. And why is this? It is because they refuse to listen to Him, for they don't care to know the truth! So then, if He were to speak directly to them, they would still reject Him! But in your case it's different. That's

---

46 John 14:12
47 John 14:13-15
48 John 14:16, 17

because you, within your hearts, have recognized the sound of His voice and have responded to it in a positive way. And accordingly, in a very real sense, He has been abiding in your lives ever since . . . and shall continue to do so—even forever!" [*Harmony* 16:52][49]

Continuing to discuss the ministry of the Holy Spirit, Jesus added, "You can be sure that you will not be treated as orphans when I leave you. For you see, through the Holy Spirit, I will still be in your midst. Yes, in a little while I will be gone out of this world, and its people will no longer see Me in person. [*Harmony* 16:36, 56] But in your case, through the Spirit, you will still see Me in your hearts and minds. And because I will be alive in your being, you shall also be alive, spiritually, through the Spirit. As a result, everything that you have experienced while I was physically with you, you will continue to experience through the ministry of the Holy Spirit, in My absence. Now, when the Holy Spirit comes upon you, you will know for sure that I am with My Father, for We, together, will have sent the Spirit to you. [*Harmony* 16:48] This way, by the Spirit's power, you will be able to continue to abide with Me, and I with you. Do you understand that?"[50]

> A mere seven weeks later, on the Day of Pentecost [Acts 2:1-4], the Holy Spirit was to be poured out on the disciples. At that point, they would know for sure that Jesus was then with the Father, for both the Father and Son on that day had sent the Spirit to be with them.

The Lord continued with His explanation of the work of the Spirit. He said, "And, how can all this happen for you? When you take hold of My commandments and cherish them, it will be a clear indication that you indeed love Me. And the one who loves Me shall be loved by the Father who sent Me. And I will continue to show My appreciation for this love by loving you all the more, and will reveal Myself to you through the Holy Spirit and His ministry within your lives. That's how it will work!"[51]

Then, Judas—not Judas Iscariot, the betrayer—said to Jesus, "Lord, please explain what You mean when You say You are about to reveal Yourself to us, but not to the world? What does that mean?" [*Harmony* 16:49][52]

---

49 John 14:17
50 John 14:18-20
51 John 14:21
52 John 14:22

Jesus answered, "Again, if anyone shows his love for Me by following My words, then My Father will love him all the more. And, through the Holy Spirit, We—the Father and the Son—will come to that person and dwell within him. That's clear, isn't it? Now, on the other hand, if there are those who do not love Me and thus refuse to follow My words—and remember, the words that I have spoken to you are not from Me, but from the Father—We will not abide with them. Of course, you, my disciples, have responded to the Father and to Me as you ought. Therefore, We will reveal ourselves to *you* through the Spirit. But the people of the world have not responded as they should have. Therefore, We will *not* reveal ourselves to them through the Spirit. So then, this is what I meant when I said, 'I will reveal Myself to you, but not to the world.' [*Harmony* 7:43; 16:49][53]

"I have spoken all these things to you while I have been in your presence," Jesus continued. "During the years of My ministry, I have taught you many things. But when I will have left you, the Holy Spirit—the Comforter—whom the Father will send to you at My request, in My name, will teach you even more things than I have taught you. Not only that, He will remind you of the really important things that I have taught you while I was still in your presence."[54]

Jesus paused. He could tell that his disciples were very distressed by what He was saying to them. "I can tell that you are frightened that I am leaving you [*Harmony* 16:36]," Jesus then observed. "Well, don't be! In reality, when I go away from you, I will give you a very special gift. That gift is My peace that will provide calm assurance for all of you. Yes, through the Spirit, I will give this peace to you. But it's not the kind of peace that the world gives. No way! It is so much better than that! So then, don't allow your heart to get carried away with emotional distress or sorrow at My leaving. Please, don't allow yourselves to become timid with fright!" [*Harmony* 12:63/][55]

To give the disciples greater comfort, the Lord explained more about the work of the Holy Spirit. He declared, "You have heard Me tell you over and over that I am going away from you, but I have also told you that I will come back to you through the Holy Spirit. Isn't that right? [*Harmony* 16:50] Now if you love Me the way that you should, you would rejoice that I am going back to the Father, rather than becoming upset about that fact. And why is that? Because

[53] John 14:23, 24

[54] John 14:25, 26

[55] John 14:27

the Father is greater than I am! Therefore, the Spirit whom He will send in My place will be able to do an even greater work than I, for He will come in the power of the Father who, again, is greater than I. I tell you all this before it actually happens—when you find it impossible to believe—so that when it actually does happen, you might believe that I have been telling you the truth from the beginning. Yes, again, you will to go on to victory, even though I am not physically in your midst." [*Harmony* 16:86][56]

> When Jesus said that the Father was greater than Himself, He was talking about Himself in His *human form*. When Jesus was on this earth, He had laid his divine powers aside. [Philippians 2:5-8] Again, this was what He meant when He said that the Father was greater than He. Furthermore, when Jesus spoke about the Holy Spirit doing a "greater work" than Him, He was talking about the amount of work, as opposed to the quality of the work. What is meant by that? When Jesus dwelt on this earth, most of the work that was accomplished during His ministry primarily took place precisely where He was at any given time. But when He left this earth, the work would expand greatly because each of His followers—scattered throughout the world—would do great things in the power of the Spirit wherever they might be, even separated from each other. [*Harmony* 16:46]

"Unfortunately," Jesus said as He interrupted His own statement regarding the Holy Spirit, "I must conclude this conversation with you, for the devil, who self-styles himself to be the ruler of this world, is coming to get Me! Of course, he is not, in any way, one of My followers! Instead he is My mortal enemy! But don't worry, all that I am facing in My battle with the devil must happen so that the world will know for sure, that, in loving the Father, I have done everything which the Father has commanded Me to do for Him and the world. And, in the final analysis, because of the love of the Father, and My allegiance to His love, the world will be saved.[57]

"Rise up! We need to be going," Jesus said in closing. He and His disciples followed the custom of singing a hymn at the conclusion of their Passover Supper. This hymn was based upon portions of Psalms 115 through 118. Then they all

---

56 John 14:28, 29

57 John 14:30, 31

left for the Mount of Olives, as this was often the place where they spent the night. Of course, Judas, the betrayer, knew this. [*Harmony* 14:23; 16:35, 35/][58]

### On the Way to Gethsemane
### < Thursday Night, Nisan 14, Spring, A.D 31 (7/7) >
### (Matthew 26:31-35; Mark 14:27-31; Luke 22:31-38; John 13:36-38; 15:1-17:26)

#### —Jesus Warns the Disciples and Especially Peter
#### < Thursday Night, Nisan 14, Spring, A.D. 31 (7/7) >
#### {Matthew 26:31-35; Mark 14:27-31; Luke 22:31-38; John 13:37, 38}

The Lord and His remaining eleven disciples made their way through the darkened streets of Jerusalem. Soon they were outside the city on a path that led to the Mount of Olives. Jesus began to speak again, explaining, "All of you will be offended because of Me tonight. It will be as it is written in the Scripture: 'I will smite the Shepherd, and the sheep will be scattered.' [Zechariah 13:7] But don't worry. After I am raised from the dead, I will go before you into Galilee. There you are to meet Me. Please remember this!" [*Harmony* 18:17, 60][59]

But Peter protested. Pointing to the other ten disciples, he triumphantly declared, "Even though all of these others may be offended because of You, You can be assured that I never will be!"[60]

To show the seriousness of His response, Jesus, in answering His disciple, used his given name, saying, "Simon! Simon! Listen! Satan has been demanding to shake you out of your faith like a farmer sifts the useless chaff from the good wheat! But, I can assure you, I've been praying for you that your faith in Me might not utterly fail, and that you will not quit in despair. Yes, you will temporarily fail Me in spite of your present declaration of loyalty. [*Harmony* 17:28, 29, 40-44] Nevertheless, when you will turn back to Me—and you *will* turn back—I want you to help your fellow disciples to remain faithful. They will be able to learn from your mistakes."[61]

However, Peter was still unconvinced that he would actually deny his Lord. He earnestly declared, "But, Lord, I am ready to go to prison, and . . . even to

---

58 Matthew 26:30; Mark 14:26; Luke 22:39; John 14:31

59 Matthew 26:31, 32; Mark 14:27, 28

60 Matthew 26:33; Mark 14:29

61 Luke 22:31, 32

death for You! And You can be sure that I will lay down my life for You, if I must."[(q)] [62]

Jesus answered, "So you will lay down your life for Me? Indeed, Peter, I tell you—and it is a fact—that during this day, even this very night, before the rooster crows two times, you will have denied Me on three separate occasions, refusing to acknowledge that you are a disciple of Mine!" [*Harmony* 17:28, 29, 40-44][(r)] [(s)] [63]

Not at all surprisingly, Peter refused to accept the Lord's prediction. The disciple continued to protest, solemnly declaring, "No! No! I tell You, if I must die with You, I will do it! But, there is no way that I will ever deny You!" And, in a like manner, the other ten disciples made the same declaration.[64]

Changing the subject, Jesus asked the disciples, "Do you remember when I sent you out, two-by-two, to witness for Me? [*Harmony* 8:37, 58] Do you remember that I sent you without a money belt, a bag of additional clothes, or extra sandals? So, let Me ask you, when you were on this mission for Me, did you lack anything?"[65]

"No! Nothing!" the disciples readily agreed.[66]

"That was because everything was provided for you, isn't that right?" Jesus replied. "Well, from now on, things will be different. Starting soon, when you witness for Me, you will need to take your own money with you. You will also need your own extra clothes and sandals. You will even need your own knives to cut up your food to eat. No one will do it for you anymore. Neither will they provide it for you. In fact, I suggest that you sell one of your own coats to purchase a knife. Yes, things will be different from now on. The days of relative popularity will be over. You will be, for the most part, on your own.[67]

"I tell you, that which has been written about Me will be fulfilled, where the Scriptures read, 'He was considered as one of the transgressors.' [Isaiah 53:12] Yes, I will be considered a sinner. Things will run their course. Indeed, many

---

62 Luke 22:33; John 13:37

63 Matthew 26:34; Mark 14:30; Luke 22:34; John 13:38

64 Matthew 26:35; Mark 14:31

65 Luke 22:35

66 Luke 22:35

67 Luke 22:36

will despise Me. And because they will hate Me, you can count on it, they will hate you, too. Because of Me, there will be very few who will show any kindness toward you anymore."[68]

Now, the disciples were totally confused as to what Jesus was saying to them. So, among the group of disciples, they found two short swords that could be serve as cutting knives. Holding them up before Jesus, they exclaimed, "Look here, we already have two swords, Lord!"[69]

"That will be plenty!" Jesus answered. "You will not need them now. Save them for later."[70]

> Clearly, the disciples did not understand as to when they would need the knives! Of course, Jesus was talking about a time later on, when they would begin their work of witnessing after the Lord had ascended into heaven. Because of their lack of understanding on this matter, Jesus had no choice at the time but to drop the subject. What exactly Jesus was trying to tell them would become much clearer to them at a later date. [*Harmony* 17:19][(t)] [1]

**— The Parable of the Grapevine**
**< Thursday Night, Nisan 14, Spring, A.D. 31 (7/7) >**
**{John 15:1-17}**

> What followed next was one of the most important parables Jesus ever told. By it, He illustrated the kind of relationship He wanted to have with all His disciples—then and now. It described a vital, growing, and totally life-altering relationship with Him. It is based upon an "abiding" experience with the Lord, wherein the Savior abides in His disciples, and His disciples abide in Him. It is the best illustration that can be found anywhere within the Scriptures of this kind of relationship.[2]

As Jesus and His eleven disciples were making their way toward the Garden, they passed through a vineyard. Looking at the grape vines there, Jesus began to talk to the disciples, saying, "Let Me give you an illustration of what My relationship with you should be, and what it should accomplish in your lives. Listen, this relationship can be compared to a grapevine—such as the ones that

---

68 Luke 22:37
69 Luke 22:38
70 Luke 22:38

you see here. In this illustration, I am the Vine of Gospel truth. My Father is the Owner of the Vineyard. And you? You are the branches of the Vine. And every 'branch' that does not bear fruit in its relationship with Me—the Vine—the Father will tear away from the Vine, because it is worthless. [*Harmony* 5:40/2; 7:50][71]

"And of those of you who *are* bearing fruit," Jesus continued, "the Father prunes away all the energy-sucking portions of the branches—that is, your sins—so that you might bear even more fruit! Now, in my illustration, you have already been pruned, so to speak, by the words that I have been teaching you the past three plus years. Yes, it is clear that the words I have spoken to you have certainly changed your lives. Indeed, you are growing in grace, being transformed into My likeness, by putting sin out of your lives. That is what I mean by the pruning process of the Father. [*Harmony* 7:52][72]

"Let Me continue with My illustration. Just as it is in the case of branches that stay connected to the main grapevine, you have borne fruit because you have faithfully remained 'connected to' Me and My teachings. But you must continue to remain connected to *Me*, so that I can remain connected to *you*! And obviously, just as a branch on a grapevine cannot continue to bear grapes unless it remains connected to the vine, no more can you unless you continue to remain connected to Me. It's just that simple! [*Harmony* 11:81/; 16:81][73]

"So again," the Lord went on, "I am the main Vine, and you are the branches. So . . . let's stay connected! It's a fact that if you remain connected to Me by faith, and I remain connected to you, you will continue to bear an abundance of fruit! But I warn you: If you lose that connection with Me, then you will not bear any fruit whatsoever. And again, those who break their relationship of faith with Me, will be cast aside as a worthless branch which has borne no fruit. As you know, the discarded branches of a grapevine will end up shriveled and dead. Accordingly, they are then gathered into a heap and burned in a fire. So it will be in the final judgment with those who have lost their connection with Me, and have stopped bearing fruit." [*Harmony* 7:51][74]

---

71 John 15:1, 2
72 John 15:2, 3
73 John 15:4
74 John 15:5, 6

In a practical way, to "stay connected" with Jesus involves at least three things: First, a study of the Scriptures—especially as they relate to Jesus—will empower the human heart to be victorious over sin. [*Harmony* 16:112] Second, a vibrant prayer life patterned after that of the Lord will strengthen the soul. [1 Thessalonians 5:17] And third, sharing one's faith—when combined with Bible study and prayer—will significantly energize one's spiritual life. [Revelation 12:11] All this is accomplished through the power of the Holy Spirit dwelling within the lives of the Lord's disciples of the world today, as it has been done through the centuries.

"Furthermore," Jesus added, "if you stay connected to Me, and you remain faithful to the words which I have taught you, you can ask of Me anything you desire in the Gospel experience, and I will do it for you. As a consequence, you will bear much fruit for the Father and Me! And the Father is greatly honored when you bear fruit for Him. In fact, bearing fruit is really the true test of your loyalty and connection to Me as My disciples." [*Harmony* 16:80, 81][(u)] [75]

In the Lord's parable of the Vine, the "bearing of fruit" represents both character development and the winning of souls for the kingdom of heaven. And any genuine follower of Jesus will bear fruit of this nature. Conversely, if one does not bear this kind of fruit, he is not a genuine follower of the Lord. It's just that simple!

Then Jesus added more important counsel regarding the presence of genuine love in the lives of His disciples. He said, "This process that I have been describing to you started with the Father's love for Me. It continued when I first began to love you with the same love the Father bestowed upon Me. Now, to keep all this going, you must respond to My love for you, by continuing to love Me in return. You may be wondering how to continue in My love. Well, it is by keeping all the commandments that I have given you. You see, the same thing was true for Me: I have consistently followed and obeyed the Father's commandments which He gave to Me and thus have remained in His favor and love. You must do the same by obeying Me. Again, that's the meaning of bearing of fruit: obedience to My commandments![76]

---

75 John 15:7, 8
76 John 15:9, 10

"Friends," the Savior continued, "I have given you these words of counsel so that the joy that I have in you may continue to abide in you. And in the final analysis, your joy will be complete if you follow exactly all this advice I've been giving you. Real joy will come to you when you sincerely love one another in the same manner that I have loved you.[77]

"Now, speaking of My love for you," Jesus went on, "let Me say that there is no greater love in the universe than the love that can be shown when one lays down his life for his friends! And that is what I will do for you. You can count on it. [*Harmony* 16:81][78]

"And, speaking of friendship, you are My friends when you do everything that I have commanded you to do. Yes, you are My friends, indeed! In fact, I no longer will call you merely servants of Mine. As you know, servants don't know what their master's plans entail. But now you know My plans. Therefore you have become much more to Me than servants. So then, from now on, I will call you My friends, because the plans that My Father had for Me, I have explained to you."[79]

> While Jesus from then on would call His disciples "friends," it didn't change the fact that they were still His servants. In reality, the true follower of Jesus, while a "friend" of Jesus, also continues to remain a servant of His. In reality, the Lord's followers are *both* friends and servants, for each of these words describes different attributes of a disciple's relationship with Jesus.

"My friends," Jesus concluded, "remember, you did not initially choose Me. Instead I have chosen you, and have called you to do a special work for Me! I have planted you, as it were, as a Vineyard. Remember the grapevine illustration? [*Harmony* 16:71-75] Well, as a fruitful vine, you must go out and bear a lot of 'grapes' for the cause of the Gospel. And I trust that your fruit will remain forever fresh and never spoil. This will take place because the Father will give you all that you shall ask of Him."[80]

Then, speaking once more about love, Jesus added, "You can be sure of one thing: If you have the kind of relationship with the Father—the kind of which

---

77 John 15:11, 12
78 John 15:13
79 John 15:14, 15
80 John 15:16

I've been describing to you in My illustration of the Vineyard—you will love one another exactly as you should. In truth, it will be the best proof of the viability of a vibrant, 'stay connected' relationship [*Harmony* 16:73] with Me." [*Harmony* 5:74/, 75, 75/1, 2; 16:76-78][81]

**— A Warning of Coming Persecution**
**< Thursday Night, Nisan 14, Spring, A.D. 31 (7/7) >**
**{John 15:18-25}**

The Lord continued to explain additional things to His disciples. He said, "There's more I need to say about love and hate, especially as it relates to the world. Now to clarify, by the designation, 'world,' I mean those in the world who think and act like those in the Jewish church who have rejected Me and are actively planning My death. So then, this is what I want you to know: If the world hates you—and it certainly will—you can rest assured that it had already hated Me in the first place! [*Harmony* 16:87] Of course, if I thought and acted like the world—that is, the way Jewish leaders act—then, in that case, they would have loved you, because the world loves its own kind. But obviously, even though I originally chose you out of the world, the world will hate you, because you no longer belong to it as you once did. But don't be distressed that you will experience this kind of tension with the world. Remember what I told you a short time ago, 'A slave is not better than his master.' [*Harmony* 16:19] This means, in part, that if they persecuted Me, they will certainly persecute you! You can see that, can't you? [*Harmony* 16:85/, 87][82]

"On the other hand, if the world had kept My word—which, of course, they haven't done—it likewise would keep your words. Obviously, they will certainly never do that! And why? Simply because of the fact that the world never tried to know the Father—the One who sent Me in the first place. Because they didn't know Him, they persecuted Me. Accordingly, because they don't know Me, they will persecute you for taking upon yourselves My name.[83]

"Now," Jesus further explained, "if I had never come into the world and told them the truths which I did, then I wouldn't hold their sin of rejecting Me against them. Why? For they would not have known any better! But because over the last several years I have openly shared the truth with them, they are certainly

81 John 15:17
82 John 15:18-20
83 John 15:20, 21

without any excuse for their wickedness. Thus, I must confess, in hating Me they have shown that they equally hate the Father, whom, quite ironically, they claim that they love so much!"[84]

Jesus concluded, "Yes, if I had not performed the many miracles I did in their presence—the kind of miracles no one else could have performed, I might add—then, I would not hold them responsible for their evil actions. [*Harmony* 13:31-34] But they refused to accept the genuineness of the many miracles I performed right in front of their eyes—to say nothing of the fact that they also hated My Father. For this reason I will certainly hold them completely responsible for every single one of their sinful, wicked actions! No exceptions! Certainly, all this fulfills the word of prophecy written in their own law, which reads, 'They hated Me without any real or just cause.'" [Psalm 35:19; 69:4][85]

> These same concepts apply in the world of today. There are those who have rejected the message of Jesus—much like the Jewish leaders of the Lord's day. In that sense, then, the definition of the word, "world," that Jesus used [*Harmony* 16:82], applies also to many throughout the history of Christianity.

**— The Coming of the Comforter**
**< Thursday Night, Nisan 14, Spring, A.D. 31 (7/7) >**
**{John 15:26-16:33}**

Changing the subject a bit, the Lord said, "I wish to explain to you again the work of the Holy Spirit within your lives. [*Harmony* 16:46-56] I mention the Spirit to you again, for He will be the One who will help you get through your times of persecution when your enemies are after you. So, when the Spirit comes to you, I want you to think of Him as a Comforter—that is, One who will, in my place, 'stand by your side.' As I have said before, I will send Him to you by asking the Father to send Him. [*Harmony* 16:48] Thus the Comforter will come to you directly from the Father at My request. And when He comes, the Spirit will bear witness to the truths which I will share with Him. Accordingly, through Him you will also bear witness to the world regarding Me. I know that I can trust you to do this in spite of persecution, because you have been closely following

---

84 John 15:22, 23
85 John 15:24, 25

Me from the very first time that you became acquainted with Me through the preaching of John the Baptist." [*Harmony* 2:3, 4][86]

But the Lord cautioned His disciples further regarding persecution, adding, "Let me remind you once more: You will be persecuted for your faithfulness in following Me. [*Harmony* 16:82-85] I am telling you this now, so that you will not be surprised or shocked when the severe persecutions begin! This way you will not become overly discouraged. Now specifically, here are some of the things that will happen to you: First, they will throw you out of the church. Following that, they will do even worse things, even to the extent of killing you! In fact, the hour is soon coming that when they kill you, they will actually think that they are doing the will of God! Yes, indeed, they will think that they have done God a great service in killing you. [Acts 6:13, 14] That's how twisted their thinking will become! And don't forget, they will do this to you because they do not believe in either the Father or Me. And, if they don't believe Us, how can they possibly believe in you? I tell you these things once more, so that when they actually happen to you, you will remember that I have already warned you regarding them.[87]

"During the course of My ministry," Jesus added, "when I was with you on a full-time basis, it was not necessary for Me to have told you all these things. But now that I am leaving you and returning to be with the Father, it is necessary that I forewarn you about what is going to happen in My absence, so that you might be prepared."[88]

Jesus looked closely at His disciples. He could see that they were very upset. So He said to them, "I can see that all this talk about persecution has caused you to stop asking of Me, 'Where are You going?' [*Harmony* 16:38] Obviously, the thought of persecution is scaring you! I can understand that. And, I can understand that My emphasis upon its coming reality is making matters worse for you.[89]

"But there is another way of looking at this. To do so, I return to the previous subject of My leaving you. And yes, this will surprise you! You see, I declare to you that it is to your great advantage that I am leaving you, even if you will be

86 John 15:26, 27
87 John 16:1-4
88 John 16:4, 5
89 John 16:5, 6

persecuted! And why is this? If I don't leave you, the Comforter will not come to be with you. But because I am going, then He will come to you at My bidding. In other words, having the Comforter with you, even during persecution, is much better than not having the Spirit dwelling among you without the persecution. Certainly you can see that!"[90]

> The Lord's point to His disciples, here, was threefold: First, He would be leaving them. Second, after He was gone, they would be persecuted. And third, they were not to fear the persecution, because the Holy Spirit—as the Comforter—would be with them. Not only would He be with them, but through the Spirit's ministry, they would continue to do fruitful work for the Lord.

"So, in the face of persecution, why is the Comforter's ministry so important to you?" the Lord asked. "It is because, when He comes, He will perform three essential tasks for you: First, He will convict the world regarding sin—what people need to *stop* doing. Second, He will convict the world concerning righteousness—what people need to *start* doing. And third, He will convict the world about the judgment—that the time is fast approaching for an absolute decision by all who have heard the truth of the Gospel. Indeed, this is an urgent time.[91]

"I'll be more specific," Jesus further explained. "The Comforter will convict the world regarding sin, because most people right in My presence have stopped listening to Me altogether. The Spirit, too, will convict the world regarding righteousness, because I will no longer be dwelling among them to show them how to live their lives. And, the Holy Spirit will convict the world regarding the judgment, because the devil is already under condemnation for his murderous wrath against Me. And those who follow the devil will be judged for being complicit with his evil acts."[92]

> Here Jesus clearly taught that, in spite of persecution, the mission of the church would move ahead triumphantly. This was because the Holy Spirit would be with His disciples, even without the Lord's visible presence among them.

---

90 John 16:7
91 John 16:8
92 John 16:9-11

The Lord added, "Besides the Spirit's ability to give you good success in the face of persecution, He will also help you in other areas. You see, there are many things which I would love to tell you, but, in truth, you are not yet ready to bear them at this time. So, the Comforter, when He comes, will inform you of these other things. Yes, He will direct you into all the truth that is necessary for you, as My disciples, to know.[93]

"And what He tells you will not be His own words. Rather, He will tell you what I ask Him to explain to you. Again, it will be at My request that the Comforter will announce to you all the things that are coming that you need to know. Indeed, the Holy Spirit will constantly honor Me by telling you what I ask Him to say. Because everything the Father has also belongs to Me, when I ask the Comforter to tell you certain things, He will be speaking not only on My behalf, but also on behalf of the Father—indeed, both of Us!"[94]

> These promises were fulfilled in part by the many prophecies recorded in the New Testament, especially the book of Revelation written by the disciple John who was present when Jesus spoke these words. But also, the Holy Spirit personally ministered through the apostles and other church leaders in the establishment and advancement of the work of the early Christian church. [Acts 8:29; 13:2, etc.]

Jesus paused and then changed the subject, "Ah, in a little while, you will not see Me, for I will have gone to be with the Father. A little while after that, you will see Me once again."[95]

His disciples were puzzled by these words and began to talk among themselves. They said to one another, "What is Jesus trying to say to us? What do the words, 'In a little while you will not see Me;' and then, 'A little while later you will see Me.' Also, what does He mean by saying, 'I go to the Father'? What is this 'little while' stuff all about? We cannot understand what the Lord is telling us."[96]

Jesus, knowing that they wanted to ask Him the meaning of these things, answered them on His own, by saying, "Are you looking to each other for an answer to your various questions? Do you wonder why I said, 'A little while and

---

93 John 16:12, 13
94 John 16:13-15
95 John 16:16
96 John 16:17, 18

you will not see Me, and again, in a little while you will see Me'? It is certainly a fact when I declare to you that a time is fast approaching when you will wail and lament over what has happened. And, at the same time, the world would be rejoicing while you are weeping. But then . . . all of a sudden . . . your grief will be turned into great joy![97]

"It's like a woman who has cried out in pain while in labor, giving birth to her child. But when her son is born, she quickly forgets the pain she has suffered because of the joy she feels as she realizes that her child has come into the world. That is the way it will be with you: You will grieve when I am taken from you, but when you see Me again, your heart will be, oh, so happy—and that happiness will never be taken from you again!"[98]

> Jesus did not answer their questions specifically. But here, in a cryptic manner, Jesus referred to His death—which, of course, would cause the disciples to grieve, and the Lord's enemies to rejoice—and also His resurrection—which would cause His disciples to rejoice, while His enemies would now weep. After His resurrection, Jesus went to the Father in heaven [*Harmony* 18:28, 29], and quickly returned to the earth again to be with His disciples for yet a while longer. This is what the Lord meant when He told them that they would not see Him, and then, they would see Him again after He had gone to the Father. It is not likely at the time that the disciples really understood what Jesus was talking about, but they did not question Him further on the subject. So Jesus dropped the subject and began to discuss the work of the Comforter once again.

Jesus said, "From the day that the Holy Spirit will have come into your midst, you will have no need to personally question Me regarding anything. This is true because after you have asked for the Holy Spirit to come, the Spirit will reveal to you all the things that you need to know. At the present, you have no concept of what the Father or I will reveal to you through the Spirit. But when the Comforter comes, you will ask, and the Spirit will dramatically answer your questions. You'll see! The result will be that your happiness and confidence in the Lord will be made complete." The New Testament experiences—especially those

---

97 John 16:19, 20
98 John 16:21, 22

recorded in the book of Acts—were, to a great extent, a fulfillment of this great promise. [Acts 13:1-3, etc.][99]

"You will have noticed, I am sure, that throughout a large part of My ministry with you I have spoken to you in parables. But the hour will come, when the Comforter arrives, that I will no longer speak to you in such allegories. Through the Spirit, the will of the Father will be made very plain to you. In addition, in those days, you will ask things of the Father in My name, and I will not need to plead with Him to respond in a positive way to your request. And why? Because He will do so automatically! You see, this is because the Father loves you just as much as I do! Yes, He will quickly respond to your requests, because you have loved Me and have trusted My words when I said that I have come from the Father." The New Testament writings, most in non-parable form, fulfilled this promise in part.[100]

"Indeed," the Lord concluded, "it is true that I have come from the presence of God. It is also true and that I have come to this earth as a human being, and that I will soon be leaving this earth and returning to the divine position I had with the Father before My coming to this world in the first place." [*Harmony* 1:1][101]

His disciples answered Him, "Yes! Now you are speaking to us in plain words, and are no longer using cryptic sayings to make Your point. We are also convinced that You know all things, and that no one can successfully question Your knowledge and wisdom! This is because we are positive that You speak with the authority of heaven, knowing that You have come from the presence of the Father."[102]

> Even though the disciples affirmed their faith in Jesus as the Messiah, He could see that they misunderstood His statements as to the timing of when He would speak to them plainly, as opposed to speaking to them through allegories. They apparently thought He was referring to that very moment as compared to some later date. Of course, Jesus was referring to the time when, after He was ascended into heaven, the Holy Spirit would arrive to aid them. [Acts 2:1-4]

---

[99] John 16:23, 24
[100] John 16:25-27
[101] John 16:28
[102] John 16:29, 30

Jesus answered, "So you really understand and believe now?" But to indicate that they really didn't understand and believe as much as they thought, the Lord added, "With certainty I declare that very soon you will all run away from Me to take care of your own selves. You will leave Me completely alone! I say alone, but, in truth I will not really be alone, because the Father will remain with Me." Of course, Jesus was talking about when His disciples would flee from Him when He was arrested a short time later in the Garden of Gethsemane. [*Harmony* 17:23] But beyond this statement, the Lord did not discuss this issue further with His disciples.[103]

Then, in summary of His entire discussion with His disciples that night, Jesus concluded His words of counsel by saying, "I have shared all these concepts with you so that you can possess a positive and peaceful confidence in Me as your Savior. Even though, while in this world as My followers, I can assure you that you will be placed in very stressful and afflicting situations, I want you to be encouraged . . . not discouraged. And why? Because, remember, My friends, I have overcome the world!" [*Harmony* 12:63/][104]

### — The Lord's Intercessory Prayer for His Disciples
### < Thursday Night, Nisan 14, Spring, A.D. 31 (7/7) >
### {John 17:1-26}

Then Jesus, lifting up His eyes toward heaven, began to pray, "Father, My hour of sacrifice is quickly approaching. Honor Me as Your Son, as I sacrifice Myself for the salvation of the entire world. In doing so, Father, I will be honoring You when I die for the sins of all mankind!" [*Harmony* 11:70; 14:140][105]

> Here, Jesus declared that not only would He be highly honored by dying for the sins of the world, but He would also honor God by fulfilling His mission as the Divine Sacrifice for all mankind!

"You gave Me complete authority over all humanity," Jesus prayed on, "and every one of those who followed Me, You have given to Me. Accordingly, I will provide eternal life for every single one of them. And this is basis of their eternal life: That they may surely have a personal relationship with You, the only True

---

[103] John 16:31, 32
[104] John 16:33
[105] John 17:1

God, and also a personal relationship with Me, Jesus Christ, the One whom You have sent."[106]

> The Lord clearly stated here that those who have a relationship with both the Father and the Son, could be assured of eternal life—a life that He, through His sacrifice, provided for all those who would seek it.

Jesus continued with His prayer, "By successfully finishing the work that You gave Me to perform on this earth, I have given You great honor. Because of that, Father, I ask that You personally honor Me by bestowing upon Me once again the greatness of the glory that We had with each other long before the creation of the world." [*Harmony* 2:31/2; 3:56; 14:140, 153/; 18:98][107]

> Jesus asked that when His work was finished on this earth, He would receive the highest honor of all: that of having His original glory reinstated. [*Harmony* 1:1]

"Indeed," Jesus continued, "I have accurately revealed Your divine character to the disciples whom You gave to Me from out of the world. They were Yours in the first place. And I am happy to say that once You gave them to Me to teach, they have learned to faithfully keep Your commands. They have finally understood that everything You have told Me to do was, in fact, Your will for Me. All the instructions that You have given to Me I have passed on to them. They have received them, for they know that I was once by Your side and that You have sent Me here to work for You.[108]

"At this moment, I pray for them, My disciples, but not now for those of the world who have rejected Me. Again, I pray for those whom You gave Me, for they are really Yours. It is true that everything I have, I originally received from You. And everything that You gave to Me, I have shared with them, My disciples. I am honored by the faithful obedience of My disciples, for they have followed what I have directed them to do and to be.[109]

"But, for all practical purposes," Christ added, "I am no longer a part of this world, but they—My disciples—still are! As I will shortly come to live where You are, I ask that You keep them—those whom You have given to Me—faithful

---

106 John 17:2, 3
107 John 17:4, 5
108 John 17:6-8
109 John 17:9, 10

to Your character. I further desire that they be unified with one another, just as We are unified as one. While I have been with them in this world, I have kept them true to Your good Name. I have closely guarded and protected those whom You gave to Me. Not one of them is lost—excepting, of course, the son of perdition, Judas—so that when he betrays Me, and I suffer at the hands of My enemies, the Scriptures which predicted My suffering would be accurately fulfilled." [*Harmony* 17:16][110]

> Jesus was not saying that Judas, in betraying His Lord, was fulfilling the will of God, but that, because God in His foreknowledge had revealed that Judas would betray the Lord, the prophecies of that betrayal would be accurately fulfilled.

"Now," Jesus prayed, "as I am about to return into Your presence, I have shared all things with My disciples who will remain behind in this world. I want them to be filled with the same joy which I have had in doing Your will. This is in spite of the fact that the world will hate them. Because I have given Your word to them, they will be hated, for they are really not of this world, just as I am not really a part of this world. No, I'm not praying that they be taken out of the world. Rather, I pray that they will not give in to the evils of this world. Again, they are not of this world, just as I was not of this world.[111]

"Make them holy in the truth, Father. Set them aside for a special work. All Your instructions are the truth that will make them righteous, as they have been set aside to work for You. This will prepare them to face the sinful world into which I will send them—the same world into which You sent Me. I have remained righteous and faithful to You. I have done so, in part, in order to give them an example of how they, too, might be made righteous by following that same truth which I followed—the truth that is contained in Your word." [*Harmony* 16:74/][112]

> In this portion of His prayer, Jesus interceded on behalf of His disciples. He made it clear that not only had He faithfully performed His mission of teaching them the correct Gospel truth, but also that they had effectively learned and practiced the truth He had taught them. Further, because He was leaving His disciples behind on this earth, He asked

---

110 John 17:11, 12
111 John 17:13-16
112 John 17:17-19

the Father that they might be sustained and kept faithful to Him and their mission. Jesus pleaded that they might be unified, bound together in the same of kind of joy He had experienced in faithfully completing His own work. The Lord also requested that His closest followers might stand for the truth, even while they must live in this wicked world. He desired that the power of the truth would transform them into holiness, carefully and continuously refining their characters.

"Furthermore," the Lord went on in His prayer, "I pray, not only for My disciples here, but also for those who will believe in Me and the Gospel through My disciples' ministry." [*Harmony* 11:149; 14:149/2][113]

This request, of course, was in behalf of all those of the Christian faith who followed the words of the disciples, either those to whom they spoke in person or those who accepted the Gospel through the words they wrote in Scripture. In reality this includes everyone who has, throughout the ages, accepted Jesus as a personal Savior!

Jesus continued with His prayer, saying, "What I really want is for all of them—the disciples, and those who believe because their testimony—to be one in unity, even as We also are one, as You are in Me, Father, and I am in You. May their unity be the result of being unified, not only with each other, but also with Us. This way, the world will be able to believe that it was You who sent Me, for such unity can be accomplished only through the indwelling of the power of God. [*Harmony* 16:115][114]

"I have also given them the same type of honor for doing their work faithfully that You have given Me for doing My work faithfully. All this will help secure the kind of unity We desire for them—the same kind of unity, again [*Harmony* 16:114], that We have with each other, Father. May it all work out perfectly: I in them, and You in Me, leading to a perfect unity among them. This will guarantee that the world can, if it chooses, recognize that You have sent Me, and that You have loved My disciples to the same extent that You have loved Me.[115]

"Father, I also desire that those whom You have given Me will ultimately be able to live with Me in heaven. This way, they will be able, on a firsthand basis, to see the glorious honor which You have given Me, because You have loved Me

113 John 17:20
114 John 17:21
115 John 17:22, 23

even before the foundation of the world was laid. Back then, Holy Father, the world did not, and still does not, recognize who You are. But I knew You back then before the world was created. And the disciples have now recognized the fact that I have been sent to the world at Your direction. I also made Your spotless character clear to them—and will continue to do so—so that, as I dwell in them, Your love will also abide in them. Amen." [*Harmony* 1:50/][116]

> It was the Lord's passionate desire that His disciples experience the same kind of unity with one another that He had with His Father, and that they honor God the same way that He had. And further, the Lord wanted His disciples to ultimately be with Him in heaven to see His glory and experience it themselves on a personal, firsthand basis. Also, in this part of the prayer, Jesus made it clear that He had been with the Father, even before the creation of the world. In making this statement, the Lord obviously verified His divinity. [1]
>
> Thus Jesus concluded His prayer for His disciples. This was, by far, the longest recorded prayer of Jesus found anywhere in the Gospel record. [*Harmony* 8:35][2]

**Supplementary Notes:**

**(a) [16:0+]** There is an apparent discrepancy among the Gospel records as to when the Passover was celebrated in the year of the Lord's death. It seems from the records of Matthew, Mark, and Luke that the Passover was kept the same night (Thursday), as when Jesus had the Lord's Supper with His disciples in the upper room. But according to John, the Passover was celebrated the next night (Friday). Even though there are a number of possibilities that *might* explain this apparent contradiction, we really don't know the correct answer. Extra-Biblical records of the time do not help us much. In any case, the answer to this dilemma is well beyond the scope of this book. But whatever the answer may be, it does not really detract from the overall message of the Gospel story. For myself, I would suggest that maybe the Lord celebrated the Passover one night earlier than the regular date because He knew that he would be dead on the actual Passover day. If that is the case, I think there is nothing in the record that would contradict this approach to the problem. In the long run, however, I suppose it is not that important. It is quite likely that this problem will never be resolved.

---

116 John 17:24-26

**(b) [16:2]** (See above.)

**(c) [16:2]** The Feast of Unleavened Bread (which lasted one week) immediately followed the Passover Festival—that is, it began the next day. Therefore, it became a practice to use the term Unleavened Bread to refer in general to the Passover, and vice versa. In other words, these designations could be interchangeable. In this portion of the Gospel record, the designation "Unleavened Bread" no doubt refers to the Passover.

**(d) [16:4]** The mystery surrounding how Jesus knew what would happen when He sent two of His disciples to set up the Passover Feast in the upper room is very similar to the events involved in the Triumphal Entry (*Harmony* 14:27, 28). Whether these events were miraculous in nature, or whether Jesus had privately set everything up, is unknown. Also, why Jesus handled these events in such a mysterious way is equally unknown.

**(e) [16:5]** (See above.)

**(f) [16:11]** The fact that Jesus specifically washed Judas's feet is not mentioned in the text, but such an assumption is implied in *Harmony* 16:18. Accordingly, I stated so.

**(g) [16:23/2]** Was the "wine" used at the Last Supper fermented or unfermented? In truth, the Greek word translated "wine" can be interpreted as being *either* fermented *or* unfermented. I believe it to have been unfermented—in short, grape juice. I find it hard to believe, considering the amount of wine that was drunk during the Passover, that it was fermented wine. Such a quantity, should it have been fermented, could have easily led to drunkenness, and drunkenness is clearly condemned in the Bible (Proverbs 20:1).

**(h) [16:24]** (See above.)

**(i) [16:25]** The well-known words of 1 Corinthians 11:23-26 are actually the words of Jesus which, apparently, the Lord directly gave (probably in vision) to Paul at some time during his ministry. And, as the reader should note, in "red letter" editions of the Bible (where the words of Jesus are printed in red ink), the words found in these texts are, accordingly, usually printed in red. The way they are written there indicates that they were a part of the actual words Jesus spoke in the upper room during the Passover celebration with His disciples. Therefore, I included all the concepts contained in these verses as though they were a part of the Gospel record of Matthew, Mark, Luke, and John.

**(j) [16:26]** (See **Note "g"** above.)

**(k) [16:26]** (See **Note "i"** above.)

**(l) [16:26/]** (See **Note "g"** above.)

**(m) [16:35]** It has been suggested that when Judas left the upper room, he still had a morsel of unleavened bread in his mouth! The text does not say that, but considering that the Lord had just given him a morsel of bread (*Harmony* 16:31), and that it takes a while to chew unleavened bread, and further, that Judas left very soon after that, it is possible.

**(n) [16:35/]** While the text does not specifically say so, it seems logical that it was at this time that Judas finalized his plans with the Jewish leaders to betray Jesus. That is why I recorded it that way I did in the *Harmony.*

**(o) [16:40]** In order to make the *Harmony* and its events read smoothly and logically, I have split John 13:37 in half, placing the first half here, and the second half under *Harmony* 16:62, combining it with John 13:38 under *Harmony* 16:63. While I was not completely comfortable with this split (for John, of all the Gospel writers is the most strictly sequential), I still consider it to be the most logical way to interpret the proper sequence of events, when the parallel accounts of Matthew, Mark, and Luke are included.

**(p) [16:47]** The impression is given that if we *ask anything* from the Lord He will do it. However, the reality of life tells us that such is hardly the case! There can be no doubt that the Lord intended that there will be some limitation placed upon this promise. However, just what that limitation may be, is unclear. I would suppose, though, that to ask within the confines of the *Lord's will* would be that reasonable limitation that could be implied in the verse. Beyond that, though, just how to interpret this verse within the constraints of the reality of life, remains unclear to me.

**(q) [16:62]** (See **Note "o"** above.)

**(r) [16:63]** (See **Note "o"** above.)

**(s) [16:63]** Matthew, Luke, and John declare that Jesus told Peter that before the rooster crowed (He didn't say how often), he would deny the Lord three times. Mark says that before the rooster crowed *twice*, Peter would deny Jesus three times. Accordingly, I went with Mark's account for the *Harmony*, considering it the most likely scenario.

**(t) [16:70/]** This story (Luke 22:35-38), quite simply, is, by far, the *strangest* story in the entire Gospel record, perhaps even in the complete Bible! While I am not comfortable with what I interpreted it to mean, I know of no other possible interpretation that would make any sense at all. It is clear (*Harmony* 17:19-21), though, that Jesus did *not* want them to actually purchase a sword for self-defense, or to be used as a weapon! So, whatever Jesus *actually* meant, as recorded in this strange event, one thing is certain: The disciples did not understand what the Lord had in mind. I suppose, neither do we!

**(u) [16:75]** (See **Note "p"** above.)

# CHAPTER SEVENTEEN

## THE PASSION WEEK: THE LAST SUFFERINGS OF JESUS

**From Jesus Prays in the Garden, to the Crucifixion of Christ**

**(Passover, Spring, A.D. 31)**

**The Gethsemane Experience[a]**
**< Thursday, Before Midnight, Nisan 14, Spring, A.D. 31 (7/7) >**
**(Matthew 26:36-56; Mark 14:32-52; Luke 22:40-53; John 18:1-12)**

**—Jesus Prays in the Garden**
**< Thursday, Before Midnight, Nisan 14, Spring, A.D. 31 (7/7) >**
**{Matthew 26:36-46; Mark 14:32-42; Luke 22:40-46; John 18:1}**

After Jesus concluded His prayer to His Father [*Harmony* 16:105-116], the group—Jesus and eleven of His disciples—continued on their way to the Mount of Olives. A garden was located there. It was called Gethsemane—a name that meant "oil press," for, no doubt, the garden was where olives were crushed to make oil. Along with His disciples, the Lord entered Gethsemane.[1]

To eight of His disciples, Jesus said, "You sit here while I go on a bit further to pray." Then He took with Him His three closest disciples, Peter, along with James and John, the two sons of Zebedee. [*Harmony* 8:18; 10:62,63/,69/] As they walked on, it became obvious that Jesus was extremely distressed and troubled. The Lord revealed to the trio of disciples the agonies of His heart, saying, "My entire soul is unbelievably grieved, as though I were about to die. Please remain here, while I go on a bit further. But do stay awake and pray with Me. Please, I need your help! [*Harmony* 17:5][2]

---

1 Matthew 26:36; Mark 14:32; Luke 22:40; John 18:1

2 Matthew 26:36-38; Mark 14:32-34

"Also," he added, "pray not only for Me, but for yourselves, that you will not be overwhelmed with temptation and despair."[3]

> At that moment, Jesus was beginning to go through a unique experience. As the Sin Bearer—the "Lamb of God," who was to carry upon Himself the sins of the world [*Harmony* 2:49]—He began to have placed upon Him the entire burden of all the guilt, of all the sins, of all humanity . . . even of all time! What a thought! In addition to that, the Savior was faced with the single biggest decision of His entire life: Would He actually complete the plan of salvation—to suffer and die for the sins of the world? [Isaiah 53:3-11] Would He be willing to experience the separation from His Father that an eternally lost sinner will experience? Already, on at least two separate occasions [*Harmony* 2:33, 35/; 10:56, 57], Jesus had been tempted to shrink from the awesome responsibility of being the Sin Bearer of the world. And now, on this third occasion, the final decision to face this incredible challenge must be taken by the Lord.

After going about a stone's throw beyond the three disciples—but still close enough so that they could hear what He was saying—Jesus knelt down upon the ground, and, as He began to pour out His soul to His Father in prayer, He fell down on His face. He pleaded with the Father, asking if the trial just before Him could be avoided. "Abba—Father!" He cried out, "If it is remotely possible, remove this cup of death from Me! That's what I desire. However, what You desire for Me is what is really important. So, may Your will be done!" [*Harmony* 2:34; 10:57/][(b)][4]

> Here Jesus compared the struggle He was called upon to face, to the drinking of a cup of poison that means certain death to the one drinking it. This statement was based upon the custom of the ancient world, in which condemned people were sometimes required to drink poison which would quickly lead to their death. [*Harmony* 17:21]

After praying for a while, Jesus presently came back to where the three disciples were supposed to be praying for Him. Indeed, He needed encouragement from them. But, alas, He found them fast asleep! Awakening Peter, He questioned him, "Simon, have you already fallen asleep? Could all of you not stay awake

---

3 Luke 22:40

4 Matthew 26:39; Mark 14:35, 36; Luke 22:41

and pray with Me for just one hour? That's all I'm asking! I told you to stay awake and pray so you would not be overcome with temptation and sleepiness." [*Harmony* 17:2] And then, almost as if to make excuse for the three of them, the Lord added, "Of course, I know that the spirit is willing, but the flesh is, oh, so weak!"[5]

Jesus left them for a second time to continue to pray alone. Once again He pleaded, "My Father, if there is no way that this trial can pass from Me, and I must drink this cup of death, then may Your will be done! I will do it!"[6]

Once more He discovered the disciples sleeping when He returned to them. Their eyes were heavy with tiredness. The three were speechless when He awakened them yet again.[7]

So, completely alone, Jesus went and prayed yet a third time, repeating what He had said on the first two occasions. The Lord finally resolved to do what His Father had willed Him to do, that is, to die for the sins of the world. The final decision to suffer the death of the cross for all mankind was now firmly made. This time, an angel from heaven came to strengthen Him for the terrible struggle that was before Him. Still in great agony, the Lord continued to pray for the strength He needed to go on with the trial that He was about to face. In fact, so severe was His agony that He actually sweat large drops of blood which fell to the ground where He prayed![8]

> There have been cases in medical science, though rare, of people who have been under such great mental and emotional stress that they have actually "sweat blood." This is the result of small capillaries in the forehead breaking down, emitting blood from under the skin.

Once more Jesus arose from the place of His agonized praying, and returned to where the three disciples were. Not surprisingly, though, they were asleep yet again—for the third time! Seeing the Lord in so much sorrow had wearied them beyond their ability to stay awake. With disappointment, He awakened them one last time, and declared with some irony, "Sleep on! Take your rest in the time that remains!" Then, with a touch of sadness, He added, "Could you have not arisen and prayed with Me so that you would have not been tempted to fall

---

5 Matthew 26:40, 41; Mark 14:37, 38
6 Matthew 26:42; Mark 14:39
7 Matthew 26:43; Mark 14:40
8 Matthew 26:44; Luke 22:42-44

asleep?" But Jesus concluded, saying, "It's enough! There is no more time for discussion of the matter! For behold, the hour has already come for the Son of Man to be betrayed into the hands of sinful men. Indeed, let us arise and go, for the one who is betraying Me has almost arrived at the garden!"[9]

### —Jesus Is Arrested in the Garden
### < Thursday, Just Before Midnight, Nisan 14, Spring, A.D. 31 (7/7) >
### {Matthew 26:47-56; Mark 14:43-52; Luke 22:47-53; John 18:2-12}

Immediately, while the Lord was saying these words, Judas—sadly, one of His own twelve closest disciples—had arrived. He was leading a huge crowd who were carrying swords and big sticks. This rabble came to the garden under the direction the chief priests, elders, and scribes—the so-called spiritual leaders of the Jewish people! Judas was leading the way because he had a good idea that Jesus would be in the garden that night for the Lord had frequently met with His disciples at the same place. The crowd who came with Judas included Roman soldiers and officers, who, at the request of the Jewish leaders and Pharisees, brought their lanterns, torches, and various weapons of war. Jesus, of course, knew all this was going to happen just as it unfolded.[10]

The Lord went out to meet the crowd as they came toward Him. With Judas standing out in front of the crowd, Jesus asked them, "Who is it that you want?"[11]

They answered, "Jesus, the Nazarene—the One from Nazareth!"[12]

Jesus responded, "I am He!" At that very instant, when Jesus said, "I am He!" the entire crowd fell back from the bright light emanating from the angel who had just been ministering to the Lord. [*Harmony* 17:8] The brightness literally threw the entire mob to the ground, including Judas who was standing there with them! Shortly, though, the light faded, and the crowd regained their composure. (c) 13

Once more Jesus asked, "Who do you want?"[14]

---

9 Matthew 26:45, 46; Mark 14:41, 42; Luke 22:45, 46
10 Matthew 26:47; Mark 14:43; Luke 22:47; John 18:2-4
11 John 18:4
12 John 18:5
13 John 18:5, 6
14 John 18:7

Again they responded, "Jesus, the Nazarene!" [*Harmony* 17:12][15]

"I told you before that I am Jesus," was His simple reply. Then pointing to His disciples, He asked of the angry crowd, "Because you want only Me, let these other people go safely on their way." This request was a fulfillment of a prophecy He had given a short time before, in which He said, "Of all those whom You have given Me, I will not lose even one." [*Harmony* 16:110][16]

Now Judas stepped forward. He had made an agreement with the leaders of the mob, saying, "The Person whom I kiss is the One! Quickly grab hold of Him! Don't let Him escape from the firm grip of the soldiers, so that you can take Him away!" So, true to his promise, Judas walked up to the Lord. He greeted Him, saying, "Hail, Rabbi!" Then, of all things, Judas actually kissed Jesus! [*Harmony* 9:49][17]

> Why did Judas kiss the Lord? Perhaps he wanted to send a message to Jesus that he was really not His enemy, for Judas never thought that Jesus would actually allow Himself to be arrested—and certainly not to be killed! [*Harmony* 14:21/1-6] The betrayer had hoped that the Lord would assert Himself, and declare that He was, in fact, the Messiah. In that case, perhaps Judas's kiss would be a signal to Jesus that Judas, as a "faithful" disciple, was really on His side.[(d)]

But the Lord responded to Judas's kiss with the words, "Friend, why are you here?" Then Jesus added, "But really, Judas, do you betray the Son of Man with a kiss?" At that moment, as they had been instructed by Judas, the Roman guard grabbed hold of Jesus, firmly securing Him. [*Harmony* 2:34/2][18]

> Jewish law did not allow for the arrest of anyone as the result of the words of a betrayer. In doing so in this case, the Jewish leaders purposely went against their own principle of law.[(e)]

At that moment, some of the disciples, seeing what was about to happen, cried out to Jesus, "Lord, should we fight back with swords?" Peter, not waiting for Jesus to give a reply, grabbed his sword from its sheath and swung wildly at the person standing nearest to him—one who was a part of the crowd who

---

15 John 18:7
16 John 18:8, 9
17 Matthew 26:48, 49; Mark 14:44, 45; Luke 22:47
18 Matthew 26:50; Mark 14:46; Luke 22:48

had seized Jesus. [*Harmony* 16:65-70] The sword hit Malchus, the High Priest's servant, slicing off his right ear. [*Harmony* 17:43][19]

Jesus immediately interrupted the attack, declaring, "Stop it! We'll have none of that!" Then, Jesus gently touched the wounded ear of Malchus and it was instantly healed![20]

Turning to Peter, the Lord said, "Put your sword back in its sheath! For those who fight with a sword will end up dying by a sword. But really, Peter," the Lord added, "don't you think that I could ask My Father, and He would, within an instant of time, give Me more than twelve legions of angels to use in any way that I choose?" (That would have been one legion for each of the Lord's twelve closest disciples, with a total of no fewer than 80,000 angels!) "But if I were to do that," Jesus concluded, "then how would the Word of God be fulfilled that has decreed that I must suffer? [Isaiah 53:3-11] That cup of 'poison' which the Father has asked Me to drink . . . should I not drink it to completion?" [*Harmony* 17:4/][21]

Turning now to the crowd—which included many of the chief priests, officers of the Temple, and the scribes—Jesus challenged them, asking, "Have you actually come all the way out to this place to arrest Me with swords and clubs, as though I were a common thief? Why, I used to sit in the Temple court virtually every day—in public view no less. Yet, with your hands you never seized Me there! [*Harmony* 11:120] But I should not be surprised! This hour of darkness—here, in the middle of the night—suits perfectly your dark and evil purposes! But again, all this has happened so that the Scriptures can be fulfilled." [Isaiah 53:3-11][22]

> It should be noted that an arrest in the darkness of night was in strict violation of Hebrew law. So, in doing so, the Jews had broken their own legal code.[f]

At that point, the Roman guard and its commander, along with the Jews, arrested Jesus. They also tied the Lord's hands. Even though it was illegal for Jews to bind a man yet to be found guilty in a court of law, they bound Him anyway. Then they led Jesus back into Jerusalem. Distraught, the eleven disciples—including Peter [*Harmony* 16:60-62]—fled for their lives, leaving the

---

19 Matthew 26:51; Mark 14:47; Luke 22:49, 50; John 18:10

20 Luke 22:51

21 Matthew 26:52-54; John 18:11

22 Matthew 26:55, 56; Mark 14:48, 49; Luke 22:52, 53

captured Jesus alone with His enemies . . . even those who were determined to kill Him. [*Harmony* 16:103][23]

It so happened that there was a certain young man there that night who had followed the crowd into the garden. His name was John Mark, a follower of Jesus—the eventual writer of the Gospel of Mark. He, along with the disciples, fled from the scene of the arrest. At the time, he was wearing nothing but a linen sheet over his body. Someone seized him. But John Mark left the sheet behind in his captor's hand and ran back to the city completely naked!(g) [24]

## The Court Trials of Jesus
## < Early Friday Morning, After Midnight Through Early Daylight, Nisan 14, Spring, A.D. 31 (7/7) >
## (Matthew 26:57-27:31; Mark 14:53-15:20; Luke 22:54-23:25; John 18:13-19:16)

### — The Lord's Hearing Before Annas
### < Early Friday Morning, After Midnight, Nisan 14, Spring, A.D. 31 (7/7) >
### {Matthew 26: 58, 69-71; Mark 14:54, 66-68; Luke 22:54-57; John 18:13-24}

What followed next was that Jesus went through six trials, all travesties of justice. There were three trials under the Jews, and three with the Romans. The Jewish trials included a preliminary investigation before Annas, a trial before Caiaphas and a smaller portion of the Sanhedrin, and the final Hebrew trial before the Great Sanhedrin, the highest Jewish court in Israel. The Roman trials, which followed shortly afterward, involved two trials before the Roman governor, Pontius Pilate, with a hearing before Herod Antipas sandwiched in between. All of these trials were strikingly distinguished by their gross illegalities and their unspeakable cruelties. This was especially sad, considering the fact that Hebrew law was written in such a way as to give an accused individual as much of the benefit of the doubt as possible. This was primarily true when a capital offence—one that required the death penalty—was involved. In fact, Jewish law was written in such a way that made it virtually impossible for an innocent man—such as Jesus—to be unjustly condemned and

---

23 Matthew 26:56; Mark 14:50; John 18:12

24 Mark 14:51, 52

> executed. Seen another way, when an innocent man *was* executed, it was because there was a conscious effort by the courts of law to murder him! This would clearly prove to be the case with Jesus.[(h)]

The rabble first took Jesus to be interrogated by Annas. Now Annas, the retired High Priest, was the father-in-law of Joseph Caiaphas, the sitting High Priest that year. It was Caiaphas who had previously observed that it was better for one man to die than for the whole nation to be destroyed by the Roman government. [*Harmony* 13:33][25]

> The decision to take Jesus to Annas initially was because Caiaphas was considered to be, perhaps, too weak to stand up to the Master. It was felt that someone who was better recognized for his toughness should question Him first. Annas, it was believed, met that requirement. Such a preliminary trial, however, was against Jewish law, because it would place a defendant at an unfair disadvantage.[(i)]

By this time, a couple of the disciples, Peter and John, had regained enough courage to follow along, albeit at a great distance, to see what would happen to their Master. John was partially known by Caiaphas, so he was able to enter the court—or palace—of the High Priest, where Jesus was in the process of being questioned. But Peter had to stand outside the door. However, John convinced the doorkeeper, a servant girl, to allow Peter to come into the courtyard with him. [*Harmony* 2:34/2][(j) 26]

As Peter entered the palace complex, the servant girl of the High Priest—the same one who served as the doorkeeper—for a moment carefully scrutinized Peter's face as though she recognized him. A number of other servants and various officers were either standing or sitting around a fire of burning charcoal. The fire was located in the middle of a lower level, outside the main part of the palace where Jesus was being questioned. At the fire, people were warming themselves from the chill of the night air. Peter edged closer to the fire. After standing there for awhile, he casually sat down. He was pretending to act indifferently to what was going on, as though he didn't care. There, he decided to wait and see what would be the final conclusion of the interrogation of his Lord.[(k) 27]

---

[25] John 18:13, 14

[26] Matthew 26:58; Mark 14:54; Luke 22:54; John 18:15, 16

[27] Matthew 26:58; Mark 14:54, 67; Luke 22:55, 56; John 18:18

As Peter warmed himself by the fire, the servant girl who had taken a long look at his face when she first let him through the doorway, boldly walked up to him and stared into his face again. Finally, she challenged him, declaring, "You are one of this Man's disciples, aren't you? Yes, I know that you were with Jesus, the Galilean, the One from Nazareth!" Pointing him out to others standing by, she announced, "Look! This man was with the One called Jesus!"[(l) 28]

Instantly, Peter denied her claim by defiantly protesting to them, saying, "I am not! I have no clue as to what you're talking about!" Looking at the girl, he lied, exclaiming, "I frankly don't comprehend a word you are saying! Young lady, I have never seen this Man before!" Then Peter heard a rooster crow! Remembering the words of Jesus that he would deny his Lord [*Harmony* 16:61, 63, 64], Peter, embarrassed, left the fire and stood alone on a nearby porch, somewhat apart from the rest of the crowd. [*Harmony* 17:40-44][(m) 29]

At the same time, Jesus continued to be questioned by Annas. Now, two legal charges had to be established against the Master if the Jewish leaders were to secure His death. First, they had to prove that the Lord was guilty of blasphemy. This would be the only way that they could have Him killed and still keep the confidence of the people who had shown faith in Him as the possible Messiah. Second, they needed to prove that Jesus was a threat to the Roman authorities. Without such proof of sedition—or rebellion against Rome—the Jews would not be able to secure the required permission from the Romans to execute the Lord. Therefore, Annas, in his questioning, first tried to establish proof of the second charge, the one of sedition. [*Harmony* 14:85][30]

The former High Priest repeatedly questioned Jesus regarding His teachings and the work of His disciples. He tried to elicit information about the activities of Jesus that would give good reason for the Roman authorities to think that the Lord was secretly planning some traitorous act against the empire. But Annas made no progress in this line of questioning.[31]

Finally, after some time, Jesus declared, "I have always spoken in an open manner to the world. As you well know, I have often been in the synagogues and the Temple. There, publicly and openly, I have shared My beliefs with anyone in

---

28 Matthew 26:69; Mark 14:66, 67; Luke 22:56; John 18:17

29 Matthew 26:70; Mark 14:68; Luke 22:57; John 18:17

30 John 18:19

31 John 18:19

the Jewish nation who might have gathered there. In short, I never spoke these things in a secret manner. So then, why do you question Me this way? If you really want to know what I've said, just ask anyone who has heard Me teach or preach! If you listen to them, they will tell you!"[32]

> Jesus, by this statement, was actually claiming His legal rights. Under Jewish law, the accused was not required to defend himself when questioned. And further, the law required that the testimony against an accused individual had to come from at least two eyewitnesses who would be in total agreement with each other. In this case, Jesus was, in effect, demanding that such witnesses be brought forward to testify against Him. Or if no such witnesses should appear to accuse Him, the Lord clearly implied that He should be promptly released.[(n)]

The Lord's bold response deeply embarrassed Annas because he was afraid that the secret plot of the Jews to kill Jesus might be publicly exposed. [*Harmony* 14:22-25] Also, Annas was quite distressed that the Lord's protest had revealed the illegal nature of this shameful hearing. It was clear to everyone present that the retired High Priest was red-faced. Noticing the priest's troubled response, one of the court officers standing close by, slapped Jesus on the face with the palm of his hand, yelling, "How dare You answer the High Priest in such a disrespectful way?"[33]

> The court officer knew that the law was being broken by the way that Jesus was being unfairly questioned. By striking the Lord he was trying to cover up its illegalities. But in doing so, he shamefully added to the injustice and mockery of this hearing.

Jesus, not surprisingly, responded to the officer, asking, "If I have answered in a rude manner, explain to Me My rudeness. But if I have answered in a correct manner"—which was clearly the case—"then why did you hit Me?" Now Jesus had every right, under the law, to ask such a question, for He was obviously being unlawfully treated.[(o) 34]

---

32 John 18:20, 21
33 John 18:22
34 John 18:23

Frustrated by this, and unable to make further progress in his questioning, Annas sent Jesus, still illegally bound, to another part of the palace, to appear before Caiaphas, the High Priest, and the Jewish court, the Sanhedrin.[35]

## —Jesus Is Tried at Night Before Caiaphas and the Sanhedrin < Early Friday Morning, After Midnight, Nisan 14, Spring, A.D. 31 (7/7) > {Matthew 26:57, 59-68, 71-75; Mark 14:53, 55-65, 69-72; Luke 22:54, 58-65; John 18:24-27}

Accordingly, Jesus was taken to appear before Caiaphas, the incumbent High Priest. As High Priest, Caiaphas was in charge of the Great Sanhedrin—the highest legal authority in the nation of Israel. Ever since Jesus had cast the moneychangers out of the Temple three and a half years earlier [*Harmony* 3:1-5], the Sanhedrin had been diligently seeking to find some way of putting an abrupt end to the ministry of the Lord. Thus, everyone who was important in the Jewish national leadership—especially those who were seeking the Lord's death—was present that night. This included a significant number of the chief priests, scribes, and elders.[36]

> The Great Sanhedrin was composed of 71 members, usually with the High Priest as the chairman. In court trials, the witnesses against the accused served as the prosecutors, while the Sanhedrin itself served as the defenders of the accused. There were no official prosecutors or defense advocates. Hebrew law required that the members of this legal body were to be men of compassion and of the highest moral character. This was essential, for the members of the Sanhedrin served not only as the judges in the cases brought before the court but also as defenders of the accused. Indeed, by law, they were to do everything they could to make sure that an accused person would get a fair trial and receive as much of the benefit of the doubt as possible. [*Harmony* 2:37][(p)] [[1]]
>
> When the court usually convened, the members of the Sanhedrin would sit in a semi-circle, with the chairman in the center. They would sit cross-legged, and bare-footed. Each judge wore a turban. A quorum consisted of 23 members. Most likely, at this particular meeting of the Sanhedrin, perhaps only the minimum number of the members were

---

35 John 18:24

36 Matthew 26:57; Mark 14:53; Luke 22:54; John 18:24

present—those who especially hated the Lord. Without doubt, those on the Sanhedrin who had a tendency to be supportive of the ministry of Jesus—such as Joseph of Arimathea [*Harmony* 18:6, 8], and Nicodemus [*Harmony* 3:10-24; 11:30; 18:8]—were not present. But, in any case, Jewish law was violated by the conduction of this session in the middle of the night.[(q)] [2]

For some time, the members of the Sanhedrin had tried to find witnesses who would bear false testimony against Jesus so that they could pin upon Him a charge that was worthy of death—that is, something that would show that Jesus was plotting the overthrow of the Roman government. But according to Jewish law, the witnesses—and there had to be more than one—were to come forward on their own. They were not to be solicited by the court. In any case, it was obviously quite illegal to have false witnesses of any kind to appear before the Sanhedrin. Nevertheless, in this case, these false witnesses were presented before the court to accuse Jesus. Even though a number of these witnesses appeared before the Sanhedrin, their testimony was so inconsistent with each other that no sustainable charge could be found. According to the law, because of their inconsistent testimony, Jesus should have been immediately released. However, of course, He wasn't.[(r)] [37]

But later on, two witnesses were brought forward on a different charge altogether. One such witness declared, "We heard this Man say, 'I am able to destroy the awesome Temple of God and within three days, I can build it back the exact same way it was before I destroyed it.'" The other witness stood up to claim, saying, "We heard, with our own ears, this Man say, 'I am able to demolish the Temple built with hands, and then, within three days, I will able to construct another Temple in its place, without using hands.'"[38]

Now, if these charges—certainly thin in nature—could be proven, it just *might* serve a double purpose. First, the Jews could condemn Jesus as worthy of death by making such a blasphemous claim regarding the Temple which was held to be holy and sacred by all the people in Israel. Second—even though it was quite a stretch—the Romans could charge Jesus with a death sentence for making a foolish claim regarding the Temple which they themselves had helped renovate. Indeed, both the Jews and the Romans considered the Temple to be a very special place

[37] Matthew 26:59, 60; Mark 14:55, 56
[38] Matthew 26:60, 61; Mark 14:57, 58

of personal and national pride. But nevertheless, even a casual observer could see that even if such a charge against Jesus were true, it was hardly a crime worthy of the severe death penalty!

Unfortunately for the Jewish leaders, it was obvious that these two testimonies, while similar, did not agree sufficiently with each other, thus negating them as valid charges against Jesus. Once again, according to the law, Jesus should have been instantly released. But of course, again, He wasn't.[(s) 39]

While all this was transpiring, and sometime after he first denied His Lord [*Harmony* 17:28, 29], Peter returned to the fire to warm himself. While he was standing there by the gate, another one of the servant girls looked intently at him. She declared to the other bystanders, "This man was with Jesus the Nazarene! Yes, he is definitely one of His disciples!" Then, turning to Peter, she said directly to him, "You are also one of them. Indeed, you are one of His disciples, aren't you?"[(t) 40]

All the people at the fire, egged on by the charge of the servant girl, also demanded of Peter, saying, "Aren't you one of His disciples? Tell us, man!"[(u) 41]

Once more, Peter denied this accusation, but this time with an oath, affirming, "I do not know this Man! No, I am not one of His disciples! Don't you get it?" [*Harmony* 16:61, 63][(v) 42]

About an hour later, another servant, a relative of Malchus—the one whose ear Peter had cut off [*Harmony* 17:19]—began to insist, saying, "It is a fact that this man was with the One named Jesus! There is no doubt that he, too, is a Galilean!" To Peter, the servant added, "Wasn't it you whom I saw in the Garden of Gethsemane with Him? Yes, it was you! I'm sure it was! I can tell by your accent that you are a Galilean, just like Jesus!" And others standing nearby made the same kind of charges against Peter.[(w) 43]

Peter now started to curse and swear. "Don't you get it? I do not know this Man!" he cried out. "Man, I do not know what you're talking about!" While Peter was still speaking these lying words, he heard a rooster crowing yet a second

---

39 Mark 14:59

40 Matthew 26:71; Mark 14:69; Luke 22:58; John 18:25

41 John 18:25

42 Matthew 26:72; Mark 14:70; Luke 22:58; John 18:25

43 Matthew 26:73; Mark 14:70; Luke 22:59; John 18:26

time. At that very second, standing some distance away, Jesus turned and looked directly at Peter. The disciple sadly remembered the words of the Lord which He had spoken to him a few hours previously, saying, "Before a rooster crows two times, you will have denied Me three times!" [*Harmony* 16:63] Distraught, Peter left the courtroom area, openly bewailing his failure to remain faithful to His Lord![(x) 44]

A short time later, back in the Sanhedrin courtroom, the High Priest stood up, came close to Jesus, and challenged Him, "Why are You refusing to answer these charges? Can't You give a satisfactory answer to us regarding what these witnesses have been testifying against You?" But Jesus did not answer with a single word! Finally, a frustrated Caiaphas demanded of Him, saying, "I command of You, by the Name of the living God, to tell us if You are the Christ, the Son of God—the Blessed One—even the Messiah!" [*Harmony* 17:51][45]

Jesus answered back to Caiaphas in clear a tone, "Yes! I am! You have said it correctly. However, I must tell you that in the future, you will see the Son of Man sitting on the right hand of power—with all His glory and authority—coming in the clouds of heaven!" By this, Jesus clearly claimed to be the Son of God who would exhibit the dramatic power of full divinity at His Second Coming in the yet distant future.[46]

Tearing his robes, Caiaphas exclaimed, "Blasphemy! He has blasphemed! We don't need any more witnesses! Listen! With your own ears you have heard this blasphemy. Don't you all agree?"[47]

And, indeed, all the members of the Sanhedrin agreed with Caiaphas, as they condemned Jesus, by crying out in unison, "Yes! He certainly deserves death!" [*Harmony* 18:6][48]

> Several illegal things had just taken place. First, Jesus as the accused could not be convicted on His own testimony. That was clearly against the law. Second, the High Priest was forbidden by Biblical law to tear his robes—robes which represented the righteousness of God. And when doing so, a High Priest was to be put to death. [Leviticus 10:6] Third,

---

44 Matthew 26:74, 75; Mark 14:71, 72; Luke 22:60-62; John 18:27

45 Matthew 26:62, 63; Mark 14:60, 61

46 Matthew 26:64; Mark 14:62

47 Matthew 26:65, 66; Mark 14:63, 64

48 Matthew 26:66; Mark 14:64

Hebrew law said that if *all* the members of the Sanhedrin should declare a defendant guilty, he must go free! This seemingly strange law was put in place because the members of the court served as the defendant's advocates. And so, if there were not at least one member of the court to vote to acquit the accused, it was thought that the defendant had not been given a fair trial—that is, the court was stacked against him. Fourth, the vote to condemn or to acquit a defendant was to be made by one person at a time, starting with the youngest and ending with the oldest. A vote was not to be given in unison, or by acclamation. This is because the law forbade anything that seemed like mob rule. Fifth, Jewish law declared that, before a judgment was made, the members of the court had first to present statements—or evidence—in favor of the accused, so that he would get all the benefit of the doubt. But in this particular trial, none of these procedures were followed, not one![y]

At this point, those who had been keeping guard of Jesus began to ridicule Him with cruel, hateful words. They also began to beat Him with their fists! Some spat in His face. Others slapped His face with their hands! Someone blindfolded the Lord, and sarcastically asked Him, "Prophesy to us—You who claim to be the Christ—who it was that just slapped You!" And there were others who said even more terrible, blasphemous things to Jesus. Obviously, all such shameful treatment was illegal in the extreme.[z] [49]

## —Jesus Is Tried in the Daytime Before Caiaphas and the Sanhedrin < Friday Morning, After 5:30 a.m., Nisan 14, Spring, A.D. 31 (7/7) > {Matthew 27:1-10; Mark 15:1; Luke 22:66-71}

Early that same morning after sunrise, the entire Sanhedrin, along with the other leaders of the Jews—composed of chief priests and scribes—quickly held another council meeting among themselves. Because it was illegal for the Sanhedrin to meet at night, they must, in order to have their decree of death against the Lord considered valid by the Roman authorities, have a second trial during the daylight hours. As this extra daytime meeting was convened, Jesus was brought before the Sanhedrin again. However, even if the first trial had been legal—which of course, it wasn't—this second trial, according to the law, was to be conducted at least a day later, not just an hour or so after the first trial.[aa] [50]

[49] Matthew 26:67, 68; Mark 14:65; Luke 22:63-65

[50] Matthew 27:1; Mark 15:1; Luke 22:66

During this court session, the members of the Sanhedrin continued to ply Jesus with questions as they had done earlier. They demanded of Him, saying, "If you claim to be the Messiah, then tell us!" [*Harmony* 17:45][51]

At first, Jesus said nothing. But as the members of the court persisted in their questioning, Jesus, finally, with some exasperation, replied, "If I were to tell you that I am the Messiah, you would not believe Me. And should I ask you a question, neither would you answer Me. But I will tell you this: Soon after this trial, the Son of Man will sit down at the right side of the throne of God, even the position of power in heaven!" Here, Jesus referred to the time when He would ascend into heaven and dwell again with His Father. [*Harmony* 18:98][52]

Together, the court cried out to Jesus, "So then, by Your own statement, do You claim to be the Son of God?"[53]

Jesus answered, "Yes! I do!"[54]

At this, the whole Sanhedrin concurred, saying, "Why do we need to bring any more witnesses? We have heard from His own mouth that He claims to be the Christ!" Accordingly, they openly condemned Jesus to death. [*Harmony* 18:6][55]

> This final trial before the Sanhedrin was riddled with illegalities. First, as in the initial trial, Jesus was condemned by His own testimony, not by that of witnesses. This was absolutely against the law. Second, no one spoke in the Lord's favor. This too, was prohibited by law. Third, the vote, as in the first trial, was by acclamation, not by a one-by-one open vote. Fourth, in the case of a death sentence, a second trial had to be held to ratify the fairness of a proposed execution. However, such a second trial was not to be held until, at least, the afternoon of the second day—not just an hour or so after the first trial, as this one was. This was to provide the judges a chance for quiet reflection on their initial decision. And furthermore, before a death sentence could be ratified, Jewish law required a very elaborate procedure to make sure that the defendant was truly deserving of death. Because life was considered very

---

51 Luke 22:66, 67
52 Luke 22:67-69
53 Luke 22:70
54 Luke 22:70
55 Luke 22:71

sacred to the Hebrews [Exodus 20:13], Jewish law was set up to give an accused person every benefit of the doubt, and every opportunity to be found innocent. Under this system of law, executions were very rare among the Jews. That was the direct intent of the law. Obviously, this procedure was hardly followed in the case of Jesus! In short, it was the determination of the court that the Savior would be condemned—legally or not!(bb) [1]

Judas, who had betrayed Jesus, now realized that, after the Lord's condemnation by the court, He was not going to do anything to save Himself. Accordingly, Judas began to have grave doubts whether he had done the right thing in betraying his Lord. It was never his intention that Jesus should die. He had hoped that once Jesus was brought before trial the Lord would declare Himself to be the true Messiah of Israel, and take power to Himself. Judas had felt that Jesus was not assertive enough—that He needed someone to help Him out. Judas also believed that when Jesus was forced to declare Himself the Messiah, He would give Judas the credit for engineering the whole thing. He further believed that, to honor Judas's wise action, Jesus would appoint him to be the chief of His advisors, or to be one of His associate leaders. And, to top it all off, Judas reasoned that he would walk away with not only a position of power *and* the Lord's praise, *but also* with 30 pieces of silver in his purse! Judas thought that he had a fool-proof plan! It could not fail. But, alas, the Lord did not react to the trial the way that Judas figured He would. Indeed, everything seemed to collapse around the betrayer.(cc) [2]

Then suddenly, after Jesus was condemned, Judas—the traitorous disciple—came forward dramatically to return the 30 pieces of silver he had received from the Jews as payment for the betrayal of his Lord. [*Harmony* 14:24] To the chief priests and elders, he cried, "I'm a sinner! I have betrayed the innocent blood of this Man!"(dd) [56]

But they shot back at him, "So what? Can't you see that we don't care?" The betrayer threw the pieces of silver into the Temple area, and left the presence of the court. Immediately, Judas went out and hanged himself! But, when hanging himself, Judas fell heavily to the ground. When he did, his abdomen ruptured. [Acts 1:18](ee) [57]

---

[56] Matthew 27:3, 4

[57] Matthew 27:4, 5

(Later on, the chief priests took the money which Judas had returned and counseled among themselves. They reasoned, saying, "It is quite against the law to put such money into the Temple treasury box, because it was used to buy someone's death!" [Deuteronomy 23:18] Instead, they decided to use the silver to purchase a potter's field as a burial site for those paupers who had no known relatives. For this reason, this cemetery was called for some years, Hakeldama [Acts 1:19]—the "Field of Blood"—a place purchased by the betrayal of the Lord's "blood." This event was a fulfillment of the prophecies of Jeremiah and Zechariah, who had said, "I took the 30 pieces of silver, the price of which had been set by the sons of Israel, and with it, purchased a Potter's Field, as God had instructed me." [Jeremiah 18:2-12; 19:1-15; Zechariah 11:13] It was also a fulfillment of a prophecy in Psalms, which said, "Let his place of living to remain desolate. May no one live there." [Psalm 69:25; Acts 1:20])[(ff)] [58]

Now that Jesus was officially convicted before the Sanhedrin, the officers of the court led Jesus, still bound, to the court of Pilate, the Roman governor. It was necessary for the governor to ratify their sentence of death upon the Lord. That is because, under the occupation of Rome, Israel had no authority to execute anyone without the empire's direct consent.[59]

### — The Lord's First Trial Before Pilate
### < Friday Morning, Nisan 14, A.D. 31 (7/7) >
### {Matthew 27:2, 11-14; Mark 15:1-5; Luke 23:1-7; John 18:28-38}

It was very early in the morning as the angry crowd followed a condemned Jesus [*Harmony* 17:55] to the official Jerusalem residence of the governor, Pontius Pilate. Normally, Pilate lived in Caesarea—the official Roman capital of Judea—which was a Mediterranean seacoast city, some 50 miles to the northwest of Jerusalem. But because it was the time of the Passover, Pilate was in Jerusalem to make sure that peace was preserved in the city that was the center of Jewish worship. His residence in Jerusalem was called the Praetorium, which means "pertaining to a praetor," or a Roman magistrate. However, the Jews refused, themselves, to enter the Praetorium, staying rather in the court outside. This was because they were to eat the Passover meal later that day, and to enter a non-Jew's house on the Passover would defile them, thus prohibiting them from celebrating

---

58 Matthew 27:6-10

59 Matthew 27:2; Mark 15:1

the Passover! [*Harmony* 17:61] Thus it was that Jesus stood inside the Praetorium with Pilate while the crowd remained outside its doors. [*Harmony* 13:36](gg) 60

> Who was the Roman governor, Pontius Pilate? Pilate had been appointed governor of Judea about five years previously. He was a ruthless man, noted for his inflexible actions. Because of his impulsive nature he had caused a great deal of trouble for himself by doing things that unnecessarily upset both the Jews and non-Jews of Palestine. [*Harmony* 12:67] Already, the Roman emperor, Tiberius, was upset by some of his foolhardy actions. Any more problems Pilate might have with the Jews could easily lead to his removal as governor. To be sure, Pilate was well aware of this fact.[1]
>
> Further, it is impossible to conceive that Pilate did not already have a basic knowledge of who Jesus was and what His ministry entailed. First, as the Roman governor of Judea, his main responsibility was to preserve order throughout the province. Thus, any possibility of an insurrection against Rome would have been reported to him. Certainly, the Jewish leaders, who hated Jesus, would have made the work of Jesus known to Pilate, in the hope that the Roman governor, on his own, might step in and end the Lord's ministry. In fact, the Jews had been trying for some time to find a reasonable cause for the Roman authorities to halt the work of the Lord. [*Harmony* 14:85-91] Up until this time, of course, they had failed. Second, there were Roman soldiers present when Jesus was arrested in the garden. [*Harmony* 17:10] These soldiers, no doubt, were there at the command of Pilate, or, at least, at the command of someone who would have reported directly to the governor, for the Jewish leaders had no authority to give orders of any kind to these soldiers. So then, all told, Pilate clearly had to have a working knowledge of the Lord and His ministry.[2]

When Pilate came out into the court to meet the crowd standing outside [*Harmony* 17:60], he asked them, "What charge do you bring against this Man?"[61]

Because they did not have a real charge to bring against the Lord—one that would satisfy a Roman court, that is—the Jewish leaders sidestepped the

---

60 Matthew 27:2; Mark 15:1; Luke 23:1; John 18:28

61 John 18:29

question and answered indirectly, saying, "If we didn't have a charge against this criminal, we would have not brought Him to you, would we?"[62]

> The Jewish leadership was surprised at Pilate's demand that they bring a specific charge against Jesus. They had been used to having him make judicial decisions—even pronounce death sentences—without closely inspecting the truthfulness of the charges brought against an accused individual. But this time it was different. There was something about the bearing of Jesus, as well as what he had heard about the Lord, that caused the governor, on this particular occasion, to dig deeper into finding out the real truth regarding this accused Man. Indeed, this time Pilate would not be railroaded.

Because the Jewish leaders gave an evasive response to His question, Pilate then sought, in a roundabout way, to understand their true thinking. He said to them, "So you won't tell me the specific charges against this Man! Well, then, in that case, pass judgment upon Him based upon your own law. Leave me out of it altogether!"[63]

Now the Jews were being forced to give a specific answer to Pilate's question. But even at that, they still hesitated. After discussing the matter among themselves, they finally answered Pilate, saying, "By the law of the Romans, we cannot put anyone to death without your approval." By giving this answer, the Jews admitted that they believed that Jesus had done something worthy of death . . . yet, they still refused to say what the Lord's supposed crime was! Also, when the Jews implied that they wanted Pilate to ratify a death sentence upon Jesus, they were referring to an execution by crucifixion—the common Roman execution process of the day. In doing so, they were fulfilling a prediction of Jesus [*Harmony* 13:99] regarding the manner of His own death.[64]

But Pilate still insisted that a specific, detailed charge be made against the Lord. Finally, then, having no real choice, the Jewish leadership came up with a series of charges—of course, all patently false. They accused Jesus, saying, "First, we have found this Man subverting the entire nation. Second, He has forbidden the people to pay taxes to Caesar. [*Harmony* 14:85-92] And third, He has made Himself to be a King—in clear opposition to Caesar. He has called Himself the

---

62 John 18:30

63 John 18:31

64 John 18:31, 32

Messiah." However, while Jesus would later claim to be a King [*Harmony* 17:66, 67], it certainly was not the kind of kingship that was any real threat whatsoever to Caesar.[65]

Turning back toward the Praetorium, Pilate, responding to the third charge, faced Jesus and asked Him directly, "Are *You* the King of the Jews?"[66]

"It is as you say!" was the Lord's simple reply. [*Harmony* 17:65] At this admission, the chief priests and elders shouted accusations at the Savior. However, besides this simple admission, the Lord remained totally silent, giving no response in rebuttal to His vicious accusers.[67]

Surprised at this, Pilate further questioned Jesus, asking, "Do You hear what they're saying against You? Do You have nothing else to say in response to their charges? Why, listen to all the terrible things they are saying about You!" Still Jesus said nothing. Now Pilate was quite amazed at the Lord's total refusal to respond further to even one of the charges that were being leveled against Him.[68]

So, declaring that he would interview Jesus privately away from the noise of the crowd, Pilate reentered the Praetorium. Once alone with Jesus, Pilate said to Him, "Are You really the King of the Jews? That is, do the Romans have anything to fear from Your public work?"[69]

Jesus answered by asking Pilate a question. He inquired, "Do you ask this question of Me for your own personal information? Or, do you ask, simply because they have told you that I claim to be the King of the Jews?" Jesus was, in effect, by His first question, asking if Pilate was personally curious about the purpose of the Lord's ministry, so that he could better understand what salvation would mean to him.[70]

Surprised—and stung—by the Lord's penetrating question, Pilate shot back, "I'm not a Jew, am I? I'm not interested in Your nation's religion. Remember, it is Your own people and their religious leaders who have brought You here to

---

65 Luke 23:2
66 Matthew 27:11; Mark 15:2; Luke 23:3
67 Matthew 27:11, 12; Mark 15:2, 3; Luke 23:3
68 Matthew 27:13, 14; Mark 15:4, 5
69 John 18:33
70 John 18:34

me. So, tell me: What terrible thing have You done to cause them to do this to You?"[71]

Jesus answered, "My kingdom does not belong to this world. If My kingdom were of this realm, then My disciples would fight as hard as they could to prevent the Jews from turning Me over to you. But again, My kingdom does not belong to this world. So, you have nothing to fear from Me as far as leading a rebellion against Rome."[72]

Still puzzled, Pilate asked, "So are you a King . . . or not? Is that what You claim . . . or not? If so, what, then, is the nature of Your Kingship?"[73]

Jesus calmly replied, "Yes! I am a King, as you have indicated—but not in the earthly sense. My purpose when I was born into the world was to bear witness to the truth of God and His gift of salvation. [*Harmony* 17:101] And everyone who is interested in understanding the truth of salvation will listen to My voice as I speak the truth." Clearly, here, Jesus was appealing to the heart of Pilate.[74]

In fact, the governor asked Jesus, "What, then, is this truth of which You speak?"[75]

But before Jesus could answer Pilate's amazing inquiry, the governor, hardening his heart, left Jesus and returned back to the crowd. While Pilate had personally rebuffed Jesus, nevertheless, he, as the governor, was determined to set Him free. He was now convinced, beyond any reasonable doubt that, whatever the kingdom of Jesus entailed, it was not in any way a threat to the secular sovereignty of Rome. So the governor announced to the chief priests and the crowd, officially declaring, "After examining the Accused, I find no fault at all in this Man. He does not deserve death." Pilate had declared that Jesus was clearly innocent of all the charges which the Jews had brought against Him, the first such declaration in the whole farcical trial. [*Harmony* 17:78/, 82, 94][76]

---

71 John 18:35
72 John 18:36
73 John 18:37
74 John 18:37
75 John 18:38
76 Luke 23:4; John 18:38

But undeterred by Pilate's firm declaration of the Lord's innocence, the crowd still clamored for the Savior's death by crying out, "This Man has agitated all the people, from Galilee, even to Judea." When Pilate heard that Jesus had labored for awhile in the northern province of Galilee, he questioned the Jewish leaders further about that. It was then that he discovered that the Lord was actually from Nazareth in the province of Galilee, and that He had spent most of His time during His ministry laboring there.[77]

So Pilate, now knowing for certain that Jesus was from Galilee, sent the Master to appear before Herod, who was, at the time, also in Jerusalem for the Passover celebration. This was because Galilee was under the jurisdiction of Herod Antipas, the tetrarch—a ruler on a slightly lower level than that of a king.[78]

> By doing so, Pilate hoped to pass the responsibility of what to do with Jesus on to Herod. And too, Pilate should have promptly released Jesus. After all, he had firmly declared the Lord to be innocent! [*Harmony* 17:76]

### —Jesus Is Tried Before Herod Antipas
### < Friday Morning, Nisan 14, Spring, A.D. 31 (7/7) >
### {Luke 23:8-12}

Herod Antipas was most happy when he first saw Jesus standing before him, for he had heard a lot about the Lord and His ministry. For a long time he had wanted to see Jesus for himself. [*Harmony* 8:74] He especially wanted to see the Lord work a miracle in his presence. [*Harmony* 12:86/][79]

> This was the same Herod, the tetrarch who had executed John the Baptist. [*Harmony* 8:66-70] Herod had thought for some time that maybe Jesus was John resurrected from the dead! [*Harmony* 8:74] But, in any case, by doing something nice for Jesus, he hoped that he might be able to expunge from his conscience the guilt for having ruthlessly executed John.

Accordingly, Herod questioned Jesus for a long time. He had all sorts of sick and infirm people brought before the Master. By doing so, Herod tried to force the

---

77 Luke 23:5, 6

78 Luke 23:7

79 Luke 23:8

Lord to perform a miracle for him. But Christ said absolutely nothing in response to Herod's demands. Neither did the Lord do anything—He just stood there! All this time, the Jewish religious leaders—the chief priests and scribes—were watching nearby, viciously condemning the Lord. Angry at Christ's refusal to answer his questions, or to even recognize him as a ruler, Herod increased his threats toward Jesus. Finally, Herod had the Savior decked out in a splendid king-like robe, and he allowed the soldiers to taunt and ridicule the Savior as the supposed King of the Jews. However, Herod, though angered by Jesus, did not have the nerve to pass a death sentence upon Him. But neither did he release the Lord, as he clearly should have done. So, the tetrarch had Jesus sent back to Pilate for the Roman governor to once again take care of the matter.[(hh)] [80]

Nevertheless, a benefit for Herod was gained that day. Previously, Herod and Pilate had been at variance with each other. Because Pilate showed great honor to Herod by sending Jesus to him, Herod and Pilate became good friends from that time onward.[81]

### —Jesus Is Tried a Second Time Before Pilate
### < Friday Morning, Nisan 14, Spring, A.D. 31 (7/7) >
### {Matthew 27:15-31; Mark 15:6-20; Luke 23:13-25; John 18:39-19:16}

When Pilate, clearly frustrated, heard that Jesus was sent back to him for judgment, he was determined to quickly release the Lord, which was consistent with what he had previously ruled. [*Harmony* 17:76] So the governor declared to the Jewish leaders—the chief priests and officers—as well as the entire crowd who were demanding the Lord's death, "This Man, whom you have brought to me, you have accused of encouraging the masses to rebel against Rome. Well, as you know, I have already carefully questioned the Accused. And, as I have previously told you [*Harmony* 17:76], I have declared that all your charges against Him have no foundation whatsoever—certainly nothing worthy of death, as you demand. Not only that, Herod has interrogated the Prisoner and has sent Him back to me without declaring Him guilty of anything worthy of punishment—certainly not death." This was the second time that Pilate had declared Jesus to be innocent of all charges. [*Harmony* 17:76, 94] But then . . . Pilate made a disastrous mistake when he added, "Therefore, I will scourge Him and then release Him!"[82]

---

80 Luke 23:9-11

81 Luke 23:12

82 Luke 23:13-16

> But, if Pilate really believed—as he twice declared—that Jesus was innocent, why then did he propose that Jesus be repeatedly beaten with a whip? Obviously, a judge should release a person who was declared innocent, and certainly, an innocent man should not be scourged! The Jews now knew that Pilate was cracking. If, they reasoned, Pilate was willing to whip an innocent Man, then, with some more pushing, he might be willing to kill that same Man!

Instead of being pacified by Pilate's proposal, the Jews cried out even more dramatically for the death of Jesus! While sitting on his judgment seat, and pondering how to respond to this latest predicament, Pilate received a message from his wife. It said, "Have nothing to do with this innocent Man! In a dream that I had last night, I suffered a great deal regarding Him!"[(ii) 83]

> With this new perspective, Pilate was even more committed to releasing Jesus. But how could he accomplish this when the Jews were so persistently clamoring for the Lord's crucifixion? Then a plan came to his mind.

It was a custom, during the Passover season, for the Roman governor—in order to show good will toward the Jews—to release one criminal whom the people chose to be set free. As of yet, Pilate had not released any such prisoner.[84]

It so happened at this time that there was a convict in custody with a notorious reputation. His name was Barabbas—a name meaning, "father's son." This evil man had recently been captured. He was part of a plot of insurrection against both the Romans and the Jews in the city of Jerusalem. His violence against the people had resulted in robbery and even murder! The entire nation was relieved that this dangerous criminal was off their streets. Barabbas had been convicted and he, along with two of his cohorts, were to be crucified that same day. Certainly, Pilate reasoned, the Jews would not want Barabbas walking the streets again, committing even more vicious criminal acts! If they had to choose, they most definitely would want Jesus to go free, and not Barabbas! Anyway, that is what Pilate logically reasoned![(jj) 85]

So, the governor addressed the people whom he had gathered before him, saying, "You have this custom that I release one prisoner during your Passover

---

83 Matthew 27:19

84 Matthew 27:15; Mark 15:6; Luke 23:17

85 Matthew 27:16; Mark 15:7; Luke 23:19; John 18:40

festival. As of yet, I have released no one. So now, I will let you choose. Which one do you want me to release back into your society? Do you want me to release Barabbas? Or do you want me to release Jesus, who is called the Christ, the King of the Jews?" Even though Pilate knew that the Jews had Jesus arrested because of their jealousy of Him, he was sure that they would prefer having Jesus go free rather than the violent Barabbas. The people had previously requested that, according to custom, a prisoner be released. So certainly, Pilate thought, they would request such freedom for Jesus![86]

That is why Pilate was justifiably shocked when the chief priests and the elders incited the crowd to cry out Barabbas's name, and not the Lord's. This meant that the crowd wanted Barabbas to be released and Jesus to be killed! In fact, the Roman governor was so shocked by their response that he thought that they must have misunderstood his initial question! So Pilate again said to the Jews, "No! No! I don't mean which one do you want me to *execute*, but rather, which one do you want me to *release*? So once more, which one do you want me to *release*: Barabbas . . . or Jesus?"[87]

But the crowd had heard Pilate correctly, for they cried back at him, "No! Don't release this Man, Jesus! Away with this Man! Instead, we want Barabbas released!"[88]

Amazed, Pilate asked of them again, "Tell me once more, what is it that you want me to do with Jesus, your Messiah—the One you have called the King of the Jews?"[89]

In unison, they screamed their verdict, "Let Him be crucified!"[90]

Nevertheless, Pilate, undeterred by the crowd's loud demand, remained determined to release Jesus. He tried to argue with the crowd, but they were not listening to him anymore. Instead they continued to chant, "Crucify Him! Crucify Him! Crucify Him!"[91]

---

86 Matthew 27:17, 18; Mark 15:8-10; John 18:39
87 Matthew 27:20, 21; Mark 15:11
88 Matthew 27:21; Luke 23:18; John 18:40
89 Matthew 27:22; Mark 15:12
90 Matthew 27:22; Mark 15:13
91 Luke 23:20, 21

Above the noise Pilate bellowed out, "But why? What wrong has He committed?"[92]

Never letting up a bit, they cried out with even more impassioned fervor, "Let Him be crucified!"[93]

For a third time [*Harmony* 17:76, 82], Pilate declared that Jesus was innocent, saying, "Why? I ask you again, why? What evil has He committed? As I have repeatedly said, I find that He has done nothing that warrants crucifixion! Once again, I say that I will scourge Him, and then release Him!" But the crowd became deafening in their demand that Jesus be crucified. Their relentless yelling continued to wear the governor down even further. The people were sensing that Pilate was on the verge of giving in to their hateful demands.[94]

In a last-ditch effort to change the thinking of the crowd, Pilate had Jesus scourged in front of the people. [*Harmony* 17:111][95]

> Just maybe, Pilate reasoned, this cruel torture would silence their demand that Jesus be crucified. According to Roman law, only a condemned person could be scourged. The fact that Jesus—three times declared to be innocent [*Harmony* 17:76, 82, 94]—was scourged, was a gross miscarriage of justice. But Pilate had hoped that such a scourging would satisfy the thirst of the Jews for punishing the Lord. Instead, it had the opposite effect. Once they saw the flowing blood of Jesus, they wanted more blood! That is why they remained relentless in their calls for the Lord's death.[1]
>
> The Roman scourge was a terrible means of torture. It consisted of a whip made of several leather strips. The strips were embedded with metal objects, or bones, for the purpose of deeply cutting the flesh when administered by a man expert in the cruel craft of scourging. So cruel was this punishment that the Jews, under their law, limited the strokes of a single scourging to 39 lashes. However, the Romans had no such limit to the amount of times one might be beaten. Jesus was scourged by the Roman method. Often in a scourging the skin and muscles were deeply torn, which led to significant bleeding. According to the Roman

92 Matthew 27:23; Mark 15:14
93 Matthew 27:23; Mark 15:14
94 Luke 23:22, 23
95 John 19:1

custom, a criminal was scourged just short of the point of death. Also, a condemned person might be beaten on any part of the body—even the face![2]

After the Lord's scourging was completed, some of the Roman soldiers placed Jesus in the center of the Praetorium for all to see. With the entire contingent of soldiers surrounding the Lord, they stripped Him, and dressed Him in a purple robe. After fashioning a crown of thorns, they placed it upon His brow. With a reed placed in His hand, they all bowed down before Him as though He were a king, and they mockingly cried out, "Hail to the King of the Jews!" Then they spat on Him. Taking the reed from His hand, they used it to beat the thorns deep into His head! They followed up that abuse with many slaps and punches to His face! Amazingly, all this was done to One who had been declared, on three separate occasions, to be totally innocent! [*Harmony* 17:76, 82, 94][96]

After subjecting the Lord to all this indescribable agony and disgrace, Pilate came out to the people and declared, "Behold! I bring this Man out to you, so that you shall know that I find Him to be completely innocent!" Apparently, Pilate still believed—although foolishly—that the Lord's sufferings showcased in front of the people would arouse compassion within the hearts of the Jewish mob. Thus, Jesus was brought out and placed directly in front the entire crowd. They, close at hand, could now see the Savior, beaten and bleeding, still dressed in the purple robe, with the crown of thorns on His head. Then Pilate, pointing to Him—and with no little drama—loudly announced for all to hear, "Behold! The Man!"[97]

Standing next to Jesus was Barabbas. The contrast between the two men was striking. The one was a vile, hardened murderer. The other one was the gentle Savior of the world. There could be no real doubt as to which one was worthy of death . . . and which one should be released!(kk)

Would the governor's plan work? Obviously not! For, when the crowd saw Jesus paraded before them, they, along with the chief priests and officers, cried out all the more, "Crucify Him! Crucify Him!"[98]

---

96 Matthew 27:27-31; Mark 15:16-20; John 19:2, 3

97 John 19:4, 5

98 John 19:6

In frustration, and with no little sarcasm, Pilate answered back, "You take Him then and crucify Him! And why? Because I find Him innocent!"[99]

The Jews realized that Pilate was not yet fully determined to have Jesus crucified. They knew that they must still convince him to sentence the Lord to death. Therefore, they argued with him, saying, "We Jews have a law against blasphemy. [Leviticus 24:15, 16] And that law says this Man must die because He has made Himself to be the Son of God! [*Harmony* 11:171, 172] And under our law, blasphemy is a sufficient cause for the death penalty!"[100]

> Normally, this type of reasoning would have had no impact on a Roman governor. Blasphemy was a religious crime—certainly not a political one. And Rome was not particularly interested in religious issues involving the Jews. However, in this case, things were different. The spirit of anger being generated by the Jewish leaders was reaching a fevered pitch. Of course, Pilate could easily put down any rebellion with a show of force. But, with his methods of control already being questioned by Caesar, Pilate knew that any rebellion—even one that had been successfully quelled—could still lead to his premature removal from office.

Fully aware that the Jews were resolute in their determination to kill Jesus, Pilate was genuinely frightened by the prospect that he was on the verge of executing an innocent Man who had claimed to be sent from God! [*Harmony* 17:74] Indeed, he knew that he must have a better understanding of what was happening in his own courtroom.[101]

Entering again into the Praetorium with Jesus, Pilate took Him aside and began earnestly to question Him once more. The governor, now sensing that he was standing in the presence of a divine Being, demanded of Jesus, "Where have You come from?" But this time, Jesus gave no answer. Irritated, the governor responded to the Lord's silence by saying, "Do You refuse to speak to Me? Have You forgotten that I have the authority to set you free . . . or to have You executed, if I so choose?"[102]

Hearing this, Jesus told the governor, "You really do not have any authority whatsoever, unless such authority be given to you from the God of heaven.

---

99 John 19:6
100 John 19:7
101 John 19:8
102 John 19:9, 10

Nevertheless, those who have brought Me here for your sentencing have committed a far greater sin than you, for they have known much better." At this point, Pilate left Jesus and returned to the crowd.[103]

Now Pilate was clearly afraid to execute Jesus. So he made yet other efforts to release Him. But all his efforts only caused the Jews to cry all the more for the Lord's death. The Jewish leaders charged, "If you don't have this Man killed, you are no friend of Caesar. Remember, every man who makes himself a king is in opposition to Caesar!" Hearing these words, Pilate became deeply concerned. As said before, because he was already in some trouble with Caesar, he could ill afford more stress involving the dictatorial Roman emperor. There was no telling what could happen to him if the Jews decided to complain to the Caesar. Even at that, Pilate would try one more time to save Jesus. His conscience was telling him that he must.[104]

Because the Jews had refused to enter the Praetorium with him, Pilate brought Jesus outside its gates to a place named "The Pavement"—which is called "Gabbatha" in the Hebrew language. There, the governor sat on a specially prepared elevated judgment seat in front of the people, so that all could have an unobstructed view and be able to hear distinctly every word he was about to speak. It was at least 6 a.m. when Pilate continued to plead with the angry crowd. Pointing to Jesus, he cried out, "Behold! Your King!"[(ll)] [105]

But they repeatedly cried back, "Crucify Him! Away with Him! Away with Him!"[106]

Pilate answered, "But do you really want me to crucify your King?" [*Harmony* 13:123/][107]

The chief Jewish priests loudly declared, "We have no king but Caesar!"[108]

For the Jews to declare that they had no king but Caesar shows the depth of their hatred for Jesus. In truth, they hated Caesar—they wanted him

---

103 John 19:11
104 John 19:12
105 John 19:13, 14
106 John 19:15
107 John 19:15
108 John 19:15

dead, too! But shockingly, it was now clear that they actually wanted Jesus dead even more than they did Caesar!

It was now patently apparent to Pilate that all was useless. There was no real hope left! The crowd was on the edge of complete anarchy. Pilate called for a bowl of water to be brought to him, and, with the entire crowd looking on, he publicly washed his hands in the water, as a sign of his own lack of complicity in pronouncing a death sentence upon the Lord—an innocent Man! The governor firmly declared, "I am innocent of this Man's blood! You see to that!"[109]

The crowd, now filled with a totally irrational rage, answered back, "Don't you worry! His blood will be upon both us and our children!"[(mm)] [110]

Only after hearing this did Pilate finally pronounce the sentence of death upon Jesus, so that the mob might be appeased. He knew that all was hopeless. So accordingly, he released Barabbas—the one who had been convicted of insurrection and murder—and had Jesus scourged a second time. [*Harmony* 17:95] This was because, under Roman law, any condemned criminal was to be scourged just prior to execution. They took off the kingly robe Jesus was wearing and dressed Him is His regular clothes. Next, Pilate delivered Jesus up to the crowd to do with Him as they wished. The angry mob grabbed hold of the Lord and jostled Him toward the place of crucifixion. [*Harmony* 10:72/; 17:118][(nn)] [111]

## The Crucifixion
## < Friday, About 8 A.M. Through 3 P.M., Nisan 14, Spring, A.D. 31 (7/7) >
## (Matthew 27:32-52, 54; Mark 15:21-41; Luke 23:26-49; John 19:17-30)

### — On the Way to the Crucifixion
### < Friday, About 8 A.M, 14 Nisan, Spring, A.D. 31 (7/7) >
### {Matthew 27:32; Mark 15:21; Luke 23:26-32; John 19:17}

After seizing Jesus, the crowd led Him away to be crucified. They required the Lord to carry His own cross to the place of the crucifixion. What Jesus carried was probably not the entire cross, but, rather, the cross bar that was to be fastened to the upright wooden beam that would be dropped into the ground. But because Jesus had been scourged severely, not once but twice [*Harmony*

---

109 Matthew 27:24

110 Matthew 27:25

111 Matthew 27:26, 31; Mark 15:15, 20; Luke 23:24, 25; John 19:16

17:95, 111], He was unable to bear the cross by Himself. So, they found in the crowd a man named Simon, the father of Alexander and Rufus. Simon was from the city of Cyrene, located in the nation of Libya in northern Africa. They compelled Simon to carry the Lord's cross as he walked behind the badly weakened Jesus.(oo) [112]

A huge multitude watched as Jesus staggered on. Among the crowd were women, who, seeing the suffering of the Savior, began to weep and mourn because of His obvious human anguish. Noticing the women, Jesus turned to them and said, "Daughters of Jerusalem, don't weep for Me! Rather cry for yourselves and all your children. Behold, the day will come when it will be said, 'Blessed are those who have no children, and the breasts that have never nursed!' That is when they will command the mountains, saying, 'Fall on us!' and to the hills, 'Cover us up!' [Revelation 1:7] My dear women, if they will do this to a green tree, just think what they will do to a dry one?"[113]

> What did Jesus mean by these cryptic words regarding a "green tree" and a "dry one"? In effect, Jesus was saying, "If this is the kind of suffering that will happen to One who has done no evil—the 'green tree'—just consider what will happen to those who are grave sinners—a 'dry tree'!" Also, earlier in His statement, Jesus referred to the time of the horrible siege and destruction of Jerusalem that would take place in A.D. 70, 39 years hence. He also referred to the time when those of Israel who had plotted and called for His death would face the Lord at His Second Coming. [Revelation 1:7]

As Jesus made His way to the crucifixion location, two other men, also condemned to death, went along with Him. [*Harmony* 17:116; 18:2](pp) [114]

### — The Crucifixion of Jesus
### < Friday, 9 A.M. — 3 P.M., Nisan 14, Spring, A.D. 31 (7/7) >
### {Matthew 27:33-52, 54-56; Mark 15:22-41; Luke 23:33-49; John 19:17-30}

Finally the entourage arrived to a certain place of execution called "The Place of the Skull" which is in Hebrew, "Golgotha." The Latin word for Golgotha is "Calvary." It was there that the Lord would be crucified. Obviously, being

112 Matthew 27:32; Mark 15:21; Luke 23:26; Luke 19:17

113 Luke 23:27-31

114 Luke 23:32

crucified was an excruciatingly painful experience. So, to help deaden the pain of a crucifixion slightly, those who were about to be executed were given some wine mixed with frankincense. But when this was offered to Jesus, He refused to drink it after barely tasting it. This was because He did not want anything to numb His sensibilities during the difficult hours ahead. He could not afford to face with a clouded mind, the temptation to free Himself from this terrible, unbelievable agony. [*Harmony* 2:34/2; 17:123. 131][(qq)] [115]

> Four Roman soldiers bore the responsibility of actually crucifying Jesus. According to custom, the clothes of the executed became the property of the executioners. So, just before Jesus was crucified, they removed the Lord's garments from Him. [*Harmony* 17:119]

And there, on Golgotha, they crucified Jesus by nailing His hands and feet to the cross! [*Harmony* 11:121; 18:47] It was about 9 o'clock, Friday morning. [*Harmony* 17:128] The two convicts who went to the place of execution with Him [*Harmony* 17:114] were crucified with Him, one on either side of Him. [*Harmony* 18:2] Thus the Scripture was fulfilled which says, "And He was counted among transgressors." [Isaiah 53:12] And, when He was actually being nailed to the cross, Jesus was overheard saying, "Father, forgive them! They are really unaware of what they are doing!"[116]

> Crucifixion was one the cruelest forms of torture and execution—possibly the worst—ever devised by man. It was calculated to be humiliating and extremely painful. Indeed, the person being crucified could live a long time in incredible agony. Not only was the pain extreme and unrelenting, it was also protracted, frequently lasting for days.[1]

> Most likely, the form of crucifixion that Jesus experienced was this: He was nailed by the wrists and the heels. His wrists were nailed to a crossbar that was fastened to a pole—or rough-hewn plank—that was dropped upright into a hole in the ground. His heels were fastened with a single nail to the upright plank between his heels. The upright plank was not more than six or seven feet tall. The entire cross, when fastened together, looked like a "T" or a "+" in appearance. Because the cross was relatively short, the Lord hung at about the eye level of those who were watching. The wounds from the scourging, the nails, the unnatural

---

115 Matthew 27:33, 34; Mark 15:22, 23; Luke 23:33; John 19:17

116 Matthew 27:35, 38; Mark 15:24, 25, 27, 28; Luke 23:33, 34; John 19:18, 24

position of the body, the exposure to the elements, and the taunts of the bystanders, all intensified the agony and humiliation of the Lord. Breathing was labored, and the pain excruciating. Thus, did Jesus, the Savior of the world, suffer.[(rr)] [(ss)]

Pontius Pilate commanded that a placard be attached to the cross, above the head of Jesus. It read, "THIS IS JESUS, THE NAZARENE, THE KING OF THE JEWS." So that all could understand this message, the inscription was written in three languages: Hebrew, Latin, and Greek—the main languages understood in that part of the world at the time. Indeed, many people were there to read the inscription, for the place of the crucifixion was close to the main part of Jerusalem. Upset that the placard gave the impression that the Jews were killing *their* King, the chief priests of the Jews pleaded with Pilate, saying, "Do not write, 'THE KING OF THE JEWS!' but only that He *claims to be*, 'I AM THE KING OF THE JEWS!'"[117]

But Pilate, obviously guilt-ridden over his unwarranted pronouncement of the death sentence on Jesus, insisted, "The words I have written will stay there, just as they are!" This way, the sign would embarrass the Jewish leaders who had, according to his perception, virtually forced him to execute the Lord. [*Harmony* 17:105-111][118]

The four soldiers who were responsible for the actual process of crucifying Jesus divided the Lord's clothing among themselves. [*Harmony* 17:115/] The clothes included the headgear, sandals, girdle, and the outer garments. However, the fifth piece, an inner tunic, was made without seams. Not wanting to tear this fifth piece into four parts, they reasoned with each other, saying, "Let's not tear it. Rather, let's cast dice for it. The winner gets the entire tunic." This event fulfilled a portion of Scripture which says, "They divided up my clothes among themselves, and for My clothing they cast lots." [Psalm 22:18] Thus the four soldiers unknowingly acted according to prophecy. After dividing up the Lord's garments, the soldiers sat down at the base of the cross to guard Jesus from there lest any of the Lord's friends or disciples try to free Him from the cross.[(tt)] [119]

Many stood at the cross watching. Others were just passing by, abusing the Lord with their words. Some, wagging their heads in contempt, sarcastically cried

---

117 Matthew 27:37; Mark 15:26; Luke 23:38; John 19:19-21

118 John 19:22

119 Matthew 27:35, 36; Mark 15:24; Luke 23:34; John 19:23-25

out to Jesus, saying, "Aha! You, who were going to destroy the Temple and rebuild it again in three days, save Yourself now! Come down off that cross!" Others said, "If You really are the Son of God, come down off that cross!" Still others cried out, "If You are the King of the Jews, why don't You save Yourself? Ha! Ha!"[120]

Adding to these searing words of the crowd, the head priests, scribes, and elders also mocked Jesus by saying various things among themselves. They said, "He has saved others, but He cannot save Himself!" "He says He trusts God—His supposed 'Father.' Well, then, let God deliver Him now—that is, if He truly takes pleasure in Him! After all, He did claim, 'I am the Son of God!'" "Let this so-called Christ—the Messiah—who is supposedly the King of Israel, come down off that cross, so that we may believe in Him!"[121]

Even the two convicts who were being crucified along with Jesus began to hurl insults at Him. [*Harmony* 17:124, 125][122]

The soldiers also mocked the Lord. For, as they came up to offer Him sour wine to drink—to lessen the pain—they said, "If you are the King of Jews, save Yourself!" But as before, Jesus refused to drink of the pain-deadening potion. [*Harmony* 17:115, 131][123]

After the passing of some time, one of the thieves crucified alongside of Jesus [*Harmony* 17:122] hurled still another insult at the Lord, declaring, "Are You really the Christ? If that's the case, then why don't you save Yourself and us too?"[124]

But the second thief had watched with amazement the calm way that Jesus faced His destiny of death. The Lord's demeanor sobered the criminal's attitude. Thus he responded to the first criminal with a rebuke, "What's the matter with you? Aren't you afraid of facing God in the judgment? You are under the same penalty of death as I am. And we deserve the death sentence placed upon us! Based upon what great evil we have done, it's only fair. But this other Man between us has done nothing wrong!" Then, sensing that the Lord was his divine

120 Matthew 27:39, 40; Mark 15:29, 30; Luke 23:35
121 Matthew 27:41-43; Mark 15:31, 32; Luke 23:35
122 Matthew 27:44; Mark 15:32
123 Luke 23:36, 37
124 Luke 23:39

Savior, he turned to Jesus, and pleaded with Him, saying, "Jesus, please think of me when You come into Your kingdom!"[125]

And Jesus, without hesitating, gave him the solemn assurance, "It is an absolute fact, when I tell you this very day, that you will be there with Me in Paradise!"[(uu) 126]

Among those standing near the cross were Mary, the Lord's mother; His aunt—Mary's sister—the wife of Cleophas; and Mary Magdalene. [*Harmony* 17:136] When Jesus noticed His mother there, standing next to His beloved disciple, John, the Lord said to His mother, "Mother, behold your son!" And to John, the Lord said, "Behold, your mother!" So then, from that moment on, Mary became a member of John's family. [*Harmony* 1:57][(vv) 127]

After Jesus had spent three hours on the cross—from 9 o'clock in the morning unto 12 noon [*Harmony* 17:116]—a mysterious darkness, shutting out the sun, settled down over the entire area. This darkness lasted for another three hours, until 3 p.m. [*Harmony* 17:135][128]

> This darkness was most unusual. It was as if nature were shutting out people from seeing the suffering of its Creator! [*Harmony* 17:135/]

Then, at that hour—about 3 o'clock—Jesus gave an agonizing cry, "Eloi! Eloi! Lama sabachthani?" Translated from the Aramaic language—the language spoken by Jesus—this meant "My God! My God! Why have You rejected Me?" [Psalm 22:1] The Savior, as the bearer of all the sins of humanity, felt totally alone on the cross . . . separated, even from His Father! That is why He cried out in such agony of mind. Of course, His Father *was* there, but Jesus did not sense His presence. [*Harmony* 2:34/2][(ww) 129]

But some standing at the foot of cross heard these words—especially the "Eloi! Eloi"—a different way. Because in their language [*Harmony* 2:58], the word for "God" and "Elijah" sounded similar, they thought that Jesus was calling

---

125 Luke 23:40-42
126 Luke 23:43
127 John 19:25-27
128 Matthew 27:45; Mark 15:33; Luke 23:44, 45
129 Matthew 27:46; Mark 15:34

for Elijah to come from heaven to save Him. [2 Kings 2:11] They said, "Behold, He is asking for Elijah to come and help Him!" [*Harmony* 17:132][(xx)] [130]

But at that very moment, knowing that He had been victorious over the temptation to remove Himself from the cross, and that the plan of salvation was secure—in fulfillment of the Scripture [Psalm 69:21]—Jesus cried out, "I'm thirsty!" [*Harmony* 17:115, 123] Instantly, a soldier dipped a sponge into a jar that was sitting there, which was filled with wine, mixed with frankincense. And placing the moistened sponge on the end of a stick, he lifted it up to the Lord's mouth.[(yy)] [131]

At that time, some cried out, "Let's see now if Elijah will come to take Him down!" [*Harmony* 17:130] But of course, Elijah did not come.[132]

When He had finished drinking the wine mixed with frankincense, Jesus cried out again with a loud voice, "It is finished!" This meant that the plan of salvation was secure! For indeed, by His death He would pay the penalty for the sins of the whole world, for everyone who had accepted Him—or would accept Him in the future. [Isaiah 53:10, 11] Then Jesus added, "My Father, I commit My breath of life into Your hands." After this, the Savior bowed His head upon His chest and breathed His last! For indeed, the Savior of the world was dead! [*Harmony* 18:3][133]

At that very instant, the heavy, ornate Temple veil separating the Holy from the Most Holy Place was miraculously torn from top to bottom.[134]

> This amazing event indicated that the purpose of the entire ritual and sacrificial service was ended. The true "Lamb of God"—Jesus—had died for the sins of the world. [*Harmony* 2:49] To be sure, no longer would there be any need for the people to bring animal sacrifices, for the real Sacrifice had been offered and died! [Hebrews 10:1-12]

---

130 Matthew 27:47; Mark 15:35

131 Matthew 27:48; Mark 15:36; John 19:28, 29

132 Matthew 27:49; Mark 15:36

133 Matthew 27:48, 50; Mark 15:36, 37; Luke 23:46; John 19:30

134 Matthew 27:51; Mark 15:38; Luke 23:45

At the moment of the Savior's death, the earth shook violently! Large rocks were moved out of their places! And many tombs were opened! [*Harmony* 17:128; 18:33][135]

> Again [*Harmony* 17:128/], it was as if nature was agonizing over the death of its Creator! There was something supernatural taking place—way beyond the ordinary.

Among those observing all these events surrounding the crucifixion were those who personally knew Jesus. There were women there, standing a good distance away. They were Mary Magdalene [*Harmony* 14:3; 17:127]; Mary, the mother of James the Less and Joses; and Salome, wife of Zebedee and the mother of the Lord's disciples, James and John. [*Harmony* 13:101] When Jesus was in Galilee, some of these women had been His followers. [*Harmony* 6:19] They also served Him in His ministry. In fact, many other women standing at the cross, as well as other individuals, had followed Jesus all the way from Galilee when He went to Jerusalem. [*Harmony* 18:10, 13][(zz) 136]

Standing guard at the cross—right in front of Jesus—was a Roman centurion. Seeing all these events—the earthquake and the way Jesus that died—the centurion, as well as some others who were guarding the cross, cried out with fear, saying, "There can be no doubt that this Man was, indeed, the Son of God!" The centurion further praised God by saying, "Certainly, this was an innocent Man!" The entire multitude, who had been standing and watching at the cross, after seeing and feeling all these things, began to run back toward Jerusalem, beating their breasts in total and unrelenting fear! [*Harmony* 18:7][137]

> Thus, the plan of salvation was successfully completed by the death of Jesus on the cross. It is now up to each individual to accept that death as complete payment for his or her sins.

## Supplementary Notes:

**(a) [17:0+]** It was quite a challenge, at times, to follow the proper sequence of events found in this chapter. Merging together the details of the various Gospel accounts, especially as they relate to the sequence of the Lord's legal

---

135 Matthew 27:51, 52

136 Matthew 27:55, 56; Mark 15:40, 41; Luke 23:49

137 Matthew 27:54; Mark 15:39; Luke 23:47, 48

trials, was not easy. However, I trust that I've done reasonably well in that regard.

**(b) [17:4]** Jesus called His heavenly Father, "Abba." This is the intimate Aramaic word for "father." Without doubt, because Jesus spoke Aramaic, this was the exact word He used when He began His prayer in the garden. When the Gospel writer Mark used this actual designation in his record, he probably wanted the reader to get a personal, more passionate understanding of the actual word Jesus spoke when He began His prayer. (For more on the Aramaic language, see *Harmony* 2:58/.)

**(c) [17:13]** The record does not tell us that a bright, shining angel struck down the crowd. However, considering the fact that an angel had very recently been present, and that angels can, with power and brightness, strike people down (*Harmony* 18:14), it seemed reasonable to suggest this possibility in the *Harmony*.

**(d) [17:17/]** I gave this suggestion as to why Judas kissed Jesus. And the more I think about it, the more I consider it likely.

**(e) [17:18/]** Throughout this chapter, from time to time, I have included references to the illegalities of the various court trials of Jesus, especially those before the Jewish Sanhedrin. I found much of the information regarding these illegalities in a marvelous little book, entitled, *Behold the Man!* written by Taylor G. Bunch. It is a great book! In this chapter, I have also included several brief descriptions of how the Sanhedrin was to function. I also found this information in this book. This information helps to understand more clearly what was happening to Jesus at any given time.

**(f) [17:22/]** (See above.)

**(g) [17:24]** It is traditionally assumed that the character in this interesting episode was the actual recorder of the event, John Mark. Accordingly, I said so in the *Harmony*.

**(h) [17:24/]** (See **Note "e"** above.)

**(i) [17:25/]** (See **Note "e"** above.)

**(j) [17:26]** The details—albeit minor—of Peter's three denials of the Lord, as recorded in the Gospels, are quite difficult—even impossible—to harmonize with complete certainty. I did my best!

**(k) [17:27]** (See above.)

**(l) [17:28]** (See **Note "j"** above.)

**(m) [17:29]** (See **Note "j"** above.)

**(n) [17:32/]** (See **Note "e"** above.)

**(o) [17:34]** (See **Note "e"** above.)

**(p) [17:36/]** (See **Note "e"** above.)

**(q) [17:36/2]** (See **Note "e"** above.)

**(r) [17:37]** (See **Note "e"** above.)

**(s) [17:39]** (See **Note "e"** above.)

**(t) [17:40]** (See **Note "j"** above.)

**(u) [17:41]** (See **Note "j"** above.)

**(v) [17:42]** (See **Note "j"** above.)

**(w) [17:43]** (See **Note "j"** above.)

**(x) [17:44]** (See **Supplementary Note "s"** in Chapter 16.)

**(y) [17:48/]** (See **Note "e"** above.)

**(z) [17:49]** (See **Note "e"** above.)

**(aa) [17:50]** (See **Note "e"** above.)

**(bb) [17:55/]** (See **Note "e"** above.)

**(cc) [17:55/2]** (See *Harmony* 14:21/1-6, and corresponding **Supplementary Note "l"**.)

**(dd) [17:56]** It seemed logical to me that Judas admitted his sin at this point in the Gospel story—even though the actual timing of his confession is uncertain. Accordingly, that is why I included it here in the *Harmony.*

**(ee) [17:57]** The details of Judas's final fate is mentioned, almost in passing, in Acts 1:18. I included these details here in the *Harmony.*

**(ff) [17:58]** These Old Testament texts are examples of Matthew using them as *secondary* applications, or using them as *illustrations.* (See **Supplementary Notes "j"** and **"s"** in Chapter 1.)

**(gg) [17:60]** (Regarding the timing of the actual Passover day, see **Supplementary Note "a"** in Chapter 16.)

**(hh) [17:80]** The record does not say that Herod brought sick people in for Jesus to heal them. However, in order for Herod to see Jesus work a miracle (Luke 23:8), it is logical to assume that sick individuals would have had to have been brought into the Lord's presence in order to satisfy the king's desire. Accordingly, I included this idea in the *Harmony.*

**(ii) [17:83]** It would be interesting to know the details of Pilate's wife's dream. I wish that such details were found in the Gospel record! Her use of the words that she "suffered many things" (KJV) in a dream regarding Jesus, shows that it was quite a dramatic event for her. It does appear that this dream was of divine origin, and that God actually wanted Pilate to refuse to execute Jesus! One wonders what would have happened next had Pilate actually released the Lord!

**(jj) [17:85]** The Gospel record does not state that the two thieves crucified with Jesus were part of Barabbas's group of insurrectionists. However, Mark 15:7 does come reasonably close to saying so. Further, one could logically assume that Barabbas and his cohorts were about to be crucified that day. So, that being the case, when Barabbas was released, it appears logical that Jesus took his cross!

**(kk) [17:97/]** The record does not say that Barabbas was present when Pilate declared, "Behold! The Man!" However, such a dramatic moment implies that Pilate *could have had* Barabbas there to emphasize the contrast between the two men: the Savior and the murderer. I admit that I took some liberty here in the *Harmony,* but I'm comfortable with my decision.

**(ll) [17:105]** The Scripture says that is was at the "sixth hour" (KJV) when Pilate addressed the crowd with the words, "Behold your King!" When is the sixth hour? Most likely, according to Roman reckoning, that would be 6 a.m., with 12 midnight being the first hour. However, considering all that had taken place thus far, it seems that it would have been later than 6 a.m. Nevertheless, I am not sure what other hour it might have been. Because of my uncertainty, I left the timing to be 6 a.m. in the *Harmony.*

**(mm) [17:110]** One would wonder what God's reaction was to these strong words of the Jews who so dramatically clamored for the death of Jesus! On one hand, Jesus prayed that His Father would forgive them (*Harmony* 17:116). On the other hand, the Bible indicates that those who were responsible for killing Jesus will, *in person*, be present to actually see Him arrive in the heavens at His Second Coming (Revelation 1:7). How God will actually judge those who were directly responsible for the death of Jesus, I will leave up to Him!

On a slightly different subject, the actual death of Jesus was the result of a co-operative action between the Jewish leaders and Pilate, the Roman governor. But the greater truth is that Jesus, of His own accord, allowed Himself to be killed (*Harmony* 11:119)! Therefore, unless the Lord had submitted Himself to the evil men who wanted to kill Him, He would never have died. And, too, He died for all the sins of the world; so then, in a very real sense, all sinners were responsible in part for the death of Jesus! Indeed, we then, as sinners, all had an active part to play in this evil event! Therefore, in summary, we must conclude, that it was the *Jewish leaders of A.D. 31, in conjunction with Pilate, the Roman governor*, who were *directly* responsible for the *actual* death of Jesus. Jews before and after the time of Jesus were *not* responsible, any more than any other people are, for the death of Jesus. *However, every sinner, Jew or non-Jew, has played a role in the death of Jesus as the world's Sin Bearer!*

**(nn) [17:111]** Was Jesus scourged a second time (with John 19:1 indicating the first time)? In fact, according to Roman law, when a criminal was convicted, he was to be scourged. That is what the references in Matthew 27:26 and Mark 15:15 indicate. These texts *may* be referring to the first scourging of John 19:1, but, based upon the timing, I think it was, indeed, a second scourging. If that is the case, the depth and severity of suffering the Lord endured is beyond our comprehension!

**(oo) [17:112]** (See *Harmony* 17:116/2 for more details on the probable method of the Lord's crucifixion.)

**(pp) [17:114]** (See **Note "jj"** above.)

**(qq) [17:115]** It is not clear whether the name Golgotha—"the place of a skull"—referred to the shape of the hill or to the fact that people died there.

**(rr) [17:116/2]** Even though we talk a lot about the cross and the crucifixion, it is amazing how little we really know about how this form of execution was actually performed. A number of theories prevail. Elaborate efforts at research, and even re-creations of crucifixions have been attempted. However, it is quite possible that our whole view of the crucifixion procedure was forever affected—especially as it relates to the nailing of the heels of the victim to the cross—when the skeletal remains of a man who had been crucified was discovered near modern Jerusalem. It appears as though the crucified victim had his legs turned to one side, and that there was a small seat upon which he could rest his body. Then a nail was driven through both heels, placed together, as they were connected to the front side of the cross. But, even at that, there are, I suppose, different ways of interpreting this archeological find. Of course, too, it is possible that the mode of crucifixion could have been different at various times. In any case, a final, definite conclusion about the true mode of the Lord's crucifixion simply cannot be determined. However, I trust that what I suggested in the *Harmony* is reasonably accurate.

**(ss) [17:116/2]** Was Jesus naked during His crucifixion? Some have assumed, based upon what is known about crucifixions—albeit little (see **Note** above)—that He was naked. The Bible does not tell us. However, there is a reasonably strong possibility that He *wasn't* naked. Public nakedness was a taboo among Jews. And, considering the fact that Jesus was crucified on the Passover day, when many more people—including many women and children—would have been town for this celebration, it is very possible that the Romans, to placate the Jews, would have allowed Jesus to have a little clothing on Him. I think that such a circumstance is quite possible—even likely.

**(tt) [17:119]** The elaborate description of the clothes of Jesus, and how they were distributed, as written in the *Harmony*, is not found in the Gospel record. In my studies, though, I came across this description and thought it would be good to include it in the *Harmony* as an interesting sidelight.

**(uu) [17:126]** The placing of commas in Scripture came many, many years after the original text was written. The placing of the comma in this verse determines its true meaning. In the KJV, the text reads, "Verily I say unto thee, To day shalt thou be with me in paradise." This rendering indicates that that Jesus *and* the thief were in Paradise that very day. There is certainly no Biblical evidence for this! (See Ecclesiastes 9:5; John 20:17.) However, the repositioning of the comma in this same verse entirely changes its meaning. Note the following: "Verily I say unto thee today, shalt thou be with me in paradise." This indicates that, as Jesus and the thief hung upon the cross—*that very day*—Jesus promised him that he would be with Him in Paradise. And, based upon Scripture, one's arrival in Paradise will take place at the resurrection at the end of the world (1 Thessalonians 4:13-18), and not before. Consequently, this is the position I took in the *Harmony.*

**(vv) [17:127]** While the direct the use of the word "woman" (as found in the Gospel record) is a sign of respect in some cultures, to our ears, it is appears disrespectful. So, to make the statement sound better to us, I used the designation "Mother" instead when Jesus directly addressed Mary, His mother.

**(ww) [17:129]** (See *Harmony* 2:58/ for more information about the Aramaic language.)

**(xx) [17:130]** (See above.)

**(yy) [17:131]** What does it mean when, as John 19:28 (KJV) states, Jesus asked for something to drink, it was in order "that the scripture might be fulfilled"? It almost appears that the Lord asked for a drink, just to fulfill what Psalm 69:21 had predicted! But considering the honest nature of Christ, that can hardly be the case! I am convinced that Jesus made His request *as a fulfillment of Scripture,* as opposed to making the request *in order to fulfill Scripture.* Accordingly, that is the way I stated it in the *Harmony.*

**(zz) [17:136]** Even though it is a small point, there is some debate regarding the man referred to as "James the Less" in this verse. First of all, the designation "Less" probably indicates that this James was either short in stature or young in age. Perhaps, too, he might be called the "Less," because was considered to be lesser in importance! Second, even though there are various theories as to whom this James was, we really don't know; so I make no definite conclusion as to his identification.

# CHAPTER EIGHTEEN

## FROM TRAGEDY TO TRIUMPH—
**From The Burial of the Savior, to Epilogue**

**(Friday, Just Before Sunset, Nisan 14 -**
**Thursday, Iyyar 25, Spring, A.D. 31)**

### Jesus in the Tomb
**< Friday, Just Before Sunset, Nisan 14, A.D. 31 -**
**Early Sunday Morning, Nisan 16, Spring, A.D. 31 (7/7) >**
**(Matthew 27:57-66; Mark 15:42-47; Luke 23:50-56; John 19:31-42)**

### — The Burial of Jesus
**< Friday, Just Before Sunset, Nisan 14, Spring, A.D. 31 (7/7) >**
**{Matthew 27:57-61; Mark 15:42-47; Luke 23:50-56; John 19:31-42}**

By now it was late Friday afternoon, and the sun would be setting soon, which, according to Biblical reckoning, would mark the beginning of a new day. In this case, it would be the weekly seventh-day Sabbath rest day, Nisan 15 of the Jewish calendar. Friday was a day the Jewish people used to prepare for the Sabbath rest. Therefore, it was called the Preparation Day. The Jewish leaders were very anxious to make sure that no one would remain on the cross during the Sabbath hours. This was especially true because this particular Sabbath was also the first day of the Feast of the Unleavened Bread, which made it a ceremonial—or ritual—Sabbath. When a weekly Sabbath, and a ritual Sabbath, fell on the same day, it was called a High Sabbath. To have Jesus hang on the cross on such an important day, with so many visitors in town for the Passover, was quite unacceptable to them.[a] [1]

Accordingly, the Jewish leaders asked Pilate, the Roman governor, that the legs of the three crucified men—Jesus and the two criminals—be broken. [*Harmony* 17:114, 116] When the legs of those on crosses were broken, besides

1 Luke 23:54; John 19:31, 42

the obvious increase of pain, the support for the body was greatly weakened. This placed a heavier burden on the arms, causing more pressure upon the heart and lungs. All this obviously hastened the death of those being crucified. Thus, their dead bodies could be removed before the seventh-day Sabbath began.[2]

So Pilate sent soldiers to break the legs of the three crucified men. But, when they came to the place of the crucifixion, they discovered that Jesus was already dead! [*Harmony* 17:133] They did, however, break the legs of the two criminals, while leaving the Lord's legs intact.[3]

But to make sure that Jesus was really dead, a soldier thrust a spear into His side, piercing the Lord's abdomen, just below the ribs. [*Harmony* 18:47, 54] Out of the wound flowed a mixture of blood and water. It is unclear what the cause of this dual flow from the Lord's body might be.[(b) 4]

The Lord's disciple, John, was nearby and saw this event. He was able to verify its exact details. On the strength of his witness, all can safely believe that this was an accurate description of what actually took place. These proceedings served to fulfill the Scriptures which said, "Not a single bone of the Lord's body will be broken," [Psalm 34:20] and "They will look on Him, the One whom they have pierced." [Zechariah 12:10][(c) 5]

Then, just before sunset that Friday—the day before the Sabbath—a certain rich man named Joseph went into action. He was a prestigious member of the Sanhedrin—the same Jewish court that had, just hours before, pronounced a death sentence upon Jesus. [*Harmony* 17:48, 55] Joseph was from the town of Arimathea, located about 22 miles northwest of Jerusalem. Joseph, a righteous and noble man, was a secret follower of the Lord. In fact, he had been looking for the coming of the true kingdom of the Messiah. But Joseph, for the most part, kept his faith in Jesus quiet because he was fearful that if his belief in the Lord had become too public, he would most certainly be thrown out of the Sanhedrin. Joseph was opposed to what the Jewish leaders had done to Jesus. No doubt he was not in attendance at the Sanhedrin, which earlier in the day had condemned Christ. [*Harmony* 17:36/1, 2] But now that Jesus was dead, Joseph

---

2 John 19:31
3 John 19:31-33
4 John 19:34
5 John 19:35-37

built up enough nerve to approach Pilate publically and beg that the body of the Savior to be committed to his care.[6]

Pilate was amazed that Jesus was already dead, so he inquired of the centurion who had been standing guard at the cross if the Master had in fact died. [*Harmony* 17:137] After being informed that He was indeed already dead, Pilate commanded that the body of Jesus be turned over to Joseph.[7]

Taking a clean linen cloth with him, Joseph, along with Nicodemus, went to the site of the crucifixion. This was the same Nicodemus who, three years earlier, had visited the Lord by night. [*Harmony* 3:10-24] He—another member of the Sanhedrin—was also a secret follower of the Savior. He had once spoken out in favor of giving Jesus a fair hearing before He should be condemned. [*Harmony* 11:30] Nicodemus, too, probably was not at the Sanhedrin session which condemned the Lord. [*Harmony* 17:36/1, 2] Nicodemus brought with him about 72 pounds of very costly myrrh and other aromatic spices to embalm Jesus. They took the body of the Messiah from off the cross. According to Jewish custom, they wrapped the lifeless Savior in a linen sheet which Joseph had just purchased specifically for this purpose. [*Harmony* 14:7][8]

Close by the crucifixion site was a garden. Coincidently, in this very garden, Joseph recently had had a tomb cut out of rock, to be used for his own burial. Before anyone else could use the tomb, Joseph and Nicodemus laid Jesus there along with the embalming spices Nicodemus had brought. Just before the sun was completely set, they finished their task by rolling a huge stone in front of the tomb's opening. Then Joseph and Nicodemus left the site.[9]

Some women from Galilee [*Harmony* 17:136] who had believed in Jesus while He ministered in that province had followed along as the body of the Lord was carried to the tomb. Arriving at the place, they sat directly across from the grave. They carefully watched as their Lord was entombed. Mary Magdalene was there, and also Mary, the mother of Joses. [*Harmony* 17:136] Returning to the city, they began to prepare additional spices and perfumes with which to anoint the Lord's body. They rested according to the Sabbath commandment [Exodus

---

6 Matthew 27:57, 58; Mark 15:42, 43; Luke 23:50-52; John 19:38

7 Matthew 27:58; Mark 15:44, 45

8 Matthew 27:59; Mark 15:46; Luke 23:53; John 19:39, 40

9 Matthew 27:60; Mark 15:46; John 19:41, 42

20:8-11], planning to return to the tomb on Sunday morning to complete their task. [*Harmony* 18:13][10]

## — Jesus Rests in the Guarded Tomb Over the Sabbath
## < Sabbath, Nisan 15, Spring, A.D. 31 (7/7) >
## {Matthew 27:62-66}

The seventh-day Sabbath—the day after the Preparation [*Harmony* 18:1]—had already begun when the head priests and the Pharisees had a meeting with Pilate. They said to him, "Sir, we remember that when this deceiver was still alive, He was heard saying, 'After three days, I will rise again!' [*Harmony* 10:84] So therefore, Governor, please give orders that the tomb be made extra secure until the third day. This way His disciples will not be able steal Him away from the tomb at night and then falsely declare, 'He has risen from the dead, just as He promised!' If that should happen, then His last deception would be much worse than all His other previous deceptions combined!"[11]

So Pilate, not wanting any more trouble with either the Jews or his Roman employers, gave permission, by saying, "You will have your guard! Go now, and make the tomb as secure as possible!" They immediately made the tomb as secure as they were able to do so by posting a large contingent of soldiers there and fastening a Roman seal upon the stone—a seal that could be broken only by permission of the Roman authorities.[12]

## The Resurrection of Jesus
## < Early Sunday Morning, Through Sunday Afternoon, Nisan 16, Spring, A.D. 31 (7/7)>
## (Matthew 27:52, 53; 28:1-15; Mark 16:1-11; Luke 24:1-12; John 20:1-18)

Just before sunrise on Sunday—the next morning—Mary Magdalene began to make her way to the tomb. She came with the hope of further anointing the body of Jesus with spices. [*Harmony* 18:10] Meanwhile, a number of other women were also traveling to the tomb to anoint the Lord with spices of their own. Two of these women were Mary, the mother of James, and also Salome. [*Harmony* 17:136][13]

---

10 Matthew 27:61; Mark 15:47; Luke 23:55, 56
11 Matthew 27:62-64
12 Matthew 27:65, 66
13 Matthew 28:1; Mark 16:1, 9; Luke 24:1; John 20:1

But before they arrived, an angel had come from heaven. There had been a severe earthquake! The angel then rolled the stone away from the front of the tomb, and sat upon it. His face had shined like the lightning, his clothing glistening as bright sunlight reflected from newly fallen snow! The entire group of soldiers guarding the tomb was stunned, and fell to the ground as though dead! [*Harmony* 11:121][14]

> It is an interesting fact of Scripture that there is no direct account of the actual resurrection of Jesus! All that is recorded is the scant report of the soldiers who were posted at the tomb to guard it. From the Biblical perspective, the resurrection of Jesus is considered an assumed fact. No other details whatsoever regarding it are recorded! During the Lord's most trying and humiliating time—the crucifixion—He was seen by hundreds, perhaps even thousands. But during His most dramatic and triumphal time—the resurrection—no one was there except some pagan soldiers who were later paid to lie about it! [*Harmony* 18:31] Soon after Jesus was resurrected, He disappeared from the area, leaving the tomb empty.

After the Lord's resurrection, and when Jesus and the angel had left the empty tomb, the soldiers hurried back to the city to tell the governmental officials what had happened. Very soon after that, Mary Magdalene arrived at the tomb. [*Harmony* 18:13] The sky was still dark, but she could see that the stone had been rolled away and that the tomb was empty. Mary quickly ran back toward Jerusalem to tell two of the Lord's closest disciples, Simon Peter and John—the disciple whom Jesus loved—what she had discovered.[15]

It was right after the sun had risen on Sunday morning that the other women, who were also to bring spices [*Harmony* 18:10], arrived at the tomb. On the way there, they said to each other, "Who will roll the stone away from the opening of the sepulcher for us?" But when they arrived at the grave, they noticed that the stone had already been removed, even though it was quite large. There was an angel sitting on the stone, for by now he had returned to the tomb. [*Harmony* 18:15] This was the same angel who had rolled away the stone in the first place, and whose brightness had struck down the burly soldiers. [*Harmony* 18:14][16]

---

14 Matthew 28:2-4

15 John 20:1, 2

16 Matthew 28:2; Mark 16:2-4; Luke 24:2

Understandably frightened, the women turned to leave, but the angel restrained them, saying, "Now don't be afraid! I know that you are looking for the crucified Jesus. But, as you can see for yourselves, He is not here! He has risen—just as He said He would! Remember?" [*Harmony* 13:99] Directing the women toward the opened tomb, the angel further declared, "Come! See for yourselves. Don't be afraid! Look at the place where He lay! Then, go quickly and tell His disciples that He has, indeed, risen from the dead! Say to them, 'Look! Jesus is going on to Galilee. [*Harmony* 16:59, 18:29, 60] There you will see Him again.' [*Harmony* 18:60-86] Now remember what I have just told you! Go now and share the good news!"[17]

The women entered the tomb, and it was just as the angel had said: Jesus was gone! Another angel was seated to the right. His garment was shiny white! Terrified and amazed, the women bowed their heads close to the ground. Both angels sought to comfort them. The angels told them, "Don't be shocked or afraid! We know that you are seeking Jesus of Nazareth, who was crucified. As you readily see, though, He is not here, for He has risen! Look! See the place where He was laid! But why is it that you seek the Living One among those who are dead? Again, He is not here, for He has risen! Remember how He explained all of this to you when you were with Him in Galilee. He had explained back then, saying, 'The Son of Man must be seized by evil men and then be crucified by them. But He will rise again on the third day.' [*Harmony* 13:99] Do you remember that? Now go quickly and tell His disciples—and especially Peter—that He is, indeed, raised from the dead!" In fact, the women did remember these same words. Immediately, with a strange mixture of emotions—fear, astonishment, and indescribable joy—the women fled from the tomb. Afraid to tell anyone else about what they had seen, the women began to search out the remaining eleven disciples.[(d)] [18]

By now the soldiers who had been guarding the tomb had reported the events of the resurrection of Jesus to the Jewish leaders. A meeting of all the chief priests and leaders was immediately called to discuss how to handle the matter.[19]

Meanwhile, Mary Magdalene arrived back in the city. She found Simon Peter and John—the disciple whom Jesus loved—and exclaimed, "Someone has

---

17 Matthew 28:5-7

18 Matthew 28:8; Mark 16:5-8; Luke 24:3-8

19 Matthew 28:11

taken the Lord out of the tomb! But I don't know where they have put Him!" Immediately, Peter and John rushed to the tomb themselves, with Mary following some distance behind. John ran faster than Peter, and thus arrived at the tomb first. The sun had already risen, casting its light into the opening of the tomb.[20]

John stooped down and, without entering, peered into the sepulcher. In the dim light, all he could see were the Lord's grave clothes lying there where Jesus had been laid. Simon Peter arrived shortly after. He looked into the tomb. There he not only saw the grave clothes lying there, he also spied the special burial face covering neatly folded in a place by itself, separate from the other burial clothes. John then entered the tomb to be with Peter. Both of them were now assured that Jesus was, indeed, nowhere to be found in the tomb. Without a doubt, He was gone! But they saw no angels, either in or around the gravesite. They, too, did not yet understand the meaning of the Scripture that had indicated that it was essential that Jesus be resurrected. [Psalm 16:10; compare with Acts 2:31] And because they did not understand the meaning of the Lord's statement that He would rise the third day [*Harmony* 13:99], Peter and John returned to their homes wondering about what the Lord's disappearance from the tomb might mean. [*Harmony* 18:40][21]

By now, Mary Magdalene had arrived back at the tomb for the second time. She lingered there for a while. Not knowing what had happened or what she should do, Mary began to cry. Walking over to the tomb, she stooped down and looked into the sepulcher once more. Inside, she saw two angels, dressed in white, sitting at the place where the body of Jesus once lay. [*Harmony* 18:18] One of the angels was seated at the head of the burial slab, the other one at the foot. They said to Mary, "Woman, why is it that you are weeping so?"[22]

She responded, "Because someone has taken my Lord away and I don't know where they have put Him!" After saying this, and not waiting for the angels to give an answer to her frustrated statement, Mary turned and left the tomb.[23]

In front of her, standing in her way, was a Man. Because of the tears in her eyes, she did not recognize who this Man was. But He asked her, "Woman, why are you weeping? Whom do you want?"[24]

---

20 Luke 24:12; John 20:2-4
21 Luke 24:12; John 20:5-10
22 John 20:11-13
23 John 20:13, 14
24 John 20:14, 15

At first, Mary thought that this Man was the caretaker of the garden and its tomb, so she asked of Him, "Sir, if it was You who have removed Him from the tomb, please tell me where You have placed Him, so that I can take Him away!"[25]

Just then the Man spoke her name, saying, "Mary!" It was then that she instantly recognized the sound of His voice. It was Jesus![26]

She fell at His feet and grabbed hold of Him as she cried out, "Rabboni!"—which means "Teacher" in the Hebrew language.[27]

After a brief time, Jesus said to her, "Stop clinging to Me! I need to be going, for I have not yet ascended to the Father to see if My death on the cross has succeeded in securing the plan of salvation for the world. But go and tell My disciples that I said, 'Behold! I am ascending to your Father and to My Father, and to My God, and your God!'" And so it was that the first person to whom Jesus revealed Himself after His resurrection was Mary Magdalene out of whom He had cast seven devils! [*Harmony* 6:19, 98/][28]

Very soon after this, Jesus ascended to heaven and just as speedily returned to earth. It was then that He met the other women still on their way back to the city to find the disciples. When He met them with the words, "Greetings to you all!" the women fell down before Him. They took hold of His feet, as Mary had previously done and continued to worship Him. He said, "Please don't be afraid! Go now, and bear the good news to My disciples. Tell them to go on to Galilee. There they will see Me." [*Harmony* 18:17, 60] The women, obeying the Lord, continued on the way back to the city to tell the disciples the exciting news of the Lord's appearance to them.[(e) 29]

When all the women excitedly told the remaining eleven disciples what they had heard and observed, the disciples simply did not believe them! There was Mary Magdalene. She was the first to see Jesus after His resurrection. Also, there was Mary the mother of James, and Joanna, and the other women. It didn't even matter that Mary Magdalene kept declaring to them, "I have seen the Lord!" She also told them everything Jesus had said to her. The disciples—the remaining

---

25 Mark 16:9; John 20:15

26 Mark 16:9; John 20:14-16

27 Mark 16:9; John 20:16

28 Mark 16:9; John 20:17

29 Matthew 28:9-11

eleven, as well as other followers of Jesus [*Harmony* 18:34]—were in such a state of mourning and extreme sorrow over the Lord's death and the apparent kidnapping of His body that it seemed just so much nonsense to them! In short, they refused outright to accept the testimony of any of the women! [*Harmony* 18:59][30]

By this time, the Jewish leaders had assembled to discuss the dramatic report of the guard of soldiers at the tomb regarding the resurrection of Jesus. They had counseled with each other as to how they were going to handle this crisis. They knew that the truth of the resurrection had to be kept secret! Accordingly, they bribed the soldiers [*Harmony* 18:15] with a huge sum of money, telling them, "If anyone asks, you are to say, 'His disciples came during the night, and, while we were sleeping, they stole Him from the tomb.' And should Pilate, the governor, hear of this, don't worry. We will convince him that it is best to keep all this hush-hush. Believe us, the governor is no more desirous for the truth of what happened to get out than you are. We'll make sure that you will be kept out of any trouble." [*Harmony* 3:7/][31]

Indeed, it took a good sum of money to silence the guards, because for them to actually have fallen to sleep while on duty would, under normal conditions, have cost them their lives. The soldiers took the money and both did and said just as they had been instructed. Nevertheless, not surprisingly, the details of the story leaked out and were spread everywhere among the Jewish people of that day.[32]

Another amazing event took place that same day that helped to publicize the resurrection of Jesus far and wide. When Jesus died on the cross on Friday afternoon, there had been a huge earthquake. [*Harmony* 17:135] Graves had been ripped open and dead bodies of some of the saints from the old days had been exposed. When Jesus was resurrected, many of the bodies of these saints were raised too! These resurrected people went into Jerusalem and appeared to many of its inhabitants, telling people of the resurrection of Jesus. However, there is no clear Biblical record as to the names of any of these resurrected people or what ultimately happened to them. [*Harmony* 3:90/][(f)][33]

---

30 Mark 16:9-11; Luke 24:9-11; John 20:18

31 Matthew 28:11-14

32 Matthew 28:15

33 Matthew 27:52, 53

## Jesus Meets With the Disciples Over the Next Few Weeks < Sunday, Late Afternoon and Evening, Nisan 16 and 17, Through the Month of Iyyar, Spring, A.D. 31 (7/7) > (Mark 16:12-14; Luke 24:13-49; John 20:19-21:23)

### — The Meeting on the Road to Emmaus < Sunday, Late Afternoon, Nisan 16, Through Evening, Nisan 17, Spring, A.D. 31 (7/7) > {Mark 16:12; Luke 24:13-33}

Much later that same day, two of the Lord's disciples—who were not a part of the Twelve—were walking to the village of Emmaus, located in the country eight miles northwest of Jerusalem. As they walked, they discussed with each other the events that had taken place over the last several days. [*Harmony* 18:30][34]

And so it was, while they were talking and reasoning with each other, that Jesus Himself came up to them and began to walk with them. He appeared to them in a form different from the one they had previously known. Thus they did not recognize Him as the Lord.[35]

Jesus said to them, "What are you discussing with each other as you are walking along? And why do you appear to be so sad-faced?"[36]

One of them named Cleopas answered, "What? Are you just a stranger in town that you haven't heard about all the things that have happened here recently?"[37]

Jesus queried, "What things are you talking about?"[38]

They replied, "The things regarding Jesus, the Nazarene, of course! He was a Man—even a Prophet—mighty in His actions and words before both God and the people. Well," they continued, "this Man was delivered by the chief priests and our rulers to the Roman authorities to be condemned to death. In fact, He was crucified! Alas! We had come to believe that He was the One who would redeem

---

34 Mark 16:12; Luke 24:13
35 Mark 16:12; Luke 24:14-16
36 Luke 24:17
37 Luke 24:18
38 Luke 24:19

the entire nation of Israel. We believed that He might be the long-promised Messiah. And it is now the third day since all these terrible things took place.[39]

"But there's more!" they continued to explain. "Some of our own women have shocked us by telling us that, when they went to the tomb early this morning, they found it to be totally empty! Furthermore, they have told us that they saw a vision of angels who explained to them that Jesus was actually alive—that He was, in fact, resurrected from the dead! Some of us—even His closest disciples [*Harmony* 18:20, 21]—went to the tomb to see for themselves whether the women's testimony was true. Sure enough, they found the tomb empty, just as the women had declared. The Lord was nowhere to be found. We just can't make any sense out of all of this!" [*Harmony* 18:59][40]

Jesus responded, "Oh, how foolish you are! How slow you are of heart to believe all the things that the prophets have said! Let Me ask you: Wasn't all this necessary for the Messiah to suffer as He did and then be resurrected with a glorious body?" And then, starting at the beginning of the Scriptures—with the books of Moses—and continuing through all the Prophets, Jesus began to explain to them all the many prophecies regarding Himself.[(g)] [41]

After the passing of some time, as the three of them were approaching Emmaus, it appeared as though Jesus was going to continue on beyond the town. But the other two compelled Him to stop, saying to Him, "Please stay here with us! It is near the evening, and the sun will be setting soon." So, He went into the house with them.[42]

They sat at the table to eat a loaf of bread. As Jesus pronounced a blessing upon the meal, the eyes of the two disciples were opened and they immediately recognized Him as the Lord! But at that instant, Jesus miraculously disappeared from their sight! They said to one another, "Isn't it a fact that our hearts were set ablaze within us as He spoke to us while we were walking together, especially when the Lord opened up our minds to understand the true meaning of those Scriptures He quoted?" Rising from the table, they rushed the eight miles back to Jerusalem in the dark.[43]

---

39 Luke 24:19-21

40 Luke 24:22-24

41 Luke 24:25-27

42 Luke 24:28, 29

43 Luke 24:30-33

## — Jesus Appears to Ten of the Disciples in the Upper Room
## < Sunday Evening and Night, Nisan 17, Spring, A.D. 31 (7/7) >
## {Mark 16:12, 13; Luke 24:33-49; John 20:19-23}

The two disciples from Emmaus made their way to the room where ten of the remaining disciples were congregated. Thomas, one of the Twelve, wasn't there at the time. [*Harmony* 18:53] (Perhaps there were other disciples there, too, besides these ten.) The disciples met in secret that Sunday evening. They had locked the doors, because they were afraid that the Jews might do something evil to them just as they had done to Jesus.[(h)] [44]

When the two disciples were admitted to the room, they excitedly said to the others congregated there, "The Lord has really been raised from the dead! We have seen Him with our own eyes!" They added, "The Lord's appearance to Simon Peter is for real!" [*Harmony* 18:59][45]

> Apparently, Jesus had appeared to Peter earlier that day—the timing of which is unknown. The disciples must already have known of this appearance, because Peter would have told them. However, up until now, they must have doubted the testimony of Peter regarding this appearance. Perhaps Peter's emotional state—after his three denials of the Lord [*Harmony* 17:26-29, 40-44] and the horrors of the crucifixion—was such that the disciples must have questioned the veracity of his statement. Also, because Jesus had not yet personally revealed Himself to them, they might have felt somewhat slighted, further leading to their questioning of Peter's testimony.

The two disciples continued to relate the details of their meeting with Jesus: the visit along the road, the blessing of the loaf of bread, and the Lord's disappearance. However, the disciples in the room still did not believe the words of these two men. Suddenly Jesus Himself stood in their midst! He said to them, "Peace be to all of you!" But they were all filled with great fear, for they thought they had seen a spirit . . . and not their actual Lord![46]

Trying to calm their fears, Jesus said to them, "Why are you so upset? Why is there so much doubt arising within you? See My hands and My feet! You can see that it is I, isn't that right? Touch Me and see for yourselves. A spirit does not

---

44 Mark 16:13; Luke 24:33; John 20:19

45 Mark 16:13; Luke 24:34, 35

46 Mark 16:12, 13; Luke 24:35-37; John 20:19

have flesh and bones, as you can readily see that I have." He then showed them His wrists, His hands, and His feet, where the nails had been driven. [*Harmony* 17:116] He also showed them His side into which the spear had been thrust. [*Harmony* 18:4] After touching Jesus for themselves, they still had a hard time believing that it was the Lord—it just seemed too good to be true! But they nevertheless marveled at it all, being filled with joy, trying hard to believe that it was actually true what they saw with their own eyes![(i)] [47]

"Have you anything here that I can eat?" Jesus asked them. They gave Him a portion of a broiled fish and some honey, which the Lord ate in front of them.[48]

Then Jesus said to them, "Remember the words that I spoke to you before My crucifixion: how I said at that time that all the things that have been written about Me and My ministry in the Holy Scriptures—the books of Moses, the Prophets and the Psalms—must be fulfilled." [Isaiah 53:3-11][49]

The Lord then began to explain the Scriptures to them. This explanation opened their minds to understand more clearly what had happened and why. In conclusion, Jesus said, "So, as you can see, just as the Scriptures have recorded, the Christ—the Messiah—must suffer, and die [Isaiah 53], and be resurrected on the third day." [*Harmony* 3:7][(j)] [50]

> On occasion Jesus had spoken about being resurrected on the third day. [*Harmony* 13:99] But is there any place in Scripture, where Jesus might have understood the concept that He would be resurrected this way? Actually, the resurrection of Jesus—on "the third day"—*was* illustrated by a part of the Passover celebration detailed in the Old Testament Scriptures. The Passover lamb was to be slain on the 14th day of the month of Nisan. The next day, the 15th, was to be a ritual Sabbath, the first day of the Feast of Unleavened Bread. The following day, the 16th—the third day of the Passover and Unleavened Bread celebration—was the time of the wave sheaf offering. This was when a sheaf of recently harvested grain was to be waved before the Lord in the Temple. [Leviticus 23:5-11] The sheaf was considered to be the "first fruits" of the grain harvest of the year. *This sheaf symbolized the resurrection of Jesus as the "first fruits" of*

---

47 Luke 24:38-41; John 20:20
48 Luke 24:41-43
49 Luke 24:44
50 Luke 24:45, 46

> *the resurrection of all the saints.* [1 Corinthians 15:20-26] On the Sunday of the Lord's resurrection, the Jews, as part of the Passover celebration, actually waved such a sheaf before the Lord. Thus, this waving of the sheaf represented the resurrection of Jesus which had taken place earlier that day! It is probable, then, that the Lord's declaration that He would rise on the third day was based on the "weave sheaf" ritual of the Feast of Unleavened Bread celebration.[1]
>
> The resurrection was of great importance for the establishment of the faith of the disciples as well as of anyone who would follow Jesus and His teachings after that. In fact, the resurrection was to be, and would remain to be, the foundation of the Christian faith. Why is this? First, it would prove that Jesus was really alive—that He, as God, had power over death. Second, the resurrection would give all the followers of Jesus—those in His day as well as those who would come afterward—the faith to believe that they too would be resurrected at the end of the world. For without this hope, they really would have no real hope at all. [1 Thessalonians 4:13-18][2]

Once again, Jesus said to them, "Peace be to you! Just as the Father has sent Me to do work for Him, so I will send you to do work for Me." The Lord came extremely close to them and as He spoke they could feel His breath on them. He said, "Receive the Holy Spirit upon you all. Under the influence of that power, you and I will work closely together again. When you follow Me as you should, I will recognize your authority on earth as though it were Mine. This means, that when you as a corporate group of My followers forgive the wrongs which repentant individuals have committed, I will also forgive them. But when hardened sinners refuse to repent, despite your efforts to turn them from their evil ways, I, too, would continue to hold their sins against them." The last part of the Lord's statement here—regarding forgiveness—was consistent with what He had said to His disciples on a earlier occasion. [*Harmony* 10:109-111][(k)] [(l)] [51]

The Lord further added, "Indeed, I am sending you to preach, in My Name, the truth of repentance and the forgiveness of sins to every nation . . . beginning first in Jerusalem. And you, My disciples, have been witnesses to all these things! So, listen carefully! I am placing upon you the promise and the gift of the Holy Spirit who will be given to you by My Father. But remember, you are to wait in Jerusalem until you are showered with an even greater measure of the Spirit's

---

[51] John 20:21-23

power which will come directly from heaven." This special outpouring of the Holy Spirit occurred on the Day of Pentecost—another Jewish holiday—some weeks later. [Acts 2:1-4][52]

## —Jesus Meets With the Disciples Again, Eight Days Later
## < Sunday Evening, Nisan 24, Spring, A.D. 31 (7/7) >
## {Mark 16:14; John 20:24-29}

One of the original twelve disciples, Thomas—known as the "Twin"—was not with the rest of them when they met with Jesus in the upper room that Sunday evening after the resurrection. [*Harmony* 18:44] Later on, when informed of the event, Thomas refused to believe the story of the other ten disciples. Of course they insisted it was true, and they firmly declared to Thomas, "But we truly did see the Lord!"[53]

In spite of their strong testimony, Thomas replied with some passion, "No! No! I must be able to see the nail wounds in His body with my own eyes. I must also be able to place my finger into the nail wounds themselves, and thrust my hand into His side where the spear entered His body. [*Harmony* 18:4] Only then will I believe. Until I do all those things, I simply cannot believe what you have told me! No, indeed!"[54]

It was a week later—on the next Sunday night—that the disciples were once again gathered together in the upper room. This time Thomas *was* with them. When the door to the room was shut and barred and they were sitting and eating, Jesus suddenly appeared before them, standing in their midst. He gently declared, "May My peace abide with you!"[(m)] [55]

Turning to Thomas with His hands outstretched to him, the Lord invited, "Reach here, Thomas, and with your fingers touch the wounds in My wrists and hands!" And turning His side toward the doubting disciple, Jesus said, "Reach here with your hand and touch the spear wound in My side! Stop your unbelieving, Thomas." After Thomas both saw and felt the Lord's wounds, Jesus asked him, "Now, do you believe?"[(n)] [56]

---

52 Luke 24:47-49

53 John 20:24, 25

54 John 20:25

55 Mark 16:14; John 20:26

56 John 20:27

Only after Thomas had done as the Master directed, he, overwhelmed with the indescribable reality that it was, indeed, the Messiah before him, exclaimed with great emotion, "Oh! My Lord . . . and my God!"[57]

Jesus chided him gently, "Thomas, do you now believe because you have seen Me? Well, that's good. But blessed are those who believe . . . though they have not been able to see Me with their own eyes as you have!"[58]

> Such a strong statement was important for Thomas—and the other disciples to understand—for the many Christians, throughout the ages, would have to believe the story of the resurrection by faith, not sight. Also Thomas's response was profound in that he recognized Jesus as his *Lord* and his *God*. By his declaration, Thomas understood clearly that Jesus was divine in nature, and consequently, the ultimate authority in his life.

As they all reclined at the table in the room, it was now unequivocally clear to all eleven disciples that their Lord was truly alive. Indeed, it was He! There could be no doubt whatsoever. Then Jesus chided them for their previous unbelief, saying, "Did you believe the testimony of those to whom I revealed Myself the day of resurrection? [*Harmony* 18:34-43, 45, 45/] No, you didn't! Now, if you expect people to believe your testimony, you first must be willing to trust the testimony of others." The Lord continued to strongly chide them for their harsh, hard-hearted, unbelieving attitude toward those—especially the women [*Harmony* 18:30]—who had originally shared the good news of the resurrection with them.[59]

## —Jesus Appears to the Disciples on the Bank of the Sea of Galilee
## < Sometime in the Month of Iyyar, Spring, A.D. 31 (7/7) >
## {John 21:1-23}

Sometime after this event, some the Lord's disciples went to the northern province of Galilee. It was there that Jesus had told them, on several occasions to go, so that they might meet with Him there. [*Harmony* 16:59; 18:17, 29] So it was that Jesus revealed Himself again to the apostles at the Sea of Galilee—sometimes known as Tiberias. This is how this particular appearance occurred: Simon Peter,

57 John 20:28
58 John 20:29
59 Mark 16:14

Thomas the "Twin," Nathanael from Cana of Galilee, the sons of Zebedee, John and James, and two other unnamed disciples, were fellowshipping together.[60]

As night approached, and unsure of when the Lord would appear to them, Peter said, "I want to go fishing like in the old days!"[61]

"Okay, we'll go fishing with you," the others replied. They all entered the boat. But all night long they caught nothing![62]

Now, as dawn was approaching, Jesus was standing on the beach. However, the disciples did not recognize that the Person standing there was the Lord. Jesus called out to them, inquiring, "Young men, you haven't caught any fish to eat, have you?"[63]

Still not aware that it was Jesus talking to them, they simply replied, "No, we haven't!"[64]

"Why don't you cast your fishing net over the right side of the boat?" the Savior suggested to them—for they had been fishing over the left side of the boat. "There you will find a good catch!" Without debating with the One who was talking to them, they did as He instructed them. Immediately, the net was filled with fish! In fact, there were so many fish that they were not able to easily pull the net back into the boat![65]

Recognizing that a miracle had just taken place, John—the disciple whom Jesus especially loved—declared to Peter, "It's the Lord! It's the Lord!" Now knowing that the Stranger was the Lord, Simon Peter put his outer garment on, for he had removed it in order to more comfortably do his fishing. No doubt, Peter wanted to meet Jesus more respectably dressed! Once completely clothed, Peter dove into the sea and swam to shore, leaving the remaining disciples to wrestle with the bulging net of fish.[66]

Meanwhile, the other disciples continued to struggle with the over-loaded net of fish, dragging it with their small boat. It took some time, even though they

60 John 21:1, 2
61 John 21:3
62 John 21:3
63 John 21:4, 5
64 John 21:5
65 John 21:6
66 John 21:7

were not that far from the shore—about a distance of about 100 yards. When they finally made it to land, they noticed that Jesus had started a fire. On the fire of burning coals were some fish as well as some bread.[67]

Jesus called out to them, "Bring some of the fish that you've caught over here!" So Peter helped the men to pull the net onto land, for it was full with large fish. In fact, they caught no fewer than 153 fish! But, even though this was a huge catch for their net, it was not damaged in the slightest. They brought some of these fish to add to those already on the coals[68]

The Lord invited them, saying, "Come and have some breakfast."[69]

By now, all the disciples knew that it was Jesus who was talking with them. They did not need to ask Him, "Who are you?" In fact, they did not say a single word to Him at all. No doubt overwhelmed to be in the presence of their resurrected Master again, they silently did just as He directed them. Jesus, once again assuming the role of a servant, took some of the bread and the fish with which Peter had provided Him, and gave this to the disciples.[70]

This was the third time that the Lord had met with His apostles after His resurrection. The first time was the night of that day in the upper room. [*Harmony* 18:44-52] The second time, a week later, was also in the upper room. [*Harmony* 18:53-59] And the third time, was here at the lake.[71]

When they had all finished their breakfast, Jesus asked Simon Peter, "Simon, son of John, do you love Me more than the other disciples?"[72]

"Lord, You know I love you!" Peter answered. But, in saying this, Peter did not suggest that he loved Jesus more than the others. He had allowed himself to get into trouble for being boastful before. [*Harmony* 16:59-64] He would not make that mistake again![73]

---

67 John 21:8, 9
68 John 21:10, 11
69 John 21:11
70 John 21:12, 13
71 John 21:14
72 John 21:15
73 John 21:15

Jesus then said, "Take care of My lambs—the ones who will follow after Me."[74]

For a second time, the Savior asked Peter, "Simon, son of John, do you love Me?"[75]

Once more, Peter answered, "Yes, Lord! You know that I love You!"[76]

Jesus added, "Be a good shepherd to My sheep."[77]

And yet a third time, Jesus asked Peter, "Simon, son of John, do you love Me?"[78]

By now Peter was quite upset that the Lord felt it necessary to ask him a third time, "Do you love Me?" With some frustration, Peter replied for the third time, saying, "Lord, You have knowledge of all things. You must know, then, that I do love You!"[79]

"Well, then," Jesus replied, "Feed My sheep. Take care of those who will follow after Me!" Jesus publicly asked this question of Peter three times, to make up for the three times he had openly denied His Lord. [*Harmony* 17:26-29, 40-44][(o) 80]

> This event took place in the presence of the other disciples so that they might know that Peter, who had publically denied His Lord, was fully accepted again by Jesus as one of the disciples, with all the privileges and responsibilities such a position entailed.

The Lord took Peter apart from the other disciples, and continued to talk with him as they walked along the shore. "It is a certain fact, I tell you," Jesus said, "that when you were young, you used to dress yourself and go wherever you wished to go. But when you are old, you will stretch out your arms and allow someone else to dress you. And, they will bring you to a place that you do not

---

74 John 21:15
75 John 21:16
76 John 21:16
77 John 21:16
78 John 21:17
79 John 21:17
80 John 21:17

desire to go." By these cryptic words, Jesus indicated the way that Peter would glorify his Master in death—that is, by being crucified.[81]

> This meant that when being crucified Peter would no longer be able to take care of himself, even to dress himself. Someone else would have to do that for him. And he would stretch out his arms to be fastened to the cross. And of course, all this would be against his wishes.

The Master concluded His remarks to Peter with the simple injunction, "Follow Me!" From that moment on, Peter was to follow His Lord, no matter where Jesus would lead him. And, never again would he deny His Savior![82]

Peter turned around and noticed that John—the disciple whom Jesus especially loved—was following behind the two of them. John was the disciple who, reclining at the Passover supper table, had leaned back on the Lord's chest, and asked Him, "Who is it that will betray You?" [*Harmony* 16:29, 30][83]

So, when Peter saw John following close behind them, he asked the Lord, "What is it that will happen to this man?"[84]

Jesus replied, "If it is My will that he stay alive until I come back from heaven, what difference is that to you? You are to follow Me and not be worried about anybody else."[85]

Because of this interesting exchange, a rumor went around the church that Jesus would come before John died. However, that is not what Jesus actually said. Rather, He declared, "*If I will* that he not die until I come, what is that to you?"[86]

### The Gospel Commission
### ‹ Sometime in the Month of Iyyar, Spring, A.D. 31 (7/7) ›
### (Matthew 28:16-20; Mark 16:15-18; Acts 1:4, 5)

Some time after this, the eleven disciples, along with 500 other followers [1 Corinthians 15:6], met with Jesus on a certain mountain in the province of

---

81 John 21:18, 19
82 John 21:19
83 John 21:20
84 John 21:21
85 John 21:22
86 John 21:23

Galilee, at a location which He had chosen. When He appeared to them, they all fell down and worshipped Him. Nevertheless, there were some in the group who still had doubts that this was really Jesus.[87]

Moving closer to them so that all could clearly hear His words, Jesus told them, "I have been given all authority in both heaven and earth. Therefore, go and disciple people from all the nations on earth. Yes, you are to go into the whole world, to preach the Gospel to the entire human creation. You are to baptize"—by immersion in water—"all the converted ones. You are to baptize them in the name of the Father, and of the Son, and of the Holy Spirit. [*Harmony* 1:22/3] And indeed, those who believe and are baptized will be saved. But those who refuse to believe will be condemned in the day of judgment. Beyond this, you are teach those who believe in Me to obey everything which I have commanded you to do. And remember, I will be with you in this noble work, even unto the end of the world." [*Harmony* 9:12/][88]

Jesus instructed His disciples further, saying, "You will know that I am with you, for miracles will accompany those who accept My teachings and preach them. They will cast out demons. They will also speak in different languages. [Acts 2:4] At times, they will pick up snakes, and not be fatally bitten. Also, on occasion, they will be forced to drink poison, but will not be killed. They will also lay hands on sick people and see them healed." [Acts 3:1-9, etc.][89]

> Miracles of this kind played an especially prominent part of the early Christian Church. These manifestations were necessary to confirm the faith of the early believers, and give them confidence that the Lord's disciples were genuine. This was especially true before the church was firmly established. After that, miracles were not as necessary. Thus, they would occur less frequently. Faith is to be the foundation of the Gospel, not the manifestation of miracles. On the other hand, on many occasions, there are miracles that do take place as part of the ministry of the Gospel. The Lord provides enough miracles to form a basis for one's faith, but not so many that people would become dependent upon them.[(p)]

---

87 Matthew 28:16, 17

88 Matthew 28:18-20; Mark 16:15, 16

89 Mark 16:17, 18

In addition, Jesus gave specific counsel as to what they should do to prepare for the promised coming of the Holy Spirit. "You are not to leave Jerusalem," He said. "Rather, you are to wait there until the Father sends you the Holy Spirit of whom you have also heard Me tell you. [*Harmony* 16:48] John the Baptist baptized people with water. But you will be baptized with the Holy Spirit, not many days from now." [Acts 2:1-4][90]

> The *baptism of the Holy Spirit* is somewhat different from the *work of the Holy Spirit* in one's life at the time of conversion. The *work of the Spirit*—that which is symbolized by the baptism of "water"—deals with the change that takes place in the heart when a person experiences the "new birth." The *baptism of the Spirit* describes the power of the Holy Spirit in the life that empowers one to share one's faith effectively with others, in the spreading of the Gospel message.

## The Ascension
## < Thursday, Iyyar 25, Spring, A.D. 31 (7/7) >
## (Mark 16:19, 20; Luke 24:50-53; Acts 1:2, 3, 6-12)

The time period between the crucifixion of Jesus and His ascension into the heavens was forty days. During that time, Jesus appeared as the living Lord to His disciples as well as to many other followers. While with them, through the power of the Holy Spirit, He gave various instructions to the apostles—that is, the ones whom He had chosen and specifically sent to witness for Him. These instructions involved issues regarding the spreading of the Gospel message of the kingdom of God into the whole world. The Lord also gave many proofs and evidences that He was truly alive and that He was, indeed, the One whom they had known throughout the years of His ministry. The proofs which He presented to them were indisputable. Indeed, there could be no doubt: He was certainly the Lord![91]

Finally, the day of His ascension arrived. It was on Thursday, the 25th day of the month of Iyyar. Jesus, along with His remaining eleven disciples, climbed the Mount of Olives which was near Jerusalem. To the west of the mountain was Jerusalem. To the east was Bethany. As they made their way up the mountain,

---

[90] Acts 1:4, 5

[91] Acts 1:2, 3

the disciples questioned Jesus, "Lord, is this the time that You will restore the kingdom to God's people?"(q) [92]

The Savior explained, "It is not for you to know the specific details of the timeline of God's plan. By His own authority He has fixed the time of the establishment of the kingdom. Don't be concerned about that." By the establishment of the kingdom, Jesus referred to His Second Coming.[93]

> It is bit surprising that the disciples, even at this late date, were still confused about when the Lord would establish His eternal kingdom. It should have been abundantly clear to them that the establishment of the Lord's glorious kingdom was still in the distant future. But confused, nevertheless, they were!

"But you are to be concerned about something else," Jesus continued. "You will receive special power when the Holy Spirit is poured out upon you. And, as a result, you shall be witnesses to Me, to personally testify of the Gospel. Your field of labor will be twofold. First, you will begin your work in Jerusalem and Judea, to work primarily among the Jews. Then, second, you are to expand your labor to the Gentiles of Samaria. In fact, ultimately, you must spread the Gospel message to the very remotest parts of the entire earth, so that all the peoples of the whole world will have an opportunity to know the truth!" [*Harmony* 11:24, 149/][94]

After saying these words, Jesus lifted up His hands before them and pronounced a blessing upon them. As He blessed them, Jesus—the Messiah, the disciples' Lord, Master, Savior, and Teacher—was lifted from off the earth! And while the disciples continued to stare at Him, a cloud carried Him completely out of their view. And while they still continued to peer intently into the heavens, hoping to catch a last glimpse of their Lord, suddenly, two angels in white clothing stood beside them. [*Harmony* 11:121][95]

The angels told them, "Men of Galilee! Why is it that you are standing here looking into the heavens? This very same Jesus, whom you have just seen return to heaven, will come back the same way that you have seen Him go into heaven."[96]

---

92 Luke 24:50; Acts 1:6
93 Acts 1:7
94 Acts 1:8
95 Mark 16:19; Luke 24:50, 51; Acts 1:9, 10
96 Acts 1:11

Falling down on the ground they worshipped their departed Savior. Then leaving the Mount of Olives, they returned the short distance from the mountain to Jerusalem, which is just about two-thirds of a mile. This is commonly called a "Sabbath day's journey"—the distance the legalistic Jews had declared they could walk on the Sabbath day without violating its sanctity. They entered the city with great happiness and joy. Awaiting the outpouring of the Holy Spirit which would take place ten days from then, the disciples could often be seen in the Temple praising God![97]

And Jesus, once ascended into heaven, sat down, at the right hand of His Father—that is, a position of honor that represents the strength and authority which the Lord received upon His official arrival in heaven. [*Harmony* 9:47; 16:107; 17:52][98]

Thus had ended the life and ministry of Jesus here on this earth. But the work of His disciples had just begun. From Jerusalem they and those who followed them ultimately went out and preached the Gospel everywhere—even to the ends of the earth. Jesus, through the Holy Spirit, was with them, confirming the words of their message by miracles that were performed through them—miracles of the body . . . and, more importantly, miracles of the conversion of the human heart![99]

—

## *The Timeline of the Ministry of Jesus, SUMMARY: Autumn, A.D. 27—Spring, A.D. 31*[(r)]

It was now the Spring of A.D. 31, and three and a half years had passed since the Lord began His public ministry in the Autumn of A.D. 27. **(1/7):** During the first six months—Autumn, A.D. 27 through Spring, A.D. 28—Jesus was baptized, was tempted in the wilderness, called His first disciples, and worked His first miracle. No further details are given regarding this time period. It was a "getting started" time for Jesus. [*Harmony* 2:22-77][[1]]

**(2/7):** During the next six months—Spring, A.D. 28 through Autumn, A.D. 28—Jesus ministered in the southern province of Judea. It all started when He cleansed the Temple of the moneychangers, which led to the beginning of a

97 Luke 24:52, 53; Acts 1:12

98 Mark 16:19

99 Mark 16:20

great struggle between the Jewish leaders and Him. The Lord labored in Judea for only a short period of time, with His disciples baptizing a number of people. [*Harmony* 3:34] While Jesus worked miracles in Judea, no specific details of these miracles are mentioned. [*Harmony* 3:8] It was in Judea, too, that Jesus had His famous night visit with Nicodemus. [*Harmony* 3:10-24] But tension with the Jewish leaders and, to a lesser extent, with John the Baptist's remaining disciples—who were somewhat skeptical of Jesus—finally led to the Lord cutting short His overall work in Judea. This meant that almost all of the rest of His ministry—with the exception of the festival seasons—was spent in places other than Judea. This was necessary because most of the Jewish leaders, who despised Jesus, lived in that province. Had the Lord labored so close to these leaders, they would have made life completely unbearable for Him as well as for the people who were listening to Him. [*Harmony* 3:1-33] In summary, not much is known about the extent and breadth of the Lord's Judean ministry.[2]

**(3/7):** The next six months—Autumn, A.D. 28 through Spring, A.D. 29—the Lord spent in the northern province of Galilee. While on His way there, He had His well-known encounter with a non-Jew—the woman at Jacob's Well. [*Harmony* 3:34-61] Overall, though—with the exception of the healing of the nobleman's son [*Harmony* 3:63-68]—the record of that entire time period is very sketchy and incomplete. Without question, most of this time was spent in the private instruction of His disciples in preparation for the beginning of their ministry in Galilee.[3]

**(4/7):** The next six-month period—Spring, A.D. 29 through Autumn, A.D. 29—was a very busy time for the Lord. It was when He actually began His ministry in earnest. There are many events of this time period that are a part of the Gospel record. During a trip to Jerusalem for the Passover, Jesus healed a paralytic by the Pool of Bethesda. [*Harmony* 3:72-81] This led to His strong defense of His ministry before the Sanhedrin. [*Harmony* 3:82-99] Soon after that, Jesus officially began His ministry in Galilee which was distinguished by many miracles and powerful preaching. [*Harmony* 4:23-31, 35-47, 57-62; 6:1-17, etc.] But Jesus had a very negative experience with His own people in Nazareth. [*Harmony* 4:4-10] However, on the positive side, during this time period the Lord officially called His twelve disciples [*Harmony* 4:14-22] and ordained them. [*Harmony* 4:67-79] This was followed by His famous "Sermon on the Mount" discourse. [*Harmony* 5:1-86] And, it was during this time period that the Lord conducted what is known as His "First Evangelistic Tour of Galilee." [*Harmony* 4:32-79] The level of the Lord's popularity with many people during this time segment was quite high. In many respects, it was the high point of the Lord's entire ministry. [*Harmony* 3:72-6:17][4]

**(5/7):** The next six-month period of the Lord's ministry—Autumn, A.D. 29 through Spring, A.D. 30—started very well but ended somewhat negatively. On the positive side, the Lord conducted His "Second Evangelistic Tour of Galilee" [*Harmony* 6:18, 19] which included His resurrection of the son of the widow of Nain. [*Harmony* 6:20-23] It was during this time, too, that Jesus started to use parables as a method of teaching the people. [*Harmony* 7:22-55] Jesus performed a number of miracles of great note. [*Harmony* 7:61-74; 8:9-19; 9:1-24, etc.] But, on the negative side, He experienced increasing difficulties with the Jewish leaders who were constantly harassing Him nearly everywhere He went, even in Galilee. [*Harmony* 7:2-17; 9:14-24; 8:1-4, etc.] During this time period, Jesus sent the twelve disciples out on their own, to minister two by two. This, along, with the Lord's own ministry, comprised His "Third Evangelistic Tour of Galilee." [*Harmony* 8:37-58] Moreover, because so many people were following Him for the wrong reasons—primarily as a result of His physical miracles, such as the feeding of the 5,000 [*Harmony* 9:1-13]—Jesus gave His famous "Bread of Life" teaching in the synagogue in Capernaum. In it Jesus urged His listeners to look beyond the mere physical qualities of His miracles to the more important spiritual aspects of His ministry. After that, sadly, many of His extended group of disciples no longer followed Him as the Messiah. [*Harmony* 9:25-54] This time segment marked a definite turning point in His ministry. However, not the least of what happened during this time period was the death John the Baptist, who, after being in prison for about a year, was brutally and shamefully executed. [*Harmony* 8:63-74][5]

**(6/7):** The next six-month segment of the Lord's ministry—from Spring, A.D. 30 through Autumn, A.D. 30—was focused primarily on ministering to Gentiles. Thus it was that the Lord labored in areas where the population of Gentiles was greater. It started with the Lord's healing of the demon-possessed daughter of a Gentile woman. [*Harmony* 10:14-22] It continued with the miraculous feeding of 4,000 non-Jews. [*Harmony* 10:27-32] Interspersed with other miracles, Jesus' ministry met with constant resistance by the usual hateful Jewish leaders. [*Harmony* 10:1-13, 33-43, 86-93, etc.] However, Jesus spent time alone with His disciples, including the time when He asked them who they thought He was [*Harmony* 10:47-61], as well as the time He was transfigured. [*Harmony* 10:62-85] Also, Jesus began to emphasize to His disciples the fact that He would soon suffer at the hands of the Jewish leaders. [*Harmony* 10:84, 85] Jesus started to give strong, practical counsels to His disciples as to how they should relate to one another as fellow workers in the Gospel ministry. [*Harmony* 10:94-118] Overall, this was a time period wherein Jesus concentrated on work among the Gentiles and on practical instruction of His disciples.[6]

**(7/7):** The next—and final—six-month segment of Christ's life—from Autumn, A.D. 30 through Spring, A.D. 31—was primarily spent in giving counsel and advice to the closest of His followers. This advice would be invaluable to them as they would begin to learn how to minister to the church and the world without Jesus physically present among them. [*Harmony* 12:1, 2, 16-18, 67-71, 78-85, 105-110, 151-158, etc.] However, this was also the time period when the Lord's struggles with the Jewish leaders reached a fevered pitch. [*Harmony* 11:56-78; 12:19-31, 124-150, etc.] Much of this contention was the result of the fact that Jesus attended three of the Jewish Festivals—the Feast of Tabernacles [*Harmony* 11:1-121], the Festival of Lights (or Dedication) [*Harmony* 11:165-175], and, of course, the Passover [*Harmony,* chapters 14-17]—during which He had frequent encounters with the angry and frustrated leadership of Israel. Also, Jesus sent the "Seventy" Gospel workers to minister to mainly the Gentiles. [*Harmony* 11:133-149] During this time period, too, Jesus performed His most dramatic miracle: the resurrection of Lazarus. [*Harmony* 13:1-38] Then, near the end of this time segment, the Lord brought His ministry to an end. In fact, about one fourth of the entire Gospel record tells the story—in a virtual day-by-day account—of the Lord's final week leading up to and including His trials and crucifixion. [*Harmony,* chapters 14-17] After the Lord's burial, He rose from the dead, met with His disciples, and gave them pertinent instructions. Some weeks later, He ascended into the heavens to be with the Father and to prepare for His Second Coming, at which time He would receive His people to be with Him forever. [*Harmony,* chapters 17 and 18] Overall, indeed, it was a glorious and triumphant conclusion to the entire ministry of Jesus, the true Messiah of the world![7]

**Thematic Review of the Ministry of Jesus:**[s]

In truth, the Lord successfully completed His ministry. While there were many people who rejected Him—especially among the Jewish leadership—the Lord, nevertheless, achieved the three main goals He originally had for His ministry. First and foremost, He vanquished the devil, providing the gift of eternal life for anyone who truly believes in Him as the Messiah. [*Harmony* 2:29-36; 3:22, etc.] Second, the Lord presented a powerful and relatively concise set of teachings which comprise what could be called the "everlasting Gospel." [*Harmony* 5:1-86] These teachings were calculated to change not only the lives of people but also the direction of the whole world! And third, Jesus trained a small but dynamic group of followers who, after He left this earth, would take the Gospel message to the whole world—just as He had commanded them to do. [*Harmony* 4:67-79; 8:37-58; 11:133-149; 18:97-97, etc.] It would be impossible to overestimate the impact of these three aspects of Christ's ministry![8]

Related directly to the above, there were many things that the Lord accomplished and taught during the course of His ministry. Indeed, the things which He emphasized over and over again became thematic during His time on this earth. While some of these repeated concepts were *doctrinal* in nature, most of what the Lord taught, dealt with the *practical* nature of His work and ministry. In regard to doctrinal issues, Jesus often discussed the reality of the resurrection of the dead [*Harmony* 3:87, 90, 92; 14:93-99, etc.], the correct perspective on marriage and divorce [*Harmony* 5:30, 31; 12:141; 13:62-71], and the true significance of the seventh-day Sabbath. [*Harmony* 4:51, 56; 12:91, etc.][9]

Beyond the aforementioned issues, there were two main fundamental concepts the Lord constantly emphasized, thus making them paramount among His teachings. First, He always talked about *His* extremely close relationship with God—the One whom He called His Father. [*Harmony* 3:82-99; 11:17, 45; 16:101, etc.] For example, when He was arraigned before the Sanhedrin early in His ministry because of the healing of the paralytic at the pool of Bethesda, the Lord gave a detailed, point-by-point essay-like presentation on this vital issue. [*Harmony* 3:82-99] There were a number of other times, too, that Jesus discussed this subject. In fact, from the Lord's perspective, this relationship with His Father formed the very foundation of the fact that He was, indeed, the Messiah of the world. While Jesus really did not specifically claim in public that He was the Messiah, there is no doubt that Jesus considered Himself to be such. [*Harmony* 10:47-54, etc.] Further, His insistence in discussing His relationship with the Father became a constant sore spot between Him and the Jewish leaders who rejected Him as the Messiah. [*Harmony* 11:61-66, 75-78, etc.] Ultimately, it became the single most important point of contention that led to their unrelenting determination to kill Jesus. [*Harmony* 11:171, 172, etc.][(t)] [10]

The second principal truth that the Savior very, very often discussed was the meaning and nature of what He usually called the "kingdom of heaven" or the "kingdom of God." There were two aspects to this "kingdom." First, there was what might be called the "kingdom of grace." This teaching dealt with the spiritual relationship every person should have with Jesus as his or her personal Savior. This aspect of the "kingdom" includes forgiveness of sins, growing in grace, and ultimate victory over sin. Second, there was what could be designated the "kingdom of glory." [*Harmony* 7:23, 23/; 13:43/, 44, etc.] This aspect of the "kingdom" deals with the establishment of the Lord's eternal and glorious "kingdom" at His Second Coming, when He will ultimately take complete charge of this earth forever.[11]

It should be noted that most—but not all—of the Lord's teachings on these two parts of the "kingdom" was through the medium of parables. [*Harmony* 7:23; 13:43, etc.] As far as the "kingdom of grace" was concerned, the Master emphasized the fact that the power of the Gospel grows within the lives of those who persistently and sincerely seek to experience it. Its growth is continual and its impact dramatic. Everything in the life is changed. Nothing remains the same. [*Harmony* 7:29-31] One's relationship with the Lord is the most valuable possession one can have. [*Harmony* 7:32, 33] It is worth every effort and struggle to obtain it. Nothing else can compare to its value. [*Harmony* 7:32, 33] On the other hand, Jesus emphasized that there are people who are not sincere in their claim to know the Lord. In that case, such a relationship can be lost, or, perhaps, it was never truly found in the first place. [*Harmony* 7:23] The bottom line is that the "kingdom of grace" must be the focus of everyone who seeks to be a true follower of the Lord. It cannot be obtained by chance, luck, or erratic effort. Indeed, its pursuit must be the primary passion of the life. [*Harmony* 7:37, etc.] [12]

When Jesus talked about the "kingdom of glory"—the establishment of His eternal "kingdom" at the end of the world—He stressed—again, often through the medium of parables—the importance of always being ready for His coming. [*Harmony* 7:24-28] It will be a time of judgment. [*Harmony* 7:34, 35] It will be when rewards—including eternal life—are given to His faithful followers. [*Harmony* 13:120-133, etc.] It will also be when punishments—specifically hell-fire—are meted out to the wicked. [*Harmony* 15:51-58] At the judgment, too, the Lord will especially hold accountable those who claimed to be leaders of God's people. [*Harmony* 15:42-50] Overall, then, being ready for the establishment of the "kingdom of glory" and its judgment process, is a serious, sobering issue—one that certainly cannot be ignored, without severe risk, by anyone. [*Harmony* 7:24-28; 14:79-84, etc.][13]

In preparation for the dramatic, earth-altering experience of the establishment of His "kingdom of glory," the Lord very often gave to the people practical advice that would be most useful in their everyday lives. The Lord's purpose in making this emphasis was that people should prepare for that day by living out the principles of the Gospel which He had taught them. Indeed, the actions of His followers must be consistent with their profession of faith in the Gospel message. In short, they must practice what they preach! Again, the Christian experience of His followers should be much more than a mere profession of faith, but rather, a living, vibrant experience that affects every part of their inner souls as well as their outward lives. [*Harmony* 7:31; 12:77] In this regard, the Lord railed against dependence upon the outside trappings of religion, which are merely a show. [*Harmony* 5:42, 44, 54] He fought against greed [*Harmony* 14:112, 113, 119], legalism [*Harmony* 14:125, 126], and a judgmental mindset. [*Harmony* 5:68-71] Instead, He emphasized love [*Harmony* 5:40, 75], forgiveness [*Harmony* 5:53], and genuine compassion for one another [*Harmony* 11:150-161], especially the less fortunate. [*Harmony* 12:97, 98] He constantly upheld the sincerity and piety of the poor [*Harmony* 14:134, 135] as well as of those who many considered to be nothing more than "sinners." [*Harmony* 8:2, 30] On the other hand, He constantly condemned the hypocrisy of those who flaunted their possessions and piety [*Harmony* 12:97, 98] and considered themselves to be more worthy than others. [*Harmony* 13:58-61] While, clearly, Jesus was not a political revolutionary [*Harmony* 17:72], He certainly sought to "shake up" the church and condemn all of its humanly-devised false teachings and practices. [*Harmony* 10:1-4] The Lord made it abundantly clear that salvation was given to those who placed their faith in Him. Salvation was not given just to the members of one particular church, race, or nationality. Rather it was to be given to *anyone, anywhere,* who reached out in *genuine* faith to God. [*Harmony* 3:22] In this regard, the Lord often praised the faith of those who were condemned by the religious snobs, [*Harmony* 7:15, 16], while, on the other hand, He condemned the lack of faith of those who should have had the most knowledge, and, accordingly, been the most faithful. [*Harmony* 14:132][14]

To help His followers to live consistent, Christ-like lives, the Lord stressed the need to understand the deep, spiritual nature of the Law—even the Ten Commandments. Indeed, Jesus taught a strict adherence to the whole Law. [*Harmony* 5:19-22] But true obedience, as Jesus taught it, was much more than merely keeping the "letter of the law." Rather, He taught that the Gospel's adherents needed to live out the deeper, spiritual aspects of the Law. Further, the Lord taught that the foundational principle of the spirit of all good law is love—love to God and love to mankind. [*Harmony* 11:152, 153] The Lord's most dramatic exposition of this theme was presented in the "Sermon on the Mount." [*Harmony* 5:1-86] These concepts were calculated to teach the true meaning of the spiritual basis of each of the Commandments. [*Harmony* 5:23-29] In a practical sense, this is best experienced by having a personal relationship with God and a loving relationship with one another. [*Harmony* 11:152, 153] Thus is exhibited by the way one truly worships God—both privately and publicly. [*Harmony* 5:42-55] Throughout the remainder of His ministry, Jesus often returned to these themes, re-emphasizing them over and over again. In summary, then, the Lord constantly talked about the necessity of having one's religious experience flow from the depths of one's heart. The Lord made it clear that one's actions are changed by what is in the heart, rather than the other way around. [*Harmony* 10:8][15]

Such victory in one's life is accomplished by having a close, personal relationship with God. [*Harmony* 16:71-74] While during His ministry, the Lord talked about the need of His followers to "believe" in Him [*Harmony* 3:22], He make it abundantly clear that, in the long run, a mere *intellectual* belief was not sufficient. Instead, He emphasized the necessity of His followers to possess an on-going personal, growing experience with Him. This could be called an "abiding relationship" with the Lord. No finer discussion on this theme can be found anywhere in the Scriptures than Christ's dramatic illustration of the vine and its branches. [*Harmony* 16:71-73][16]

Unfortunately, though, Jesus had to spend a lot of time during His ministry trying to correct several misunderstandings the people—and even His disciples—had regarding His work. Two areas stood out. First, the Lord had to discuss quite often the "suffering servant" aspect of the Messiah's work. [*Harmony* 10:84, 85] Indeed, this part of His ministry was gravely misunderstood. Throughout their lives, the Jews had been living under the delusion that the Messiah would have a glorious and peaceful reign, easily conquering all His *political* foes—such as the Romans. They had little or no concept of the necessity of the Messiah, as the Sin Bearer of the world, to suffer and die. [*Harmony* 10:85] So strong was this misunderstanding that, in spite of the Lord's constant emphasis on this subject, even the disciples never fully grasped its reality until Jesus actually died. [*Harmony* 18:40, 41][17]

Second, Jesus was forced to deal with the misunderstanding of the nature and purpose of His miracles. Every one of His miracles served to meet a human need and was a natural result of the Lord's love and compassion. Moreover, His miracles were intended to create in His followers a sense of faith and trust in Jesus—the Messiah—as a powerful Miracle Worker. It was important, though, for them to realize that these miracles had another even more important purpose. Most people never understood that all His miracles were to have a spiritual application, as opposed to the mere *physical* reality of the actual miracles themselves. [*Harmony* 9:30] That is, many people viewed them only as dramatic miracles of the *body*. The blind were able see. The lame could walk. The dead were raised, and so forth. They failed to appreciate that, through these miracles, Jesus was primarily teaching them that as He healed the physical body *He could also heal the soul*. In fact, these spiritual aspects of His miracles were more important than the physical miracles themselves. [*Harmony* 9:30-32] Finally, Jesus had no real choice but to meet this misunderstanding head-on. This happened when He made His "Bread of Life" presentation in the synagogue in Capernaum. [*Harmony* 9:25-48] So distasteful was this concept to many of the people that, at the time, Jesus lost many—perhaps even a majority—of His followers. [*Harmony* 9:50][18]

Also, throughout the Lord's ministry, He spent a lot of time at social gatherings. [*Harmony* 2:69-77; 8:1-4; 12:19-31, etc.] Thus, He was much more than a preacher, teacher, or healer. He was a social being! He especially enjoyed spending time with those who were considered by the religious leaders of the time to be the outcasts of society. This included tax-collectors, prostitutes, and sinners of every sort. [*Harmony* 8:30; 13:108-112, 120, etc.] There is no telling just how many people were led to a correct understanding of the Gospel message through the social gatherings Jesus had with the people. Jesus, who never once sinned, spent much time with people who truly enjoyed His company in such social settings. This is an amazing fact when one considers that these people—sinners of every sort and variety—were completely comfortable with Him, and He with them.[19]

Working with people of all sorts was a huge part of the ministry of Jesus. Basically the Lord ministered to roughly four groups of people. With some He had great success, with others He had less success, if any at all. The latter was especially true with the Jewish leaders, the first of the four groups for whom He labored. In fact, the boiling-over of tensions between these leaders and the Lord represents, perhaps, the most uncharacteristic aspect of the overall ministry of Jesus. [*Harmony* 12:25-31] However, with the second group to whom He ministered—the common people—the Lord had much better success. But, because of the negative influence of the Jewish leaders upon the lives of the common people, the Lord's relationship with them was not nearly as effectual as it might have been. [*Harmony* 9:46, 47] They, because of what they had been taught by the errant Jewish leaders, were blinded to the truth of the Gospel that Jesus taught. [*Harmony* 14:120] Nevertheless, the Lord continued to exercise patience with them. Of course, with the third group, His own disciples, the Lord's relationship was close and cordial. To be sure, there were some tense moments. [*Harmony* 10:84, 85, 94] Considering all the things that they had to "unlearn," one should not find that surprising. But in spite of their considerable shortcomings, the Lord's experience with His closest followers was rewarding. [*Harmony* 16:108] This is due to a large extent to that fact that no matter what, Jesus continued to believe in them, trust them, and love them. [*Harmony* 17:9] Finally, with the fourth group, the Gentiles—or non-Jews—the Lord had great success. In spite of their limited understanding of many concepts of the Gospel, they, nevertheless, had a tendency to reach out to the Lord with faith and firmly grasp the concepts He taught them. [*Harmony* 3:60, 61; 10:27-31, etc.] Jesus treated each group of people differently, relating to them according to what they understood, or *should have* understood. It could be said that the Lord was more than fair with people![20]

Laboring with and training His disciples—especially His closest "Twelve"—involved a large portion of the Lord's entire ministry. He began to call them to work with Him early on in His ministry. The first members of this group were originally disciples of John the Baptist. With this being the case, they already had an understanding—though incomplete—of the basic purpose of the ministry of the Messiah. As time progressed Jesus called other men to join His growing group of disciples. With the exception of Judas, Jesus had hand-picked them all. [*Harmony* 4:67-79] At first they followed the Lord on a part-time basis for up to about 18 months. [*Harmony* 4:79/2] It was only then that He asked them to become His disciples on a full-time basis. He wanted to make sure that they were truly ready to forsake all and follow Him. During these months, they had a chance to observe the Lord's ministry on a firsthand basis. They worked closely with Him. It was only after they were officially called and ordained, that He began to send them out to work on their own. [*Harmony* 4:67; 8:37-58] They served as close associates of His in spreading the message of the Gospel. For the remaining couple of years of the Lord's ministry, Jesus continued to instruct them in the work of the Gospel. [*Harmony* 10:86-118] When an additional number of extended disciples were chosen—called the "Seventy"—the Twelve served as leaders among them. [*Harmony* 11:133-149] He placed strong confidence in all His disciples. He made it clear that His followers must give account of their responsibilities as disciples of His. He would not tolerate indolence or neglect of duty. [*Harmony* 12:59-61] Besides the men who were His fellow workers, Jesus had a number of women who followed Him and assisted in His ministry. [*Harmony* 6:19] In fact, the Lord firmly upheld and expanded the place of women in the work of the Gospel and the church. [*Harmony* 18:28, 29, 59] He praised the power of their faith and criticized those who didn't believe their testimony. In a society that dramatically downplayed the role of women, such an emphasis was radical in the extreme! Part of the instruction the Lord gave to His followers was how they might, on a practical, day-to-day basis, cooperate with one another in the Gospel work, no matter how tough the circumstances might become. He told them to treat one another with tenderness and patience, always showing a forgiving spirit. [*Harmony* 10:96, 97] Further, the Savior gave specific counsel as to how deal with problems that might arise among its members and workers within the growing church. [*Harmony* 10:109-111] The Lord prepared His disciples for the long haul, not just for a short period of time. His counsel was timeless, practical for every age of history. Finally, the Lord commissioned all His disciples, in His stead, to take the message of the Gospel to the whole world, to both Jews *and* non-Jews—or Gentiles. [*Harmony* 18:88] To accomplish this awesome task, Jesus gave them the promise of the Holy Spirit who would empower them. [*Harmony* 18:90] Jesus was very organized in His plan of discipling His followers. He knew what He was doing. And His overall plan met with dramatic success![[21]]

—

## The Epilogue to the Gospel Story (Matthew 28:20; Mark 16:20; Luke 24:53; John 20:30, 31; 21:24, 25)

There were many other things that Jesus did—including the performance of miracles—in the presence of His disciples, that have not been included in the Gospel record. But, regarding the record that does exist, those who described these events did so for all to read and understand. And these Gospel recorders—Matthew, Mark, Luke, and especially John—were willing to certify that the words written in their record were completely accurate and reliable. All can be assured that their testimony is the truth.[(u)] [100]

[100] John 20:30, 31; 21:24

Besides the things that were written in the Gospel record, there are many things that could be said about Jesus and what He did. In fact it is supposed that the earth is not large enough to contain all the books so written![(v)] [101]

However, the things that are included in this written story were recorded so that you might have complete confidence that Jesus was—and is—the Christ, the Messiah, both the Son of God and the Son of Man. And because of your belief in the Lord, you can possess eternal life within the power of His name![102]

Amen![(w)] [103]

**Supplementary Notes:**

**(a) [18:1]** The 14th day of Nisan—the "preparation" of John 19:31 in the KJV (our Friday in the *Harmony*) was the Passover Day. The 15th day of Nisan—which began when the sun set on the 14th—was the first day in the week-long celebration of the Feast of Unleavened Bread. Therefore, the "high day"—also of John 19:31 in the KJV (the "High Sabbath" of the *Harmony*)—referred to the first day of the Feast of the Unleavened Bread, which was a ritual Sabbath day (Leviticus 23:6, 7).

**(b) [18:4]** There have been attempts to explain the blood and water mixture that came from Jesus when He was pierced with the spear, including the supposition that Jesus "died of a broken heart." I consider such a suggestion to be improbable. While I am clearly not a medical expert (or even an amateur one!), I've been told, over and over, by several medical personnel, under normal conditions, such a flow would indicate that Jesus was suffering from some kind of *long-standing* illness involving the heart and lungs. (Such a possibility is extremely unlikely; it is impossible to believe!) Further, I am told, an immediate medical situation, *no matter how traumatic,* would not produce such a result. Thus, for the time being, *based upon what I've been told by others,* I believe that we just don't know what actually caused this unusual mixture of the flow that came from His body. It is anyone's *guess!* For myself, I decided *not* to guess!

**(c) [18:5]** The phrase, "he that saw it" (John 19:35 KJV), without any doubt, refers to the disciple (or Apostle) John, the author of the Gospel of John.

---

101 John 21:25
102 John 20:31; 21:24
103 Matthew 28:20; Mark 16:20; Luke 24:53; John 21:25

And further, I suspect the purpose of the John's elaborate explanation in this verse has *less* to do with the water and blood mixture he describes in John 19:34, but rather, *more* to do with the fact that none of the Lord's bones were broken and that He was, in fact, pierced—both of which are fulfillments of specific Bible prophecies (John 19:36, 37), as are recorded in *Harmony* 18:5.

**(d) [18:18]** The details of this paragraph are a bit confusing to figure and harmonize. However, I am satisfied with the results as found in the *Harmony*.

**(e) [18:29]** I am not completely comfortable with the overall timing of these events, but it is the best that I can figure. Here is the projected sequence of events: (1) Mary Magdalene leaves the city, arrives at the tomb for the first time, and finds it empty (*Harmony* 18:13). (2) Other women are on their way to the tomb, but have not arrived there yet (*Harmony* 18:13). (3) Mary returns to the city to tell Peter and John about the empty tomb (*Harmony* 18:15). (4) The other woman come to the tomb and likewise found it empty. There they meet two angels who instruct them to tell the disciples that Jesus is risen (*Harmony* 18:16-18). (5) Mary, now in the city, tells Peter and John of the empty tomb (*Harmony* 18:20). (6) Both Peter and John arrive at the tomb, find it empty, and return to the city (*Harmony* 18:20, 21). (7) Mary arrives at the tomb the second time, and sees two angels. Then, she meets Jesus, and He tells her that He needs to ascend into heaven. Finally, Mary returns to the city to inform the disciples (*Harmony* 18:22-28). (8) Jesus ascends into heaven to see the Father (*Harmony* 18:29). (9) Finally, Jesus descends from heaven and greets the women *still returning to the city*—sequence Number 4 (*Harmony* 18:29). To me, however, there is not enough time between the women's return to the city and the time Jesus actually meets with them. For, during that time period, Peter and John come to the tomb and go back into the city; Mary returns to the tomb and meets Jesus; Jesus ascends into heaven and then returns to meets the women *still* returning to the city. The way I see it, they must have been slow walkers! Perhaps there is better sequence than the one I suggest. To be sure, though, I'm sure that there was a good bit of confusion on the day of the resurrection regarding the things that happened—when they happened, and to whom—rendering the account a bit fuzzy, not only to us, but also to them who experienced it! The reality of the various events is of more importance than their sequence.

**(f) [18:33]** It has been suggested by some scholars that the "four and twenty elders" of Revelation 4:4, described as being in "God's Throneroom" in heaven, are part of the group of those who were resurrected when Jesus was, and were also later taken to heaven when Jesus arrived there. The Bible does not specifically say that these resurrected ones went to heaven; however, one might reasonably make this assumption. Personally, I do ascribe to the above suggestion.

**(g) [18:41]** We would wish that the Gospel record had shared with us some of the Old Testament Scriptures Jesus quoted to the two disciples during this event. Unfortunately we are forced to speculate. Perhaps—maybe even likely—some of these texts were the ones that some weeks later were quoted by Peter in his sermon on the Day of Pentecost. They can be found in Acts 2. (See also **Note "j"** below.)

**(h) [18:44]** Of course there were only ten of the disciples in attendance that day, with Judas Iscariot now dead and Thomas missing.

**(i) [18:47]** I included the word "wrists" (in addition to "hands") in this portion of the *Harmony*. This is because I make the usual modern assumption that the wrists were nailed to the cross, not the hands, as such. This assumption is based on two concepts: (1) It is believed that the nailing of the actual hands would be insufficient to hold someone's weight on a cross, thus, the nailing of wrists was practiced. And (2), in *Bible times,* when referring to hands, the wrists were considered a part of the hand structure; thus, the use of the word "hands" in the Biblical record *to include the wrists* is technically correct. So, in order to make the wording of the *Harmony* more understandable for our age, I used the additional word "wrists." Considering all these things, then, I think this is an accurate rendering.

**(j) [18:50]** Unfortunately the actual texts that Jesus quoted here are not given. I would think, though, some of these texts are included among those that Peter himself later quoted on the Day of Pentecost, as contained in Acts 2:25-28, 34, 35 (Psalm 16:8-11, 110:1). (See also **Note "g"** above.)

**(k) [18:51]** The phrase that states that Jesus "breathed" on the disciples is intriguing. Of course, there could be debate on the issue as to its true meaning. However, I really like the interpretation I made in the *Harmony*. It truly expresses the Lord's intimacy with His followers!

**(l) [18:51]** What is the meaning of the forgiving of sins comment in John 20:23? It seems to me that Jesus, in part, referred to the sins one might *commit against the disciples*, as opposed to the forgiving of sins in *general.* On the other hand, it seems clear to me from the Gospel record that Jesus referred to something more than this. He referred, I think, to a persistent attitude of rebellion, to refuse to deal with *open sins that have stained the name of the church and God.* This includes sins committed by those who persistently and rebelliously remain in the state of sin by refusing to confess them or seek forgiveness for them. These are the kind of sins that the Lord had earlier generally referred to in *Harmony* 10:109-111, and, as an example, the kind that Paul specifically mentions in 1 Corinthians 5:1-5. To be sure, though, I am convinced that Jesus did not refer to the *general forgiving of one's personal sins.* These sins are to be taken directly to the Lord, not to the church. Accordingly, based upon all this, that is why I interpreted the text the way I did in the *Harmony.*

**(m) [18:55]** The phrase "after eight days" in John 20:26 in the KJV, based upon the inclusive reckoning of the Jews, would mean "one week later." How did I arrive at this conclusion? This is how "eight days" of inclusive reckoning is calculated in this verse: (1) The *first* Sunday, (2) Monday, (3) Tuesday, (4) Wednesday, (5) Thursday, (6) Friday, (7) Saturday, and (8) the *second* Sunday— a total of eight different days. In this case, then, based on John 20:19, this was "eight days after" the "first day of the week" (or our Sunday), when Jesus *first* met with the disciples after His resurrection. In other words, Jesus met with the disciples the next (or the *second)* Sunday. So then, in reality, these "eight days" really means exactly seven days later! That is why I interpreted the text the way I did in the *Harmony.*

**(n) [18:56]** (See **Note "i"** above.)

**(o) [18:80]** There have been intricate efforts made to explain the Lord and Peter's use of various forms of the word "love." Perhaps they are valid. I suspect that they are not. That is why I interpreted the text the way I did.

But for what it is worth, here is what some have suggested: In the first two instances Jesus questioned Peter, using the Greek words "agape" (the strong Greek word for "love"). Because Peter felt that he could not aspire to such an exalted form of love, he, in response, used "phileo" (the weaker word for "love"). Then, in Jesus' final question, He conceded to Peter's response and used Peter's own term, accepting this form of love as the disciple's best service and sincere commitment. However, I am told, that in normal conversation it was common practice to use interchangeably both of these words. Besides, Jesus and Peter were speaking to each other in Aramaic, not Greek. Furthermore, I'm not convinced that either Jesus or Peter would have communicated to each other in the way suggested above.

**(p) [18:89/]** There is a tendency for people to rely too heavily on the miracles of the body—such as physical healings. Of course, we are always pleased when we actually see miracles of the healing of the body. But I believe that that should not be our main emphasis. Nevertheless, miracles are one of the identifying features of the ministry of the church. However, such are to be mainly the miracles of the conversion of the human heart rather than those of the body. (See *Harmony* 9:25-54 for more information on this subject.)

**(q) [18:92]** From the way this text is written (Acts 1:3), the specific date for the Ascension was 40 days after the Lord's *resurrection* on the first day of the week. This explains the date chosen in the *Harmony* for the Ascension.

**(r) [18:99+]** This is the eighth of eight insertions in the *Harmony* that places the events of the three-and-a-half-year ministry of Jesus on a "timeline," divided into seven six-month segments. The other segment insertions can be found in the following locations: Segment One, *Harmony* 2:21/; Two, *Harmony* 3:0; Three, *Harmony* 3:33/2; Four, *Harmony* 3:71/; Five, *Harmony* 6:17/; Six, *Harmony* 10:0; and Seven, *Harmony* 11:0. And, as can be seen in the listing of the seven six-month segments, of the Lord's three-and-a-half years' ministry in this section, I designate the standard 1/7 through 7/7 numbering for each time of the seven time periods.

**(s) [18:99/7+]** The **Thematic Preview of the Ministry of Jesus** parallels the **Thematic Review of the Ministry of Jesus** (*Harmony* 2:21/5-18). For more information on how the **Thematic Preview** and the **Thematic Review** are to be used, please refer to "Thematic Preview of the Ministry of Jesus" and "Thematic Review of the Ministry of Jesus" in "Features for Using the *Harmony* as a Reference Book," which follows this chapter.

The subjects that I chose for both the **Thematic Preview** and **Review** came to me as I prepared this book. They were the things that stood out in my mind. It is not by any means a complete list. I am confident, though, that the key events in the ministry of Jesus are adequately covered. Also, the **Cross**

**References** in the *Harmony* that I chose to document the points I make in the **Thematic Review** are only a few of the references I could have used.

**(t) [18:99+/10]** Why did Jesus not openly proclaim His Messiahship? For an answer to this question, please refer to *Harmony* 10:54, 54/.

**(u) [18:100]** While I listed all the various names of the Gospel writers when it comes to verifying their accounts, the Biblical record mentions only John.

**(v) [18:101]** John made the statement (in the KJV) that, should all that Jesus did during His ministry be recorded, he "suppose[ed] that even the world itself could not contain the books that should be written." Such a declaration is a strong hyperbole—an exaggeration for the purpose of emphasis. It seems to me that John was expressing a real frustration that so many more things could have been said by the four Gospel writers about the Lord's ministry. Indeed, many things, of necessity, had to be left out.

To give some perspective to this amazing statement of John, consider the following two comparisons: (1) The recorded story of the last six months of the Lord's ministry comprises roughly one half of the entire written record of His public ministry of three and a half years. If the first three years of His ministry had received the same treatment as the last six months, the Gospel record would have been no less than three and a half times its present length. (2) The written record of the final week of the Lord's ministry takes up about one fourth of the Gospel record. If each week in the Lord's ministry (about 186 weeks) had received the same treatment in the written record, the Gospel account would be no less than 45 times its present length! (It should be noted, too, that even the final week of the Lord's life is probably told in a condensed version of what the Lord said and did.)

And remember, the entire written record of the Lord's early life until He was thirty years of age (when He began His public ministry) comprises only a relatively few pages of the entire Gospel story. Indeed, so much more could have been said!

**(w) [18:103]** At this point in the *Harmony,* I wish to take some space to share with the reader my personal reflections on what I discovered as I wrote this book. The things I list here are those items that surprised—and even shocked—me as I put this volume together. I trust that my observations will be of some interest to the reader.

**First,** by far and away the most amazing thing I discovered is how tough Jesus was. We often measure the ministry of Jesus by the fifteen or so hours that He, without complaint or resistance, suffered and died as the Sin Bearer of the world. But that tells only part of the story. The truth is that throughout the course of His public ministry the Lord always stood up, in word and action, to both the devil and the constantly belligerent Jewish leaders. He never gave in at all. He was in charge at all times. If a tough-mindedness was called for, He provided it. If a strong word needed to be said, He spoke it. Yet, one senses that He never lost control of Himself during any situation into which He might be placed.

**Second,** it was fascinating to me to discover the large emphasis the Lord placed upon working for Gentiles. It can be assumed—incorrectly, I might add—that Jesus spent all His time with Jews. But such is not the case. For those of us who can be classified as "Gentile Christians" this is especially gratifying. The Lord appreciated the demonstration of faith Gentiles showed to Him and His ministry. He never cast away as unimportant those who were not a part of the Jewish church. He was just as excited to provide salvation to Gentiles as He was to Jews.

**Third,** the amount of time the Lord devoted to discussing His personal relationship with God the Father is striking to me. He not only talked about His personal, direct communication with the Father, He also discussed His unique relationship within the confines of the Godhead. He was never afraid to let people know that *He* intimately knew the Father, and that He *always* had. In short, the reality of the Lord's divinity was very important to Him—so important that He talked about it often.

**Fourth,** I was surprised by how organized the Savior was in the way He went about His ministry. One might get the idea that Jesus just went around in His ministry to people with no particular program in mind. Not so! There was a definite structure in His approach to His work. Taking His ministry as a whole, one can quickly see just how well-organized it was. It had a clear beginning, a definite emphasis throughout, and an obvious and dramatic ending.

**Fifth,** I was truly impressed by how patient Jesus was with His disciples. In spite of the troubles they seemed always to be getting into, the Lord never gave up on them. He encouraged them when they needed encouragement. He chided them when they needed discipline. Yet, at all times, He seemingly never lost His patience with them. Humanly speaking, it seems to me that He could have easily—and often—given up on them. Yet, He never did. Yes, He expected much of them; but when they fell short of His goal for them, He always gave them another chance to redeem themselves.

# FEATURES FOR USING THE *HARMONY* AS A REFERENCE BOOK

Using the *Harmony* as reference book (or a commentary) can be very rewarding. In that regard, here are some situations that might occur when the *Harmony* would be of significant help:

When someone is reading the *Harmony* and, for comparison purposes, wants to find that particular reference (or references, in the case of multiple accounts) in any particular Bible or translation

When someone is reading the Gospel story in a Bible and wants to find how a particular account is recorded and/or interpreted in the *Harmony*

When someone is thinking of a particular story, word, or concept, and wishes to see how such is characterized or interpreted in the *Harmony*

When someone wishes to see how a particular story relates in timing or meaning to another story or event

There are a number of features this book contains that, once understood, can enhance significantly the value the reader can attain from the *Harmony* in the case of all of the above situations. Below, listed alphabetically, are those features. All direct reference to any of these features are in bold print. On occasion, to completely understand how to use one feature, it may be necessary to refer to another feature found elsewhere in this listing. At first, reading the foregoing list may seem a bit confusing; but if patient, the reader will soon, with some experimentation and exploration, become accustomed to their various meanings and will discover how truly easy it is to find one's way around within the *Harmony.*

## Alphabetical Index:

The **Alphabetical Index** located near the end of the book contains a large indexing of events and persons involved in the life of Jesus, as well as the various sayings and teachings of Christ. The purpose of this index is to help the reader to quickly find certain events, sayings, or portions of the life and ministry of Jesus. All entries in this index are followed by the appropriate **Harmony Reference Number.** (See the introduction to the **Alphabetical Index** to learn more on how to effectively use this index.)

## Chapter Titles:

The titles of the various 18 chapters of the *Harmony* are found at the top of the page at the beginning of each chapter. Each title is practical in nature. This means that the chapter titles allow the reader to know, in brief, what that particular part of the book is about. Also, under the main title of each chapter is the *opening* and *closing* **Event of the *Harmony*** contained in that chapter, so that the reader can know the range of events covered. Finally, the range of **Dating** for the entire chapter is listed.

## Chronological Index:

This part of the index contains an entire reproduction (in chronological order, of course), of all the parts of the *Harmony*: **Chapter Titles, Sections, Sub-sections, Timeline Segments,** and both the **Thematic Preview** and **Review of the Ministry of Jesus.** In addition to this, all the **Harmony References Numbers** for each of the appropriate above items are listed. This index is useful is seeing how particular events relate to each other in time sequence. (See the introduction for this index to learn more on how to effectively use this particular index.)

## Cross References:

The approximately 1,600 **Cross References** of the *Harmony*—similar in function to the marginal references of many Bibles—are found interspersed throughout the entire text of the *Harmony*. **Cross References** are of the following types: (1) Old Testament references; (2) New Testament references (beside those found in Matthew, Mark, Luke, John, and Acts 1:2-12); and (3) References (including **Explanatory Notes**) within the *Harmony* itself (where the reference, designated by a **Harmony Reference Number,** is written in a "chapter-and-verse-style"). In all cases, when a particular text is referred to in the *Harmony*, the **Cross Reference** is listed within brackets (within the main text of the *Harmony*), or within parentheses (in the **Supplementary Notes** section).

## Dating:

One of the unique features of this particular harmony of the Gospels is the placing of the entire life and ministry of Jesus on a timeline. This is accomplished by **Dating** *every* **Event of the *Harmony*.** The **Dating** procedure of the *Harmony* is listed in the following places: (1) At the end of **Chapter Titles** (within parentheses); (2) In **Sections** (within "less than" and "greater than" symbols [< >]); (3) In **Sub-sections** (also within "less than" and "greater than" symbols); and (4) In the **Timeline Segments** (within the text of each segment). In short, with the exception of the general introduction and conclusion to the entire **Harmony Text** of the *Harmony,* virtually *everything* in the *Harmony* has a **Dating** designation. This is particularly useful when looking up any one event or concept. (See **Timeline Segments** for more details on how and where these segments are placed throughout the *Harmony.*)

(It should be noted that the **Dating** procedure used in the *Harmony* presented some interesting issues that had to be considered and resolved. To understand these issues better, please refer to the special note, "Dating Issues of the *Harmony,*" located at the end of the Introduction to the *Harmony* at the beginning of the book.)

### Events of the *Harmony:*

The **Events of the *Harmony*** are the individual stories, introductions, and/or events that took place during the life and ministry of Jesus, as are recorded in the Biblical Gospel record. There are about 180 of such event entries in the *Harmony,* making up the bulk of the entire *Harmony.* Each of these events is listed under the individual **Sections** or **Sub-sections** of the individual chapters.

### Explanatory Notes:

The **Explanatory Notes** are found in fully indented paragraphs throughout the *Harmony.* There are nearly 700 of these notations in the *Harmony.* These notes are the author's brief commentary (or explanatory) notations on the **Harmony Text** that either preceded it, or, in some cases, follow it. These comments are in *addition to* the embedded comments that have been placed within individual **Harmony Texts.** On occasion, too, **Explanatory Notes** can be summaries of various points made within the *Harmony.* Each **Explanatory Note** is numbered, based upon the **Harmony Text** that *immediately* precedes it. To distinguish the note from the **Harmony Text,** a forward slash (/) was added when they are found in the **Alphabetical Index** listings, or in the **Harmony Textual Range.** Should there be *more than one* consecutive **Explanatory Note** listed in the **Harmony Text,** then each of these notes will be numbered by a superscripted number in brackets at the end of the note (such as [1], [2], etc.). When listed in the **Alphabetical Index,** these multiple **Explanatory Notes** listings are indicated by a forward slash and their numbering. In the *Harmony,* the numeric listing of the multiple **Explanatory Notes** continues until there is another **Harmony Text,** even if there are **Sections** or **Sub-sections** interspersed between.

### Footnotes:

The **Footnotes** are listed at the bottom of the pages in the *Harmony* when a particular **Harmony Text** *ends* on that page. When **Harmony Texts** begin on a page, but end on the next page, the **Footnote** will be listed on that second page. The **Footnote** number is superscripted at the end of each **Harmony Text.** Listed in each **Footnote,** in chronological order, are the various texts in Matthew, Mark, Luke, John, or Acts, used for the **Harmony Text.** The **Footnotes** provide easy access to the Bible references as well as the parallel accounts of the four Gospel writers. All the **Footnotes** serve as the basis of the **Scriptural Index** at the back of the *Harmony.*

### Harmony Text:

The **Harmony Text** is the main part of the entire *Harmony.* There are no less than 1,818 such **Harmony Texts.** Each text is based upon the verses (or portions of them), that are listed as **Footnotes** numbers at the bottom of the page, where the number of each **Footnote** corresponds to the superscripted number at the end of each **Text.** The message of each **Harmony Text** is based upon an expanded paraphrase and/or interpretation of the Biblical verses referred to. Each of the **Harmony Texts** is assigned a **Harmony Reference Number** (similar to the chapter and verse designation found in all Bibles). Such a designation is to be used for quick research purposes. (If there is more than one sentence of explanation or interpretation at the end of a text, it is usually placed within the following **Explanatory Note,** rather than in the **Harmony Text** itself.)

### Harmony Reference Numbers:

The **Harmony Reference Numbers** are the way that the *Harmony* identifies each paragraph of the **Harmony Text.** This identification is made by listing the chapter and paragraph (or "verse") by a number at the end of each paragraph of the **Harmony Text.** *This is done the same way that the chapters and verses of a regular Bible are made, except, of course, they are listed at the* ***end*** *of the "verse" instead at the beginning.* The **Harmony References Numbers** provide the way that things can be easily and quickly found anywhere in the *Harmony. All* entries in the **Alphabetical Index, Scriptural Index, Cross References** (involving the **Harmony Texts**), as well as many parts of the **Supplementary Notes,** are in the form of **Harmony Reference Numbers.** In reality, the **Harmony Reference Numbers**—as in the case of a regular Bible—are the way that the vast majority of things are quickly found in the entire *Harmony.* (Refer to **Explanatory Notes, Timeline Segments,** and the **Thematic Preview** or **Review** to learn how they are referenced and found.)

### Harmony Textual Range:

The **Harmony Textual Range** is listed at the top of each page. The purpose of this listing is to help the reader to quickly find a certain **Harmony Reference Number** in the *Harmony.* This designation, very similar to regular chapter and verse references found in almost all Bibles, includes all the **Harmony Texts** that are fully, or *partially*, contained on a certain page. This means that the **Harmony Textual Range** for an particular page includes, not only any **Harmony Text** that *ends* on that page, but also includes one that *begins* but does not end on that page. However, in the case when an *entire* page contains **Explanatory Notes,** the **Harmony Textual Range** for that page will be followed by a forward slash (/) which corresponds to the number of the *first* **Explanatory Note** in that particular sequence. In some cases, the **Harmony Textual Range** on a page may contain the specific numbers for the **Explanatory Notes** on that page.

### Scriptural Index:

To make any true harmony of the Gospel story practical, such an index is absolutely necessary. The primary purpose of this index is to find a specific place in the *Harmony* when one is reading any part of the Gospel record in the Scriptures themselves. In short, this index contains all the **Footnotes** found in the entire *Harmony.* It is located at the back of the book for easy reference. (Refer to the introduction of this index to understand more about how to use it.) The value of this particular index cannot be overestimated!

### Sectional References:

The **Sectional References** are those texts of the Gospel record in the Bible that were used to make up a particular **Section** of the *Harmony.* These references are enclosed within parentheses. These references also include all **Sectional References** and **Sub-sectional References** from the Gospel record that may be a part of any **Sub-section** found under a **Section.**

## Sections:

Each chapter of the *Harmony* is divided into **Sections.** The titling of the **Sections** is centered on the page. Each **Section** contains the following parts: (1) An explanatory title for the **Section**; (2) The **Dating** and **Segmental Placement Number** of the events contained within the **Section**; and (3) The **Sectional References** used for the text of the entire **Section.**

## Segmental Placement:

Every event during the three-and-a-half year public ministry of Jesus (from His baptism to His ascension) has such a **Segmental Placement,** recorded within parentheses. These three and a half year years are divided into *seven* **Timeline Segments** of six months a piece. Each is assigned a consecutive number, 1-7, to distinguish it from the other segments. At the end of the **Dating** of all **Events of the *Harmony*,** such a number is placed to allow the reader to know when the events took place during the entire public ministry of the Lord. These placement numbers are appropriately listed as 1/7 through 7/7 respectively. (This means, for example, that an event that has a 7/7 **Segmental Placement** number took place sometime during the last six months of the Lord's public ministry.)

## Sub-sectional References:

The **Sub-sectional References** are those texts that were used from the Gospel record in the Bible to make up that particular **Sub-section.** These references are placed within "wavy brackets" ({ }).

## Sub-sections:

Often under the **Sections** of the *Harmony* are **Sub-sections.** These **Sub-sections** make up portions of the **Sections.** These **Sub-sections** are listed at the left hand of the various pages, and are preceded by an extended hyphen (—), followed by a space and then the title of that **Sub-section**. Each **Sub-section** contains the following components: (1) An explanatory title for the **Sub-section**; (2) The **Dating** and **Segmental Placement Number** for the events of the **Sub-section**; and (3) The **Sub-sectional References** from the Gospel record in the Bible that are used in making up the entire text of the **Sub-section.**

## Supplementary Notes:

There are about 450 **Supplementary Notes** found within the 18 chapters of this book. These notes discuss various issues, observations, or problems that were encountered in the interpretation of some of the **Harmony Texts.** These notes are located at the end of each chapter, and are indicated by a superscripted letter within parentheses at the end of the paragraph that is being discussed. In some cases, there is more than one such entry for a particular paragraph. Each **Supplementary Note** listed at the end of a chapter is preceded, in brackets ([ ]), by the appropriate **Harmony Reference Number** or **Explanatory Note Number.**

## Thematic Preview of the Ministry of Jesus:

This feature of the *Harmony* previews the major themes of the ministry of Jesus—the items that the careful reader of the story of Jesus needs to look for when studying this book. The **Thematic Preview of the Ministry of Jesus** (also called the **Thematic Preview**) can be found at the conclusion of the first **Timeline Segment** in Chapter 2. (At the end of the eighth **Timeline Segment** in Chapter 18, the **Thematic Review of the Ministry of Jesus** can be found.) For reference purposes, each paragraph of the **Thematic Preview** is numbered with a superscripted number within brackets, based upon the nearest **Harmony Text** that preceded it. In the **Alphabetical Index,** such references are indicated by a forward slash, followed by the appropriate number (or numbers) of the paragraph (or paragraphs).

## Thematic Review of the Ministry of Jesus:

The **Thematic Review of the Ministry of Jesus** (also called the **Thematic Review**) is a follow-up to the **Thematic Preview of the Ministry of Jesus,** which can be found at the end of the first **Timeline Segment** in Chapter 2. This feature of the *Harmony,* found near the end of Chapter 18, takes a look at the same things that are a part of the **Thematic Preview of the Ministry of Jesus;** but this time, various **Harmony References** (as **Cross References**) are listed in brackets ([ ]), so that the reader can look up the facts presented in the each section of the **Thematic Review.** For reference purposes, each paragraph of the **Thematic Review** is numbered with a superscripted number within brackets, based upon the nearest **Harmony Text** that preceded it. In the **Alphabetical Index** (found under "Timeline segments"), such references are indicated by a forward slash, followed by the appropriate number (or numbers) of the paragraph (or paragraphs).

### Timeline Segments:

There are eight **Timeline Segments** entries in the *Harmony*, which describe a portion (or portions) of the ministry of Jesus. The public ministry of Jesus, which lasted for three and a half years, has been divided into seven segments of six months a piece. These sections make up the **Timeline Segments.** The first seven of these are placed at the beginning of each segment. The eighth such segment is placed at the end of the seventh segment, serving as a review of the Lord's whole ministry. For reference purposes, each paragraph of all **Timeline Segments** is numbered with a superscripted number within brackets, based upon the nearest **Harmony Text** that preceded it. In the **Alphabetical Index,** such references are indicated by a forward slash, followed by the appropriate number (or numbers) of the paragraph.

### *Additional Note:*

Except for **Supplementary Notes,** *every paragraph* of the *Harmony* is labeled in some way, either by a superscripted number within brackets (as in the case of **Harmony Texts**), a forward slash (as in the case of a single **Explanatory Note**), a forward slash plus a number or numbers within brackets (in the case of multiple **Explanatory Notes, Timeline Segments,** and either the **Thematic Preview** or **Review of the Ministry of Jesus**). These reference numbers, of one sort or another, can be found in various places throughout the entire *Harmony.* This makes the finding of any of the above items very easy to accomplish! ***Special notes:*** If a **Timeline Segment** or an **Explanatory Note** is placed at the *beginning* of a chapter, its reference number in the **Supplementary Notes** section at the end of a chapter is a zero [0]; if an **Explanatory Note** is placed at the end of a **Section** title, it is designated by a plus mark (+); and if such an **Explanatory Note** is placed at the end of a **Sub-section** title, it is designated by two plus marks (++).

**Also,** it will be useful to study the introduction of each of the three indexes of the index section to fully understand how to effectively use them.

# — ACKNOWLEDGEMENTS AND SOURCES —

## — Acknowledgements —

The writing of a book such as this, while it took about seven years of relatively concentrated effort, is really the result of nearly a lifetime of studying the life of Jesus. Books that I have read (including the classic volume, *The Desire of Ages,* by Ellen G. White), classes in school that I took (including a college course on the Life of Jesus), as well as my continual personal study of the Gospel story, have deeply affected me and the various interpretations I have placed in the book.

In addition, as a pastor, I have preached many sermons that have been the result of a careful study of the story of Jesus as recorded in the Bible. Throughout the years, too, in different places, I have preached the same sermons over and over again on particular subjects from the Gospels. Several portions of this book reflect strongly the gist of these sermons. This is particularly true in the case of Chapter 5, concerning the "Sermon on the Mount"; Chapter 7, which contains the events of a single day in the life of the Savior; Chapter 9, on the subject of the Bread of Life Teaching; Chapter 17, dealing with the Legal Trials of Jesus and the Crucifixion (which is also my favorite chapter); Chapter 18, which discusses the events between Jesus' Resurrection and Ascension; and the combination of Chapters 14-17, outlining the events of the so-called Passion Week of Jesus. Several other chapters in the *Harmony* became new and special projects of mine as I worked on the book. This includes the last part of Chapter 10, detailing the Lord's effort to get through to His 12 disciples when they were frustrated with each other; and Chapters 11 and 12, where Jesus had to deal with His quickly deteriorating relationship with the Jewish leaders.

In my preaching I have developed the style of paraphrasing the words of Scripture in an attempt to explain the meaning of various texts. This habit of mine was put to continued use in the writing of this book.

When I finally set my mind to produce this book, I determined that my primary source of information would be the actual words of the four Gospels. In that regard I used several Bible translations. I used the standard work, the 1611 version of the *King James Bible* (referred to on occasion in the Supplementary Notes section of the *Harmony* as KJV). I also used the *New American Standard Bible*—the Bible I have been preaching from for over 30 years. In that regard, in most cases I used the modern spellings for places and individuals that are a part of this bible. And too, from time-to time I referred to *The Word: The Bible From 26 Translations,* edited by Curtis Vaughan. The basic text I used, however, was *The Interlinear Greek-English New Testament,* edited and translated by Jay P. Green, Sr. In all cases, though, my main use of these Bibles was to make sure that I did not miss any part of the Gospel story. It was always my intent and effort to express the Gospels in my own words.

In addition to these Bibles, I used a certain Bible commentary that was of great value to me. That being the case, I wish to thank the *Review and Herald Publishing Association* in Hagerstown, Maryland, who gave me permission to use the excellent Harmony of the Gospel they produced many years ago that is a part of the *Seventh-day Adventist Bible Commentary.* Also, they gave me permission to use the Chronology of the Gospel story that is a part of their Harmony. Without the diligent efforts of those who produced the Harmony and its Chronology, the writing of my book would have been much, much more difficult—if not impossible—than it actually was. The publishing house additionally gave me permission when I occasionally used ideas suggested by the commentary when interpreting some portions of the Gospel story. Overall, this involved the following sources: *Volume 5* of the commentary (containing the four Gospels), *Volume 6* (which includes the book of Acts). In all cases, however, I used my own words in the expression of the interpretation of any verse. I also used *Volume 8* (the *Bible Dictionary* of the same commentary series), from which I obtained information regarding distances and locations of various places in and around the land of Israel during the time of Jesus. In the final analysis, though, I bear responsibility for the interpretations I made on any verse or concept.

I also wish thank TEACH services, for the use of the book *Behold the Man!* (Copyright 2005 by TEACH Services, Inc., and used with permission; located on the Web at http://www.teachservices.com), originally written by Taylor G. Bunch in 1940. TEACH Services allowed me to use information from that book that was extremely useful in the production of Chapter 17 in my book, when I discussed the illegalities of the various court trials of Jesus. As was always the case, I put everything into my own words.

I want, too, to take this opportunity to thank a few individuals who have been of assistance to me in the writing of this book. First and foremost, I want to thank my wife, Janice, who patiently allowed be to spend untold hours working on this project. In addition, on occasion, she encouraged me to finish my effort.

I wish to thank Alice Cronje', who proofread the book on two separate occasions. Her words of advice and encouragement were invaluable to me.

I also thank Leigh Chacon, who fairly early on in the project, proofread the book, and gave words of encouragement to me.

## — Sources for this Harmony of the Gospels —

The following Bibles and books were used for research purposes; they are neither directly nor intentionally quoted in the *Harmony*:

Bibles —

The King James Bible, 1611 edition (KJV)

The New American Standard Bible (NASB), The Lockman Foundation, Anaheim, California, 92816

The Interlinear Greek-English New Testament, Jay P. Green, Sr., Editor and Translator, Henrickson Publishers, Peabody, Massachusetts 01961-3473

The Word: The Bible from 26 Translations, Curtis Vaughn, Th.D., General Editor, Mathis Publishers, Inc., 3401 McNair Street, P.O. Box 8621, Moss Point, Mississippi 35963

Reference Books —

The Seventh-day Adventist Bible Commentary, Volume 5, Matthew-John, 1956 edition

The Seventh-day Adventist Bible Commentary, Volume 6, Acts-Ephesians, 1957 edition

The Seventh-day Adventist Bible Dictionary, Volume 8 (of the Seventh-day Adventist Bible Commentary series), 1960 edition, all published and copyrighted by the Review and Herald Publishing Association, 55 West Oak Ridge Drive, Hagerstown, Maryland 21740

# — INDEXES —

# CHRONOLOGICAL INDEX TO THE EVENTS OF THE *HARMONY*

The Chronological Index is a complete chronological listing of all the Parts, Chapter Titles, Sections, Subsections, and Timeline Segments of the *Harmony*. Included with this index are the *Harmony* Scriptural references. Those references for each chapter are both **<u>bolded and underlined</u>**. The sectional references are **bolded**. And, the sub-sectional references are ***bolded and italicized***. The primary purpose of this index is to find the various events and stories of the Gospel record as they relate to each other in time and chronology.

**PART I — Beginnings: From the Birth of Jesus Through the Lord's First Miracle (6 B.C. - A.D. 28)**

*Chapter* ONE: The Early Years of the Messiah — From the Mission of the WORD, to Jesus Grows Up in Nazareth (Autumn, 6 B.C. — Autumn, A.D. 27) — **<u>Harmony 1:1-84 and 1:1-14 (Supplementary Notes)</u>**

The Mission of the WORD! (John 1:1-5, 9-14, 16-18) — **Harmony 1:1-6**

— The WORD as God, Creator, and Light {John 1:1-5, 9} — ***Harmony 1:1, 2***
— The WORD as Savior {John 1:10-14, 16, 17} — ***Harmony 1:3-5***
— The WORD Speaks on Behalf of God {John 1:18} — ***Harmony 1:6***

The Recording of the Gospel Story (Luke 1:1-4) — **Harmony 1:7, 8**

Two Miracle Babies < Autumn, 6 and 5 B.C. > (Luke 1:5-80) — **Harmony 1:9-37**

— Gabriel Gives Zacharias Some Good News < Autumn, 6 B.C. > {Luke 1:5-25} — ***Harmony 1:9-17***
— Gabriel Gives Mary Some Great News < Spring, 5 B.C > {Luke 1:26-38} — ***Harmony 1:18-23***
— The Mothers of the Two Miracle Babies Meet < Spring, 5 B.C. > {Luke 1:39-56} — ***Harmony 1:24-28***
— The Birth of John the Baptist < Summer, 5 B.C. > {Luke 1:57-80} — ***Harmony 1:29-37***

The Birth and Infancy of the Messiah < 5 and 4 B.C.> (Matthew 1:1-2:23; Luke 2:1-40; 3:23-38) — **Harmony 1:38-76 and Harmony 1:1-14 (Supplemental Notes)**

— An Angel Visits Joseph < Summer or Autumn, 5 B.C. > {Matthew 1:18-25} ***— Harmony 1:38-42***

— The Messiah Is Born < Autumn, 5 B.C. > {Luke 2:1-7} — ***Harmony 1:43-45***

— The Angels Visit the Shepherds < Autumn, 5 B.C. > {Luke 2:8-20} — ***Harmony 1:46-50***

— Jesus Is Circumcised < Autumn, 5 B.C. > {Matthew 1:25; Luke 2:21} ***Harmony 1:51***

— Jesus Is Dedicated in the Temple < Autumn, 5 B.C. > {Luke 2:22-38} — ***Harmony 1:52-59***

— The Genealogy of Jesus {Matthew 1:1-17; Luke 3:23-38} — ***Harmony 1:60 and Harmony 1:1-14 (Supplemental Notes)***

— The Visit of the Magi < Winter, 4 B.C. > {Matthew 2:1-12} — ***Harmony 1:61-68***

— The Family of Jesus Flees Into Egypt < Winter, 4 B.C. > {Matthew 2:13, 14, 16-18} — ***Harmony 1:69-71***

— Jesus and His Family Return to Nazareth < Summer, 4 B.C. > {Matthew 2:15, 19-23; Luke 2:39, 40} — ***Harmony 1:72-76***

The Childhood and Young Manhood of Jesus < Spring, A.D. 9-A.D. 27 > (Luke 2:41-52) — **Harmony 1:77-84**

— Jesus' First Passover Visit < Spring, A.D. 9 > {Luke 2:41-50} — ***Harmony 1:77-82***

— Jesus Grows Up in Nazareth < Spring, A.D. 9 — < Autumn, A.D. 27 > {Luke 2:51, 52} — ***Harmony 1:83, 84***

*Chapter* TWO: The Early Ministry of Jesus — From the Ministry of John the Baptist, to the Lord's First Miracle (Autumn, A.D. 27 — Spring, A.D. 28) — **Harmony 2:1-77**

The Ministry of John the Baptist < Summer and Autumn, A.D. 27 > (Matthew 3:1-12; Mark 1:2-8; Luke 1:80; 3:1-18; John 1:6-8, 15, 28) — **Harmony 2:1-21**

**The Timeline of the Ministry of Jesus, Segment ONE:**
**Autumn, A.D. 27 — Spring, A.D. 28**
**Thematic Preview of the Ministry of Jesus**

The Lord's Baptism < Autumn, A.D. 27 (1/7) > (Matthew 3:13-17; Mark 1:1, 9-11; Luke 3:21-23) — **Harmony 2:22-28**

The Temptations of Jesus in the Wilderness < Autumn, A.D. 27 (1/7) > (Matthew 4:1-11; Mark 1:12, 13; Luke 4:1-13) — **Harmony 2:29-36**

Jesus Officially Begins His Ministry < Late Autumn, A.D. 27 (1/7) > (John 1:19-51) — **Harmony 2:37-68**

— John the Baptist is Questioned by the Jewish Leaders < Late Autumn, A.D. 27 (1/7) > {John 1:19-28} — ***Harmony 2:37-48***
— John Declares Jesus to be "The Lamb of God" < Late Autumn, A.D. 27 (1/7) > {John 1:29-34 — ***Harmony 2:49-52***
— Jesus Calls His First Disciples < Late Autumn, A.D. 27 (1/7) > {John 1:35-51} — ***Harmony 2:53-68***

The Lord's First Miracle: Turning Water Into Wine at Cana < Late Autumn, A.D. 27 (1/7) > (John 2:1-12) — **Harmony 2:69-77**

## PART II — Public Ministry: The Judean and Galilean Ministries (Passover, Spring, A.D. 28 — Passover, Spring, A.D. 30)

*Chapter* THREE: The Judean Ministry of Jesus — From the First Cleansing of the Temple, to the Lord's Defense Before the Sanhedrin (Passover, Spring, A.D. 28 — Passover, Spring, A.D. 29) — **Harmony 3:1-99**

### The Timeline of the Ministry of Jesus, Segment Two: Spring, A.D. 28 — Autumn, A.D. 28

The Lord Begins His Ministry in Judea < Passover, Spring, A.D. 28 (2/7) > (John 2:13-3:36) — **Harmony 3:1-33**

— The First Cleansing of the Temple < Passover, Spring, A.D. 28 (2/7) > {John 2:13-25} — ***Harmony 3:1-9***
— The Night Visit of Nicodemus < Passover, Spring, A.D. 28 (2/7) > (John 3:1-21) — ***Harmony 3:10-24***
— John the Baptist Defends the Lord's Ministry in Judea < Spring through Winter, A.D. 28 (2/7) > {John 3:22-36} — ***Harmony 3:25-33***

### The Timeline of the Ministry of Jesus, Segment Three: Autumn, A.D. 28 — Spring, A.D. 29

A Brief Sojourn Into Galilee < Winter and Spring, A.D. 29 (3/7) > (Matthew 14:3-5; Luke 3:19, 20; John 3:23; 4:1-54) — **Harmony 3:34-71**

— The Conversion of the Samaritan Woman at Jacob's Well < Winter, A.D. 29 (3/7) > {John 4:1-42} — ***Harmony 3:34-61***

— Jesus Heals the Nobleman's Son <Winter, A.D. 29 (3/7) > {John 4:43-54} ***— Harmony 3:62-68***

— John the Baptist Is Imprisoned < Spring, A.D. 29 (3/7) > {Matthew 14:3-5; Luke 3:19, 20; John 3:23} ***— Harmony 3:69-71***

**The Timeline of the Ministry of Jesus, Segment Four: Spring, A.D. 29 — Autumn, A.D. 29**

Jesus at the Passover Again < Spring, A.D. 29 (4/7) > (John 5:1-47) — **Harmony 3:72-99**

— The Healing of the Invalid at the Pool of Bethesda < Spring, A.D. 29 (4/7) > {John 5:1-15} ***— Harmony 3:72-81***

— The Lord's Defense Before the Sanhedrin < Spring, A.D. 29 (4/7) > {John 5:16-47} ***— Harmony 3:82-99***

*Chapter* FOUR: The Early Galilean Ministry of Jesus — From the Opening of the Lord's Galilean Ministry, to the Official Appointment of the Twelve Disciples (Spring, A.D. 29 — Late Summer, A.D. 29) — **Harmony 4:1-79**

The Lord's Ministry in Galilee < Spring, A.D. 29 (4/7) > (Matthew 4:12-22; 8:14-17; Mark 1:14-34; Luke 4:14-41; 5:1-11) — **Harmony 4:1-31**

— The Opening of the Lord's Galilean Ministry < Spring, A.D. 29 (4/7) > {Matthew 4:12; Mark 1:14, 15; Luke 4:14, 15} ***— Harmony 4:1-3***

— The Lord's First Rejection in Nazareth < Late Spring, A.D. 29 (4/7) > {Luke 4:16-30} ***— Harmony 4:4-10***

— Jesus Moves to Capernaum < Late Spring, A.D. 29 (4/7) > {Matthew 4:13-17; Luke 4:31} ***— Harmony 4:11-13***

— The Disciples Are Called By the Sea < Late Spring, A.D. 29 (4/7) > {Matthew 4:18-22; Mark 1:16-20; Luke 5:1-11} ***— Harmony 4:14-22***

— The Healing of the Demoniac in the Synagogue < Late Spring, A.D. 29 (4/7) > {Mark 1:21-28; Luke 4:31-37} ***— Harmony 4:23-26***

— Peter's Mother-in-law Is Healed, and Other Sick Are Healed that Evening < Late Spring, A.D. 29 (4/7) > {Matthew 8:14-17; Mark 1:129-34; Luke 4:38-41) ***— Harmony 4:27-31***

The Lord's First Major Galilean Evangelistic Tour < Late Spring through Late Summer, A.D. 29 (4/7) > (Matthew 4:23-25; 8:2-9; 9:2-9; 12:1-21; Mark 1:35-2:14; 2:23-3:19; Luke 4:42-44; 5:12-28; 6:1-16) — **Harmony 4:32-79**

— The Beginning of the Lord's First Galilean Evangelistic Tour < Late Spring, A.D. 29 (4/7) > {Matthew 4:23-25; Mark 1:35-39; Luke 4:42-44} — ***Harmony 4:32-34***

— Jesus Heals His First Leper < Summer, A.D. 29 (4/7) > {Matthew 8:2-4; Mark 1:40-45; Luke 5:12-16} — ***Harmony 4:35-39***

— The Healing of the Paralytic Lowered Through the Roof < Summer, A.D. 29 (4/7) > {Matthew 9:2-8; Mark 2:1-12; Luke 5:17-26} — ***Harmony 4:40-47***

— Levi Matthew Is Called to be a Disciple < Summer, A.D. 29 (4/7) > {Matthew 9:9; Mark 2:13, 14; Luke 5:27, 28} — ***Harmony 4:48-50***

— The Disciples Pluck Grain on the Sabbath Day < Summer, A.D. 29 (4/7) > {Matthew 12:1-8; Mark 2:23-28; Luke 6:1-5} — ***Harmony 4:51-56***

— The Healing on the Sabbath of the Man with the Withered Hand < Summer, A.D. 29 (4/7) > {Matthew 12:9-14; Mark 3:1-6; Luke 6:6-11} — ***Harmony 4:57-62***

— The Lord's Popularity in Galilee < Summer, A.D. 29 (4/7) > {Matthew 12:15-21; Mark 3:7-12} — ***Harmony 4:63-66***

— The Official Appointment of the Twelve Disciples < Late Summer, A.D. 29 (4/7) > {Mark 3:13-19; Luke 6:12-16} — ***Harmony 4:67-79***

*Chapter* FIVE: The Early Galilean Ministry of Jesus —The Sermon on the Mount (Late Summer, A.D. 29) — **Harmony 5:1-86**

The Sermon on the Mount < Late Summer, A.D. 29 (4/7) > (Matthew 5:1-8:1; Mark 3:13, 14; Luke 6:13, 17-49) — **Harmony 5:1-86**

— Jesus Prepares for His Most Important Sermon < Late Summer, A.D. 29 (4/7) > {Matthew 5:1, 2; Mark 3:13, 14; Luke 6:13, 17-20} — ***Harmony 5:1, 2***

— Blessings of Growth for Those Who Accept the Gospel of Jesus: "The Beatitudes" < Late Summer, A.D. 29 (4/7) > {Matthew 5:3-12; Luke 20:20-23} — ***Harmony 5:3-11***

— Woes Upon Those Who Reject the True Gospel Message < Late Summer, A.D. 29 (4/7) > {Luke 6:24-26} — ***Harmony 5:12-15***

— God's Plan for You—His People

— To Be the Salt of the Earth < Late Summer, A.D. 29 (4/7) > {Matthew 5:13} — ***Harmony 5:16, 17***

— To Be the Light of the World < Late Summer, A.D. 29 (4/7) > {Matthew 5:14-16} — ***Harmony 5:18***

— The Gospel Will Change Your Lives Forever

— The Gospel Reveals the True Spirit of the Law and Scriptures < Late Summer, A.D. 29 (4/7) > {Matthew 5:17-20} — ***Harmony 5:19-22***

— The True Meaning of the Sixth Commandment: You Shall Not Kill < Late Summer, A.D. 29 (4/7) > {Matthew 5:21-26} — ***Harmony 5:23-27***

— The True Meaning of the Seventh Commandment: You Shall Not Commit Adultery < Late Summer, A.D. 29 (4/7) > {Matthew 5:27-30} — ***Harmony 5:28, 29***

— The Only Justification for Divorce < Late Summer, A.D. 29 (4/7) > {Matthew 5:31, 32} — ***Harmony 5:30, 31***

— How to Make Vows < Late Summer, A.D. 29 (4/7) > {Matthew 5:33-37} — ***Harmony 5:32-35***

— The True Meaning of the Laws of Justice: "An Eye for an Eye . . ." < Late Summer, A.D. 29 (4/7) > {Matthew 5:38-42; Luke 6:29, 30} — ***Harmony 5:36, 37***

— The True Meaning of Love: To Love Your Enemies < Late Summer, A.D. 29 (4/7) > {Matthew 5:43-47; Luke 6:27, 28, 32-35} — ***Harmony 5:38-40***

— In Summary: The True Meaning of Mercy and Perfection < Late Summer, A.D. 29 (4/7) > {Matthew 5:28; Luke 6:36} — ***Harmony 5:41***

— The Gospel Will Also Change the Way You Worship God

— The Proper Motives for Good Deeds < Late Summer, A.D. 29 (4/7) > {Matthew 6:1-4} — ***Harmony 5:42, 43***

— The Proper Way to Pray < Late Summer, A.D. 29 (4/7) > {Matthew 6:5-13} — ***Harmony 5:44-52***

— The Requirement for Divine Forgiveness < Late Summer, A.D. 29 (4/7) > {Matthew 6:14, 15} — ***Harmony 5:53***

— The Proper Way to Fast < Late Summer, A.D. 29 (4/7) > {Matthew 6:16-18} — ***Harmony 5:54, 55***

— How to Accomplish the Gospel Experience

— The Proper Attitude Toward Possessions < Late Summer, A.D. 29 (4/7) > {Matthew 6:19-21} — ***Harmony 5:56, 57***

— Your Attitude Toward Heavenly and Earthly Things Is the Key < Late Summer, A.D. 29 (4/7) > {Matthew 6:22, 23; Luke 6:39} — ***Harmony 5:58, 59***

— Your Must Be Totally Committed to Securing the Gospel Experience < Late Summer, A.D. 29 (4/7) > {Matthew 6:24} — ***Harmony 5:60***

— If You Are Focused on Obtaining the Gospel, You Must Not Worry About Obtaining the Necessities of Life < Late Summer, A.D. 29 (4/7) > {Matthew 6:25-34} — ***Harmony 5:61-67***

— When You Are Focused on Growing in the Gospel, You Will Not Have Time to Judge Others < Late Summer, A.D. 29 (4/7) > {Matthew 7:1-6; Luke 6: 37, 38, 41, 42} — ***Harmony 5:68-72***

— How to Live the Victorious Life < Late Summer, A.D. 29 (4/7) > {Matthew 7:7-11} — ***Harmony 5:73, 74***

— The Gospel Experience Will Affect the Way You Relate to People < Late Summer, A.D. 29 (4/7) > {Matthew 7:12; Luke 6:31} — ***Harmony 5:75***

— It's Decision Time! < Late Summer, A.D. 29 (4/7) > {Matthew 7:13, 14} — ***Harmony 5:76***

— A Warning! < Late Summer, A.D. 29 (4/7) > {Matthew 7:15} — ***Harmony 5:77***

— You Can Distinguish Between the False and True Teachers of the Gospel < Late Summer, A.D. 29 (4/7) > {Matthew 7:16-23; Luke 6:40, 43-46} — ***Harmony 5:78-82***

— Conclusion and Appeal: The Parable of the Wise Man and the Foolish Man < Late Summer, A.D. 29 (4/7) > {Matthew 7:24-27; Luke 6:47-49} — ***Harmony 5:83, 84***

— Jesus Concludes His Sermon < Late Summer, A.D. 29 (4/7) > {Matthew 7:28-8:1} — ***Harmony 5:85, 86***

*Chapter* SIX: The Mid-Galilean Ministry of Jesus — From the Healing of the Centurion's Servant, to the Resurrection of the Widow of Nain's Son (Autumn, A.D. 29) — **Harmony 6:1-23**

Various Miracles of Jesus < Autumn, A.D. 29 (4/7) > (Matthew 8:5-13; 9:27-34; Luke 7:1-10) — **Harmony 6:1-17**

— The Healing of the Centurion's Servant < Autumn, A.D. 29 (4/7) > {Matthew 8:5-13; Luke 7:1-10} — ***Harmony 6:1-9***

— The Healing of Two Blind Men < Autumn, A.D. 29 (4/7) > {Matthew 9:27-31} — ***Harmony 6:10-14***

— The Healing of a Dumb Demoniac < Autumn, A.D. 29 (4/7) > {Matthew 9:32-34} — ***Harmony 6:15-17***

**The Timeline of the Ministry of Jesus, Segment Five: Autumn, A.D. 29 — Spring, A.D. 30**

The Beginning of the Lord's Second Galilean Evangelistic Tour < Autumn, A.D. 29 (5/7) > (Matthew 9:35; Luke 7:11-17; 8:1-3) — **Harmony 6:18-23**

— Jesus Starts His Second Galilean Evangelistic Tour < Autumn, A.D. 29 (5/7) > {Matthew 9:35; Luke 8:1-3} — ***Harmony 6:18, 19***

— The Resurrection of the Widow of Nain's Son < Autumn, A.D. 29 (5/7) > {Luke 7:11-17} — ***Harmony 6:20-23***

*Chapter* SEVEN: The Mid-Galilean Ministry of Jesus: The Lord's Busy Day — From Christ's Family Is Concerned About Jesus, to the Healing of the Demoniacs of Gadara (Autumn, A.D. 29) — **Harmony 7:1-74**

Jesus Heals a Blind and Dumb Demoniac and Talks About the Unpardonable Sin; the Lord's Mother and Brothers Come to Visit Him < Autumn, A.D. 29

(5/7) > (Matthew 12:22-50; Mark 3:20-35; 6:3; Luke 8:19-21; 11:14-32) — **Harmony 7:1-21**

— The Lord's Busy Day
— Christ's Family Are Concerned About Jesus < Autumn, A.D. 29 (5/7) > {Mark 3:20, 21; 6:3} — ***Harmony 7:1***
— The Healing of a Demon-possessed Man < Autumn, A.D. 29 (5/7) > {Matthew 12:22, 23; Luke 11:14} — ***Harmony 7:2***
— Contention with the Pharisees over the Lord's Healings of Demon-possessed People < Autumn, A.D. 29 (5/7) > {Matthew 12:24-30; Mark 3:22-27; Luke 11:15-23} — ***Harmony 7:3-8***
— The Unpardonable Sin < Autumn, A.D. 29 (5/7) > {Matthew 12:31-45; Mark 3:28-30; Luke 11:24-26, 29-32} — ***Harmony 7:9-17***
— Jesus Identifies His True Family < Autumn, A.D. 29 (5/7) > {Matthew 12:46-50; Mark 3:31-35; Luke 8:19-21; 11:27, 28} — ***Harmony 7:18-21***

The Sermon of Parables Given by the Sea < Autumn, A.D. 29 (5/7) > (Matthew 13:1-53; Mark 4:1-34; Luke 8:4-18) — **Harmony 7:22-55**

— Jesus Teaches by the Sea < Autumn, A.D. 29 (5/7) > {Matthew 13:1-3; Mark 4:1, 2; Luke 8:4} — ***Harmony 7:22***
— The Sower and the Soils < Autumn, A.D. 29 (5/7) > {Matthew 13:3-9; Mark 4:2-9; Luke 4:4-8} — ***Harmony 7:23***
— The Wheat and the Weeds < Autumn, A.D. 29 (5/7) > {Matthew 13:24-30} — ***Harmony 7:24-28***
— The Growing Seeds < Autumn, A.D. 29 (5/7) > {Mark 4:26-29} — ***Harmony 7:29***
— The Mustard Seed < Autumn, A.D. 29 (5/7) > {Matthew 13:31, 32; Mark 4:30-32} — ***Harmony 7:30***
— The Yeast < Autumn, A.D. 29 (5/7) > {Matthew 13:33} — ***Harmony 7:31***
— The Buried Treasure < Autumn, A.D. 29 (5/7) > {Matthew 13:44} — ***Harmony 7:32***
— The Expensive Pearl < Autumn, A.D. 29 (5/7) > {Matthew 13:45, 46} — ***Harmony 7:33***
— The Fishing Net <Autumn, A.D. 29 (5/7) > {Matthew 13:47-50} — ***Harmony 7:34, 35***
— The Lamp < Autumn, A.D. 29 (5/7) > {Mark 4:21-25; Luke 8:16-18} — ***Harmony 7:36, 37***
— The Lord Concludes His Parables < Autumn, A.D. 29 (5/7) > {Matthew 13:51-53; Mark 4:53} — ***Harmony 7:38-40***

The Third Galilean Evangelistic Tour: The Mission of the Twelve Apostles < Winter to Spring, A.D. 29-30 (5/7) > (Matthew 9:36-11:1; Mark 6:7-13; Luke 9:1-6) — **Harmony 8:37-58**

The Lord's Second Rejection at Nazareth < Spring, A.D. 30 (5/7) > (Matthew 13:54-58; Mark 6:1-6) — **Harmony 8:59-62**

The Execution of John the Baptist < Spring, A.D. 30 (5/7) > (Matthew 14:1-4, 6-12; Mark 6:14-29; Luke 9:7-9) — **Harmony 8:63-74**

*Chapter* NINE: The Later Galilean Ministry of Jesus: Trouble in Galilee — From the Feeding of the 5,000, to the Bread of Life Teaching (Just before Passover, Spring, A.D. 30) — **Harmony 9:1-54**

The Feeding of the Five Thousand < Spring, A.D. 30 (5/7) > (Matthew 14:13-22; Mark 6:30-45; Luke 9:10-17; John 6:1-15) — **Harmony 9:1-13**

Jesus Walks on Water! < Spring, A.D. 30 (5/7) > (Matthew 14:23-33; Mark 6:46-52; John 6:15-21) — **Harmony 9:14-24**

The "Bread of Life" Teaching < Spring, A.D. 30 (5/7) > (Matthew 14:34-36; Mark 6:53-56; John 6:22-7:1) — **Harmony 9:25-54**

**PART III — Instruction: The Respite from Ministry Among Jews and the Ministry to the Gentiles (Passover, Spring, A.D. 30 — Passover, Spring, A.D. 31)**

*Chapter* TEN: Working Among Gentiles — From the Contention About Tradition and Ceremonial Washings, to the Lord's Teaching on Humility and Forgiveness (Just Before Passover, Spring A.D. 30 — Autumn, A.D. 30) — **Harmony 10:1-118**

**The Timeline of the Ministry of Jesus, Segment Six:**
**Spring, A.D. 30 — Autumn, A.D. 30**

Contention Regarding Human Tradition and Ceremonial Washings < Spring, A.D. 30 (6/7) > (Matthew 15:1-20; Mark 7:1-23) — **Harmony 10:1-13**

The Lord Among the Gentiles < Spring and Summer, A.D. 30 (6/7) > (Matthew 15:21-39; Mark 7:24-8:10) — **Harmony 10:14-32**

— The Lord's Withdrawal to Phoenicia; the Healing of a Gentile Woman's Daughter < Spring, A.D. 30 (6/7) > {Matthew 15:21-28; Mark 7:24-30} — ***Harmony 10:14-22***

— The Healing of a Deaf-mute and Other Miracles in Decapolis < Spring and Summer, A.D. 30 (6/7) > {Matthew 15:29-31; Mark 7:31-37} — ***Harmony 10:23-26***

— The Feeding of the Four Thousand < Summer, A.D. 30 (6/7) > {Matthew 15:32-39; Mark 8:1-10} — ***Harmony 10:27-32***

The Lord's Critics Demand a Sign < Summer, A.D. 30 (6/7) > (Matthew 16:1-12; Mark 8:11-21) — **Harmony 10:33-43**

Jesus Heals a Blind Man Near Bethsaida < Summer, A.D. 30 (6/7) > (Mark 8:22-26) — **Harmony 10:44-46**

Withdrawal to Caesarea Philippi — The Great Confession < Summer, A.D. 30 (6/7) > (Matthew 16:13-28; Mark 8:27-9:1; Luke 9:18-27) — **Harmony 10:47-61**

An Amazing Couple of Days: The Transfiguration and the Healing of a Demon-possessed Boy < Late Summer, A.D. 30 (6/7) > (Matthew 17:1-21; Mark 9:2-29; Luke 9:28-43) — **Harmony 10:62-85**

— The Transfiguration < Late Summer, A.D. 30 (6/7) > {Matthew 17:1-13; Mark 9:2-23; Luke 9:28-36} — ***Harmony 10:62-72***

— The Healing of a Demon-possessed Boy < Late Summer, A.D. 30 (6/7) > {Matthew 17:14-18; Mark 9:14-27; Luke 9:37-43} — ***Harmony 10:73-83***

Jesus Makes a Secret Journey Through Galilee < Late Summer, A.D. 30 (6/7) > (Matthew 17:22, 23; Mark 9:30-32; Luke 9:43-45) — **Harmony 10:84, 85**

The Tribute Money Incident; and the Lord Teaches About Humility and Forgiveness < Late Summer, A.D. 30 (6/7) > (Matthew 17:19-21, 24-18:35; Mark 9:33-50; Luke 9:46-50) — **Harmony 10:86-118**

— The Confused Disciples and the Tribute Money Incident < Late Summer, A.D. 30 (6/7) > {Matthew 17:19-21, 24-27; Mark 9:28, 29} — ***Harmony 10:86-93***

— The Lord's Teaching on Humility and Forgiveness < Late Summer, A.D. 30 (6/7) > {Matthew 18:1-35; Mark 9:33-50; Luke 9:46-50} — ***Harmony 10:94-118***

*Chapter* ELEVEN: Contentions With Jews and Success Among Gentiles — From Jesus Visits the Feast of Tabernacles, to Jesus at the Feast of Dedication (Autumn, A.D. 30 — Early Winter, A.D. 30) — **Harmony 11:1-175**

## The Timeline of the Ministry of Jesus, Segment Seven: Autumn, A.D. 30 — Spring, A.D. 31

Jesus Visits the Feast of Tabernacles < Autumn, A.D. 30 (7/7) > (John 7:2-10:21) — **Harmony 11:1-120**

— Jesus Debates With His Brothers Regarding a Visit to the Feast of Tabernacles < Autumn, A.D. 30 (7/7) > {John 7:2-13} — ***Harmony 11:1-7***
— The Lord's Teaching in the Temple During the Feast of Tabernacles < Autumn, A.D. 30 (7/7) > {John 7:14-8:1} — ***Harmony 11:8-32***
— The Lord Defends the Woman Caught in Adultery < Autumn, A.D. 30 (7/7) > {John 8:2-11} — ***Harmony 11:33-41***
— Jesus Declares Himself to be the "Light of the World" < Autumn, A.D. 30 (7/7) > {John 8:12-30} — ***Harmony 11:42-55***
— An Argument Regarding Who Has Descended from Abraham < Autumn, A.D. 30 (7/7) > {John 8:31-59} — ***Harmony 11:56-78***
— The Healing of a Man, Blind from Birth < Autumn, A.D. 30 (7/7) > {John 9:1-41} — ***Harmony 11:79-109***
— The "Good Shepherd" Teaching < Autumn, A.D. 30 (7/7) > {John 10:1-21} — ***Harmony 11:110-120***

The Lord's Ministry Continues Among the Gentiles < Autumn and Early Winter, A.D. 30 (7/7) > (Matthew 19:1, 2; Mark 10:1; Luke 9:51-10:42) — **Harmony 11:121-164**

— Jesus Wraps Up His Galilean Ministry, and Begins His Samaritan-Peraean Ministry < Autumn, A.D. 30 (7/7) > {Matthew 19:1, 2; Mark 10:1; Luke 9:51-56} — ***Harmony 11:121-125***
— The Test of Discipleship < Autumn, A.D. 30 (7/7) > {Luke 9:57-62} — ***Harmony 11:126-132***
— The Mission of the "Seventy" < Autumn and Early Winter, A.D. 30 (7/7) > {Luke 10:1-24} — ***Harmony 11:133-149***
— Who Is Our Neighbor? The Story of the "Good Samaritan" < Early Winter, A.D. 30 (7/7) > {Luke 10:25-37} — ***Harmony 11:150-161***
— Jesus In the Home of Mary and Martha < Early Winter, A.D. 30 (7/7) > {Luke 10:38-42} — ***Harmony 11:162-164***

Jesus at the Feast of Dedication < Early Winter, A.D. 30 (7/7) > (John 10:22-40) — **Harmony 11:165-175**

*Chapter* TWELVE: Controversy and Instruction — From Jesus Goes Into the Wilderness, to the Teaching on Forgiveness, Faith, and Service (Winter, A.D. 30 — Late Winter, A.D. 31) — **Harmony 12:1-158**

The Peraean Ministry of Jesus: The Lord's Various Experiences and Teachings While Sojourning in Peraea < Winter, A.D. 30 — 31 (7/7) > (Luke 11:1-13, 33-54; 12:1-17:10; John 10:40-42) — **Harmony 12:1-158**

— Jesus Goes Into the Wilderness < Winter, A.D. 30 (7/7) > {John 10:40-42} — ***Harmony 12:1, 2***

— The Lord's Instruction on Prayer < Winter, A.D. 30 (7/7) > {Luke 11:1-13} — ***Harmony 12:3-15***

— The Inner Light Illustration < Winter, A.D. 31 (7/7) > {Luke 11:33-36} — ***Harmony 12:16-18***

— Jesus Dines With a Pharisee < Winter, A.D. 31 (7/7) > {Luke 11:37-54} — ***Harmony 12:19-31***

— Jesus Warns His Followers Regarding the Pharisees < Winter, A.D. 31 (7/7) > {Luke 12:1-12} — ***Harmony 12:32-39***

— The Folly of Riches Is Condemned < Winter, A.D. 31 (7/7) > {Luke 12:13-34} — ***Harmony 12:40-54***

— Being Ready for the Master's Return < Winter, A.D. 31 (7/7) > {Luke 12:35-59} — ***Harmony 12:55-66***

— Divine Mercy and Justice < Winter, A.D. 31 (7/7) > {Luke 13:1-9} — ***Harmony 12:67-71***

— The Healing of a Crippled Woman on the Sabbath < Winter, A.D. 31 (7/7) > {Luke 13:10-17} — ***Harmony 12:72-75***

— Growing Within the Kingdom of Heaven < Winter, A.D. 31 (7/7) > {Luke 13:18-21} — ***Harmony 12:76, 77***

— What It Takes to be Saved < Winter, A.D. 31 (7/7) > {Luke 13:22-30} — ***Harmony 12:78-85***

— A Warning of Divine Justice < Winter, A.D. 31 (7/7) > {Luke 13:31-35} — ***Harmony 12:86-89***

— Jesus Heals on the Sabbath While Eating in the Home of a Pharisee < Winter, A.D. 31 (7/7) > {Luke 14:1-24} — ***Harmony 12:90-104***

— The Cost of Discipleship < Winter, A.D. 31 (7/7) > {Luke 14:25-35} — ***Harmony 12:105-110***

— The Lost Sheep, Coin, and Son Parables < Winter, A.D. 31 (7/7) > {Luke 15:1-32} — ***Harmony 12:111-123***

— The Dishonest Steward, and the Rich Man and Lazarus Parables < Winter, A.D. 31 (7/7) > {Luke 16:1-31} — ***Harmony 12:124-150***

— Forgiveness, Faith, and Duty < Winter, A.D. 31 (7/7) > {Luke 17:1-10} — ***Harmony 12:151-158***

*Chapter* THIRTEEN: The Final, Slow Trip to Jerusalem — From the Raising of Lazarus, to the Parable of the Nobleman and His Money (Late Winter, A.D. 31 — Just Before Passover, Spring, A.D. 31) — **Harmony 13:1-134**

The Raising of Lazarus; the Jewish Leaders Plot the Death of Jesus; the Lord Relocates to Ephraim < Late Winter, A.D. 31 (7/7) > (John 11:1-57) — **Harmony 13:1-38**

— The Raising of Lazarus < Late Winter, A.D. 31 (7/7) > {John 11:1-46} — ***Harmony 13:1-30***
— The Jewish Leaders Plot the Death of Jesus < Late Winter, A.D. 31 (7/7) > {John 11:47-53} — ***Harmony 13:31-34***
— Jesus Relocates to Ephraim < Late Winter, A.D. 31 (7/7) > {John 11:54-57} — ***Harmony 13:35-38***

The Lord's Roundabout Journey to Jerusalem for His Final Passover < Early Spring, A.D. 31 7/7 > (Matthew 19:3-20:34; Mark 10:2-52; Luke 17:11-19:28) — **Harmony 13:39-134**

— Jesus Heals Ten Lepers < Early Spring, A.D. 31 (7/7) > {Luke 17:11-19} — ***Harmony 13:39-43***
— The Lord Explains the Words, "The Kingdom of God" < Early Spring, A.D. 31 (7/7) > {Luke 17:20-37} — ***Harmony 13:44-53***
— The Parable of the Unjust Judge < Early Spring, A.D. 31 (7/7) > {Luke 18:1-8} — ***Harmony 13:54-56***
— The Parable of the Pharisee and the Publican < Early Spring, A.D. 31 (7/7) > {Luke 18:9-14} — ***Harmony 13:57-61***
— Jesus Discusses Marriage and Divorce < Early Spring, A.D. 31 (7/7) > {Matthew 19:3-12; Mark 10:2-12} — ***Harmony 13:62-71***
— Jesus Blesses the Children < Early Spring, A.D. 31 (7/7) > {Matthew 19:13-15; Mark 10:13-16; Luke 18:15-17} — ***Harmony 13:72-74***
— Jesus Converses with the Rich Young Ruler and the Parable of the Workers in the Vineyard < Early Spring, A.D. 31 (7/7) > {Matthew 19:16-20:16; Mark 10:17-31; Luke 18:18-30} — ***Harmony 13:75-97***
— Jesus Foretells His Own Death < Early Spring, A.D. 31 (7/7) > {Matthew 20:17-19; Mark 10:32-34; Luke 18:31-34} — ***Harmony 13:98-100***
— James and John Make a Special Request < Early Spring, A.D. 31 (7/7) > {Matthew 20:20-28; Mark 10:35-45} — ***Harmony 13:101-107***
— The Lord Talks with Zaccheus, Heals Two Blind Men, and the Parable of the Nobleman and His Money < Early Spring, A.D. 31 (7/7) > {Matthew 20:29-34; Mark 10:46-52; Luke 18:35-19:28} — ***Harmony 13:108-134***

**PART IV — The End . . . and the Beginning (Passover, Spring, A.D. 31 — Just Before Pentecost, Spring, A.D. 31)**

*Chapter* FOURTEEN: The Passion Week: Friday through Tuesday Afternoon — From Simon's Feast, to the Final Rejection by the Jewish Leaders (Just Before Passover, Spring, A.D. 31) — **Harmony 14:1-154**

Celebration and Betrayal < Friday (The Preparation), Nisan 7 through Saturday Night, Nisan 9, A.D. 31 (7/7) > (Matthew 26:3-16; Mark 14:1-11; Luke 7:36-50, 22:1-6; John 12:1-11) — **Harmony 14:1-25**

— Simon's Feast < Saturday Night, Nisan 9, Spring, A.D. 31 (7/7) > {Matthew 26:6-13; Mark 14:3-9; Luke 7:36-50; John 12:1-9} — ***Harmony 14:1-18***

— Judas's Betrayal Plot < Saturday Night, Nisan 9, Spring, A.D. 31 (7/7) > {Matthew 26:3-5, 14-16; Mark 14:1, 2, 10, 11; Luke 22:1-6; John 12:10, 11} — ***Harmony 14:19-25***

Triumph and Sadness < Sunday Afternoon and Early Evening, Nisan 9, Spring, A.D. 31 (7/7) > (Matthew 21:1-11; Mark 11:1-11; Luke 19:29-44; John 12:12-19) — **Harmony 14:26-41**

A Curse and a Cleansing < Monday, Nisan 10, Spring, A.D. 31 (7/7) > (Matthew 21:12-19; Mark 11:12-19; Luke 19:45-48) — **Harmony 14:42-51**

— Jesus Curses the Fruitless Fig Tree < Monday, Nisan 10, Spring, A.D. 31 (7/7) > {Matthew 21:18, 19; Mark 11:12-14} — ***Harmony 14:42, 43***

— Jesus Cleanses the Temple for the Second Time < Monday, Nisan 10, Spring, A.D. 31 (7/7) > {Matthew 21:12-17; Mark 11:15-19; Luke 19:45-48} — ***Harmony 14:44-51***

A Day of Judgment for Israel < Tuesday, Nisan 11, Spring, A.D. 31 (7/7) > (Matthew 21:19-24:1; Mark 11:20-12:40; Luke 20:1-47) — **Harmony 14:52-133**

— The Fruitless Fig Is Withered < Tuesday, Nisan 11, Spring, A.D. 31 (7/7) > {Matthew 21:19-22; Mark 11:20-26} — ***Harmony 14:52-54***

— The Jewish Leaders Challenge the Lord's Ministry < Tuesday, Nisan 11, Spring, A.D. 31 (7/7) > {Matthew 21:23-32; Mark 11:27-33; Luke 20:1-8} — ***Harmony 14:55-66***

— The Story of the Evil Vine-growers < Tuesday, Nisan 11, Spring, A.D. 31 (7/7) > {Matthew 21:33-46; Mark 12:1-12; Luke 20:9-19} — ***Harmony 14:67-78***

— Jesus Tells the Parable About a Man Without a Wedding Garment < Tuesday, Nisan 11, Spring, A.D. 31 (7/7) > {Matthew 22:1-14} — ***Harmony 14:79-84***

— The Lord Is Tested: Should a Jew Pay Tribute to Caesar? < Tuesday, Nisan 11, Spring, A.D. 31 (7/7) > {Matthew 22:15-22; Mark 12:13-17; Luke 20:20-26} — ***Harmony 14:85-92***

— The Lord Is Tested a Second Time: Is There a Resurrection? < Tuesday, Nisan 11, Spring, A.D. 31 (7/7) > {Matthew 22:23-33; Mark 12:18-27; Luke 20:27-38} — ***Harmony 14:93-99***

— Jesus Is Tested a Third Time: Which Is the Greatest Commandment? < Tuesday, Nisan 11, Spring, A.D. 31 (7/7) > {Matthew 22:34-40; Mark 12:28-34; Luke 20:39, 40} — ***Harmony 14:100-106***

— Finally, Jesus Silences His Critics < Tuesday, Nisan 11, Spring, A.D. 31 (7/7) > {Matthew 22:41-46; Mark 12:35-37; Luke 20:41-44} — ***Harmony 14:107-110***

— Jesus Pronounces His Woes on the Pharisees < Tuesday, Nisan 11, Spring, A.D. 31 (7/7) > {Matthew 23:1-24:1; Mark 12:38-40; Luke 20:45-47} — ***Harmony 14:111-133***

The Lord's Final Contact with the People in the Temple Court < Tuesday, Nisan 11, Spring, A.D. 31 (7/7) > (Mark 12:41-44; Luke 21:1-4; John 12:20-50) — **Harmony 14:134-154**

— The Widow's Two Tiny Copper Coins < Tuesday, Nisan 11, Spring, A.D. 31 (7/7) > {Mark 12:41-44; Luke 21:1-4} — ***Harmony 14:134, 135***

— The Lord Conversation with Greek Visitors, and Comments on the Encounter < Tuesday, Nisan 11, Spring, A.D. 31 (7/7) > {John 12:20-36, 44-50} — ***Harmony 14:136-149***

— The Reasons Behind the Jewish Leaders' Rejection of Jesus < Tuesday, Nisan 11, Spring, A.D. 31 (7/7) > {John 12:37-43} — ***Harmony 14:150-154***

*Chapter* FIFTEEN: The Passion Week: Tuesday Afternoon through Wednesday — From the Signs of the Lord's Second Coming, to the Parable of the Sheep and the Goats (Just Before Passover, Spring, A.D. 31) — **Harmony 15:1-60**

Jesus Gives Signs of His Glorious Second Coming, and Illustrates the Preparation Needed for this Climatic Event < Tuesday Evening and Night, Nisan 12, Spring, A.D. 31 (7/7) > (Matthew 24:1-25:46; Mark 13:1-37; Luke 21:5-36) — **Harmony 15:1-58**

— Signs of the Lord's Second Coming < Tuesday Evening and Night, Nisan 12, Spring, A.D. 31 (7/7) > {Matthew 24:1-51; Mark 13:1-37; Luke 21:5-36} — ***Harmony 15:1-31***

— Parable One: The Ten Maidens < Tuesday Night, Nisan 12, Spring, A.D. 31 (7/7) > {Matthew 25:1-13} — ***Harmony 15:32-41***

— Parable Two: The Talents < Tuesday Night, Nisan 12, Spring, A.D. 31 (7/7) > {Matthew 25:14-30} — ***Harmony 15:42-50***

— Parable Three: The Sheep and the Goats < Tuesday Night, Nisan 12, Spring, A.D. 31 (7/7) > {Matthew 25:31-46} — ***Harmony 15:51-58***

Jesus Predicts His Death Again < Tuesday Night, Nisan 12, Spring, A.D. 31 (7/7) > (Matthew 26:1, 2; Mark 14:1) — **Harmony 15:59**

A Summary of the Lord's Activities of the Past Couple of Days < Monday and Tuesday, Nisan 11 and 12, Spring, A.D. 31 (7/7) > (Luke 21:37, 38) — **Harmony 15:60**

*Chapter* SIXTEEN: The Passion Week: Thursday Afternoon and Night — From the Preparation for the Passover, to the Lord's Intercessory Prayer (Just Before Passover, Spring, A.D, 31) — **Harmony 16:1-116**

The Lord's Final Passover < Thursday Afternoon and Evening, Nisan 13 and 14, Spring, A.D. 31 (7/7) > (Matthew 26:17-30; Mark 14:12-26; Luke 22:7-30, 39; John 13:1-37; 14:1-31) — **Harmony 16:1-58**

— Preparation for the Celebration of the Passover Feast < Thursday Afternoon, Nissan 13, Spring, A.D. 31 (7/7) > {Matthew 26:17-19; Mark 14:12-16; Luke 22:7-13; John 13:1} — ***Harmony 16:1-5***

— The Lord's Final Passover Celebration Begins < Thursday Evening, Nisan 14, Spring, A.D. 31 (7/7) > {Matthew 26:20; Mark 14:17; Luke 22:14-16; John 13:2} — ***Harmony 16:6, 7***

— Jesus Washes His Disciples' Feet < Thursday Evening, Nisan 14, Spring, A.D. 31 (7/7) > {Luke 22:24-30; John 13:3-17} — ***Harmony 16:8-20***

— The Lord Celebrates the Passover with His Disciples < Thursday Night, Nisan 14, Spring, A.D. 31 (7/7) > {Matthew 26:26-29; Mark 14:22-25; Luke 22:17-20; John 13:18-20} — ***Harmony 16:21-26***

— Jesus Reveals His Betrayer < Thursday Night, Nisan 14, Spring, A.D. 31 (7/7) > {Matthew 26:21-25; Mark 14:18-21; Luke 22:21-23; John 13:21-30} — ***Harmony 16:27-35***

— Jesus Gives Counsel to the Remaining Eleven Disciples < Thursday Night, Nisan 14, Spring, A.D. 31 (7/7) > {Matthew 26:30; Mark 14:26; Luke 22:39; John 13:31-37; 14:1-31} — ***Harmony 16:36-58***

On the Way to Gethsemane < Thursday Night, Nisan 14, Spring, A.D. 31 (7/7) > (Matthew 26:31-35; Mark 14:27-31; Luke 22:31-38; John 13:37, 38; 15:1-17:26) — **Harmony 16:59-116**

— The Lord's First Trial Before Pilate < Friday Morning, Nisan 14, Spring, A.D. 31 (7/7) > {Matthew 27:2, 11-14; Mark 15:1-5; Luke 23:1-7; John 18:28-38} — ***Harmony 17:60-78***

— Jesus Is Tried Before Herod Antipas < Friday Morning, Nisan 14, Spring, A.D. 31 (7/7) > {Luke 23:8-12} — ***Harmony 17:79-81***

— Jesus Is Tried a Second Time Before Pilate < Friday Morning, Nisan 14, Spring, A.D. 31 (7/7) > {Matthew 27:15-31; Mark 15:6-20; Luke 23:13-25; John 18:39-19:16} — ***Harmony 17:82-111***

The Crucifixion < Friday, About 8 A.M. through 3 P.M., Nisan 14, Spring, A.D. 31 (7/7) > {Matthew 27:32-52, 54; Mark 15:21-41; Luke 23:26-49; John 19:17-30} — ***Harmony 17:112-137***

— On the Way to the Crucifixion < Friday, About 8 A.M., Nisan 14, Spring, A.D. 31 (7/7) > {Matthew 27:32; Mark 15:21; Luke 23:26-32; John 19:17} — ***Harmony 17:112-114***

— The Crucifixion of Jesus < Friday, 9 A.M. — 3 P.M., Nisan 14, Spring, A.D. 31 (7/7) > {Matthew 27:33-52, 54-56; Mark 15:22-41; Luke 23:33-49; John 19:17-30} — ***Harmony 17:115-137***

*Chapter* EIGHTEEN: From Tragedy to Triumph — From the Burial of the Savior, to The Epilogue of the Gospel Story (Friday, Just Before Sunset, Nisan 14 — Thursday, Iyyar 25, Spring, A.D. 31) — **Harmony 18:1-103**

Jesus in the Tomb < Friday, Just Before Sunset, Nisan 14 — Early Sunday Morning, Nisan 16, Spring, A.D. 31 (7/7) > (Matthew 27:57-66; Mark 15:42-47; Luke 23:50-56; John 19:31-42) — **Harmony 18:1-12**

— The Burial of Jesus < Friday, Just Before Sundown, Nisan 14, Spring, A.D. 31 (7/7) > {Matthew 27:57-61; Mark 15:42-47; Luke 23:50-56; John 19:31-42} — ***Harmony 18:1-10***

— Jesus Rests in the Guarded Tomb Over the Sabbath < Sabbath, Nisan 15, Spring, A.D. 31 (7/7) > {Matthew 27:62-66} — ***Harmony 18:11, 12***

The Resurrection of Jesus < Early Sunday Morning, Through Sunday Afternoon, Nisan 16, Spring, A.D. 31 (7/7) > (Matthew 27:52, 53; 28:1-15; Mark 16:1-11; Luke 24:1-12; John 20:1-18) — **Harmony 18:13-33**

Jesus Meets With the Disciples Over the Next Few Weeks < Sunday, Late Afternoon and Evening, Nisan 16 and 17 — Through the Month of Iyyar, Spring, A.D. 31 (7/7) > (Mark 16:12-14; Luke 24:13-49; John 20:19-21:23) — **Harmony 18:34-86**

— The Meeting on the Road to Emmaus < Sunday, Late Afternoon, Nisan 16, Through Evening, Nisan 17, Spring, A.D. 31 (7/7) > {Mark 16:12; Luke 24:13-33} — ***Harmony 18:34-43***

— Jesus Appears to Ten of the Disciples in the Upper Room < Sunday Evening and Night, Nisan 17, Spring, A.D. 31 (7/7) > {Mark 16:12, 13; Luke 24:33-49; John 20:19-23} — ***Harmony 18:44-52***

— Jesus Meets with the Disciples Again, Eight Days Later < Sunday Evening, Nisan 24, Spring, A.D. 31 (7/7) > {Mark 16:14; John 20:24-29} — ***Harmony 18:53-59***

— Jesus Appears to the Disciples on the Bank of the Sea of Galilee < Sometime in the Month of Iyyar, Spring, A.D. 31 (7/7) > {John 21:1-23} — ***Harmony 18:60-86***

The Gospel Commission < Sometime in the Month of Iyyar, Spring, A.D. 31 (7/7) > (Matthew 28:16-20; Mark 16:15-18; Acts 1:4, 5) — **Harmony 18:87-90**

The Ascension < Thursday, Iyyar 25, Spring, A.D. 31 (7/7) > (Mark 16:19, 20; Luke 24:50-53; Acts 1:2, 3, 6-12) — **Harmony 18:91-99**

**The Timeline of the Ministry of Jesus, SUMMARY:**
**Autumn, A.D. 27 — Spring, A.D. 31**
**Thematic Review of the Ministry of Jesus**

The Epilogue to the Gospel Story (Matthew 28:20; Mark 16:20; Luke 24:53; John 20:30, 31; 21:24, 25) — **Harmony 18:100-103**

# ALPHABETICAL INDEX

This index contains, in alphabetical order, a listing of the events, most of the people, and teachings and sayings of Jesus, that are found in the Gospel story. Obviously, because so much of the message of the Gospels directly involves the life and ministry of Jesus, it is hard to include things in this index that don't involve Jesus in some way. So to make sure that the entire index was not under a single listing for "Jesus Christ," it, in part, was broken down into different categories that are mostly exclusive of each other. They are as follows:

"Disciples of Jesus"—this includes all things in the Gospel record that specifically mentions the disciples, individually as well as collectively; but it does not generally include things Jesus taught them.

"Jesus Christ" (events in the life of)—this includes the various *events* in the life of Jesus, as well as *things that happened to Him*. However, this list does *not* generally include the things Jesus taught and said. Also included in this list, under individual names, are the events involving various people who related directly to Him.

"Miracles of Jesus"—this includes all the miracles of Jesus, including those that took place on the Sabbath.

"Parables of Jesus"—this includes all the parables of Jesus and their interpretations. Also included are many of the illustrations Jesus used that are not usually considered parables as such.

"Sabbath"—this includes all the events involving Jesus (including miracles) that relate to the seventh-day Sabbath. This also includes the things Jesus said about the Sabbath.

"Sayings and teachings of Jesus"—*except* items involving the Sabbath, this includes the many things that Jesus said, as well as taught the people, including His disciples.

"Social events in the ministry of Jesus"—this includes the events in the life of Jesus that involved some type of social event.

On occasion, some of the things listed above may be found in one of the other categories; however, it will be easier to find an item listed under a category that specifically involves such an event or teaching.

In two other categories, "Jewish leaders," and "John the Baptist," some of the events listed there do directly involve Jesus, while others do not. In addition, all other listings in this index will involve specific people and things that do not, necessarily, have a direct bearing on Jesus, or what He said.

This index includes, not only the events of the Gospel story that are contained in the *Harmony*, but also the following:

All the Explanatory Notes founding the *Harmony*. In the index, they are *usually* listed as an "explanation of." These Notes are always listed as with an "(E)" designation, to denote that it is an Explanatory Note. Also, these entries are listed with a slash mark (/) to indicate that they are Explanatory Notes. (See "Explanatory Notes" in "How to Use the *Harmony* as Reference Book" section to understand more about Explanatory Notes.)

All eight Timeline Segments.

Both the Preview and Review of the Ministry of Jesus Sections.

In spite of the extensiveness of this index, it might be that one still might not be able to find a particular desired item. In that case, the reader is directed to the Scriptural Index which follows this one, where an item can be found in conjunction with the use of a concordance.

## ALPHABETICAL INDEX:

## John the Baptist

# SCRIPTURAL INDEX

The Scriptural Index is the link that connects any Bible the reader might be using to the *Harmony*, and vice versa. By using this index, the reader can easily move from the *Harmony* to the Bible, and *especially* from the Bible to the *Harmony*. Such an index is absolutely necessary if the reader is to use the Bible and the *Harmony* as companion books. In reality, this index contains the chronological listing of all the 1,818 footnotes found within the 18 chapters of the *Harmony*.

The uniqueness of this index is that every reference is listed separately for all parallel readings in the Gospel record. This means if there are up to four different accounts of a particular event, all of these are listed under the various Gospels. For example, find Matthew 3:1 below, found in *Harmony* 2:2. There, the reader will see this listing plus the ones for also Mark (Mark 1:4), Luke (Luke 1:80; 3:3), and John (John 1:28). In this index under Mark 1:4, the reader will find that one, plus the same ones for Matthew, Luke, and John. The same is additionally true for both Luke references, and also that of John. And should a particular reference skip a verse (or verses) in its sequence, there are additional listings for that reference. For example, see Matthew 2:15, 19, 20 below, as well as Matthew 2:19, 20 (15) listed below that.

Please note, though, that if a particular verse is used more than one time for the *Harmony*, it is left up to the reader to determine which portion of the verse has be used for any particular part of the *Harmony*.

And, in spite of the extensiveness of the preceding Alphabetical Index, should the reader still be unable to find a particular event or concept in the *Harmony*, there is a certain way of doing so with this index. How is this accomplished? Look up any word, event, or concept in a good concordance (*Strong's Exhaustive Concordance* is highly recommended). When the desired word, event, or concept is found in the concordance, refer to the Scriptural Index and find the appropriate *Harmony* location. Then look up that reference in the *Harmony*. It's just that simple!

**MATTHEW**

**Matthew 5:23, 24 — *5:26***
**Matthew 5:25, 26 — *5:27***
**Matthew 5:27, 28 — *5:28***
**Matthew 5:29, 30 — *5:29***
**Matthew 5:31 — *5:30***
**Matthew 5:32 — *5:31***
**Matthew 5:33 — *5:32***
**Matthew 5:34, 35 — *5:33***
**Matthew 5:36 — *5:34***
**Matthew 5:37 — *5:35***
**Matthew 5:38 — *5:36***
**Matthew 5:39-42 (Luke 6:29, 30) — *5:37***
**Matthew 5:43-45 (Luke 6:27, 28) — *5:38***
**Matthew 5:46, 47 (Luke 6:32-34) — *5:39***
**Matthew 5:48 (Luke 6:36) — *5:41***
**Matthew 6:1, 2 — *5:42***
**Matthew 6:3, 4 — *5:43***
**Matthew 6:5 — *5:44***
**Matthew 6:6 — *5:45***
**Matthew 6:7-9 — *5:46***
**Matthew 6:9 — *5:47***
**Matthew 6:10 — *5:48***
**Matthew 6:11 — *5:49***
**Matthew 6:12 — *5:50***
**Matthew 6:13 — *5:51***
**Matthew 6:13 — *5:52***
**Matthew 6:14, 15 — *5:53***
**Matthew 6:16 — *5:54***
**Matthew 6:17, 18 — *5:55***
**Matthew 6:19 — *5:56***
**Matthew 6:20, 21 — *5:57***
**Matthew 6:22, 23 — *5:58***
**Matthew 6:24 — *5:60***
**Matthew 6:25 — *5:61***
**Matthew 6:25 — *5:62***
**Matthew 6:26 — *5:63***
**Matthew 6:27 — *5:64***
**Matthew 6:28-30 — *5:65***
**Matthew 6:31, 32 — *5:66***
**Matthew 6:33, 34 — *5:67***
**Matthew 7:1 — *5:68***

**Matthew 16:7 (Mark 8:16) — *10:37***
**Matthew 16:8, 9 (Mark 8:18, 19) — *10:39***
**Matthew 16:10 (Mark 8:20) — *10:41***
**Matthew 16:11, 12 (Mark 8:21) — *10:43***
**Matthew 16:13 (Mark 8:27) — *10:47***
**Matthew 16:13 (Mark 8:27; Luke 9:18) — *10:48***
**Matthew 16:14 (Mark 8:28; Luke 9:19) — *10:49***
**Matthew 16:15 (Mark 8:29; Luke 9:20) — *10:50***
**Matthew 16:16 (Mark 8:29; Luke 9:20) — *10:51***
**Matthew 16:17 — *10:52***
**Matthew 16:18, 19 — *10:53***
**Matthew 16:20 (Mark 8:30; Luke 9:21) — *10:54***
**Matthew 16:21 (Mark 8:31, 32; Luke 9:22) — *10:55***
**Matthew 16:22 (Mark 8:32) — *10:56***
**Matthew 16:23 (Mark 8:33) — *10:57***
**Matthew 16:24, 25 (Mark 8:34, 35; Luke 9:23, 24) — *10:58***
**Matthew 16:26, 27 (Mark 8:36, 37; Luke 9:25) — *10:59***
**Matthew 16:28 (Mark 9:1; Luke 9:27) — *10:61***
**Matthew 17:1 (Mark 9:2; Luke 9:28) — *10:62***
**Matthew 17:2 (Mark 9:2) — *10:63***
**Matthew 17:2, 3 (Mark 9:3, 4; Luke 9:29-32) — *10:64***
**Matthew 17:4 (Mark 9:5, 6; Luke 9:33) — *10:66***
**Matthew 17:5, 6 (Mark 9:7; Luke 9:34, 35) — *10:67***
**Matthew 17:7, 8 (Mark 9:8; Luke 9:36) — *10:68***
**Matthew 17:9 (Mark 9:9; Luke 9:36) — *10:69***
**Matthew 17:10 (Mark 9:11) — *10:71***
**Matthew 17:11-13 (Mark 9:12, 13) — *10:72***
**Matthew 17:14 (Mark 9:14, 15; Luke 9:37) — *10:73***
**Matthew 17:14, 15 (Mark 9:17, 18; Luke 9:38, 39) — *10:75***
**Matthew 17:15, 16 (Mark 9:18; Luke 9:39, 40) — *10:76***
**Matthew 17:17 (Mark 9:19, 20; Luke 9:41, 42) — *10:77***
**Matthew 17:18 (Mark 9:25; Luke 9:42) — *10:82***
**Matthew 17:18 (Mark 9:26, 27; Luke 9:42, 43) — *10:83***
**Matthew 17:19, 24 (Mark 9:28) — *10:86***
**Matthew 17:20, 21 (Mark 9:29) — *10:87***
**Matthew 17:22, 23 (Mark 9:30, 31; Luke 9:43, 44) — *10:84***
**Matthew 17:23 (Mark 9:32; Luke 9:45) — *10:85***
**Matthew 17:24 — *10:88***
**Matthew 17:24 (19) (Mark 9:28)**
**Matthew 17:25 — *10:89***
**Matthew 17:25 — *10:90***

**Matthew 19:21 (Mark 10:21; Luke 18:22) — *13:81***
**Matthew 19:22 (Mark 10:22; Luke 18:23) — *13:82***
**Matthew 19:23, 24 (Mark 10:23-25; Luke 18:24, 25) — *13:83***
**Matthew 19:25 (Mark 10:26; Luke 18:26) — *13:84***
**Matthew 19:26 (Mark 10:27; Luke 18:27) — *13:85***
**Matthew 19:27 (Mark 10:28; Luke 18:28) — *13:86***
**Matthew 19:28, 29 (Mark 10:29; Luke 18:29, 30) — *13:87***
**Matthew 19:30 (Mark 10:30, 31; Luke 18:30) — *13:88***
**Matthew 20:1, 2 — *13:89***
**Matthew 20:3, 4 — *13:90***
**Matthew 20:5, 6 — *13:91***
**Matthew 20:7 — *13:92***
**Matthew 20:7 — *13:93***
**Matthew 20:8 — *13:94***
**Matthew 20:9-12 — *13:95***
**Matthew 20:13-15 — *13:96***
**Matthew 20:16 — *13:97***
**Matthew 20:17 (Mark 10:32; Luke 18:31) — *13:98***
**Matthew 20:18, 19 (Mark 10:33, 34; Luke 18:31-33) — *13:99***
**Matthew 20:20 (Mark 10:35) — *13:101***
**Matthew 20:21 (Mark 10:36) — *13:102***
**Matthew 20:21 (Mark 10:37) — *13:103***
**Matthew 20:22 (Mark 10:38) — *13:104***
**Matthew 20:22 (Mark 10:39) — *13:105***
**Matthew 20:23 (Mark 10:39, 40) — *13:106***
**Matthew 20:24-28 (Mark 10:41-45) — *13:107***
**Matthew 20:29 (Mark 10:46; Luke 19:1-4) — *13:108***
**Matthew 20:29, 30 (Mark 10:46, 47; Luke 18:35-38) — *13:113***
**Matthew 20:31 (Mark 10:48; Luke 18:39) — *13:114***
**Matthew 20:32 (Mark 10:49; Luke 18:40) — *13:115***
**Matthew 20:32 (Mark 10:50, 51; Luke 18:40, 41) — *13:117***
**Matthew 20:33 (Mark 10:51; Luke 18:41) — *13:118***
**Matthew 20:34 (Mark 10:52; Luke 18:42, 43) — *13:119***
**Matthew 21:1 (Mark 11:1; Luke 19:29; John 12:12) — *14:26***
**Matthew 21:1-3 (Mark 11:1-3; Luke 19:29-31) — *14:27***
**Matthew 21:4, 5 (John 12:14, 15) — *14:40***
**Matthew 21:6 (Mark 11:4-6; Luke 19:32-34; John 12:14) — *14:28***
**Matthew 21:7, 8 (Mark 11:7, 8; Luke 19:35, 36; John 12:12-14) — *14:29***
**Matthew 21:9 (Mark 11:9, 10; John 12:13) — *14:30***
**Matthew 21:10 (Mark 11:11) — *14:37***
**Matthew 21:11 — *14:38***

**Matthew 22:16 (Mark 12:14; Luke 20:21) — *14:86***
**Matthew 22:17 (Mark 12:14, 15; Luke 20:22) — *14:87***
**Matthew 22:18 (Mark 12:15; Luke 20:23) — *14:88***
**Matthew 22:19, 20 (Mark 12:15, 16; Luke 20:24) — *14:89***
**Matthew 22:21 (Mark 12:16; Luke 20:24) — *14:90***
**Matthew 22:21 (Mark 12:17; Luke 20:25) — *14:91***
**Matthew 22:22 (Mark 12:17; Luke 20:26) — *14:92***
**Matthew 22:23 (Mark 12:18; Luke 20:27) — *14:93***
**Matthew 22:23-27 (Mark 12:18-22; Luke 20:27-32) — *14:94***
**Matthew 22:28 (Mark 12:23; Luke 20:33) — *14:95***
**Matthew 22:29 (Mark 12:24) — *14:96***
**Matthew 22:30 (Mark 12:25; Luke 20:34-36) — *14:97***
**Matthew 22:31, 32 (Mark 12:26, 27; Luke 20:37, 38) — *14:98***
**Matthew 22:33 — *14:99***
**Matthew 22:34, 35 (Mark 12:28) — *14:100***
**Matthew 22:35, 36 (Mark 12:28) — *14:101***
**Matthew 22:37-39 (Mark 12:29-31) — *14:102***
**Matthew 22:40 (Mark 12:31) — *14:103***
**Matthew 22:41, 42 (Mark 12:35) — *14:107***
**Matthew 22:42 — *14:108***
**Matthew 22:43-45 (Mark 12:35-37; Luke 20:41-44) — *14:109***
**Matthew 22:46 (Mark 12:37) — *14:110***
**Matthew 23:1 (Mark 12:38; Luke 20:45) — *14:111***
**Matthew 23:2, 3 (Mark 12;38; Luke 20:46) — *14:112***
**Matthew 23:4 (Mark 12:40; Luke 20:47) — *14:113***
**Matthew 23:5, 6 (Mark 12:39) — *14:114***
**Matthew 23:7, 8 (Mark 12:38; Luke 20:46) — *14:115***
**Matthew 23:9, 10 — *14:116***
**Matthew 23:11, 12 — *14:117***
**Matthew 23:13 — *14:118***
**Matthew 23:14 — *14:119***
**Matthew 23:15 — *14:120***
**Matthew 23:16 — *14:121***
**Matthew 23:17 — *14:122***
**Matthew 23:18, 19 — *14:123***
**Matthew 23:20-22 — *14:124***
**Matthew 23:23 — *14:125***
**Matthew 23:24 — *14:126***
**Matthew 23:25, 26 — *14:127***
**Matthew 23:27, 28 — *14:128***
**Matthew 23:29-33 — *14:129***

**Matthew 25:21 — *15:46***
**Matthew 25:22 — *15:47***
**Matthew 25:23 — *15:48***
**Matthew 25:24, 25 — *15:49***
**Matthew 25:26-30 — *15:50***
**Matthew 25:31-33 — *15:51***
**Matthew 25:34-36 — *15:52***
**Matthew 25:37-39 — *15:53***
**Matthew 25:40 — *15:54***
**Matthew 25:41-43 — *15:55***
**Matthew 25:44 — *15:56***
**Matthew 25:45 — *15:57***
**Matthew 25:46 — *15:58***
**Matthew 26:1, 2 (Mark 14:1) — *15:59***
**Matthew 26:3, 4 (Mark 14:1; Luke 22:1, 2) — *14:19***
**Matthew 26:5 (Mark 14:2) — *14:21***
**Matthew 26:6 (Mark 14:3; Luke 7:36; John 12:1, 2) — *14:1***
**Matthew 26:7 (Mark 14:3; Luke 7:37) — *14:3***
**Matthew 26:7 (Mark 14:3; Luke 7:37, 38; John 12:3) — *14:4***
**Matthew 26:8, 9 (Mark 14:4, 5; John12:4-6) — *14:5***
**Matthew 26:10, 11 (Mark 14:6-8; John 12:7, 8) — *14:6***
**Matthew 26:12, 13 (Mark 14:8, 9; John 12:7) — *14:7***
**Matthew 26:14 (Mark 14:10; Luke 22:3, 4) — *14:22***
**Matthew 26:15 — *14:23***
**Matthew 26:15, 16 (Mark 14:11; Luke 22:5, 6) — *14:24***
**Matthew 26:17 (Mark 14:12; Luke 22:7, 8) — *16:2***
**Matthew 26:17 (Mark 14:12; Luke 22:9) — *16:3***
**Matthew 26:18 (Mark 14:13-15; Luke 22:10-12) — *16:4***
**Matthew 26:19 (Mark 14:16; Luke 22:13) — *16:5***
**Matthew 26:20 (Mark 14:17; Luke 22:14-16) — *16:6***
**Matthew 26:21 (Mark 14:18; Luke 22:23; John 13:21, 22) — *16:27***
**Matthew 26:22 (Mark 14:19) — *16:28***
**Matthew 26:23, 24 (Mark 14:20, 21; Luke 22:21, 22) — *16:32***
**Matthew 26:25 — *16:33***
**Matthew 26:25 (John 13:27, 30) — *16:34***
**Matthew 26:26 (Mark 14:22; Luke 22:19) — *16:25***
**Matthew 26:27-29 (Mark 14:23-25; Luke 22:20) — *16:26***
**Matthew 26:30 (Mark 14:26; Luke 22:39; John 14:31) — *16:58***
**Matthew 26:31, 32 (Mark 14:27, 28) — *16:59***
**Matthew 26:33 (Mark 14:29) — *16:60***
**Matthew 26:34 (Mark 14:30; Luke 22:34; John 13:38) — *16:63***

**Matthew 27:15 (Mark 15:6; Luke 23:17) — *17:84***
**Matthew 27:16 (Mark 15:7; Luke 23:19; John 18:40) — *17:85***
**Matthew 27:17, 18 (Mark 15:8-10; John 18:39) — *17:86***
**Matthew 27:19 — *17:83***
**Matthew 27:20, 21 (Mark 15:11) — *17:87***
**Matthew 27:21 (Luke 23:18; John 18:40) — *17:88***
**Matthew 27:22 (Mark 15:12) — *17:89***
**Matthew 27:22 (Mark 15:13) — *17:90***
**Matthew 27:23 (Mark 15:14) — *17:92***
**Matthew 27:23 (Mark 15:14) — *17:93***
**Matthew 27:24 — *17:109***
**Matthew 27:25 — *17:110***
**Matthew 27:26, 31 (Mark 15:15, 20; Luke 23:24, 25; John 19:16) — *17:111***
**Matthew 27:27-31 (Mark 15:16-20; John 19:2, 3) — *17:96***
**Matthew 27:31 (26) (Mark 15:15, 20; Luke 23:24, 25; John 19:16) — *17:111***
**Matthew 27:32 (Mark 15:21; Luke 23:26; John 19:17) — *17:112***
**Matthew 27:33, 34 (Mark 15:22, 23; Luke 23:33; John 19:17) — *17:115***
**Matthew 27:35, 36 (Mark 15:24; Luke 23:34; John 19:23-25) — *17:119***
**Matthew 27:35, 38 (Mark 15:25, 27, 28; Luke 23:33, 34; John 19:18) — *17:116***
**Matthew 27:37 (Mark 15:26; Luke 23:38; John 19:19-21) — *17:117***
**Matthew 27:38 (35) (Mark 15:24, 25, 27, 28; Luke 23:33, 34; John 19:18, 24) — *17:116***
**Matthew 27:39, 40 (Mark 15:29, 30; Luke 23:35) — *17:120***
**Matthew 27:41-43 (Mark 15:31, 32; Luke 23:35) — *17:121***
**Matthew 27:44 (Mark 15:32) — *17:122***
**Matthew 27:45 (Mark 15:33; Luke 23:44, 45) — *17:128***
**Matthew 27:46 (Mark 15:34) — *17:129***
**Matthew 27:47 (Mark 15:35) — *17:130***
**Matthew 27:48 (Mark 15:36; John 19:28, 29) — *17:131***
**Matthew 27:48, 50 (Mark 15:36, 37; Luke 23:46; John 19:30) — *17:133***
**Matthew 27:49 (Mark 15:36) — *17:132***
**Matthew 27:50 (48) (Mark 15:36, 37; Luke 23:46; John 19:30) — *17:133***
**Matthew 27:51 (Mark 15:38; Luke 23:45) — *17:134***
**Matthew 27:51, 52 — *17:135***
**Matthew 27:52, 53 — *18:33***
**Matthew 27:54 (Mark 15:39;Luke 23:47, 48) — *17:137***
**Matthew 27:55, 56 (Mark 15:40, 41; Luke 23:49) — *17:136***
**Matthew 27:57, 58 (Mark 15:42, 43; Luke 23:50-52; John 19:38) — *18:6***
**Matthew 27:58 (Mark 15:44, 45) — *18:7***
**Matthew 27:59 (Mark 15:46; Luke 23:53; John 19:39, 40) — *18:8***
**Matthew 27:60 (Mark 15:46; John 19:41, 42) — *18:9***
**Matthew 27:61 (Mark 15:47; Luke 23:55, 56) — *18:10***

## MARK

**Mark 1:35-37 (Luke 4:42) — *4:32***
**Mark 1:38, 39 (Matthew 4:23; Luke 4:43, 44) — *4:33***
**Mark 1:40 (Matthew 8:2; Luke 5:12) — *4:35***
**Mark 1:40 (Matthew 8:2; Luke 5:12) — *4:36***
**Mark 1:41, 42 (Matthew 8:3; Luke 5:13) — *4:37***
**Mark 1:43, 44 (Matthew 8:4; Luke 5:14) — *4:38***
**Mark 1:45 (Luke 5:15, 16) — *4:39***
**Mark 2:1, 2 (Luke 5:17) — *4:40***
**Mark 2:3, 4 (Matthew 9:2; Luke 5:18, 19) — *4:42***
**Mark 2:5 (Matthew 9:2; Luke 5:20) — *4:43***
**Mark 2:6, 7 (Matthew 9:3; Luke 5:21) — *4:44***
**Mark 2:8, 9 (Matthew 9:4, 5; Luke 5:22, 23) — *4:45***
**Mark 2:10-12 (Matthew 9:6, 7; Luke 5:24, 25) — *4:46***
**Mark 2:12 (Matthew 9:8; Luke 5:26) — *4:47***
**Mark 2:13 — *4:48***
**Mark 2:14 (Matthew 9:9; Luke 5:27) — *4:49***
**Mark 2:14 (Matthew 9:9; Luke 27, 28) — *4:50***
**Mark 2:15 (Matthew 9:10; Luke 5:29) — *8:2***
**Mark 2:16 (Matthew 9:11; Luke 5:30) — *8:3***
**Mark 2:17 (Matthew 9:12, 13; Luke 5:31, 32) — *8:4***
**Mark 2:18 (Matthew 9:14; Luke 5:33) — *8:5***
**Mark 2:19, 20 (Matthew 9:15; Luke 5:34, 35) — *8:6***
**Mark 2:21 (Matthew 9:16; Luke 5:36) — *8:7***
**Mark 2:22 (Matthew 9:17; Luke 5:37-39) — *8:8***
**Mark 2:23, 24 (Matthew 12:1, 2; Luke 6:1, 2) — *4:51***
**Mark 2:25, 26 (Matthew 12:3, 4; Luke 6:3, 4) — *4:52***
**Mark 2:27, 28 (Matthew 12:8; Luke 6:5) — *4:56***
**Mark 3:1 (Matthew 12:9, 10; Luke 6:6) — *4:57***
**Mark 3:2 (Matthew 12:10; Luke 6:7, 8) — *4:58***
**Mark 3:3, 4 (Luke 6:8, 9) — *4:59***
**Mark 3:5 (Matthew 12:11, 12; Luke 6:10) — *4:60***
**Mark 3:5 (Matthew 12:13; Luke 6:10) — *4:61***
**Mark 3:6 (Matthew 12:14; Luke 6:11) — *4:62***
**Mark 3:7, 8 (Matthew 12:15) — *4:63***
**Mark 3:9, 10 (Matthew 12:15) — *4:64***
**Mark 3:11, 12 (Matthew 12:16) — *4:65***
**Mark 3:13, 14 (Luke 6:13, 17-19) — *5:1***
**Mark 3:13-15 (Luke 6:12, 13) — *4:67***
**Mark 3:16 (Luke 6:14) — *4:68***
**Mark 3:17 (Luke 6:14) — *4:70***
**Mark 3:17 (Luke 6:14) — *4:71***

**Mark 7:31 — *10:23***
**Mark 7:32-35 — *10:24***
**Mark 7:36, 37 — *10:25***
**Mark 8:1-3 (Matthew 15:32) — *10:27***
**Mark 8:4 (Matthew 15:33) — *10:28***
**Mark 8:5 (Matthew 15:34) — *10:29***
**Mark 8:5 (Matthew 15:34) — *10:30***
**Mark 8:6-9 (Matthew 15:35-38) — *10:31***
**Mark 8:9, 10 (Matthew 15:39) — *10:32***
**Mark 8:11, 12 (Matthew 16:1) — *10:33***
**Mark 8:12, 13 (Matthew 16:2-4) — *10:34***
**Mark 8:14 (Matthew 16:5) — *10:35***
**Mark 8:15 (Matthew 16:6) — *10:36***
**Mark 8:16 (Matthew 16:7) — *10:37***
**Mark 8:17, 18 — *10:38***
**Mark 8:18, 19 (Matthew 16:8, 9) — *10:39***
**Mark 8:19 — *10:40***
**Mark 8:20 — *10:42***
**Mark 8:20 (Matthew 16:10) — *10:41***
**Mark 8:21 (Matthew 16:11, 12) — *10:43***
**Mark 8:22, 23 — *10:44***
**Mark 8:24 — *10:45***
**Mark 8:25, 26 — *10:46***
**Mark 8:27 (Matthew 16:13) — *10:47***
**Mark 8:27 (Matthew 16:13; Luke 9:18) — *10:48***
**Mark 8:28 (Matthew 16:14; Luke 9:19) — *10:49***
**Mark 8:29 (Matthew 16:15; Luke 9:20) — *10:50***
**Mark 8:29 (Matthew 16:16; Luke 9:20) — *10:51***
**Mark 8:30 (Matthew 16:20; Luke 9:21) — *10:54***
**Mark 8:31, 32 (Matthew 16:21; Luke 9:22) — *10:55***
**Mark 8:32 (Matthew 16:22) — *10:56***
**Mark 8:33 (Matthew 16:23) — *10:57***
**Mark 8:34, 35 (Matthew 16:24, 25; Luke 9:23, 24) — *10:58***
**Mark 8:36, 37 (Matthew 16:26, 27; Luke 9:25) — *10:59***
**Mark 8:38 (Luke 9:26) — *10:60***
**Mark 9:1 (Matthew 16:28; Luke 9:27) — *10:61***
**Mark 9:2 (Matthew 17:1; Luke 9:28) — *10:62***
**Mark 9:2 (Matthew 17:2) — *10:63***
**Mark 9:3, 4 (Matthew 17:2, 3; Luke 9:29-32) — *10:64***
**Mark 9:5, 6 (Matthew 17:4; Luke 9:33) — *10:66***
**Mark 9:7 (Matthew 17:5, 6; Luke 9:34, 35) — *10:67***

**Mark 10:16 (Matthew 19:15) — *13:74***
**Mark 10:17 (Matthew 19:16; Luke 18:18) — *13:75***
**Mark 10:18 (Matthew 19:17; Luke 18:19) — *13:76***
**Mark 10:19 (Matthew 19:18, 19; Luke 18:20) — *13:79***
**Mark 10:20 (Matthew 19:20; Luke 18:21) — *13:80***
**Mark 10:21 (Matthew 19:21; Luke 18:22) — *13:81***
**Mark 10:22 (Matthew 19:22; Luke 18:23) — *13:82***
**Mark 10:23-25 (Matthew 19:23, 24; Luke 18:24, 25) — *13:83***
**Mark 10:26 (Matthew 19:25; Luke 18:26) — *13:84***
**Mark 10:27 (Matthew 19:26; Luke 18:27) — *13:85***
**Mark 10:28 (Matthew 19:27; Luke 18:28) — *13:86***
**Mark 10:29 (Matthew 19:28, 29; Luke 18:29, 30) — *13:87***
**Mark 10:30, 31 (Matthew 19:30; Luke 18:30) — *13:88***
**Mark 10:32 (Matthew 20:17; Luke 18:31) — *13:98***
**Mark 10:33, 34 (Matthew 20:18, 19; Luke 18:31-33) — *13:99***
**Mark 10:35 (Matthew 20:20) — *13:101***
**Mark 10:36 (Matthew 20:20) — *13:102***
**Mark 10:37 (Matthew 20:21) — *13:103***
**Mark 10:38 (Matthew 20:22) — *13:104***
**Mark 10:39 (Matthew 20:22) — *13:105***
**Mark 10:39, 40 (Matthew 20:23) — *13:106***
**Mark 10:41-45 (Matthew 20:24-28) — *13:107***
**Mark 10:46 (Matthew 20:29; Luke 19:1-4) — *13:108***
**Mark 10:46, 47 (Matthew 20:29, 30; Luke 18:35-38) — *13:113***
**Mark 10:48 (Matthew 20:31; Luke 18:39) — *13:114***
**Mark 10:49 (Matthew 20:32; Luke 18:40) — *13:115***
**Mark 10:49, 50 — *13:116***
**Mark 10:50, 51 (Matthew 20:32; Luke 18:40, 41) — *13:117***
**Mark 10:51 (Matthew 20:33; Luke 18:41) — *13:118***
**Mark 10:52 (Matthew 20:34; Luke 18:42, 43) — *13:119***
**Mark 11:1 (Matthew 21:1; Luke 19:29; John 12:12) — *14:26***
**Mark 11:1-3 (Matthew 21:1-3; Luke 19:29-31) — *14:27***
**Mark 11:4-6 (Matthew 21:6; Luke 19:32-34; John 12:14) — *14:28***
**Mark 11:7, 8 (Matthew 26:7, 8; Luke 19:35-36; John 12:12-14) — *14:29***
**Mark 11:9, 10 (Matthew 21:9; John 12:13) — *14:30***
**Mark 11:11 (Matthew 21:10) — *14:37***
**Mark 11:11, 12 — *14:39***
**Mark 11:12, 13 (Matthew 21:18) — *14:42***
**Mark 11:13, 14 (Matthew 21:18, 19) — *14:43***
**Mark 11:15 (Matthew 21:12; Luke 19:45) — *14:44***
**Mark 11:15-17 (Matthew 21:12, 13; Luke 19:45, 46) — *14:45***

**Mark 12:38 (Matthew 23:1; Luke 20:45) — *14:111***
**Mark 12:38 (Matthew 23:2, 3; Luke 20:46) — *14:112***
**Mark 12:38 (Matthew 23:7, 8; Luke 20:46) — *14:115***
**Mark 12:39 (Matthew 23:5, 6) — *14:114***
**Mark 12:40 (Matthew 23:4; Luke 20:47) — *14:113***
**Mark 12:41, 42 (Luke 21:1, 2) — *14:134***
**Mark 12:43, 44 (Luke 21:3, 4) — *14:135***
**Mark 13:1 (Matthew 24:1; Luke 21:5) — *15:1***
**Mark 13:2 (Matthew 24:2; Luke 21:5, 6) — *15:2***
**Mark 13:3, 4 (Matthew 24:3; Luke 21:7) — *15:3***
**Mark 13:5-7 (Matthew 24:4-6; Luke 21:8, 9) — *15:4***
**Mark 13:8 (Matthew 24:7, 8; Luke 21:10, 11) — *15:5***
**Mark 13:9, 10 (Luke 21:12, 13) — *15:7***
**Mark 13:11 (Luke 21:14, 15) — *15:8***
**Mark 13:12, 13 (Luke 21:16, 17) — *15:9***
**Mark 13:14 (Matthew 24:15, 16; Luke 21:20-22) — *15:12***
**Mark 13:15, 16 (Matthew 24:17, 18) — *15:13***
**Mark 13:17, 18 (Matthew 24:19, 20; Luke 21:23) — *15:14***
**Mark 13:19, 20 (Matthew 24:21, 22) — *15:16***
**Mark 13:21-23 (Matthew 24:23-25) — *15:18***
**Mark 13:24, 25 (Matthew 24:29; Luke 21:25) — *15:17***
**Mark 13:25-27 (Matthew 24:29-31; Luke 21:26-28) — *15:21***
**Mark 13:28-31 (Matthew 24:32-35; Luke 21:29-33) — *15:22***
**Mark 13:32 (Matthew 24:36-39) — *15:23***
**Mark 13:33 (Matthew 24:42-44) — *15:25***
**Mark 13:34 (Matthew 24:45) — *15:26***
**Mark 13:35-37 — *15:29***
**Mark 14:1 (Matthew 26:1, 2) — *15:59***
**Mark 14:1 (Matthew 26:3, 4; Luke 22:1, 2) — *14:19***
**Mark 14:2 (Matthew 26:5) — *14:21***
**Mark 14:3 (Matthew 26:6; Luke 7:36; John 12:1, 2) — *14:1***
**Mark 14:3 (Matthew 26:7; Luke 7:37) — *14:3***
**Mark 14:3 (Matthew 26:7; Luke 7:37, 38; John 12:3) — *14:4***
**Mark 14:4, 5 (Matthew 26:8, 9; John 12:4-6) — *14:5***
**Mark 14:6-8 (Matthew 26:10, 11; John 12:7, 8) — *14:6***
**Mark 14:8, 9 (Matthew 26:12, 13; John 12:7) — *14:7***
**Mark 14:10 (Matthew 26:14; Luke 22:3, 4) — *14:22***
**Mark 14:11 (Matthew 26:15, 16; Luke 22:5, 6) — *14:24***
**Mark 14:12 (Matthew 26:17; Luke 22:7, 8) — *16:2***
**Mark 14:12 (Matthew 26:17; Luke 22:9) — *16:3***
**Mark 14:13-15 (Matthew 26:18; Luke 22:10-12) — *16:4***

**Mark 14:16 (Matthew 26:19; Luke 22:13) —** ***16:5***
**Mark 14:17 (Matthew 26:20; Luke 22:14-16) —** ***16:6***
**Mark 14:18 (Matthew 26:21; Luke 22:23; John 13:21, 22) —** ***16:27***
**Mark 14:19 (Matthew 26:22) —** ***16:28***
**Mark 14:20, 21 (Matthew 26:23, 24; Luke 22:21, 22) —** ***16:32***
**Mark 14:22 (Matthew 26:26; Luke 22:19) —** ***16:25***
**Mark 14:23-25 (Matthew 26:27-29; Luke 22:20) —** ***16:26***
**Mark 14:26 (Matthew 26:30; Luke 22:39; John 14:31) —** ***16:58***
**Mark 14:27, 28 (Matthew 26:31, 32) —** ***16:59***
**Mark 14:29 (Matthew 26:33) —** ***16:60***
**Mark 14:30 (Matthew 26:34; Luke 22:34; John 13:38) —** ***16:63***
**Mark 14:31 (Matthew 26:35) —** ***16:64***
**Mark 14:32 (Matthew 26:36; Luke 22:40; John 18:1) —** ***17:1***
**Mark 14:32-34 (Matthew 26:36-38) —** ***17:2***
**Mark 14:35, 36 (Matthew 26:39; Luke 22:41) —** ***17:4***
**Mark 14:37, 38 (Matthew 26:40, 41) —** ***17:5***
**Mark 14:39 (Matthew 26:42) —** ***17:6***
**Mark 14:40 (Matthew 26:43) —** ***17:7***
**Mark 14:41, 42 (Matthew 26:45, 46; Luke 22:45, 46) —** ***17:9***
**Mark 14:43 (Matthew 26:47; Luke 22:47; John 18:2-4) —** ***17:10***
**Mark 14:44, 45 (Matthew 26:48, 49; Luke 22:47) —** ***17:17***
**Mark 14:46 (Matthew 26:50; Luke 22:48) —** ***17:18***
**Mark 14:47 (Matthew 26:51; Luke 22:49, 50; John 18:10) —** ***17:19***
**Mark 14:48, 49 (Matthew 26:55, 56; Luke 22:52, 53) —** ***17:22***
**Mark 14:50 (Matthew 26:56; John 18:12) —** ***17:23***
**Mark 14:51, 52 —** ***17:24***
**Mark 14:53 (Matthew 26:57; Luke 22:54; John 18:24) —** ***17:36***
**Mark 14:54, 67 (Matthew 26:58; Luke 22:54; John 18:15, 16) —** ***17:26***
**Mark 14:54 (Matthew 26:58; Luke 22:55, 56; John 18:18) —** ***17:27***
**Mark 14:55, 56 (Matthew 26:59, 60) —** ***17:37***
**Mark 14:57, 58 (Matthew 26:60, 61) —** ***17:38***
**Mark 14:59 —** ***17:39***
**Mark 14:60, 61 (Matthew 26:62, 63) —** ***17:45***
**Mark 14:62 (Matthew 26:64) —** ***17:46***
**Mark 14:63, 64 (Matthew 26:65, 66) —** ***17:47***
**Mark 14:64 (Matthew 26:66) —** ***17:48***
**Mark 14:65 (Matthew 26:67, 68; Luke 22:63-65) —** ***17:49***
**Mark 14:66, 67 (Matthew 26:69; Luke 22:56; John 18:17) —** ***17:28***
**Mark 14:67 (54) (Matthew 26:58; Luke 22:55, 56; John 18:18) —** ***17:27***
**Mark 14:68 (Matthew 26:70, 71; Luke 22:57; John 18:17) —** ***17:29***
**Mark 14:69 (Matthew 26:71; Luke 22:58; John 18:25) —** ***17:40***

## LUKE

**Luke 4:4 (Matthew 4:4) — *2:31***
**Luke 4:5-7 (Matthew 4:8, 9) — *2:34***
**Luke 4:8 (Matthew 4:10) — *2:35***
**Luke 4:9-11 (Matthew 4:5, 6) — *2:32***
**Luke 4:12 (Matthew 4:7) — *2:33***
**Luke 4:13 (Matthew 4:11; Mark 1:13) — *2:36***
**Luke 4:14 (Matthew 4:12; Mark 1:14) — *4:1***
**Luke 4:14 (Mark 1:14, 15) — *4:2***
**Luke 4:14, 15 — *4:3***
**Luke 4:16-19 — *4:4***
**Luke 4:20, 21 — *4:5***
**Luke 4:22 — *4:6***
**Luke 4:23 — *4:7***
**Luke 4:23 — *4:8***
**Luke 4:24-27 — *4:9***
**Luke 4:28-30 — *4:10***
**Luke 4:31 (Matthew 4:13) — *4:11***
**Luke 4:31, 32 (Mark 1:21, 22) — *4:23***
**Luke 4:33, 34 (Mark 1:23, 24) — *4:24***
**Luke 4:35 (Mark 1:25, 26) — *4:25***
**Luke 4:36, 37 (Mark 1:27, 28) — *4:26***
**Luke 4:38 (Matthew 8:14; Mark 1:29, 30) — *4:27***
**Luke 4:39 (Matthew 8:15; Mark 1:31) — *4:28***
**Luke 4:40 (Matthew 8:16; Mark 32, 33) — *4:29***
**Luke 4:40, 41 (Matthew 8:16; Mark 1:34) — *4:30***
**Luke 4:42 (Mark 1:35-37) — *4:32***
**Luke 4:43, 44 (Matthew 4:23; Mark 1:38, 39) — *4:33***
**Luke 5:1-3 — *4:16***
**Luke 5:4 — *4:17***
**Luke 5:5 — *4:18***
**Luke 5:6, 7, 10 — *4:19***
**Luke 5:8-10 — *4:20***
**Luke 5:10 — *4;21***
**Luke 5:10 (6, 7) — *4:19***
**Luke 5:10, 11 — *4:22***
**Luke 5:12 (Matthew 8:2; Mark 1:40) — *4:35***
**Luke 5:12 (Matthew 8:2; Mark 1:40) — *4:36***
**Luke 5:13 (Matthew 8:3; Mark 1:41, 42) — *4:37***
**Luke 5:14 (Matthew 8:4; Mark 1:43, 44) — *4:38***
**Luke 5:15, 16 (Mark 1:45) — *4:39***
**Luke 5:17 — *4:41***

**Luke 6:20 (Matthew 5:1, 2) — *5:2***
**Luke 6:20 (Matthew 5:3) — *5:3***
**Luke 6:21 (Matthew 5:4) — *5:4***
**Luke 6:21 (Matthew 5:6) — *5:6***
**Luke 6:22, 23 (Matthew 5:11, 12) — *5:11***
**Luke 6:24 — *5:12***
**Luke 6:25 — *5:13***
**Luke 6:25 — *5:14***
**Luke 6:26 — *5:15***
**Luke 6:27, 28 (Matthew 5:43-45) — *5:38***
**Luke 6:29, 30 (Matthew 5:39-42) — *5:37***
**Luke 6:31 (Matthew 7:12) — *5:75***
**Luke 6:32-34 (Matthew 5:46, 47) — *5:39***
**Luke 6:35 — *5:40***
**Luke 6:36 (Matthew 5:48) — *5:41***
**Luke 6:37, 38 — *5:70***
**Luke 6:39 — *5:59***
**Luke 6:40 — *5:82***
**Luke 6:41, 42 (Matthew 7:3-5) — *5:71***
**Luke 6:43, 44 (Matthew 7:16-20) — *5:78***
**Luke 6:45 — *5:79***
**Luke 6:46 (Matthew 7:23) — *5:81***
**Luke 6:47, 48 (Matthew 7:24, 25) — *5:83***
**Luke 6:49 (Matthew 7:26, 27) *5:84***
**Luke 7:1, 2 (Matthew 8:5, 6) — *6:1***
**Luke 7:3, 4 (Matthew 8:5, 6) — *6:2***
**Luke 7:4, 5 — *6:3***
**Luke 7:6 — *6:5***
**Luke 7:6 (Matthew 8:7) — *6:4***
**Luke 7:6-8 (Matthew 8:8, 9) — *6:6***
**Luke 7:9 (Matthew 8:10-12) — *6:7***
**Luke 7:10 (Matthew 8:13) — *6:9***
**Luke 7:11, 12 — *6:20***
**Luke 7:13-15 — *6:21***
**Luke 7:16 — *6:22***
**Luke 7:17 — *6:23***
**Luke 7:18 (Matthew 11:2) — *8:20***
**Luke 7:19 (Matthew 11:2) — *8:21***
**Luke 7:20 (Matthew 11:3) — *8:22***
**Luke 7:21-23 (Matthew 11:4-6) — *8:23***
**Luke 7:24-27 (Matthew 11:7-10) — *8:24***

**Luke 9:62 — *11:132***
**Luke 10:1 — *11:133***
**Luke 10:1, 2 — *11:134***
**Luke 10:3 — *11:135***
**Luke 10:4 — *11:136***
**Luke 10:4 — *11:137***
**Luke 10:5, 6 — *11:138***
**Luke 10:7 — *11:139***
**Luke 10:8-11 — *11:140***
**Luke 10:12-14 — *11:141***
**Luke 10:15 — *11:142***
**Luke 10:16 — *11:143***
**Luke 10:17 — *11:144***
**Luke 10:18 — *11:145***
**Luke 10:19, 20 — *11:146***
**Luke 10:21 — *11:147***
**Luke 10:22 — *11:148***
**Luke 10:23, 24 — *11:149***
**Luke 10:25 — *11:150***
**Luke 10:26 — *11:151***
**Luke 10:27 — *11:152***
**Luke 10:28 — *11:153***
**Luke 10:29 — *11:154***
**Luke 10:30 — *11:155***
**Luke 10:31, 32 — *11:156***
**Luke 10:33, 34 — *11:157***
**Luke 10:35 — *11:158***
**Luke 10:36 — *11:159***
**Luke 10:37 — *11:160***
**Luke 10:37 — *11:161***
**Luke 10:38, 39 — *11:162***
**Luke 10:39, 40 — *11:163***
**Luke 10:41, 42 — *11:164***
**Luke 11:1 — *12:3***
**Luke 11:2 — *12:4***
**Luke 11:2 — *12:5***
**Luke 11:2 — *12:6***
**Luke 11:3 — *12:7***
**Luke 11:4 — *12:8***
**Luke 11:4 — *12:9***
**Luke 11:5, 6 — *12:10***

**Luke 11:7 — *12:11***
**Luke 11:8 — *12:12***
**Luke 11:9, 10 — *12:13***
**Luke 11:11, 12 — *12;14***
**Luke 11:13 — *12:15***
**Luke 11:14 (Matthew 12:22, 23) — *7:2***
**Luke 11:15, 16 (Matthew 12:24; Mark 3:22) — *7:3***
**Luke 11:17, 18 (Matthew 12:25, 26; Mark 3:23-26) — *7:4***
**Luke 11:19 (Matthew 12:27) — *7:5***
**Luke 11:20 (Matthew 12:28) — *7:6***
**Luke 11:21, 22 (Matthew 12:29; Mark 3:27) — *7:7***
**Luke 11:23 (Matthew 12:30) — *7:8***
**Luke 11:24-26 (Matthew 12:43-45) — *7:17***
**Luke 11:27 — *7:19***
**Luke 11:28 — *7:20***
**Luke 11:29 (Matthew 12:39, 40) — *7:14***
**Luke 11:30, 32 (Matthew 12:41) — *7:15***
**Luke 11:31 (Matthew 12:42) — *7:16***
**Luke 11:32 (30) (Matthew 12:41) — *7:15***
**Luke 11:33 — *12:16***
**Luke 11:34, 35 — *12:17***
**Luke 11:36 —*12:18***
**Luke 11:37 — *12:19***
**Luke 11:38 — *12:20***
**Luke 11:39-41 — *12:21***
**Luke 11:42 — *12:22***
**Luke 11:43 — *12:23***
**Luke 11:44 — *12:24***
**Luke 11:45 — *12:25***
**Luke 11:46 — *12:26***
**Luke 11:47, 48 — *12:27***
**Luke 11:49 — *12:28***
**Luke 11:50, 51 — *12:29***
**Luke 11:52 — *12:30***
**Luke 11:53, 54 — *12:31***
**Luke 12:1 — *12:32***
**Luke 12:1 — *12:33***
**Luke 12:2, 3 — *12:34***
**Luke 12:4, 5 — *12:35***
**Luke 12:6, 7 — *12:36***
**Luke 12:8, 9 — *12:37***

**Luke 12:9, 10 — *12:38***
**Luke 12:11, 12 — *12:39***
**Luke 12:13 — *12:40***
**Luke 12:14 — *12:41***
**Luke 12:15 — *12:42***
**Luke 12:16, 17 — *12:43***
**Luke 12:18, 19 — *12:44***
**Luke 12:20 — *12:45***
**Luke 12:21 — *12:46***
**Luke 12:22, 23 — *12:47***
**Luke 12:24 — *12:48***
**Luke 12:25, 26 — *12:49***
**Luke 12:27 — *12:50***
**Luke 12:28 — *12:51***
**Luke 12:29, 30 — *12:52***
**Luke 12:30-32 — *12:53***
**Luke 12:33, 34 — *12:54***
**Luke 12:35, 36 — *12:55***
**Luke 12:37, 38 — *12:56***
**Luke 12:39, 40 — *12:57***
**Luke 12:41 — *12:58***
**Luke 12:42-44 — *12:59***
**Luke 12:45, 46 — *12:60***
**Luke 12:47, 48 — *12:61***
**Luke 12:49, 50 — *12:62***
**Luke 12:51-53 — *12:63***
**Luke 12:54, 55 — *12:64***
**Luke 12:56 — *12:65***
**Luke 12:57-59 — *12:66***
**Luke 13:1 — *12:67***
**Luke 13:2, 3 — *12:68***
**Luke 13:4, 5 — *12:69***
**Luke 13:6, 7 — *12:70***
**Luke 13:8, 9 — *12:71***
**Luke 13:10-13 — *12:72***
**Luke 13:14 — *12:73***
**Luke 13:15, 16 — *12:74***
**Luke 13:17 — *12:75***
**Luke 13:18, 19 — *12: 76***
**Luke 13:20, 21 — *12:77***
**Luke 13:22, 23 — *12:78***

**Luke 15:22-24 — *12:120***
**Luke 15:25-27 — *12:121***
**Luke 15:28-30 — *12:122***
**Luke 15:31, 32 — *12:123***
**Luke 16:1 — *12:124***
**Luke 16:2 — *12:125***
**Luke 16:3, 4 — *12:126***
**Luke 16:5 — *12:127***
**Luke 16:6 — *12:128***
**Luke 16:6 — *12:129***
**Luke 16:7 — *12:130***
**Luke 16:7 — *12:131***
**Luke 16:7 — *12:132***
**Luke 16:8 — *12:133***
**Luke 16:9 — *12:134***
**Luke 16:10-12 — *12:135***
**Luke 16:13 — *12:136***
**Luke 16:14 — *12:137***
**Luke 16:15 — *12:138***
**Luke 16:16 — *12:139***
**Luke 16:17 — *12:140***
**Luke 16:18 — *12:141***
**Luke 16:19 — *12:142***
**Luke 16:20, 21 — *12:143***
**Luke 16:22, 23 — *12:144***
**Luke 16:24 — *12:145***
**Luke 16:25, 26 — *12:146***
**Luke 16:27, 28 — *12:147***
**Luke 16:29 — *12:148***
**Luke 16:30 — *12:149***
**Luke 16:31 — *12:150***
**Luke 17:1 — *12:151***
**Luke 17:2 — *12:152***
**Luke 17:3, 4 — *12:153***
**Luke 17:5 — *12:154***
**Luke 17:6 — *12:155***
**Luke 17:7 — *12:156***
**Luke 17:8, 9 — *12:157***
**Luke 17:10 — *12:158***
**Luke 17:11 — *13:39***
**Luke 17:11-13 — *13:40***

**Luke 21:25 (Matthew 24:29; Mark 13:24, 25) — *15:17***
**Luke 21:26-28 (Matthew 24:29-31; Mark 13:25-27) — *15:21***
**Luke 21:29-33 (Matthew 24:32-35; Mark 13:28-31) — *15:22***
**Luke 21:34, 35 — *15:30***
**Luke 21:36 — *15:31***
**Luke 21:37, 38 — *15:60***
**Luke 22:1, 2 (Matthew 26:3, 4; Mark 14:1) — *14:19***
**Luke 22:2 — *14:20***
**Luke 22:3, 4 (Matthew 16:14; Mark 14:10) — *22:22***
**Luke 22:5, 6 (Matthew 26:15, 16; Mark 14:11) — *14:24***
**Luke 22:7, 8 (Matthew 26:17; Mark 14:12) — *16:2***
**Luke 22:9 (Matthew 26:17; Mark 14:12) — *16:3***
**Luke 22:10-12 (Matthew 26:18; Mark 14:13-15) — *16:4***
**Luke 22:13 (Matthew 26:19; Mark 14:16) — *16:5***
**Luke 22:14-16 (Matthew 26:20; Mark 14:17) — *16:6***
**Luke 22:17, 18 — *16:24***
**Luke 22:19 (Matthew 26:26; Mark 14:22) — *16:25***
**Luke 22:20 (Matthew 26:27-29; Mark 14:23-25) — *16:26***
**Luke 22:21, 22 (Matthew 26:23, 24; Mark 14:20, 21) — *16:32***
**Luke 22:23 (Matthew 26:21; Mark 14:18; John 13:21, 22) — *16:27***
**Luke 22:24-27 — *16:8***
**Luke 22:28-30 — *16:9***
**Luke 22:31, 32 — *16:61***
**Luke 22:33 (John 13:37) — *16:62***
**Luke 22:34 (Matthew 26:34; Mark 14:30; John 13:38) — *16:63***
**Luke 22:35 — *16:65***
**Luke 22:35 — *16:66***
**Luke 22:36 — *16:67***
**Luke 22:37 — *16:68***
**Luke 22:38 — *16:69***
**Luke 22:38 — *16:70***
**Luke 22:39 (Matthew 26:30; Mark 14:26; John 14:31) — *16:58***
**Luke 22:40 — *17:3***
**Luke 22:40 (Matthew 26:36; Mark 14:32; John 18:1) — *17:1***
**Luke 22:41 (Matthew 26:39; Mark 14:35, 36) — *17:4***
**Luke 22:42-44 (Matthew 26:44) — *17:8***
**Luke 22:45, 46 (Matthew 26:45, 46; Mark 14:41, 42) — *17:9***
**Luke 22:47 (Matthew 26:47; Mark 14:43; John 18:2-4) — *17:10***
**Luke 22:47 (Matthew 26:48, 49; Mark 14:44, 45) — *17:17***
**Luke 22:48 (Matthew 26:50; Mark 14:46) — *17:18***
**Luke 22:49, 50 (Matthew 26:51; Mark 14:47; John 18:10) — *17:19***

**Luke 23:34 (Matthew 27:35, 36; Mark 15:24; John 19:23-25) — *17:119***
**Luke 23:35 (Matthew 27:39, 40; Mark 15:29, 30) — *17:120***
**Luke 23:35 (Matthew 27:41-43; Mark 15:31, 32) — *17:121***
**Luke 23:36, 37 — *17:123***
**Luke 23:38 (Matthew 27:37; Mark 15:26; John 19:19-21) — *17:117***
**Luke 23:39 — *17:124***
**Luke 23:40-42 — *17:125***
**Luke 23:43 — *17:126***
**Luke 23:44, 45 (Matthew 27:45; Mark 15:33) — *17:128***
**Luke 23:45 (Matthew 27:51; Mark 15:38) — *17:134***
**Luke 23:46 (Matthew 27:48, 50; Mark 15:36, 37; John 19:30) — *17:133***
**Luke 23:47, 48 (Matthew 27:54; Mark 15:39) — *17:137***
**Luke 23:49 (Matthew 27:55, 56; Mark 15:40, 41) — *17:136***
**Luke 23:50-52 (Matthew 27:57, 58; Mark 15:42, 43; John 19:38) — *18:6***
**Luke 23:53 (Matthew 27:59; Mark 15:46; John 19:39, 40) — *18:8***
**Luke 23:54 (John 19:31, 42) — *18:1***
**Luke 23:55, 56 (Matthew 27:61; Mark 15:47) — *18:10***
**Luke 24:1 (Matthew 28:1; Mark 16:1, 9; John 20:1) — *18:13***
**Luke 24:2 (Matthew 28:2; Mark 16:2-4) — *18:16***
**Luke 24:3-8 (Matthew 28:8; Mark 16:5-8) — *18:18***
**Luke 24:9-11 (Mark 16:9-11; John 20:18) — *18:30***
**Luke 24:12 (John 20:2-4) — *18:20***
**Luke 24:12 (John 20:5-10) — *18:21***
**Luke 24:13 (Mark 16:12) — *18:34***
**Luke 24:14-16 (Mark 16:12) — *18:35***
**Luke 24:17 — *18:36***
**Luke 24:18 — *18:37***
**Luke 24:19 — *18:38***
**Luke 24:19-21 — *18:39***
**Luke 24:22-24 — *18:40***
**Luke 24:25-27 — *18:41***
**Luke 24:28, 29 — *18:42***
**Luke 24:30-33 — *18:43***
**Luke 24:33 (Mark 16:13; John 20:19) — *18:44***
**Luke 24:34, 35 (Mark 16:13) — *18:45***
**Luke 24:35-37 (Mark 16:12, 13; John 20:19) — *18:46***
**Luke 24:38-41 (John 20:20) — *18:47***
**Luke 24:41-43 — *18:48***
**Luke 24:44 — *18:49***
**Luke 24:45, 46 — *18:50***
**Luke 24:47-49 — *18:52***

## JOHN

**John 7:2 — *11:1***
**John 7:3, 4 — *11:2***
**John 7:5 — *11:3***
**John 7:6-9 — *11:4***
**John 7:10 — *11:5***
**John 7:11 — *11:6***
**John 7:12, 13 — *11:7***
**John 7:14, 15 — *11:8***
**John 7:16-18 — *11:9***
**John 7:19 — *11:10***
**John 7:20 — *11:11***
**John 7:21-23 — *11:12***
**John 7:23, 24 — *11:13***
**John 7:25 — *11:14***
**John 7:25, 26 — *11:15***
**John 7:27 — *11:16***
**John 7:28, 29 — *11:17***
**John 7:30 — *11:18***
**John 7:31 — *11:19***
**John 7:32 — *11:20***
**John 7:33, 34 — *11:21***
**John 7:35 — *11:22***
**John 7:36 — *11:23***
**John 7:37-39 — *12:24***
**John 7:40-42 — *11:25***
**John 7:43, 44 — *11:26***
**John 7:45 — *11:27***
**John 7:46 — *11:28***
**John 7:47-49 — *11:29***
**John 7:50, 51 — *11:30***
**John 7:52 — *11:31***
**John 7:53, 8:1 *11:32***
**John 8:1 (7:53) — *11:32***
**John 8:2 — *11:33***
**John 8:3 — *11:34***
**John 8:4, 5 — *11:35***
**John 8:6 — *11:36***
**John 8:7, 8 — *11:37***
**John 8:9 — *11:38***
**John 8:10 — *11:39***
**John 8:11 — *11:40***

**John 8:11 — *11:41***
**John 8:12 — *11:42***
**John 8:13 — *11:43***
**John 8:14 — *11:44***
**John 8:15-18 — *11:45***
**John 8:19 — *11:46***
**John 8:19 — *11:47***
**John 8:20 — *11:48***
**John 8:21 — *11:49***
**John 8:22 — *11:50***
**John 8:23, 24 — *11:51***
**John 8:25 — *11:52***
**John 8:25 — *11:53***
**John 8:26, 27 — *11:54***
**John 8:28-30 — *11:55***
**John 8:31 — *11:56***
**John 8:31, 32 — *11:57***
**John 8:33 — *11:58***
**John 8:34 — *11:59***
**John 8:35, 36 — *11:60***
**John 8:37, 38 — *11:61***
**John 8:39 — *11:62***
**John 8:39, 40 — *11:63***
**John 8:41 — *11:64***
**John 8:42, 43 — *11:65***
**John 8:44 — *11:66***
**John 8:45-47 — *11:67***
**John 8:48 — *11:68***
**John 8:49 — *11:69***
**John 8:49, 50 *11:70***
**John 8:51 — *11:71***
**John 8:52 — *11:72***
**John 8:53 — *11:73***
**John 8:54, 55 — *11:74***
**John 8:56 — *11:75***
**John 8:57 — *11:76***
**John 8:58, 59 — *11:77***
**John 8:59 — *11:78***
**John 9:1, 2, 14 — *11:79***
**John 9:3-5 — *11:80***
**John 9:6, 7 — *11:81***

**John 18:25 (Matthew 26:71; Mark 14:69; Luke 22:58) — *17:40***
**John 18:25 (Matthew 26:72; Mark 14:70; Luke 22:58) — *17:42***
**John 18:26 (Matthew 26:73; Mark 14:70; Luke 22:59) — *17:43***
**John 18:27 (Matthew 26:74, 75; Mark 14:71, 72; Luke 22:60-62) — *17:44***
**John 18:28 (Matthew 27:2; Mark 15:1; Luke 23:1) — *17:60***
**John 18:29 — *17:61***
**John 18:30 — *17:62***
**John 18:31 — *17:63***
**John 18:31, 32 — *17:64***
**John 18:33 — *17:69***
**John 18:34 — *17:70***
**John 18:35 — *17:71***
**John 18:36 — *17:72***
**John 18:37 — *17:73***
**John 18:37 — *17:74***
**John 18:38 — *17:75***
**John 18:38 (Luke 23:4) — *17:76***
**John 18:39 (Matthew 27:17, 18; Mark 15:8-10) — *17:86***
**John 18:40 (Matthew 27:16; Mark 15:7; Luke 23:19) — *17:85***
**John 18:40 (Matthew 27:21; Luke 23:18) — *17:88***
**John 19:1 — *17:95***
**John 19:2, 3 (Matthew 27:27-31; Mark 15:16-20) — *17:96***
**John 19:4, 5 — *17:97***
**John 19:6 — *17:98***
**John 19:6 — *17:99***
**John 19:7 — *17:100***
**John 19:8 — *17:101***
**John 19:9, 10 — *17:102***
**John 19:11 — *17:103***
**John 19:12 — *17:104***
**John 19:13, 14 — *17:105***
**John 19:15 — *17:106***
**John 19:15 — *17:107***
**John 19:15 — *17:108***
**John 19:16 (Matthew 27:26, 31; Mark 15:15, 20; Luke 23:24, 25) — *17:111***
**John 19:17 (Matthew 27:32; Mark 15:21; Luke 23:26) — *17:112***
**John 19:17 (Matthew 27:33, 34; Mark 15:22, 23; Luke 23:33) — *17:115***
**John 19:18, 24 (Matthew 27:35, 38; Mark 15:24, 25, 27, 28; Luke 23:33, 34) — *17:116***
**John 19:19-21 (Matthew 27:37; Mark 15:26; Luke 23:38) — *17:117***
**John 19:22 — *17:118***

## ACTS

CPSIA information can be obtained
at www.ICGtesting.com
Printed in the USA
BVHW031935120620
581302BV00001B/3